THE
RIVER
BATTLES

CANADA'S FINAL CAMPAIGN
IN WORLD WAR II ITALY

MARK ZUEHLKE

THE
RIVER
BATTLES

Douglas & McIntyre

DOUGLAS AND MCINTYRE (2013) LTD.
P.O. Box 219, Madeira Park, BC, VON 2HO
www.douglas-mcintyre.com

Editing by Kathy Vanderlinden
Cover typesetting by Shed Simas / Onça Design
Typesetting by Shed Simas / Onça Design
Maps by Stuart Daniel
Cover photographs: *top:* Courtesy of Seaforth Highlanders Regimental Museum;
bottom: Photographer unknown, LAC e999920233-u
Printed on 100% recycled paper
Printed and bound in Canada

Canada

Douglas and McIntyre (2013) Ltd. acknowledges the support of the Canada Council for the Arts,
the Government of Canada, and the Province of British Columbia through the BC Arts Council.

LIBRARY AND ARCHIVES CANADA CATALOGUING IN PUBLICATION
Title: The river battles : Canada's final campaign in World War II Italy / Mark Zuehlke.
Names: Zuehlke, Mark, 1955- author.
Series: Canadian battle series (Vancouver, B.C.)
Description: Reprint. Originally published 2019. | Includes bibliographical references and
    index.
Identifiers: Canadiana 20210183829 | ISBN 9781771623124 (softcover)
Subjects: LCSH: Canada. Canadian Army. Canadian Corps, I—History. | LCSH: Canada.
    Canadian Army—History—World War, 1939-1945. | LCSH: World War, 1939-1945—
    Campaigns—Italy—Emilia-Romagna. | LCSH: World War, 1939-1945—Riverine
    operations—Italy—Emilia-Romagna. | LCSH: World War, 1939-1945—Canada.
Classification: LCC D763.182 E45 2021 | DDC 940.54/2154—dc23

THE CANADIAN BATTLE SERIES*

The Cinderella Campaign: First Canadian Army and the Battles for the Channel Ports

Forgotten Victory: First Canadian Army and the Cruel Winter of 1944–45

Tragedy at Dieppe: Operation Jubilee, August 19, 1942

Breakout from Juno: First Canadian Army and the
Normandy Campaign, July 4–August 21, 1944

On to Victory: The Canadian Liberation of the Netherlands, March 23–May 5, 1945

Operation Husky: The Canadian Invasion of Sicily, July 10–August 7, 1943

Terrible Victory: First Canadian Army and the Scheldt Estuary
Campaign, September 13–November 6, 1944

Holding Juno: Canada's Heroic Defence of the D-Day Beaches, June 7–12, 1944

Juno Beach: Canada's D-Day Victory, June 6, 1944

The Gothic Line: Canada's Month of Hell in World War II Italy

The Liri Valley: Canada's World War II Breakthrough to Rome

Ortona: Canada's Epic World War II Battle

A CANADIAN BATTLE SERIES COMPANION*

Through Blood and Sweat: A Remembrance Trek Across
Sicily's World War II Battlegrounds

OTHER MILITARY HISTORY BOOKS BY MARK ZUEHLKE

The Canadian Military Atlas: Four Centuries of Conflict
from New France to Kosovo (with C. Stuart Daniel)*

Brave Battalion: The Remarkable Saga of the 16th Battalion
(Canadian Scottish) in the First World War

The Gallant Cause: Canadians in the Spanish Civil War, 1936–1939

For Honour's Sake: The War of 1812 and the Brokering of an Uneasy Peace

Ortona Street Fight

Assault on Juno

*Available from D&M (2013) Publishers Inc.

Six and twenty panther tanks
Are waiting on the shore,
But Corps intelligence has sworn
That there are only four.

We must believe there are no more,
The information comes from Corps,
So onward to Bologna—
Drive onward to the Po!

On our way to Venice, we had a lovely time
We drove a bus from Rimini right through the German line.
Then to Bologna we did go
We all went swimming in the Po.

We are the D-Day Dodgers, in sunny Italy.

> —*Verses from the Canadian version of "We Are the D-Day Dodgers," added during the fall of 1944. Sung to the melody of "Lili Marlene."*

Harry, you'll like Italy. It has good food, willing ladies, and pretty country—whenever it stops raining.

> —*Chris Vokes to Harry Foster*

To a man, we had one goal, and that was to return to Canada and our families in about the same physical condition we had brought with us to Italy. Nothing more—nothing less.

> —*Private Stan Scislowski, Perth Regiment*

[CONTENTS]

Preface   1
Acknowledgements   4
Maps   8

INTRODUCTION   Ace High   17

PART ONE   THE PROMISED LAND

1   Get Ahead Fast   25
2   A Frightful Nightmare   41
3   Not a Leader   58
4   Somewhat Depressing   73
5   Wholehearted Co-operation   89
6   We'll Take a Chance   106
7   Absolutely Browned Off   124
8   You Miss, You're Dead   141
9   Cardinal Sin   158
10   A Sorry Mess   174

PART TWO   TAKING RAVENNA

11   Command Shuffle   187
12   Virtually Unending   203
13   A Grim Task Indeed   220
14   Cheerful to the End   236
15   A Ghastly Failure   252

PART THREE MONTONE TO THE SENIO

16 Exiled to Italy 269
17 My Fucking Nerves 286
18 Well Done Indeed 303
19 No Braggadocio 321
20 Hard Going 337
21 So Ended 1944 353
22 Hordes of the Enemy 364
23 It Hasn't Been a Picnic 381
24 The Winter Line 394

EPILOGUE The River Battles in Memory 411

APPENDIX A Principal Commanders in the River Battles 415

APPENDIX B The Canadian Army in the River Battles 417

APPENDIX C Canadian Infantry Battalion 420

APPENDIX D Canadian Army and German Army Order of
Ranks 421

APPENDIX E Canadian Army Decorations 423

Notes 424
Bibliography 450
General Index 457
Index of Formations, Units, and Corps 466
About the Author 470

O N A WARM spring day in 2006, I sat in the sun-drenched living room of Loyal Edmonton Regiment veteran John Dougan's Saanich Peninsula home near Victoria. Across Haro Strait, Mount Baker's snow-cloaked volcanic cone thrust into a brilliantly blue sky. I had come to interview Johnny for my fourth book on the Italian Campaign—*Operation Husky*. It seemed fitting to us that we were looking out at a volcano while talking of a time when Johnny had marched under a searing sun across the battlefields of Sicily with another volcano—Mount Etna—looming on the eastern flank of the Canadian line of advance. Over the years, I had interviewed Johnny several times, and a friendship had developed. After a couple of hours, his memories and thoughts on the Sicilian campaign concluded, conversation turned from the beginning of Canada's World War II experience in Italy to the months before its end. I mused that there might not be enough in that story to justify a book. Johnny, who had returned from the war to be chosen in 1946 as Alberta's Rhodes Scholar and then to pursue a long and distinguished career in the Department of External Affairs, with many overseas postings, was a thoughtful and intelligent man. I had come to respect his insights. He mulled the question over for a while and then nodded. "There wasn't a lot of forward movement. Things were mostly static. I'm not sure it could carry a book."

It was not just Johnny's observation that dissuaded me. Discussions with historians at the Department of National Defence's Directorate of History and Heritage and elsewhere led to the same conclusion. Those months from late September 1944 to February 1945 had, it was true, seen hard fighting under the bitterest circumstances of weather. But very little ground had been won, and this for little apparent strategic gain. That was the gist of virtually every conversation.

Consequently, I set aside thoughts of writing a book about that period. That is where things might have rested had it not been for an unexpected email message on July 24, 2014, from Mariangela Rondinelli of Bagnacavallo. I had met Mariangela the previous year at the Canadian Embassy in Rome during an event leading up to the launch of "Operation Husky 2013"—the remembrance trek marking the seventieth anniversary of Canada's participation in the Sicily Campaign. That, however, was not the reason for her email. She wrote that 2014 was also the seventieth anniversary "of the liberation of many towns in our province, Ravenna . . . All the towns were liberated by Canadian Regiments towards the end of 1944." A local history institute based in Ravenna and the city administration planned to host a small conference on December 4—the day that Ravenna had been liberated in 1944—and hoped I would be the keynote speaker.

Such requests from European countries in which Canadians fought in World War II are not entirely uncommon. Usually, however, they fade away once the problem of how to finance such an appearance is raised. This time, however, the Istituto Storico della Resistenza e dell'età Contemporanea in Ravenna e Provincia offered to cover all expenses. The subject of my talk was to be the last months of the war in the Italian theatre, between November 1944 and January 1945.

Despite having concluded that the events during that time did not warrant a book, I thought there was surely sufficient grist for a thirty-minute presentation. Having accepted the invitation, I set about researching and writing the talk—and soon found myself forced to condense details to fit the allotted time frame. Left out were so many accounts of fierce battles fought in a complex landscape criss-crossed by myriad rivers and canals. I came across countless stories of individual courage and sacrifice.

At the beginning of December 2014, I flew to Bologna and drove to Ravenna. In discussions with Mariangela and Giuseppe Masetti—the head of the Istituto Storico—I was further encouraged to look beyond the limited scope of ground won to recognize the significance of what 1 Canadian Corps had achieved in this period. Giuseppe particularly emphasized that the Canadians won more ground from the Germans than any other Allied units. He also maintained that they achieved this while braving the worst of fighting conditions and extreme German opposition.

After the conference, I spent several days visiting the entire battlefield. It was December, so I was able to stand on dykes overlooking the mud-soaked fields and vineyards in conditions mirroring those the Canadians endured in 1944–45. Using topographic maps, I hunted down the exact spot next to a little church where Seaforth Highlander Private Smokey Smith earned his Victoria Cross. Walking away from that church in a cold rain, I realized the hook was in. A fifth volume would be added to the Canadian Battle Series books on the Italian Campaign.

The River Battles is the result. Fortunately, as I dug into the research, a wealth of material came to hand. Buried well away in the Department of National Defence's Directorate of History and Heritage archives and the army files held at Library and Archives Canada were hundreds of historical records chronicling the intense fighting of those hard, last months. Although few veterans remained, there were enough voices in oral history collections and other interviews conducted in earlier years to enable me to create the "you are there" experience that has marked the other Canadian Battle Series titles. This aspect is critical, as it enables *The River Battles* both to tell the story of the soldiers who fought there and to honour them.

ACKNOWLEDGEMENTS

SO MANY PEOPLE stepped forward to assist with the research and writing of *The River Battles*. I hope not to forget anyone.

First to thank, as has been the case for many years, is my Dutch colleague, Johan van Doorn. He is a gifted expert at mining massive archival catalogue databases for the relevant documents, which are always spread over a vast array of files. Mining complete, he then produces excellent and essential Excel spreadsheets that enable me to follow a navigable course through the material. As so little has been written about this period of Canada's participation in the Italian Campaign, we had expected slim pickings within the official records. What we found was completely the opposite—likely the most detailed and expansive collection of material ever generated for any period of the war. Without Johan's assistance, I might still be in Ottawa blundering my way through another thousand boxes of documents!

In Ottawa, the staff at Library and Archives Canada went out of their way to facilitate my work. Recognizing that I came from the other side of the country and had limited time, they made sure that upon my arrival, all would be in readiness to enable me to immediately get to work. Photo research was greatly assisted by Karine Gélina, who manages the Digi-Lab. At Directorate of Heritage and History, Department of National Defence, Dr. Steve Harris and staff also offered sterling assistance.

Due to a glitch on my part, I returned from Ottawa to discover that somehow, among the many thousands of digital photographs taken, none were of the war diaries for the three regiments from 2nd Canadian Infantry Brigade. This conundrum was rectified with the assistance of Karen Storwick in Calgary, who connected me with the right people at the Military Museums and also the Loyal Edmonton Regiment Military Museum in Edmonton. Colonel Peter C. Boyle and Princess Patricia's Canadian Light Infantry Regiment's archivist, Jim Bowen, ensured that the diaries for that regiment were pulled together. Anna Hebert, friend and a guest on the Liberation Tours 100th Vimy Ridge Commemorative trip, then photographed them. In Edmonton, Executive Director Terry Allison provided the war diaries of the Loyal Eddies. Seaforth Highlanders' Honorary Colonel Rod Hoffmeister linked me up with James Calhoun, the curator and archivist at Vancouver's Burrard Street Armoury, who supplied the regiment's war diaries for the period and some supplementary documents.

As time goes by, some regimental histories are increasingly difficult to source. This proved to be the case with those of the Irish Regiment and Governor General's Horse Guards. Jerry Scislowski—son of Perth Regiment's Stan Scislowski—filled this gap by giving me access to his copies. Captain Mike Gray of the Princess Louise Fusiliers also provided additional information on their role in these battles, as did Tim Sugrue for the 4th Princess Louise Dragoon Guards. Mike Blanchett and Linda Webb did likewise for the 8th Princess Louise's New Brunswick Hussars.

My colleague at Liberation Tours and expert on the German side of the war, Mark Proulx, helped sift through events that led to 'A' Company of the Irish Regiment being overrun on the night of September 27–28, 1944, at the Fiumicino River.

For all the years I have been working on the Canadian Battle Series, the late Ken MacLeod always willingly shared his many veteran interviews collected over a number of years. Several of those interviews were essential here. So, too, were many of the interviews held in University of Victoria's Military Oral History collection—particularly the long and rich interview with Lieutenant Colonel Jim Stone of the Loyal Eddies.

In Italy, Dr. Giuseppe Masetti—head of Ravenna's Istituto Storico—provided valuable insights into the importance of 1 Canadian Corps's operations during this period. Mariangela Rondinelli was a gem—driving me to several key battle sites in the Bagnacavallo and Russi area, as well as helping me sketch out the rest of the essential battlefield tour I conducted in December 2014. Also in Ravenna, Manuela Farneti volunteered to translate for me expertly during the conference commemorating the city's 1944 liberation. I'm not sure what the Italian conference delegates thought of it, but I think we provided a stirring duet of "We Are the D-Day Dodgers." Manuela also waded into the thick of Italian police bureaucracy to rescue me from having to pay innumerable traffic violation fines in Ravenna due to the failure of hotel staff to register with the local authorities that I was driving in and out of the city's limited vehicle access zone. Without her assistance, I'd likely be a fugitive felon in Italy or a pauper after paying the fines!

My agent, Carolyn Swayze, continues to keep the business side of my career running smoothly. Douglas & McIntyre (2013) staff, from the editorial and production side to marketing and publicity, are always professional and quick to respond to any issues that arise. They are a pleasure to call colleagues. So, too, is Kathy Vanderlinden—my now long-term editor on the Canadian Battle Series. We make a good team. As part of what we dub the Zuehlke team, I was happy to welcome back again copy editor Merrie-Ellen Wilcox. Mapmaker C. Stuart Daniel has been a stalwart companion almost since the beginning of my book-writing career. The maps for this period of the war—with so much action taking place within a very small canvas—presented a particular challenge in achieving both accuracy and clarity. On the subject of maps, many small hamlets and villages named in this volume no longer exist. The residents either moved away after the war or the places were absorbed into expanding nearby towns. Spellings also often varied, and we have generally gone with how they were known by 1 Canadian Corps staff and mapmakers.

Final and most appreciated thanks must go to my partner in this journey, Frances Backhouse. Whether walking far-flung battlefields with me or here at home, as I work on this series that has grown into a life's vocation, Frances is always solid in her loving support. And that makes life all the more worthwhile.

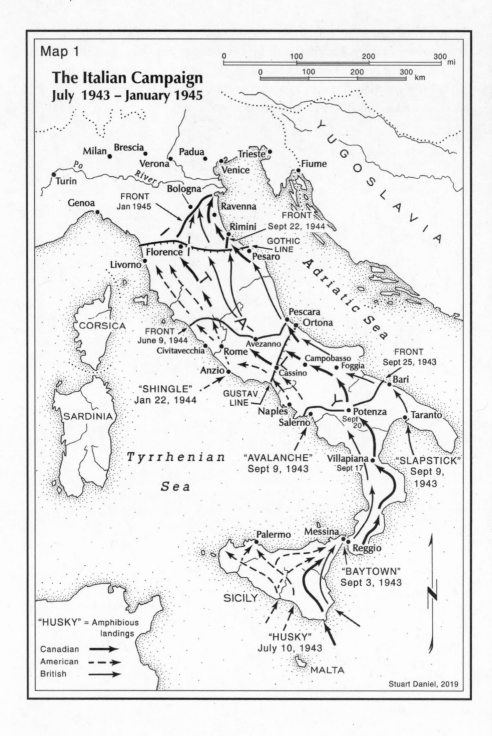

Map 1

The Italian Campaign
July 1943 – January 1945

Stuart Daniel, 2019

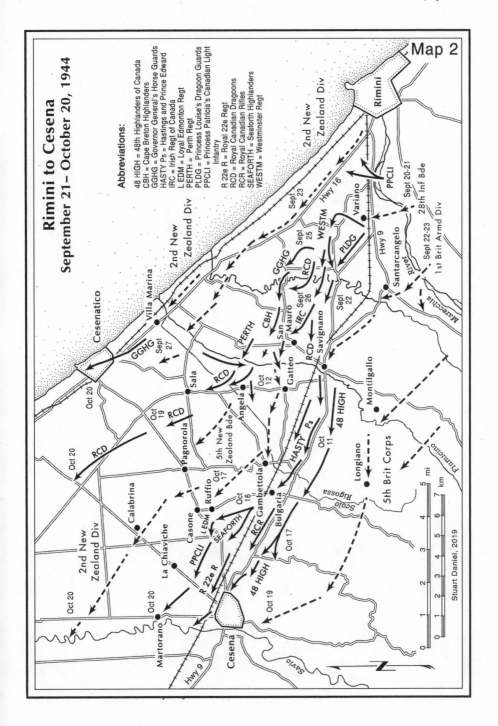

Rimini to Cesena
September 21– October 20, 1944

Abbreviations:

48 HIGH = 48th Highlanders of Canada
CBH = Cape Breton Highlanders
GGHG = Governor General's Horse Guards
HASTY Ps = Hastings and Prince Edward
IRC = Irish Regt of Canada
L EDM = Loyal Edmonton Regt
PERTH = Perth Regt
PLDG = Princess Louise's Dragoon Guards
PPCLI = Princess Patricia's Canadian Light
  Infantry
R 22e R = Royal 22e Regt
RCD = Royal Canadian Dragoons
RCR = Royal Canadian Rifles
SEAFORTH = Seaforth Highlanders
WESTM = Westminster Regt

Map 2

Stuart Daniel, 2019

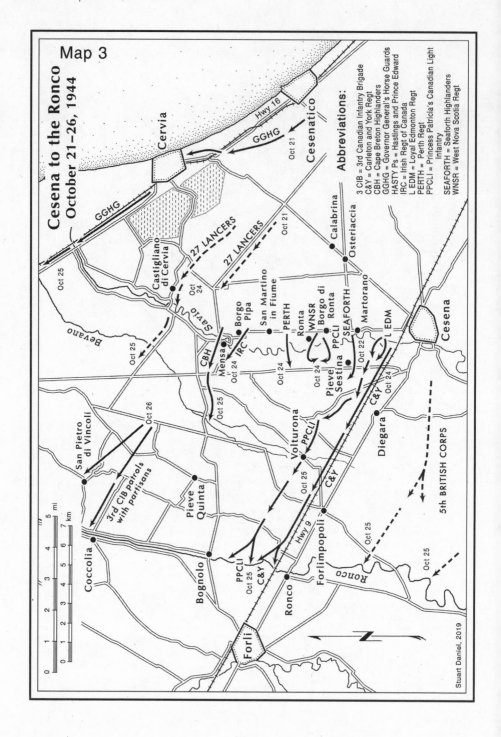

Map 3

Cesena to the Ronco
October 21–26, 1944

Abbreviations:

3 CIB = 3rd Canadian Infantry Brigade
C&Y = Carleton and York Regt
CBH = Cape Breton Highlanders
GGHG = Governor General's Horse Guards
HASTY Ps = Hastings and Prince Edward
IRC = Irish Regt of Canada
L EDM = Loyal Edmonton Regt
PERTH = Perth Regt
PPCLI = Princess Patricia's Canadian Light
    Infantry
SEAFORTH = Seaforth Highlanders
WNSR = West Nova Scotia Regt

Stuart Daniel, 2019

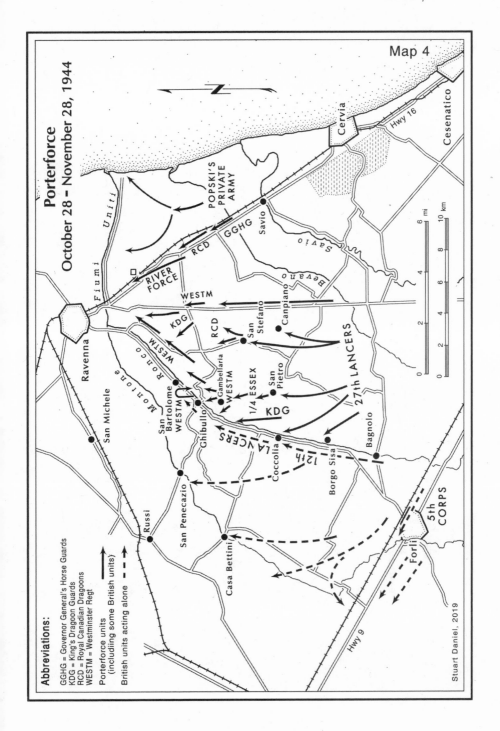

Map 4

Porterforce

October 28 – November 28, 1944

Abbreviations:

GGHG = Governor General's Horse Guards
KDG = King's Dragoon Guards
RCD = Royal Canadian Dragoons
WESTM = Westminster Regt

→ Porterforce units
(including some British units)

⇢ British units acting alone

Stuart Daniel, 2019

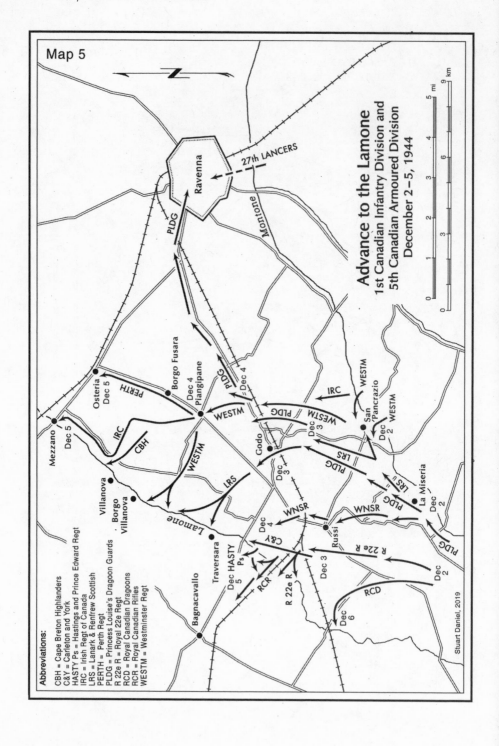

Map 5

27th LANCERS

Ravenna

PLDG

Montone

Advance to the Lamone
1st Canadian Infantry Division and
5th Canadian Armoured Division
December 2–5, 1944

0   1   2   3   4   5 mi

0   3   6   9 km

Osteria
Dec 5

PERTH

Borgo Fusara

Dec 4
Piangipane

PLDG = Dec 4

Mezzano
Dec 5

IRC

CBH

WESTM

IRC

WESTM

San
Pancrazio
Dec 2

WESTM

WESTM

Dec 3

Godo

PLDG

WESTM

WESTM

Villanova

Borgo
Villanova

WESTM

LRS

Lamone

LRS

Dec
3

Dec 4

WNSR

WNSR

LRS

PLDG

PLDG

La Miseria
Dec 2

LRS

PLDG

Russi

R 22e R

Traversara

C&Y

Dec HASTY
5   Ps

RCR

R 22e R

Dec 3

Dec
2

Bagnacavallo

R 22e R

RCD

Dec
6

Stuart Daniel, 2019

Abbreviations:
CBH = Cape Breton Highlanders
C&Y = Carleton and York
HASTY Ps = Hastings and Prince Edward Regt
IRC = Irish Regt of Canada
LRS = Lanark & Renfrew Scottish
PERTH = Perth Regt
PLDG = Princess Louise's Dragoon Guards
R 22e R = Royal 22e Regt
RCD = Royal Canadian Dragoons
RCR = Royal Canadian Rifles
WESTM = Westminster Regt

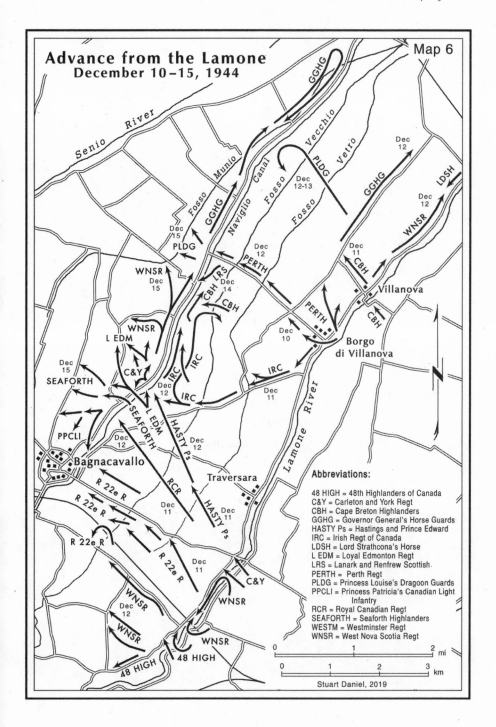

Advance from the Lamone
December 10–15, 1944

Map 6

Senio River

GGHG

Vecchio

Munio

Fosso

GGHG

Dec 15

PLDG

Naviglio Canal

Fosso

Dec 12-13

PLDG

Vetro

Dec 12

GGHG

WNSR

Dec 12

LDSH

Fosso

WNSR
Dec 15

PLDG

PERTH

Dec 12

CBH LRS
Dec 14

WNSR
Dec 15

CBH

CBH

Dec 11

CBH

Villanova

PERTH

CBH

L EDM

WNSR

Dec 10

PERTH

Dec 15

SEAFORTH

C&Y

IRC

IRC

Dec 12

Borgo
di Villanova

Lamone River

IRC

Dec 11

PPCLI

Dec 12

SEAFORTH

L EDM

IRC

HASTY Ps

Dec 12

Bagnacavallo

RCR

Traversara

R 22e R

Dec 11

HASTY Ps

Dec 11

R 22e R

R 22e R

Dec 11

C&Y

R 22e R

WNSR
Dec 12

WNSR

WNSR

WNSR

48 HIGH

48 HIGH

Abbreviations:

48 HIGH = 48th Highlanders of Canada
C&Y = Carleton and York Regt
CBH = Cape Breton Highlanders
GGHG = Governor General's Horse Guards
HASTY Ps = Hastings and Prince Edward
IRC = Irish Regt of Canada
LDSH = Lord Strathcona's Horse
L EDM = Loyal Edmonton Regt
LRS = Lanark and Renfrew Scottish
PERTH = Perth Regt
PLDG = Princess Louise's Dragoon Guards
PPCLI = Princess Patricia's Canadian Light
           Infantry
RCR = Royal Canadian Regt
SEAFORTH = Seaforth Highlanders
WESTM = Westminster Regt
WNSR = West Nova Scotia Regt

0   1   2 mi

0   1   2   3 km

Stuart Daniel, 2019

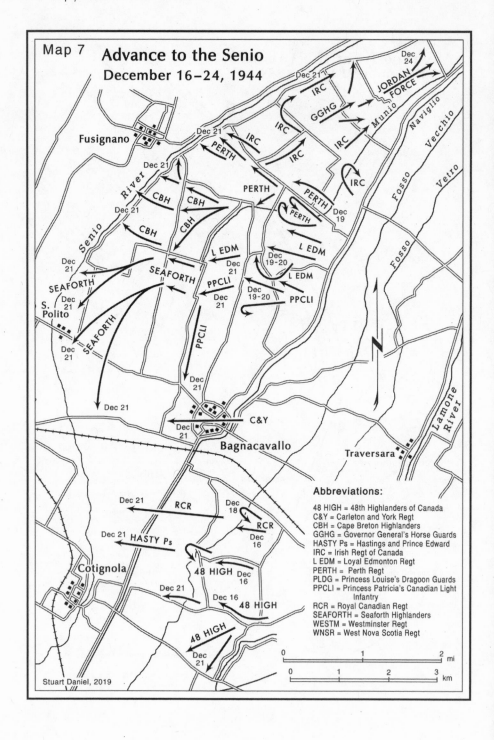

Map 7 **Advance to the Senio**
December 16–24, 1944

Fusignano

IRC

GGHG

JORDAN FORCE

Dec 24

Dec 21

Dec 21

IRC

IRC

IRC

IRC

IRC

Dec 21

PERTH

PERTH

PERTH

PERTH

PERTH

Dec 19

Munio

Fosso Naviglio Vecchio

Fosso Vetro

Dec 21

River

Senio

CBH

CBH

CBH

CBH

Dec 21

Dec 21

L EDM

L EDM

L EDM

Dec 19–20

Dec 21

SEAFORTH

SEAFORTH

SEAFORTH

Dec 21

Dec 21

S. Polito

Dec 21

PPCLI

PPCLI

PPCLI

Dec 21

Dec 19–20

Fosso

Dec 21

Dec 21

Dec 21

Lamone River

Dec 21

C&Y

Dec 21

Bagnacavallo

Traversara

Dec 21

RCR

Dec 18

RCR

Dec 16

Dec 21 HASTY Ps

Cotignola

48 HIGH Dec 16

Dec 21

Dec 16

48 HIGH

48 HIGH

Dec 21

Abbreviations:

48 HIGH = 48th Highlanders of Canada
C&Y = Carleton and York Regt
CBH = Cape Breton Highlanders
GGHG = Governor General's Horse Guards
HASTY Ps = Hastings and Prince Edward
IRC = Irish Regt of Canada
L EDM = Loyal Edmonton Regt
PERTH = Perth Regt
PLDG = Princess Louise's Dragoon Guards
PPCLI = Princess Patricia's Canadian Light
        Infantry
RCR = Royal Canadian Regt
SEAFORTH = Seaforth Highlanders
WESTM = Westminster Regt
WNSR = West Nova Scotia Regt

0   1   2 mi

0   1   2   3 km

Stuart Daniel, 2019

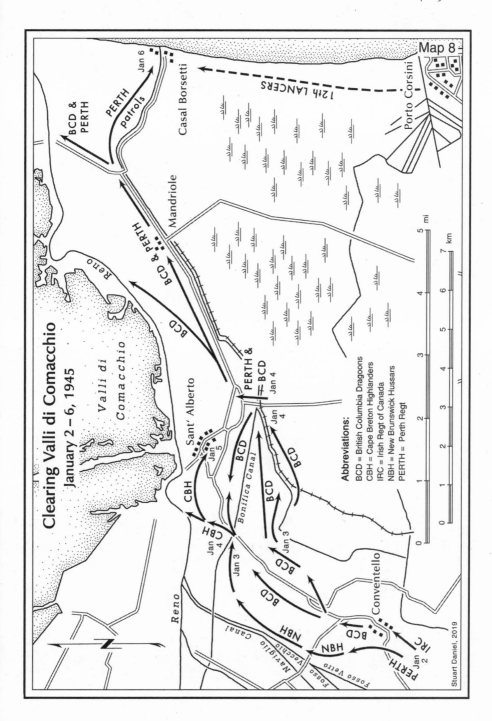

Map 8

Clearing Valli di Comacchio
January 2–6, 1945

Valli di Comacchio

Porto Corsini

Casal Borsetti

12th LANCERS

PERTH patrols

Jan 6

BCD & PERTH

BCD & PERTH

Mandriole

Reno

BCD

PERTH & BCD

Jan 4

Sant' Alberto

BCD

Jan 4

BCD

BCD

Jan 5

CBH

CBH

Jan 4

Jan 3

Bonifica Canal

BCD

Jan 3

BCD

NBH

NBH

BCD

Reno

Navigilo Vecchio Canal

Fosso Vetro

Conventello

BCD

IRC

PERTH

Jan 2

Abbreviations:
BCD = British Columbia Dragoons
CBH = Cape Breton Highlanders
IRC = Irish Regt of Canada
NBH = New Brunswick Hussars
PERTH = Perth Regt

Stuart Daniel, 2019

0   1   2   3   4   5 mi

0 1 2 3 4 5 6 7 km

Ace High

L IEUTENANT SYD FROST and his seventeen survivors from 'D' Company's No. 18 Platoon were out in the blue. Not only were they on point for the Princess Patricia's Canadian Light Infantry, but they were literally at the very tip of the Canadian advance across the Marecchia River. Gaining the river's north bank was considered the first step by 1 Canadian Corps into the broad, fertile plains of the Emilia–Romagna region. It was about 0730 hours on September 22, 1944, and the tall twenty-two-year-old platoon leader thought it likely this foray beyond the Marecchia was going to end with them all dead. In the past few minutes, the white-stoned, two-storey farm building in which Frost had established his platoon headquarters the evening before had been struck repeatedly by 88-millimetre shells. Chunks of stone, wood, and plaster flew about the large downstairs room where his headquarters section and one section of men hunkered. The other two platoon sections were out in the farmyard, dug into slit trenches that Frost hoped were carved deep. A lance corporal whom Frost had posted upstairs as an observer crashed down the stairs, head smeared with blood. "Christ, those were big ones," he shouted. "The front room is a shambles."

More shells pounded the building, while five-pound explosive rounds from probably an entire battery of six-barrelled Nebelwerfer rocket launchers pounded the yard with so many explosions that

Frost could see no sign of his men through the thickening smoke. Deciding there was nothing he could do for those outside, Frost turned his attention to the wounded lance corporal. Although a large gash on the man's forehead bled fiercely, Frost saw that the wound was superficial. A bandage stemmed the bleeding. Once the shock of the wound passed, the man should be able to continue functioning.

Frost wished he knew these men better. But he had only returned to the regiment on the 19th and had immediately taken them into battle. On October 26 the year before, while leading a patrol along a road in southern Italy, he had had most of his jaw torn off by a bullet. The wound was so grievous that Frost had not expected to survive. Long months of highly experimental facial reconstruction surgery at a hospital in England had followed. What had been a ruined face was slowly reassembled to near normalcy, with just a little paralysis in the right cheek. Frost had eventually been declared fit to return to the regiment in Italy.

He arrived just as the bloodiest battle the Canadians fought in Italy was ending. Since August 25, 1944, 1 Canadian Corps had been slugging its way up the Adriatic coast through the last major German defences in Italy—the vaunted Gothic Line. More than 4,500 casualties were suffered in an advance from just south of Pesaro to the Marecchia River—a little north of Rimini. The Patricias had been in the thick of the last fighting on San Fortunato Ridge, west of Rimini, when Frost arrived.

Counting himself and the men of No. 18 Platoon, 'D' Company now numbered only about 60 soldiers. It should have numbered about 130. Its commander, Captain Sam Potts, was the only other officer. San Fortunato Ridge crowded up close to the south bank of the Marecchia, and Potts had led the company down its flank under cover of darkness on the night of September 21–22. After the intense heat and dust that had prevailed during the Gothic Line Battle, that night brought a cool rain, and the clay underfoot turned slimy. Only a little water ran down a series of shallow channels in the riverbed that were separated by ridges of sand and gravel. But nobody had to get their feet wet, as the Germans had damaged, but failed to blow, a wooden bridge.

Although the Germans had tried to stem the advance, their efforts were disorganized and disconnected. A couple of strongpoints established in small hamlets were easily bypassed, the Tiger tanks and infantry holding them left to be dealt with later. 'D' Company's priority was to cut Highway 9 (the Via Emilia), which paralleled the river about five hundred yards to the north and ran in a virtually straight line from Rimini to Bologna. Well before dawn, 'D' Company had dashed across the highway and established a holding position. Guarding the rest of the company's left flank, No. 18 Platoon had stormed a white farmhouse and taken five confused Germans prisoner. Potts and the other two platoons were in buildings to the east. 'A' Company was also in the vicinity, but about five hundred yards back and just north of the river. This left No. 18 Platoon out front with its left flank entirely exposed. Shortly after dawn, the rain ceased. The sky cleared, and a brilliant sun brought back the summer heat.

The Patricias had been told they would be relieved on the morning of September 22 by elements of 2nd New Zealand Armoured Division, which was taking over the frontage from 1st Canadian Infantry Division. The Canadians were to withdraw for a well-deserved rest and refit. It seemed, however, the Germans had other ideas and were intent on killing Frost and his men before the relief occurred. Undoubtedly, this battering by artillery and Nebelwerfers was a prelude to a combined attack by infantry and tanks. The platoon might stop the infantry, Frost thought, but with only two PIAT anti-tank launchers, it had little hope of knocking out even one of the Tigers lurking in the bypassed hamlets.

Unable to see anything out the first-floor windows, Frost called for a volunteer to go upstairs and watch for the Germans. The volunteer barely made it to the top of the stairs when several shells smashed into the upper storey and sent him tumbling down. Gamely regaining his feet, the man started back up, but Frost told him to stop. More shells tearing into the upper storey convinced Frost to abandon it.

Another volley of Nebelwerfer fire crashed into the farmyard. Frost dashed to the back door, intent on finding his section leaders. One hurtled through the door as he opened it. "God Almighty, the bastards are throwing everything they've got at us. Never seen anything like it." The man had a broken arm gushing blood. As Frost dressed the wound and rigged an ad hoc sling, the soldier urged him to get the sections outside into the house's dubious shelter. Looking out the back door, Frost spotted the other section leader looking his way and signalled him to retreat.

Moments later, the entire platoon was crowded into the ground floor of the house. Frost considered the situation. With the New Zealanders expected and 5th Canadian Armoured Division also supposedly coming up on the left flank, it was possible the Germans would abandon an actual attack. Even if they retook the house, they would soon be overwhelmed. Survive the shelling for a few more hours, then. And just hope the house held together until help arrived.

This was a big hope, because more shells had torn the upper storey clean away, and the 88-millimetre guns now battered the main floor. Its three rooms had stouter outside walls than the upstairs, and for now the shells were failing to penetrate. But if a shell or mortar round lobbed down upon the ruined upper storey, it could easily penetrate the first floor's thin ceiling.

How to deploy the men? The big room serving as his headquarters was in the centre and more protected, but did it make sense to keep everyone together? As he considered whether to divide men between rooms, a mortar round dropped into the eastern one, and its outside wall collapsed. Two rooms now. Frost thought about poker and his "phenomenal luck" with cards. No chance at a full house. "That's shot to hell," he wrote later. "Do I keep my pair or throw one away and draw a straight? I feel like I am on a high induced by sodium pentothal after one of my operations. I'll let the pair go and try for a straight."

A good decision. Seconds later, a 105-millimetre shell from a new gun entering the game demolished the second room. That was it for the house's outer stone walls. As Frost bent to speak to a wounded soldier, an armour-piercing round tore through the main room's interior wall, passed directly over him, and punched out the wall on the other side. Everybody flattened down on the earthen floor. Nebelwerfer rounds, mortar bombs, and artillery shells started slamming into the rapidly crumbling house. Whole sections of ceiling crashed down, but the stout beams on which the upper storey had been built held.

Everyone was covered in debris. Through gaping holes in the ceiling Frost saw blue sky. The room filled with smoke and plaster dust. A man sobbed hysterically, pulled out a bible, and started to pray. "There is no hope. We are doomed. We must confess our sins to Him before we are all blown straight to hell," he cried.

"No one is going to be blown to hell in this platoon," Frost shouted, shaking the man's shoulders and striking him lightly with the back of a hand. The soldier calmed. "Anyone else think he's going to hell?" Frost snapped.

A badly wounded man whimpered. Frost spoke with him quietly and administered a shot of morphine. The shelling seemed to slacken. Frost peered out a shattered window. Another armour-piercing round punched a hole through the wall. "Will it never stop?" he whispered.

Then from the exposed flank came a dreaded sound—the clank of tank tracks. Panicky, Frost rushed to the rear door. Through a cloud of dust a troop of tanks emerged, headed directly for the house. Panic turned to elation. Frost ran into the open, waving and shouting at the Churchill tanks of the 2nd New Zealand Division. "I have just drawn my straight—ace high," he thought.[1]

The New Zealanders had arrived. An Allied toehold on the Marecchia's north shore was firm and would provide the start point for British Eighth Army—with 1 Canadian Corps under command—to begin its advance into the Romagna. That advance, higher command believed, would be the beginning of an armoured romp across open plains that would liberate northern Italy and bring the long Italian Campaign to a victorious end.

PART ONE

THE PROMISED LAND

1

Get Ahead Fast

O N SEPTEMBER 22, 1944, Brigadier John S. Lind, commanding
5th Canadian Armoured Division's 12th Canadian Infantry
Brigade, gathered his three battalion commanders and that of the
attached supporting tank regiment—Lord Strathcona's Horse—on
the heights of San Fortunato Ridge to examine their next field of battle.[1] Before them, a vast sprawling plain stretched to the far horizon.
This was what the division's tankers and the motorized infantry of
the Westminster Regiment had longed for since their November 1943
deployment in Italy. The rugged terrain the Canadians encountered
during their advances up either flank of the Apennines, which
formed a hard spine in the country's centre, had prevented this kind
of mobile warfare. Now, however, the Apennines had doglegged westward to the French Alps and stood behind them. It seemed they had
reached that final ridge and were ready to "emerge in flat country
where the Tedeschi [Germans] would not be looking down (and accurately directing fire) from higher points further back." Westminster
Regiment's Lieutenant Colonel Gordon Corbould returned to his battalion headquarters "fairly beaming. 'As far as you can see from up
there, it's as flat as a pool table,'" he reported.[2]

The Lord Strathcona's Horse's Lieutenant Colonel Jim McAvity
was equally elated. At long last, 5th Division was ready to "debauch
on to the Po Valley. For weeks, we had been looking forward to this

occasion; for weeks, we had been pounding over hill after hill, reminded by the senior commanders . . . that beyond these hills lay
'The Promised Land,' the 'wide open spaces' where our tanks could
run wild in their mad gallop to the Po."[3]

Indeed, as 1 Canadian Corps Lieutenant General Eedson L.M.
"Tommy" Burns had often explained, the "struggle to break the Gothic
Line" and then push the Germans back to the Marecchia River at
such bloody cost "had been seen as opening the way to a decisive
series of blows against [a] defeated and retreating enemy. This would
be possible in open country with the Eighth Army's superiority in
armour and air support." Map and aerial reconnaissance photography
study encouraged Burns and the other British Eighth Army superior
officers to consider this outcome inevitable.[4]

Even Eighth Army's common soldiers had caught the excitement,
adding a new lyric to the popular self-mocking "We Are the D-Day
Dodgers," sung to the melody of the wartime favourite "Lili Marlene":

> We shall debouch into the Valley of the Po,
> Jump off from the Gothic Line and smash the cringing foe;
> We shall debouch into the Po,
> And this we know
> 'Cause Corps says so;
> Forward to Bologna—drive onward to the Po.

They had sung the song lustily while marching through the dust
en route from one firefight in the Gothic Line Battle to the next.[5]

When 1st Canadian Infantry Division began the move into corps
reserve at the end of this battle, one army historian wrote, many of its
infantrymen "believed they had fought their last battle in Italy. The
man with the red patch on his arm standing on top of San Fortunato
Ridge on [September 21] and watching the armour and cars of
[2nd New Zealand Armoured Division] go through towards the great
plain beyond—this man, tired though he was, could vigorously wave
them on, for he believed that his job was done, that the scout cars and
carriers and Shermans and Churchills would sweep into the plain,
taking all before them. But had he looked down at his feet, he would

have seen that they were wet and muddy and might have taken their condition as an omen."[6]

There were other signs, even as the great breakout plan was being finalized, that caused unease among the senior officers. Yet the possibility of finally routing the Germans and mercilessly pursuing them—denying any opportunity to establish yet another defensive line that must be broken at great cost in time and lives—was so beguiling. Easier to brush aside worrisome details about the topography of the plain ahead. Better to trust the intelligence appreciations that the level expanse would enable the armoured formations to ruthlessly pursue a slower-moving enemy. One could ignore the fact that the favourable appreciations had been developed by studying the sector of plain around inland Bologna, rather than this Romagna area on the plain's coastal and southeastern apex. From San Fortunato Ridge the officers had seen the plain, and doctrine said such terrain provided ideal tank country. The coming advance must surely prove this.

THE DAY BEFORE Brigadier Lind held his meeting on San Fortunato Ridge, General Harold Alexander, commander of the Allied Armies in Italy, had telephoned London and spoken with Chief of the Imperial General Staff Field Marshal Sir Alan Brooke. Despite the Gothic Line victory, Alexander was deeply worried that the desired breakout into the Romagna plain might be unachievable. His concerns were based not on topography but on the overall weakness of Allied forces in Italy. On June 7, 1944, Alexander had been ordered to withdraw by phases all three divisions of U.S. VI Corps and the four-division-strong French Expeditionary Corps. These formations were assigned to Operation Anvil (later renamed Operation Dragoon)—the invasion of southern France near Marseilles. This invasion was meant to strengthen the Allied presence in France following the Normandy landings. Dragoon had been launched on August 15, 1944, while the Allies in Italy had been mustering their assault on the Gothic Line.

To soften the loss of seven divisions, Allied Supreme Command had promised Alexander major reinforcements. But he received only enough men to form one and a half divisions. This included the 78th British Infantry Division, which would not be capable of deployment until the first week of October. That left Alexander with a net loss of five and a half divisions.

Alexander had foreseen this manpower crisis in April when, after receiving 13,000 infantrymen from the United Kingdom, he was warned there would be no more. Assuming that the coming battles would see high attrition, he had predicted this quota would be fully committed by July's end. Alexander's only recourse had been to create more reinforcements from troops already in Italy. Disbanding light anti-aircraft units deemed surplus, now that the Allied air forces had gained superiority over the remaining Luftwaffe squadrons, provided thousands of soldiers. Eliminating some Royal Armoured Corps units—tanks being less necessary than infantry—added several thousand more. This in-theatre pool numbered 17,000, and 9,000 went to the infantry. At the end of August, Alexander converted 5,000 more artillerymen into infantry. But the Gothic Line Battle sucked up so many infantrymen that Eighth Army emerged in September again desperately short-handed.

Eighth Army's General Sir Oliver Leese considered the fighting his troops had faced at the Gothic Line as bitter as that of North Africa at Alamein or during the protracted Monte Cassino and Liri Valley battles. While Leese claimed Eighth Army had "severely mauled" eleven German divisions and taken more than 8,000 prisoners, its own butcher's bill had surpassed 14,000 casualties, with at least half from British infantry units. To rebuild the infantry, Alexander had to take another unwelcome step and disband 1st British Armoured Division, while reducing a 56th British Infantry Division brigade to cadre status. All remaining British infantry battalions were reorganized into three rifle companies rather than the normal four.

Since May, the Germans had lost divisions as well. Commander-in-Chief Southwest Generalfeldmarschall Albert Kesselring, Alexander advised Brooke during the phone call, had been forced to transfer three of his original twenty-three divisions to other fronts and had disbanded another to strengthen those remaining. But this loss had been more than compensated for by the infusion of ten divisions and a reinforcement pool equivalent in strength to three divisions. Although one of the new divisions had recently been disbanded,

Kesselring still had twenty-eight German divisions and two fascist Italian divisions. The latter were at least capable of internal security duties that freed up German forces.

Alexander explained that he was left fighting with about twenty divisions, which had all endured long periods of battle and were badly worn. Although the Allies were inflicting heavy losses on the Germans and making steady, though slow, progress, his casualties continued to be high. Further, the country his two armies were fighting in was so difficult that for successful operations, the basic military axiom that an attacking force should outnumber the defender by three to one was apt. It would not be surprising, he warned, if the Allies in Italy failed to win a decisive victory when they were up against an equally matched opponent.

There would, of course, be no slackening of effort. Alexander realized that within the grand strategy of the war, the role of his armies in Italy was to prevent as many German divisions as possible from being transferred to Northwest Europe or the Russian front. It was in either or both of those two theatres that the war would lead to an invasion of Germany and its then-inevitable defeat. By comparison, the war in Italy was less about winning strategic ground than pinning down and grinding up as many German forces as possible. But because of Alexander's own losses, continuing to batter the Germans to keep the pressure on would eventually become impossible without a suspension of operations.

With the Gothic Line Battle concluded, Alexander could not afford a pause. The advance into the plains must begin immediately in order to deny the Germans time to regroup and develop further strong and well-prepared defensive lines. His two armies—the U.S. Fifth Army under General Mark Clark and General Sir Oliver Leese's British Eighth Army—were too weak, however, for Alexander to be confident of achieving more costly breakthroughs.[7]

"WE CANADIANS WERE feeling the manpower pinch also," Lieutenant General Burns wrote. Infantry reinforcements were "drying up" despite "remustering the surplus reinforcements for other arms into infantry. Heavy drain on reinforcements caused by the fighting in the Normandy bridgehead and the break-out had obliged Canadian Military Headquarters in England to reduce the numbers sent to Italy."[8]

The Gothic Line Battle had exacted a heavier casualty rate than any other campaign in Italy. In addition to the 4,511 casualties, another 1,005 men were evacuated because of illness—a disproportionate ratio of these being battle exhaustion cases. Casualties in the infantry battalions far outstripped those in the armoured or artillery regiments. The three infantry brigades of 1st Canadian Infantry Division alone reported 2,162 casualties.[9] Major General Chris Vokes told Burns that his division's "cutting edge has been blunted," with the heaviest loss among company, platoon, and section leaders. These were the men with the most combat experience. While Burns knew he had sufficient reinforcement to physically replace these leaders, he could "not replace their battle-craft, their knowledge of what could be done, and how it could be done in the conditions of close combat. So although the ranks of the formations could be filled with some difficulty, neither of the divisions had the same offensive power they had when they crossed the Metauro" to attack the Gothic Line. "This had a depressing effect on everybody's spirits."[10]

Burns knew his Canadians badly needed a rest, but he could only give one to 1st Division. Both Alexander and Leese were eager to have Eighth Army keep the Germans running, with 1 Canadian Corps advancing up the Adriatic and v British Corps to its left. Using Highway 9 for the axis of its advance, v Corps was to drive northwest, with the Apennines crowding up against its left flank, toward Bologna—approaching the city from the east while the U.S. Fifth Army advanced toward it through the Apennines via a poor road network coming from Florence. The Canadians, meanwhile, retaining 2nd New Zealand Armoured Division under command, would advance north close to the coast and secure bridgeheads across the Po River. On the right flank, the Kiwis could concentrate their advance on Highway 16—the ancient Via Adriatica of Roman times—from Rimini to Ravenna and then on to Ferrara. On their left, 5th Canadian Armoured Division was restricted to local dirt roads that led to farms and small hamlets.

Passing out of a bridgehead established across the Marecchia River by 4th British Infantry Division, Major General Bert Hoffmeister's plan was to push 5th Canadian Armoured Division's 12th Canadian Infantry Brigade forward in three bounds. The first would take it to San Vito, a village adjacent to the Uso River. Once this river was bridged, a second bound two miles to the Salto River would follow. From the Salto, the advance would continue through to the Fiumicino River—considered by most historians quite likely to be the Rubicon that Julius Caesar had crossed unopposed two thousand years earlier in his march on Rome. Once this river was crossed, the division's 11th Infantry Brigade would move to the front and lead the way to the Po itself. The distance from the Marecchia bridgehead to the Fiumicino was about seven miles.[11]

In the aftermath of the Liri Valley Campaign in early June 1944, 5th Canadian Armoured Division had failed to quickly overcome stiff German resistance and achieve a breakout because of its inherent weakness in infantry. The division had been set up according to the unit organization used by the British in North Africa, which consisted of one armoured brigade and one infantry brigade, with each comprising three regiments. Added infantry mobility was provided by the motorized Westminster Regiment, which fell directly under divisional command and was deployed as needed to work alongside the tanks.

Early in the Italian campaign, the British had recognized that the North African model no longer worked. The rugged terrain, frequent river barriers, and dense foliage of olive groves and vineyards offered the Germans too many defensive positions that had to be overcome in turn. By the time 5th Armoured Division deployed to Italy, the British armoured divisions had been bolstered with an additional infantry brigade. In July 1944, Burns decided the Canadian division had to be similarly strengthened. When a request for sufficient reinforcements from Canada to be sent to Italy for this purpose was scuttled by the Imperial General Staff's Field Marshal Sir Alan Brooke, Burns decided to cobble together an infantry brigade from units already in theatre. The 4th Princess Louise Dragoon Guards—1st Division's armoured reconnaissance regiment—and 1st Canadian Light Anti-Aircraft Regiment were accordingly stripped of their respective armoured cars and anti-aircraft guns and handed rifles. Adding the Westminster Regiment to the brigade provided a seasoned infantry regiment. A number of non-commissioned officers from other infantry regiments were also assigned to the renamed 1st Light Anti-Aircraft Battalion. Sergeant Fred Cederberg and several comrades were sent from the Cape Breton Highlanders.

Cederberg and the others were soon serving as drill sergeants, setting up "bayonet drills [and] demonstrations highlighting the functions of our own and enemy minefields." Also, "crude bazooka and rifle ranges were built, [and] all ranks were trained on the rifle, Bren, Tommy gun, two-inch mortar and grenades." While such training was important, Cederberg and the others kept hammering home basic survival skills. "Most of you think your weapon is your key to survival," Cederberg's friend Corporal Albert MacNeil said. "Well it isn't. And don't laugh when I tell you it's your friggin' shovel. Don't go anywhere without it."[12]

The new brigade had seen some tough fighting during the Gothic Line Battle, particularly in the bloody struggle for Coriano Ridge. But as they formed up for the advance to the Uso, neither of the newly formed battalions could be considered truly combat hardened.

"Two main facts . . . have a large bearing in the employment of this brigade as an infantry brigade," the 12th Brigade's war diarist commented as the orders to advance were issued. First, two of its battalions had only "six weeks training as infantry." This meant the Westminster Regiment "must be saved as much as possible to push through in support of the armour in the event that a break occurs on any part of the front. Obviously all three battalions must be employed in a brigade show and when a hard fight is indicated the Westminster, being the best trained and most experienced, bear the brunt."

In the current task, the idea was "to get ahead fast, bypassing and picketing centres of resistance, leaving [11th Brigade] to mop them up as they catch up to us." Supporting arms for the operation would be provided by tanks of the Lord Strathcona's Horse, artillery of the 14th Field Regiment, the anti-tank guns of the 96th (towed) and 16th (self-propelled) Anti-Tank Batteries, and the engineers of 14th Field Company.[13]

As these forces mustered during the night of September 22, Strathcona's Lieutenant Colonel McAvity attended a final Orders Group held by Brigadier Lind in a barn serving as brigade headquarters. Spirits were running high, the "Promised Land" beckoning. "All of us . . . confidently expected to find open, flat country—and conservative estimates . . . as to the number of days it would take us to reach the Po River did not exceed 12."[14]

ON SEPTEMBER 22, 2ND NEW Zealand Armoured Division had advanced from Rimini up coastal Highway 16. Encountering unexpectedly stiff resistance, its leading troops paused for the night before the Canale Viserba, only a mile north of Rimini. This, however, put the Kiwis on a line roughly parallel with the start point for 12th Canadian Infantry Brigade's planned advance the following morning.

Major General C.E. "Steve" Weir, temporarily commanding the New Zealanders in the absence of Lieutenant General Bernard Freyberg, who had been injured in a plane crash early in September, told Burns that the Germans were "making a rather determined stand" behind the canal. Repeated attempts to win a crossing on September 23 were thrown back. Weir finally abandoned daylight operations with a plan to establish a bridgehead during the night and then renew the advance on September 24.

Leaving the New Zealanders to it, Burns visited 12th Brigade. He was displeased to learn that 4th British Infantry Division's reports that its units in the bridgehead were no longer in contact with the Germans had proven false.[15] As the Princess Louise Dragoon Guards (the Plugs) and the Strathconas entered the bridgehead, they found the infantrymen of 2nd Somerset Light Infantry and supporting tanks of the North Irish Horse "lying 'doggo' under extremely heavy shelling and mortaring, and with enemy infantry only a few hundred yards away."[16]

The Plugs advanced through the battered village of San Giustina. Despite now serving as infantry, they continued to refer to subunits as composed of squadrons and troops rather than companies and platoons. Lieutenant Colonel Bill Darling had two squadrons forward, with 'A' on the right and 'C' to the left. As these squadrons exited the village, they came under intense artillery fire. The advance slowed to a crawl. Back in San Giustina, meanwhile, the remaining Plugs and most of the accompanying supporting arms were subjected to such heavy fire that further forward movement became impossible.[17]

Struggling onward alone, 'A' and 'C' Squadrons crossed a railway track about 250 yards north of the village, only to be immediately pinned down by drenching artillery and mortar fire that included heavy-calibre shells and salvos of Nebelwerfer fire. Several machine guns also opened up from thickets of vines, seldom more than fifty yards apart, that formed boundaries around fields barely exceeding four hundred square yards. Fire also came from two hamlets north of the railway—Casale to the west and the smaller house cluster of Variano to the east. By this time, each forward Plug squadron was being supported by a troop of three Strathcona Shermans, but the dense vegetation hampered visibility. "Olive trees and farm buildings added to the difficulty. It was impossible for the squadron commanders to exercise control in the usual manner with troops supporting one another forward," Strathcona's McAvity reported.[18]

To find and destroy the machine guns raking the infantry, 'C' Squadron's Nos. 1 and 3 Troops crossed the tracks. No. 1 Troop's lead tank, commanded by Lieutenant Edward Ralston, quickly mired in a muddy shell crater. Realizing the tank was a sitting duck, Ralston ordered his men out. Sergeant William John Costello swung his tank around and hooked a cable to the stuck Sherman to pull it free. From out of nowhere, an 88-millimetre shell slammed into Costello's tank. It burst into flame, killing Costello and Trooper Lawrence Stonefish. Corporal E.E. Copper was critically wounded.[19]

Ralston, meanwhile, had taken over command of the troop's third Sherman from Corporal R. Lake, who joined the lieutenant's crew next to the bogged-down tank. A second 88-millimetre shell soon wrecked the stuck tank and badly wounded Lake and Trooper H.E. Davidson. No. 1 Troop reduced to one Sherman, Ralston joined up with No. 3 Troop. German sniper and mortar fire lashed the four tanks, making it impossible for crew commanders to raise their heads out of the turret hatches to search for targets. After a few minutes of this, the four tanks retreated to the protective cover provided by the raised railway.[20] It was 1225 hours, and the advance was stalled.[21]

Bursting out of Casale, 29th Panzer Grenadier Division troops counterattacked the platoon guarding 'C' Squadron's left flank. Seeing the platoon commander was among several men struck by fire, Captain Kenneth William Eagan—an 11th Field Regiment forward observation officer—realized he was unable to direct fire onto the Germans without endangering the platoon. Contacting Darling by wireless, Eagan asked for permission to assume platoon command and extract it from danger. Darling immediately agreed. Running to the platoon, Eagan skilfully organized the withdrawal of its casualties and then led the remaining soldiers to a better position. With the Germans still pressing in, Eagan arrayed the platoon to meet the attack, while also calling in artillery fire that shattered the Panzer Grenadier attack. Eagan's Military Cross citation credited him with "saving the lives of the platoon and destroying many of the enemy opposing it."[22]

The Plugs were so disorganized by now, however, that Darling advised Brigadier Lind that he needed to pause and reorganize. He also reported that Casale and Variano were heavily held strongpoints. The battalion's casualties numbered nine officers and seventy-one men. Lind ordered the Plugs to dig in and stay put.

While this advance had been under way, the Westminster Regiment had crossed the Marecchia and come up behind the Plugs to be ready to take over the lead. Lind decided to have the Westies move a thousand yards east of San Giustina and carry out a wide sweep to the northeast, then hook west over to San Vito and gain a crossing over the Uso. 'A' Company was to lead the advance, with the Strathcona's 'B' Squadron in support. The advance began at 1500 hours.[23]

LEAVING THEIR TRUCKS and Bren carriers behind, 'A' Company was just approaching Highway 9 on foot when it encountered a minefield, which, Lieutenant James Oldfield noted, was "laid, ironically enough, around a walled cemetery." While the tanks of the Lord Strathcona's Horse supporting 'B' Squadron were unable to proceed until a path was cleared, the infantry managed to pass through the field by advancing in single file. When the Bren carrier hauling the company's wireless set tried to follow the same path, it ran over two adjacent Teller mines and "was knocked completely upside down by the terrible concussion." Signaller Private Jim Nichols was killed and the carrier's driver badly wounded.[24]

Westminster Regiment commander Lieutenant Colonel Corbould, meanwhile, requested that the Strathcona's 'A' Squadron hook around the minefield to catch up with his 'A' Company. Starting off at "good speed," Major F.C. Braithwaite's squadron had nearly reached the infantry when its leading troop entered another minefield. All three tanks blew up, and then two more from another troop were disabled a minute later. The rest of the squadron stalled at the minefield's edge.[25] Steel-cased and shaped like a covered cooking pan, the Teller mines in these minefields were detonated by a pressure-activated fuse and loaded with about twelve pounds of explosives.

Night had fallen by the time Lieutenant Jack Cambridge's Westminster anti-tank platoon reached the second minefield to begin the dangerous task of detecting and neutralizing sufficient mines to clear a path for the tanks and other supporting vehicles. Although the area was being heavily shelled, Cambridge hooked a long wire to his carrier and then entered the minefield, the wire pulling up mines as he went. Having lifted at least 100 mines, Cambridge cleared a 400-yard-long lane through which the tanks and anti-tank guns safely passed. Cambridge's actions garnered a Military Cross.[26] Just as he finished the job, the lieutenant was severely wounded by shellfire.[27]

Once through the minefield, 'A' Squadron rolled in single file along the route taken by the Westies—a narrow country road with deep, soft ditches on either side. Two tanks were lost when they edged too close to either roadside and became stuck. This left just eight operational Shermans by the time the Strathcona squadron reached the infantry.[28]

By dawn, having been slowed more by the need to clear lanes through several more minefields than by German resistance, the Westminster's 'A' and 'C' Companies were dug in astride the road about six hundred yards from San Vito. Across the breadth of their frontage, however, it was clear the panzer grenadiers were heavily entrenched, with tanks lurking in the village and hidden among the adjacent vineyards.[29]

Realizing that pushing the Germans back across the Uso was not going to be easy, Brigadier Lind and Major General Hoffmeister had spent the night putting an expanded operation into motion for September 24. On the brigade's left flank, the Princess Louise Dragoon Guards were to clear Variano and Casale and to gain the river immediately west of San Vito. Following the same route taken by the Westies, 1st Light Anti-Aircraft Battalion advanced into a supporting position. Their task was either to pass through the Westies once a river crossing was won at San Vito, or to expand the frontage on one side if a set-piece attack became necessary. The division's reconnaissance regiment, the Governor General's Horse Guards—with bridging equipment and supporting engineers attached—was also to move via the route opened by the Westies and then hook about three thousand yards north of San Vito to effect another Uso River crossing.[30]

During the night, a squadron of Plugs crossed the railway track and occupied Variano without incident. A patrol then tried to creep westward into Casale but was thrown back by heavy small-arms fire. Lieutenant Colonel Darling decided to put in a full squadron attack on the town with tank support at 0600 hours, preceded by a rain of heavy shelling by medium artillery.[31] Lieutenant F.N. Clifford's Shermans of 'C' Squadron's No. 4 Troop supported the Casale attack, with Lieutenant Ralston tagging along in the single tank left from his No. 1 Troop. The force was dogged by heavy shell and mortar fire the entire way. When a heavy-calibre shell or mortar round exploded on top of his Sherman's turret, Ralston was instantly killed. The twenty-four-year-old from Westmount, Quebec, had joined the Strathconas only three weeks earlier.[32]

Pushing on through thickening artillery and mortar fire, the Plugs' 'D' Squadron found that the defending Germans in and around Casale were confined to a few machine-gun positions that the tanks were able to subdue. By 0715, Casale was taken. And yet the Plugs and tankers in its ruins continued to endure heavy shelling.[33]

With all 12th Infantry Brigade battalions and the Strathconas facing heavy shelling and mortaring, progress was slow. Despite Brigadier Lind urging haste, the Westies of 'A' and 'C' Companies were only ready to attack San Vito at 1030 hours. Just as they started moving, the Germans counterattacked with infantry supported by tanks coming from the north, west, and south. Well hidden in the thick vegetation, the German tanks kept their distance while pounding the infantry with high-explosive rounds and sniping at the Strathcona's tanks with armour-piercing shells. When it began to look like the closing infantry were going to overrun the forward positions, the Westies hunkered low in their slit trenches, and the Strathconas let loose with their 50-calibre bow machine guns. The counterattack dissolved quickly, but two of the Shermans were struck by high-velocity shells and started burning.[34] Seeing that either the driver or co-driver was wounded and unable to escape through the front hatch, Westminster snipers Privates Joseph Plecas and Edward Andrew French jumped onto the Sherman to pull the man free. Struck by machine-gun fire, Plecas and French were both killed, and the crewman also perished.

Although the counterattack had been broken, the relentless artillery, mortar, and tank fire ended any thoughts of a successful attack being mounted at San Vito. Seeking better cover, some men took shelter in a farmhouse, which was soon "virtually demolished by a sudden shelling." Sergeant Ed Quamme and Corporal Adam Gillies were killed, while Lieutenants Ross Newton, Pete Skrimshire, and Jack Frisby all suffered wounds.[35]

Using a farm building for shelter also proved Lieutenant Cambridge's undoing. From the cover of a house, the anti-tank gun platoon commander was trying to spot an 88-millimetre gun when its crew detected him first. A shell cracked into the building, and Cambridge was badly cut by flying bricks and mortar.[36]

Because of road obstructions, blown culverts, and minefields, the Westminster stretcher-bearers were unable to get Bren carriers up to evacuate the wounded. In the late afternoon, Medical Officer Ed Wilder and a couple of aides arrived on foot. Setting up an emergency Regimental Aid Post in an old barn, Lieutenant Oldfield noted "how they efficiently administered blood plasma and emergency first-aid in the most unsanitary surroundings." By nightfall, a route had been cleared that enabled Bren carriers to evacuate about twenty casualties.[37]

When the Westminster attack crumbled, Brigadier Lind ordered 1st Light Anti-Aircraft Battalion to hook through to the Uso on the stalled battalion's eastern flank. The Strathcona's No. 4 Troop of 'B' Squadron and three 16th Anti-Tank Battery M-10 self-propelled guns (SPGS) advanced ahead of the leading infantry to clear German machine-gun positions. After eliminating several positions, the armour reached an intersection that marked the attack's halfway point. Suddenly, armour-piercing fire set Lieutenant Bill Guest's and another Sherman on fire. Both crews managed to escape, but both drivers were wounded. Behind the armour, the infantry was pinned down by heavy mortar and machine-gun fire. The arrival of another 'B' Squadron troop failed to tip the balance. As night fell, the infantry dug in, and 'B' Squadron and the M-10s withdrew five hundred yards to a more sheltered area. "It was anything but a quiet or restful night," Lieutenant Colonel McAvity reported. "The squadron had to move to an alternative harbour when two M-10s were hit, one of them caused to burn, by the heavy and accurate shelling that persisted."

Lind ordered a joint effort by the Westies and 1st Light Anti-Aircraft Battalion launched at midnight after an intense artillery barrage. This attack also fizzled out well short of the river because of "an incredible hail of lead from machine guns and mortars . . . As they withdrew to their original positions, the Westminsters were followed by the fanatical enemy, and . . . 'A' Squadron had a long, but fortunately uneventful, 'stand to.' The [Anti-Aircraft Battalion] won their second objective during this action, which they held. Both battalions were by now within 1,000 yards of the Uso."[38] After two days of intense fighting, 12th Infantry Brigade was still well short of the river. During these two attempted advances, German dead were found to be from 1st Fallschirmjäger Division. These elite paratroops were old foes whom the Canadians had first fought in Sicily and then in every major battle thereafter. Intelligence officers at 12th Brigade considered their presence "a good explanation of the severity of the opposition they were encountering."[39]

To the right of 12th Brigade, 'B' Squadron of the Governor General's Horse Guards had spent much of September 24 heavily engaged with the paratroopers and some supporting tanks. As a recce regiment, Horse Guard squadrons were equipped with a mix of Shermans providing firepower, and lighter, faster Stuarts providing speed for reconnaissance. Striking out on the regiment's assigned northeastward line toward the Uso, 'B' Squadron was soon halted, a thousand yards beyond Highway 9, by a dense belt of minefields and a ditch. No. 4 Troop was on point, and its commander's Sherman rolled over while trying to cross the ditch. The troop's two Stuarts were then disabled by mines.

Ordered to press on and turn the flank of the paratroopers, Captain Chas Brown replied that the plan was not feasible because the enemy shelling was too heavy and the ground on that route impassible. 'B' Squadron was fast losing tanks—most of them hitting mines or getting stuck in the increasingly boggy ground. By 1330 hours, it had just six serviceable Shermans and the same number of Stuarts. Approaching a cluster of farmhouses, the Horse Guards caught some paratroopers in the open, and the lead tank killed about six with a burst of machine-gun fire. As the rest fled into the houses, a Panther tank appeared on a road fifty yards away and backed in behind one of the buildings. Troop leader Lieutenant John Munro Murray edged his Sherman forward to situate the Panther in order to call artillery fire down on it. Unsuccessful, he finally just had artillery plaster the buildings in hope of a random hit.

At 1500 hours, the Horse Guards were suddenly confronted by two Panthers firing from positions next to the buildings. As Murray jockeyed to attain a firing angle on one of the Panthers, two rounds punched through his turret. Murray was killed and two of his crew wounded. That finished 'B' Squadron's advance. Brown ordered a withdrawal to a position about 1,500 yards east of San Vito and a mile north of Highway 9.[40]

2

A Frightful Nightmare

D URING THE EARLY morning hours of September 25, the
4th Princess Louise Dragoon Guards' 'D' Squadron sent three
small patrols from Casale toward San Vito. Although each bumped
into Germans outside the village, it was decided that San Vito could
be taken by a full-squadron assault. By 0745 hours, the Plugs had
come up alongside San Vito and the Uso River. A thin trickle of
water ran along its gravel bed.[1] Although resistance had been light,
'D' Squadron commander Captain Robert A. White was wounded in
the chest. Captain Lorne Ogilvie rushed from battalion headquarters
to take over.[2]

Just before dawn, all of 12th Canadian Infantry Brigade was fully
committed. The 1st Light Anti-Aircraft Battalion was on the right,
with two companies in enemy contact and the other two guarding the
brigade's right flank. The Westminster Regiment was in the centre,
with two companies at the road intersection three hundred yards
east of San Vito. The Plugs had 'D' Squadron next to the river, one in
Casale and the other two back in San Giustina.

Deciding the time was ripe to win a river crossing, Brigadier John
Lind ordered the two flanking battalions forward. The Plugs were
to take San Vito, while 1st Light Anti-Aircraft Battalion advanced
to the northeast to gain control of a road paralleling the Uso, which
would serve as a jumping-off point for the crossing. In the centre,

the Westies would sit tight as a reserve. Once the Uso was crossed, they would pass through and lead the way to the Salto River.[3] The Governor General's Horse Guards' 'A' Squadron was to support 1st Light Anti-Aircraft Battalion's left flank squadron.[4] The battalion's right flank squadron would be supported by the Lord Strathcona's Horse's 'B' Squadron, while 'C' Squadron worked with the Plugs.

Just after dawn, two 'B' Squadron troops joined 1st Light Anti-Aircraft Battalion's 'B' Company advance. The going was very slow, owing to mines, craters in the narrow road, and fire from anti-tank guns across the Uso. By 1400 hours, the entire tank squadron had to dismount to work with engineers on clearing mines and rendering the road serviceable, and the advance stalled.[5]

To the right, 'A' Company fared better. By 1030 hours, it had secured a road intersection just short of the river.[6] The Horse Guards' 'A' Squadron left Nos. 1 and 3 Troops to provide fire support for the infantry, while the rest of the squadron turned north to effect its own crossing farther out on the 5th Canadian Armoured Division's right flank. There was "nothing to prevent the squadron from making a rapid advance," the Horse Guards' historian recorded. "There were no mines in the area, so they deployed off the road and advanced northwards; but shortly before 1100 hours they were spotted by the enemy and began to come under fire." No. 4 Troop encountered some German paratroopers and, without slowing, sent them running with machine-gun fire.

But the thickening shellfire from across the Uso led to the squadron stopping to return fire. It was soon determined that the culprit was an SPG being directed by German observers in nearby houses. Because of intervening tall vines, the tankers were unable to identify any targets, until a team—including an accompanying artillery forward observation officer—set up in the top storey of an adjacent building. From this perch, "the whole flat terrain could be easily observed. Artillery was brought down on all houses from which Germans were operating, and the squadron opened up with their own 75-mm main tank guns. By 1130 hours, the target was neutralized and the troops resumed the advance."

The relatively clear sailing ended abruptly as the tanks rolled into a maze of ditches and shell craters. After gaining a few hundred yards, the squadron ground to a standstill before a tangle of ditches no tanks could cross, while the nearby road was too badly cratered for use. Probing about, No. 2 Troop discovered a small stone bridge spanning the largest ditch. Soon Nos. 2 and 4 Troops were hurrying onward. Suddenly, they could see the Uso, but another minefield blocked their way. Although a foot patrol found that the Germans had abandoned the east side of the river, Italian civilians reported them holding the opposite bank in strength. Following the tracks of German tanks, the patrol found a manageable ford. Spotting what appeared to be two paratroop companies covering the ford, however, the patrol withdrew unseen. A minefield also blocked the approach. If the tankers were going to force a crossing, they needed infantry support.

When Lieutenant Colonel Allan Kitchener Jordan advised Major General Bert Hoffmeister of the situation, the divisional commander ordered a Westminster Regiment company to join the Governor General's Horse Guards. After some confusion, with guides from the Horse Guards and Westies failing to locate each other, 'B' Company turned up at about 1715 hours.[7] A probe toward the Uso confirmed that the ford was strongly defended, and the infantry company's commander decided to dig in for the night about a thousand yards back. This left them exposed to heavy machine-gun and mortar fire that dogged the Westies through the night.[8] The Horse Guards harboured nearby. A combined tank-infantry attack would be put in at first light.

WHILE THE TWO Governor General's Horse Guards' 'A' Squadron troops operating on the right flank were advancing toward the Uso River, the remaining squadrons joined 1st Light Anti-Aircraft Battalion's 'C' Company as it advanced from a start point at the crossroads toward the river. By late morning, 'C' Company had patrols over the river. At 1730 hours, both 'C' and 'A' Companies had crossed the river, but the advance stalled 150 to 200 yards beyond it.[9]

A heavy drizzle had started. Sergeant Fred Cederberg expected the battalion's anti-tank platoon to move its guns across a culvert-style bridge that 14th Field Company's engineers had quickly cobbled together. By the time the platoon arrived, however, the Uso had risen rapidly and washed out the bridge. With tanks and anti-tank guns stranded on the shore behind the platoon, Cederberg later wrote, the "menacing German Tigers and heavy machine-gun fire stopped us cold." Just before nightfall, some of the two companies, including Cederberg's platoon, fell back over the river to establish a protective circle around the tanks. German shelling was at first desultory, leading most of Cederberg's men to dig slit trenches that were too shallow. His insistence that they keep digging elicited more grousing than compliance. Suddenly, two 88-millimetre airburst shells "tore the darkness apart, angrily spewing sheets of flame and shrapnel. Then one of the tanks, its hatch open, erupted in a sheet of flame, followed by a series of explosions as its ammo went up. The glare from the burning Sherman lit up the vineyards." The tankers, brewing evening tea nearby, scattered to cover.

One clearly burning tank was sure to lead the Germans to hit hard in hope of knocking out others. Cederberg looked skyward and then shouted, "Dig! Everybody dig like you've never dug before!" Two minutes later, "we cowered in half-finished slits, rolling mud balls with feverish fingers and cursing while exploding 88s marched back and forth, crisscrossing the vines in crazy tic-tac-toe patterns." During lulls, the men dug deeper. When the shells began hammering the area again, they cowered, prayed, and cursed. "Christ," Cederberg mumbled at one point, "there's no escape." As the night went on and the shelling continued, the sergeant was surprised to find himself sleeping through periods of explosions. At times, the 88-gun crews turned the job over to the Nebelwerfers, whose rockets earned the nickname Moaning Minnies, as "they sobbed hysterically" in clusters that "howled and danced through the lines."

Eventually, Cederberg awoke to warm sunlight. The guns had fallen silent. Relieved, he roused his platoon section and sent a man to waken a new recruit apparently still sleeping in a shallow trench next to a haystack. The man, named Norm, bent over, lifted a blanket, and yanked on a foot. "The leg came away in his hand and he nearly went over backwards."

"'My God, come here! The poor bugger's cut in two.' Norm flung the cold, hairy leg back on the blanket," wiping his hands on his trousers. If he had dug just a foot deeper, another man observed, the recruit would have been okay. "Poor, sad bastard!"[10]

Back on the other side of the Uso, the rest of the 'C' and 'A' Companies had spent the night reorganizing. Battalion commander Lieutenant Colonel W.H. "Buck" Buchanan had, meanwhile, ruled against any attempt at a stealthy infiltration because of the strong presence of German troops on both flanks. Buchanan told Brigadier Lind his morning's plan was to mount a deliberate attack with both companies. Lind agreed, insisting Buchanan "make every possible effort to improve the situation by an advance of 300 to 400 yards by first light." To give the infantry some firepower, Buchanan was to ensure that the anti-tank platoon got its guns across. Lind promised full support by engineers attached to the brigade, which would include an armoured bulldozer to carve out ramps on either riverbank. The real estate the battalion had won across the Uso, Lind emphasized, "was essential to further progress."

The brigadier was generally content with how the September 25 push to force the Uso had developed. In the centre, Buchanan's battalion had established a bridgehead—albeit one that would only be secure if deepened. To the left, the Princess Louise Dragoon Guards had encountered ever-lightening resistance.[11] At 1400 hours, a platoon of Plugs in company with Lieutenant A.S. Hutchings's No. 3 Troop of 'C' Squadron had entered the shot-up ruins of San Vito and found the village abandoned except for nine German stragglers, who were taken prisoner. The Lord Strathcona's Horse troop soon engaged and silenced machine-gun positions firing from across the river. By last light, the Plugs had two companies consolidated inside the village. A frantic search for crossing points ensued. Strathcona Lieutenant F.N. Clifford moved alongside the river on foot. The Uso was obviously prone to flooding. Both sides of the fifty-foot-wide river had been dyked, and the banks were up to ten feet high. They were also extremely slippery, and the heavy drizzle steadily worsened the situation. By midnight, however, Clifford had found a spot that might work and soon led No. 4 Troop across.[12] They joined the Plugs' 'B' Squadron, which had crossed thirty minutes earlier.

By dawn of September 26, all four Plug squadrons were over the Uso, and Lieutenant Colonel Bill Darling's tactical headquarters (Tac HQ) was in San Vito. A hard push toward the Salto River—about two miles distant—began. 'D' and 'C' Squadrons led. Progress was again slow, the Germans doggedly fighting from the cover of the vines surrounding each small field.[13] Hutchings's No. 3 Troop was following a narrow road right up with the leading infantry when a Mark IV tank appeared directly ahead at a range of four hundred yards. The German tank snapped off a round that disabled Corporal F. Thiessen's tank. Hutchings immediately punched a 75-millimetre armour-piercing round through the Mark IV's armour, and it burst into flames.[14] By mid-morning, the advance was halted a thousand yards from the Uso.

To the right, meanwhile, 1st Light Anti-Aircraft Battalion had kicked off its deliberate attack at 0435 hours. Because the Uso was running high, the Strathconas were unable to move any tanks across. Although the infantry's anti-tank platoon had been ordered to get its guns forward, the men were able to manhandle only one of them to the other side. With just this six-pounder for support, the lead companies halted about a thousand yards from the Uso and dug in at 1300 hours. The company on the right flank soon reported six German tanks and about forty infantrymen closing on its position. As five of the tanks were reported as being either Tigers or Panthers, the single six-pounder was no match. Buchanan, however, was able to summon medium artillery support. The "first salvo fell right among [the tanks] and we did not see them again," a battalion report stated.[15] Late in the afternoon, the engineers deployed a scissors bridge, and the Strathcona's 'B' Squadron and the rest of the anti-tank platoon crossed over. One 16th Anti-Tank Battery troop had, meanwhile, found its own crossing point and managed to drive three M-10 SPGs through to the infantry.

ALL ACROSS 12TH INFANTRY Brigade's front on September 26, advances still failed to meet the expectations of both Brigadier Lind and Major General Hoffmeister. Right of 1st Light Anti-Aircraft's toehold, the Westminster Regiment had pushed two companies across the river at 1230 hours and then dug in on the opposite bank. When the Governor General's Horse Guards' 'A' Squadron attempted to cross, the Stuart leading the way blew up on a mine while climbing up the cutting on the opposite bank and blocked its further use. Under heavy machine-gun fire, with mortars and artillery also weighing in, engineers from the 5th Canadian Armoured Brigade's Assault Troop laboured to clear the mines. At 1345 hours, 'A' Squadron was able to put one troop across. When the remaining two troops moved to follow, however, "there suddenly occurred an explosion of terrible violence," the Horse Guards' historian wrote. "To observers on the near side of the stream it appeared to lift the entire floor of the gully. Our . . . troop was hopelessly trapped and sustained tragically high casualties with sixteen men killed and five wounded. The whole incident took place with such shattering suddenness that no one will ever know exactly what happened. The survivors were dazed and their theories ranged from trip wires to the idea that it was detonated by enemy observers. It was impossible to discover the exact method by which the calamity was precipitated."

This crossing point would be useless until the Assault Troop engineers could clear the wreckage and thoroughly sweep the area for more mines. At 1400 hours, however, the Westies discovered a workable crossing to the south. The commander of 'A' Squadron nevertheless thought the distance far enough that he might as well wait for the crossing before him to be opened again. But an hour later, with only slow progress made, he changed his mind and asked Lieutenant Colonel Jordan's permission to head for the southern crossing. Jordan refused, having decided to send 'C' Squadron there instead. In the end, the south crossing proved unusable, however, because of mines and the ever-deepening muddy approaches. The Horse Guards finally moved over to the scissors bridge east of San Vito and then back along the riverbank to the originally planned crossing point.[16]

Despite the lack of tank support, the Westies managed some forward progress. Major George Johnson's 'B' Company had crossed the Uso about two thousand yards to the left of the battalion's main force, consisting of 'C' and 'A' Companies. Lieutenant Colonel Gordon Corbould's plan was for 'B' Company and 'C' Company to link up at a road junction about a thousand yards short of the Salto River and then advance together, with 'A' Company following in reserve.[17] While 'B' Company's main body struck out cross-country toward the junction, Corporal Ernest Frederick Dayton led his section of men along the riverbank. They quickly found a series of caves carved into the high bank facing the water. A maze of telephone wires dangled out of them. "Must be an abandoned headquarters," Dayton thought, as he led his men past. Looking back, Dayton was shocked to see Germans emerging stealthily. A close-range firefight erupted. Casting about for a defendable position, Dayton spotted a stout house. The hoped-for shelter, however, proved to be an enemy ammunition dump. Realizing that "sitting on a veritable powder keg of small-arms ammunition and 'potato mashers'" invited disaster, Dayton and his men hastily broke contact with the Germans and rejoined the rest of 'B' Company.[18]

When the link-up at the junction was effected, the Westies were five hundred yards short of the Salto. It was 1630 hours, and all battalions of 12th Brigade were informed that they were to be relieved during the night by 11th Brigade. The four-day struggle to simply gain a shallow bridgehead across the Uso had left the brigade's battalions exhausted, so Major General Hoffmeister decided to bring 11th Brigade into action sooner than planned. This brigade would push on to the Salto and as far beyond as possible.

"Our battalions . . . are very tired as a result of their strenuous and very good work," the 12th Brigade's war diarist reported. But "we do not expect to be out of the line for long this time as the progress at present is slow and very fatiguing, and [11th Brigade] too will need a rest shortly. Furthermore, should the front become more fluid and the chances of a breakthrough greater we expect to be called upon to assist in an armoured thrust by our division."

Although actual close combat had been less fierce than during the Gothic Line Battle, "the unprecedented amount . . . of artillery and self-propelled guns in this sector and the close nature of the ground made every foot gained a difficult and well-earned one." The opposing Germans had been a grab bag from three divisions—1st Fallschirmjäger, 29th Panzer Grenadier, and

20th Luftwaffe Field Division. While the Canadians had taken quite a number of deserters prisoner—particularly from the 20th Luftwaffe—"on the whole the enemy fought well and stubbornly and made the fullest use of every natural feature and all vegetation to conceal himself and so surprise us with hidden anti-tank guns, MGS, snipers, and minefields."

Despite this, the brigade's casualty rate was surprisingly low, with just 30 other ranks from all three battalions killed and 13 officers and 207 other ranks wounded.[19]

As 12th Brigade handed over the forward lines to 11th Brigade's battalions on the night of September 26–27, the supporting Lord Strathcona's Horse also passed the torch to the 8th Princess Louise's New Brunswick Hussars. In a heavy rainstorm, the Strathconas struggled through deepening mud to a seemingly even more mud-soaked harbour on the eastern edge of San Giustina. Lieutenant Colonel Jim McAvity thought "the hectic four days of action . . . had been a frightful nightmare." Earlier thoughts of reaching the Po River in twelve days at most were shredded. "Now, at the end of the fourth day, we had crossed only the first of the score of rivers and ditches between us and the legendary Po. In this veritable jungle, the enemy had fought cleverly, expending lavishly and accurately the ammunition from the dumps built up on his line of withdrawal, and employing small groups of infantry and tanks so sited as to bring murderous cross-fire on our advancing infantry." McAvity no longer believed in mad tank gallops to the Po. He saw nothing ahead but a grim and costly slog.[20]

LIEUTENANT GENERAL TOMMY Burns and 1 Canadian Corps intelligence staff had also recognized that the expected armoured dash to the Po had been based "on a too superficial inspection of the maps and air photos." Now they took a long, hard look at the real topography.[21] What they saw was water. Water that came in almost every imaginable form—rivers, creeks, canals, drainage ditches, swamps, and marshes. Yes, they faced a great plain, but it was one divided into two sectors by the defining waterways. The most northerly sector was entirely dominated by the mighty Po River, fed by tributaries flowing out of both the Alps and the Apennines. With one of the most complex deltas in Europe, the Po boasted at least fourteen river mouths and had a long history of causing devastating floods. As the Po was about a hundred miles north of Rimini, this sector of the plains was of no immediate concern.

It was the southerly sector Burns and his staff now investigated closely. The whole area, they discovered, was a great reclaimed swamp formed by lower courses of numerous rivers flowing out of the northwesterly curving reaches of the Apennines. So many rivers—with the Uso being the first principal one. It was followed by, in order, the Fiumicino, Savio, Ronco, Montone, Lamone, Senio, Santerno, Sillaro, and Idice. Between these rivers ran hundreds of smaller streams, canals, and irrigation ditches. Throughout the Roman and medieval eras, the great swamp had been patiently drained to create cultivable land—but some patches of swamp remained. The soil throughout this region was clay, a fine-grained sediment that compacted when drained. As the ground between rivers sank, high dykes were required to prevent their spilling over the natural banks—especially during heavy rainstorms and spring snowmelt. These dykes had been gapped in many places to divert water into the canals and irrigation ditches. Most of these subsidiary water courses were also dyked and equipped with pumps to control water volumes. Regular pumping was all that kept the lowest lands bordering the sea from returning to swamp.

Clay and military operations go together poorly. In dry weather, marching troops and vehicle convoys stir up thick clouds of choking dust. The Canadians had experienced this throughout most of the Gothic Line Battle. Now, however, they were learning clay's other side. Even a slight shower turned the clay treacherously slick. With the weather certain only to worsen, Burns and his staff realized the ground around them was going to turn into a morass capable of sucking men down to their knees and vehicles to their axles.[22]

Staff at 5th Armoured Division's 12th Infantry Brigade had developed an even more damning appreciation of the new battleground. Although the ground was flat, they reported, "contrary to the prevailing impression, it is not by any manner of means ideal for offensive operations." What roads existed were "bordered by dykes, canals or ditches, seriously restricting movement off them . . . The area is further interspersed with streams and rivers, many of which are wide and deep and have steep banks anywhere up to 25 feet high and which all run straight across our axis of advance, thus forming excellent defensive lines and delaying positions for the enemy. In addition, visibility is strictly limited by thick vegetation. Tank commanders are handicapped as turret-high trees and shrubs hinder observation and operations are difficult to find due to the flatness of the country. Also the ground is liberally strewn with all type of mines.

"In short, the fighting in this region is very difficult."[23]

The unfavourable terrain would not have mattered had the Germans conformed to expectations and withdrawn to a line anchored behind the Po River. In fact, decoded telegram and Enigma transmission intercepts had suggested that following the Gothic Line collapse, the Germans had decided on a retirement to the Alps. The Japanese ambassador in Berlin had advised his government of this by telegram after a September 4 meeting with Hitler and Foreign Minister Joachim von Ribbentrop. This Alpine line, the ambassador's intercepted telegram reported, could be held with small forces and enable transfer of several divisions from the Italian theatre to other battlefronts.

Allied intelligence staff had additional reasons to believe that Commander-in-Chief Southwest Generalfeldmarschall Albert Kesselring was readying for a major withdrawal under the code name Operation Herbstnebel ("autumn mist"). One intercept stated that, should Herbstnebel be initiated, all river-crossing equipment and bridges up to and including the Po were to be destroyed. Seeing such detailed instructions transmitted back and forth by Enigma was assumed to mean that German preparations for such a withdrawal were well advanced.

On September 25, General Harold Alexander's staff received several additional Herbstnebel-related decrypts. These indicated that with Rimini lost, the Allies having crossed the Marecchia River, and the U.S. Fifth Army having broken the Futa Pass fortifications north of Florence, the Germans were incapable of re-establishing a coherent defensive line. Indications that a thinning of strength adjacent to the French–Italian border was under way were also interpreted as an essential preliminary step toward a general withdrawal.[24]

The battering that Kesselring's Tenth Army suffered during the Gothic Line Battle had shaken him. When he agreed to a withdrawal across the Marecchia on September 20, Kesselring had glumly written in his diary, "I have the terrible feeling that the thing is beginning to slide." But LXXVI Panzer Korps commander General der Panzertruppen Traugott Herr, whose divisions were fighting the Canadians before the river, thought withdrawing onto the plain was "no less favourable, as our positions there cannot be seen so well as now, where they are spread out before the eyes of the enemy on the hills."[25]

Little reassured, Kesselring sent a courier carrying the Herbstnebel plan to Berlin along with a request that Hitler approve its implementation. Still, he was uncertain this was the right strategy. "As we had failed to hold the Apennines," he wondered, "should a retirement behind the Po be made now or not until immediately before the Allied offensive, or should the decisive battle be accepted where we now stood more by accident than by choice?" By the time Hitler rejected immediate implementation of Herbstnebel, Kesselring was more relieved than disappointed. The operational plan had been hurried—arising out of an August 30 planning conference at Tenth Army headquarters. "To start it at once," he reflected, "would indeed have been against my deepest conviction—so difficult an operation had to be carefully and calmly thought out and put on paper with an exact time schedule." If need be, Kesselring was certain he could push the matter and win Hitler's assent to it.[26]

For reasons that baffled many of his colleagues, particularly Generalfeldmarschall Gerd von Rundstedt, Kesselring enjoyed a rare immunity from Hitler's interference in his strategic and tactical planning. Instead, as one Canadian intelligence officer put it, Hitler had allowed Kesselring to "fight his battles on sound military lines, giving up ground when he chose to do so, and apparently free to dispose his forces as he saw fit."[27]

The fifty-eight-year-old general habitually exuded an air of cheerful and unfailing optimism that earned him the nickname

Smiling Albert. But he also possessed a steely personal confidence that enabled him to implement operations with an unwavering iron hand. His Allied adversaries conceded that Kesselring's handling of German and Italian forces in the campaign justified his reputation as a brilliant defensive strategist.[28]

With the path ahead uncertain, Kesselring decided to conduct "a kind of 'delaying strategy,'" he later wrote. "I purposely say 'a kind of' because circumstances would have to determine whether the battle assumed the character more of defence or retirement." For now, he hoped the line held by his Tenth and Fourteenth Armies, which stretched across Italy, could be retained until winter arrived with only minimal loss of ground. Significant military operations in northern Italy's winter climate, Kesselring expected, would prevent any significant military action. So the job was to stall the Allies until weather closed the campaign season. In the meantime, the Germans must stop U.S. Fifth Army from thrusting out of the Apennines south of Bologna. Only here, Kesselring reasoned, was there true opportunity for the Allies to decisively punch through his line, because the Americans could then break the seam between his two armies and turn Tenth Army's right flank. If that happened, a hurried retreat to the Po or even the Alps would be necessary. As for the ground east of Bologna, Kesselring felt that if "the enemy attacked and penetrated our line or improved his own positions [there,] it would only be of local importance."[29]

Kesselring's thinking accorded with the strategy he had implemented in Italy from the beginning. Knowing he could not defeat the Allies, Kesselring opted to bleed them through a campaign of slow, carefully controlled actions that maximized the defensive characteristics of Italy's terrain. As the Allies battered their way slowly northward, the Germans used the time gained to create major defensive lines designed to force costly set-piece battles. The Canadians' first experience of this had come in December 1943 in and around Ortona. On the other side of Italy, the much bloodier and protracted battles at Cassino had begun in January 1944 and raged until the liberation of Rome on June 4. The Canadians had waded into that nightmare in May and by the time Rome fell had lost about 800 men killed, 2,500 wounded, and 4,400 hospitalized for sickness and battle exhaustion. But that was a small percentage of the almost 105,000 Allied casualties and estimated German losses of about 80,000.[30]

The Gothic Line had followed, and with its loss Kesselring was left with no major defensive lines. But the watery plain north of Rimini should let him bleed the Allies for an unforeseen duration—even until winter set in.

DESPITE THE STIFF resistance 12th Canadian Infantry Brigade had encountered in forcing a crossing over the Uso River, Lieutenant General Burns still anticipated a major breakout by 5th Canadian Armoured Division and 2nd New Zealand Armoured Division. He believed the Germans were "carrying out a general withdrawal, covered by rearguards." Corps intelligence staff reported "no indication that [they] would make a real stand on any line." Consequently, Burns ordered both divisional commanders "to press their advance night and day in an effort to maintain contact with the enemy main body." His September 27 message instructed that wherever "the general advance is slowed up by river lines, crossings will be made with a force adequate to penetrate deep into the enemy defences in order to ensure maintenance of contact. Where it is NOT possible to get supporting arms across obstacles immediately in rear of assaulting infantry, the infantry must be prepared to push ahead without supporting arms, particularly at night when the value of the enemy's close support weapons is greatly reduced."[31]

As 11th Infantry Brigade, with the tanks of 8th Princess Louise's New Brunswick Hussars in support, relieved 12th Brigade, Irish Regiment of Canada Captain Gordon Wood wrote that they were to support "a tank drive, which it was hoped would send us across the plains in the direction of Forli and Bologna, to meet the [U.S.] Fifth Army who were also making a drive from the western side of the country."[32]

Even as Wood was writing, Irish patrols and those of the adjacent Cape Breton Highlanders reported on the night of September 26–27 that the Salto River before them presented "a definite tank obstacle." Running midway between the Uso and Fiumicino Rivers, the Salto had a u-shaped bed that was twelve to thirty-five feet wide and bordered by partially tree-lined banks ranging in height from four to seven feet.

Shortly after dawn, the brigade's advance was led by the Irish on the left and Cape Breton Highlanders on the right. Each battalion had a squadron of Hussars in support. The Irish objective was to cross the Salto, advance through the village of San Mauro, and then establish a bridgehead across the Fiumicino River. After crossing the Salto, the Highlanders were to ford a couple of narrow intervening creeks—the first named the Vena—and secure a bridge in the village of Fiumicino.[33]

The Irish Regiment's 'B' Company, under Major Bill Armstrong, quickly marched to the Salto. Finding it undefended, Armstrong's men forded the river and led the way toward San Mauro. Halfway to the village, Captain Pat O'Brien's 'A' Company took over the lead and by midday reached the village's outskirts. As O'Brien's men searched the buildings, they came under sniper fire. Anxious to avoid getting tangled up in a house-to-house fight, Brigadier Ian Johnston ordered Lieutenant Colonel Bobby Clark to bypass the village and cross the Fiumicino as soon as possible. O'Brien immediately swung his company past San Mauro's western flank and headed for the river. A few minutes later, "due to a peculiar atmospheric condition in this area," Clark lost wireless contact with the company. 'A' Company was out in the blue.[34]

From the moment the Irish pushed off toward the Salto, they had rapidly outpaced the 8th Hussars' 'C' Squadron. "Beneath the crumbling weight of their tanks," the regiment's historian reported, "the soil was soft and sucking and almost liquid. Across the land, like some vast communication's net, the vines and fruit trees were a web and wall of passive resistance." Major Cliff McEwen reported that the Irish crossed the Salto "and kept on, but for the tanks it wasn't that simple. The stream had risen far beyond its normal size. It was flowing fast and a way had to be made across. We hollered for the bulldozers and the engineers to come up and break down the bank, pushing the earth into the water until there was something we could cross."

Night had fallen by the time 'C' Squadron had two troops and part of McEwen's headquarters troop across. German artillery spotters had targeted the crossing point and it was being so heavily shelled that McEwen ordered the rest of the squadron to pull back. He led the tanks that had crossed the Salto about three hundred yards away from the road in an attempt to elude the spotters. But "all night long they plastered the road and the [ford] and all around them. It was shelling like we'd never seen before."

Hoping to find Armstrong's 'B' Company headquarters, McEwen set out on foot. "It was as dark and terrifying as the most exclusive dungeons of Hell," he wrote. Armstrong was supposed to be on the outskirts of the artillery-ruined San Mauro, so McEwen blundered toward the still smouldering village. Suddenly, a sound like a railway boxcar careening in his direction rent the air. "'Cliffie, this is for you,' McEwen gasped. "I could see a little fold in the ground. I jumped for it but there was a fence and I hit that and then the dirt. That shell picked me clear off the ground and threw me as though I were a toy." McEwen survived that blast and, after dodging more artillery fire, returned to his tanks.

Making another attempt, he and Lieutenant George Pitt finally managed to reach Armstrong's headquarters. "They were in a farmhouse. The shelling was heavy. The place was ripped and battered. They were sitting there trying to figure out how to do a company's job with half enough men. The men were dug in up ahead in the mud towards the river and every so often someone else would be hit. There was an artillery forward observation officer with Bill, and we had some wine." Armstrong's 'B' Company was to advance to the river at midnight and possibly also find the missing 'A' Company. McEwen promised that 'C' Squadron would follow at first light.[35]

To the right of the Irish Regiment, the Cape Breton Highlanders had been badly delayed as engineers struggled to install a Bailey bridge across the now very swollen Uso River. Because the site was under heavy artillery fire, the work was carried out in fits and starts whenever the rate of shelling decreased for a few minutes. When the bridge was finished, at 1300 hours, 'A' Company led the advance and soon left the 8th Hussars' struggling 'B' Squadron well behind. Moving quickly through the cold late-afternoon rain, the Highlanders forded the Salto, found an unblown crossing over the Vena, and were closing on Villa Grappa, about five hundred yards short of the Fiumicino, when they were halted by stiffening sniper and machine-gun fire from the hamlet.[36]

Back at the Salto at about 1800 hours, a bridge was completed that enabled the regiment's Bren carriers bearing the advancing companies' wireless sets to catch up to their respective units. 'B' Squadron also crossed, but its progress was slow owing to the boggy ground and the engineers carefully sweeping the road ahead of them for mines. The best the tankers could promise Highlanders commander Lieutenant Colonel Boyd Somerville was to have a troop alongside each company by early morning.

This was of little help, as Brigadier Johnston had ordered the Irish and Highlanders to cross the Fiumicino that night and establish crossings that the brigade could use for a full-scale advance shortly after dawn. "The day," Johnston reported to Major General Hoffmeister, "had been one of steady progress slowed down by the difficulties of the crossings, the persistency of the enemy's resistance, and the extremely close nature of the country." However, the Irish and the Highlanders were still going forward. The Perth Regiment had come out of reserve and was situated about a half mile east of the Highlanders to broaden the brigade's front.

Left of the Irish, the Princess Louise Dragoon Guards had been retained for the morning under Johnston's command to guard that flank. Their foot patrols up to the Salto had found the area clear of enemy. At 1330 hours, the Plugs were relieved by the Royal Canadian Dragoons, 1st Infantry Division's armoured reconnaissance regiment. The Dragoons entered country so close that it was necessary to frequently dismount from their Daimler Dingo scout cars and Staghound armoured cars to patrol on foot. By late afternoon, however, they had two squadrons across the Salto and consolidated for the night eight hundred yards south of San Mauro. They were well positioned to guard the flank of the Irish Regiment's night push past the village to the Fiumicino.[37]

3

Not a Leader

CREEPING OUT FROM where it had bypassed San Mauro, the Irish Regiment's 'A' Company had continued toward the Fiumicino River on the night of September 27–28. Major Bill Armstrong's 'B' Company was trying to catch up but remained out of contact with Captain Pat O'Brien's men. Armstrong's instructions were to find 'A' Company and either reinforce it or take over the lead if required. Visibility limited by the persistent rain, Armstrong's forward scouts had still not found 'A' Company by dawn. Nor could Armstrong or Lieutenant Colonel Bobby Clark raise O'Brien by wireless, and it was presumed that atmospheric conditions still blocked communications.[1]

In the early hours of September 28, O'Brien's company had waded across the Fiumicino. Leaving a section of men to guard the ford, O'Brien advanced the rest about three hundred yards to secure a road junction. It was not, however, until 0925 hours that the company's location was reported to 12th Canadian Infantry Brigade by a wireless message from the Royal Canadian Dragoons. 'A' Company's position was reportedly under heavy shelling, but the Dragoons added that two troops of 8th Princess Louise's New Brunswick Hussars tanks had reached the Irish position. This claim was quickly denied by the Hussars' 'C' Squadron, which reported all its tanks still one hundred yards short of the Fiumicino and "not across the river."[2]

What the Dragoons had unwittingly seen was 'A' Company being overwhelmed by a superior force of 26th Panzer Division tanks and infantry, which had attacked at about 0830 hours. Soon after the attack began, O'Brien sent a runner, who found Armstrong's 'B' Company just as it reached the Fiumicino. The runner told Armstrong that 'A' Company was "hard pressed by enemy infantry and tanks." Armstrong immediately crossed the river with one platoon. His plan was to establish contact with O'Brien and see what assistance was required. To re-establish communications, Armstrong took along signaller Lieutenant J.J. Asselstine and a more powerful wireless set than the standard infantry company model.[3]

Major Cliff McEwen's 'C' Squadron, meanwhile, was frantically trying to find a way across a river now running "swift and bloated." The nearest bridge had been blown, but enough structure remained that McEwen assumed this was how 'A' Company had got across and then Armstrong and his platoon. He ordered Lieutenant George Pitt's troop to make for the bridge and determine if it might be passable. The troop rolled into a minefield, and Pitt's tank was knocked out. "Its gun suddenly was pointing one way and it was heading another," McEwen wrote. "I put one troop to the left and another to the right to look for a crossing. We were stretched out along the banks, three troops abreast trying to find a way across. There were a lot of vines. On the other side there was a farmhouse and behind it a clump of woods and out of the woods, very suddenly, there came a German self-propelled gun and a Tiger."

The Tiger's appearance was a nasty surprise, because 26th Panzer Division had none in its armoured regiment. But the Germans had two independent heavy tank battalions—Schwere Panzer-Abteilung (S.Pz.-Abt.) 504 and 508—in Italy. The Tigers of the 504th had been scattered among the German divisions holding the line along Highway 9 from the Adriatic to Bologna. To provide the Tiger's excellent tank-killing ability along this entire front, the 504th was never deployed in squadron or troop strength. Rather, its tanks were scattered about as necessary in penny packets. Even more common was to attach only a single Tiger to support the lighter tanks of a Panzer Division. While deployment in this manner violated German armoured doctrine, in the restrictive countryside of the plains a single Tiger—weighing about 54,000 kilograms, with armour up to 120 millimetres thick and mounting an 88-millimetre gun—often proved capable of defeating heavy Allied attacks with deadly efficiency.[4] This was a fact that 'C' Squadron now learned the hard way.

"Lieutenant Dave Gass and Sergeant [Warren] Rosa began to fire at them. You could see them ranging with tracers and then they began to shell. They got the S.P. Stopped it cold. But the Tiger kept on coming. Kept on firing. We were firing at it with shells and even machine-guns but it didn't make much difference. I could hear Gass on the radio: he'd had his suspension cleaned off. I told Rosa to get the crew out. They got out and into Rosa's tank and he took them back.

"Then No. 2 tank of four troop called: they had a casualty. I said, 'Get back.' We'd been hitting the Tiger but it didn't matter. The shells just bounced off, like peas off a wall. We'd never seen anything like that before."

Pitt's No. 4 Troop tank had been disabled by a shell. While his crew scrambled to safety, Pitt contacted McEwen by wireless. "Cover me, Sir, and I'll take a grenade and throw it into her," he offered. "Stay where you are," McEwen snapped.

In another No. 4 Troop tank, Lance Corporal Jim MacGillvray found himself in command while also having to load and fire the gun and operate the wireless because of other crew members suffering wounds. He kept punching 75-millimetre rounds into the Tiger—to no avail. "In one way, we had a grandstand seat," he said later. "Some of us could see the infantry over the river, getting up and then going down again when the shells came. And then we could see them in a helpless position with the Germans around them and the Irish with their hands up, surrendering."[5]

By the time Armstrong's patrol reached the intersection, only nine corpses and one wounded man remained. "The wounded man," 5th Canadian Armoured Division's historical officer wrote later, "had not much to tell except that they had been strongly counterattacked by infantry and tanks and finally overrun." An initial German wireless intercept reported thirty-four Irish taken prisoner, but that number was soon raised to fifty-three.[6] When Armstrong reported his findings to Lieutenant Colonel Clark, he was ordered to pull back across the river.[7]

McEwen's Hussars had lost four tanks before he broke contact with the Tiger by having Lieutenant Len Goucher's troop fire a covering smokescreen. Armstrong's 'B' Company went with them. McEwen thought the Irish were "stricken . . . pale, shaken men and boys." But tankers and infantry soon rallied. Returning to the river, they found the Tiger gone. The damage had been done, McEwen recognized. "If there ever had been an authentic bridgehead across the river, it had perished with the capture of the orphaned company. The river rolled profanely before the tanks, and there was no crossing it . . . Instead, along the twisting banks of this inflated stream, the 5th Division front lurched to a halt."[8]

WHILE THE IRISH REGIMENT was meeting with disaster, 11th Canadian Infantry Brigade's other two battalions had closed on the Fiumicino River to the right. The Cape Breton Highlanders' objective was a bridge in the village of Fiumicino. A half mile to the east, the Perth Regiment was to reach the riverbank. Both battalions were subject to almost continual artillery and mortar fire. Unsure if he could even get a company to the river, Highlanders Lieutenant Colonel Boyd Somerville ordered 'D' Company's Major C.P. MacPherson to first send a patrol through. If it succeeded, the entire company was to follow. Encountering no enemy, the patrol returned at 0650 hours. A tactical air reconnaissance report also advised that the bridge still stood. Somerville immediately ordered 'D' Company "to consolidate along the river and secure the bridge." Shortly after pushing off, the company was stopped by heavy mortar and machine-gun fire. Hoping to break the impasse, Somerville sent 'B' Company forward at 0840 hours and 'A' Company a few minutes later. Soon all three companies were heavily engaged by opposing 29th Panzer Grenadier Division units. "The enemy is certainly trying hard to slow us up. He is also shelling us almost continuously," intelligence officer Captain J.R. Johnston wrote.[9] The advance ground to a halt at 1100 hours, still well short of the Fiumicino.[10]

At 0630 hours, meanwhile, the Perth's 'B' and 'C' Companies had crossed the Salto River and secured a start line for the battalion's

planned drive to the Fiumicino. That day, the four company commanders had been designated Left Out of Battle to give the second-
in-commands leadership experience. So battalion intelligence officer
Lieutenant L. Thompson and the second-in-commands set out on a
recce toward the river. The party was quickly driven back by sniping,
machine-gun fire, and heavy shelling. But the company second-in-
commands mustered their men and pushed forward. The soldiers
trudged through deepening mud created by the increasingly heavy
rain. Despite the opposition the officer recce had encountered, the advancing force reached the river without a fight. As they were digging in,
however, heavy artillery fire resumed. 'A' Company's position was especially hard hit, and second-in-command Captain Franklin B. Kennedy
and a platoon commander, Lieutenant Frederick James Culliton, were
killed. In an attempt to escape the shellfire, an entire 'A' Company platoon crowded into a building that proved to have been booby-trapped.
The ensuing explosion caused heavy casualties that accounted for most
of the Perth's three men killed and twenty-seven wounded that day.[11]

The Fiumicino had swollen into a thirty-foot-wide torrent. As the
regiment's historian noted, "There was nothing to do but dig into the
sticky clay, and sit" under the continuing shelling.[12]

Both Major General Bert Hoffmeister and Brigadier Ian Johnston
had other ideas. At 1600 hours, 11th Brigade's Johnston convened
an Orders Group and told his battalion commanders to force the
Fiumicino that night. The Highlanders had still not reached the village of Fiumicino, but as soon as night fell, 'D' Company pushed
forward and by 2200 hours had secured it. The bridge, however, had
been destroyed sometime that morning.

As the rain worsened after nightfall, Johnston conceded that
conditions were deteriorating so fast that the night attack was impossible.[13] His order cancelling it was particularly welcomed by the
Highlanders, who, Lieutenant Thompson recorded, "did not feel
much enthusiasm for an attack after the past two days' hardship."
Somerville summoned Major MacPherson to his Tac HQ to report on
the situation in Fiumicino. Arriving at 0105 hours on September 29,
MacPherson said his company was in "bad shape due to cold, wet,
and lack of food," but they were settling in as best they could. At

0130 hours, MacPherson walked back to his company through the ever-worsening deluge.[14]

Shortly after dawn on September 29, 1 Canadian Corps commander Lieutenant General Tommy Burns acknowledged that the rain had rendered "conditions impossible for operations in the low-lying country." Bringing the senior officers and staff together at 2nd New Zealand Armoured Division's headquarters later that morning, Burns outlined a planned assault by both the Kiwis and 5th Canadian Armoured Division to get over the Fiumicino. But he admitted "it was obvious these operations would not be able to take place until the ground had dried up."[15] The only road in the corps sector that the rains had not made unusable was the coastal highway. In the New Zealand sector, two brigades were up to the riverbank—the attached 3rd Greek Mountain Brigade and 5th New Zealand Infantry Brigade. As 11th Canadian Infantry Brigade had veered inland toward Fiumicino and San Mauro, a gap of almost two miles existed between the two divisions that required regular patrolling along the riverbank to prevent German incursions. The 1 Canadian Corps front stretched along the east bank of the Fiumicino for about five miles, from the Adriatic to San Mauro. Left of San Mauro, v British Corps had made less progress, with only its 56th Infantry Division keeping pace with the Canadians and reaching the Fiumicino at the town of Savignano on September 27. They found the town and a low ridge just east of the river heavily defended, and their attack that night failed to dislodge the Germans. Finally the rain made further attempts impossible. But as the Canadians had gained the river at San Mauro, the Germans abandoned Savignano and the ridge on the night of September 29–30. This allowed the British to then advance to the Fiumicino.

Farther inland, however, the 46th British Infantry Division and 4th Indian Division met heavy opposition in the Apennine foothills, and progress remained very slow. The expectation was that it would be several days into October before the Germans were forced to cede the ground there and fall back behind the Fiumicino.[16]

Along the Canadian-held front, patrols set out to gather information on enemy positions and locate potential crossings. Perth patrols reported that no vehicles could possibly cross the river without a bridge. They also confirmed two fords that infantry could use. While one ford appeared undefended, the one on the battalion's left flank proved to be guarded by Germans on both sides of the river. Heavy enemy fire drove the Perth patrol away before it could thoroughly inspect this ford. Throughout the day, the Germans continued to heavily shell and mortar the entire battalion position, while machine-gun posts and snipers across the river immediately fired on anybody who strayed into range.[17]

Although the intensity of German fire varied from one battalion to another, the stalled situation 11th Brigade faced along the river-bank was similar across the front. At 0920 hours, Brigadier Johnston advised the battalion commanders that there would be no offensive action until the ground dried, and the current job was to improve defensive positions along the river.[18] Each battalion was supported by an 8th Hussars squadron, with 'C' still backing the Irish, 'B' the Highlanders, and 'A' having joined the Perths.[19] The Hussars, their historian recorded, "sat there, unable to do much more than the odd shoot at houses looming through the murk and the rain across the river. Enemy bazookas [Panzerfausts] struck back and knocked out two tanks. A third had to be evacuated for repairs from the effects of the shellfire. The shellfire was such at times that even when the supply lines brought up hot food and the crews were told it was there, they didn't get out to get it. And in the mud, the farmhouses, the fields, the infantry put their heads down and took it, and the casualties grew."[20]

IN THE EARLY afternoon of September 28, Canada's Minister of National Defence, Colonel J. Layton Ralston, arrived at 1 Canadian Corps headquarters after a two-day trip that included flights from New York to Casablanca and then on to Naples. Ralston advised Lieutenant General Burns that he wanted to visit as many of the troops as possible to gather an informal understanding of problems they faced and whether he could personally do anything to improve conditions for the front-line troops. A Great War veteran, Ralston was particularly keen to visit the Cape Breton Highlanders, who perpetu-ated his old command—the 85th Battalion. After dinner that night, Burns and Ralston discussed the manpower problem. Ralston had been accompanied to the front by Brigadier E.G. Weeks, who commanded the Naples-based Canadian permanent headquarters. Weeks had been crunching casualty-rate numbers and cautioned that if recent trends continued, the reinforcement pool in Italy would run dry by October 10. This might force the Canadians to mirror the British and reduce infantry battalions to three companies. Neither Burns nor Ralston liked that idea.[21]

But Weeks also guessed that the front was about to "become a quiet sector with an active defence," wherein 1 Canadian Corps "will not have many casualties and our reinforcement situation will tend to improve." Less optimistic, Burns argued that the infantry "under his command must be maintained at full [strength], ready to fight as the situation demands."[22]

The "main sore point with the men," Burns said, "was that they knew reinforcements were running low and many of the units were under strength, yet there were many thousands of men called up under the National Resources Mobilization Act [NRMA] who had refused to volunteer for service outside Canada. The general servicemen contemptuously called them 'Zombies.'" In his opinion, "the troops would not feel that the government and the country was supporting them wholeheartedly if, while it possessed the power to send these potential reinforcements overseas by order-in-council, it allowed them to sit safely and comfortably in Canada, seeming to defy the general will."

Over the next two days, Ralston embarked on a whirlwind tour—probing and prodding officers and other ranks alike for information and opinions. Common beefs regarded how few men were granted leave back to Canada after three years of overseas service, problems that led to inconsistency in the policy that a soldier thrice wounded would be returned to Canada, and a shortage of Canadian beer reaching the front lines.[23]

During the morning of September 30, Ralston and Burns travelled to the front lines in an armoured scout car to visit the Highlanders. The day was like those before it, the Germans shelling and mortaring. One supporting tank was knocked out by a shell.[24] Apparently expecting something akin to the front during the Great War, a puzzled

Ralston asked where the communication trenches leading from the rear to the soldiers in the forward trenches were located. Battalion staff quickly explained how the fluidity of this war was not conducive to such permanent construction. As Ralston walked among the soldiers—taking in the sodden conditions and their sparse numbers—"tears ran down his face."[25] Because of the sporadic shelling, which seemed to bother Ralston not at all, Burns was much relieved to get the defence minister back in the armoured car and safely returned to corps headquarters.[26]

Not content to gather information only from Canadians, Ralston met with General Sir Oliver Leese and asked his opinion on one option to resolve the manpower issue. This was to eliminate one of 1st Canadian Infantry Division's brigades and put those men into the reinforcement pool. Leese was aghast. The 1st Division, he told Ralston, "was undoubtedly the best in the Eighth Army . . . could always be relied upon to take on a tough job successfully, and that any reduction in its infantry would be a mistake."[27]

Ralston said nothing to Burns about the tour's effect on his thinking. On October 4, he flew to England and four days later met with Lieutenant General Guy Simonds, acting commander of First Canadian Army, which was then heavily engaged in the Scheldt Estuary Campaign. Although Simonds reported that infantry companies were all short of men due to casualties, he did not think this was impairing "fighting efficiency." But the reinforcement data provided for Northwest Europe added to Ralston's concerns. At current rates of loss, First Canadian Army staff expected that the "pool of infantry reinforcements overseas would soon be empty." The only other source, Ralston knew, was to draw on NRMA men. And in his notes coming out of the meeting with Simonds, he jotted down that it "wouldn't be easy."[28]

Returning to Canada, Ralston initiated a push to force Prime Minister Mackenzie King to send NRMA men overseas for combat service involuntarily. King—realizing such a move would unleash a political storm, especially in Quebec, where memories of the Great War conscription crisis remained strong—had no intention of doing so. Igniting a political crisis, he believed, would more negatively impact the war effort than would the Canadian army's overseas manpower shortage. On November 1, he fired Ralston and replaced him with General Andrew McNaughton, who thought it possible to persuade NRMA men to volunteer. When that strategy fell flat, King would eventually agree to a limited involuntary draft for overseas. But this move came far too late to have any effect on the operations in Italy. The Canadians there would fight on with far too few men to ever bring the infantry battalions up to full strength.

"I AM TO be an Army Group Commander—a Commander in Chief—with a Union Jack!" General Sir Oliver Leese wrote in his diary on September 28. "Starting in India, to Command the British Armies in the final fight against the Japanese . . . It's a wonderful command in war time, and I pray for strength and wisdom and guidance to carry it through." General Harold Alexander "told me this morning on the beach [south of Rimini.] He was so nice about it and said I was the only person."[29]

It was not as simple as that. Chief of the Imperial General Staff Field Marshal Sir Alan Brooke had never thought Leese up to commanding British Eighth Army. He considered Leese's failure to win a decisive victory at the Gothic Line "a serious disappointment" that left an "impression of stickiness and lack of thrust." At Brooke's suggestion, Prime Minister Winston Churchill had agreed to Leese's replacement.[30] Firing an army commander could, however, adversely affect the morale of both the nation and those serving in the army's ranks. So Leese was promoted to a job that gently removed him from combat command to an administrative posting.

Brooke's impressions of Leese stood at complete odds with the reputation he had built since taking over Eighth Army's command from Field Marshal Bernard Montgomery. Harold Macmillan, the British resident minister for the Central Mediterranean, whose job it was to pinch-hit for Churchill when problems arose in Italy, described Leese as "a very popular figure," who conducted the war "like an election campaign." Leese struck him as the epitome of a modern army commander. A "youngish man, in shorts and open shirt, driving his own jeep, and waving and shouting his greetings to the troops, as he edges his way past guns, tanks, trucks, tank carriers, etc., in the crowded and muddy roads, which the enemy may actually be shelling as he drives along."[31]

Major General Chris Vokes of 1st Canadian Infantry Division found the perpetually cheerful Leese "a complete extrovert with a ribald sense of humour. His favourite form of dress was khaki plus-fours, a khaki shirt and a woolen pullover, topped by the red-banded general's hat worn by all general officers in the British Army. At all times he attired himself for personal comfort and never to the regulation pattern."[32] Leese, Vokes later declared, was "the best British General I served under in World War II and they were all good."[33]

After the Liri Valley Campaign, Leese had sent a letter to all Eighth Army ranks commending them for winning such a great victory. Major General Hoffmeister saved the message, adding a marginal note that read, "A very inspiring message from our much loved and respected army commander."[34]

Both Vokes and Hoffmeister preferred the British Eighth Army command style over that of their Canadian superiors. Whereas Canadian army, corps, and divisional commanders tended to assume a top-down approach in which they micromanaged operations, the British generally set out the objective to be attained and some general guidelines they thought should be followed, and then left it to subordinates to shape a final plan and execute it. Leese and the other British commanders Hoffmeister served under "*always* came up to my HQ and together we made a recce of the ground," he said. "The orders were verbal, informal and never firm until my opinions were given and considered." It was an effective system and one Hoffmeister—and to a lesser extent Vokes—utilized in handling their divisions. As one analyst described the system, "From their subordinates, commanders obtained well-considered analyses for each stage of a given operation—the sort of analyses they could not do on their own—and that, in turn, ensured a thorough and proper examination of the tactical problem. It also fostered what Hoffmeister called the 'great mutual confidence' that he enjoyed with British commanders in the Eighth Army. Being a part of the planning process gave Hoffmeister a stake in the plan."

When Hoffmeister put the same practice into action at a divisional level, the results were duplicated. Brigadier Ian Johnston said that when Hoffmeister gave his 11th Brigade a job, "he wouldn't tell me how to do it; he would tell me what had to be done, but he wouldn't tell me what troops to use or anything like that." For his part, Leese held Hoffmeister and Vokes in the same high regard they afforded him. "Hoffmeister," he wrote, "is always in the forefront of the battle . . . he has that inestimable asset, the will to get on at all costs." Vokes also "did very well, with a little direction and an occasional prod."[35]

The two divisional commanders respected each other's abilities and were friends despite having dramatically different personalities. Prone to bluster, possessed of a fiery Irish temper, and vulgar-mouthed, the forty-year-old Vokes always adopted a gruff, no-nonsense approach when addressing the other ranks. "Go in there and kick 'em in the crotch," he liked to say before sending troops into battle. It was a line that always drew a cheer.[36] Having joined the Seaforth Highlanders of Vancouver as a cadet at twelve, the thirty-four-year-old Hoffmeister had worked his way up through the regiment's ranks. In 1939, he held the rank of major and went overseas with command of a company. By October 1942, the Seaforths were his. A year later, Hoffmeister took over 2nd Infantry Brigade from Vokes, who moved up to 1st Infantry Division command and led that formation through the house-to-house Ortona street fight. On March 20, 1944, Hoffmeister was promoted to major general and to command of 5th Canadian Armoured Division. This unique rise from the rank of private gave him an unusual perspective toward the other ranks. Unlike many senior officers, including Vokes, he never talked down to them. Understanding "how soldiers thought and reacted and how they wanted officers to treat them," Hoffmeister was able to draw out the best in each soldier.[37] Before an action, he strove to ensure that everyone in the division understood the job ahead and its importance. His respect for the men was returned in kind, and they took to calling themselves "Hoffy's Mighty Maroon Machine" after their divisional shoulder patches.

There was, however, an increasingly festering weak link in 1 Canadian Corps at the end of September 1944—Lieutenant General Tommy Burns. At forty-seven, Burns was the oldest Canadian active field commander when he took over from Lieutenant General Harry Crerar on March 20, 1944. As he headed off to lead First Canadian Army, Crerar had insisted that Burns succeed him. But although superiors and colleagues recognized Burns's high intelligence and talents as an administrator, they were also aware of his liabilities. One was that he lacked true combat experience. A six-week stint commanding 5th Division just before moving up to corps command didn't really count, as it had been a period of only static operations.[38]

His most serious handicap, however, was his personality. Former minister of national defence Ralston believed that despite his "exceptionally high qualifications," Burns "was not a leader." He was "a difficult man to approach, cold and sarcastic. Will never secure devotion of his followers."[39] He had a sour demeanour, seemed deadly serious about everything, and rarely laughed or smiled. Mocking the British army wireless convention whereby formation and unit commanders were referred to as Sunray, the troops nicknamed him Smiling Sunray.

Rumours and stories soon swirled throughout the corps of "Burns disciplining troops coming out of the line with their battledress jackets unbuttoned" and constantly criticizing "someone or something." The corps mess became a silent, gloomy place, made so by Burns's refusal to engage in light conversation. Hoffmeister, Vokes, and many other senior officers avoided him unless contact was absolutely necessary.

Leese had come out of the Liri Valley Campaign thinking Burns had to go and told General Alexander so on June 28. Alexander concurred, cabling their concerns to Brooke. There is, he said, "no doubt at all that the present position regarding Command is unsatisfactory . . . I am not sure if you know Burns well. He is intelligent and easy to work with but he is sadly lacking in tactical sense and has very little personality and no (repeat no) power of command. It might be possible in time to develop a tactical sense in him but personality and power of command are, as you know, qualities which simply cannot be taught to a man of his age."[40]

Alexander thought the crisis so serious that the corps should be dissolved and the two Canadian divisions absorbed into a British corps. Before Brooke could act on this cable, however, a copy came to the attention of Crerar, who acted quickly and astutely to alert higher Canadian authorities. From Canadian Military Headquarters in London, Major General Kenneth Stuart immediately flew to Italy. Both Vokes and Hoffmeister frankly told Stuart they lacked confidence in Burns. Vokes went further, saying that Burns "seldom appears cheerful and his 'sad sack' manner repels subordinates and senior commanders alike . . . He seems to lack the human touch . . . necessary in the successful command of troops. All the British corps commanders in Italy are cheerful extroverts as part of their stock-in-trade. By comparison General Burns is a drab commander." Despite all this, Vokes promised Stuart he would serve Burns loyally.[41]

Hoping to save Burns, Stuart concocted out of this a sanitized report that the divisional commanders respected his tactical knowledge and decision making and were happy to go into the next operation with him at the helm. Particularly if Stuart counselled Burns to improve his "manner and personality."[42] Neither Alexander nor Leese was able to muster a convincing counter-argument, so Burns survived to lead the corps through the Gothic Line and out onto the plains.

Now it was Leese who was out, while Burns remained in place. Burns was aware of his negative reputation among some of his British superiors, but he thought the 1 Canadian Corps performance during the Gothic Line Battle should lead them to change their minds about him.[43]

On October 1, Leese bade Eighth Army farewell with a personal message distributed through the units. "This message is to say goodbye to you all," it began and reported his being given command of an army group. Eighth Army, he said, had fought its way in nine months from Cassino to Rimini and had now "smashed the Gothic Line and broken out into the Plains." Leese said he handed off to Lieutenant General Richard McCreery "with complete confidence . . . I leave our great Eighth Army . . . with real regret. This Army has, and always will have, a spirit of comradeship all its own. I shall always remember with pride your friendliness and cheerfulness in good times and bad, and the confidence you have placed in me throughout our battles."[44]

Richard "Dick" McCreery was considered by many in the British military to be the last real cavalryman, and it was true he was a passionate horseman. Before this promotion, he had commanded the 'X' British Corps—which served as part of General Mark Clark's U.S. Fifth Army. At forty-six, McCreery was a Great War veteran, who had headed up an armoured brigade in May 1940 through to the British Expeditionary Force's evacuation at Dunkirk. In 1942, he was posted to Cairo as an armoured adviser. Falling into disfavour with General Claude Auchinleck, McCreery had been dismissed in July 1942. Rescued by Alexander, McCreery became his chief of staff and was subsequently given 'X' Corps command. Having led it ashore at Salerno on September 9, 1942, McCreery commanded the corps with distinction through the Gari River, Cassino, and Gothic Line operations.

Alexander believed that the Salerno amphibious landing and hard fighting that followed when the Germans nearly threw the Allies back into the sea typified the kind of challenges McCreery had since faced. Time and again, McCreery had succeeded while working with limited resources, fighting in terrain unsuited to the offence, and having to constantly adjust his tactics. McCreery, Alexander thought, was a scientific general who had masterfully used strategic deceptions to outwit the Germans at the Gari River. Alexander had seen McCreery's work up close when the latter had been his chief of staff during the fighting at Alamein and then the drive to victory in Tunisia. As a result, Alexander believed the new Eighth Army commander had a natural gift for planning and executing offensive actions.[45]

Arriving at his new headquarters, McCreery soon observed in his diary, "Things are very much bogged down and at a standstill at the moment . . . Today we have had [two] inches of rain . . . The Po valley will be an absolute morass, the poor tanks find Italy almost impossible."[46] McCreery was aware of how successful 1 Canadian Corps had been in the Gothic Line Battle, but he had also been apprised of the controversy surrounding Burns. He was quick to note the "decreased esprit de corps and . . . frustration between the division commanders and their superior." He sensed that the corps "was quickly becoming dysfunctional; efficiency suffered, tension was thick, and everyone from the division commanders to the enlisted men appeared uneasy."[47]

[4]

Somewhat Depressing

As NIGHT FELL on September 30, the 11th Canadian Infantry
Brigade troops beside the Fiumicino River had a more concrete
reason for unease than that caused by rumours of friction between
commanding generals. Across the front, German tanks and infantry
were heard moving. In the Irish Regiment's sector, 'D' Company had
only to make a short move eastward along the front to link up with
the Cape Breton Highlanders and "deny the enemy access to our side
of the river," Captain G.S. Horgan recorded in the regiment's war
diary, when several German planes streaked across the pre-dusk sky
and launched a "spectacular air-bombing and strafing" raid. Ending
in seconds, the raid was immediately followed by "intensive shelling
and mortaring all along the front." A flurry of wireless signals warned
the Irish that tanks and infantry had crossed the river at Savignano
and in the Perth Regiment's sector on the brigade's far-left flank.[1]

The 17th Field Regiment was supporting the brigade, and its headquarters was inundated by messages from forward observation officers (FOOS) that a counterattack was under way. Soon several German
aircraft roared over the regiment's position, scattering bombs across
it. While the resulting explosions caused no casualties or damage to
the guns, most phone lines connecting the batteries to headquarters
were severed. As crews rushed to make repairs, all the FOOS were
calling for repeated defensive fire missions. Headquarters' operators

scrambled to "receive and pass on a continuous stream of fire orders" that resulted in sixteen defensive fire tasks being fired. One Uncle Target (both of 5th Canadian Armoured Division's field regiments firing in unison), three Mike Targets (all three 17th Field Regiment batteries firing together), and two single-battery eight-gun fire tasks were also carried out.[2]

In the Irish sector, 17th Field's Major G. Wright called for rapid artillery fire. The battalion's 3-inch mortar platoon also fired continuously, while Bren gunners raked the opposite bank. The unified action created "a wall of bursting shells, bombs, and bullets" across the Irish front. A supporting Saskatoon Light Infantry platoon chimed in with its 4.2-inch mortars, unleashing five hundred rounds in just two hours. Such was the weight of fire that any German threat to the Irish was stopped cold.[3]

The real threat to 11th Brigade's line, however, lay in the still open gap between the Cape Breton Highlanders and the Perth Regiment sectors. Just left of the Perths—in ground secured only by both battalions conducting small patrols—was an undetected footbridge. Crossing in single file, a small German infantry force closed on the Perth lines while heavy shellfire from several SPGs across the river masked its approach.[4]

Both 'A' and 'D' Company positions along the riverbank were hit hard by the shelling. When wireless contact with 'A' Company was lost, the worst was feared. A runner's arrival at battalion headquarters did little to assure Lieutenant Colonel Maurice Andrew that the company had not been overrun, as the soldier "was shell-shocked and unable to give any coherent information."

By midnight, the situation across the brigade front quieted. But it remained unclear whether the Germans were counterattacking. In an attempt to improve its position, 'D' Company sent a section to occupy a building in the gap, which turned out to be booby-trapped. The resulting explosion wounded six men. In the morning, Andrew sent a patrol to 'A' Company's position. The company's commander, Lieutenant George Alvin Gallagher, reported that the supposed counterattack had been overblown. His company had encountered no German infantry. An enemy SPG firing across the river, however, had knocked apart the house occupied by his leading platoon.[5] The platoon had suffered six casualties.[6] Intelligence staff at 5th Division headquarters decided that just a handful of Germans had actually crossed the river, only to be scared off by the rapidity and scale of the Canadian artillery response.[7]

The German air attack and shelling binge of September 30, however, left 11th Brigade unsettled. Even its headquarters in a sprawling villa well away from the front had been strafed, a bomb narrowly missing the building. At noon, a barrage of shellfire wounded three men. The salvo damaged several vehicles, four reduced to burning wrecks. One round also started a fire in the villa.[8]

Morning of October 1 found 11th Brigade's infantrymen weary, wet, and dispirited. Yet they were still expected by 1 Canadian Corps to win a bridgehead over the Fiumicino the following day and advance two miles to a drainage canal called the Scolo Rigossa.[9] Because of the high casualty rate suffered when 'A' Company had been overrun and mostly captured on September 28, the Irish Regiment was withdrawn a mile from the front and replaced by 12th Canadian Infantry Brigade's 1st Light Anti-Aircraft Battalion. Out of the line, Irish Regiment Captain Horgan wrote, "the companies were able to get the men under cover, which was pleasant after the last few days. The day was spent in cleaning up and arrangements were made to bring up the men's small packs, blankets and hot meals." 'A' Company was also rebuilt with a draft of reinforcements under command of Captain D.A. Smith.[10]

At 1100 hours, Major General Bert Hoffmeister met Brigadier Ian Johnston at 11th Brigade headquarters.[11] As the rain had ceased, he reported that the division's engineers were now improving the road leading to the river and starting to remove mines along the bank. Although the soft ground meant difficult going for the tanks, Hoffmeister's staff believed "the prospects of the ground drying out enough by the evening of [October 2] seemed good," and the attack was consequently set for 2000 hours that evening.

The night of October 1–2, however, brought heavy rain that eclipsed that of the last days of September. Scrapping the attack, Hoffmeister decided to use the enforced postponement to relieve all of 11th Brigade.[12]

On the division's left front and holding the line between Savignano and San Mauro were the Royal Canadian Dragoons, whose war diarist summed up the situation. 'B' Squadron was right up on the river with the rest of the regiment deployed farther back. As the day progressed, 'B' Squadron's armoured cars soon could no longer move without getting stuck. The squadron "ceased pretending to be employed and bowed its head, with impatient misery, to the torrents of water which fell. The remainder of the regiment did likewise."[13]

Still hoping 11th Brigade would be able to launch an attack in a few days, Lieutenant General Tommy Burns ordered 5th Division's lines shortened to concentrate its strength. Accordingly, he had 2nd New Zealand Armoured Division shift leftward to take over the ground held by the Perth Regiment. At 2030 hours, the 5th New Zealand Infantry Brigade's 22nd Battalion entered the Perth perimeter, and by 2330 hours the handover was complete.[14] In the brigade centre, the 4th Princess Louise Dragoon Guards finished relieving the Cape Breton Highlanders at 2335 hours. Both reliefs went smoothly—the continuing deluge having apparently dampened German enthusiasm for shelling and mortaring across the river.[15]

Mud had presented its own problems. When the Plugs had approached their trucks parked in open fields, they found them sunk so deeply in muck that tow trucks were required to pull them free. The Plugs consequently marched through the deluge on foot to relieve the Highlanders.[16]

Despite a few brief lulls that raised spirits, which were quickly dashed, the rain was largely unrelenting. Beside the river, the Royal Canadian Dragoons "sank deeper and deeper into the mud" on October 3. The following day, they were "enduring the rain in idleness, thinking hard thoughts of the oncoming winter." Two days later, the "rain continued, the mud grew deeper." A German shell scored a direct hit on a Daimler scout car and "produced remarkable results on the vehicle—results which gave some concern to those who had previously considered the vehicle proof against even direct hits by light calibre high-explosives." By October 8, the war diarist reported, the heavy rain was producing "heavier despair."

October 9 saw "the military situation . . . satisfactory only to the German Command, and the weather to neither side . . . In each sector, plans of attack, cancellations of the plans, reliefs, concentrations, dispersals of the troops took place with bewildering rapidity."[17]

Earlier, on October 5, 11th Brigade had relieved 12th Brigade of the front line to the right of the Dragoons in order to prepare for another planned attack. Two battalions were stationed on the river—the Irish Regiment on the right and Cape Breton Highlanders on the left. The Perth Regiment was in reserve.

BRITISH EIGHTH ARMY commander Lieutenant General Richard McCreery had been champing at the bit since assuming command on October 1, but the rain kept washing away each offensive plan. McCreery wanted to decisively break the German hold on the Fiumicino River and drive them back behind the Scolo Rigossa. To do so, he envisioned a two-corps attack, with 1 Canadian Corps busting across the Fiumicino to gain the canal, while v British Corps to the west would clear the ground south of Highway 9 and then cross the Fiumicino to secure the town of Gatteo.

Both 2nd New Zealand Armoured Division and 5th Canadian Armoured Division were to lead the 1 Canadian Corps advance. The Kiwis would be responsible for a front extending from just west of the village of Sant' Angelo to the sea, while 5th Division crossed the Fiumicino immediately to the southwest. A three-phased attack, the first would win a bridgehead over the Fiumicino, the second establish crossings of the Rigossa, and the third advance north beyond the canal.

McCreery had set the attack for the night of October 6–7. But the ground was so mucky "that cross-country movement" was "practically impossible." Pushing things back a night achieved little for 1 Canadian Corps, as the rain in its sector was so heavy that any movement was hopeless. Operating in the rugged Apennine foothills, v Corps fared better, with its 10th Indian Division on the far left crossing the Fiumicino and capturing the 1,600-foot Mount Farneto. In the v Corps centre, 46th British Infantry Division also managed to cross the river next to Montilgallo. Capitalizing on this success,

McCreery shifted the 43rd Independent Gurkha Infantry Brigade from 56th British Infantry Division to reinforce the 10th Indian Division. This left the 56th Division on the 1 Canadian Corps's left too weak to support its operations.

McCreery breathing down his neck, Lieutenant General Burns knew some advance—even a limited one—had to be made. So he teed up an attack for the night of October 8–9 whereby the Kiwis would cross the Fiumicino and advance 1,500 yards to the Rio Baldona, which paralleled the Scolo Rigossa a short distance to its front. In the Canadian sector, 11th Brigade was to win a bridgehead extending from Sant' Angelo on the Kiwis' left flank west to about a thousand yards short of San Mauro. Directly west of San Mauro, meanwhile, 12th Brigade would establish a "shallow bridgehead" over the Fiumicino. This done, the corps would force the crossing over the Rigossa the following night.

Even this modified plan, however, had to be scuttled early on October 8, when "excessively heavy rain during the night and day made it absolutely impossible to carry out the planned attack." Exasperated, Burns convened a meeting at 5th Division headquarters. Major General Hoffmeister and his divisional artillery commander Brigadier H.A. Sparling, 1st Canadian Infantry Division's Major General Chris Vokes, and 2nd New Zealand Armoured Division's Major General Steve Weir and his divisional artillery commander all attended.[18]

"All divisional commanders," Burns recorded in his diary afterward, "pointed out the very bad going, and expressed the opinion that we might be drifting into the carrying on of an offensive in similar conditions to those of last autumn and winter, where the hard fighting and numerous casualties resulted in no great gain." He had icily retorted "that the general situation required the offensive action of this corps, and that other troops in Italy and on the Western Front were attacking despite bad weather conditions and mud."[19] Having delivered this rebuke, Burns nevertheless agreed to ask McCreery to postpone the attack for forty-eight hours.[20]

McCreery accepted the proposal, but only because it fit a new plan he had devised on October 7. He had decided to capitalize on the gains won by v Corps by shifting the weight of Eighth Army left. With 1 Canadian Corps mired in the muddy plains, McCreery realized that the Apennine foothills provided more stable ground for offensive operations. But v Corps was in rough shape. Its 56th Infantry Division had suffered heavy casualties reaching the Fiumicino and needed to be withdrawn to reorganize. Then the 78th British Infantry Division had been pulled by General Harold Alexander on October 2 and sent to bolster U.S. Fifth Army. For his plan to work, McCreery needed to concentrate what v Corps strength remained.

On the afternoon of October 8, shortly after Burns met his divisional commanders and heard their complaints, McCreery appeared at 1 Canadian Corps headquarters. Burns, he said, must extend his front to the left to about one thousand yards south of Highway 9. This would necessitate 1st Canadian Infantry Division relieving the beleaguered 56th Division, which could then form the army's reserve.

McCreery's sights were set on the town of Cesena, just where Highway 9 ceased to border the Apennine foothills and struck out into open country toward Bologna. The Savio River flowed past Cesena to the west, and McCreery intended to cross the river on the town's outskirts.

On October 9, Burns ordered McCreery's plan for the Canadians put into effect. The corps was to take over the sector held by 56th Division and on the night of October 11–12 establish a bridgehead over the Fiumicino to enable an advance up Highway 9 toward Bologna. The 56th Division would hold in place until 1st Canadian Infantry Division's leading brigade relieved it. At the same time, 2nd New Zealand Armoured Division would thin out from its existing front to pass through 5th Canadian Armoured Division and then advance across the Fiumicino on a line north of the Rimini–Bologna railway, which closely paralleled Highway 9. Once the Germans had been pushed back from 5th Division's front, the division would pass into corps reserve.

McCreery's general idea for 1 Canadian Corps was that 1st Division, with the New Zealanders providing a strong flank guard in the sodden plain to the right, would advance along Highway 9. The coastal section abandoned by the Kiwis would be screened by an ad hoc unit dubbed Cumberland Force because it was to be commanded by 5th Canadian Armoured Brigade's Brigadier Ian Cumberland.[21]

"Cumberland Force," wrote Brigadier Cumberland, "was one of those set-ups so peculiar to the Eighth Army. A mixed force holding a wide front which, while the most important sector to the troops fighting on it, was not very vital to the Army plan." Deployed in the late morning of October 10, Cumberland Force was responsible for guarding a front stretching along the Fiumicino for four miles to where it spilled into the Adriatic. The coastal sector was primarily held by 3rd Greek Mountain Brigade. The Greeks were strengthened by a New Zealand tank squadron and two troops from an anti-tank battery, as well as some Canadian anti-tank batteries. In the centre was a subunit dubbed Wilder Force—a group of New Zealand armour and artillery units serving as infantry. On the left flank, the Royal Canadian Dragoons had also dismounted to guard the river frontage there. Cumberland grouped the Dragoons under command of the armoured car regiment's Lieutenant Colonel Keith Landell.[22]

"WE ARE TO go into the line to relieve 5 Cdn Armd Div who with the soft and boggy ground are hopelessly mudded down," 1st Canadian Infantry Division's war diarist wrote on October 10. "Our lads greeted the prospects with mixed feelings, our rest period had been most enjoyable and the thought of action again, particularly in the type of weather we shall meet, is somewhat depressing."

The "torrential downpour" that morning did little to lift spirits.[23] When Lieutenant General Burns appeared at 5th Canadian Armoured Division headquarters to coordinate its operations with 1st Division, he was struck by how the heavy rains had "water-logged" the surrounding countryside. The situation was so bad, Burns decided that "at least two clear, fine days would be necessary before the ground [might] sufficiently dry for infantry and tanks to operate."

Returning to corps headquarters, Burns met with McCreery. With V Corps experiencing "relatively better going," McCreery wanted 1 Canadian Corps to only "adopt a follow-up role, opening up Route 9 and, if the weather improved, put in a secondary attack on the German positions." This meant the corps was "merely to keep pace with any enemy withdrawal, maintaining contact at all times," rather than attempt a breakout.[24]

By 2200 hours on October 10, 5th Division had withdrawn to reserve positions—except for the Princess Louise Dragoon Guards and the division's units assigned to Cumberland Force. The Plugs relieved the Irish Regiment during the night and were attached to 5th New Zealand Infantry Brigade, which was to guard the right flank of 1st Canadian Infantry Division's push across the Fiumicino River. The 46th British Infantry Division of v Corps would be operating on the Canadian left.[25]

Because of the sodden ground in the Canadian sector, the only viable part of the plain for operations was bounded by the railway running past the north side of Savignano to a point one thousand yards south of Highway 9.[26] The breadth of this two-thousand-yard-wide front would barely change until the Pisciatello River—six miles distant—was gained. Major General Vokes decided there was only room for his 1st Brigade to carry the advance to the Pisciatello. Thereafter, the next mile and a half offered a wider front, and he would have 2nd Brigade take the right with 3rd Brigade to its left to reach the Savio River at Cesena. While 1st Brigade would be supported by the Lord Strathcona's Horse drawn from 5th Division, a regiment from the British 21st Tank Brigade would assist the two-brigade advance.[27]

Once Vokes passed his plan to 1st Brigade, Brigadier Allan Calder assembled all its officers and non-commissioned officers at his headquarters for a briefing. Determined to stamp out any grousing about the return to action, Calder stressed the "necessity of maintaining enthusiasm at [a] high pitch." This message was to be rammed home at the battalion level.[28]

Calder's battalion commanders faced an uphill battle on the enthusiasm front. "The 48th Highlanders were as glum as the gray glower of the Adriatic sky when their [trucks] carried them down to ... the flatlands in the depressing drizzle of October 10," the regimental historian recorded.[29] Morale was even lower among the Hastings and Prince Edward Regiment (Hasty Ps), tasked with the main advance up the highway. Battalion intelligence officer Lieutenant Farley Mowat ruefully noted that there was "growing disillusionment with all authority that lay immediately beyond the boundaries of the Regiment."[30]

Rather than engage in pep talks, the battalion commanders focused on getting the men prepared for the job ahead. Already the plan was changing, but this time due to positive developments. On October 10, the British 44th Reconnaissance Regiment that the Hasty Ps were to relieve had pushed a squadron across the Fiumicino. Although the Germans were still heavily mortaring and shelling Savignano and other positions south of the river, the squadron met only light contact with the enemy. The 44th commander's reports to 56th Infantry Division's headquarters were so encouraging that an effort to bridge the river was put into play for that night.[31]

On receiving this news, Calder decided to throw caution to the wind. Instead of conducting a phased relief of 56th Division, the brigade would pass through it to bring all battalions up alongside the Fiumicino. If no Germans were met there, the Hasty Ps would cross the bridge and advance alone until they met serious resistance. As the ground was considered still too muddy for tanks, the battalion would go it alone.[32]

The morning of October 11 dawned fair and cool, an auspicious start to the operation. By 0930 hours, the Hasty Ps were over the British bridge and within a half hour had established a two-thousand-yard-deep bridgehead. Two companies were forward, with 'B' Company off the road near the rail tracks and 'A' Company up to where Highway 9 intersected a road running to the northeast. Only one 'B' Company patrol encountered any Germans when it entered some farm buildings. A short firefight ended quickly, with four Germans dead and an equal number taken prisoner for no loss.

It was 1100 hours, and Calder pushed Lieutenant Colonel Don Cameron to keep the Hasty Ps moving until they met some serious opposition. Cameron had come to the regiment as a replacement during the fighting around Ortona in 1943 and on April 9, 1944, had been promoted to regimental command. Well respected, he was considered an officer who would not take unnecessary risks. This advance entailed more risk than Cameron would have liked. Lacking tank support, the battalion "was solely dependent upon its own resources," with both flanks entirely exposed. Cameron suspected that contact with the Germans would come when the Hasty Ps reached either the Scolo Rigossa or the Pisciatello. Both were a long way off, so Cameron decided to pass his companies forward one by one. The moment one company reached a designated point, it would send patrols out on the flanks, while the next company leaped forward. Cameron's Tac HQ, in two vehicles loaded with wireless equipment, was tucked in close to the rear of the advancing companies. He had an artillery FOO team and the battalion's 3-inch mortar platoon with him. A wireless team from the mortar platoon switched from one leading company to the next, ready to call in fire as needed.

From the foothills to the left and, likely, from the village of Gambettola to the right, Cameron suspected they were under German observation—a suspicion confirmed by the increasing weight of shelling thrown their way. Three men were hit. One, thirty-two-year-old Private George David Caswell, died. 'B' Company had just passed through 'C' Company and was entering a cluster of buildings immediately south of the Rigossa when it met the first serious resistance. "A fierce fight ensued" before the enemy withdrew. They left behind several dead and another four men taken prisoner. As the Germans pulled back, they blew a culvert to block the road. The Hasty Ps also saw ahead four "formidable" roadblocks. Each had been booby-trapped. The battalion's pioneer platoon rushed forward to defuse the explosive charges. It was 1600 hours. 'D' Company edged around the roadblocks to gain the Fiumicino while the pioneers did their work. Reaching a badly damaged stone bridge, the company commander reported that a serious weight of small-arms fire from buildings about two hundred yards behind the canal's opposite bank indicated that considerable German forces lay ahead.[33] 'A' Company, meanwhile, had slipped off south of the road in another attempt to reach the Rigossa. Two hundred yards short of the canal and with night falling, it was driven to ground by "small-arms fire and a blistering fall of shells and mortar bombs."[34] Cameron halted the advance, intending to try pushing across the Rigossa in the morning. The battalion had suffered only five casualties, Caswell being the one fatality.

During the night, 'B' Company sent a couple of patrols across the Fiumicino, which were both driven back immediately by heavy fire from nearby buildings.[35]

ALTHOUGH THE HASTY PS had advanced well out on 1st Brigade's point, they had not crossed the Fiumicino River entirely alone. In the late morning, the 48th Highlanders of Canada had also passed into the bridgehead and advanced to the left. Aware that the Canadians were across the river, the Germans heavily shelled and mortared the bridgehead. Shortly after Lieutenant Colonel Don Mackenzie established his Tac HQ inside it, the area was subjected to heavy fire that killed one man, wounded six others, and destroyed one of the battalion's anti-tank guns.[36]

The 48th's advance followed a line about a half mile south of, and parallel to, Highway 9. Fighting their way through tangled vineyards, the leading companies utilized Mackenzie's favoured tactical method, which he called "winkling." During an Orders Group the day before, Mackenzie had reinforced the men's understanding of how winkling worked. "We must abide strictly to the principle of one foot on the ground, and advance almost as a drill. The scouts will recce; then one platoon forward, then up the company. Then we'll play leap-frog."[37] And so they did. When one company reached an assigned point, it was joined by another, and both sent out patrols. Once the flanks were found clear, another company passed through to the next point.

Major D.B. Deeks's 'C' Company was advancing with scouts forward when a German machine gun was detected guarding a roadblock thrown across a muddy track that ran out of the mountains to Highway 9. The lead platoon quickly moved up, surrounded the startled gun crew, and took all five Germans—identified as from 90th Panzer Grenadier Division—prisoner. This was the only contact the 48th Highlanders encountered. With only "very vague" reports of where the 46th British Infantry Division's nearest units to his left flank were located, Mackenzie had his company commanders move warily forward for fear of blundering into friendly forces or Germans lying in ambush. Neither situation occurred. By nightfall,

'B' Company had reached a point about two and a half miles out from Savignano.[38]

Whatever contact the Hasty Ps and 48th Highlanders had with the enemy on October 11 provided 1 Canadian Corps intelligence staff with a better picture of the opposition. It helped explain the thickening nature of the artillery and mortar fire that the Hasty Ps and the bridgehead were experiencing. Beyond the railway and on the north bank of the Scolo Rigossa, the small manufacturing town of Gambettola was believed to be held by 26th Panzer Division's 9th Panzer Grenadier Regiment. On the side of the railway facing the Hasty Ps, the immediate adversary was confirmed as a battalion of 361st Panzer Grenadier Regiment from 90th Panzer Grenadier Division. In an ideal world, the New Zealanders, operating on the Canadian right, would have cleared Gambettola soon after the Hasty Ps reached the river. But they had been halted in front of a strong outpost inside the village of Sant' Angelo and were now two and a half miles back.[39]

The lagging Kiwis caused Brigadier Calder sufficient concern that he ordered the Royal Canadian Regiment out of reserve. Two of the battalion's companies crossed to the north side of the railway, while the other two pushed out from the bridgehead on a line between the tracks and Highway 9. The RCR task was to protect the Hasty Ps' right flank. Until the New Zealanders caught up, 1st Brigade must take care of itself.

How exposed the brigade was to German artillery observers was immediately made clear when 'B' Company came under heavy shelling as it crossed the railway. Two men were wounded before Captain Len Courtin could get the men dug in. Courtin had felt ill all day and at 1600 hours agreed to be evacuated to hospital. The diagnosis was a recurring bout of malaria. Captain E.M. Hills took over.

As had the Hasty Ps and 48th Highlanders, the RCR continued to be shelled well into the night. The companies dug in deep, while Lieutenant Colonel Jim Ritchie's Tac HQ took shelter "in a stout building in the centre" of Savignano.[40]

During the night, a 1st Field Company engineering officer appeared at Lieutenant Colonel Cameron's Tac HQ to report that in the

morning his men would take over from the Hasty Ps pioneers the job
of clearing the roadblocks off Highway 9 and also deploy an Ark MK
II bridge across the Rigossa. The Ark MK II was a bridging system
designed and built by British engineers in Italy. Replacing the turret
of a Churchill tank with steel decking and then attaching fifteen-
foot-long front and rear ramps made from American steel-treaded
pontoon bridge components, the system offered a quick way to create
crossings over relatively narrow rivers or canals. The tank would be
driven into the river, the ramps dropped, and the bridge would be
ready to go.

While the 1st Field Company officer was talking with Cameron,
two others had been investigating the possibility of deploying a
second Ark across the Rio Baldona—a small drainage canal about a
mile east of the Rigossa. Approaching the canal just after midnight,
Lieutenant William Archibald Reid was wounded in the abdomen.
Racing to the nearest dressing station, the driver of their armoured
reconnaissance vehicle took a wrong turn and plunged into a gap
left by a blown bridge. The driver survived the crash, but Reid and
Lieutenant John Albert MacDonald were both killed.[41]

GIVEN THE FIRE thrown at the Hasty Ps from the other bank of
the Scolo Rigossa, Lieutenant Colonel Cameron realized that the
Germans considered the canal an important defensive obstacle. They
also still had significant strength south of the Rigossa concentrated in two building clusters opposite Gambettola. Deciding these
Germans needed to be dealt with, Cameron teed up artillery to cover
an attack by 'D' Company. At the same time, 'A' Company was to hook
back onto Highway 9 and establish a bridgehead across the Rigossa.
At 0930 hours on October 12, Lieutenant Don Kennedy's No. 16
Platoon led 'D' Company's advance, with both the battalion's 3-inch
mortars and supporting artillery firing high-explosive and smoke
rounds to provide protective cover. 'D' Company was soon embroiled
in a stiff house-to-house fight, each building having to be taken in
turn. The battle raged through the entire morning. At its end, twenty
Germans were either dead or wounded. Several more surrendered.[42]
'A' Company, meanwhile, had waded across the swollen Rigossa. After

silencing two German defensive posts on the riverbank, the company dug in under heavy artillery and mortar fire. Although a narrow bridgehead was won, the relentless German bombardment made further expansion impossible.[43] What the Hasty Ps needed were supporting tanks, but that required a bridge.

Behind and to the left of the Hasty Ps, the 48th Highlanders experienced a day of confusion. After crossing the Rio Baldona, the lead companies were caught in an exchange of small-arms fire with an undetermined number of Germans at 1130 hours. As the volume of enemy fire increased, Lieutenant Colonel Mackenzie decided to clear the Germans off with a one-company attack, supported by the battalion's 3-inch mortars, that would go in at 1800 hours. At 1700 hours, while he was teeing this up with Major Deeks of 'B' Company, a signal arrived advising that 46th British Infantry Division was putting in a major assault to the 48th's left with support provided by 1st Canadian Infantry Division's artillery. To thicken this support, Mackenzie was ordered to add his 3-inch mortars to the mix. Thirty minutes later this order was rescinded, but the artillery appeared to still be committed to helping the British. Not knowing when he could get artillery support for his own attack, Mackenzie pushed it back an hour.

'B' Company's plan was to attack two closely grouped German positions, with each assigned to one of two platoons, while a third platoon provided covering fire. As the two attacking platoons moved from their forming-up points, 'C' Company was to replace them in order to maintain control over the ground the 48th had already won. When Mackenzie's order to push the attack back an hour failed to be communicated to the two platoon leaders, they headed out as earlier scheduled. It was 1835 hours when Deeks reported that his two platoons were leaving for their objectives and the start point was unprotected. A 'C' Company platoon was immediately dispatched to secure the abandoned ground.

The situation went from bad to worse in minutes, as German infantry jumped 'B' Company, causing its platoons to scatter toward the main 48th position. Arriving at the 'B' Company start point at about 1845 hours, the 'C' Company platoon found it already occupied by the enemy. When the platoon leader reported being greeted by

heavy machine-gun and mortar fire, Major F.G. MacLaren ordered it
to fall back to rejoin the company's main body. He then established a
firm defensive base into which 'B' Company's scattered platoons retreated. After Deeks reorganized his men, 'B' Company attacked the
Germans holding their start position and retook it at 0100 hours on
October 13. Retrieving the situation caused by faulty communications
had cost the 48th seven hours.[44]

During the afternoon of October 12, meanwhile, 1st Field
Company had managed to clear the roadblocks and start bridging
the Rigossa. It was late evening before the demolition booby traps had
been removed from the last roadblock. Like the other three, this roadblock had been constructed by piling together wine barrels filled with
stones, fallen trees, farm carts, and concrete blocks. As an armoured
bulldozer moved in to dismantle the obstacle, its operator found the
dark and restricted vantage from his seat made doing the job impossible. Although the bulldozer was drawing intense German artillery
fire and also small-arms fire from across the river, Lieutenant Victor
Alexander Moore jumped onto the vehicle. Standing outside of the
protective cage surrounding the driver, Moore provided directions.
At times, he hopped down from the bulldozer and walked alongside
it to direct the driver in removing a specific part of the roadblock. It
took three hours to finally disassemble the obstacle and open the way
for the Ark bridge's move to the river. Moore's courage garnered a
Military Cross.[45]

The Ark soon entered the Rigossa. In the darkness, however,
the engineers had misjudged the width and depth of the stream.
As the Ark struck bottom, it sank into the mud and overturned. A
second bridge was sent for, but until it arrived, the two troops of
Lord Strathcona's Horse's 'A' Squadron tasked with supporting the
Hasty Ps were unable to cross.[46] Hopes of any major advance by
1st Brigade on October 12 fizzled.

5

Wholehearted Co-operation

ON THE MORNING of October 12, Irish Regiment Padre David Rowland visited the site where 'A' Company had been over-run on September 28. He soon determined that the men had got about four hundred yards from the Fiumicino River to a few houses bordering Highway 9. In the second house, Rowland reported, he "found about fifteen pieces of equipment consisting of webbing, rifles, and ammunition piled in a heap with an Irish bonnet resting on top. I moved from there to the third and last house on the west side of the highway at a 'T' junction . . . In the house I found another pile of equipment consisting of Bren magazines, rifles, and steel helmets. West of the house about fifty yards and piled against a hay stack I found a similar pile. This equipment has since been identified by numbers and names printed on it as the property of men of 'A' Company. In my preliminary search I found the bodies of men of the Irish Regiment, these four men were identified by identity discs and pay-books.

"Since the area was heavily mined, I returned the next day with a party of men and detectors. We made a careful search of the area, and working from the directions of an Italian civilian found the buried bodies of five men of 'A' Company. These were disinterred and identified by pay books, rings, and letters. Later I found another 'A' Company man about two hundred yards west of the highway and a hundred yards from the north bank of the river. From the condition of these bodies it would appear that with one exception the men were killed by shell fire.

"During my investigation of the houses in this area, I concluded that: (a) Equipment which was found was left in such a manner that it indicated . . . the soldiers who had placed it there had done so under orders. (b) Lack of casualties from small-arms fire might indicate that any battle which had taken place was neither intense nor prolonged, unless our wounded were evacuated by the enemy.

"My personal opinion is that 'A' Company occupied the house at this locality to give protection during the impending attempt to bridge the river, and to protect their exposed flanks. From lack of battle signs, and my knowledge of the fighting spirit of the company, I am convinced that either the company was totally surrounded by a numerically superior force of the enemy, or else tanks with an excellent highway to work on and the knowledge that the bridge was still blown and that our tanks were not across the river, moved swiftly in on them."[1] The actual fate of the company was never determined.

Even as the padre was concluding his investigation, 'A' Company got a new commander, Captain T.A. Popplewell. Captain D.A. Smith, who had rebuilt the company with reinforcements after the debacle, remained as second-in-command.

THE IRISH, HOWEVER, were out of the line on October 13—settling into quarters near the seaside town of Riccione, while 1st Canadian Infantry Division's 1st Brigade continued expanding the narrow bridgehead across the Scolo Rigossa established the day before by the Hastings and Prince Edward Regiment. Before dawn, 'C' Company crossed the Rigossa to the right of Highway 9 and advanced about 1,000 yards before being stopped by heavy machine-gun fire coming from Bulgaria, a curiously named hamlet a third of a mile away. The company set up amid a cluster of buildings. Left of the highway, 'A' Company—dogged by artillery and mortar fire—managed to extend its narrow bridgehead no more than 450 yards before being forced to take cover in some farm buildings. The advances by these two companies, however, did provide sufficient cover to enable

'B' Company to also cross the Rigossa and anchor the bridgehead by digging in astride Highway 9. Under fire from the heavily defended town of Gambettola, 'D' Company only managed to edge forward a short distance to cover offered by a raised road close to the Rigossa.

Hoping to break the German hold on Bulgaria, 1st Brigade's Brigadier Allan Calder—taking advantage of the blessedly clear skies that had arrived on October 12—called in four Desert Air Force fighter-bomber strikes that the Hasty Ps reported did "an excellent job with direct hits every raid." But the Germans refused to loosen their grip, and 'C' Company was unable to renew its advance. At 1400 hours, Lieutenant Colonel Don Cameron ordered all four companies to hold in place. Although little ground was gained, the three companies across the Rigossa had carved out a salient about three-quarters of a mile wide by three-quarters of a mile deep.[2] This provided a base upon which to build a set-piece attack for October 14.

Twice during the day, Major General Chris Vokes had visited Calder's headquarters to learn why the advance was stalled. Both men recognized the dire need to get tanks across the Rigossa to support the Hasty Ps.[3] Plans were put into place for 1st Field Company engineers to launch another Ark bridge. The Lord Strathcona's Horse's 'A' Squadron had moved up to the Rigossa during the afternoon, where Major F.C. Braithwaite confirmed that the narrow, deep ditch was "tank proof." Even though the heavy rains had at least momentarily ceased, fields were still sodden. Any advance by tanks was going to be confined to roads. On October 12 and 13, Lieutenant Colonel Jim McAvity had overseen several trials in which tanks were fitted first with rubber and then steel tracks to test the ground in several fields. Each time, the test tank had to be dragged out after immediately sinking into the mud. Even as the Shermans were hauled free, McAvity looked enviously at German Panther track marks. As "their track was considerably wider than ours . . . they appeared to have had no difficulty in going cross-country."[4]

While improved weather had the war diarist at 1st Division headquarters musing that "two or three such days will harden the ground and enable tanks to function off the roads," the immediate future was grim. Weather forecasters had predicted rain for late October 13, which failed to materialize despite clouds forming during the afternoon.

Vokes and Calder agreed that Bulgaria was the key to unlocking the German defences facing the Rigossa. Both the road and the railway track that provided avenues of supply to Gambettola passed the hamlet. Its loss would render the German hold on Gambettola untenable. Although the 23rd Battalion of 5th New Zealand Infantry Brigade had closed up alongside the Canadians, they remained stuck behind the Rigossa with little prospect of putting in a successful attack on Gambettola until its German garrison was isolated.[5]

Taking Bulgaria promised to be difficult, even if the Strathconas were able to get forward to support the Hasty Ps. The hamlet, wrote Lieutenant Farley Mowat, consisted of "a straggling group of houses . . . The upper stor[eys] of the stone buildings, emerging from the thick cover of olive groves were heavily manned and each house held at least one machine gun sited to sweep the intervening spaces."

Given Bulgaria's importance, Lieutenant Colonel Cameron expected it to be held by at least a company of 90th Panzer Grenadier Division's 361st Panzer Grenadier Regiment. While the German hold on the Rigossa was strong, there was a flaw. The soldiers in Bulgaria were from a different division than those holding the opposite side of the railway and Gambettola. Divisional boundaries tended to be sacrosanct. So the troops of the 26th Panzer Division's 9th Panzer Grenadier Regiment in Gambettola were unlikely to threaten the weakly held right flank of the Hasty Ps, as this would mean sending men into the 90th Division's boundary.[6]

At 2000 hours, Cameron held an Orders Group to set out the battle plan. Present were the commanders of 'B' and 'C' Companies, Major Braithwaite of the Strathconas, and officers from various supporting arms. There would be two phases. 'B' Company would first drive out of the salient up Highway 9 for a mile to seize the junction with the road leading to Bulgaria. 'C' Company would then pass through, carry out the half-mile advance along the road to Bulgaria, and clear the hamlet. Artillery support would be lavish—all divisional field regiments plus a medium regiment and 11th Field Regiment. The Saskatoon Light Infantry provided one 4.2-inch mortar platoon and a heavy machine-gun platoon. To convince the Germans that the Hasty Ps were attacking Bulgaria directly, the 4.2-inch mortars would fire smoke and high-explosive rounds into the hamlet in conjunction with similar fire by some of the artillery units.[7]

Essential to the attack were the Strathcona tanks. The whole show would be cancelled if they were unable to cross the Scolo Rigossa. As the entire salient was under direct observation from Gambettola, Braithwaite wanted 1st Field Company's engineers to install a workable bridge before first light. After the briefing, Braithwaite and his troop leaders reconnoitred a route to the planned crossing. They were dismayed to find the earlier deployed Ark turned on its side and unusable.[8]

DURING THE EARLY morning hours of October 14, 1st Field Company deployed a second Ark adjacent to the overturned one. Although this effort succeeded, when the first Strathcona troop began to cross, the second tank in line bogged down in mud and blocked the exit ramp. Nearby, Highway 9's masonry bridge had been partially destroyed by German demolitions. Although the arch was intact, the supporting sides were destroyed. Despite the officer commanding 1st Field Company warning Major Braithwaite that the bridge was unsafe for tanks, the Strathconas decided to gamble. Every man in 'A' Squadron knew the Hasty Ps were relying on them.

It was already 0600 hours—the set time for the attack to begin. Lieutenant Colonel Cameron pushed things back ninety minutes to 0730 to give the tankers a chance to reach his companies. One by one the Shermans of Nos. 1 and 2 Troops carefully squeezed onto the shaky, narrow bridge and clanked to the other side.

At 0730 hours precisely, Lieutenant B.D. Richards—who had just joined the regiment on September 30—moved No. 2 Troop out ahead of 'B' Company and rolled toward the Highway 9 junction with the road leading to Bulgaria. Buildings were clustered around the junction, and others between it and the attack's start point were likely German strongpoints, so the three Shermans advanced with machine guns blazing. Twenty minutes later, as No. 2 Troop and 'B' Company reached the junction, German infantry were spotted fleeing either into houses on its north side or toward Bulgaria. As the leading Hasty Ps set about clearing each house, they were fired on by Germans a hundred yards away. Dashing into the nearest house for cover, the men tripped a booby-trap bomb. Two men were killed and two injured. By 1100 hours, however, the junction was secure and No. 2 Troop was released to join the advance on Bulgaria.

Having exhausted most of its machine-gun ammunition, No. 2 Troop was granted a pause to restock before the attack would be renewed. At 1130 hours, Richards reported being ready to go. Cameron then advised 'C' Company's Captain Max Porritt that the artillery would drench Bulgaria at 1210 hours. The artillery support would occur in two phases, with the first consisting of a twenty-minute program focused on Bulgaria and the road leading to it. At 1230 hours, the artillery would lift to pre-arranged targets three hundred yards beyond the hamlet.

As soon as the first shells started exploding, 'C' Company swung through the junction to pick up two tank troops.[9] "Perhaps never before or since, in the experience of the Regiment," Lieutenant Colonel McAvity wrote, "has there been such a spontaneous demonstration of genuine, whole-hearted cooperation between infantry and tanks." Based "solely upon a four-day acquaintance and a vague respect which each unit had for the other's fine reputation, the good spirit was almost incredible. As 1st Troop led off up the road, 'shooting up' the farms from which M.G. fire had come, the 'Hasty Ps' loped along in the roadside ditches . . . and would say to a tank commander: 'That's enough, we'll take over that house.' Typical of this spirit was a remark passed over the wireless by Lieutenant Richards to his squadron HQ—in what was intended as a routine 'Sitrep.' 'Hello King 2—have made another 300 yards—shooting up small opposition in houses with no difficulty—our little brothers are doing a really terrific job—King 2—Over.'"[10]

During the approach to Bulgaria, No. 2 Troop advanced along the road, while No. 1 Troop moved through fields sufficiently dry to support the Shermans. All six tanks were surrounded by Hasty Ps to protect them from infantry armed with Panzerfaust anti-tank launchers. As a building was approached, an infantryman would assign the target to the tank with the best angle of fire on it. The tank would then slam the building with a high-explosive round, rake it with machine-gun fire, and finish with a smoke round to cover the infantry assault. As the building was being cleared, the rest of the attackers continued toward Bulgaria.

Despite heavy resistance, the Hasty Ps and Strathconas entered the hamlet just before 1300 hours. Since the house-clearing method used during the approach had been so successful, Richards and Porritt decided to tackle Bulgaria the same way. But the hamlet's houses were closer together and more stoutly constructed, and clearing them turned into a slow, deadly business. In most cases, the tank fire succeeded in driving the Germans out of a building, but they only withdrew to dugouts about twenty yards away. The tankers responded by firing smoke shells on the dugouts and raking them with machine-gun fire until the infantry closed in to overrun the position.

When a group of panzer grenadiers refused to budge from one building, Porritt's men at first tried driving them out by throwing in Type 36 grenades. But the explosion and resulting shrapnel fragments proved of little use against men fighting from the second storey. Switching to No. 77 grenades largely solved this problem. A twelve-ounce tin with a fuse that ignited when it struck a hard surface, the No. 77 grenade was loaded with white phosphorous that scattered widely and ignited spectacularly when it came into contact with air. Even a slight amount of phosphorous contacting skin could cause deep, severe burns. Not surprisingly, the German soldiers, who had no equivalent weapon, found the grenades terrifying and frantically fled the confines of the building.[11]

As the brutal afternoon fight wore on, the number of panzer grenadiers killed, wounded, or taken prisoner grew rapidly. But the fight was not entirely one-sided. Thirty-four-year-old Private Huron Eldon Brant—a Mohawk from Ontario's Bay of Quinte, who had received a Military Medal for bravery in Sicily—was killed, along with his entire six-man section, when it was caught by a long machine-gun burst fired from a nearby ditch.[12] At 1630 hours, Porritt signalled Cameron that Bulgaria was clear of enemy and 'C' Company was consolidating its hold. Sixty panzer grenadiers had surrendered, and Porritt estimated that about a hundred had been killed or wounded in the fight. The Hasty Ps counted eight dead and seven wounded. Two of the latter died later. The Strathconas suffered no casualties.

Given Bulgaria's size, Cameron feared the Germans might try infiltrating back in after dark. Detaching a platoon from 'D' Company, which was in reserve, provided sufficient numbers to occupy all the buildings. An attempt to send the battalion's anti-tank platoon to the hamlet was stopped at the road junction by heavy artillery and mortar fire. While the platoon dug in alongside 'B' Company, a troop of M-10s from the 1st Anti-Tank Regiment managed to work through the shellfire and formed alongside the Strathcona tanks. Richards and Lieutenant James John Black of No. 1 Troop had set up west of Bulgaria in order to remain on call should the Hasty Ps require them.

At 1700 hours, a 'B' Company patrol spotted a German Panther approaching Bulgaria and reported four more closing on the railway from Gambettola with supporting infantry in tow. Belatedly, the 29th Panzer Division troops in the fortified town had realized the threat that Bulgaria's loss meant and were trying to rescue the situation. Alerted, the Strathconas quickly advanced to guard positions in front of the town.[13]

As the tankers tried to spot the leading Panther, a high-velocity round snapped out of an orchard and blew away a tank seat strapped to the back of No. 2 Troop Corporal M.J. Farrall's Sherman. Corporal H.J. Lodwick immediately engaged the Panther with his 75-millimetre while contacting Sergeant Gordon Fraser Johnson by wireless for help. At the end of September, Johnson had exchanged his regular Sherman for a new one mounting the more powerful 17-pounder gun. Designated a Firefly, the new tank was capable of going head-to-head with the Panther's long-barrelled 75-millimetre or even a Tiger's 88-millimetre gun. Firing at a range of four hundred yards, Johnson's gunner punched the Panther with four armoured-personnel rounds. Although the Panther failed to burst into flame, it was knocked out.

"After seeing this example of fine marksmanship and alertness," Lieutenant Colonel McAvity wrote, "the commander of the German tanks must have changed his plans, for, from that moment, nothing

more was seen or heard except for spasmodic shelling and mortaring."[14] The Hasty Ps posted several men to prevent the Germans
from attempting to recover the Panther until the battalion's pioneers
arrived to wreck it with explosives. Apart from heavy shelling, mortaring, and some harassing machine-gun fire against 'C' Company's
perimeter in Bulgaria, the night passed in what the Hasty Ps now
considered a quiet manner.[15]

WHILE THE HASTY PS had been winning Bulgaria, the 48th
Highlanders had kept pace on their left flank. So close to the
Apennines, they moved against the normal grain of the land. All
roads ran across their line of advance rather than in line with it. The
roads also meandered. "At best," the war diarist wrote, due to the zig-
zagging route, "our lines of communication would not have been first
class, but with 'blows' from demolitions and shelling and mines laid
in considerable density, the [movement of] supplies and evacuation of
casualties was a constant problem."[16]

When the 48th's lead companies halted for the night on October 14,
the battalion's Tac HQ received jumbled wireless reports that the
Germans were massing a Panther-led counterattack. Lacking tank
support, the two company commanders on the sharp end urgently
requested that the anti-tank platoon be brought forward. Two veteran sergeants of the platoon went up to Captain George Fraser's
'A' Company to select positions for the guns. Twenty-nine-year-old
Sergeant George Adams and twenty-four-year-old Sergeant Bob Shaw,
who had been awarded a Military Medal on October 2 for his bravery during an action in the Liri Valley, found Fraser's headquarters
in a jam factory surrounded by mines. Fraser had already marked
positions for two guns with white tape. As the two men headed back
along a route deemed safe and across which 'A' Company's Lieutenant
Andy LeMeseurier had walked several times, one triggered a box
mine. Both men were killed.

Still worried about the possible counterattack, 'C' Company's
Major F.G. MacLaren kept asking for anti-tank guns. But, he reported,
the "road's pitted with mines; it will have to be swept." Pioneer platoon Sergeant Ed Ralph came forward to look the situation over. If

the platoon swept the required section of road now that it was day-light and Germans could observe them from the foothills to their left, heavy casualties would result, he told MacLaren. It was 0800 hours on October 15, the sky was clear, and his men would be perfectly exposed. Mulling it over, Ralph decided to just do the job alone. Crawling on his hands and knees, prodding the road with a knife, while being fired on by mortars zeroing in like snipers with rifles and the occasional 88-millimetre shell thrown his way to boot, Ralph calmly and deliberately worked away. He lifted twenty-two mines to clear a two-hundred-yard stretch of road. Some of these had been booby-trapped to explode if tampered with and required more sensitive deactivation. Job done, Ralph strolled off. The anti-tank guns were soon brought through to 'C' Company.[17] His Military Medal citation stated that Ralph "showed not only a courage and coolness of the highest order, but also a concentration of mind and effort at time of extreme peril, which caused the admiration and enthusiasm of all."[18]

As the 48th renewed their advance, the Royal Canadian Regiment passed through the Hasty Ps on October 15 to continue the push along Highway 9. Right of the Canadians, the New Zealanders had crossed the Scolo Rigossa in the morning and found the Germans at Gambettola gone. The 5th New Zealand Infantry Brigade was soon across the Rigossa in strength all along its front and matching pace with 1st Brigade.

The RCR's 'C' Company, under Captain J.M. Gregg, headed straight along Highway 9 with Captain E.M. Hills's 'B' Company out several hundred yards to the right. It soon became clear that after the previous days' fierce artillery pounding, the Germans were now offering no more than light rearguard resistance before the panzer grenadiers would fall back to another temporary position. At times, wrote Major Strome Galloway—who was in temporary command of the battalion effective that day—"the battlefield was as silent as the tomb."[19] Lieutenant Colonel Jim Ritchie had passed command to Galloway at Brigadier Calder's insistence. "Give Galloway the battalion for a couple of days and see what he can do," Calder said. The twenty-nine-year-old Galloway was already an RCR legend. Attached to the 2nd London Irish Rifles in early 1943, he had served with it for two months in Tunisia under a plan to give some Canadian officers battle experience. Landing with the RCR in Sicily, he had fought with distinction in all the battalion's many battles since. When giving Ritchie his instructions about Galloway, Calder had also said it was about time someone in the RCR got a Distinguished Service Order. Ritchie told Galloway that he had replied, "We don't get DSOS in the RCR, Sir. We only do our job." This reluctance to reward was a bone of contention between Ritchie and Galloway.

When the previous battalion commander had been reassigned after the Liri Valley Campaign, Galloway had not expected to take over the RCR. The battalion was one of 1st Infantry Division's three Permanent Force units, and Galloway had come into the army through the militia. But it had galled him when Ritchie—who was Permanent Force but lacked combat experience—arrived from a rear-area administrative posting to assume command on May 31, 1944. Since then, Ritchie had steadfastly refused to put any officers forward for either the Military Cross or the DSO. Galloway suspected that Ritchie's reasoning was that nobody was going to get a medal before he did. Only two officers, Lieutenant Benny Potts and Lieutenant Geoff Wright, had slipped past Ritchie's barrier, with Military Crosses awarded on August 8 and October 2, respectively, for actions in the Liri Valley during May. In each case, however, the paperwork had advanced well up the command chain before Ritchie arrived and could not be blocked.[20]

Galloway, now mightily relieved to at least briefly escape the tethers of battalion second-in-command, wherein one was almost perpetually at the rear headquarters while the commander was up at Tac HQ overseeing operations, was determined to get close to the sharp end. At 1430 hours, Gregg reported 'C' Company was meeting stiffer resistance and not keeping aligned with 'B' Company. Realizing 'B' Company's good pace was also putting Hills out of wireless range with his headquarters, Galloway formed a small command group and sought to catch up to Gregg. He could then chivvy 'C' Company forward while maintaining better wireless contact with 'B' Company.

As Galloway passed his small group—which consisted of Potts acting as his intelligence officer, the Tac HQ wireless signallers, a runner, and a corporal and private as guards—through the forward lines of the Hasty Ps, it came under shellfire and momentarily went to ground until the shrapnel stopped flying. When Galloway caught up to 'C' Company, he ordered Gregg to speed up by pushing Lieutenant A.D. Egan's platoon out forward with instructions to overrun and occupy any strongpoint encountered. The immediately following platoon would then pass to the lead and repeat the process.

At 2230 hours, joined by 2nd Field Regiment's Captain Ross Zavitz and his small forward observation party, Galloway continued along the road close behind Gregg's men. Seeing a house that might serve well as a Tac HQ, Galloway led the party into a small lane, where "a burst of Spandau streaked across the yard and the group doubled into the house . . . in quick order." The house appeared empty but had so many outdoor openings that blacking the place out for the night would be impossible. Galloway opted to set up his HQ in the next house along the way, which was already occupied by Lieutenant A.M. Ferguson's No. 15 Platoon of 'C' Company. Just before midnight, ten Germans were spotted running from the building Galloway had rejected. A patrol revealed that they had been lying "doggo on the top floor" while the command group had inspected the lower floor. Galloway sent Ferguson's men to join the rest of 'C' Company and had 'D' Company come forward to form up around his Tac HQ. This put the battalion in a solid position for the night.

The plan for October 16 was to adhere to the standard infantry battalion method of advancing two companies forward and continue along Highway 9 toward the Pisciatello River. As the advance began, at 0500 hours, a terrific artillery concentration mixed with Nebelwerfer fire slammed down on 'D' Company and the Tac HQ. One Nebelwerfer round blasted apart an outside wall.[21] Galloway and the others inside were thrown to the ground. There were no injuries, but the wireless equipment was knocked out of commission, severing Galloway's link back to 1st Brigade headquarters. When contact was re-established after several hours, Brigadier Calder firmly ordered Galloway to be more cautious and move his HQ "some 1,500 yards to the rear!"[22]

ON OCTOBER 16, LIEUTENANT General Tommy Burns issued orders setting the winning of bridgeheads over the Savio River and the capture of Cesena as the immediate 1 Canadian Corps objective. Phase one entailed 2nd New Zealand Armoured Division and 1st Canadian Infantry Division establishing crossings over the Pisciatello River. The 5th New Zealand Infantry Brigade's left flank would advance to the east of a road running from Bulgaria to the village of Ruffio, just short of the Pisciatello. In the Canadian sector, 1st Brigade would continue along Highway 9 and to its left, while 2nd Brigade came up on the right and advanced to the right of the railway.

The day before, Burns had met at 1st Division headquarters with Major General Chris Vokes and Lieutenant General Bernard Freyberg—who had recovered from the injuries suffered in his September airplane crash and resumed command of the New Zealanders. Discussion centred on how best to advance the two divisions to the Pisciatello. Burns emphasized the need for "gaining contact with the enemy, driving in his outposts, and, if his resistance stiffened, mounting an attack."

Hoping to improve his line of approach east of Highway 9, Vokes proposed that 2nd Brigade be allowed to use the Bulgaria–Ruffio road. At first Freyberg agreed with this plan, but within a few hours the New Zealander insisted that his division "could advance rapidly adhering to the original boundary," and Vokes lost access to the road.[23]

Burns was increasingly ruing Freyberg's return. His relationship with Freyberg's replacement, Major General Steve Weir, had been excellent. Because of Freyberg's elevated status—and despite the fact that he got along well with the New Zealander—Burns was often left tiptoeing around an officer he commanded. During the Great War, Freyberg had earned a DSO at Gallipoli and then a Victoria Cross at the Somme in 1916. Freyberg added a bar to the DSO in September 1918 and then earned a second DSO when his unit seized a bridge at Lessines a minute before the armistice was declared. In the interwar years, Freyberg had been promoted to major general before heart issues forced his retirement in late 1937. Shortly after the new war broke out, Freyberg offered his services and was soon appointed to command 2nd New Zealand Armoured Division. Given command of the ill-fated Allied garrison on Crete, his handling of its defence until the island fell to German forces was subject to much criticism. But what damage this did to his reputation was largely dispelled by his leadership of 2nd New Zealand Division during the desert campaign of 1941–43. Eschewing an offer of corps command to adhere to his promise not to leave the Kiwis, he led them through the battle for Cassino—playing a key role in having the famous abbey atop Monte Cassino bombed into oblivion to deny its use as a German observation post and fortress.[24]

By the time Freyberg came under Burns's command, even the most senior officers in Italy had learned that to get his compliance it was better to ask rather than bluster about with commands. So even though Burns would have preferred to implement Vokes's plan for 1st Division to take over the Bulgaria–Ruffio road, he was not about to impose that on Freyberg. Despite Freyberg's unquestionable "extreme personal bravery," Burns considered him "not a great 'thruster'; he tended to take a less optimistic view of some of the operations planned . . . He certainly remembered the difficulties the New Zealanders had had the previous winter at Cassino, and did not relish the prospect of again battling rain and mud, as well as the Germans."[25] Burns could only hope that Freyberg would ensure that his troops kept pace with the Canadian advance.

Fortunately, after the Germans abandoned Gambettola on October 15, they offered the 5th New Zealand Infantry Brigade ever-slackening resistance. By last light on October 16, the brigade had reached a road paralleling the Pisciatello from Ruffio east to Castellaccio.[26] Broadening the line the Kiwis had established to the right of 1st Infantry Division, the Royal Canadian Dragoons serving with Cumberland Force had sent two squadrons across the Fiumicino River on October 16 and advanced to Sant' Angelo on the Baldona River and relieved the Kiwis there.

As soon as the Dragoons had consolidated, 'D' Squadron crossed the Baldona and advanced up the road toward Castellaccio. "It was not much fun," the regiment's historian recorded. "The first patrol crept ahead down the muddy ditches or along lines of trees, in constant danger of mines. It was shelled and mortared constantly, for the

German always covers his retreats by fire. Then, when it got up to the house, it always had to rush a hundred yards or more across absolutely open and level ground to the objective. That took courage—to get up out of the ditch and dash over a field as flat and clear of shelter as a billiard table, straight at a house that might pour fire out from every window. Sometimes whole patrols were lost in this charge, and nearly always there were one or two casualties, because the German generally left small rearguards in positions from which he had withdrawn his main strength.

"After the charge, it was kick down the doors, jump aside while someone tossed in a grenade, rush the rooms, set up the telephone and then hurry outside to dig weapon pits. Occasionally the German would let a patrol into a house without a fight and then blast the house down by fire from a self-propelled gun ramped up on a dyke a thousand yards away.

"As the advance went on, more and more canals and ditches stretched across the lines of communications, for no one could be spared for bridging. The houses, too, were generally from 500 to 1,000 yards apart so that posts could seldom by made to support each other. Thus the squadron would sit, with big holes in its defence, virtually cut off at the rear, with no reserves and limited artillery support in case the enemy counterattacked."27

The Dragoons' advance to Castellaccio was part of a full-scale Cumberland Force push across the Fiumicino. On the Adriatic coast, however, an attempt by Wilder Force's 3rd Greek Mountain Brigade to advance beyond the river was driven back by a counterattack. This was the Greeks' last action in Italy, as they were ordered to stand down to return to their homeland and assume occupation duty.

With the Greeks gone, Cumberland Force was left with only three armoured units serving as infantry and the tanks of 5th Canadian Armoured Division's British Columbia Dragoons. Confined to the roads because of the still muddy countryside, the tanks could do little but provide support fire as directed by the nearby infantry. Meanwhile, 5th Division's reconnaissance regiment, the Governor General's Horse Guards, took over responsibility for the coastal sector, with the British 27th Lancers Cavalry Regiment holding the ground between the two Canadian regiments. The Horse Guards were assigned to hold the coast, the 27th Lancers the centre, and the Royal Canadian Dragoons the left flank. Although Brigadier Ian Cumberland recognized the shortage of men in these three reconnaissance regiments, he "felt confident of [their] being able to do the job satisfactorily." With 5th New Zealand Infantry Brigade to Cumberland Force's left making steady gains, the brigadier was also determined to keep prodding the enemy before him. As the German situation became increasingly untenable, Cumberland expected that even his limited force should be able to push them back.[28]

FOR IST CANADIAN INFANTRY Brigade's Royal Canadian Regiment, the advance along Highway 9 on October 16 was a hard day's slog to the Pisciatello River. Joined by No. 3 Troop of the Lord Strathcona's Horse's 'A' Squadron, 'C' Company led the advance along the road, with 'B' Company operating out to the right. In the late morning, about a mile short of the river, the tankers and 'C' Company were stopped by Germans defending a built-up area around a road junction. Panzerfaust rounds fired from the houses caused sufficient damage to convince the tankers to withdraw while the infantry cleared the houses. Lieutenant A.D. Egan's No. 14 Platoon quickly broke left off the road to seize a house on the flank, from which Germans firing Panzerfausts and machine guns dominated the junction.[29] "After a spirited fight," Major Galloway wrote, they "killed and captured a number of enemy and put the remainder to flight. Lieutenant Egan . . . attempted to halt the enemy's withdrawal by firing a 2-inch mortar from the upper window of one of the houses just seized but was unsuccessful."[30]

A short distance away, Private Norman Rauta, number-two man on a Bren gun team, had run well forward to find a good position to fire at the retreating Germans. As he reached a small stream, Rauta suddenly faced four Germans just ten feet away. Two were armed with Schmeisser submachine guns and the other two carried rifles. One German shouted, "You are my prisoner!" Another fired a Schmeisser burst at the private, but missed. Firing his Lee-Enfield from the hip, Rauta shot and wounded the German with the Schmeisser. From a nearby house, a heavy machine gun opened fire on Rauta. Ignoring this, Rauta "continued to shoot it out with his original opponents. He wounded a second German and the other two fled to cover." The Germans in the house also broke and fled what could have been a formidable and costly position for No. 14 Platoon to clear. "The gallant action of this soldier," Rauta's Military Medal citation declared, "thus resulted in the wounding of two Germans and the routing of the remainder."[31]

As it was getting dark and the road beyond the junction was blocked, the tanks withdrew. Captain Gregg ordered 'C' Company to carry on alone. After taking a couple more German prisoners, the company finally reached the Pisciatello—which proved to be nothing more than a small trickle running through a culvert under the road.[32]

To 'C' Company's right, meanwhile, 'B' Company had become entangled in a hard fight to clear a house cluster, beginning at 1100 hours and lasting seven hours. As the company renewed its advance, it was plastered by extremely heavy mortar fire. Lieutenant Alfred Hubert Poirier and two men were killed, and Lieutenant X.W. Boucher and seven others were wounded. After recovering from this tragedy, the company pressed on to reach the river at 2200 hours.[33]

While the RCR had been carrying out 1st Brigade's main thrust of the day, the 48th Highlanders had kept pace on the left flank. The Germans gave ground only grudgingly, and numerous short, sharp engagements were required to push them along.[34] Lieutenant Colonel Don Mackenzie was constantly on the move, his Tac HQ moving in two jeeps. At 1100 hours, he was in the lead jeep that passed along a stretch of road reportedly swept of mines. The following jeep, driven by Private Bruce Lloyd, blew up on a mine and was demolished. A stretcher-bearer rushed to the scene and found Lloyd with blood flowing from wounds on his face and other parts of the head. Lloyd was in shock and losing blood fast, but the stretcher-bearer was able to bandage the injuries and stem the loss of blood.[35] Twenty-year-old Signaller Kenneth William Bud Jesshope, who had also been in the jeep, died of his wounds.

6

We'll Take a Chance

AT 1230 HOURS ON October 16, Major General Chris Vokes briefed Lieutenant Colonel Pat Bogert at 2nd Canadian Infantry Brigade headquarters in Savignano. An acting brigade commander, Bogert had not yet been promoted to brigadier. The 1st Canadian Infantry Division was to increase the pressure from the east on the Germans in Cesena while also crossing the Savio River north of the town. To the right, 2nd New Zealand Armoured Division would also drive to the river. On the left, v British Corps would secure the high ground southwest of Cesena to cut off any retreat in that direction. "The whole effect is that of a large pincer movement," brigade intelligence officer Captain Ed Bradish later wrote. Within 1st Division, 1st Brigade was to continue along Highway 9 toward Cesena, while 2nd Brigade would thrust around to the east and secure crossings over the Savio that would enable it to link up with v Corps and surround the town. The 2nd Brigade's first phase of advance would be made by the Seaforth Highlanders, with the objective of reaching the Pisciatello River and establishing a bridgehead on its north bank near Ponte della Pietra. If the Seaforths met too much resistance while gaining the Pisciatello, the Loyal Edmonton Regiment (Eddies) would pass through to force the actual crossing. The Princess Patricia's Canadian Light Infantry would be in reserve. 'B' Squadron of the British 12th Royal Tank Regiment would support the Seaforths. Also accompanying the Seaforths would be a reconnaissance party of engineers to determine crossing sites over the Pisciatello.[1]

Lieutenant Colonel Henry Ogle "Budge" Bell-Irving had the Seaforths moving by 1620 hours, with 'C' and 'D' Companies leading from a holding position established by the Hastings and Prince Edward Regiment astride Highway 9. The position was well to the rear of the still-advancing Royal Canadian Regiment and 48th Highlanders. The Seaforths soon left Highway 9 and moved northeast toward the Pisciatello by way of two rough farm tracks. Although no opposition was met, progress was slow. About every hundred yards, the leading companies and supporting armour would reach an irrigation ditch that the tanks had to carefully cross. Although the infantry could have easily moved well ahead of the British tankers, Bell-Irving had "issued strict orders . . . that they, at no time would leave the tanks, who, in such close country would be easy prey for [Panzerfaust-firing] infantry," a Seaforth report noted.

'C' Company's route soon deteriorated so badly that it became impassable to tanks. By swinging to the right and passing through where 'D' Company was settling on its objective, Major Stewart Lynch was able to keep the tanks and his company together. At 2310 hours, 'C' Company anchored the battalion's left flank and sent a patrol to establish contact with the Royal Canadian Regiment.

By this time, Captain Tony Staples had passed 'B' Company to the front on the battalion's right flank and soon reached its objective, about six hundred yards from the Pisciatello. En route, 'B' Company's supporting tank troop had encountered a large crater blocking the road and were unable to get around it. With adjacent fields too muddy, the tanks were left behind. Major Robert Clark's 'A' Company had also been following this route, but hearing of the crater, Clark stopped well short and sent out patrols to find a cross-country route that was tank friendly.

Having met no opposition or artillery fire during the October 16 phase of the advance, the Seaforth's luck ran out in the early morning hours of the following day. Ignoring the darkness, German artillery pounded all roads and tracks in the area with shellfire.[2] At 0230 hours, with 'A' Company still stuck on the road and now being lashed by machine-gun fire from across the Pisciatello, Bell-Irving ordered Lynch to advance 'C' Company to the river and attempt a two-platoon crossing, with the tanks and battalion anti-tank guns providing fire support. Captain Thomas Edwin Woolley, who commanded the battalion support company, was already moving toward 'C' Company's assigned crossing point next to where the railway bridged it. He had the battalion's medium machine guns loaded on Bren carriers, with the six-pounder anti-tank guns in tow behind. Before reaching the crossing point, Woolley's little column came under fire, and the twenty-four-year-old officer was killed.

At 0415 hours, 'C' Company dug in 150 yards short of the Pisciatello. When Lynch tried sending a patrol across the river in advance of the planned two-platoon effort, it was driven back by direct 88-millimetre gun and machine-gun fire from the opposite bank. About four hours later, 'A' Company and its supporting tanks finally reached its objective across from Ponte della Pietra—digging in behind the high dyke that bordered the river. "A patrol attempting to cross the river," the Seaforth war diarist reported, "met a similar fate as 'C' Company. The enemy was evidently firmly entrenched and had so sited his MGs that they completely covered any crossing." Clark's 'A' Company was also fending off German infantry infiltration attempts. To thicken 'A' Company's position, Bell-Irving had a 'D' Company platoon join it.[3]

The Seaforths and the engineering party that had accompanied them were beginning to understand that bridging the Pisciatello was going to be difficult. At one possible crossing, the stream was about forty yards wide and four feet deep. From the cover of a high brick wall running along the opposite bank, German machine guns fully covered the crossing site.[4]

Bell-Irving realized that the 2nd Brigade plan for crossing the Pisciatello was impossible. The Germans obviously intended to maintain their grip on the opposite bank. If infantry crossed the river without tanks, they would suffer extremely heavy casualties and likely be driven back. Now that it was daylight, it was also apparent by the weight and accuracy of the mortar and artillery fire falling on the Seaforth positions that the Germans enjoyed excellent observation points.

From their positions behind the dyke, the forward company commanders reported to Bell-Irving that they could see a palatial mansion near Cesena. They suspected that the German observers were in its upper storey. Pinpointing it on his map, Bell-Irving asked Desert Air Force to hit it with aerial strikes. As there were fighters and fighter-bombers circling overhead in what was designated as cab rank formation, the strikes were almost immediate. He also had the building pounded by artillery. Although from a distance the thick-walled building appeared largely unscathed after these attacks, the fire falling in the Seaforth's area noticeably lessened.

Soon after, Captain W.L. Roberts and his 4-inch mortar platoon set up about 500 yards from the Pisciatello and engaged suspected and known German positions.[5] A Saskatoon Light Infantry platoon also brought up its Vickers medium machine guns and between 1400 and 1630 hours hosed the German positions with 21,000 rounds. With both sides now engaged in a fierce artillery and mortar duel, movement along either riverbank was nearly impossible. By 2000 hours on October 17, the Seaforths had suffered six men killed and another fifteen wounded.[6] Despite the hazards of travelling through the shell-fire striking the roads, the Regimental Aid Post's stretcher-bearers raced in Bren carriers to the front whenever required to evacuate dead and wounded. In the evening, each company's Bren carrier also brought a hot meal to the troops.[7]

With the Seaforths virtually pinned in place, Vokes and Bogert decided at 1430 hours to pass two companies of the Loyal Edmonton Regiment through to secure a crossing just to the right of the railway track. It would be a silent attack put in after dark, at 2030 hours.[8]

LEFT OF THE Seaforth Highlanders, the Royal Canadian Regiment had also pushed up to the Pisciatello on October 17, encountering initial stiff resistance from a number of machine-gun positions covering Highway 9. These had to be silenced by artillery fire directed by 2nd Field Regiment's Captain Ross Zavitz.[9] In the late afternoon, 'A' Company gained the river just to the left of the railroad, and No. 9 Platoon, led by Corporal James Ettels Bain, attempted to win a crossing. Quickly wading the stream, Bain and his men occupied a two-storey, two-roomed railway building, only to be attacked by a group of Germans heavily armed with Panzerfausts. One Panzerfaust round ripped the upstairs floor away, where Bain was with two other men. Bain and one man "fell ten feet into a heap of debris on the floor below. The Germans then rushed the house, led by an officer." The third man upstairs had managed to get astride a naked rafter, and from this position he shot the officer dead. In a moment, two other men in Bains's group were on their feet and, joined by the remainder of the section, they fought off the Germans, losing one man killed and four wounded in the process, but "ringing themselves with three dead Germans and several wounded ones."[10]

In the middle of the fight, 'A' Company's runner, Private William Bertrand, arrived to find out what was going on, because the platoon's No. 38 wireless set appeared not to be working. With another German counterattack mustering and the platoon's ammunition nearly exhausted, Bain said they needed to withdraw. Bertrand volunteered immediately to report the situation to company headquarters and ensure that covering fire was available. "Although the position was now completely dominated by the enemy," his Military Medal citation reported, "Private Bertrand insisted that he should be allowed to go alone. He left the house and crossed 350 yards of open ground to Company headquarters through severe mortar and aimed small-arms fire. He then gave the company commander a complete and clear picture of the situation and plan of the platoon commander, as a result of which supporting artillery and small-arms fire was brought down in such a manner as to enable the platoon to be withdrawn and reorganized in a dominating position on the river line. Had it not been for Private Bertrand's brave action . . . the platoon of twenty-two all ranks would have been completely overwhelmed."[11]

Learning that 2nd Brigade's Loyal Edmonton Regiment was to put in a night attack on the opposite side of the tracks from 'A' Company's position, Major Strome Galloway—still commanding the battalion—decided to push 'B' Company through this position to establish a bridgehead. The attack would be timed to coincide with that of the Eddies. At 2330 hours, however, Captain E.M. Hills reported that he had sent a 'B' Company patrol through 'A' Company's position and discovered the crossing point well defended. The Germans were in fact sweeping the ground almost continuously with machine-gun fire from positions along the railway. Galloway decided "to wait before occupying the area and see if the Edmonton's attack would ease the pressure on 'B' Company's objective."[12]

Over the course of October 17, the 48th Highlanders on 1st Brigade's left flank had also reached the Pisciatello, which on their side of Highway 9 was called the Donegaglia. The 48th's orders were to match the timing of their nighttime crossing to that of the RCR. At 1500 hours, meanwhile, a divisional intelligence report advised Lieutenant Colonel Don Mackenzie that a time bomb had reportedly been hidden in a building that proved to be in 'B' Company's area.[13] A large three-storey *casa* on a hill, it was serving as 'B' Company's headquarters. Having been in the house for three hours, Captain Mike George and Lieutenant John Milling of No. 10 Platoon were at first dubious. There was, the regiment's historian wrote, "so little worry that a card game" played by members of Milling's platoon "continued, the players scornfully [insisting] they had heard those jittery staff rumours before."

George, however, began to worry, and told several men armed with flashlights to search the wine cellar. "It was a dungeon-like basement, with heavily-walled vaults, an ideal spot to take cover or to plant a fiendish contrivance."[14] At 1600 hours, a stick of plastic high-explosive was found in a cistern in the wine cellar. Sergeant Arnold Lea and Corporal Al Payton volunteered to conduct a further investigation as soon as the other personnel cleared the house. "At 1605 hours, after removing the debris from the well, some 50 boxes of HE with 25 sticks in a box were removed and carried outside. When some 20 of these had been removed gun cotton charges were discovered—enough of these were removed to fill completely, a 3 feet high and 2 feet in diameter 'flour bin.' By this time the well had been searched and cleared to a depth of approximately 36 inches," the 48th Highlander official report on the incident recorded.

"Under these charges 20 rounds of 88-millimetre HE had been placed . . . with the nose caps removed. In the centre of these was a timed charge, wrapped in cloth, and under this again more gun cotton charges. The time clock was set . . . with the clock window uppermost . . . A white bag was placed over it." Private Arthur Trudel, who had taken a course on time mechanisms, deactivated the clock. It was set to explode one day and twenty-one hours after Trudel's deactivation. "The enemy had evidently placed his charge to catch a command post or a HQ. The building was large and had been occupied by the enemy. The basement was undoubtedly impregnable to shellfire and therefore an attractive spot . . . The three men who took part continued in the search and disposal and estimated that 100–150 pounds of explosives was placed in the well."[15]

DURING THE EARLY afternoon of October 16, there had been a light shower. On the 17th, cloudy skies prevailed. Then, in the late afternoon, it began raining lightly and steadily. Amidst growing concern that the heavy rains that had halted operations at the end of September were returning, Loyal Edmonton Regiment's Lieutenant Colonel Jim Stone sent a reconnaissance patrol to the selected assault point next to the Pisciatello railroad crossing. The patrol leader soon returned and told Stone that the "banks were very slippery" and the ground next to the river was "just straight mud."

The thirty-six-year-old Stone had entered the war as a private after enlisting at the Loyal Edmonton Regiment's recruitment centre in Grande Prairie. Having served in the British militia before he immigrated to Canada, Stone was soon recognized as a soldier with potential. Promoted to corporal, he was sent to England for specialized small-arms training. By April 1940, Stone was a sergeant and had been further promoted to company sergeant major by the time he participated in the August 1941 raid of Spitsbergen, Norway. Two months later, he was selected for officer training. Assigned to serve as one of 1st Division's beach masters in Sicily, Stone spent Operation Husky supervising the offloading of ships onto the Canadian beach and grimly contemplating "jumping ship" to get back to the regiment and into the fight. Just before the Canadians joined the British Eighth Army invasion of the Italian mainland, in September 1943, Stone was promoted to captain and achieved his long-desired goal of commanding an infantry company. By the Gothic Line Battle, Stone was second-in-command and serving under Lieutenant Colonel Bell-Irving. When Bell-Irving had been given command of the Eddies after the Liri Valley Campaign, Stone had angrily demanded a transfer. Bell-Irving, however, had calmly met the six-foot-five man's eyes and told Stone that he "*was* the Edmonton Regiment." The two soon became fast friends and managed the battalion command like teammates. On October 7, however, the Seaforth's commander, Lieutenant Colonel Syd Thomson, was transferred out of the division after clashing with 2nd Brigade's Brigadier Graeme Gibson. Being an original Seaforth, Bell-Irving replaced Thomson. Gibson was ostensibly replaced by Pat Bogert due to illness, but the real reason was that Lieutenant General Tommy Burns had lost faith in his leadership because of a series of clashes with the brigade's battalion commanders. Amid this shuffling, Stone got command of the Eddies. "I was joyful," he said later, "because I had commanded it a couple of times before. I also felt a great sense of satisfaction, because I had joined the Eddies as a private and now commanded them." To some degree, Stone felt the command was his due, for he was "probably one of the most experienced officers in Italy, as no wounds or sickness had kept me out of the line."

Stone's level of experience was such that Vokes trusted his judgment. Consequently, when Stone called the divisional commander and told him about the poor ground conditions, Vokes said it was up to him whether to launch the attack that night. "He knew I would go if I could," Stone remembered. After a couple of minutes' thought, Stone said, "We'll take a chance on it."[16]

The attack plan Stone hammered out with Bogert at 1630 hours called for a single company of Eddies to cross silently east of the railroad. It would then swing right and seize a house about four hundred yards away. A single platoon would then move to another house, also four hundred yards east of the crossing point but almost adjacent to the Pisciatello. This would give the company a narrow bridgehead guarding a second ford, halfway between the railroad and Ponte della Pietra, that had been identified as likely suitable for tanks. The rest of the battalion would stand ready to cross into the bridgehead either at the new ford or at the crossing adjacent to the railroad. If the first company met stiff resistance, Stone planned to pass another company over and have it seize the second house. As soon as the tanks crossed at the designated ford, Stone would take Ponte della Pietra. The hamlet itself was of no significance, but next to it was a demolished stone bridge, and it was here that divisional engineers planned to erect another bridge alongside it.

The assault was to be lavishly supported by a platoon each of the Saskatoon Light Infantry's heavy machine guns and 4.2 mortars, a troop of 1st Anti-Tank Regiment M-10 SPGS, a squadron of 12th Royal Tank Regiment, and artillery on call. At 1800 hours, Stone signalled that "the attack was on."

'C' Company, under Major H.A. Tucker, walked to the river through darkness, thick fog, and pouring rain. At 2215 hours, Tucker's men waded the shallow stream undetected. Swinging right, they headed for the first building. They were closing on it at 2300 hours when several German machine guns opened up with long bursts of fire. A close-quarters gunfight erupted around the building.

As soon as Tucker reported that 'C' Company was caught in a fight, Stone ordered Captain L.E. Taplin's 'B' Company to join the battle. By 0045 hours on October 18, Taplin reported just crossing the river and coming into "immediate contact with the enemy." At 0100 hours, Tucker reported that the house was won. But 'C' Company was still closely engaged. He also advised that Germans had infiltrated between the two Edmonton companies. Stone later wrote that "within a limited bridgehead of 500 yards square, around the ford, the battle continued until daylight. Enemy patrols repeatedly counterattacked and were beaten back by determined opposition."[17]

As the battle raged, Stone was working on getting tanks to his men. But an engineering reconnaissance party and officers from 1st Anti-Tank Regiment reported at 0500 hours that crossing the M-10s at the ford was "impossible . . . because of the soft sandy nature of the river bottom." Thirty minutes later, 'B' and 'C' Companies reported that they had linked up, were "consolidated together along the river bank," and had several prisoners. They were also having their wounded carried or walked back across the crossing by either the railroad or the ford. As daylight broke, the German artillery shelling that had been hammering all lines of approach to the river decreased. But the Germans kept pounding the ford itself.[18]

When Bogert learned that the ford was unusable, he sent a message urging Stone to have 'B' and 'C' Companies "hold their present gains . . . if possible." Bogert added that this "order . . . was not mandatory." If Stone wished, he could pull one company out. To provide some support, Bogert also ordered 1st Anti-Tank Regiment to send a troop of M-10S "to the river's edge." From there they could at least provide fire support to the companies on the other side.

At 0800 hours, Bogert and his intelligence officer, Captain Bradish, arrived at the stone farmhouse Stone was using for a Tac HQ. They found Stone "quite satisfied with the situation with 'B' Company . . . and 'C' Company with the areas clear of enemy, although they were being subjected to considerable MG and sniper fire both from the front and flanks." Bogert advised Stone that the situation on 2nd Brigade's flanks "was quite gratifying." Although 1st Brigade's attempts to cross the river had been driven back, Bogert expected the situation to improve because 3rd Brigade was to take over that front in the evening. That would put fresh troops into the mix. On the extreme left flank, 46th British Infantry Division was descending rapidly from the Apennine foothills, only about a mile and a half from Cesena. To the right, 5th New Zealand Infantry Brigade had reached Ruffio on October 16. The Kiwis were now closing on the Pisciatello across from the village of Casone and were less than three-quarters of a mile to the right of the Seaforth Highlanders.[19]

ALTHOUGH LIEUTENANT COLONEL Stone had evinced nothing but confidence in the Loyal Edmonton Regiment's two-company bridgehead, he was concerned about his men's ability to hold on without direct armour support. With him at Tac HQ was Captain Bullock, a 12th Royal Tank Regiment liaison officer. Bullock decided at 0930 hours to personally check conditions at the ford. Accompanied by two Edmonton scouts, Bullock quickly decided that the earlier report had been wrong and the Pisciatello was fordable. While the party was at the river, the scouts rounded up four German prisoners, whom they escorted back to Stone's headquarters.[20] "I can wade it with my tanks," Bullock told Stone, who realized the risk the tanker was willing to take. If one of the Churchills got stuck in the ford, it would be vulnerable to destruction by either artillery fire or panzer grenadiers infiltrating into Panzerfaust range.[21]

The additional four prisoners brought the total at Stone's head-quarters to nine, so he ordered Lieutenant Bill Foster to escort them to a prisoner cage farther back. En route, Foster was wounded by mortar fire and later died at the Regimental Aid Post (RAP). He was the second Edmonton officer to be killed while well back from the front lines, Captain Thomas Patrick Gentles having also fallen victim to mortar fire the same day.

Across the Pisciatello, 'C' Company had pushed out to seize the house that had been its original objective. Trying to keep pace, 'B' Company reported at noon that it was under increasingly heavy machine-gun fire. Stone knew the two companies could be moving into real trouble. He ordered 'D' Company to accompany the troop of Churchills across the ford at 1330 hours, but this was pushed back thirty minutes because the tanks were having problems with their tracks. When 'D' Company and its three supporting Churchills forded the river, the force quickly established contact with 'B' Company with-out meeting any opposition. Thirty minutes later, the British squad-ron commander crossed with his remaining two troops of Churchills.

The fight turned decisively in the Eddies' favour, and 'C' Company's Major Tucker reported that "several casualties had been inflicted upon the enemy by our tanks." With each company supported by a tank troop, a concerted push toward Ponte della Pietra began. At 1430 hours, 'B' Company reached its objective. Stone ordered it to stay put to provide a firm base for 'D' Company to pass through and lead the drive to Ponte della Pietra.[22] 'C' Company, meanwhile, was pushing out on the battalion's left flank toward a group of houses, with No. 13 Platoon under Corporal Gerald Elwood Kingston lead-ing. Kingston had taken over the platoon when its leader had been wounded early in the operation. As the platoon approached the build-ings, "it came under intense machine-gun and grenade fire from well concealed and dug-in enemy positions which were screened from the view of [the] supporting tanks."

Kingston shouted "Charge" and pelted ahead of his men across fifty yards of open ground to close on the German dugouts. A panzer grenadier officer tried to break the Edmonton charge by throwing grenades, but Kingston shot him dead at a range of just five yards with a burst from his Thompson submachine gun. Having lost their officer, the remaining Germans hunkered deep into their dugouts. Here they were "quickly disposed of by hand grenade." Although wounded in the opening moments of the charge, Kingston continued to lead the platoon until all the buildings were cleared. No. 13 Platoon rounded up twenty-one prisoners and reported four Germans killed. One of the prisoners was a German artillery officer with a wireless set, who had been "directing the heavy and accurate artillery fire" on the ford to prevent its use as a vehicle crossing. Kingston's subsequent Distinguished Conduct Medal citation credited his "courage, initiative, and leadership" for the success of 'C' Company's attack. The capture of the artillery officer also "enabled supporting arms to cross the river and this ensured the breaking of the enemy's defences in the battalion sector."[23]

Learning there were a good number of wounded Eddies who needed evacuating to the RAP, which was 1,800 yards from the Pisciatello, Private Joseph Charles Bohemier volunteered to take a carrier and get them. Arriving after the British tank squadron had crossed, he found the ford reduced to a virtual quagmire. It was also still being hit by accurate artillery and mortar fire. Bohemier proceeded to cross the ford five times to bring twenty wounded men to safety. On his way to one of the forward companies, a shell, pierced in several places by shrapnel, landed only a few yards from the carrier. The explosion's flash and a spray of mud temporarily blinded Bohemier. Inching on through heavy mortar fire, his sight gradually returning, Bohemier reached the company, loaded three seriously wounded men aboard the carrier, and drove it back to the RAP. Bohemier's Military Medal citation declared that "his gallant action in the face of great danger and difficulties undoubtedly saved the lives of several men."[24]

'D' Company met some opposition but reached Ponte della Pietra at 1830 hours. Although the Germans had abandoned the hamlet, they had dynamited a large crater in its central road that made it impossible for the tanks to pass through. Until the crater was filled, the planned advance by 'A' Company on the road running north from the hamlet would lack tank support. Stone rushed the battalion's pioneer platoon to the scene, but they reported that it would take a bulldozer to repair the damage. While there had been no further rain during the day, the surrounding countryside remained sodden and largely impassable to the Churchills.

Major Bill Longhurst's 'A' Company marched out of Ponte della Pietra alone at 2100 hours on an advance that was to carry it a thousand yards. Met by heavy machine-gun fire, Longhurst pulled back to the village and then hooked out cross-country to the northeast. Despite meeting several machine-gun positions along the way, Longhurst reported his men firmly in control of the road objective at 0015 hours on October 19.[25]

The weather remained cloudy but clear of rain. However, the ground off the roads was "still very muddy and soft," the Edmonton's war diarist recorded. At the ford, the troop of M-10s from 1st Anti-Tank Regiment attempted a crossing. The first one made it and trundled off to join 'D' Company at Ponte della Pietra, but the remaining two "became stuck in the sandy river bottom." With the ford blocked to any further vehicles, the ammunition and rations sent forward to the infantry companies had to be "man-packed" across the river and up to the troops.

Just before dawn, Stone, his batman, and a signaller hitched a ride aboard one of the Bren carriers bringing rations up to the ford. The carrier was followed by a 3-ton lorry of 3rd Field Company, Royal Canadian Engineers. Their route was via a road running from Ruffio to the blown bridge at Ponte della Pietra. About two hundred yards short of the Pisciatello, both vehicles triggered mines. Of the eight men present, all but Stone were injured.[26]

"I made a big curve through the air and landed in a ditch. Got up completely unshaken. The signaller was in the ditch lying on top of the wireless. Batman had a broken leg."[27] Carrier driver Private Maurice James Mather died of his injuries two days later.[28]

Despite this mishap, Stone was determined to cross the river to see what was happening. He headed along the road, which was

bordered by hedges on both sides. It was pitch black. Stone had the
.45-calibre Colt revolver he had parlayed out of an American during
a drink somewhere along the way. For once, "Big Jim Stone," as the
Eddies called him, was scared and shaking—thinking this might not
have been the brightest notion on the part of a battalion commander.
The bridge had been blown apart, but enough of it protruded from
the water that Stone was able to pick his way across. He was soon relieved to have a corporal call out a password. Stone had the man take
him up to the 'D' Company commander, who reported that he had
the tanks with him and everything was under control.[29]

By the time Stone returned to the river, 3rd Field Company sappers were well along in building an eighty-foot Bailey bridge next
to the demolished stone one. At 0830 hours, the bridge opened to
traffic, and Stone had his Tac HQ moved to a house on the north
side of the hamlet, which derived its name from the wrecked bridge.
The Princess Patricia's Canadian Light Infantry, tasked with leading
2nd Brigade's drive to the Savio River, began crossing the bridge
and moving past the Eddies. Their three-day battle at the Pisciatello
over, the Eddies counted casualties. Six men were killed and thirty-
five wounded—at least some of these surviving as a result of Private
Bohemier's rescue efforts. How many Germans had died was never
determined, but the Eddies sent eighty prisoners back to the rear.

In his report on the action, Stone concluded that this kind of night
attack was the "most practical and safest way to cross a river." As for
the engineers and anti-tank regiment officers who had deemed the
ford impassable, Stone declared that "tracks must attempt possible
crossings before saying that they are impractical." Had not the British
liaison officer "taken a chance, no armour would have been over the
river and the result may have been much different." The decision to
first task just two companies with winning the bridgehead he considered a wise move. Committing a larger number of troops into "a
small area only results in heavy losses from mortar and shell fire.
Two companies only were committed in this case and although slow,
proved ample for mopping up in the original forward bridgehead . . .
For conclusion, a good plan on all levels, vigorously carried out will
always be successful."[30]

TO THE LEFT of 2nd Brigade, the battalions of 3rd Brigade had relieved 1st Brigade by midnight on October 18. The Royal 22e Régiment (Van Doos) relieved the Royal Canadian Regiment, the West Nova Scotia Regiment took over from the 48th Highlanders, and the Carleton and York Regiment replaced the Hastings and Prince Edward Regiment in Bulgaria.

The Royal 22e Régiment's commander, Lieutenant Colonel Jean Allard, had been instructed by Brigadier Paul Bernatchez to relieve the Royal Canadian Regiment literally "down to individuals relieving their opposite numbers. Our task," Allard told his officers, "is to keep in touch with the enemy and work our way forward piece by piece." When his briefing concluded, Allard went directly to the RCR Tac HQ and took over from Lieutenant Colonel Jim Ritchie, while his company commanders met the officers they were to replace and reconnoitred the new positions. In the process, 'A' Company's Captain L. Deniset was wounded by shellfire, and Lieutenant Paul Emile Vincent replaced him.

Allard had no intention of just establishing his companies along the Pisciatello River by the railway. Instead, 'C' Company was to put "a strong fighting patrol" across the river and five hundred yards along Highway 9 to a T-junction. If little or no opposition was met, a 'B' Company patrol led by Lieutenant C. Bouchard would move along the river to the railway crossing. By 0035 hours on October 19, the Van Doos were in place and the two patrols headed out. At 0155 hours, Bouchard reported he was alongside the railway crossing and no enemy were present. Bouchard had even fired some rifle grenades in hopes of drawing German fire, but nothing was returned. Three minutes later, 'C' Company's Major Louis F. Trudeau informed Allard that his patrol had reached its objective unopposed. Allard ordered Trudeau to advance his whole company to the patrol's position, with 'D' Company moving up to 'C' Company's river position. He also instructed Major Pierre Potvin at 0400 hours to send a new patrol about six hundred yards to a large building identified as Casa Calandrini, midway between the railroad and Highway 9. Allard was getting the sense that the Germans were withdrawing fast and the Van Doos could gain ground quickly. By 0600 hours, this appeared to be the case. as all companies had reached their new objectives without incident.

Thirty minutes later, Bernatchez signalled Allard. "The situation appears to have calmed down on our front and our flanks. You will push forward." The new objective was another junction on Highway 9 about one thousand yards north of the T-junction that 'C' Company had reached. Allard hurried up to 'C' Company's position with his intelligence officer and artillery forward observation officer in tow to develop a new plan. He decided to send 'A' and 'B' Companies along both sides of the highway, with 'D' and 'C' Companies out on the flanks.[31]

It was about 0700 hours. The Loyal Edmonton Regiment was alongside on the right with the Princess Patricia's Canadian Light Infantry readying to push through for an advance to the Savio River. Immediately to the left, the West Nova Scotia Regiment was reporting no enemy contact. Behind the Van Doos, the Carleton and York Regiment remained in Bulgaria. But Bernatchez planned to bring the Carletons forward in the afternoon and pass them through either the Van Doos or the West Novas.[32]

The Van Doos continued a steady unopposed advance. At 1010 hours, Bernatchez arrived at Allard's Tac HQ with more instructions and waited impatiently for the battalion commander to return from consulting with the company commanders. "All intel reports collected in the last twelve hours tend to indicate a general withdrawal of the enemy on the natural line of defence of the Savio River," he said. Forward elements of 46th British Infantry Division were probing Cesena from the southwest. Accordingly, 3rd Brigade was to gain the east bank of the Savio and the eastern side of Cesena. The brigade advance was to see the West Novas proceed only about a mile from the Pisciatello and then stop to form a blocking line running from Highway 9 left to the 1st Canadian Infantry Division's boundary with the 46th Division. Allard would advance north of Cesena to gain the Savio and restore contact with the Germans. The Carletons, meanwhile, would prepare to pass through the West Novas and come up left of the Van Doos to push up Highway 9 past Cesena to the river.[33]

By noon, the West Novas had halted, "entirely surrounded by friends," as the battalion war diarist put it.[34] Meanwhile, as the Van Doos continued their steady advance, Allard increasingly expected trouble. He kept the advance narrow, with 'A' and 'C' Companies leapfrogging each other at regular intervals. The Bren carrier platoon followed, ready to provide support as necessary. A troop of 12th Royal Tank Regiment Churchills also lurked a quick bound back from the two leading companies. Moving with 'C' Company was a Royal Canadian Horse Artillery forward observation officer—ready to call up the guns. Behind the tanks and carriers, 'B' and 'D' Companies were also close behind, ready to pass to the front at any time. Allard was also moving with the troops, having created a mobile command post, linked to his Tac HQ by wireless and runners.

At 1530 hours, Allard's expectations were fulfilled when the entire battalion came under heavy shelling from 105-millimetre and 88-millimetre guns, Nebelwerfers, mortars, and medium machine guns. The German fire extended as far back as the Tac HQ, which Allard kept advancing to new positions to ensure that it kept within wireless range of the forward companies. At 1600 hours, he told its personnel to set up in a filthy stable Allard had passed with his mobile command post.

Twenty-five minutes later, 'A' Company reached the road that ran straight as an arrow east from Cesena to a mile and a half south of Cervia on the Adriatic coast. Here, the company was subjected to intense fire from a position about three hundred yards to the north. Allard ordered the artillery to engage the German position and the troop of tanks to join 'A' Company. Trudeau soon reported that he was running short of ammunition. Allard sent a Bren carrier to resupply him.

Major Potvin took 'B' Company forward to come up on 'A' Company's right flank. He was soon reporting meeting heavy resistance and taking casualties. All contact with 'C' Company, meanwhile, had been lost when it was still a few hundred yards short of the Cesena–Cervia road. Allard decided at 1700 hours to send a signaller with a No. 48 wireless set and two scouts under command of 'B' Company's Lieutenant F. Turgeon to find 'C' Company and re-establish its communications. Soon after the party left, the Tac HQ signallers managed to re-net 'C' Company into the communications loop. The company commander reported being north of the road now. Turgeon's party soon joined 'C' Company, reporting that they had been dodging shellfire the entire trip forward.

As night fell, the Van Doos halted a short distance beyond the road. At 2200 hours, carriers began evacuating the wounded. The German shelling eased. About three thousand yards to the west beyond Cesena, two big explosions were heard and their flashes were clearly visible. Allard took this as a sign that the Germans were retreating across the Savio. The Van Doos buttoned down for a brief reorganization, with patrols active to intercept any attempted counterattacks.[35]

7

Absolutely Browned Off

AT 1550 HOURS ON October 19, the Carleton and York Regiment had moved out from behind the Royal 22e Régiment to advance on its left toward Cesena via Highway 9. The Van Doos were drawing away to the east and concentrating on a line of advance immediately right of the railroad. As the Van Doos were still a short distance ahead, they protected the Carletons' eastern flank somewhat, while 46th British Infantry Division—closing on Cesena—covered their western flank. Unable to find any weak points to exploit, the Germans in front of the Carletons melted away. At 2340 hours, all four Carleton companies were just short of Cesena—ending, as their war diarist noted, "a day of movement."

Twenty minutes into October 20, 'B' Company's Major L.A. Watling sent a patrol into Cesena.[1] With a population of about sixteen thousand, Cesena boasted several fine palaces and a Renaissance library. On its southwestern flank, the old fortress called Rocca Malatestiana stood. The Madonna del Monte Abbey perched on a hill south of the city.[2]

As the patrol closed on the city centre, it was engaged by MG42 machine guns firing on fixed lines and hastily withdrew. When 3rd Canadian Infantry Brigade headquarters was advised of this, the Carletons were ordered to have 'B' Company send "a contact patrol to the friends on our left." Watling sent men out, and they soon reported having met a patrol of the 46th Division's 6th Black Watch Regiment. By dawn, Watling's company controlled a good portion of the city's southeastern part.[3] At 0800 hours, Lieutenant Colonel Jack P. Ensor figured the Germans had given up Cesena, and he headed toward the city centre with his adjutant, Captain W.C. Ott. Half an hour later, Ensor was back at his Tac HQ, happily reporting having been "royally welcomed as a liberator by the citizens of Cesena." Ensor told Brigadier Paul Bernatchez that not only was Cesena clear, but elements of the 46th Division were consolidating within. Bernatchez immediately ordered the Carletons and Van Doos to press on to the Savio River and seek viable crossings.

Captain D.A. Crutcher's 'D' Company moved out immediately. Passing through Cesena, it soon reached the Highway 9 bridge. It was blown, and the company drew machine-gun fire from across the Savio. Crutcher told Ensor the river here looked unfordable, but a road bridge half a mile south seemed still intact. As this bridge lay in V British Corps's sector, Crutcher could only observe it from 3rd Brigade's designated western boundary. From this distance, he could see "piers of an old Roman bridge which had survived Allied bombing and German demolitions." These offered a likely foundation for a Bailey bridge.

By mid-morning, 'D' Company was joined by 'C' Company. 'B' Company was a few hundred yards back in Cesena and 'A' Company farther back still, on the city's southern outskirts. The battalion spent the remainder of the day getting a sense of the river and the German defences across it.[4]

While the Carletons's advance had gone smoothly and without notable casualties, the Royal 22e Régiment faced stiffer resistance during its early-morning advance. The Van Doos were often more understrength than other 1 Canadian Corps infantry battalions because of difficulty finding new French Canadian reinforcements. Consequently, as a result of the fighting to close on the river, 'C' Company reported a fighting strength of just thirty-eight men. Shortly thereafter, Major Pierre Potvin advised Lieutenant Colonel Jean Allard that 'B' Company numbered sixty-six men and had one man killed, three wounded, and two missing. The Van Doos kept pushing forward cautiously, pushing back the gradually thinning German rearguard. By 0940 hours, Potvin's 'B' Company had reached the Savio.

A patrol sent where the railway spanned the river reported a thirty-yard gap blown in the bridge there. The patrol leader thought the river fordable at this point by both infantry and tanks. Getting tanks down to the riverbed was another matter, as the dyke was steep. Still, he believed a tank could probably slide down without burying its nose in the river bottom. The German side of the river sloped up fairly gently so could be easily mounted. About twenty to thirty yards wide, the Savio appeared to be only three to four feet deep with "a good, firm bottom." Along the Canadian bank, a wire ran north of the railroad tracks for about a hundred yards, and attached to it were signs reading "*Minen*." Before any tanks approached the river, the patrol leader advised the engineers to sweep the area for mines.[5]

TO THE RIGHT of the Van Doos, 2nd Brigade's Princess Patricia's Canadian Light Infantry had crossed the Pisciatello River via the Ponte della Pietra Bailey bridge in the early morning of October 19. At 0850 hours, Captain N. Featherstone's 'A' Company, with a troop of 12th Royal Tank Regiment Churchills, led the advance out of the Loyal Edmonton Regiment's bridgehead. The company's intermediate objective was 800 yards due north. 'B' Company under Major Colin MacDougall followed, while the other two companies and Lieutenant Colonel R.P. "Slug" Clark's Tac HQ were farther back. The Patricias were to reach the Savio River, clearing Sant' Egidio village en route. This village stood on the south side of the Cesena–Cervia road, about 1,000 yards northeast of Cesena, and was also designated as a boundary marker for 2nd and 3rd Canadian Infantry Brigades.

All went smoothly until 1415 hours, when Major Pat Crofton's 'D' Company—having leapfrogged to the lead—was 300 yards east of its objective, a built-up intersection on the Cesena–Cervia road, code-named Upperchurch. The lead platoon was pinned down by fire from the buildings. Moments later, two of the three supporting Churchills were knocked out by a self-propelled or anti-tank gun.

Realizing the lead platoon was so close to the Germans that it would be unsafe to call in artillery, Crofton extracted it and then pulled back 1,200 yards. He then had artillery pound the intersection. Clark, meanwhile, had dispatched the battalion's anti-tank platoon to protect 'D' Company's exposed right flank. Although the 4th New Zealand Armoured Brigade was advancing to the Patricia's right, its battalions were about three miles back.

Determined to keep the advance going, Clark ordered Featherstone's 'A' Company to execute a left hook and seize Sant' Egidio, which was 300 yards southwest of Upperchurch. He hoped this would relieve the pressure on 'D' Company. At 1800 hours, Featherstone's men and their three supporting tanks swept through Sant' Egidio without incident.

With medium artillery hammering Upperchurch in an attempt to put the German infantry and SPG to flight, Clark ordered 'A' and 'D' Companies to launch a pincer attack. At 1820 hours, 'A' Company would strike from the southwest and 'D' Company the east.[6] Crofton's 'D' Company was quickly stopped 500 yards short of the buildings by heavy machine-gun fire, and the fighting patrol leading Featherstone's company was also halted the moment it reached the intersection's buildings. The continued artillery fire on the intersection and Canadian infantry showing up on two flanks, however, snapped the German determination to hold. As the fire eased, Crofton led his men in among the buildings. A quick house-to-house clearing operation met little resistance. At 2350 hours, Crofton reported 'D' Company snug in Upperchurch. The day ended with the Patricias having suffered no casualties.

By midnight it was raining.[7] In the dark, early-morning hours of October 20, the Patricia's historian wrote, Major Sam Potts and 'C' Company "filed silently across the sodden fields and dripping pastures to a crossroads about [1,000] yards west of La Chiaviche." This put them about 300 yards short of the Savio. Patrols to the river "were fired on from the opposite bank and a number of Germans were seen emerging from dugouts to man nearby weapon pits. The Canadian artillery immediately began to pound the area."[8]

THE ADVANCES BY 1st Canadian Infantry Division and 2nd New Zealand Armoured Division to the Savio River on October 19–20 left the Germans facing Cumberland Force in an untenable position. Accordingly, on the night of October 19–20, LXXVI Panzer Korps commander General der Panzertruppen Traugott Herr ordered 1st Fallschirmjäger Division's General der Fallschirmtruppe Richard Heidrich to withdraw to the Savio. He would then transfer the division to control by LI Gebirgskorps (mountain corps), which was holding the line to the right of Herr's Korps. Always professional, the paratroopers were gone by dawn. "In the morning," Brigadier Ian Cumberland wrote, "it became evident the enemy had withdrawn a long way. Preliminary confirmation soon came from a deserter who stated that the Germans had gone back to the Savio. Little or no opposition was encountered during the day."[9]

Crossing the Fiumicino River, the Governor General's Horse Guards headed up Highway 16 for Cesenatico. The leading troops soon encountered large groups of Italians, who reported the Germans had fled all the way back to Cervia. Commandeering bicycles, Lieutenant Colonel Allan Jordan and several Tac HQ officers pedalled merrily up the highway, rode into Cesenatico, "and were acclaimed as liberators by the civil population."[10]

The Germans had, however, done a thorough job of rendering the coastal highway impassable for vehicle use. All bridges were blown, long sections of road had been cratered by explosives, and any off-road movement left vehicles stuck in the adjacent "soft, marshy ground."

Inland, the Royal Canadian Dragoons, still operating on foot and supported by tanks of the British Columbia Dragoons, easily advanced five miles to the Granarolo River, which flowed into the Adriatic a little south of Cervia. Here, the Royal Canadian Dragoons were relieved by the British 27th Lancers Cavalry Regiment and went into reserve. Cumberland's intention for the following days was to push hard for the Savio, which drained into the Adriatic about five miles north of Cervia.[11]

On Cumberland Force's left flank, 2nd New Zealand Division's advance beyond the Pisciatello River had started on the early morning of October 19 and progressed rapidly, until the 18th and 20th Regiments of 4th New Zealand Armoured Brigade—which had led the drive once the Pisciatello was bridged—met heavy resistance at the Cesena–Cervia road between Calabrina and Osteriaccia. These two villages were barely a mile apart, and the New Zealanders had aimed to shoot like an arrow through the gap between. Reorganizing during the night, the Kiwi armour ground into the gap on the morning of October 20 and swept through minimal resistance to gain the Savio in front of the hamlet San Martino. Heavy machine-gun fire from across the river greeted them. The 2nd New Zealand Division's job was complete. They were to be relieved by 5th Canadian Armoured Division either on or shortly after October 21.[12]

Although 5th Canadian Armoured Division was returning to the line, British Eighth Army's Lieutenant General Richard McCreery intended to soon give all 1 Canadian Corps a rest. On October 19, McCreery had advised Lieutenant General Tommy Burns that once the Savio River crossings were won, he foresaw the Canadians holding just beyond the river to protect Eighth Army's right flank from Highway 9 to the Adriatic.[13] The corps would have no "tasks beyond this, except possibly to follow up with light reconnaissance forces to a limited distance."

Burns, however, was anxious to finish the job. On the morning of October 20, he visited 1st Division's headquarters and instructed Major General Chris Vokes to establish a bridgehead across the river forthwith.[14] Vokes had planned for 2nd Brigade to do precisely that. Relations between Burns and his two Canadian divisional generals were reaching the breaking point. In a hand-written letter to a friend at Canadian Military Headquarters in London, Vokes had just scribbled, "Things have reached a crisis here . . . but whether any action is taken by parties responsible at your end is impossible to predict. If nothing is done & quickly, [Major General] Bert [Hoffmeister] and I . . . are prepared to adopt the only course possible. Personally I am absolutely browned off. In spite of no able direction we have continued to bear the cross for an individual who lacks one iota of personality, appreciation of effort or the first goddamn thing in the application of book learning to what is practical in war & what isn't. I've done my best to be loyal but goddammit the strain has been too bloody great."

Vokes cited several senior corps and divisional officers who felt the same. The brewing storm of likely insubordination or outright mutiny within the corps had become so glaringly apparent that Brigadier E.G. Weeks, responsible for the Canadian rear area and reinforcement pools in Italy, had visited the front to investigate the situation. In a cabled report to London, Weeks said, "On 16 Oct Hoffmeister informed me relationship with Burns was becoming intolerable. During recent ops, Hoffmeister stated had lost all confidence in Burns. Gave as examples remarks at conferences, tendency interfere forward commanders.

"Hoffmeister found himself in spite best intentions inclined to be insubordinate to Burns with result Hoffmeister feels that either he or Burns should be relieved. On 18 Oct I proceeded Corps by air. On arrival [Corps Assistant Adjutant and Quartermaster General Lieutenant Colonel W.P.] Gilbride informed relationships between Hoffmeister and Vokes with Burns becoming intolerable. [Brigadier, General Staff] Des Smith, Gilbride, [Commander, Corps Royal Artillery Brigadier E.C.] Plow, [Corps Chief Engineer Brigadier C.A.] Campbell informed me individually that they were considering parading before McCreery in order to bring attention Burns attitude and remarks conferences arguments with Hoffmeister and Vokes lack dignity unpleasant embarrassment. Also tendency on part of Hoffmeister and Vokes ignore Burns direction."

When Weeks spoke with McCreery, the Eighth Army commander was fully aware of the bad blood between Burns and his divisional generals. He told Weeks the situation was "intolerable" and set up a meeting between the brigadier and General Harold Alexander.[15] Burns was becoming a marked man.

On October 20, however, Vokes had more important irons in the fire. He badly wanted 2nd Brigade across the Savio. To his right, the New Zealanders were sitting tight and awaiting relief by Hoffmeister's division. But on the left, v British Corps had already crossed the river. On the 19th, battalions of 46th British Infantry Division had entered Cesena and then been relieved by 4th British Infantry Division. In the early morning hours of October 20, a battalion of 4th Division's 12th Brigade waded the Savio five hundred yards south of Cesena and gained a foothold. Despite determined counterattacks, the foothold was held and considerably expanded. Meanwhile, descending from the foothills, 10th Indian Division won two bridgeheads adjacent to Highway 71.[16] Vokes knew the Canadians needed to get into the game.

Whenever Vokes rushed things, he defaulted to a one-battalion attack without regard to opposing German strength. His instructions to Lieutenant Colonel Pat Bogert accordingly called for the Patricias to bounce the Savio with two companies. They would advance from the cover of the village of Martorano, wade the river, and push out eight hundred yards to establish a shallow bridgehead. Once this was done, the Seaforth Highlanders would pass through and extend the bridgehead to a depth of a mile, with its outer boundary reaching the village of Pieve Sestina. This would provide room for the engineers to securely do their bridging work. Where the bridge would be built was not yet determined. When a Patricia patrol accompanied an engineering party to the Savio at 1140 hours, machine-gun fire from the opposite bank forced a hurried withdrawal. With time for only a brief glimpse of the river and its banks, the engineers learned nothing more than that any bridge building must be done in daylight.[17]

SOON AFTER THE assault on the Hitler Line during the Liri Valley Campaign, it had been realized that Canadian infantry battalions had nothing to match the tremendous rate of fire the Germans could deliver with their MG42s. The answer had been for each battalion to add a medium machine-gun platoon (MMG platoon) to the support company, which already provided a pioneer platoon, an anti-tank platoon, and 3-inch mortar platoon. At first glance, an MMG platoon seemed a duplication of the machine-gun platoons of Saskatoon Light Infantry that normally supported 1st Division's battalions during attacks. But the SLI's Vickers machine guns mainly provided indirect fire from positions considerably distant from the forward companies or were used to cover a battalion's flanks. The inherent MMG platoon worked more closely. Each MMG platoon consisted of twenty-nine men and was organized into two sections and a headquarters team. Seven men, including the commander, made up the headquarters, and the rest were divvied between the two sections. Each section was armed with two Vickers machine guns, which were normally moved aboard Bren carriers.

Not long after his involvement in winning a crossing over the Marecchia River on September 22–23, Lieutenant Syd Frost took command of the Patricia's MMG platoon. He quickly learned that its primary role was not so much to deal out death and destruction but to influence "morale. Bolster ours and destroy theirs."

It was to emphasize this role that Lieutenant Colonel Clark assembled a Patricias Orders Group in a shell-torn house on the outskirts of Sant' Egidio. The place was jammed, cigarette smoke filling the room. Present were the battalion's adjutant, the intelligence officer, the signals officer, the medical officer, the four company commanders, all officers of the support company, and artillery, tank, engineer, and SLI representatives. In the middle of the room were map boards. The intelligence officer, Lieutenant D.G. MacCulloch, handed out lists of code names for the attack's objectives. From an adjacent room came the screech and whine of wireless sets being netted in. Outside, German shells and Moaning Minnie rounds shook the building's walls.[18]

A 1st Division photo interpreter had provided air photos of the Savio River taken on October 18. They were not especially helpful. "Likely crossings were not apparent as even the Italians in peacetime had never put a bridge across the river on the front on which we were advancing." Based more on a hunch than anything, the engineers figured the best bridging site was close to Martorano. So that was where the attack would occur. "The air photos also showed that there were very many enemy positions covering the river. It appeared," according to a 2nd Brigade intelligence report, "that German forces were concentrated "so that we could not get a foothold on the west bank, as from the photos he did not seem to have many positions in reserve. It was apparent that he could make a very definite stand on this obstacle."[19]

A 1 Canadian Corps mapping unit noted that "from Cesena to the sea the Savio follows a meandering course north over the flat cultivated plain with its vineyards and tree bordered fields. These latter are interlaced with many irrigation ditches and canals, some of which are tank obstacles." Air reconnaissance indicated that "the river is fordable for infantry throughout its length, but only in a few places for vehicles." Except at Cesena, where the riverbed was about 120 feet wide, with water normally running through about a 60-foot width in the centre, the Savio to the east narrowed to widths between 35 and 50 feet for about five miles, with water filling the entire bed. For the last three miles to the Adriatic, the Savio widened dramatically from 70 feet to 200 feet at its mouth. The riverbed consisted of mud with interspersed gravel shoals. Its banks were wide and steep, rising to 30 feet in places. Only at Cesena and near the river mouth did the ground slope gently to the water. Dykes bordered both sides of the river, except in spots where the bank itself was high enough to prevent flooding. The riverbanks were overgrown with grass, brush, reeds, and, in some places, trees.

In the absence of bridges, the locals used fords when the river was low. The rough roads approaching these generally stopped abruptly at the top of the bank with no cuttings down to the river. For the last 200 yards leading to the river, the roads crossed soft, marshy ground that would provide no solid footing for tanks. Except at the fords, the average depth was about four feet in normal weather. But the Savio's width and depth could change rapidly. During one twenty-four-hour period of torrential rain, the river had widened in one spot from 45 feet and spilled over its banks to a breadth of 300 feet with a current hitting 20 knots. The Germans, of course, had supplemented all the Savio's natural obstacles by sowing "a belt of anti-personnel mines connected to tripwires on the near bank."[20]

Everyone in the room was digesting this rather daunting information when Lieutenant Colonel Clark arrived from getting a final briefing from Bogert. After the battalion had reached the Savio the previous night, the companies had been reorganized. Those officers who had been Left Out of Battle for the approach to the river now replaced the ones who had commanded during this push. As a result, 'A' Company was now under Major Ted Cutbill, 'B' Company Captain Andy Campbell, 'C' Company the now-Major Sam Potts, and 'D' Company Captain A.G. Robinson. With 'B' and 'C' Companies currently holding the front line, 'A' and 'D' Companies would put in the attack. Cutbill's men would thrust out of 'C' Company's position, code-named Snake and lying 1,000 yards south of Martorano, while 'D' Company sallied out from 'B' Company in the village itself, code-named Tay. Until the engineers could install a bridge, there would be no tank support. But Bogert and Clark had teed up extensive artillery, mortar, and medium machine-gun support. The attack was set for 1700 hours.

Frost already had his machine guns set up, with one section at Snake and the other at Tay. As the o Group broke up, Frost asked Clark if there were any special instructions for him. Clark said that once the two companies were across the river, he was to get the platoon over to meet any counterattack.

Only ninety minutes remained until Zero Hour when Frost hitched a ride in Campbell's jeep to 'B' Company's sector. Canadian and German artillery were hammering opposing sides of the river with increasing intensity. With Campbell at the wheel, the jeep had just cleared an intersection when it was hit by an explosion of shellfire. Then a volley of Nebelwerfer rounds struck the road fifty yards ahead. Frost feared the gunners could see them and were bracketing the jeep for a killing salvo. But suddenly Campbell slewed the jeep behind a stout building, which was immediately shaken by shells exploding in the front yard. Campbell smiled at Frost and said, "Welcome to my HQ."

Continuing on foot, Frost dodged salvoes of incoming fire to reach the house close to the river where No. 1 Section had its two Vickers machine guns in an upstairs room. The crew reported having zeroed in on various targets. Corporal W.B. Kilborn pointed out "several weapon pits and dugouts clearly visible around a large white house on the other side of the river." Thinking he saw a couple of Germans on the move, Frost started to raise his binoculars, only to be jerked back by Kilborn. Frost was "much too close to the window," he warned, and the Germans had "a couple of snipers waiting to drill anyone" who offered themselves as targets. A 'B' Company man had died earlier when he leaned on the windowsill to fire his rifle across the river.

Noticing that "both gun barrels were resting on steel bars supported by stones and that a piece of signal wire [was] attached to the traversing handle of the guns," Frost asked Kilborn, "What kind of contraption is this?"

Kilborn grinned. "You know how we don't have any proper indirect or night firing equipment. Well, I rigged up these iron bars so they will keep the guns on the right elevation for night firing. The signal wire holds the traverse handles on the line of fire."

"What about the flash from the guns?" Frost countered.

"We fire through wet blankets," came the answer. "They conceal the flash at night." Frost imagined the quartermaster's reaction to blankets shredded by bullets and singed by hot gun barrels. "Don't worry, Sir," the soldier said with a laugh, "we use liberated Itie blankets."

It was 1600 hours, and Frost still wanted to check his other gun section. As the houses of Martorano formed an unbroken line alongside the river road, Frost was able to move from one backyard to another and avoid German shelling. He found No. 2 Section as well prepared as No. 1 Section and then headed back to the battalion's Tac HQ—arriving just in time for Zero Hour.[21]

NIGHT HAD JUST fallen as Lieutenant Frost watched from the Tac HQ the entire front erupting with "one tremendous roar." Shells screamed overhead, mortar rounds chuffed across the river, the medium machine guns spewed "streams of lead. Tons of steel land[ed] on the far side and explode[d] in sheets of flame and clouds of smoke and dust."[22] To blind the Germans, the battalion's 4.2-inch mortars smothered the near bank with smoke rounds.

Five hundred yards of open ground separated 'A' and 'D' Companies from the Savio River. Deployed in arrowhead formations, with one platoon on point and the other two behind on either side, the men started forward. Behind, intelligence officer Lieutenant MacCulloch saw that the covering smoke had "pillared . . . and was too sketchy."

Too soon, the barrage lifted. As the German machine gunners opened fire, MacCulloch realized the intelligence reports had badly underestimated the number of defenders. Two companies were heading into the massed fire of an entire battalion of 26th Panzer Division's 9th Panzer Grenadier Regiment. The MG42s' ominous sheet-tearing shriek was joined by rapid small-arms fire. Only able to see 'D' Company, MacCulloch watched its men start to fall to bursts of fire scything the field. He heard, more than saw, German tanks grinding up to the edge of the opposing riverbank. Well short of the river, 'D' Company hit the ground.[23]

On the left, Major Cutbill's men pressed on through the deadly fire, only to have the leading platoon enter a minefield just short of the river. As the platoon moved left to avoid this peril, Cutbill lost contact with it. His signaller bearing the No. 18 wireless set had also disappeared with the platoon. That left him with no link to the battalion. Ahead, Sergeant A.R. Whitford had found a path through the minefield. Those men still with Cutbill carefully followed the sergeant in single file to the river. Pitifully few men gained the river-bank. Never considering stopping, Cutbill skidded down the greasy slope and waded into the surging water. He had no idea how many men followed. The water was shoulder-deep. At times Cutbill had to swim. Bullets kicked up spouts around him, but magically failed to strike home. Floundering up the far bank, Cutbill pitched down just below the rim and turned to see sixteen men alongside.

'A' Company's objective lay eight hundred yards beyond the Savio, and Cutbill's first instinct was to carry on. To test the resistance, he sent a scout forward. The soldier was immediately killed by a machine-gun burst as he started across the top of the dyke. Undeterred, Cutbill led his men southward along the riverbank toward a hedgerow that cut inland and might provide cover. Suddenly, Allied searchlights beamed back and forth across the overhead clouds to provide planned "artificial moonlight." Cutbill wished they would turn the things off, as "it was altogether too light and quiet for comfort." Why had the Germans stopped firing? "Perhaps," he later wrote, "Jerry is resting. Or maybe he is allowing the fly to walk into his parlour."

Reaching the hedge, Cutbill's little party crept along it toward a house. It was big, easily able to shelter a couple of platoons. Two men moved closer, returning to report that sentries were posted outside, with more Germans seen and heard moving about inside.

"What to do next?" Cutbill wondered. "Attack the house with the benefit of surprise (perhaps)? Sounds OK. But suppose He is strong?

Or suppose that He counterattacks at dawn? Besides we have no communication with Tac. It is doubtful if any tactical success could be achieved by holding a house in the middle of Jerryland and not be able to poke our noses outside without drawing fire."

Forgoing the house, Cutbill led his men four hundred yards north, where they encountered a manned outpost. Swiftly encircling it, the men hurled grenades and then rushed the position. Three panzer grenadiers surrendered and two others lay dead. Cutbill ordered the men back to the riverbank, where they dug in. He could have withdrawn across the river. Who would blame him? He had no more than a handful of men and no wireless communication. But damned if he was going to give up. Cutbill decided that 'A' Company would make its stand right there on the riverbank. Sergeant Frank Harris Sparrow volunteered to go back to Tac HQ and tell Clark of Cutbill's intent.[24]

AT TAC HQ, meanwhile, news of the disaster was trickling in. Lieutenant Colonel Clark called Lieutenant Frost over. "Frost, we've got to get some help to Able and Dog Companies right away," he announced. "I'm going to make another attempt to get Dog Company across the goddamn river. I want you to take the two guns and their crews now at Tay and cross the river with Dog Company. Able Company's 18 set is out, so I don't know what's happening over there: as soon as I find out, I'll send over your other two guns at Snake." It was "a tall order and a dangerous one." Both men knew it. But what was needed across the river was firepower to stop the inevitable dawn counterattack.

Throwing on web equipment, checking his Thompson submachine gun and ammo, Frost headed for the door. How the hell were his crews "going to manhandle the heavy Vickers across the swollen river?" The barrels alone weighed forty pounds, the tripod fifty, the "bloody ammunition . . . a ton." Frost was just leaving when Clark shouted for him to wait. Orders had just come in. The battalion was to hold in place. Brigade command had decided a one-battalion attack was suicide, especially when two companies had already been shredded. The Loyal Edmonton Regiment and Seaforth Highlanders would take over and attack the next night. Frost felt like a condemned man just given a reprieve from the gallows.

Curling up in a corner of one room, he tried to sleep. Outside, it was raining. The Germans were shelling the area continuously. Frost was just nodding off when Sergeant Sparrow burst into the Tac HQ, "soaked to the skin, filthy dirty and dead beat." But Frost knew that Sparrow was "one tough soldier." He quickly outlined Major Cutbill and 'A' Company's situation. Clark gave Sparrow a replacement wireless set and told him to round up any company stragglers he found and then rejoin Cutbill. Sparrow said he was confident the company could hold its tiny bridgehead until rescued by the Eddies or Seaforths.[25]

Picking up stragglers along the way, Sparrow returned to Cutbill. 'A' Company's strength on the other bank now numbered thirty-five. With the wireless, Cutbill called down a half-circle of protective defensive artillery fire whenever the Germans started forming for a counterattack.

Lieutenant MacCulloch, meanwhile, set 'A' Company's current losses at three men killed, sixteen wounded, and one missing. 'D' Company's were two dead and nine wounded. Sixteen German prisoners had been taken.

"SOON AFTER FIRST light," Major Cutbill wrote, "there is spasmodic mortar fire of the 'Moaning Minnie' variety. Jerry, I think, does not know what the score is and does not yet know that we are sitting in his lap. I get Sergeant Buckberry . . . to send out a recce patrol. It returns with the news that von Hun has some beautiful dug-in positions all around us at twenty-five yards distance and is there with flags flying, so to speak.

"Things begin to happen. Over comes the big stuff. He says to hell with twenty rounds per gun per day and just lets it slide over, with no economy at all. The worst is the 'Moaning Minnie' which is very accurate. We spit dirt. He then gets nasty and takes up a position on a wooded promontory fifty yards away and lets fly with an MG42. It's *no buono*. One of my better shots is told to keep the place peppered while we resume our watch.

"Sure enough, on the opposite flank he is trying to counterattack. We chuck the steel at him and he withdraws." From 'C' Company's area, Lieutenant Frost's No. 2 Section was firing its guns into the flat ground beyond the riverbank where Cutbill's men were dug in. "This dueling continues on and off all day. Several times the situation gets quite critical. Fortunately we are able to survive and we send out a fighting patrol under Corporal Baker to quieten other positions that are troublesome. This patrol killed four and captured six Jerries. Good Show."[26]

In the mid-morning, Lieutenant Colonel Clark asked Cutbill to send Sergeant Sparrow back with information on enemy positions. At 0900, Clark, Sparrow, and Captain Robinson went to 2nd Brigade headquarters, where Sparrow gave "much valuable information on the condition of the river and enemy positions." After this briefing, Sparrow returned to 'A' Company.[27] In broad daylight, while being fired on continuously by machine guns, Sparrow had to pass through the minefield on each of what would finally be six trips across the Savio River. On his final trip, Sparrow triggered a mine and was wounded in the leg and arm. His actions would be recognized with a Military Medal.[28]

Throughout the course of October 21, the Germans continued to batter the battalion with "extremely heavy shelling." 'A' Company was hit hardest. They were out there, Lieutenant MacCulloch recorded in the battalion war diary, coping "with rain, collapsed dug-in positions, and the uncomfortable closeness of the enemy." He would completely understand if they "were not happy."

On the Patricia's left, meanwhile, the Royal 22e Régiment had closed up with them along the Savio and were just three hundred yards from 'C' Company at Snake. The Van Doos had found the lost 'A' Company platoon "unable to move to rejoin their company because of heavy MG fire" whenever they stirred.[29]

Back at 2nd Brigade headquarters, Lieutenant Colonel Bogert finalized the new plan for winning a bridgehead across the Savio. Starting at 2000 hours, the Seaforth Highlanders would be on the right and Loyal Edmonton Regiment the left. Engineers of the 3rd and 4th Field Companies were to reconnoitre two bridge crossings—the main one in the Seaforth's area and a secondary one intended just for the Eddies to pass over their supporting arms. An elaborate fire plan "provided for blocks of targets on each battalion front which could be fired simultaneously, repeated or delayed as needed." Supporting arms included the complete Saskatoon Light Infantry, "who were firing for the first time as a battalion" all their medium machine guns and 4.2-inch mortars. Still hoping to get tanks across via the bridges, the British 145th Armoured Regiment replaced the 12th Royal Tank Regiment. The latter was sent out for a well-deserved rest. In an attempt to divert some German attention away from 2nd Brigade, 3rd Brigade to the left would put in a feint attack. But its battalions would not try to win a crossing unless there was no opposition.[30]

By the afternoon the rain had intensified. The engineers found it impossible to "even deliver bridging equipment to the proposed crossing sites, let along make the crossings." The approaches, ending well short of the river, foiled every attempt to bring forward the trucks bearing the heavy equipment. Lieutenant Sydney Charles Kenyon of 3rd Field Company was killed and Sergeant K.K. Lloyd wounded when their jeep blew up on a mine while the men were scouting for a path to the river.[31]

With the engineers frustrated, the attack plan had to be modified. There would be no tanks. The Seaforths and Eddies would have to win their bridgehead alone.

8

You Miss, You're Dead

WHEN MAJOR GENERAL Chris Vokes sent the Princess Patricia's Canadian Light Infantry across the Savio River, Seaforth Highlanders Lieutenant Colonel Budge Bell-Irving had anticipated failure. Too many times in the past, such single-battalion assaults—normally led by just two rifle companies—had been shredded by far more German defenders than expected while fighting from excellent defensive positions. Consequently, even before the attack started, Bell-Irving had directed Lieutenant Alan MacKenzie to establish the Seaforth's scout and sniper platoon in Martorano's church to create a base for the two-battalion attack now planned for October 21.[1]

In the mid-morning, Bell-Irving established his Tac HQ in the church, which stood alongside the river road a few hundred yards from the German positions on the Savio's west bank. Recognizing the potential its steeple offered for observing their dispositions, the Germans subjected the church to steady artillery and mortar fire while also frequently raking the tower with machine guns.[2]

Despite this incoming fire, Bell-Irving and his company commanders spent hours in the steeple getting "a good picture of the ground beyond the river."[3] The Seaforth plan called for 'D' Company on the left and 'B' Company the right to attack on virtually the same lines as the Patricias had taken the night before. These two companies were to advance to positions about five hundred yards beyond the river. Thereafter, 'A' and 'C' Companies would leapfrog them and advance a thousand yards farther to sever a road that ran dead straight from Cesena north to the coastal city of Ravenna.[4]

About a thousand yards upstream from the Seaforths, the Loyal Edmonton Regiment planned to put only 'A' Company across the Savio. Once 'A' Company gained a toehold, 'D' Company would cross and leapfrog to a point midway between the river and the Cesena–Ravenna road. 'B' Company, following close behind, would slip through to the road itself. Both 'C' Company and 'A' Company would then come forward to extend the battalion's grip on the road, while 'D' Company maintained a line back to the river.

At 1515 hours, Lieutenant Colonel Jim Stone sent his scout officer, Lieutenant W. Remple, with three men to recce the crossing area and test the water depth. At the riverbank, Remple's party came under intense fire from two machine-gun positions. Pinned down, they could only lie low and hope to withdraw after nightfall. Any attempt at movement brought immediate and accurate fire.[5]

Back at his Tac HQ, Stone had no idea what had happened to his scouts. But he knew their failure to report meant that he and the attacking companies would know "nothing about the river and that this was going to be an attack at night. So I said to the commanders of 'A' and 'D' Companies, 'I feel quite guilty launching you into this thing with no reconnaissance of the river, but it had been forded further downstream.' They were both brave and ready."[6] In the absence of a recce report, the company commanders resorted to aerial photographs.

At 1820 hours, the Eddies moved to their assembly area, and Stone established his Tac HQ five hundred yards from the Savio. He still wondered where Remple was and regretted the lack of a recce report. Night fell. At 1930 hours, Remple turned up to report he had learned nothing because of being pinned down.[7] Stone realized the detection of the patrol meant any element of surprise was lost.[8] Moments later, the battalion's second-in-command returned from sharing plans with the Seaforths and advised him that Bell-Irving was leading with two companies. At 1955 hours, the entire weight of 1 Canadian Corps artillery and the Saskatoon Light Infantry's 4.2-inch mortars and medium machine guns opened fire.

As planned, and on time at 2000 hours, 'A' Company headed out.9 To the right, the Seaforth's 'B' and 'D' Companies also moved. Across the Savio, Major Ted Cutbill's 'A' Company still clung to the side of the riverbank it had won during the Patricia's attack the night before. Ammunition, food, and water were desperately short. In the late afternoon, an enemy sniper had worked into a spot where the river executed one of its sharp bends and was able to fire along the bank from a range of about fifty yards. "We killed him," Cutbill said later. "Since our position was precarious we had to be watchfully aggressive." The indefatigable Sergeant Frank Harris Sparrow had alerted Cutbill to the planned Seaforth and Eddies attack. He also said that once they passed through, the plan was to send 'A' Company a full resupply to enable it to hold in place. Cutbill just hoped the Seaforths showed up before the Germans counterattacked.10

Just as he had that thought, "a barrage of terrific proportions" erupted. "Our artillery shells and MMG bullets whiz overhead and miss us by a hair's breadth," he wrote. "Let us hope there are no 'shorts.' I hope to God our own infantry don't attack us.

"We see the advancing troops some distance away, silhouetted clearly against our searchlights."11 Using a bit of high ground well illuminated by the searchlights bouncing off the clouds, Captain D.G. Duncan's 'D' Company had headed directly for Cutbill's position. Lieutenant D.H. McKay's No. 16 Platoon led. "The going was very heavy," Duncan wrote, "as the company was moving across . . . mud flats caused by the river's flooding. The Germans had deemed these . . . impassable for marching troops, as we found out later, and had no defensive fire or harassing tasks laid on. As a result there was only one casualty caused by enemy fire, Private [D.S.] Murray, who was hit in the leg by a stray burst of MG fire. When the company arrived on the other side of the river, which was chest deep at the time, they ran into [the] company of PPCLI who . . . had been pinned along the river bank all day by 6 known MG42 positions on [the] small ridge about 100 yards in front of them."12

"'D' Company of the Seaforths arrive in our territory," Cutbill wrote. "I give their company commander full particulars of the enemy and of the ground. His company moves out and is stopped by heavy MMG fire. He then calls for mortar support and covered by fire from every weapon in our company he is able to move forward from our bridgehead."[13]

In crossing the Savio, the rifles of many of McKay's platoon had become covered in mud. Seeing this, and knowing the Seaforths were going into an attack where a jammed rifle could mean death, the Patricias swapped their rifles for those of McKay's men. While the mortars had been doing their work, 'D' Company had been able to pinpoint a number of German positions from muzzle flashes. With the rest of the company and the Patricias providing covering fire, McKay sent Corporal H.R. Smith's section of No. 16 Platoon to find a position from which flanking fire could be brought against the main German defensive position ahead. Once he found a suitable spot, Smith fired a Bren gun burst. McKay rushed the rest of the platoon to Smith's position.

"The road running straight up [from our position] had good cover on the left. We proceeded up about 100 feet to an open field on our left, walked right in behind the machine-gunners, and took them without a shot," McKay wrote.[14] These guns silenced, No. 16 Platoon swept ahead to clear a nearby house that provided a concealed space where Duncan could consult his map by flashlight. Surprising the Germans inside, the platoon took twenty-five prisoners and determined that they had overrun the headquarters for the troops guarding this river sector. Duncan's map check showed that 'D' Company was only three hundred yards from its crossroad objective. Once again, McKay's platoon led, picking up more prisoners along the way. Reaching the objective, McKay sent a runner to guide the rest of the company forward. A nearby house was quickly converted into an advanced aid post by the stretcher-bearer from No. 16 Platoon. Most of the German prisoners were wounded, and the stretcher-bearer started giving them rudimentary first aid. Once the prisoners were attended to, a No. 16 Platoon section escorted them across the river. The section was also tasked with bringing back badly needed ammunition.[15]

On the right, meanwhile, Captain Tony Staples's 'B' Company had two men killed and three wounded by mortar fire before reaching the Savio.[16] Two of the wounded were signallers. That left Private Gordon Victor Carrington as the lone wireless operator. Taking the No. 18 set from the fallen men, Carrington adjusted it to fit his back. Further burdened by two satchels loaded with spare parts and batteries, Carrington rushed to catch up with his captain.[17] Realizing the Germans had his line of approach pinpointed, Staples swung the company three hundred yards north of their designated crossing site. With one platoon prone on the dyke providing covering fire, Staples led the rest of the company across. Not expecting an attack, the Germans had taken refuge in the covered portions of their dugouts to escape the heavy rain that was falling. Staples and his men slipped past these positions undetected. They then moved back to the assigned line of advance and turned toward their objective, a large farmhouse about halfway between the Savio and the Cesena–Ravenna road.

As No. 12 Platoon approached the building, it came under machine-gun fire from three positions. Reinforced by a section from No. 10 Platoon and the company PIAT team, the combined force mounted an attack but were thrown back. Several casualties resulted, including two section leaders. No. 10 Platoon then came under fire from a position halfway between the building and the river. Three men were hit, including another section leader. Deciding to leave the building, Staples set the company to clearing the ground between it and the river.[18] Carrington dogged along behind Staples, but the wireless he carried had been drenched in the river and had stopped working. With 'B' Company rushing to attack one machine-gun position after another, Carrington was unable to try repairing the set.[19] Staples and his men had soon taken fifteen prisoners from five different machine-gun posts. In the pre-dawn light, Staples turned back toward the building with No. 12 Platoon leading.[20]

Staples expected to carry the building pretty easily, but No. 12 Platoon found itself caught between two hidden dugouts from which machine-gun fire ripped. The platoon scrambled out of range. Staples sent a platoon out on either flank, intending "to pinch them off, and they were kicked back; then we brought up a couple PIATs, and . . .

fired at the building itself, because they had these emplacements out in front of the building, and [in] the basement of the building . . . they had MGS in the corner of the building, as well as these dugouts," Staples said later. "We threw several PIAT bombs through it, then tried to go through once again, and all they'd done was go down when we put the PIATS in . . . all we'd done was knock some holes in the wall . . . causing some casualties but it didn't stop them, they came back up."[21]

While this fight was under way, Private Carrington lay in an open field subject to intermittent shell and mortar fire, trying to get the wireless functioning. When he got a signal, he would flee the field for better cover. Each time, however, all reception was immediately lost. Returning to the field, an action that would earn a Military Medal, he patiently replaced more parts. After an hour of this back-and-forth process, the set started functioning reliably.[22] Carrington advised Lieutenant Colonel Bell-Irving of 'B' Company's situation and provided a running commentary, until the building was finally taken at 0630 hours. Staples reported that the company had taken fifty-one prisoners and killed four panzer grenadiers.[23]

LEFT OF THE Seaforths, the Edmonton's 'A' Company had reached the Savio River close behind the barrage. The lack of recce and loss of surprise meant the Germans knew where to expect the attack, while thirty-three-year-old Major Bill Longhurst had no idea what lay ahead. Longhurst led his men scrambling down the riverbank into the fast-flowing water. On the other side was not only a high riverbank but also an even higher dyke behind it.[24] As Longhurst reached the far side, he reported by wireless that 'A' Company was across and the river ranged from three to four feet deep. As Longhurst was filing this report, the lead platoon passed over the top of the riverbank and then, having surmounted the dyke, disappeared. Leading the rest of the company to the top of the riverbank, Longhurst was riddled by bullets and died instantly, as the German machine guns hidden along the dyke opened up with raking fire. The lead platoon, cut off and overwhelmed, were almost all taken prisoner. Suddenly leaderless, most of the company fled in disorder back across the Savio.[25]

Longhurst had enlisted on the day Canada had declared war. Of frail physique, he had been assigned to battalion headquarters and served as the orderly room sergeant. By the time the Eddies landed in Sicily on July 10, 1943, he was a lieutenant and the battalion intelligence officer. In southern Italy he became battalion adjutant but longed to be on the sharp end. Longhurst got his wish at the Moro River outside Ortona when he took over 'A' Company. During the fierce street fight in the town itself, he masterminded the idea of "mouseholing" from one connected building to another to avoid moving on the gun-swept open streets. But Longhurst was generally considered by his colleagues still too frail for combat command. Only his tenacious insistence prevented his being returned to a headquarters job.[26] Lieutenant Colonel Stone, who considered Longhurst a "particularly good friend," had given him 'A' Company because the officer was a good leader and so determined.[27]

Seeing Longhurst killed, Company Sergeant Major Wallace George Davies immediately brought the company's headquarters section and a few men on either side under his control. Just ten strong, Davies and his little command dug in on the riverbank. Davies was determined to hold, confident that the rest of 'A' Company would be reorganized and sent back to renew the attack.[28]

At 2130 hours, Captain J.R. Washburn's 'D' Company got two platoons across the river. But they were not in contact with Davies's group. Stone was desperate for information, but it was 2215 hours before a wounded Lieutenant A.F. Firth of 'D' Company and Sergeant John Goodwin Milnes of 'A' Company returned to Tac HQ. They told Stone that in front of their respective units, German defences lined the dyke that lay just a few yards back of the riverbank. Milnes explained how 'A' Company had been lured into the ambush. He also reported having rounded up men who had fallen back across the river and said they were ready to cross back.

Stone's attack plan had entailed 'B' Company following 'D' Company across. Learning of the 'A' Company remnant, Stone scrapped that idea and ordered 'B' Company to reinforce Davies and his men. Milnes and his 'A' Company men would join the effort. As the change of plan necessitated 'B' Company moving to a new start line, its advance did not begin until shortly before 2330 hours.[29]

Across the Savio, Davies's party had been clinging for three hours to their perilous position "in the face of persistent efforts by the enemy to drive them off." When it seemed one counterattack was sure to overrun his men, Davies told them to stand fast, and "inspired by his personal bravery, they made a concerted effort and drove the Germans back. A few minutes later heavy shell fire began to fall on them and continued to do so for a period of almost two hours, but through sheer dogged persistence they held the ground," reported the citation for the Distinguished Conduct Medal Davies subsequently received.[30]

Just before midnight, two 'B' Company platoons arrived. Thirty minutes later, a 'B' Company wireless signal reported "no indication that the resistance was decreasing." When Milnes's 'A' Company group reinforced Davies's group, 'B' Company was freed to push toward a group of buildings about three hundred yards away. All of Washburn's 'D' Company, meanwhile, was concentrated across the Savio and "proceeding slowly forward against increasing opposition." At 0045 hours on October 22, Washburn signalled that 'D' Company "was involved in close fighting," but was approaching a handful of houses identified on the Canadian maps as Case Gentili.

Although Stone badly wanted a bridge installed so he could reinforce his embattled companies with heavy weapons, Major A.F. Macdonald and a team of engineers and battalion pioneers reported at 0500 hours that "crossing with anything but boats was impossible." Lacking these, the Eddies had to keep wading the Savio—something becoming increasingly difficult as the heavy rain that had started after midnight was raising the water level and strengthening the current. At 0315 hours, Stone had fed 'C' Company into the battle, but it took almost an hour for all its men to struggle across the river.[31] The crossing was made even more difficult by the water being covered in heavy, black oil. Whether the Germans had deliberately pumped oil into the river with the intention of setting it on fire was unknown. Oil so saturated the uniforms of 'C' Company that they would have to be destroyed, but for now it just added to the men's overall discomfort.[32] Just before 'C' Company had entered the river, some of its men had been sent to 'B' Company with an ammunition resupply. One man, who was a strong swimmer, returned at 0430 hours to report that "wading at any point was [now] impossible," and the rest of the ammo-carrying party had opted to stay "with 'B' Company to fight."

News from the companies was discouraging. While 'D' Company seemed to be doing fairly well at closing on its objective of buildings alongside the Cesena–Ravenna road, 'B' and 'A' Companies were still locked in close-quarters fighting. There was no news of 'C' Company at all.[33]

AT 2345 HOURS, THE Seaforth's 'A' Company under Major Robert Clark headed for the Savio River to begin the battalion's second phase of advance. Major Stewart Lynch's 'C' Company soon followed. Also headed for the river was a five-man team of engineers from 3rd Field Company to check the proposed crossing site. Stumbling into a minefield by the river, three of these five men had their legs blown off.[34] When the two survivors returned to Tac HQ with the news, Medical Officer Captain Joseph Charles Portnuff volunteered to render aid. Entering the minefield, Portnuff had just completed dressing one man's wounds when a nearby mine exploded. "Mud and fragments thrown into his face caused temporary total blindness." Groping his way out of the minefield, the doctor returned to the Regimental Aid Post. His medical sergeant was able to restore Portnuff's sight to the extent that he could "distinguish the outline only of large objects. In spite of this handicap," his Military Cross citation noted, "Captain Portnuff refused to be evacuated until a relief Medical Officer arrived. Working with impaired vision and with the guidance of his staff, he administered one blood transfusion and retained control of the Regimental Aid Post until all casualties had been dressed and evacuated. He only permitted himself to be evacuated when the relief Medical Officer arrived."[35]

While Portnuff had been in the minefield, 'A' and 'C' Companies had crossed the Savio. Their objectives were two intersections where country lanes met the Cesena–Ravenna road. 'A' Company's was about four hundred yards west of Pieve Sestina, while 'C' Company's was the hamlet itself and the intersection next to its church, Chiesa di Pievesestina. The two companies advanced on parallel roads. Clark soon reported that 'A' Company was passing 'D' Company's position and was on its way.

No sooner had 'A' Company's No. 9 Platoon led off than a burst of machine-gun fire wounded four men. These were tucked into the safety of a nearby house, and the platoon carried on. Clark's orders had been to reach the intersection, bypassing any resistance points. But as one German defensive position after another was encountered, this quickly proved impossible. Eliminating these positions netted a significant number of prisoners, but also wounded two Seaforths. Both groups were returned to the house, where the earlier wounded were under the care of a stretcher-bearer and two guards.

Thirty minutes after 'A' Company had struck out from 'D' Company's lines, Clark's main force reached the intersection that was its objective. Behind it, however, ten Germans overwhelmed the two guards at the house near the start line and liberated their comrades. As some of the freed Germans headed quickly toward their lines, Clark spotted them and thought he recognized a couple. Suspicions aroused, Clark sent two men back to investigate. The men caught the Germans guarding the wounded Seaforths by surprise. Private A.L. Frocklage wounded one of them when he offered resistance. At this point, 'A' Company received an order to consolidate around the cluster of houses it had just cleared at the intersection. Dawn was breaking.

To the right of 'A' Company, Lynch's 'C' Company progressed rapidly after it left 'B' Company's position. The Seaforth's newly formed tank-hunting platoon under command of Sergeant Keith Thompson trailed close behind.[36] The idea for a dedicated tank-hunting platoon had arisen out of an incident during the Gothic Line Battle. The Loyal Edmonton Regiment had been fighting on San Fortunato Ridge and managed to knock a Tiger tank out with PIAT rounds and a chain of No. 75 Hawkins anti-tank grenades. The latter weapon could be either hand-thrown like a grenade or emplaced on the ground like a mine. Resembling a metal liquor flask, it had a screw-on cap for filling it with two pounds of either ammonal or TNT explosive and weighed three pounds in all. As the grenades were not particularly effective as thrown weapons, usually several of them were strung across a road. When a vehicle drove over a Hawkins mine, it cracked a chemical igniter that detonated the charge.

The Eddies' success using these grenades plus PIATS against the Tiger so impressed Lieutenant Colonel Stone that he decided to form a permanent platoon equipped with four PIATS, the anti-tank grenades, and Bren guns. It consisted of twenty men and was commanded by the battalion's anti-tank platoon's second-in-command. This innovation was quickly embraced by the other two 2nd Brigade battalions and several other 1st Division battalions.[37]

Unlike 'A' Company, 'C' Company encountered no resistance along the muddy farm road bordered by waterlogged fields. At about 0230 hours, 'C' Company reached the crossroads. The shell-shattered Chiesa di Pievesestina faced the Cesena–Ravenna road with the farm road alongside. All told, Lynch's force—including the tank hunters—numbered about fifty men. Lynch immediately sent No. 14 Platoon to clear a nearby house, ordered No. 15 Platoon to dig in alongside the intersection, and deployed No. 13 Platoon inside the church. 'C' Company's arrival surprised two sections of Germans, with Lieutenant Sid Dickinson's No. 14 Platoon netting nine prisoners and knocking out a truck. No. 15 Platoon pulled in ten more. Then a burst of machine-gun fire wounded Dickinson. As No. 14 Platoon silenced the machine gun, an ominous rumble of tracked vehicles approaching from Cesena was heard.[38]

Having just established his company headquarters in the church alongside No. 13 Platoon and Thompson's platoon, Lynch ordered the tank hunters into action. Thompson quickly deployed the PIAT teams of Sergeant R.P. Leon and Sergeant R. Greengrass in opposite roadside ditches, from which they had a good field of fire.[39] He then strung a chain of Hawkins grenades across the road and hurriedly concealed them.[40]

Thompson had just scrambled to cover when a Kubelwagen staff car with a driver and officer aboard roared up the road. Its wheels narrowly missed all the mines, but as the vehicle entered the intersection, 'C' Company tore into it with small-arms fire. The driver was killed, but the officer jumped out of the vehicle and began yelling a warning back toward the rapidly closing column. A burst of fire cut the officer down.

The column headed for 'C' Company consisted of three Panther tanks, one fully tracked self-propelled gun, and a half-track SPG mounting a 75-millimetre gun. About thirty infantrymen were riding on the hulls of the armour. Tankers and grenadiers were crack troops of 26th Panzer Division. The wide tracks of the leading SPG detonated one or more of Thompson's mines. One track blown off, the SPG halted and completely blocked the road. Leon and Greengrass blasted it with PIAT rounds, while some other men chucked grenades into its open hatch, killing the Germans inside.

The fight turned into a swirling brawl. Lynch later described the action as "a section commander's battle" with the outcome determined by the individual courage, discipline, and training of the men involved.[41] Thompson ran back and forth across bullet-swept ground in front of the church to get Leon's and Greengrass's PIATs sighted on the Panther that had been riding almost on the SPG's bumper. The Panther was slowly backing up to gain some room to manoeuvre and bring its weapons into play.

Another three-man PIAT team, meanwhile, had dashed across a field behind the church to the ditch on the left side of the farm lane the Seaforths had followed from the Savio. One team member was thirty-year-old Private Ernest Alvia Smith, nicknamed Smokey because during school sprinting events he had always "smoked" the competition.[42] Smith carried a Thompson submachine gun and was tasked with providing covering fire for the two-man PIAT team. In combat, Smith was reputed to be a fighter and a natural leader. This had led to several promotions to corporal and sergeant ranks. But Smith never cared for being formally in charge and tended to get into trouble whenever the Seaforths were out of the line. Demotions came quickly and frequently. In a tight situation, however, Private Smith tended to take charge—as he now did.

Smith told Private K.W. Ballard to stay put while he and Private James Tennant ran back to the church to retrieve a second PIAT.

Returning, they moved along the ditch on the opposite side of the road from Ballard to close the range on the Panther. Suddenly, the tank swung about and headed toward them with machine guns ripping fire into the ditch. Tennant was badly wounded in the leg.

"Our way was to fight from the ditches and wait until they got real close," Smith said later. "Thirty feet or less, if possible, because you don't want to fire at a tank with a PIAT and miss. Because if you miss, you're dead. They have the machine guns and they'll just eat you alive."[43]

Smith fired the PIAT. The two-and-a-half-pound, hollow-charged explosive bomb hit the Panther squarely. As the Panther's driver started frantically trying to turn around to escape the line of fire, ten panzer grenadiers piled off its back. Several charged toward Smith with Schmeissers blazing, while others threw stick grenades at him. Snatching up his Thompson, Smith stepped into the middle of the road to divert the fire from the helpless Tennant. At point-blank range, he fired a burst that killed four Germans. The rest fled.

From the Cesena–Ravenna road, a second Panther punched a round in Smith's direction. Panzer grenadiers also advanced across the intervening field. Scrambling back to the ditch, Smith retrieved spare magazines from Tennant. Reloaded, he opened fire on the infantry. Tennant was in no shape to fight. Smith was alone. He could have run, could have left Tennant, but Smith "steadfastly held his position, protecting his comrade and fighting the enemy with his Tommy gun until they finally gave up and withdrew in disorder."

Although the Panther on the road continued firing, Smith took advantage of the slight lull to help Tennant back to the church and turn him over to a first-aid man. Then Smith returned to his position to keep 'C' Company's flank protected.[44]

Unable to use the farm lane and the Cesena–Ravenna road blocked by the disabled SPG, the half-track SPG managed to break across country and then attempted to race past the church. 'C' Company let loose a hail of fire that rattled harmlessly off its armour until one of the PIAT teams that Thompson was directing scored a hit that knocked the SPG out. Suddenly, the Panther that had been firing in Smith's direction attempted to squeeze by the disabled SPG on the road, only to slide down into the water-filled ditch. As the forty-five-ton tank's tracks churned the mud vainly in search of traction, a PIAT bomb struck it. The Panther started burning. Having also become stuck in mud off the road, the crew in the third Panther bailed out. A couple of the men were shot down and the survivors fled into the night.

The entire action had lasted barely an hour.[45] Three Seaforths were wounded—Leon, Tennant, and Private W.O. Ladiceur. Major Lynch reported that 'C' Company had taken ten prisoners and killed about eight others.[46] For his courageous solitary stand, "Smokey" Smith became the third and last Canadian recipient of a Victoria Cross in the Italian Campaign. He was also the only Canadian private in World War II to be so honoured. Sergeant Thompson received a Distinguished Conduct Medal. "I can assure you, that when it came to the question of awards," Lynch wrote later, "it was a very difficult decision to favour one over the other."

Private Bill Robinson was another member of the tank-hunting platoon. "I believe Smokey was the right guy to get it," he said later of the Victoria Cross award. "He stuck his neck out further."[47]

A GREY, WATERY dawn on October 22 greeted the Seaforth Highlanders and Loyal Edmonton Regiment inside their Savio River bridgehead. Although the bridgehead was about a mile wide and a thousand yards deep, it was anything but secure. There was, in fact, grave concern at 2nd Brigade headquarters that the two battalions might not be able to hang on if the Germans counterattacked in strength. At 0500 hours, an engineering officer from the Seaforth's area reported to 2nd Brigade headquarters. He advised that "it would be impossible to bridge in that area—the banks were too steep, the river too high, and the long approaches too muddy." Things were no better in the Edmonton sector. An alarmed Lieutenant Colonel Pat Bogert immediately contacted Major General Vokes. Bogert said there was no hope of getting any supplies into the bridgehead for at least twenty-four hours. Vokes kicked the ball upstairs to 1 Canadian Corps's Lieutenant General Tommy Burns, who ordered the two battalions "to remain over the river and hold on as well as they could."

No close fire support was possible because neither tanks nor anti-tank guns could find suitable positions on the Savio's east bank, and the entire frontage was subject to frequent German artillery fire. The bridgehead was under near-constant mortar and shellfire. Air support was also impossible, owing to heavy cloud cover and rain. Both battalions were low on all ammunition, with PIAT bombs particularly badly needed. The Princess Patricia's Canadian Light Infantry companies had carrying parties organized with all the supplies needed, but nobody could figure out how to get them across the river.[48]

As Bogert signalled both battalions to hang on, a counterattack by tanks and infantry at 0615 hours fell on the Edmonton's 'D' Company inside the hamlet of Case Gentili. This attack was just beginning when the commander of 'C' Company—silent through the night—came up on the wireless and reported having reached a large building about two hundred yards northeast of the hamlet. Although able to see 'D' Company being attacked, the officer said his men could not reinforce it. With his company all but surrounded, Captain Washburn spotted 'C' Company at the large building and ordered his men to fall back to its position. Several men and the company's No. 18 wireless set were left behind and captured. Although 'D' Company numbered barely more than twenty-five men, Washburn radioed Lieutenant Colonel Stone to say that he and 'C' Company would take the hamlet back.[49]

At 0700 hours, Stone—acting on Washburn's behalf—requested that 2nd Brigade arrange a medium artillery bombardment of Case Gentili. Bogert passed the request to the British liaison officer from 3rd Medium Regiment, Royal Artillery. "I pointed out that it was a very close target" to where 'D' and 'C' Companies were, the officer said later, "but they said they appreciated that and would lie low. I arranged for the regiment to fire a small fire plan at 0715 hours."

The attack went in fast behind the shelling, and Case Gentili was quickly taken, with all the prisoners recovered and thirty-five Germans surrendering. A delighted Stone soon summoned the British officer to tell him the "the medium shoot was marvelous and that when his company entered the village . . . the place was nearly flat and there were dozens of dead Boche."[50]

As the situation in the Edmonton's sector stabilized somewhat, things heated up in the Seaforth's area in a strange way. Just after first light, the Germans manning machine-gun positions that had been bypassed in the night awoke hungry and confused. With mess tins in hand, a column trudged up to the building that had housed their unit's kitchen but that now served as Captain Duncan's 'D' Company headquarters. Fifty-six unarmed Germans were taken prisoner and went hungry. Duncan then sent a party of men to run a telephone line back to the river to try to eventually connect with Lieutenant Colonel Bell-Irving's Tac HQ. Apparently still unaware that they were now inside an enemy-held bridgehead and seeing a communication line they could not connect to, a team of German signallers showed up to repair it. These men were added to the prisoner count. The fortuitous German confusion allowed the two Seaforth companies back by the Savio to police up the few remaining machine-gun positions. Bell-Irving reported by early morning that the Seaforths had taken some 150 prisoners and were digging graves for twenty-seven dead Germans.[51]

'A' Company, having had to fight its way from the river to three buildings that looked across a wide field to the Cesena–Ravenna road, only reached them at dawn. The buildings were undefended. This put Major Clark's men about a hundred yards left of 'C' Company's position at the church. Ahead, where the lane 'A' Company had followed during the night joined the road, was a cluster of other buildings. Knowing that from their current position, 'A' Company was unable to cut German traffic using the road and therefore properly enable his company and 'C' Company to cover each other's flanks, Clark sent No. 7 Platoon to occupy the buildings at the intersection. As the platoon closed in, it was fired on by a tank from a concealed position to the west. The platoon fell back. Regrouping, Clark sent No. 7 and No. 9 Platoons forward with his company's PIAT crew attached. The buildings were taken.

In the mid-afternoon, thirty panzer grenadiers were spotted marching along the road—apparently oblivious to 'A' Company's presence. Clark organized an ambush, instructing the Bren gunners not to fire until the Germans were within twenty to thirty yards. One twitchy-fingered gunner, however, loosed a burst when the Germans were still two hundred yards away. Unharmed, the Germans took cover. The concealed tank opened up on the roadside buildings with its 75-millimetre gun and machine guns. Under this covering fire, the panzer grenadiers attacked the two platoons. After some close-quarters firing, the Seaforths retreated to the buildings across the field. Subjected to long-range main-gun and machine-gun fire from what were now two tanks, Clark abandoned thoughts of gaining control of the intersection. If the tanks and infantry mounted a coordinated assault across the field, it was unlikely 'A' Company could hold its present position. But, likely wary because of the losses inflicted by the tank-hunters with 'C' Company, the tankers kept their distance.[52]

A hundred yards to the right, 'C' Company faced a similar stalemate. There would be no more advances on the Seaforth or Edmonton front until the engineers solved the bridging problem, which would enable reinforcement by armour and anti-tank guns. For now, any advantage in the standoff lay with 26th Panzer Division.

The Germans, however, were disinclined to attempt an attack on the bridgehead. During the course of the day on October 22, one of Commander-in-Chief Southwest Generalfeldmarschall Albert Kesselring's two chief staff officers, General der Panzertruppen Hans Röttiger, called Tenth Army's chief of staff, Generalmajor Fritz Wentzel. "This is quite a mess at Crasemann's," Röttiger said, referring to 26th Panzer Division's commander Generalleutnant Eduard Crasemann. "Yes," Wentzel replied, "it was a fierce artillery shoot there during the night, and contrary to expectations, and in spite of being thrown back repeatedly, the enemy renewed his attacks with a will. He now has a bridgehead, but the thing has been stopped due to his difficulties in crossing the water with tanks and heavy weapons. We are in difficulties too, because in the counterattacks our tanks bogged down."[53]

9

Cardinal Sin

D URING A MORNING meeting at 2nd Canadian Infantry Brigade's headquarters on October 22, Major General Chris Vokes and Lieutenant Colonel Pat Bogert had sought a plan to break the Savio River stalemate. It all depended on a bridge. The Seaforth Highlanders and Loyal Edmonton Regiment's bridgehead would remain tenuous unless it could be supplied with ammunition and food. There were also the wounded and prisoners to evacuate. The news a British 145th Armoured Regiment officer brought offered a glimmer of hope. Conducting a personal recce, the officer had found a likely bridging location at Borgo di Ronta—about a mile downstream from Martorano. The site, he said, was about sixty feet wide and had "good approaches on either side for the erection of a Bailey Bridge." Vokes immediately summoned engineer Lieutenant Colonel Ted Webb for an opinion.

Webb's positive response prompted Vokes to send one company of Princess Patricia's Canadian Light Infantry with a 145th Regiment tank troop to secure the site, which was in 5th Canadian Armoured Division's new boundary. Having just returned to the front lines and relieving 2nd New Zealand Armoured Division, none of its troops had yet reached the Savio. Vokes wanted the site secured before the Germans realized the potential it presented.[1]

Even as Vokes ordered Borgo di Ronta secured, 3rd Field Company engineers had launched near the crossing point a temporary ferry operation, code-named Snake. Using Floating Bridge Equipment (FBE), the engineers constructed a temporary emergency crossing capable of bearing vehicles weighing up to ten tons. FBE bridges were constructed by joining together several folding assault boats, anchoring them to both shores, and adding wood or steel decking.[2]

It took sixteen men to carry one 870-pound folding boat, so teams of Patricias had helped the sappers unload three of these from a flatbed truck. Snake, however, proved to be under direct German observation and artillery fire. The ferry operation was consequently shifted to directly in front of Martorano, as buildings provided cover behind which to unload the boats. Sappers and Patricias then carried them to the river without drawing fire. Realizing the need for haste, the engineers ditched plans for an immediate bridge. Instead, four ropes were thrown over the Savio, which crews used to pull each boat across by hand. By mid-morning, this ferry had transferred food, ammunition, and rum into the bridgehead. The wounded and prisoners were brought out on return runs. During a lull, steel cables replaced the ropes.

In the afternoon, immediate resupply completed, the engineers turned to building a bridge. On the far bank, a steep footpath was sighted. The Patricia's pioneer platoon was ferried across to use the footpath as a starting point for a vehicle-capable ramp carved out with picks and shovels. The sappers, meanwhile, launched assault boats that were tied together and anchored to both riverbanks. Bridge decking was then installed. By early evening, four 2-pounder anti-tank guns, three medium machine guns, and a jeep had crossed into the bridgehead.[3] The anti-tank guns were manned by a 1st Anti-Tank Regiment troop. Normally, this regiment deployed 17-pounders, but these were too heavy for the boggy ground. Fitting the lighter 2-pounder with a "Little John" choke-bore adapter, the regiment's historian wrote, squeezed the shot to a smaller diameter and "jumped up the muzzle velocity to 4,000 feet-per-second . . . [W]hen sabot ammunition was used . . . this resulted in . . . correspondingly greater armour penetration."[4] Each infantry battalion was assigned two anti-tank guns, while the machine guns went to the Eddies—deemed most at threat of counterattack. The jeep towed the guns and moved supplies. Although this bridge had eased the critical situation, it did not have the strength needed to support tanks that could break the stalemate. It was hoped that the bridge they would build at Borgo di Ronta would do this.[5]

WHILE 2ND BRIGADE WAS establishing and holding the bridgehead on October 21–22, Cumberland Force pushed up Highway 16 on the coast to seize Cervia, which would bring it to within five miles of the Savio River. This position would soon allow the force to anchor 1 Canadian Corps's right flank on the river. Cervia lay about four miles north of Cesenatico, which the Governor General's Horse Guards had liberated the previous day.

At 0830 hours on October 21, 'A' Squadron advanced with Corporal J.N. Smythe's bicycle patrol out front. The rest of the squadron was on foot. Lacking motorized transport, the squadron's ammunition and other supplies were loaded, as the regiment's historian wrote, in "a weird collection of handcarts of all varieties [which they] dragged and pushed up the highway. The resulting procession was certainly most unorthodox and a sight to shock the precisionist, but it served our purpose and everyone was enthusiastic."[6]

From Rimini to Ravenna, a railroad paralleled Highway 16, with the tracks twice crossing it between Cesenatico and Cervia. At the first crossing, a mile and a half short of Cervia, a machine gun fired on the bicycle patrol. Immediately west of the highway, a salt marsh two thousand yards wide extended about five thousand yards northward. Cervia was in the centre of this marsh, which created an ideal chokepoint on which the enemy had capitalized.

To reach the German machine gun required crossing an expanse of flat bare ground. Rather than attempting such an advance, Smythe pulled back out of range. As Lieutenant Colonel Allan Jordan manoeuvred 'A' Squadron to within three hundred yards of the gun, an Italian army officer attached to Jordan's Tac HQ returned with several partisans from Cervia. They claimed to be part of a two-hundred-strong force. "Our new found friends made up for in enthusiasm, what they lacked in soldierly appearance," the regiment's war diarist recorded. The leader "offered to help us take Cervia if we would arm them. A frantic call was sent out for all the grenades, Tommy guns, and Brens we could get." Soon Tac HQ was surrounded by partisans receiving a course from Jordan in firing guns and throwing grenades.

As soon as night fell, Jordan planned to eliminate the machine gun and open the way to Cervia. At 0500 hours, the partisans—having infiltrated around to the north of the town—would attack, while 'A' Squadron approached from the south.

Under cover of darkness, Lieutenant Frank Victor Clapp crept with a platoon toward the machine-gun post. Ahead of the rest, Trooper G. Neuspiel surprised a sentry and took him prisoner. Having got their names from the prisoner, German-speaking Neuspiel lured the other three sentries "into the darkness, where they were quite surprised to feel the muzzle of [his] Tommy Gun in their backs." When the remaining Germans realized four comrades had mysteriously disappeared, they grabbed the machine gun and withdrew.

Information from the prisoners confirmed partisan reports that the Germans held Cervia in greater strength than originally believed. "This resulted in a very sudden waning in enthusiasm among our newly recruited friends." Wavering about whether to attack with 'A' Squadron alone, Jordan decided at dawn to have Major H.W.F. Appleton "push forward to ascertain what truth there was in these reports."[7] Led by a troop under Lieutenant R.W. Murray, at 0630 hours on October 22, 'A' Squadron entered Cervia to find its cathedrals ringing bells. Only when Murray's troop approached a canal connecting the salt flats to the sea was it met by scattered machine-gun and rifle fire from the opposite bank. Although the Germans had blown a highway bridge, the remaining wreckage was sufficient for Murray's troop to cross. The rest of the squadron soon followed. About five hundred yards beyond Cervia, however, fire from a German pillbox at another railway–highway crossing halted the advance. A sniper round killed Lieutenant Clapp. Armed with a PIAT, Sergeant J.P. Ross scored several hits on the pillbox, but it remained unscathed. When a bullet struck, severing a finger, Ross withdrew.

Behind 'A' Squadron, 'B' Squadron had been ensuring that Cervia was clear of opposition. The town's liberation proved "a strange compound of tragedy and rejoicing. The civilians thronged the streets and windows, cheering madly, throwing flowers, and generally announcing their delight at our arrival, but enemy, or possibly fascist, snipers were still in some . . . houses and one of them suddenly fired on Lieutenant [Laurence Edward] McCormack . . . who was instantly killed. It happened so unexpectedly that it seemed somehow unreal. Crowds of partisans assisted 'B' Squadron, and in a short time the town was clear. The highway, which formed the main street, was blocked with piles of rubble from German demolitions, and the bridge over the canal was, of course, blown, but large numbers of willing civilians, acting on their own initiative, were instantly at work clearing the rubble, and a local engineer took charge of the bridging. Big timbers were rolled into position and a bridge began to take shape."

At 1800 hours, 'B' Squadron took over the advance from 'A' Squadron. A patrol found the pillbox abandoned. Morning of October 23 saw the Horse Guards continuing toward the Savio but dogged by demolished sections of highway and German rearguards fighting from behind one narrow canal after another.[8]

IN THE MID-AFTERNOON, Princess Patricia's Canadian Light Infantry's Lieutenant Colonel Slug Clark recalled Captain A.G. Robinson from 'D' Company's holding position at Borgo di Ronta for an Orders Group. The briefing was held in the same shell-battered building on Sant' Egidio's outskirts that had housed Clark's Tac HQ since the start of the Savio River operation. At 1600 hours, Lieutenant Syd Frost was among several officers waiting for Robinson. Half asleep, he kept mulling over the "lousy" last two days. Despite the setbacks, he thought Clark had done everything right. The fault lay instead with "the staff officers at brigade, division, and corps. They . . . failed miserably to appreciate the problems involved in crossing the river. Even a cursory glance at their precious pamphlets on staff duties in the field should have warned them that the Patricia attack had no chance of success."[9]

At 1638 hours, Robinson arrived and Clark started the briefing. They were to win another Savio River crossing, but a mile downriver at Borgo di Ronta. Only Robinson's 'D' Company would be involved.

With 2nd Brigade so overextended, Major General Vokes had attached the 3rd Brigade's West Nova Scotia Regiment. While 'D' Company was to be under command of the West Novas, its task was to win the "primary bridgehead over the Savio." Adding 'D' Company to the West Novas was "to bolster a fresh, but under-strength . . . battalion," the Patricia's war diarist noted.

Once 'D' Company crossed the Savio, Clark said, two West Nova companies would expand the bridgehead to give the engineers room to work. The attack would go in at midnight with artillery on call.[10]

Frost and the other officers listened in disbelief. "The advantages the enemy had in the last attacks across the river have not changed," he thought. "In fact, the odds in favour of the enemy have increased. He is now thoroughly alerted. He knows as well as we do that we can't get tanks and vehicles across the river in the area of the present bridgehead." Poor visibility meant no air support and the rain just kept swelling the Savio. "On top of it all, the staff, not satisfied with the debacle they have already caused, are again going to commit the cardinal sin of sending one battalion to do the job of two . . . But god-dammit, the general wants his lousy bridge and he shall have it even if it takes us all winter!"

As Robinson prepared to return to 'D' Company, most of the other officers stopped to wish him luck.[11] Before leaving, Robinson contacted his Tac HQ by wireless to set up an o Group. He also ordered a patrol sent to the assigned crossing site. When Robinson reached 'D' Company, the patrol had just returned. Its leader "reported the river in [full] spate, banks steep, and enemy movement on the other side. Water [was] about breast high."[12]

While Robinson briefed his men, Lieutenant Colonel Al Saunders did likewise with the West Novas. Saunders had joined the battalion on September 25, so this would be his first real combat. It was already 2000 hours. The West Novas were in Cesena and needed to march three miles along the river road to pass through Martorano and reach Borgo di Ronta. Saunders said that once the Patricia's 'D' Company formed a shallow bridgehead, the West Nova 'D' Company would enter and expand it rightward to a depth of four hundred yards. Major R.G. Threxton's 'A' Company would then cross and push it out to the same depth on the left-hand side. Major D.W. McAdam's 'C' Company would then pass through 'A' Company and push the left flank out another three hundred yards. 'B' Company would remain on the east bank to guard the crossing and Saunders's Tac HQ.[13]

While these instructions looked well developed, they were based on no appreciation of the situation at Borgo di Ronta. Saunders and his company commanders, as the regiment's historian wrote, "had nothing more than a quick glance at an aerial photograph before setting out on their march." The battalion started for the crossing site at 2200 hours.[14]

Two hours later, the Patricia's 'D' Company bumped into a standing patrol of Germans on the Savio's east bank. Although three Germans were taken prisoner, some managed to escape. Fully alerted, the Germans raked the east side of the river with machine-gun fire. Succeeding in getting a rope across at 0200 hours on October 23, the Patricias were able to get one platoon to the other side in two assault boats. As the river was six to seven feet deep with a swift current, swimming or wading was impossible. It reportedly took thirty minutes for all of 'D' Company to make the crossing.[15]

At 0300 hours, the West Nova's 'D' Company, led by Major John Keble Rhodes, started across. In the path of intense machine-gun fire, they were an hour completing the move. Striking out to the right as planned, Rhodes and his men began slowly clearing a string of farmhouses. In the distance, German tanks could be heard, and sometimes the shouts of their crew commanders were detected.[16]

Robinson, meanwhile, had advanced most of the Patricia's 'D' Company about 250 yards from the river to secure a group of buildings and then sent Lieutenant Ernie Shone's platoon another 150 yards to the left. As 'A' Company of the West Novas had not yet crossed the Savio, the lone platoon was to extend the bridgehead on that flank until relieved.[17]

Threxton's 'A' Company started crossing in assault boats at 0415 hours, with Lieutenant A.C. Mackenzie's platoon leading. Once on the opposite bank, Mackenzie headed toward Shone's position. Mackenzie's men were immediately entangled in a sharp action by Germans dug into slit trenches near the riverbank. Eliminating the position yielded fifteen prisoners. Dawn found Lieutenant Douglas Knowles's platoon of 'A' Company still crossing the river. Half of it gained the west bank just as drenching mortar, machine-gun, and small-arms fire caught the men in the open.[18]

In front of them, the Canadians on the Savio's west bank saw a strong counterattack by tanks and infantry barrelling in. A group of tank-supported infantry sliced between Shone's platoon and the rest of 'D' Company. Seeing his platoon cut off, Robinson assumed it had either been slaughtered or taken prisoner. With the Germans so close, calling in artillery was impossible. Rather than be cut to pieces, Robinson ordered the remains of his company to retreat to the river.[19]

'A' Company's Threxton was still on the east bank when Mackenzie reported his platoon being attacked by three tanks and infantry firing from a range of about two hundred yards.[20] Threxton had just relayed this news to Saunders when the engineering party entered the West Nova's Tac HQ. "A bridge at this point is impossible," its commander told Saunders, "due to rising water and the condition of the banks of the river." Saunders was just accepting that the operation was for naught when Rhodes signalled by wireless at 0535 hours that 'D' Company had reached its objective "after having fought for every inch of the ground to get there."

With the crossing under heavy fire, Threxton ceased trying to pass more of 'A' Company across at 0650 hours. At the same time, Rhodes reported his position amid several houses being blasted by tanks. A few minutes later, Mackenzie brought the two platoons of 'A' Company back to the riverbank. The Patricias of 'D' Company also arrived, and a disorganized withdrawal by both companies followed. Shone and his twenty-eight Patricias were reported missing and believed lost.[21]

Also missing was Lieutenant Knowles. Mackenzie reported that he had last been seen "firing a rifle at an advancing tank, a gallant gesture in the face of death."[22] His body was never recovered.

Rhodes and 'D' Company were under heavy attack by tanks and infantry intent on overrunning their position. Rhodes, Royal Canadian Horse Artillery's Captain Fred Drewry, and signaller Private Alan K. Minard were in a house on the forward edge of the company area with a No. 18 wireless set. The building was being blasted continuously by both armour-piercing and high-explosive shells that ripped tiles off the roof and punched holes through the walls. Rhodes stayed put, helping Drewry to supply the artillery with coordinates for close-support fire that kept the Germans at bay. Between 0720 and 1050 hours, the Germans attempted three counterattacks on 'D' Company. Each attack was broken by shelling brought to "bear on at least five Panther and Mark iv tanks, scoring direct hits and keeping the tanks from closing the range."23

Clearly realizing that Rhodes and Drewry were operating an artillery observation post out of the house, the Germans ramped up the number of armour-piercing and high-explosive tank shells directed at it. Undaunted, the three-man team stayed put.24

Seeing that 'D' Company must eventually be overrun, Saunders ordered Rhodes to get ready to break for the Savio under cover of a smokescreen.25 Drewry and Rhodes provided ranges so the smoke would fall on the enemy for a minute. Rhodes then instructed his men "to show themselves as much as possible and for the ncos and officers to shout loudly." As the artillery fell, Rhodes wrote, the fire "had the desired effect of making [the enemy] think we were going to attack. They apparently drew back well behind the smoke to prepare for us and we were able to retire across the river with our prisoners without any casualties or interference."26

While Rhodes led the company to safety, Drewry remained behind until satisfied that the West Novas had escaped. With tanks closing on the house, Drewry slipped away. Behind, he could hear the Germans talking on their wireless sets.27 For their bravery, Rhodes received the Distinguished Service Order, Drewry a Military Cross, and Minard a Military Medal.

By 1130 hours, 'D' Company had withdrawn across the river. The platoon of Patricias was still missing. About fifty Germans had been taken prisoner. Another fifty were estimated to have been killed. In addition to Lieutenant Knowles being listed as missing, the West Novas reported seven other ranks killed and eight others wounded. All were from 'A' Company. 'D' Company, amazingly, suffered no casualties.

At 1940 hours, the Patricia's battalion headquarters received news that Lieutenant Shone and eleven men—one badly wounded—had managed to escape across the river. Another man reached the West Nova's Tac HQ at 1430 hours on October 24.[28]

After Shone rejoined the Patricias at Martorano, he "staggered" into Frost's platoon headquarters, "bedraggled, covered in mud, dead beat, but clearly alive, though he looked as if he had been resurrected from the dead . . . He and his platoon had lain doggo after the Panthers had ground through his position, forcing the rest of his company to withdraw. The platoon remained there until last light and then crept back to the river . . . It was his first real experience in action and one that he doubtless never forgot. He was very lucky."[29]

IN THE MID-MORNING of October 23, Lieutenant General Tommy Burns met Major General Vokes at 1st Canadian Infantry Division headquarters. Vokes reported that the Borgo di Ronta attack had failed. Incredibly, he then proposed a second attempt that very afternoon with the same battered troops. In the end, they settled on a postponement to feed in a fresh brigade. Returning to his headquarters, Burns phoned British Eighth Army's Lieutenant General Richard McCreery and outlined the plan. McCreery rejected committing 1st Division to another brigade-scale operation. In the v British Corps sector west of the Savio River, the way the situation had developed led McCreery to expect that LXXVI Panzer Korps must soon undertake a significant withdrawal. Accordingly, he wanted 1st Division to only maintain 2nd Brigade's bridgehead. The bridging situation in 4th British Infantry Division's sector by Cesena, he said, would soon enable tanks to cross there and then be sent to Pieve Sestina to secure the bridgehead. Burns was to instruct the rest of 1 Canadian Corps to confine front-line operations to active patrolling. Only in the centre, where 5th Canadian Armoured Division was relieving 2nd New Zealand Armoured Division, was the Savio to be reconnoitred to find a crossing point. McCreery considered the Germans in this sector of such a low calibre that a foothold on the west bank might be easily won.[30]

After Burns briefed Vokes on McCreery's instructions, the divisional commander ordered Lieutenant Colonel Bogert to concentrate on strengthening the present bridgehead. At 1430 hours, Bogert told the Seaforths and Eddies to consolidate their positions and patrol vigorously to try to discover whether the enemy was attempting to disengage. The Patricias were to cross into the bridgehead at 1800 hours and settle behind the other two battalions in readiness for an advance if opportunity arose. At the Tay crossing, 3rd Field Company engineers were to strengthen the bridging so it could bear light vehicles. The West Novas would provide carrying parties, taking that task from the Patricias.[31]

In accordance with these instructions, Seaforth's 'A' Company Major Robert Clark led a patrol in the late afternoon to find out whether the Germans still held the buildings alongside the Cesena–Ravenna road, which had been his final objective. As one platoon closed on the buildings, a second hovered off to one flank to provide covering fire. Clark and his men were almost across the open field between 'A' Company's position and the buildings when they came under heavy fire, proving that the Germans were holding in strength. Anticipating this, Clark had arranged for the 2-pounder anti-tank gun to provide covering fire if the patrol needed to make a hasty withdrawal. The gun jammed on the first round, there were no tools to clear it, and the patrol had to return under heavy fire. Although the other men reached safety, Clark was missing. His body was found the next day in the middle of the field.[32]

As night fell, the Germans at Borgo di Ronta started shelling the lane that led to the river with a 210-centimetre gun. The explosions shattered the adjacent farm buildings and set five large haystacks on fire. Wanting to see if this shelling presaged some change in the intentions of the Germans opposite, West Nova Lieutenant Colonel Saunders decided to send a patrol across the Savio. Lieutenant C.H. Smith and ten men, keeping to an olive grove and vineyard to avoid being illuminated by burning haystacks, headed for the river. On the way, Corporal William Frederick Clark triggered a mine and was killed. Reaching the river, Smith heard a tank on the opposite shore. Happening upon one of the assault boats lost during the earlier attack, the men paddled across.

Leaving four men to guard the boat, Smith and five others moved to where the Patricia's 'D' Company platoon had been cut off. This was adjacent to a large white building called Casa Porcelli. There they found several dead Patricias. The muddy soil was also chewed up by what Smith took to be Tiger tank tracks. Posting his Bren gunner outside, Smith and the other men entered the house. Inside they "found German equipment littered about the rooms but not a living soul. Smith pushed on resolutely by a series of zigzag lanes, searching various houses along the way and finding signs of recent German occupancy. Along those lanes and in the muddy fields, like the trail of gigantic reptiles in a prehistoric swamp," the regiment's historian wrote, "lay the fresh tracks of several Tiger tanks, crisscrossed with tracks of various half-tracks and wheeled vehicles, plain evidence that a mobile German force of considerable strength had assembled here very recently. In some of the houses the very smell of the German soldier still hung in the air. At length the patrol reached the hamlet of Pieve Sestina, about a mile west of the Savio and on the main highway to Forli. Here, in one of the houses they found an Italian family, who regarded them first with amazement and then with joy, and informed Lieutenant Smith that so far as they knew the last of the 'Tedeschi' had gone up the road." Realizing the import of this news, Smith raced back to report.[33]

There were other signs the Germans were abandoning their fierce defence of the Savio. In the late afternoon, the shelling of the river at Tay had so decreased that the engineers were able to start the improvements ordered by Lieutenant Colonel Bogert. Bulldozers carved ramps down the banks, and the engineers then rejigged the assault boats into proper alignment for bridge decking to be installed. At 0300 hours on October 24, they declared open a sixty-foot Class 9 FBE capable of supporting vehicles weighing up to ten tons. This meant that jeeps, Bren carriers, and anti-tank guns heavier than the 2-pounders could enter the bridgehead. The only handicap was that the exit bank was still so steep that each vehicle had to be winched up. By first light, however, several anti-tank guns and numerous vehicles loaded with ammunition and supplies were inside the bridgehead and moving about unmolested.

After dawn, 1st Division's chief engineer, Lieutenant Colonel Webb, made a recce to the Savio in the sector held by the Royal 22e

Régiment. It was a dull, cloudy day, but lack of rain the day before had caused the river to recede somewhat. The banks in this sector also seemed to be drying a little. About two hundred yards north of the destroyed railway bridge outside Cesena, a road led to what had been a rifle range next to a ford in the river. Webb decided the ford would serve for the division's main bridging site. In the centre of the river was a small island that could help support a seventy-foot Bailey bridge. Work by 4th Field Company started at noon, with a bulldozer scouring an approach from the range-keeper's house to the dyke. It then breached the dyke to access the riverbank. This two-hundred-yard approach was improved with a corduroy surface made with logs and rubble from nearby damaged buildings. The bridge itself angled gradually downward to rest on the island and then ascended to the opposite shore. At dawn on October 25, the bridge opened and two troops of British 145th Regiment tanks rolled across. As the day progressed, most of 2nd and 3rd Brigades' vehicles were passed across the Savio—a clear sign that the battle for the river was won.[34]

McCreery sent Bogert effusive congratulations on 2nd Brigade's performance. "I am convinced that your battle has been the most important factor in forcing the enemy to withdraw . . . The way your brigade secured a big bridgehead, smashed all enemy counterattacks, and surmounted all the difficulties of having no bridge behind was magnificent . . . The battle has been a great example of how determined, well-trained infantry can destroy enemy tanks with their own weapons . . . You have inflicted heavy casualties on the enemy and have captured a large number of prisoners from one of his best divisions."[35]

With the Savio River battle won by dawn on October 24, 1st Division set off in pursuit of the retreating Germans with 3rd Brigade's Carleton and York Regiment and 2nd Brigade's Patricias advancing in line. The Carletons headed straight alongside the railroad leading from Cesena to Forli. To their right, the Patricias followed rough tracks or cross-country roads. Their immediate objective was Volturona, a village on the east side of the next river, the Bevano, which proved little more than a ditch lacking dykes.

Neither battalion met opposition beyond some random shelling. Early on October 25, both crossed the Bevano without incident. Engineers were close behind and by midday had an Ark bridge installed across the ditch. By the afternoon, both battalions had reached the Ronco River. Vokes ordered recce patrols to cross it, but there would be no attempt at a full crossing. Since the Ronco ran as fast and deep as the Savio, no patrols could reach the far bank.[36] Patricia patrols northward along the east bank encountered no Germans and learned from the local farmers that the river was in full spate and two hundred yards wide. All bridges had been destroyed.[37]

WELL TO THE right of 1st Canadian Infantry Division, 5th Canadian Armoured Division had also advanced. To secure crossings over the Savio River on a broad front, Major General Bert Hoffmeister had ordered 11th Infantry Brigade to deploy the Irish Regiment and Cape Breton Highlanders at the village of Borgo Pipa, about midway between the coast and Cesena. After dark on October 23, the Irish scout platoon under Sergeant Arthur Charles Cullation swam the river, picked their way through a minefield, and entered the town of Mensa. Having determined that a full infantry company crossing would require assault boats, Lieutenant Colonel Bobby Clark put the planned October 24 attempt back to 1300 hours to allow for boats to be brought forward. Meeting no opposition, the Irish had all companies across by late afternoon. The anti-tank platoon then brought its guns over on rafts. As the platoon manhandled the guns up the riverbank, one broke free and slid into a verge that the pioneer platoon had not yet swept for mines. This accident was disastrous, as it triggered a German wooden box mine. Three men were killed instantly, two subsequently died of wounds, and eight were wounded—effectively knocking the platoon out of action.[38]

The Highlanders entered the Irish bridgehead early on October 25 and left Mensa for the Bevano River. By 0800 hours, all companies had reached their objective unopposed. Realizing that the Germans had withdrawn, Lieutenant Colonel Boyd Somerville decided at 1230 hours to push on to the Bevano. As expected, no Germans were encountered, except for four brought in as prisoners by one of the many partisan groups. By nightfall, a bridge spanned the Savio at Mensa, and all the Highlander vehicles and supporting tanks were alongside the companies.

To the right of the Highlanders and about equidistant from Highway 16, Cumberland Force's British 27th Lancers Cavalry Regiment had reached the village of Castiglione di Cervia on October 24 and waded the adjacent Savio the next night. Meeting no opposition, the Lancers advanced to the Bevano on October 25 and had a bridgehead across by day's end.[39]

On Highway 16 itself, Cumberland Force's Governor General's Horse Guards with 'B' Squadron leading advanced on October 24 from Cervia to a canal just short of the Savio. Although the day before, 1st Fallschirmjäger Division had been relieved in this sector by the much lower-calibre 114th Jäger Division, these Germans offered a fight. When a dismounted patrol was pinned down across the river, its leader, Sergeant Alexander Ellwood Chambers, was killed. Lieutenant James Lorne Chesney drove his Sherman tank into the fray. Although successful in extracting the patrol, Chesney was shot by a sniper and died instantly.

Captain J.A. McKechan ground up to the river with two Shermans. From a range of 150 yards, the tanks pounded the German position with armour-piercing and high-explosive shells while raking it with machine guns. One armour-piercing round penetrated a dugout and twelve Germans fled. "From there on," the regiment's historian wrote, "the tanks had a field day. At least six Germans were killed and the rest lost all their enthusiasm."[40]

With Cumberland Force now under his direct command, 5th Division's Major General Hoffmeister ordered 11th Brigade's Perth Regiment to send a company to take over the advance along Highway 16. Captain Robert Cole's 'A' Company paddled across the Savio in assault boats at noon on October 25. Cole led two platoons toward the Bevano, but they were stopped short by machine-gun fire from the opposing bank. Regrouping, Cole and the full company waded the five-foot-deep Bevano and established a bridgehead at 0350 hours on October 26. Dawn brought a German counterattack, which was driven off with only one Perth being wounded. Thereafter, the only opposition was harassing mortar and artillery fire.

This last skirmish marked the end of combat actions by Cumberland Force. It remained in static positions until formally disbanded at noon on October 28. Brigadier Ian Cumberland of 5th Armoured Brigade noted that its "short life" had been a brief eighteen days.[41]

10

A Sorry Mess

LIEUTENANT GENERAL TOMMY Burns could never remember whether it was October 24 "or a day or so later" when Lieutenant General Richard McCreery summoned him to British Eighth Army headquarters and told him that "he was not satisfied with me as corps commander, and had recommended that I be replaced." Burns was stunned. "I had thought that after the victories of the corps in the Adriatic offensive the higher command had revised its previously unfavourable opinion of my ability. Giving me command of divisions other than Canadian had seemed to confirm this."

Burns raised these points with McCreery. The lieutenant general, however, replied that during the previous winter—while he still commanded 'X' British Corps at the Garigliano River—poor weather had also plagued operations. When General Mark Clark had ordered McCreery to win a bridgehead across the river, he had driven the corps ruthlessly and got the job done. Burns realized the implication. He was considered to have failed as a hard-charger.[1]

There was, of course, more to it. Neither Canadian divisional commander trusted or respected Burns. Corps senior staff was increasingly mutinous. McCreery thought it was far too late for Burns to rectify matters. A competent staff officer, Burns had failed as a field commander.[2]

It little helped that Burns was openly critical of Allied strategy in Italy—a strategy dictated by Supreme Headquarters, Allied Expeditionary Force commander General Dwight D. Eisenhower. Through the coming winter, Eisenhower wanted the Germans engaged on all fronts. Consequently, despite grave shortages in personnel and material, the Allies in Italy were to remain on the offensive.

Burns had made it clear that he "did not believe it would be sound policy to continue an all-out offensive, and to incur further heavy casualties under the conditions in the Romagna, where the prospects for decisive victory during the winter months of rain, snow, and mud appeared negligible."

Knowing his earlier champion could not save him, Burns still wrote a defensive note to First Canadian Army's Lieutenant General Harry Crerar. The corps, he argued, had won "all objectives assigned to it, inflicting heavy losses on the enemy, which compromised the best divisions in Italy. Though progress was not always as rapid as desirable, nevertheless, during our period of action, we went farther and faster than any other corps."[3]

Shortly thereafter, Allied Armies in Italy commander General Harold Alexander gently sent Burns away. Struck by Alexander's "personal kindness," Burns thanked him. "It has helped a great deal," he wrote the commander.[4]

CHANGES, SOME PLANNED and others resulting from calamity, were also afoot on the German side. The period of October 20–24 had been a time of crisis. With both British Eighth Army and U.S. Fifth Army striving for major breakthroughs, Commander-in-Chief Southwest Generalfeldmarschall Albert Kesselring and Tenth Army's Generaloberst Heinrich von Vietinghoff had juggled units frantically to blunt the Allied efforts. Although Eighth Army's advances in the Romagna posed a critical threat, Fifth Army's Apennine push toward Bologna presented the gravest danger. Bologna served as the dividing boundary between Germany's Tenth Army to the east and Fourteenth Army, which held the front westward to the Tyrrhenian Sea.

Although Fifth Army's daily advances seldom exceeded two thousand yards, each loss of ground loosened the German foothold in the mountains. Generals Alexander and Clark desperately wanted Fifth Army to break free of the mountains in October to avoid being stuck there through the winter. Already the weather was rapidly deteriorating. Worsening matters, xii British Corps and its three divisions—serving under Clark's command—were exhausted. To strengthen the corps, Alexander fed in his last fresh division—the 78th British Infantry Division, just returned from the Middle East. Even this addition, Alexander feared, was too little to enable Fifth Army to escape the mountains.

With no room for manoeuvre, Clark could only bludgeon forward. In the army's centre, facing Bologna, U.S. ii Corps bulled ahead, with 85th Division immediately east of Highway 65 and the 91st Infantry Division astride the road itself. Diversionary attacks were made by the 88th Infantry Division on the right and 34th Infantry Division to the left. To the right of ii Corps, xiii British Corps had soon relieved the 88th Division with its newly deployed 78th Division.

With Fifth Army generally attacking downhill, it should have held the advantage. But the mountain structure was so complex and fragmented—with deep ravines bordered by tall summits—that the Germans withdrew from one strongpoint to another with relative ease. The abysmal rains also favoured them. Backs to the wall, the Germans resisted fanatically—morale boosted by a personal order from Hitler that the Apennines be held at all costs.

To maintain this resistance through October, Kesselring had drawn divisions from other sectors. Not wanting to weaken lxxvi Panzer Korps facing Eighth Army, he had shifted 65th Infanterie-Division from the less-threatened western sector. On October 13, he had then fed in 44th Infanterie-Division from a reserve holding position at Bologna. This left him with no remaining fresh reserves.

The next day brought a crisis that persuaded Von Vietinghoff to risk a major reverse in the Romagna by sending the 29th Panzer Grenadier Division to strengthen i Fallschirmjäger Korps. Despite this infusion, on October 20, the U.S. 88th Infantry Division had won the great massifs of Monte Grande and Monte Cerere from the

Germans. Two days later, the Americans were just four miles from severing Highway 9. On the 23rd, the 34th Infantry Division captured Monte Belmonte and stood only nine miles from Bologna.

Cutting Highway 9 east of Bologna would place Fifth Army behind Von Vietinghoff's Tenth Army. Such an outflanking would force a major withdrawal and likely mean the loss of Ravenna.[5] The situation so alarmed Kesselring that, at 0500 hours on October 23, he personally began a tour of divisional headquarters. "I . . . was able to give advice, encouragement, and in some cases assistance by allocating reserves," he wrote. As the journey progressed, Kesselring sensed that the crisis was abating and the Germans in the Apennines were holding. After visiting 29th Panzer Grenadier Division, Kesselring headed east on Highway 9 toward Forli, where LI Gebirgskorps was headquartered. Coming upon a long German column, Kesselring's driver was squeezing past when a long-barrelled self-propelled gun emerged from a crossroad and struck the car. Kesselring suffered a severe concussion and "a nasty gash on the left temple." He regained consciousness the next morning in a hospital in Ferrara, but the accident would sideline him until January 1945.[6]

Von Vietinghoff immediately replaced Kesselring as Commander-in-Chief Southwest, and Tenth Army passed to General der Panzertruppen Joachim Lemelsen, who in turn handed Fourteenth Army off to General der Artillerie Heinz Ziegler. Reviewing the situation, Von Vietinghoff decided he could only continue the desperate battle in the Apennines and hope Fifth Army ran out of steam. To keep the fight before Bologna going, however, meant moving two more divisions—the 90th panzer grenadiers and 1st Fallschirmjäger—from the Romagna. The arrival of the two best German divisions in Italy proved pivotal. As the rain intensified and was accompanied by gale-force winds, the strengthened German resistance combined with Fifth Army's increasing exhaustion prompted Clark to suggest abandoning the offensive. On October 27, Alexander reluctantly agreed. Fifth Army assumed a defensive posture.

Alexander was deeply disappointed that Bologna would not be won, but there was no alternative. Fifth Army's current casualty rate had become so acute that Clark reported its American divisions would be eight thousand infantrymen understrength by November 1. That translated into a shortage of seventy-five men per rifle company. With Eighth Army similarly weakened, Alexander conceded that the bitter October fighting likely meant that Ravenna would also remain in German hands.[7]

IN THE I CANADIAN Corps sector of the Romagna, the night of October 25–26 again brought heavy rain. At 0800 hours, 1st Canadian Infantry Division's senior engineer, Lieutenant Colonel Ted Webb, was told the Savio River was rising rapidly. Leaping into a jeep, Webb raced toward the Bailey bridge the engineers had installed two hundred yards downriver from the destroyed railway bridge. Forty-five minutes later, he bitterly watched as water "came up over the top of the bridge and washed out the decking." Then the "bridge itself started to twist and turn, and rolled three or four hundred yards down the river. The rain continued all day."

While Webb was watching the bridge's destruction, an infantry officer told him the Floating Bridge Equipment downriver at Martorano was on the verge of washing out. Webb ordered 1st Field Company to the site with orders "to yank it out before the water came up over it. As they came up to it, the water was coming . . . over the ramps and, before they could do any work, the whole bridge broke loose."

Downriver, 5th Canadian Armoured Division's bridges were also wrecked. Webb was piqued that that division's chief engineer "accused us of sabotaging their first bridge, saying that a hay stack, a dead ox, and our FBE hit it at the same time, and that the final straw was our FBE."

Hoping to prevent the approaches to the Bailey bridge site from being washed away, Webb ordered a bulldozer to fill in the breach in the dyke on the Savio's east bank that had been cut to provide access to the river. "By the time we could get a bulldozer on the job, the water was up to the level of the bottom of the dyke. We did manage to get the gap filled to a height of [five feet], but further up, the dyke had been damaged by the Germans, so the water flowing in behind the dyke made our work useless. Shortly after this, there was a raging torrent [three hundred yards] wide on the wrong side of the dyke. Water was washing up against the river side wall of the range warden's house, and spouting out the windows on the other side like water out of a flume.

"Before dark that night the water in the river was eighteen feet high." By noon, the only bridge between Cesena and the sea was one in 4th British Infantry's sector just east of Cesena. Here, British engineers had erected a Bailey atop the stout stone piers of an old Roman bridge. Although the Germans had blown the span, they left the piers intact, and the height of these kept the bridge decking from being washed away. Until the Savio returned to normal levels, this would be the only crossing for both 1 Canadian Corps and v British Corps to maintain contact with the forward troops holding on the Ronco River. On October 27, however, this bridge was closed to all but jeep traffic because heavier vehicles combined with the raging river to severely weaken the ancient piers. The following morning, engineers managed to install a new bridge where Highway 9 crossed the Savio. Although traffic capacity remained limited, no crisis in moving supplies forward developed.

In its attempts to bridge the Savio, Webb reported, 1 Canadian Corps had used up all its "bridging equipment resources . . . yet no bridges withstood the tide. During the last [two thousand] years, the natives of Italy have built good and numerous bridges, but never have they bridged the River Savio in the [seven] mile stretch from Cesena north to Mensa. This the Canadians attempted to do, and failed."[8]

AS THE CANADIAN troops miserably endured the rains that brought October to a close, their spirits were lifted somewhat by the know-ledge that dry quarters soon awaited them. Eighth Army's Lieutenant General McCreery had announced that, after two months of almost constant action, it was time to give them a deserved rest. The relief was to have started at 0600 hours on October 27 but was rescheduled for noon of the following day because of the torrential rain.[9]

Along the Ronco River, there had been little fighting. In 5th Canadian Armoured Division's sector, the Canadian presence on the river was limited to patrols sent forward by 11th Infantry Brigade from its base on the Bevano River. These patrols were mostly carried out by the Irish Regiment's 'A' and 'D' Companies, working closely with about two hundred partisans, who had started appearing on the night of October 25–26.[10]

Irish Regiment's Captain Gordon Wood wrote that "we saw girls with grenades at their waist, and men with every kind of weapon imaginable, including Berettas and Schmeissers. These courageous people infiltrated into the German lines, appearing to be civilians in their shabby and worn attire, and brought back vital information, mostly concerning the defences around the Montone River and Ravenna."[11]

On the morning of October 28, a twelve-man 'D' Company patrol accompanied by ten partisans headed for the hamlet of San Pietro in Vincoli, situated midway between the Bevano and the Ronco. Armed with three PIATS, the force set up an ambush just outside the hamlet. Soon a troop of German armoured cars emerged from the hamlet. A PIAT round knocked the lead car out and killed an officer aboard. Its other two passengers surrendered and the remaining armoured cars rapidly withdrew. The successful ambush was unique, as generally the patrols encountered no enemy.

When the patrol reached friendly lines, it found 5th Division well along in handing over its sector running from the mouth of the Savio River to the hamlet of Bagnolo on the Ronco. By noon, the Irish were gone.[12] Taking over the division front was another ad hoc unit similar to Cumberland Force and, in fact, comprising some of its battalions. Commanded by Lieutenant Colonel Andrew Horsbrugh-Porter of the British 27th Lancers Cavalry Regiment, the unit was designated Porterforce. Both the Governor General's Horse Guards and the Royal Canadian Dragoons shifted from Cumberland to Porterforce, while 5th Division's Westminster Regiment, the Princess Louise Fusiliers' mortar crews, and various artillery, engineer, and other small units were also added.

The 1st Division relief, meanwhile, was carried out by a single British cavalry regiment—the 12th Royal Lancers—who came under V British Corps command. As October 28 ended, all units of 1 Canadian Corps—save those in Porterforce—were moving to designated rest areas on the Adriatic coast.[13]

Between entering the Romagna on September 23 and the October 28 cessation of operations, 1 Canadian Corps had advanced only twenty-three miles. It was ground won at the cost of 355 officers and men killed, 1,471 wounded, and 92 lost as prisoners.[14] Predictably, the greatest losses were suffered by infantry battalions, with those in 2nd Brigade hardest hit. The brigade reported its casualties from the launch of the attack across the Savio as 40 killed, 199 wounded, and 32 missing.[15] More than a third of these were men in the Loyal Edmonton Regiment, which had 14 killed, 100 wounded, and one missing.[16] The Seaforth Highlanders ran a close second—18 killed, 61 wounded, and 12 missing.[17] Because so many bridging operations were undertaken under enemy fire, the engineers suffered significantly higher than the usual number of casualties. Thirteen engineers were killed and 77 wounded.[18]

PULLING AN ENTIRE corps out of the front lines could never happen overnight. By the end of October 28, 1st Division still had its three brigades down near the Ronco River, awaiting better weather that might dry and improve the roads. On October 30, Major General Chris Vokes and his headquarters left Cesena under a dull, cloudy sky and moved to the coastal town of Riccione.[19] The division's 3rd Brigade had moved at 1030 hours the previous day from positions about six miles northwest of Cesena. Shortly after the strung-out convoy turned south on Highway 9, it was fired on at long range by German SPGS. No vehicles were hit, and the brigade soon reached Cattolica—another coastal town south of Riccione—without further incident. By 1900 hours, brigade headquarters and the entirety of its three battalions had all found billets.[20]

The 2nd Brigade was last to leave the line. Its departure from near the Savio River was delayed by some 5th Division units being slow to respond to orders to vacate Riccione. The Princess Patricia's Canadian Light Infantry were first to be greenlighted for a move—transport arriving at 1600 hours on October 31.[21] At 0845 hours the next day, the battalion convoy set out and reached Riccione at 1130 hours. As the men were settling into assigned billets, intelligence officer Lieutenant D.G. MacCulloch observed that these "were not as good as the majority we have had in the past rest areas. Most of the buildings carry the scars of war, such as damaged roofs and walls."[22] Practically every building, Lieutenant Syd Frost noted, lacked most of their roofs, windows, and doors. Some had about a foot of rainwater sloshing about on the floors.[23] Things went from bad to worse as a gale swept in on the night of November 1–2. By morning, "all the roads and yards were miniature lakes. A goodly amount of this water found its way into the billets, and things were a sorry mess," MacCulloch wrote. "But a determined effort by all those affected soon got the situation under control."[24] Still, it took until November 4 to sufficiently repair things to get brigade headquarters and the other two battalions settled into Riccione.

November 4 also saw 5th Division's 11th Brigade depart the front after spending three days just east of the Savio in "a mud hole," where, the brigade war diarist noted, they had "no responsibility on this front [so] life is very boring and there is no entertainment available." The brigade settled in Urbino, a village about fifteen miles west of Pesaro.[25]

By November 6, all of 1 Canadian Corps was fully settled in rest areas. Corps headquarters was at Riccione, beside 1st Division's headquarters and its 1st and 2nd Brigades, while 3rd Brigade was in Cattolica. This was an ideal concentration that enabled easy communication and interaction.

Such was not the case for 5th Division. Its headquarters was in San Giovanni in Marignano, a short distance west of Cattolica and five miles from the more inland Morciano di Romagna, which housed 12th Infantry Brigade's headquarters and its 4th Princess Louise Dragoon Guards. The brigade's Westminster Regiment was in San Clemente, a couple of miles to the north of Morciano, and the 1st Light Anti-Aircraft Battalion was in Montefiore Conca. As the crow flies, this village was only about three miles from Morciano. But the only link was via a tortuous road that made the trip about ten miles.[26] The 11th Infantry Brigade was concentrated around Urbino, a village about twenty miles to the south, while 5th Armoured Brigade had remained in Cervia, thirty miles to the north. The isolation of 11th Brigade was further exacerbated by army policy that closed many secondary roads when Bailey bridges were removed in order to reuse them later on. Civilian repair efforts were proceeding at a snail's pace, so the San Giovanni–Urbino trip required a sixty-mile detour.[27]

Had 5th Division's only purpose been to rest troops, this scattering would have meant little. But, while 1 Canadian Corps had been pulled out of the line ostensibly to be rested, this was not a time for officers and troops to lie around enjoying themselves. The corps was to rest and train for a new phase of operations in November. In the meantime, Eighth Army continued offensive action, with 11 Polish Corps and v British Corps maintaining as much pressure as possible on the Germans in the Romagna. At the end of the month, "freshened and retrained," as one army report put it, "the Canadians would return to the line to take part in the all-out drive to capture Ravenna."[28]

PART TWO

TAKING RAVENNA

11

Command Shuffle

WHILE I CANADIAN CORPS had been completing its oper-
ations toward the end of October and then leaving the line
for a well-deserved rest, Allied Armies in Italy commander General
Harold Alexander had faced an increasing dilemma. The Allied of-
fensive plan was focused on a breakout from the Apennines to seize
Bologna and a simultaneous advance in the Romagna to win Ravenna.
Yet winning both cities would compromise the grander, overarching
Allied strategy for Italy. The fact was that Supreme Headquarters,
Allied Expeditionary Force (SHAEF) commander General Dwight
D. Eisenhower was less interested in winning ground in Italy than
in preventing enemy divisions there from being sent to either
Northwest Europe or the Russian front, where they could strengthen
the German defences.

If one considered only how to pin in place the maximum number
of German divisions, standing on the current Apennine line made
most sense. But if Bologna fell, the Germans would likely pull back
to a line anchored on the Po and Ticino Rivers. This would enable
them to abandon northwest Italy and transfer at least two divisions
elsewhere. A line on these two rivers was also unlikely to prove viable
for long, and a further withdrawal all the way to the Adige River
would soon follow.[1]

Once the Germans fell back to the Adige, Alexander mused gloomily, they could transfer a good number of divisions. They would also be containing the Allies in Italy, whereas at present the situation was reversed. Currently, the Germans had to keep all their divisions in Italy in line to prevent an Allied breakout.[2]

Despite the potential negative result of taking Bologna and Ravenna, the Allies had to persist in the effort. Standing still was not an option because the Germans might risk transferring divisions anyway. On October 29, Alexander convened a meeting of his two army commanders and other high-ranking staff in Florence.

Alexander reiterated why he wanted these two cities. They would serve his tactical and administrative needs. Bologna was the communication node for the entire region, and Ravenna could provide a useful base for administering the build-up for future operations in the Po Valley. If they were to be taken, it had to happen before the onset of winter brought conditions that would render major operations impossible. Yet, Alexander said, if the two cities were not taken, the Germans would be forced to hold the present line to defend them.

Once winter ended, a new offensive could be mounted in early 1945. Alexander advised that he had sent a proposal to the Combined Chiefs of Staff Committee in London calling for a February 1 start date.

General Mark Clark interjected that his four U.S. infantry divisions had suffered twenty thousand casualties and "could not go on unless he could get two or three of them rested" and assimilate available reinforcements. How to pull these divisions out of the line? To the right of U.S. 11 Corps, XIII British Corps was already overextended due to its own shortages but also plagued by bad mountain roads that created an administrative nightmare. On 11 Corps's left flank, the 6th South African Armoured Division had also suffered heavy casualties and equally needed a rest. The only apparent solution was to try to rest the Americans and South Africans in piecemeal fashion.

When the time came for the push on Bologna, Alexander promised that U.S. Fifth Army would be strengthened with the addition of 78th British Infantry Division and 11 Polish Corps. Both Clark and Lieutenant General Richard McCreery were told to mount respective offensives toward Bologna and Ravenna. Target start date would be

November 30, with termination on about December 15. The attacks, Alexander said, "would only be launched if they had a good chance of success."

McCreery advised "that it was difficult to maintain pressure over the rain sodden ground and across the swollen rivers." He realized "that pressure must be maintained as long as possible, but . . . operations by Eighth Army must end" by about December 15. "He could mount a full scale attack, which would include three fresh divisions by the end of November." Taking Ravenna could not be done by direct attack, he cautioned. That was prohibited by the "water-logged state of the coastal plain." Instead, he planned to advance "on the drier ground astride Highway 9" and capture Ravenna "by threatening the enemy's communications" to the city. Essentially, he would cut it off from the German rear and thereby force the garrison within to either withdraw or face being surrounded and destroyed in place.

This sounded good to Alexander, but he stressed that there "were certain liabilities which had to be met." Already 4th Indian Division had been withdrawn and was being sent to Greece. The 1st British Armoured Division was being disbanded, and one British infantry division "would have to be cannibalized to meet an estimated deficiency of 17,000 men by 1 February 1945. Against these liabilities, 5th Infantry Division was coming from the Middle East after a period of rest and training, but another division must go from this theatre in exchange, for internal security duties in Palestine." The 8th Indian Division and 6th South African Armoured Division "would have to go out of the line for rest when relief was possible. British Eighth Army formations must be out of the line by January and it was possible that it would be best to take over their sector initially with a corps composed of the Poles, Italians, and two Indian divisions" under command of Alexander's headquarters.

At this point in the meeting, the focus took an abrupt turn. It seemed the reason Eighth Army had to be out of the line by January was to prepare to take part in an ambitious scheme of Alexander's. He planned to make a major strategic game change in the Mediterranean for early 1945. Increasingly, he was convinced that "a frontal attack in Italy was likely to prove unprofitable." He now envisioned "a double-handed punch in conjunction with Russia and Tito's forces [as] the best answer."[3]

The Italian Campaign, Alexander explained, had always been designed to support an invasion in Western Europe—even before it began on June 6 with D-Day. With the invasion now well advanced and the Allies knocking on Germany's door, there were four possible ways to continue supporting this primary front. First, he could transfer troops directly to assist the advance into Germany. The second plan, and the one he favoured, envisioned troops from Italy being sent to Yugoslavia.[4] After Yugoslavia had been conquered by Germany in April 1941, Josip Broz—who went by the *nom de guerre* Tito—had led a growing Communist partisan army in fighting the occupation. By the fall of 1944, the People's Liberation Army, which at times numbered about 70,000 partisans, was tying down as many as 500,000 Axis troops. Sending Eighth Army into Yugoslavia would ensure that those Axis forces remained in place and might force the Germans to reinforce that theatre. Alexander's plan was to land the army at Split and other Dalmatian ports that the Germans did not occupy. The army would then advance on Zagreb, Ljubljana, and Fiume. Fifth Army would remain in Italy to fight its way across the Po and Adige. Then the two armies could advance in a pincer movement to the Gorizia and Trieste area. From there, they could "strike towards Vienna."[5] This second option appealed to the strategic general in Alexander—it was a bold, imaginative strike.

There were, however, two less imaginative options. He could continue the offensive in Italy to the limits set by exhaustion of his troops and growing material shortages. Or he could cease the offensive and rebuild with the idea of renewing the effort at a later date.

Shortly after the October 29 meeting, Alexander presented all four ideas to Eisenhower. The SHAEF commander's response was that no extra troops were needed in France, so option one was unnecessary. Option two might have some advantages, but an adventure into Yugoslavia would not affect the Western Front, and its impact on the Russian front would likely not be seen until the spring of 1945 at the earliest. Continuing the offensive in Italy, Eisenhower said, would be best. Alexander, always somewhat easy-going, amiably agreed. Despite all the handicaps, they would press on in Italy.[6]

ALTHOUGH I CANADIAN CORPS was in reserve, several battalions were still in the field with Porterforce. When this force had been formed on October 28, the Governor General's Horse Guards was initially attached with orders to advance via Highway 16 toward Ravenna. The following day, a 'B' Squadron patrol commanded by Corporal C.A. Smith advanced a couple of miles from the Bevano River to the Fosso Ghiaia—about six miles south of Ravenna. Although *fosso* translates as "ditch," the Ghiaia was more a narrow canal. The highway bridge was blown, but Smith saw no Germans on the opposite bank. Returning to the squadron's base near the Bevano, Smith was told the Royal Canadian Dragoons would relieve the Horse Guards at 1800 hours.

By 0900 hours on October 30, the Horse Guards had departed Porterforce. This, the regiment's war diarist wrote, brought "to a close an operation which was to say the least unusual. In 12 hectic days, the regiment had advanced, on foot, approximately 15 miles . . . to the F. Ghiaia . . . In order to make this advance possible, the regiment built its own bridges and maintained itself by wheelbarrow, bicycles, donkey carts, boats, rafts, and in some cases, only the long arduous man-handling of supplies. The initiative of everyone from the co down to the newest trooper was taxed to the limit and now that it is over, we look back on it with pride."[7]

The Dragoons were displeased with their new assignment. Lieutenant Colonel Keith Landell soon realized that the Germans had returned to the Fosso Ghiaia and seemed determined to block any further advance up Highway 16. Conditions were abysmal. "The enemy had opened the dykes of the Savio River," he wrote, "and flooded the area so that the road was under water in places and in others ran like a causeway across the drowned countryside. Troops and vehicles moved on that highway like targets in a penny shooting gallery, and the Germans wasted no time in taking full advantage of this fine opportunity for target practice. He was sitting quite snug across the Ghiaia . . . whose dykes were still intact, with this great sheet of water in front of him, its surface broken only by the road and a few houses built up high beside it. In its worst dreams the Regiment had never seen itself advancing in such a position."

It was not surprising that Landell disliked Porterforce's task, which was to advance to the Fiumi Uniti—a canal that drained into the Adriatic on Ravenna's southern outskirts. The force's main strength was provided by two armoured car regiments—his and the 27th Lancers Cavalry Regiment's. The Lancers were on the western flank, operating in ground bordered on their left by Highway 67 and their right by the Cesena–Ravenna road. Because of the flooding, Landell's Dragoons had little room to manoeuvre on either side of Highway 16.[8]

Eighth Army's Lieutenant General McCreery had even grander ambitions for Porterforce. His October 27 order creating it had set three objectives. First, it was to protect v British Corps's right flank as it closed on Ravenna from the west. Second, it was then to "capture and occupy Ravenna." And third, subsequent to this, Porterforce would "push on north and west, continuing to open up Route 16." Canadian units attached to it were the Dragoons, 2nd Field Regiment, 5th Medium Regiment, and the 12th Field Company's engineers. The British contributed the self-propelled 24th Field Regiment and 151st Anti-Tank Battery.[9]

On October 31, Landell launched an attempt by 'D' Squadron to reach the Ghiaia. As almost six feet of water covered the road, the armoured cars and other vehicles had to be left behind. "The whole position was fantastic," he grumbled, "but the orders were to maintain contact, and that was the only way it could be done." To keep the squadron supplied, Landell acquired several amphibious trucks known as DUKWS. Built by the Americans in 1942, boat-shaped, and driven in water by a single propeller while having a normal engine and wheels for movement on land, DUKWS were called "Ducks."[10]

Major Allen Brady's squadron managed to reach and occupy two houses about 120 yards short of the Ghiaia. Fire from a German outpost near the south bank blocked further advance. Despite the sniping and machine-gun fire, Brady led a section of men forward. When the section outflanked the Germans, they withdrew to buildings alongside the canal. Both sides settled in for the night.

The next morning, Brady led No. 3 Troop under Lieutenant George Wharton Dauphinee to the canal and occupied a house overlooking it. Here Brady established his squadron headquarters and ran a telephone line back to Landell's Tac HQ.

Brady's building was soon subjected to a shower of mortar, artillery, and sniper fire. Then an 88-millimetre self-propelled gun (SPG) lobbed rounds straight along the highway from the opposite bank. Several shells struck the building. Dauphinee and three others were killed.[11] After being hit three times by shrapnel and knocked unconscious, Brady awoke to find the SPG still pounding the building. The telephone line had been severed, so Brady had no way of seeking artillery support. Running outside, he managed to repair the line while under fire. He then directed artillery fire onto the SPG and knocked it out. With Dauphinee dead, Brady—despite "great pain" and heavy bleeding from his undressed wounds—rallied No. 3 Troop and led it to a better position alongside the river. Brady's actions were recognized with a Distinguished Service Order.[12]

'D' Squadron's hold on the south bank of the Ghiaia was secure, but the Germans were too well entrenched across the canal for any further advance up Highway 16. After relieving 'D' Squadron at last light on November 1, 'B' Squadron assumed a purely defensive role.

Hoping to turn the German flank, Landell had 'C' and 'A' Squadrons backtrack to Cervia and then cross the Savio River at Castiglione di Cervia. The countryside was again so waterlogged that 'C' Squadron's troops all dismounted and went forward as infantry. By 1300 hours on October 31, the squadron reached the Cesena–Ravenna road after covering a mile and a half of ground.[13] As this road was less flooded, the heavy Staghound armoured cars of one troop were brought up so it could support the other two troops in their infantry role.

Once this reorganization was completed on November 1, the squadron advanced about three miles, until fired on by Germans dug in at a crossroads. Quickly pulling out of gunfire range, the Dragoons smothered the crossroads with artillery fire. "Much confusion was caused to the enemy," the regiment's war diarist recorded, "and one shell-shocked German appeared madly waving his Safe Conduct Pass

[a leaflet dropped on German troops either by air or fired inside special shells into their lines]. The remainder . . . scattered in all directions, some of whom were blown up on their own minefields." Joined
by 12th Field Company, the Dragoons and engineers cleared a path
through the minefields. The advance then continued to about three
miles short of the Ghiaia, where the road was completely blocked by
a massive crater.[14]

With the Cesena–Ravenna road's condition worsening, 'A' and
'C' Squadrons pushed out of the hamlet of San Stefano on November 2
along parallel trails that were often mined and where every culvert
had been blown, toward a crossroads about a half mile short of
the Ghiaia.

'A' Squadron's advance was led by Lieutenant S.W. Bone's troop,
with two crews in armoured cars and the other working as infantry.
Closing on the crossroads, the leading armoured car drew fire from
an adjacent house. When the lead car returned fire, its main gun
jammed. Bone ordered its crew to hold and advanced his car toward
the building. When Bone's head rose slightly above the turret hatch,
it was grazed by a sniper bullet. Seconds later, the car was disabled
by a mine, and the other car was knocked out by a Panzerfaust. Both
crews dismounted and ran to a nearby building. Before they could go
inside, the owners warned them that four heavily armed Germans occupied the second floor. Bone and his troopers withdrew to a nearby
ditch and pointed their small-arms toward the building.[15]

Having abandoned their armoured cars, the troop was unable
to contact 'A' Squadron's Major Charles Victor William Vickers,
prompting him to go forward in a scout car driven by Trooper James
Morris Papps. Once on the scene, Vickers joined Bone's troop in the
ditch. Ordering them to cover him, Vickers ran to the house. Kicking
the door in, he exchanged gunfire with the Germans upstairs. All
four surrendered. Returning to the ditch, Vickers wounded another
German and took him prisoner.[16]

The ditch was now under heavy machine-gun, mortar, and shell
fire, which wounded Bone again, as well as injuring two other men.
The rest of the troop were low on ammunition. Deciding to retreat,
Vickers ordered Papps to evacuate everyone in the armoured scout car.

As the car could only hold a few men, Papps had to make repeated trips through heavy fire to reach San Stefano. As he returned for the fifth and final run, the car took a direct mortar-round hit and stalled. Papps was badly shaken and suffered shrapnel wounds to his head and shoulders. Joining the remaining men in the ditch, Papps waited for a lull in the German shelling. When it came, he dashed to the scout car. Working in the open, Papps managed to start the engine. Vickers and the others squeezed aboard and Papps drove them clear. His actions earned a Military Medal.[17]

Hoping to outflank the Germans who had stopped Bone's troop, Vickers sent 'A' Squadron out to the left. He was just about to follow when, at 1300 hours, Landell ordered him by wireless to push on immediately to the crossroads to link up with 'C' Squadron. Unable to recall the rest of his squadron, Vickers headed directly for the crossroads with his headquarters section, consisting of three armoured cars. Encountering the same heavy machine-gun and mortar fire that Bone's troop had met, Vickers ordered the section to halt short of the building from which the heaviest fire was coming. Dismounting, he ran forward alone and barged into the building. After an exchange of shots, Vickers accepted the surrender of five Germans inside.

Although the position at the crossroads was now being subjected to heavy fire, Vickers led three men on foot into the cauldron. As they dug in to create a strongpoint, some men from 'C' Squadron arrived and the link-up was achieved. Once the situation was secure, Vickers and his headquarters section returned to San Stefano. Vickers's actions were recognized with a Distinguished Service Order.[18]

ON NOVEMBER 1, PORTERFORCE had been reinforced east of the Royal Canadian Dragoons by the most unusual unit in Eighth Army— Popski's Private Army. The Belgian-born son of a Russian engineer, Vladimir Peniakoff had been managing a sugar factory in Alexandria, Egypt, when the war began. Fluent in Arabic and familiar with desert conditions, he was recruited by the British. Nicknamed Popski by his British contacts, he and twelve Arabs were soon conducting reconnaissance operations up to three hundred miles behind enemy lines. By the time Popski transferred to Italy and joined Porterforce, he held the rank of lieutenant colonel. His "army" consisted of about 120 volunteers—mostly Scots and North Country Englishmen. Using heavily armed jeeps, they routinely ranged far behind German lines by moving through country the enemy considered inaccessible. Popski also established close working relationships with the partisans. His task with Porterforce was to closely reconnoitre the densely forested coastal ground found between Cervia and Ravenna.[19] This mostly pine forest was intermingled with lowlands that were often flooded by a mixture of salt water and fresh water. The forest and lowlands stood back from a strip of low sand dunes that faced long stretches of sandy beach. Popski's operational area was heavily defended by the Germans, who anchored their defences on the many rivers and canals that drained through it. Every farmstead, haystack, and coastal dune was turned into a strongpoint, with all approaches to each protected by minefields.

While normal military tactics for overcoming these strongpoints would have entailed heavy casualties, Popski loaded jeeps and men into DUKWs that sailed up the coast at night to land behind each position in turn. When it came to attacking the Germans at the Ghiaia, Popski rushed ten jeeps—each mounting two 50-calibre machine guns—through the morning mist to the canal's south bank. The heavy fire that raked the German positions persuaded them to surrender.[20]

By November 3, the Royal Canadian Dragoons had also cleared the last Germans from the Highway 16 section of the Ghiaia and were firmly established on its southern bank. But in the Cesena–Ravenna road sector, pockets of Germans remained, often infiltrating back into positions eliminated earlier. Farther inland, the 27th Lancers had enjoyed better fighting conditions. Although the ground was muddy, it was not flooded and there was a better road network. Still, the advance was slow. Small groups of Germans offered determined resistance until each was eliminated, and reinfiltration was common.

On the night of November 3–4, a section of Dragoons from 'C' Squadron set up in a captured German position. Corporal Thomas Smith's six men settled in for what they expected to be an uneventful night. At 0400 hours, however, about thirty Germans burst out of the darkness. A fierce two-hour battle ensued. While personally manning the section's Bren gun, Smith gave instructions to the others. The Dragoons killed two Germans and wounded seven others before their ammunition began to run low. Telling his men to use their guns sparingly, Smith stepped into the open to throw grenades. Although there was no hope of being reinforced before daybreak, Smith never considered a retreat, despite being so outnumbered. At 0730 hours, the Germans melted away. Smith and his men were unscathed. The corporal's "heroism, calmness, and skill" merited a Military Medal.[21]

Such actions became all too common, and despite the addition of Popski's Army, Porterforce remained deadlocked before the Ghiaia as the first week of November closed. On November 7, the Dragoons were relieved. On Highway 16, they turned the line over to a company of the British 1st Battalion/4th Essex Regiment. This unit also relieved one squadron of the 27th Lancers. The two remaining 27th Lancer squadrons were sent to Porterforce's left flank adjacent to v Corps.

Bad weather and determined German resistance had slowed to a snail's pace the early November advance by v Corps. On November 7, however, the British launched a two-division attack between the Ronco and Rabbi Rivers south of Forli. After a fierce fight, Forli fell on November 9, and the Germans began grudgingly to give ground. They withdrew toward Ravenna.[22]

On the same day as v Corps launched its renewed offensive, 12th Canadian Infantry Brigade's Westminster Regiment was notified that it would join Porterforce as part of the relief of the Royal Canadian Dragoons. The Westies had been settling into an anticipated prolonged rest at the village of San Clemente. "This sudden news caused some flurry," the battalion's war diarist grumbled, "as there had been no previous word of a move."[23] The Westminster's Lieutenant James Oldfield added that the regiment now held "the dubious honour of being the only Canadian unit in action."[24]

ON NOVEMBER 2, STAFF at I Canadian Corps headquarters in Cesenatico learned that Lieutenant General Tommy Burns would "be leaving the theatre shortly for an unspecified appointment."

Replacing him as temporary commander was 1st Infantry Division's Major General Chris Vokes.[25]

Granted a short leave before leaving Italy for good, Burns met Brigadier George Kitching in Rome. Kitching was the incoming 1 Canadian Corps chief of staff and would replace Brigadier Desmond Smith. Burns briefed Kitching for an hour on developments in Italy, since the latter man had last been in this theatre for a short time in February 1944, commanding 11th Infantry Brigade. That February, Kitching had been recalled to England by 11 Canadian Corps commander Lieutenant General Guy Simonds to command 4th Armoured Division. During the Normandy campaign, however, Simonds had considered Kitching's performance poor and stripped him of divisional command. Kitching had then briefly commanded the 13th Infantry Brigade reinforcement pools in England. Like Burns, Kitching was a solid staff officer and had been sent to Italy in late October to prepare for his forthcoming posting to 1 Canadian Corps.

The day following his meeting with Burns, Kitching set off in a station wagon on the meandering five-hundred-mile drive from Rome to Cesenatico, arriving late on November 5. During their meeting, Burns had not mentioned that he had been sacked. and Kitching fully expected to serve under his command. Burns had even advised Kitching that he would return by air to corps headquarters on May 6. When Kitching told Smith that he had met the corps commander in Rome, the outgoing chief of staff turned and said, "Which Corps Commander?" He then cheerfully broke the news to Kitching that Vokes was temporary commander, and Smith was temporarily taking over 1st Infantry Division.[26]

Burns arrived later in the day, spent a few afternoon hours packing, and left for England that evening.[27] He landed with the rank of major general and appointment as General-Officer-in-Charge, Canadian Section, General Headquarters, 2nd Echelon, Twenty-First Army Group. Effectively, Burns oversaw all Canadian rear-area units in Northwest Europe. It was the kind of administrative duty that Burns shone at. He performed well, despite a lingering bitterness over being fired from corps command.[28]

As Burns had been leaving Italy, Vokes had been greeting Kitching "like a lifelong brother." Vokes, however, refused to discuss what had led to Burns's relief. As far as he was concerned, Vokes told Kitching, "the matter was closed."[29]

During the previous few days, General Harold Alexander and Lieutenant General Richard McCreery had both spoken to First Canadian Army's Lieutenant General Harry Crerar, recommending that corps command go to Vokes. On November 6, so far as anybody in Italy was concerned, this was how events were playing out. But Crerar was having none of it. "I consider Foulkes, not Vokes, definitely the better prospective Corps Commander," he decided. Major General Charles Foulkes, currently commanding 2nd Canadian Infantry Division in Holland, would take command, assuming the rank of lieutenant general. Crerar, knowing that Vokes and Foulkes despised each other, also decided to separate them by having Vokes exchange his post as 1st Infantry Division commander with the current commander of 4th Armoured Division, Major General Harry Foster.[30]

1 Canadian Corps, meanwhile, moved from Cesenatico to Riccione, where its headquarters was established in the former fascist municipal office building. Several nearby hotels served as messes. Riccione, wrote the corps war diarist, "should prove to be an ideal rest area, as it has two cinemas, a theatre, a senior and junior officers club, and two large recreation centres for [other ranks]."[31] Soon after the move, Vokes received a telegram from Alexander congratulating him on becoming corps commander. That evening, about fifteen senior officers hosted a celebratory dinner in Vokes's honour.[32]

Vokes tackled his new job enthusiastically. At 0800 hours on November 10, he convened a major briefing of officers at the Teatro Dante to outline "his policy for the corps." An hour later, he led these officers in a study period on how best to apply artillery fire during battle. Then senior officers of both divisions and Army Group, Royal Artillery, gave more detailed briefings on artillery procedures. As the discussion continued, it was agreed that current artillery procedures worked and nothing needed to be changed. Vokes ended the session by stressing the "necessity for an extremely flexible fire plan . . . with concentrations preferred to barrages, which presupposes that

infantry following up a barrage can maintain a steady rate of advance."
In Italy's wintery conditions, everybody agreed there was no guaran-
tee that infantry could keep pace with a creeping barrage. Better to
let the infantry commanders, even at company level, summon fire
as required.

On November 14, Kitching formally became corps chief of staff
and Brigadier Smith took over 1st Division command.[33] Vokes was
away visiting various brigades in their rest areas. At about 1700 hours,
Kitching was handed a wired signal marked, "Top Secret. General
Vokes eyes only." The message was also marked, "Operational
Immediate." With Vokes away, Kitching could open it. He was hor-
rified to read that Vokes was not only not being promoted but was
being transferred immediately to Northwest Europe and command
of 4th Armoured Division. The message concluded that Lieutenant
General Charles Foulkes would soon arrive.

This was army politics at its worst, Kitching thought. Vokes was
senior to Foulkes, "had four times the operational experience, was
well known to our troops who had confidence in him, and he was well
known at [Eighth] Army Headquarters," Kitching wrote later. Crerar's
motive, he felt, was Machiavellian. "He did not want Simonds or
Vokes to be Chief of the General Staff after the war; they both had
strong opinions and personalities. Charles Foulkes would be more
amenable to the politicians." But for Foulkes to rise that high, he
had to get corps experience during the war. So Crerar was paving
the pathway.

Two hours later, Vokes returned. Kitching passed the message and
apologized for its containing bad news. Vokes took it into his office,
closed the door, and remained there for ten minutes. Then he opened
the door and called Kitching inside. "George, who else knows about
this?" Kitching said he had told nobody. Vokes asked him to set up
a meeting of the corps officers. "George, when you lost command of
4th Armoured Division did you consider resigning your commission?"

"No," Kitching replied, "that never entered my mind although
there was a time that day when I thought I might shoot myself."
Vokes grinned.[34]

"I have often wondered," Vokes later wrote, "whether someone got the names Vokes and Foulkes mixed up . . . I . . . lost no sleep over that command shuffle, but I have sometimes speculated about what later might have been.

"No doubt about it, I was hurt for a few hours. On top of that I was transferred and I didn't want to leave the theatre. I knew the troops and they knew me. I felt like I was being forced to change horses in mid-stream. No doubt 'Uncle' Harry Crerar had assessed the need for change in the senior appointments in Italy." Vokes also realized that "the top brass knew I'd be able to stomach Foulkes even less than I had Burns."[35]

On November 15, Vokes broke the news to the corps.[36] Afterward, he directed Kitching to make sure Foulkes was greeted at the airfield with a complete guard of honour, full band, red carpet—the works. "I want every senior officer of the Corps, down to and including full colonels, to be at the airfield to meet him. I will introduce them to him and I want it to be a first class reception in every way. We will then return to this headquarters where he will take over officially from me. Is that clear?"

A signal from London gave Foulkes's arrival time as 1500 hours on November 16 at a dilapidated airfield between Rimini and Cesenatico. By 1430 hours an honour guard from the Royal Canadian Regiment—Foulkes's peacetime unit—was formed up, looking smart in fresh uniforms. A band stood ready. Thirty to forty senior officers were assembled. Time passed, no airplane appeared. By 1530 hours men were stamping feet to keep circulation moving in the cold and damp. At 1600 hours, Kitching was called to a phone. On the other end was Eighth Army's chief of staff, Brigadier Harry Floyd. Foulkes, he reported, was at Eighth Army headquarters and "hopping mad because no one was at the airport to greet him." Immediately, Vokes and Kitching headed over to pick Foulkes up. Vokes was furious at the aircrew, who had obviously landed at the wrong airfield. They arrived to find McCreery trying to smooth Foulkes's ruffled feathers. The return to corps headquarters was made in silence, Vokes and Foulkes sitting stonily in the back and Kitching up front with the driver.

As Vokes showed Foulkes his accommodation, he said, "Charles, I'll let George explain what happened this afternoon. There is no need for an official handover. Everything is in good shape. Goodbye, I'm leaving now. It's all yours."[37] Vokes climbed into the waiting car, returned to the shabby airport, and flew immediately to Florence en route to Northwest Europe.[38]

"George, what's the matter," Foulkes asked, "why weren't you at the airfield to meet me? I had a hell of a time after the captain of the U.S. Air Force Mitchell left me on the runway." Kitching explained the mix-up. The aircrew, Foulkes explained, had left him "standing on the small road that ran round the circumference of the airfield. His baggage was left on the road and he walked over to a small hanger nearby in which Canadian soldiers were working on a vehicle." Foulkes called over the senior corporal present, gave his name, and announced that he was the corps commander. The corporal said he knew Major General Chris Vokes well and was "sorry he could not help him because he was certainly not the Corps Commander." No objection or attempt to order the corporal to assist him worked, so Foulkes ended up walking to the main highway, where he was fortunate enough to hitch a ride on a Provost Corps jeep—despite once again dealing with the issue of Foulkes not being Vokes. By the time Foulkes reached Eighth Army headquarters, he was in a towering rage. Only reluctantly did he concede that the whole affair had not been a deliberate effort to show the new corps commander he was not wanted.[39]

12

Virtually Unending

THE V BRITISH CORPS November 7–9 offensive forced the
Germans east of 1 Canadian Corps into a wedge of ground bordered by the Ronco River to the southeast and the Montone River to
the northwest. At the same time, Porterforce had stepped up efforts
to win crossings over the Fosso Ghiaia for a drive on Ravenna from
the south. On November 10, Lieutenant Colonel Andrew Horsbrugh-
Porter created a subunit designated River Force, which would operate
astride Highway 16 and in the coastal country to its east. It comprised
one squadron of 27th Lancers Cavalry Regiment, a company from
1st Battalion/4th Essex Regiment, Popski's Army, and partisans.[1]
The 3rd Canadian Field Regiment supported River Force from gun
positions outside San Pietro in Campiano, about a mile southwest of
the larger Campiano. Most Italian towns and villages the Canadians
encountered bore the ravages of war to varying degrees. This time,
however, the regiment's historian wrote, it was a "delightful surprise
to find the village unmarked by war, and in the same block of buildings which house [Regimental Headquarters], a barber shop, butcher
shop, and grocery carried on business as usual."

Mostly, the regiment supported Popski's Army and the partisans.
The gunners found working with both groups a unique experience. The partisans, the regiment's historian recorded, were "well
organized and armed. They were belligerent and very active, and

included a number of women in their ranks. The sight of one of their Amazonish 'nurses' cycling down the road complete with first-aid kit, red cross armband, knife, pistol, Sten gun, and a supply of grenades hung from the belt by their pins was awe-inspiring."

As the hamlet was in such good condition, the entire regiment was comfortably quartered in buildings, and there was never any counter-fire from German artillery. The gunners would look back fondly on their time with Porterforce.[2]

Such was not the case for the Westminster Regiment, whose 'A' and 'B' Companies had relieved the Royal Canadian Dragoons on November 9. The men had just finished digging slit trenches when "a night of wild wind and rain" struck, leaving everyone drenched and miserable. At dawn, the rain ceased and was followed by a clear, cold morning. Snow was visible on the mountains and foothills to the west.[3]

Both companies were initially just outside San Stefano, north of Campiano, and a standard routine developed. During the day, Lieutenant James Oldfield wrote, "everybody lay low and got what sleep they could in preparation for active patrolling during the night."[4] The countryside was so flat that the Westies could clearly see taller buildings in Ravenna, almost eight miles distant. This visibility cut both ways. German artillery observers could see the Westies and subjected them to intermittent daytime shelling. Although few casualties resulted, sleep was often disturbed.

Patrol activity focused on trying to intercept German forces still operating south of the Ghiaia Canal in the Cesena–Ravenna road sector. The situation was extremely fluid. On November 10, for example, 'A' Company's Oldfield led a patrol almost to the canal west of the road without incident. 'B' Company's patrol, commanded by Lieutenant Thomas Ormond "Tommy" Johnson, meanwhile, headed for a building—identified as La Parsota—next to the road and about two miles from San Stefano. As the patrol closed in, it was fired on by machine guns concealed in a haystack next to the building. Johnson was killed, and the patrol retreated.[5] "Tommy Johnson was an 'old' Westie," Oldfield recorded, "who had come up the hard way through the NCO ranks. Careful, conscientious, and amiable, his loss was widely felt."

Seeking revenge, 'B' Company sent a twenty-one-man standing patrol under Sergeant Jack Laing to La Parsota to occupy the building for twenty-four hours, hoping to ambush the Germans who had killed Johnson. Reaching the building undetected, the patrol set up the ambush. But no Germans showed. At the same time, however, a heavy-fighting patrol commanded by Lieutenant Bert Stephens returned to the ground where Oldfield had found no Germans and came under intense fire from two positions. Thirty-nine-year-old Bren gunner Private Albert Koblun was killed and the patrol's sergeant wounded in an exchange of fire that lasted ninety minutes before the patrol broke contact with the Germans.[6]

Not only were the front lines fluid, but Porterforce kept shifting units as opportunities to exploit various successful gains developed. On the night of November 13–14, the King's Dragoon Guards cavalry regiment relieved 'A' and 'B' Companies. The Westies replaced 1st Battalion/4th Essex in the Gambellera sector where the British unit had just forced a crossing near the Ghiaia's headwaters. Gambellera was about a mile north of the canal. The Westies were to clear the area south of the Ronco. As per normal with Porterforce operations, this was, a Westminster report stated, "to be done by strong patrolling."[7]

WHILE THE WESTMINSTER Regiment adapted to its new operational area, the rest of 1 Canadian Corps continued resting and preparing to resume operations. On November 7, 12th Canadian Infantry Brigade headquarters had been notified that at long last the 1st Light Anti-Aircraft Battalion would be given a more notable designation. Brigadier John Lind happily informed Lieutenant Colonel Buck Buchanan that his battalion would forthwith become the Lanark and Renfrew Scottish Regiment. Since the battalion's creation on July 13, 1944, its officers had been lobbying for the battalion to be given a regimental identity that the men could serve in with pride. Preference had been for a highland regiment. Various potential highland identities had been forwarded. Eventually, as Ontario's Lanark and Renfrew Scottish had not been mobilized, that regiment was approached and offered its support to the idea. As the Lanarks had been officially allied with the Black Watch in 1927, the unit being formed in Italy was approved to wear that regiment's tartan. "This battalion has had to wait a long time for a good infantry title and it certainly earns this one," the brigade's war diarist declared.[8]

Although the news broke on November 7, it was not until Remembrance Day that the new designation became formal. Canadian Press correspondent Doug How reported that "the Scottish went into action September 2, after 29 days of training under their present colonel who is a Sicily and Italy veteran."[9]

On November 11, Buchanan paraded the battalion. "He told us," the war diarist wrote, "that we had a tradition to live up to and knew that we could do it." That evening, at an officer's mess dinner, Buchanan "gave a short talk on the better known points of the history of the Lanark and Renfrew Scottish and also passed on the praise of the corps high officials pertaining to the good work the [battalion] has done in the past," the regiment's war diarist recorded. After the King was toasted, a second toast was raised. "Gentlemen, I give you the Lanark and Renfrew Scottish Regiment of Canada," Lieutenant G.L. MacDonald called out. "To the knowledge of everyone concerned it is the first time in Lanark and Renfrew history that a toast was drunk to the unit by the battalion in the field in an operations theatre of war. The C.O. and all officers present expressed their pride and pleasure in being given such a famous name."[10]

While the officers were celebrating, Sergeant Fred Cederberg had donned his new Balmoral, climbed aboard a truck, and departed on leave to Rome. "It was Rome with an autumn nip in the air and venereal disease rife in unlicensed cathouses; where hawkers peddled dirty pictures and blessed rosaries outside the massive ruins of the Colosseum; and the jagged remains of long-ago temples where old crones and cats lay down to sleep even on chilly nights," Cederberg wrote. "During those nights, red-capped British and white-helmeted American military police patrolled the dark streets, checking for deserters, muggers and soldiers improperly dressed or drunk. And airborne troops and infantrymen fought over young prostitutes, crooked crap games or real or imagined insults."

Cederberg toured the sights as pointed out by a scrawny Italian kid named Giuseppe ("but you should calla me Joe because that's

what the Yankees all-a call me"). As a tour guide, it seemed Joe actually knew what he was talking about. Later, the hotel concierge booked
Cederberg an appointment with an English prostitute and addressed
him formally as Signori. "Fuck me," Cederberg thought, "now I'm
a *signori*! And right in the middle of a friggin' war, in the middle
of Rome, there's an English whore who works by appointment only."
When the woman took a shine to Cederberg, they ended up spending
his remaining leave together, making love, dining out, and not thinking of the future. She walked with him to the loading trucks. "Will
I see you again?" Cederberg asked. "'We'll see, love,'" she whispered,
but her eyes said no . . . 'Love, you've been fun . . . very much fun.'"
Then she "kissed me so warmly I was startled. Before I could react,
she pulled free and walked quickly down the Via Nationale without
looking back, her high heels clicking rhythmically on the pavement.

"The transport officer yelled: 'OK! Let's move 'em!'" Cederberg
found the return "long and tiring. And by the time I had checked
into the regimental orderly room, I was no longer sure of her
apartment number."[11]

Cederberg's return found the Lanarks busy practising river crossings. Buchanan warned the men, the war diarist wrote, that sometime in the next two weeks "we would be called on to do a job we had
not done before, that of crossing a river and taking a town. He said
it would be done in 5 stages of which the first 4 would be the work of
this [brigade]. He told us that it would be made in conjunction with
attacks all along the line with the 1st Division on our left. After the
completion of this task, we would then head for our winter billets.
One of the main purposes of this attack was to establish a winter
line under much more favourable conditions than encountered last
winter. He stressed security and confidence and knew that it could
be done by the Regiment. He also said that in the next few days, we
would be carrying out very intensive training from 0800 hours till
2230 hours."[12]

BY MID-NOVEMBER, PORTERFORCE was well established north of the
Ghiaia Canal. A patrol by King's Dragoon Guards and partisans even
reached the southern edge of Ravenna's airfield on November 16.[13]

On the left flank, meanwhile, the Westminster Regiment was advancing along the Ronco's southeastern bank. 'A' Company's advance on November 17 was impeded by mines that the support company had to come forward to clear. "There were a terrific number of mines in the area, cross roads, verges and ditches being very heavily mined, as well as indiscriminate mining of fields with anti-personnel mines and prepared charges."[14]

At 1130 hours on November 18, a twenty-man 'C' Company patrol led by Lieutenant Art Miller set out to cross the Ronco and clear 2,500 yards of ground between it and the Montone. It was to then test enemy strength at a known crossing over the Montone.[15] Crossing the Ronco, the patrol pressed on 1,000 yards to the Scolo Lama. Here it came under fire from Germans entrenched in several houses. Return small-arms fire killed two Germans and allowed Miller to win a building. From its shelter, he radioed firing coordinates to 3rd Field Regiment and had the other buildings blasted with shells. After this "softening up," the patrol sallied out to the canal, only to become entangled in a hot fight with Germans dug in on the opposite bank. Hitting the dirt avoided a fusillade of machine-gun fire but still exposed the men to fire from rifle grenades and light mortar rounds. Seriously wounded in the legs and hands, Miller passed control to Corporal L. Field. The patrol withdrew, carrying its casualties. Private Eugene Morin—although suffering a mortal wound—held off the pursuing Germans with a steady stream of Bren-gun fire until he fell dead. Escaping across the Ronco, the patrol counted four men killed and eight wounded. Sergeant G. Bartoletti, a partisan, was among the wounded.

After this patrol, a cat-and-mouse game along the Ronco developed. Whenever Bren carriers brought supplies to the forward companies, the Germans attempted to destroy them with artillery and mortar fire. During one such incident, a carrier loaded with ammunition had three mortar bombs land within fifty feet of it—one striking on either side and the third to the front.

More feared than the shelling, however, were the mines. "Anyone who maintains that the Germans are an unimaginative race, tied to routine, obviously has never encountered those responsible for the mine-laying efforts on the Italian front," Lieutenant Oldfield observed. "Many of their jobs were ingenious in the extreme. Where their supplies would not allow mining as heavily as they would have liked, the Jerries often substituted bricks here and there—covering them only slightly. These had to be cleared just as painstakingly as the real mines, since there was no way of knowing which bumps were more genuine and which spurious. Then, to make things more interesting, the occasional brick was laid with a real mine attached . . . beneath it. If the brick was recognized, and left in place, any vehicle crossing it would be knocked out by the mine beneath. If the brick was cleared, unless extreme care was used, the person clearing it stood a good chance of being eliminated. Perhaps the peak of devilry noted in this area was a case where a 'glass' mine was lifted, following which a carrier was knocked out by another mine lying beneath it. Whereupon the engineers came back to re-check the area and lost one of their personnel to another deeply buried 'schu' mine [shoe-mine]. The explosive power of some of the larger tank mines had to be seen to be appreciated. In one case a bridge had to be improvised from some farm wagons and barn doors, to allow passage over a 'blow' in the road."

The period November 19–24 was punctuated by a series of higher command plans cancelled as quickly as they were issued. On the 25th, when Porterforce was transferred from direct British Eighth Army command to 1 Canadian Corps, it became clear that a return to major offensive action was imminent. Sudden interest by 5th Canadian Armoured Division headquarters in whether a bridge over the Montone near San Pancrazio might support heavy traffic struck the Westies as confirming this. Oldfield and the other officers in 'A' Company, whose sector the bridge was in, were puzzled by the repeated requests for information because they possessed an aerial photograph that clearly showed the bridge had been wrecked. Yet the requests continued with mounting urgency. Finally, Major W.J. Neill sent a patrol that confirmed "the bridge was lying in pieces on the river bottom, remarkably similar to its appearance in the air oblique."[16]

By bringing Porterforce under command, 1 Canadian Corps assumed responsibility for Eighth Army's right flank from the Ronco to the sea. At the same time, Porterforce took over the area between the Ronco and the Montone south of the village of Molinaccio. This freed v Corps's 10th Indian Division to concentrate between the Montone and Lamone Rivers. Eighth Army headquarters was particularly concerned that this division should clear the Germans away from the northwest bank of the Montone in the area of a bridge at a farm called Casa Bettini. The bridge was deemed essential to the forthcoming Canadian offensive.

As the already overextended Westminster Regiment was required to fill the seven-thousand-yard space between the Ronco and the Montone, a squadron of Governor General's Horse Guards tanks was sent to help. Although the Westies were supposed to press the Germans back to the Montone and even win a crossing, the task was quickly recognized as impossible for such a small force. The Germans on both sides of the river were dug into excellent positions and responded to every probe so violently that it was clear their orders were to stand fast. The weather, which had been remarkably good for much of the month, also broke. Heavy, steady rain caused the predictable spilling of rivers and canals over dykes. A series of fragile and somewhat perilous footbridges had to be installed to enable resupply of forward troops.[17]

The scope of German determination to hold their ground was demonstrated on the cold, drizzly morning of November 30, when No. 6 Platoon of 'B' Company, under Lieutenant Vic Wilson, attempted to seize three closely clustered groups of buildings on the Montone's southeast bank. After securing the first two unoccupied clusters, Wilson and his men were heading for the third when machine guns started firing from inside the facing buildings and from across the river. Pulling back to the other two clusters, Wilson ordered the platoon to stand fast despite heavy incoming artillery and mortar fire. At 1400 hours, the German infantry counterattacked Wilson's position with several soldiers firing Panzerfausts in support. No. 6 Platoon repelled the attack, the Germans "leaving their dead and taking several wounded with them." From across the river, SPGs fired on the buildings. Any attempt to retreat meant crossing open ground swept by fire, so the platoon could only hunker down. At 1900 hours, the Germans again counterattacked. Although they were driven off, two Westies were wounded and Private Robert Thomas Watson was killed. Shortly after nightfall, Lieutenant G.B. Eatons reinforced Wilson, also delivering badly needed ammunition and rations.[18]

This action marked the end of Canadian operations under Porterforce, as all such units returned to their respective divisions on November 30. A much-reduced Porterforce—consisting mainly of the 27th Lancers and Popski's Army—continued, but under 5th Division control. "I think the operation has been a success," Lieutenant Colonel Horsbrugh-Porter wrote. "Our aim of clearing the Hun from the area bounded by R. Ronco and Ghiaia was achieved, and an additional and most difficult belt of country between the Ghiaia and Uniti Canal [the eastward extension of the Montone from Highway 16 to the sea] has been similarly deloused . . . I reckon every single man in this Force has had a damned good crack at helping the war effort."[19]

The action fought by No. 6 Platoon struck Oldfield as typifying the Westminster's time with Porterforce. "This was the sort of action that does not make the front page of either the home papers or the *Maple Leaf.*" It was "unspectacular, uncomfortable, and it seemed at the time, virtually unending."[20]

The war in Italy had been going on so long that Oldfield saw no end in sight for it, either. So the arrival of Lieutenant General Charles Foulkes at battalion headquarters bearing news "that the war would be over by Christmas" caught everybody by surprise. This declaration, the battalion diarist recorded, "was accepted rather skeptically."[21]

Making such rash announcements was hardly typical of the forty-one-year-old Foulkes, who seldom sought to inspire. Pudgy and usually dour, he had established a reputation in Northwest Europe as First Canadian Army's most unapproachable general. Major General Harry Foster, expected to shortly take over 1st Canadian Infantry Division, considered him "mean and narrow," possessed of a "hard-shelled Baptist mind" and a "sneering supercilious attitude toward anyone his own rank or below." Foulkes simultaneously had a reputation for "groveling to everybody" senior. In some ways a consummate politician, he instinctively knew how to strike the balance between servility and the self-confidence required to impress.[22]

As for the war-over-by-Christmas prediction, it was impossible to conceive how Foulkes could believe this. In the heady aftermath of the breakout from the Normandy beachhead in August, even General Dwight D. Eisenhower and Field Marshal Bernard Montgomery had dared believe in a 1944 victory. But such thoughts had been dashed by late September with the failure of Operation Market Garden and hardening resistance as the Allies closed on the German border. Serving as acting II Canadian Corps commander while Lieutenant General Guy Simonds replaced an ill Lieutenant General Harry Crerar at First Canadian Army headquarters, Foulkes had been in the middle of the Scheldt Estuary Campaign that ground to a costly and bitter end in early November. As he had prepared to depart for Italy, First Canadian Army was forming along the lower reaches of the Rhine River for a predicted long winter watch. Here the army was to rest and rebuild to be ready for a return to the offensive in late January, when the ground would be sufficiently frozen to enable a breakout into Germany's Rhineland.

In the end, perhaps his musing at the Westminster Regiment's headquarters was nothing more than an awkward attempt to boost morale by a man lacking any concept of how to do so.

ON NOVEMBER 18, TWO days after Lieutenant General Charles Foulkes assumed command, 1 Canadian Corps headquarters staff began planning its December offensive. Because the success or failure of British operations along Highway 9 would impact where the Canadian effort would be launched, three scenarios were devised.

The first assumed the Germans continued to stand on the Montone River, requiring 1st Infantry Division to force a crossing. An advance passing through the town of Russi would win a bridgehead across the Lamone River, with the thrust then continuing through Bagnacavallo and over the Senio River to win the larger town of Lugo. Once Russi was secure, 5th Armoured Division would pivot through on a northeastward track, cut Highway 16 north of Ravenna, and then secure that city.

The second plan assumed the Germans abandoned the Montone to establish a new line behind the Lamone. In that case, 1st Division would force a crossing and continue as in the first plan through to

Lugo, with 5th Division also carrying on with securing Ravenna from the north.

Plan three cautiously assumed that adverse weather left the objectives in the first two plans impossible to reach because of flooding. In that event, the corps would remain in reserve until v British Corps's advance along Highway 9 ran out of steam. The Canadians would then pass through and continue along the highway.[23]

Two days after this session, on November 20, all 1 Canadian Corps officers down to the level of battalion commanders and their second-in-commands assembled at noon in Riccione's Teatro Dante for a first formal address by Foulkes.[24]

Looking around the theatre, chief of staff Brigadier George Kitching thought at least 125 officers were present. Most had never served with Foulkes and knew nothing about him. Kitching had suggested it would be politic for Foulkes to praise the "fighting qualities" of both divisions and acknowledge the "excellent reputation" they had earned within Eighth Army.

Foulkes ignored him. He launched instead into a lecture on how tactics used in Italy were out of date and must change to employ the new equipment that was being used successfully in Belgium and Holland. The corps now, he said, was "crossing the same rivers that Caesar had and . . . using the same equipment."

Kitching "watched the faces of his audience" as Foulkes spoke. It was "obvious . . . that he had failed to win their enthusiastic support. As soldiers, of course, they would go about their duties as well as they had in the past, but there was no sparkle in Charles Foulkes' remarks and there was little interest in the eyes of his audience."[25]

One officer present knew Foulkes well. Foulkes had been Major Strome Galloway's teacher back in 1933 at the Provisional School of Infantry when he was there as a militia sergeant. Sitting in the audience, Galloway was reminded of the man's "miserable personality." And when Foulkes started hectoring them to display "spirited leadership," Galloway knew "he lost any of the personal loyalties he might have hoped to gain—if indeed he ever thought that way."

Foulkes had served as a divisional commander for less than four months and had seen no action prior to that posting. "Those of us who had experienced sixteen months of fighting in Sicily and Italy," Galloway seethed, "did not need this high-ranking tyro to tell us how to lead our men. His contempt for the fighting troops was apparent in his very face, and something that would become more evident in the weeks to come."[26]

AS NOVEMBER APPROACHED its close, General Harold Alexander consulted his two army commanders to determine the next phase of operations. "The enemy," he observed in a new operational order on November 28, "continues to contest every inch of the ground, and although he could shorten his front considerably by withdrawing his left flank to the Valli di Comacchio he shows no sign of doing so except under heavy pressure, much less of carrying out any general withdrawal voluntarily." Alexander appreciated the fact that the Germans on the left flank were conducting a fighting withdrawal. Once the Germans were forced back to what the Allies believed was their main defensive line, they would stand determined. That line ran from Bologna southeast to the Valli di Comacchio—a vast marshy lagoon system north of Ravenna. The Comacchio's southern tip stood virtually parallel to and about forty-five miles east of Bologna.

Alexander estimated that Eighth Army had sufficient resources to continue offensive operations for at best three to four weeks. The U.S. Fifth Army would only be able to return to operations on December 7 and could sustain no more than fifteen days of intense fighting. But it was imperative to the Allied war effort that the Germans again be brought to battle in Italy. To achieve this, British Eighth Army must continue pushing forward, with Fifth Army's XIII British Corps securing its left flank. Fifth Army would also continue a main thrust toward Bologna on the axis of Highway 65—starting on Alexander's order soon after December 7. As both armies had limited offensive capability, it was particularly important that the ground and weather be thoroughly considered " . . . and no attacks . . . be launched unless . . . conditions are favourable."[27]

When Alexander issued this instruction, Eighth Army was concluding a major two-corps offensive to secure Faenza and the high ground to its southwest. This would provide a starting point for the December operations. With v Corps driving up Highway 9 and II Polish Corps to its left, the advance had initially gone well. By November 26, both corps had reached the Lamone River. That day, however, it rained so intensely that further operations became impossible. This meant that the new offensive would have to start right there and not farther west, as had been desired.

Lieutenant General Richard McCreery did not consider this significant. His plan for December still envisioned a three-corps advance, with I Canadian Corps on the right, v Corps in the centre, and II Polish Corps to the left. The way the November advance had worked out did, however, mean that it was the first plan hammered out by Lieutenant General Foulkes and his staff to be implemented. The Canadians would cross the Montone, seize Russi, and get over the Lamone and then the Senio at Lugo. Along the way, an opening would be created for 5th Division to hook into Ravenna from the north. McCreery hoped that the Canadians could do even better than this. He wanted the advance to pass through Lugo and reach the next river—the Santerno. Reaching this river would align the Canadians with where he hoped his other two corps would end their advances.[28] Here, the army could pause for the winter and then renew operations as the weather improved in early 1945.

During its rest period, the Canadians in Italy were introduced to some of the new equipment that had proven effective in Northwest Europe and that Foulkes had alluded to in his November 20 speech. The 12th Royal Tank Regiment demonstrated the Crocodile flame-throwing Churchill tanks to 5th Canadian Armoured Brigade's regiments. At the same time, the infantry battalions of both divisions were issued with four Wasp Bren carriers mounting flame-throwers. Two smaller, man-packed flame-throwers called Lifebuoys were also issued to each infantry battalion. While many soldiers considered the Crocodiles, Wasps, and Lifebuoys as perilous to the operator as to the enemy, they had proven their worth in flushing Germans from pillboxes and other strongpoints.[29]

In late September, a handful of 17-pounder "Firefly" Sherman tanks had been deployed among the regiments of 5th Armoured Brigade. Each now received a full complement of sixteen of these tanks that could match Panthers and Tigers. The addition of six Shermans, each mounting a 105-millimetre howitzer, also greatly increased the regiments' ability to support infantry with indirect fire.[30]

There was no official policy on how these more powerful tanks should be integrated into the regiments. After some experimentation, the British Columbia Dragoons decided to distribute them throughout the squadrons rather than cluster them in one or two special troops.[31] Most of the regiments did similarly, generally swapping one standard 75-millimetre Sherman for a Firefly per troop.[32]

Another piece of equipment intended to assist in river crossings was a tracked amphibious carrier called a Weasel. This half-ton carrier was originally commissioned for the combined Canadian–American Special Service Force to provide a vehicle capable of traversing deep snow. But the Weasel's light construction and wide track also suited it to operating on swampy ground.[33] Its river-crossing ability, however, was quickly cast in doubt when, on November 12, 3rd Canadian Infantry Brigade's transport officer, Captain A.B. Edgar, splashed one into the Conca River. He quickly "found the traction was not sufficient to overcome the current," the brigade's war diarist recorded. "[He] was drifting rapidly towards Yugoslavia when his 'infernal machine' fortunately grounded on a sand-bar, 100 yards at sea."[34]

At the Savio and other rivers encountered in October, the engineers had faced extreme difficulty. While intensified training with normal bridging equipment and rafts helped ready the men for future operations, some new innovations were also developed. The "Olafson bridge" was a light, highly portable bridge developed by 3rd Canadian Infantry Brigade's 3rd Light Aid Detachment's Captain E.A. Olafson. It was constructed by welding together sections of half-inch pipe in fifteen- or eighteen-foot lengths. Each section weighed two hundred pounds and could be linked to other sections to span forty-five feet. Buoyancy was achieved by attaching cushions filled with kapok—a cotton-like substance obtained from trees native to Java and the Indian archipelago.[35]

On November 22, Foulkes and other senior officers attended a demonstration of the bridge where the Ventena River flowed into the sea just north of Cattolica. The river was six feet deep. Olafson's men quickly deployed a sixty-foot bridge that a line of infantrymen crossed with ease. Then everyone watched tensely as a jeep was driven over the "seemingly frail structure." Foulkes was sufficiently impressed to order lengths of Olafson bridging constructed for use by each 1st Division infantry battalion.[36]

As the worth of the tank-hunting platoons had been proven by Private Smokey Smith at the Savio, these units were now formalized. On November 19, each battalion was instructed to create an anti-tank company, drawing its personnel, weapons, and vehicles from the support company. In coming operations, the instructions read, "the arrival of heavy equipment to support the infantry is likely to be a comparatively slow procedure. Infantry must be able to hold ground gained against enemy counterattacks until the heavier anti-tank weapons can be brought forward. In this country, it is the enemy's custom to use its tanks in 'Penny-Packets,' therefore some mobile form of anti-tank defence must be made available to forward companies."

Each company was to consist of sixty-two men organized into two tank-hunting platoons under a company headquarters. These platoons would be armed with PIAT anti-tank launchers and broken into two sections and a headquarters. A third platoon would be equipped with the 2-pounder anti-tank guns. At the same time, the support company was to surrender its 6-pounder anti-tank guns, which would only be deployed at either brigade or divisional direction.

The successful deployment of the specially adapted Little John 2-pounders by 1st Anti-Tank Regiment at the Savio had so impressed 1st Division staff that it had ordered twelve of the guns formed into a special battery of three four-gun troops. This battery would serve under 1st Anti-Tank Regiment's control and be allotted to brigades by the division's senior artillery officer as needed.[37]

IN THE MIDDLE of November, partisan leader Lieutenant Arrigio Boldrini, who went by the *nom de guerre* Major Bulow, sent a wireless signal to Eighth Army's liaison to the U.S. Office of Strategic Services (OSS), Captain Alphonse Peter Thiele. Bulow commanded the 28th Garibaldi Brigade, which operated from the sanctuary of the Valli di Comacchio marshlands to the north of Ravenna. As Porterforce had closed on the city from the south, Bulow had dispatched the partisans, who had not only provided valuable intelligence but also fought alongside its units. They had developed a particularly close relationship with Popski's Army.

Realizing that Eighth Army must soon attempt to seize Ravenna, Bulow became anxious over the fate of his beloved city. Ravenna was renowned for its Byzantine art and its cathedrals, which were richly adorned with mosaics. The Germans seemed determined to retain their hold on the city, and Bulow anticipated that the Allies might bombard Ravenna from air, sea, and land prior to committing their infantry and tanks to an all-out assault. Ravenna's glories could be reduced to ruin. But Bulow had a plan to save the city. In the wireless signal to Thiele, he proposed a meeting.

Fluent in Italian and having worked closely with Adriatic region partisan groups in clandestine raiding operations, Thiele sensed an opportunity. When he passed the signal to 1 Canadian Corps's intelligence section, its officers were equally intrigued. A submarine was sent to pick Bulow up on the night of November 19. Too impatient to await the submarine, however, Bulow headed for Allied lines in a boat rowed along the Adriatic coast by a dozen fishermen. Aboard, he also had two downed American pilots, several pistols, and a large keg of wine. After rowing for thirty miles through a moonless night, Bulow and his party landed at Cervia and were taken to 1 Canadian Corps headquarters in Riccione.[38]

Bulow, the 1 Canadian Corps war diarist reported, "claims that partisans are in control of the marshland north of Ravenna."[39] Using a series of professionally prepared operational maps, Bulow proposed a multi-pronged attack on the Germans defending Ravenna. The partisans would strike from the north, and the Canadians—particularly the attached Popski's Army—the south. His operational outline was so convincing, the partisan leader was whisked off to Eighth Army headquarters, where Thiele presented him to Lieutenant General McCreery and his senior staff. McCreery quickly approved the plan, and Bulow was escorted back to Riccione.[40]

After further extensive discussions, arrangements were made to support the partisans with arms, ammunition, clothing, and food. When Bulow left after dark on November 25 for a return boat trip to the marshes, he was accompanied by Canadian intelligence officer Captain Dennis Healy. "Captain Healy will live with the partisans, reporting by wireless . . . any information about enemy movement which he can obtain," the corps war diarist wrote.[41] Thirty-three-year-old Healy had left a position as head of the University of Alberta's French Department to join the war effort. By May 1944, he was a Canadian intelligence officer.

At 2330 hours, Healy and Bulow reached the marshes. The Canadian was led through the swamps to an island where the partisan headquarters was located. Introduced to the oss signals team whose wireless Bulow had used to contact Thiele, Healy was soon sending messages providing details for air drops of supplies to the island and also reports on German positions and movements in the Ravenna area.

In order to draw troops away from Ravenna, Bulow and Healy planned a partisan attack on a German strongpoint at the site of an abandoned factory on the southern outskirts of Porto Corsini. This port served Ravenna but lay about five miles northeast of the city and was linked to it by a canal. On the night of November 29–30, 150 partisans assaulted the strongpoint. Healy was alongside Bulow with the headquarters section and helped direct the partisan fire that eliminated two of the strongpoint's three machine guns. After inflicting heavy casualties on the Germans, the partisans slipped back into the marshes. The following day, as Bulow had hoped, two hundred Germans were sent from Ravenna to reinforce the garrison at Porto Corsini.[42]

13

A Grim Task Indeed

IT WAS LIKE a bad joke. Code names for Canadian and British army operations were usually innocuous. Two past Canadian offensives had been code-named Olive and Chesterfield. Understandable, then, the raised eyebrows and outright groans that greeted Operation Chuckle. The army's official historian for the Italian Campaign traced the code name back to a plan conceived by 1 Canadian Corps in early November to capture Ravenna by an attack that involved an amphibious landing north of the city. "Someone's sense of humour gave the proposed operation the code name 'Chuckle,'" he wrote, "and when the scheme was abandoned in favour of the army group plan, the name was retained to designate the Canadian part in the Eighth Army's offensive."[1]

Corps chief of staff Brigadier George Kitching disputed this colourful claim. Code names, he said later, were issued in allotments that usually started with the same letter. In this case, the letter had been c, and top of the drawer was "Chuckle." So Chuckle it had been.[2]

On November 26, for the last time, Teatro Dante teemed with 1st Canadian Infantry Division officers for Chuckle's unveiling. Present were all brigade commanders, heads of various services of arms, Grades I and II staff officers, and all regiment commanders and their respective company and battery leaders. It was 1100 hours when the division's acting commander, Brigadier Desmond Smith, took the stage. The divisional war diarist reported that Smith de-scribed "'Chuckle' in a very precise and clear manner," using a large map to demonstrate the ground, the enemy picture, and all the stages and phases of the anticipated battle.[3]

Chuckle would kick off on December 1. Both Canadian divisions would be involved from the start. Initially, 1st Division's 3rd Canadian Infantry Brigade would enter the bridgehead established by v British Corps's 10th Indian Division. The 5th Canadian Armoured Division's 4th Princess Louise Dragoon Guards would be under brigade com-mand. As soon as the attack began, the Plugs would strike out along-side the Montone River and establish a bridgehead into which the rest of 5th Division's 12th Canadian Infantry Brigade would concentrate its drive on Ravenna.[4]

Once it crossed the Montone, 5th Division's initial objective was the village of Godo. Thereafter, the division's two infantry brigades would clear a wide swath of ground south of the Lamone River. The eastern flank of this area was bordered by the stretch of Highway 16 that ran northwest from Ravenna to Mezzano on the Lamone. The road from Godo to Bagnacavallo marked the division's western flank. Once the Lamone was reached across this frontage, 5th Division would go into reserve but remain ready to take over the advance to Medicina if 1st Division ran out of steam.

Porterforce, under 5th Division command, was to hold its ground along the Montone south of Ravenna until the order was given for its joint attack on the city by the partisans to the north. Once Ravenna was secured, Porterforce would take over the Lamone front from 5th Division, freeing it to relieve 1st Division.

Major General Bert Hoffmeister was optimistic that if 12th Brigade quickly broke out of the bridgehead anchored on San Pancrazio, "chances of isolating and destroying a substantial part of the enemy division opposing us are good."[5]

Left of 12th Brigade, meanwhile, 1st Division's 3rd Brigade would advance through Russi to reach and cross the Lamone. A squadron of the new British Crocodile flame-throwing tanks would support its move to the Lamone. Thereafter, the Crocodiles would assist 5th Division's approach on Ravenna.

As V Corps and II Polish Corps were launching simultaneous offensives, the Desert Air Force (DAF) would be badly overextended. No
close support bombing in the early stages was anticipated, however,
because the Germans did not appear to have constructed any major
strongpoints to bar the advance. Fighters and fighter-bombers would,
however, lurk in "cab ranks" to be summoned as needed. British
Eighth Army had issued an edict that individual towns were not to
be "blitzed unless there was proof that the enemy was occupying
them in strength." Potential observation posts in specific houses and
churches had been identified, but were only to be "bombed if the enemy was known to be actually occupying them." With major German
movement expected only under cover of darkness, particularly along
Highway 16, DAF "was asked to harass . . . roads from last light until
first light, by flare dropping, bombing, and strafing."[6]

The 1st Division offensive would unfold in four phases. In the
first, 3rd Brigade would establish a bridgehead across the Lamone.
Phase two would see 2nd Brigade capture Bagnacavallo and cross
the Senio River. The 1st Brigade would then launch phase three to
capture Cotignola and Lugo and gain the Santerno River. Finally,
3rd Brigade would return to the front and seize the towns of Massa
Lombarda and Medicina. At this point, 1st Division would be just
twelve miles southeast of Bologna.

The object of the offensive, Smith emphasized, was "to destroy the
enemy, not to capture ground, for the ground at Medicina is just as
bad, from a tactical point of view, at this season, as the ground where
the [Forward Defence Lines] are now located."[7]

German reaction was expected to follow the established pattern,
with "a small battle at a river line, a period of no contact, another
bump at the next river line and so on. It was expected that he would
continue these tactics until he reached the salt pan lying between
Argenta and Bologna, when he would regroup and strengthen his
position."

Smith stressed four points to be followed throughout the battle.
"There must be an alternative plan for every action of every unit and
subunit. Get patrols up to the next river obstacle immediately after
a bridgehead has been formed. Do not worry about flanks. We can

and must forget flanks right down to company and battalion level. Avoid house fighting. Bring fire down before we reach them."[8] Smith envisioned the division's role to last "a minimum of two weeks" and promised that "the division will be out of action at Christmas."[9]

Royal 22e Régiment's Lieutenant Colonel Jean Allard thought the initial plan for 3rd Brigade simple enough, but he disliked how the topography favoured the German defenders. This country had once been part of a massive marsh—of which the large Valli di Comacchio north of Ravenna remained intact. Spring runoff from the Apennines into the Montone, Lamone, Senio, and Santerno Rivers, with resulting floods, had created the marsh. Over centuries, the Italians had patiently contained the seasonal flooding by building high dykes to canalize the rivers. As these rivers crossed the plain and moved closer to the sea, however, their flow grew more sluggish. Instead of carving deeper beds, the rivers silted up and ever-higher banks were required to contain them.

Most of these dykes, Allard noted, rose to "some thirty feet above ground level [and] offered magnificent observation points, given the fairly flat topography of the region. As defensive positions . . . they were difficult to penetrate. In addition, the railway lines were also raised on embankments to the same level as the canals, and formed a grid that could not be ignored." These obstacles would slow the brigade's advance. Aerial photography had also identified two strong defensive lines. The first was a "deep-rooted" one "entrenched in a ditch ten feet wide, approximately three hundred yards south of . . . Russi. The second line was dug into the northwest embankment of the Lamone."[10]

Between the four main rivers, the flat countryside was crisscrossed with smaller streams and canals. Some were formidable barriers in their own right.

Given the region's natural defensive strength, the Germans were able to deploy fewer troops than normally would be required. The line from the Adriatic to San Pancrazio was held by 114th Jäger Division, with 356th Infanterie-Division to its right in the vicinity of Albereto. While the 114th Division was considered to be of poor quality and known to be understrength, 356th Division was up to strength and its troops good. Their continuing stubborn resistance in front of 10th Indian Division confirmed this.

Even 114th Division could make a good stand when given this terrain's defensive advantages. The Germans were also always adept at enhancing a situation. In this case, their engineers had capitalized on the inherent advantages provided by the dykes. In some places, they dug holes in the riverbanks to create underground accommodations. Tunnels were bored and riveted with stout timbers to create porthole-like openings in the banks from which machine guns could fire. As the rivers tended to meander lazily, the Germans established mutually supporting strongpoints that could rake the open ground between with crossfire. Because the dykes were so narrow, they offered poor targets for aerial or artillery bombardment. Naturally, the Germans had destroyed all bridges. The Canadian engineers building new ones would have to work on the site of the demolished structures, "since the slopes of the banks were too steep for tracked and wheeled vehicles to surmount without approaching ramps. Thus," as one report put it, "to reach these flood banks with mechanized arms presented a problem of extreme difficulty; to storm them a grim task indeed."[11]

OVER THE COURSE of November 28–29, 1 Canadian Corps lumbered toward battle. Snaking away from Riccione in a long column, 1st Division bogged down in the tight confines of Rimini's bomb-battered streets. It looked, the division's intelligence officer—who was also in charge of leading the column—wrote, "as if every lorry in Italy was trying to get through." An hour later, the column cleared the city and rolled along Highway 16. In the stretch extending twenty-eight miles from Rimini to the Savio River, the officer counted no less than a dozen Bailey bridges replacing those blown by the Germans. At the Savio, the convoy swung southeastward on a secondary road and the heavy trucks struggled through "inches of heavy sticky mud." As night fell, the column groped almost blindly forward, as headlights were prohibited this close to the front. At each junction, the intelligence officer looked hopefully for provost officers to point the column in the right direction, but none were present. "It's a strange feeling for the leader of a convoy to wonder all the time whether he's on the right road or not, but when the enemy is near enough to be a neighbour and you are going straight in his direction, in the darkest of the night and you've no flashlight to look at a map, you don't wonder what can happen if by mistake you lead an entire convoy into Jerry's lap! We've heard of Courts Martial too! However, Provost or no Provost, all went well." Divisional headquarters pulled into the grounds of Villa Pasolini, on the west side of the Ronco River, about three miles from the enemy positions across the Montone. It had taken five hours to travel fifty miles. At 2000 hours, an hour after arriving, divisional headquarters was operational.[12]

Not far away, 3rd Brigade concentrated across the Ronco at Coccolia, a village about four miles northeast of Forli. Arriving just after midnight on November 29, the brigade dispersed into several farmyards.

Brigadier Paul Bernatchez held an Orders Group at 0900 that morning. In addition to the Princess Louise Dragoon Guards, 1st Division's Royal Canadian Dragoons were under brigade command. The latter regiment would provide left flank protection, while the Plugs would advance on Godo to the right. Russi was the brigade's first objective. The West Nova Scotia Regiment on the right and Royal 22e Régiment on the left would lead the advance to it. If Russi proved strongly defended, both battalions would pass by on either side. Were it undefended, the West Novas would sweep through without stopping and continue to the Lamone at a point across from the village of Traversara.[13] The Van Doos were to seize a railway junction a thousand yards northwest of Russi. Here the railroad from Ravenna split—one line running west past Bagnacavallo to Bologna and the other southwest to Faenza. The Van Doos were to follow the one leading to Bagnacavallo—a ruler-straight line built atop a twenty-foot embankment. It was hoped the railway bridge across the Lamone might still be usable.[14]

Once the two leading battalions reached the Lamone, the Carleton and York Regiment would force a crossing. Bernatchez pointed out the new forms of available support. There would be six Crocodiles, fifteen Lifebuoy flame-throwers, and air support on call in the form of American-made Thunderbolt fighter-bombers that either fired rockets or dropped phosphorous bombs.[15]

As the day progressed, more supporting units arrived—two 1st Anti-Tank Regiment batteries, a Saskatoon Light Infantry medium machine-gun company and three of its heavy mortar batteries, the 4th Field Company's engineers, 9th Light Field Ambulance, and 12th Royal Tank Regiment's 'C' Squadron accompanied by the six Crocodiles.[16]

While 3rd Brigade gathered on November 30, 10th Indian Division capitalized on a drying trend in the weather to seize the town of Albereto with a combined infantry and tank force. A hard fight left the place in ruins and forty Germans dead. Winning the town loosened the German hold on the river crossing at Casa Bettini. Early on December 1, the Germans pulled away.[17]

Even as this fighting was going on, 3rd Brigade started entering 10th Indian Division's bridgehead on the Montone's west bank. All vehicles had to use a pontoon bridge inside Forli and then follow a narrow road along the west side of the river. Heavy rain the night before had turned the road muddy, and the traffic soon caused it to start crumbling. The Canadians soon realized that the bridgehead was shallower than expected. Their concentration area became "very crowded with troops, vehicles, tanks, and guns. All transport was road bound, due not only to the muddy condition of the fields, but also to the fact that the majority of the entrances to farmyards across the deep ditches which lined either side of the road had been destroyed by the enemy. These physical factors were to render more difficult the task of passing the brigade through the Indians," a 3rd Brigade summary reported. The West Novas and Van Doos, meanwhile, had entered the bridgehead via two footbridges.[18]

During its move, 12th Royal Tank Regiment's 'C' Squadron was misdirected by v Corps military police at the Forli bridge. Denied use of the bridge, the tankers were directed onto a road running up the Montone's eastern bank. By the time 12th RTR's commander caught up to the squadron and turned it back toward Forli, a traffic jam clogged the bridge. There was no way the squadron could get into position to support the 3rd Brigade attack. Hurried arrangements were made to have the North Irish Horse, which had been supporting the 10th Indian Division, assist the Canadians.[19]

As 3rd Brigade took over the line from four Indian battalions, 1st Infantry Division secured the loan of the King's Dragoon Guards to replace the westernmost battalion. The Royal Canadian Dragoons' 'A' Squadron, serving again as infantry, took over from the adjacent battalion, the Van Doos the next, and the West Novas the one farthest to the east.[20] With this battalion still engaged in fighting at Casa Bettini, the West Novas were unable to occupy their forward positions until the evening. The last Canadian unit to enter the bridgehead was the Princess Louise Dragoon Guards, arriving at 1730 hours.[21]

Having the King's Dragoon Guards added to 3rd Brigade's strength, its war diarist noted, made the brigade group "probably bigger than it has ever been before—four infantry and two recce battalions, with supporting arms."[22] In the fading light, the Canadians could see through the leafless grape vines the red-tiled roofs of Russi—just three miles distant.

THE SUN ROSE into a clear, blue sky on December 2. Meteorologists predicted no rain. At 0900 hours, a thick screen of smoke in front of 3rd Brigade's front lines obscured the sun. Well behind the smoke line, the Van Doos and West Novas walked into battle. Each battalion was supported by a troop of North Irish Horse.

The smoke fired by 1st Canadian Field Regiment was part of a coordinated artillery and Desert Air Force operation called a Timothy. With ideal weather, 1st Division's war diarist wrote, "DAF was able to give maximum support to the ground troops . . . A Timothy consists of a smoke screen laid by arty, on a frontage of 3,000 yards; this serves as a bomb-line for the Air Force who will attack, bomb and strafe anything beyond it for a period of 30 minutes after which the infantry continues its advance. A Timothy is normally used against stiff opposition and the bomb-line (smoke screen) is laid approximately 300 yards ahead of our forward elements. We evidently were amateurs at it today as the smoke came down a full 1,000 yards ahead of our forward troops; this because we thought 300 yards might be too close. However, we learned much by using this new type of support and no doubt will use it as it should be used in future."[23]

Despite misapplied Timothy, the advance proceeded swiftly. As anticipated, the loss of Albereto and Casa Bettini had persuaded the Germans to abandon the Montone with a night withdrawal back to a drainage canal called the Scolo Via Cupa. The canal lay about a thousand yards beyond the Canadian start lines and barred the way to Russi. About seven feet wide and bordered by five-foot-high dykes, it offered a solid defensive position.[24]

Lieutenant Colonel Jean Allard had advanced three companies of Van Doos single file toward the canal. Major Henri Tellier's 'A' Company was on point, 'B' Company in the middle, and 'C' Company trailing. Once contact was made, the two forward companies would fan out and open a path through which Major Louis Trudeau's 'C' Company could drive through to the Lamone. Allard "knew the risks we would be taking" but was counting on speed and determination to win through.[25]

All went well until Tellier's lead platoon neared the canal and came under fire from a small knoll to the left that dominated his company's line of approach. As Tellier's men hit the dirt and started returning fire, Major Pierre Potvin swung 'B' Company left to charge the hill. When the North Irish Horse tank providing fire support was knocked out, Potvin's attack stalled.

Tellier's company, meanwhile, had started moving across a field bordered by two roads, only to be stopped again by fire from blockhouses standing in front of the canal. On each road, one or more German tanks could be heard manoeuvring. Quickly reorganizing, Tellier renewed the advance and his men soon silenced the blockhouses, taking nine prisoners and killing several other Germans. But Tellier was still unable to reach the canal. By 1530 hours, 'A' Company had suffered twenty-five casualties.[26] Ten of these were fatal.[27]

Allard ordered Tellier to withdraw and Trudeau "to take his entire company and crush this defence." 'C' Company, however, was thrown back, with several men killed or wounded. One fatality was Company Sergeant Major Pierre Bérubé. He had suffered three previous serious wounds. According to army policy, a thrice-wounded soldier was to be sent back to Canada. Bérubé, Allard wrote, had opted "to remain with his friends until the end of this battle" and had thus "sealed his own fate."

Trudeau attacked twice more but was again repulsed. Allard had come forward to observe the third attempt. After examining the terrain, he sent Trudeau's company a thousand yards to the left to outflank the Germans. 'A' Company was ordered to continue pushing straight ahead to keep the enemy distracted. With artillery providing supporting fire and a smokescreen, Trudeau's men crossed the canal unopposed. 'C' Company quickly advanced about a mile, and Trudeau reported being less than two miles from the railway junction. Then Allard lost wireless contact with him.

Deciding to capitalize on Trudeau's apparent success and also re-establish contact, Allard ordered Potvin's 'B' Company to follow 'C' Company's path. To do so, Potvin had to disengage from a hot fight with the Germans on the knoll. Eliminating this strongpoint was passed over to 'D' Company.

Despite intense resistance to its front, 'A' Company managed to cross the canal at the same time as Potvin's men made another unopposed crossing. The German hold on the canal in the Van Doos sector crumbled.[28] Undaunted, the Germans fell back to strongpoints at a road junction about a mile south of Russi. In pursuit, 'B' Company was caught in a heavy artillery and mortar concentration. Several men were killed or wounded. Two of Potvin's lieutenants, Jules Armand Comeault and Paul Emile Vincent, died.[29] Night falling, Allard halted to reorganize. .

"SPEED IS TO be the keynote," a 1st Division message to the West Novas had stressed before the attack. Opting for a routine attack formation, Lieutenant Colonel Al Saunders had 'B' Company under Major Harvey Jones lead on the left, with Major Gordon Leo French McNeil's 'C' Company to the right. Following 'C' Company was Captain D.I. Rice's 'A' Company, while Major John Rhodes's 'D' Company trailed Jones's men. The following companies were to be ready "to exploit any opening that presented itself."

Despite 'C' Company being accidentally strafed by Desert Air Force fighters and having to clear Germans out of a couple of houses, the West Novas progressed well. By 1100 hours the lead companies closed on the canal. 'C' Company was stopped fifty yards short by heavy fire from machine-gun posts dug into the dyke. At the same time, Captain Rice reported that small groups of Germans appeared to be deploying into the gap between his company and 'B' Company.

Sensing an opportunity, meanwhile, Jones led 'B' Company dashing to a wrecked bridge spanning the canal. Jumping from one chunk of rubble to another, one platoon managed to reach the opposite shore and dug in under protective covering fire by the rest of the company across the canal.

To 'B' Company's right, however, Rice's company was under intense pressure from enemy positions along the canal bank, as well as Germans infiltrating his company's flank. Fearing being overrun, Rice pulled 'C' Company back to consolidate.[30]

The company's position was just ahead of the West Nova's Tac HQ. Realizing 'B' Company had been left out on a limb and could be counterattacked by Germans on both sides of the canal, Saunders ordered Jones to "hold at all costs." When night fell, he intended to launch 'A' Company through 'B' Company's tenuous bridgehead and then follow it with 'D' Company.

The wintery sun dipped below the horizon at 1630 hours, and at 1745 hours supporting artillery opened fire. At 1812 hours, the lead 'A' Company platoon clambered across the ruined bridge. Soon both 'A' and 'D' Companies were fully across. By 1907 hours, 'A' Company had advanced two hundred yards from the canal, and 'D' Company was a hundred yards farther out. At 2030 hours, both company commanders reported that they had met "enemy, apparently in large numbers." At his Tac HQ, Saunders could hear "much MG and tank fire." With the Germans so close, Saunders decided to withdraw the two companies to the "near side of the canal" to gain room to bring in artillery fire.

Brigadier Paul Bernatchez arrived just before midnight. He and Saunders planned a renewed attack through the tenuous hold 'B' Company retained on the opposite side of the canal. At the same time, 4th Field Company engineers started work on a Bailey bridge next to the wrecked one.[31]

top · Canadian and Greek Brigade troops march through Rimini in mid-September, passing a sign showing their next major objective—Ravenna—to be only fifty-two kilometres distant. Photographer unknown. LAC e999920235-u.

bottom · Saskatoon Light Infantry Vickers machine-gun crew provides fire support for 1st Infantry Division's crossing of the Marecchia River, September 22, 1944. Corporal R. Hill mans the gun, while Private A.D. Hiebert feeds the ammunition. Photographer unknown. LAC e999920213-u.

top left · A Sherman tank wallows up a dyke after crossing the Uso River at a shallow ford. Photographer unknown. LAC e999920238-u.

bottom left · On October 1, 1944, Lieutenant General Richard McCreery assumed command of the British Eighth Army and quickly realized that 1 Canadian Corps faced a crisis of command. Lt. J.E. DeGuire photo. LAC e999920212-u.

top · German prisoners carry a wounded Canadian past ruined buildings in Cesena. Photographer unknown. LAC e999920220-u.

top · A Carleton and York Regiment soldier dashes across a street in Cesena on October 20, 1944, while under fire from German snipers being engaged by a 1st Canadian Anti-Tank Regiment's 17-pounder self-propelled gun. Photographer unknown. LAC e999920219-u.

bottom · Seaforth Highlanders stand on the Savio River dyke shortly before the regiment crossed the river on the night of October 21, 1944. Padre Roy Durnford faces the camera, second from left. Photographer unknown. Photo courtesy of Seaforth Highlanders Regimental Museum.

top · Trucks cross the Savio River via Floating Bridge Equipment.
Photographer unknown. Photo courtesy of Seaforth Highlanders
Regimental Museum.

bottom · The Savio River battleground shortly after October 22, 1944.
Photographer unknown. Photo courtesy of Seaforth Highlanders
Regimental Museum.

top left · On the night of October 25–26, heavy rains caused the Emilia–Romagna region's rivers to rise rapidly, sweeping away most of the Canadian bridges, such as this one over the Marecchia. Photographer unknown. LAC e999920237-u.

bottom left · Van Doos train with collapsible canvas boats on the Conca River during the November rest period. Lt. J.E. DeGuire photo. LAC e999920226-u.

top · On November 13, Major General Chris Vokes said goodbye to 1st Canadian Infantry Division and left to assume command of 4th Canadian Armoured Division in Northwest Europe. Capt. C.E. Nye photo. LAC e999920222-u.

top left · Private A. Buck Owen and Corporal E.H. de Paiva depart the Grand Hotel Leave Centre in Riccione to return to their regiment in late November. Lt. D. Guravich photo. LAC e999920224-u.

bottom left · Brigadier Desmond Smith commanded 1st Canadian Infantry Division briefly (November 13 to December 6) and was instrumental in planning the disastrous 1st Infantry Brigade attack at the Lamone River on December 5. Capt. C.E. Nye photo. LAC e999920223-u.

top · The Irish Regiment holds a memorial service and march past at Cattolica in November in honour of their comrades who fell during the September–October fighting in the Emilia–Romagna region. Capt. C.E. Nye photo. LAC e999920200-u.

top left · On November 16, Lieutenant General Charles Foulkes took command of 1 Canadian Corps. He is pictured here (right) with Lieutenant General Richard McCreery (centre). Capt. A.M. Stirton photo. LAC e999920217.

bottom left · Canadian soldiers talk with two Bagnacavallo partisans, twenty-six-year-old Luisa and nineteen-year-old Bruno Cristofori. Their brother Italo was killed in fighting on December 5 during the 28th Garibaldi Brigade's advance on Ravenna. Capt. A.M. Stirton photo. LAC e999920228-u.

top · Soldiers clear a 7.2-inch shell that failed to explode after it hit a building in Bagnacavallo and ricocheted into the street. Capt. A.M. Stirton photo. LAC e999920229-u.

top · As the fighting raged around Bagnacavallo, about four thousand civilians hid in basement shelters like this one for as long as twenty days. Capt. A.M. Stirton photo. LAC e999920231-u.

top right · Canadian soldiers march through rain toward the next battle, sometime in January 1945. Photographer unknown. LAC e999920233-u.

bottom right · In the aftermath of the fighting for Conventello in the Valli di Comacchio salient, civilians scavenge through ruins that were heavily damaged by combined Allied air and artillery fire. In the background is a burned-out Panther tank. Photographer unknown. LAC e999920232-u.

top left · Winter on the Senio line prompted the improvisation of a variety of stoves, such as this one made by fitting a pipe to a shell box. Pictured are Gunners George Blagdon, Frank Klein, and Sergeant Leonard Tremblay. Lt. D. Guravich photo. LAC e999920203-u.

bottom left · 2nd Field Regiment artillery crew fires at Germans across the Senio from a gun position near the Lamone River. Capt. A.M. Stirton photo. LAC e999920206-u.

top · On February 18, 1945, the Carleton and York Regiment conducts a dedication ceremony at a cemetery between Russi and the Lamone River. Capt. A.M. Stirton photo. LAC e999920207-u.

top · Arrivederci, Italy. A Sherman tank is loaded aboard an American Landing Craft (Tank) at Leghorn during Operation Goldflake—the transfer of 1 Canadian Corps to Northwest Europe. Capt. A.M. Stirton photo. LAC e999920209-u.

Both 3rd Brigade battalions ended December 2 on parallel lines that were less than two thousand yards from the start line. Divisional intelligence had reported that the Germans on the left flank were going to fall back to the Lamone, so both battalions were to prepare "for a rapid advance during the remaining hours of darkness."[32]

AS 3RD BRIGADE HAD started toward Russi, 5th Division's 12th Brigade had launched its thrust eastward along the Montone River. Because the bridgehead was so narrow, Brigadier John Lind had to modify the initial plan. "You will . . . have to go on a one company front," his handwritten order to Princess Louise Dragoon Guards commander Lieutenant Colonel Bill Darling directed. After a mile, a road branched off the one paralleling the river and ran northwest to Russi. When this point was reached, Lind thought there would be sufficient room to assume the normal two-company leading formation. Although a pause to shake into this formation would be necessary, Lind cautioned Darling to ensure it lasted no more than thirty minutes. Speed was essential to keeping the Germans off balance. Lind promised enough artillery to "cover your needs. We have dumped extra ammunition, so use it. The targets are on call." In addition to artillery, Desert Air Force would have four hundred aircraft ready to support 1 Canadian Corps.

A squadron of British Columbia Dragoon tanks was to have been in support, but Lind warned Darling that they might not reach the Plugs in time to start. Nevertheless, "you must push on anyway. My intention for you is to secure Godo."[33]

Lind fussed over every detail because the Plugs would initially have no cover on either flank and would undoubtedly face well dug-in German forces. Corps intelligence staff reported that 12th Brigade faced four battalions, each averaging 250 men. Immediately beyond the start line was a 356th Infanterie-Division battalion. Its sector extended to the road where the attack was to widen out. The other three battalions were from 114th Jäger Division. This division had seven battalions stretched twelve miles from its boundary with 356th Division to the sea. The German infantry was supported by twenty-four 105-millimetre or 150-millimetre field guns. There were also five Italian assault guns, six 88-millimetre self-propelled guns, and several Panther tanks.

The Germans defending Ravenna were reportedly emplacing demolitions and in the process of evacuating base installations—a sign that a gradual withdrawal might be under way. Yet the intelligence report stated it was "abundantly clear that he would not give up Ravenna without a fight."[34]

It had been hoped that the Germans would be caught by surprise when the Plugs emerged from the bridgehead. Instead, as soon as 'C' Squadron appeared at 0900 hours it was greeted by heavy machine-gun fire. Despite some men going down dead or wounded, the squadron kept moving. At his Tac HQ, Darling discovered that all communication links back to 12th Brigade had been lost. This hampered his ability to request artillery fire on specific targets. Also, as Lind had feared, the British Columbia Dragoon tanks were no-shows. 'C' Squadron was on its own.[35]

Trying to reach the Plugs, the B.C. Dragoons' 'C' Squadron under Major John Edward Cooke was struggling through extensive minefields, cratered road patches, and countless blown culverts. "Movement off the roads was almost impossible," the regiment's historian wrote, "and even likely looking spaces where a tank might pull off the road for any reason were usually mined. At times crews had to get out of their tanks to sweep the roads for mines."[36]

At 1135 hours, the communication link to 12th Brigade was restored and artillery support greatly improved. Soon after, 'C' Squadron reached the road and 'A' Squadron quickly came up alongside at 1310 hours. Both companies came under immediate enemy fire. 'C' Squadron had so far suffered twenty casualties. At 1430 hours, the advance stalled.[37]

According to the brigade plan, the Lanark and Renfrew Scottish Regiment should have already come up beside the Plugs and filled in the ground between the road and the Montone. But when Lanark Major D.E. Jones set out on this mission with 'A' Company, it became entangled with B.C. Dragoon tanks blocking the road.[38] The delay hardly mattered. The front was still too narrow to accommodate more troops.

Lind appeared at Darling's Tac HQ at 1600 hours to discuss how to break the deadlock. A renewed attack, with heavy artillery support, was set for 1800 hours. While 'A' Squadron pulled back to reorganize, disengaging was not an option for 'C' Squadron. It was pinned down by machine-gun fire from a group of houses. The new plan called for 'D' Squadron to lead the advance, with 'A' Squadron following and 'B' Squadron behind. To the right of the Plugs, the Lanarks would try again.

"The account of the battle so far is not very dashing," the Plugs' war diarist recorded. By 1700 hours, twenty-one men had been wounded and evacuated. Three others were dead.[39]

EARLY IN THE morning on December 2, Lieutenant Colonel Gordon Corbould of the Westminster Regiment had learned from Brigadier Lind that the attack on the other side of the Montone was stalling. If his Westies could cross the river at San Pancrazio, Corbould realized, some of the pressure could be taken off the brigade's other two battalions.[40]

Corbould turned to Major Bert Hoskin of 'C' Company. "Bert, do you think you can get across with your company?" Hoskin had been thinking about how to do this for days. "Yes," he replied.

By 1000 hours, 'C' Company was ready. The dyke on their side of the river had a German communication tunnel dug through it about two feet below the top. It was well shored with timbers and high enough that most men could walk through without stooping. Morning mist still hung on the river, providing welcome cover. Sergeant J.D. Jones and No. 17 Platoon lugged an assault boat through the tunnel, slid it down the bank to the water, and paddled across undetected. Jones and his men cut a path through the wire defences and lifted any mines blocking the gap. Stringing a rope across the river allowed more boats to be brought across quickly.[41] The battalion's drivers and batmen paddled the men of 'C' Company across, and Hoskin led them over the bank, surprising the Germans guarding the river.[42] The attack ended with six Germans killed, several wounded, and others sent running. Seventeen prisoners were taken.

Mortar fire from San Pancrazio began falling, but it little delayed the crossing effort. More assault boats were carried to the river and tied side by side to provide the base for a floating bridge. Crossing on this, 'A' Company passed through Hoskin's men and headed for the long, straggling village of San Pancrazio. German resistance in the village was disorganized and sporadic. One 'A' Company patrol led by Sergeant Ralph Ballam caught a German mortar crew disassembling the weapon and took them prisoner.[43] Also taken prisoner was the sergeant commanding the garrison. Lieutenant James Oldfield learned from him "that our attack had been quite unexpected and before they could muster their defences they were beaten."[44] Although the remaining Germans seemed intent on retreating, they did so grudgingly. 'A' Company's Private Bud Mabbett was standing guard in a building's second storey when a German rifle grenade struck him in the chest. The wound would have been mortal had not a civilian physician turned up to stop the bleeding.[45]

At 2000 hours, 'B' Company entered the Westie bridgehead. By 2300 hours, all three companies were firmed up inside San Pancrazio.[46] Meanwhile, at 1800 hours, 4th Field Company engineers had started another floating bridge capable of bearing the weight of vehicles.

The Westminster assault had the desired effect. When the Lanark and Renfrew Scottish and the Princess Louise Dragoon Guards launched their advance, progress was at first slow. But as evening progressed, the pace quickened. By midnight, the Lanarks and Plugs were just a mile west of San Pancrazio. At 0525 hours on December 3, the Lanarks made contact with the Westies. Together they ensured that San Pancrazio was completely clear of enemy. Both the Plugs and Lanarks headed toward Godo at 0815 hours. Resistance was slight, and Lind ordered them "to push on with all possible speed."

This they did. By 1300 hours, the Lanarks' 'A' Company had waded the Scolo Via Cupa and was barely a mile from Godo. The Plugs, meanwhile, swerved behind the Lanarks to come up on their right flank, with orders to sever the railway and road linking Godo to Ravenna. In what a 12th Brigade report considered "a magnificent spurt" of speed, the two leading squadrons carried out a rapid cross-country march that passed the railway line running just south of Godo and were soon astride the road just east of the town. The time was 1605 hours. Soon all four squadrons were consolidating between the railway and road. By 1820 hours, the Lanarks had pushed into Godo's southern outskirts.

"This was an exceptionally successful afternoon," the 12th Brigade report concluded, "for the speed and suddenness of our advance had carried it through the enemy's delaying line east of River Lamone (which was in fact the line of railway running through Godo). Ravenna itself became badly outflanked and the enemy manning the River Montone east of San Pancrazio and south of the Godo–Ravenna railway line was faced with the choice of a very hasty and disorganized withdrawal, or the near certainty of being completely cut off."[47]

14

Cheerful to the End

———————

"THE ENEMY HAS put up a very stiff resistance all along the natural obstacle of Scolo Via Cupa," Lieutenant Colonel Jean Allard wrote on the night of December 2. "He has carried out very heavy shelling and has counterattacked all along [the front] in a manner which tends to indicate his preparing for a withdrawal tonight. He would like us to deploy in preparation for a full-scale attack on these obstacles tomorrow morning while he would withdraw safely behind a screen of strong outposts at road junctions and other tactical features. We will therefore bypass all tactical features and push straight to our initial objectives, by infiltrating in the fields and ignoring all points of resistance."

At 2030 hours, the Royal 22e Régiment commander convened an Orders Group. His plan saw Major Pierre Potvin's 'B' Company leading on the right, with Major Louis Trudeau's 'C' Company to the left. 'A' and 'D' Companies would follow and mop up the bypassed strongpoints. If resistance stiffened, the trailing companies would come up on either flank to firm up the line. The attack would start when the moon rose at 2300 hours. November 30 had seen a full moon, so the light it cast was still bright enough to provide good illumination.

Trudeau's 'C' Company proved so good at "dodging the enemy" that by 0330 hours it reached the railway junction northwest of Russi. There, however, the company "had to stop to fight it out . . . [and soon] could go no further as it had expended all ammunition in hand while advancing and had to replenish first." Having driven the Germans off, 'C' Company paused to let the rest of the Van Doos catch up.

'C' Company's successful advance was soon reinforced by the rest of the battalion. Allard realized the Germans were completely confused. The Van Doos had taken twenty-nine prisoners and the following day the Carleton and York Regiment reported bagging an additional sixty. Most of these "were soldiers who had been trying to find their leaders or who had been sleeping in houses."

Once 'C' Company had replenished its ammunition, Allard ordered Trudeau to head for the railroad bridge that spanned the Lamone River a mile away. At the same time, Potvin's 'B' Company was to try for the Godo–Bagnacavallo road bridge 1,500 yards east of the railroad span.

As the advance started at 1400 hours, the Germans had sufficiently reorganized to offer "a determined stand to screen his hastened withdrawal."[1] Having managed to overcome the military police misdirection "fiasco of the previous day," No. 1 Troop of 12th Royal Tank Regiment's 'A' Squadron had joined Trudeau's advance.

"The tanks," according to a 12th RTR report, "moved behind the rear platoon of the company so that the noise of the tracks would not bring down enemy shell fire on the leading infantry. One man from the tank troop went on foot with the company commander to act as [a] link between tanks and infantry. This liaison proved particularly successful, but accurate shooting was difficult owing to the very close country which consisted of clustered vineyards. In spite of this, the troop was able to engage enemy in houses with both 6-pounder and Besa [machine-gun fire] and supported the infantry to within 200 yards of the railway bridge, where they were held up by heavy MG and mortar fire." The Van Doos attack ran out of steam. At about 1800 hours, Trudeau's men dug in, and No. 1 Troop withdrew to the outskirts of Russi.[2]

Meanwhile, the Germans had blown the railroad bridge, and 'B' Company had come nowhere near reaching the Godo–Bagnacavallo road crossing. Potvin's men instead dug in to the right of 'C' Company at an abandoned monastery. 'A' and 'D' Companies, along with Allard's Tac HQ, were a short distance back. Allard was worried. The "regiment was . . . alone, and there was no reserve, we could be attacked at any time and from any direction. We spent the night as a lonely outpost.

"In the confusion created by [our] rapid attack a number of Germans had remained in their positions . . . I had not had the axis of advance cleared and did not feel it was necessary to waste my time doing it. I had reached my objective, and I was too far from the West Nova Scotias, who were advancing very slowly, to risk losing the ground we had won by spreading my men out."[3]

To the right of the Van Doos, the West Nova Scotia Regiment had been delayed waiting for 4th Field Company engineers to install a crossing next to the wrecked bridge that 'B' Company had used to gain a toehold across the Scolo Via Cupa. Blocked from expanding this bridgehead by fierce resistance on December 2, Lieutenant Colonel Al Saunders planned a renewed effort, with Captain D.I. Rice's 'A' Company leading and 'D' Company under Major John Rhodes following. Rice's company hooked left to strike the Germans along the canal from the rear.[4]

At 0215 hours, both companies rushed across the canal and struck out from the bridgehead. Unaware that a German withdrawal was under way and having previously found the "enemy . . . very thick on the ground," they expected a hard fight. Instead, they met little op-position.[5] As 'A' Company swept the canal, Rhodes led 'D' Company cross-country toward Russi.

Passing through the hamlet of Pezzolo, Lieutenant Don Campbell's platoon surprised a party of Germans. After a short, sharp fight, most threw down their arms and ran past Campbell's platoon "with hands up, crying in terror and heading blindly in several directions until they were booted in the direction of the West Nova rear by the follow-ing wave of 'D' Company—all . . . to the astonishment and pleasure of the Italian farmers and their families, who came from their hiding places as the fighting passed and clapped and jeered at this spectacle of Hitler's 'supermen' in defeat."[6]

'B' Company, meanwhile, had joined the push on Russi and led the way into the town at 0920 hours. Major Harvey Jones reported that the Germans there had fled. A thousand yards beyond Russi, however, the company was halted by heavy fire.[7] 'D' Company also ran into trouble from machine-gun nests "hidden in hollowed-out haystacks with the gunners dug into the ground beneath." Return small-arms fire being entirely ineffective, the West Novas tried to rush the positions but were driven back. An attempt by one soldier to ignite the haystacks with a Lifebuoy flame-thrower failed when he was unable to get into range. Finally, the Bren gunners set them ablaze with tracer rounds. As the Germans broke cover, they were shot down.[8]

While this fight was under way, 'D' Company's headquarters was struck by mortar fire that wounded Rhodes and Campbell.[9] Also hit was Royal Canadian Horse Artillery's forward observation officer Captain Fred Drewry, who succumbed to his wounds four days later.[10]

Both 'B' and 'D' Companies called for tank support. Two troops of 12th Royal Tank Regiment's 'C' Squadron reinforced 'D' Company, but none could reach 'B' Company. Even with the tanks, 'D' Company's progress was terribly slow. One No. 11 Troop Churchill tank was hit by three high-velocity, high-explosive rounds, all of which failed to knock it out. The British tankers were, meanwhile, unable to see any targets to engage.[11]

At 1230 hours, Lieutenant Colonel Saunders futilely tried to get the attack moving by signalling "that speed was essential in the attainment of their objectives." Finally, at 1630 hours, 3rd Canadian Infantry Brigade told the West Novas "to sit tight until further notice." A night attack supported by artillery would follow.

Sundown brought cold, thick mist from the nearby canals and drainage ditches. 'A' and 'C' Companies led off. Progress was again slow, this time due to poor visibility and the many deep ditches.[12] At 0130 hours on December 4, the West Novas stopped two thousand yards short of the Lamone.[13]

Even before the West Novas had started this night attempt, Brigadier Paul Bernatchez was expecting failure. At 1740 hours on December 3, he had anticipated that the Van Doos and West Novas were going to be stopped short of the river. Yet there was encouraging news from 5th Canadian Armoured Division that its 12th Infantry

Brigade had cut the railroad east of Godo and was advancing. As a result, Bernatchez sensed the German grip on the southeast side of the Lamone might become untenable. Perhaps another push could win through. He therefore ordered Lieutenant Colonel Jack Ensor to immediately pass the Carleton and York Regiment through the Van Doos and seize both the railway and road bridges that his other two battalions had failed to reach. To achieve this, the Carletons must split up—two companies heading for each bridge. If successful, the West Novas would reinforce the Carletons at the road bridge, while the Van Doos would do the same at the railway.

At 2130 hours, supported by heavy artillery fire, 'B' Company headed toward a group of buildings that overlooked the railroad bridge, while 'D' Company thrust toward the road bridge. A thick fog blanketed the ground. There was little opposition until 'B' Company closed on the railway bridge at about midnight and came under heavy machine-gun fire. 'D' Company was soon also encountering pockets of resistance that had to be eliminated in turn. A stalemate looming, Ensor sent 'C' Company on a right flanking movement through the West Novas. Realizing the threat, the Germans facing 'D' Company gave way. By dawn on December 4, the Carletons were advancing rapidly. At 0700 hours, 'B' Company reached the blown railway bridge and came under heavy fire from Germans dug in on the opposite bank. 'D' Company met similar resistance when it came up to the demolished road bridge.[14]

ON THE MORNING of December 4, the mood at 1st Canadian Infantry Division headquarters was heady. The Carletons, the war diarist recorded, "had crashed through the German defences and . . . reached the Lamone." On the right, the West Novas were closing in. The next step was to send 1st Brigade's Hastings and Prince Edward Regiment "to try and force a crashing of the river."[15]

What sounded simple to Brigadier Desmond Smith and his staff seemed entirely the opposite to Lieutenant Colonel Don Cameron. A decision by 1st Brigade's Brigadier Allan Calder only worsened matters. Calder had been pressing Cameron to let Hasty Ps' second-in-command, Major Stan Ketcheson, lead a battalion attack. Believing it his duty to command the men in battle, Cameron had steadfastly refused. As December began, Calder ordered Cameron to comply. "I suggest that Ketcheson's first battle be an easy one—an approach to combat, for instance," Cameron had pleaded. Calder insisted that the untried officer oversee the attempted "crashing" attack. Adding to Cameron's concern, Ketcheson's inexperience would not be unique— three company commanders had also seen little or no combat.[16]

Things were terribly rushed. Returning from brigade headquarters with his instructions at 1120 hours, Ketcheson was to send 'A' Company across the Lamone at 1250. Their start line was a ditch 150 yards from the river.

Desert Air Force began strafing and bombing the Germans across the river at noon and medium artillery joined in soon after. Despite the distance to the start line, 'A' Company reached it at 1300 hours and Captain Max Porritt led the men forward without pause. Fifty yards from the river they were struck by intense mortar and machine-gun fire and could go no farther.

At 1400 hours, Porritt called for artillery concentrations on buildings immediately across the river. The shells started falling at 1410 hours and continued for ten minutes.[17] Porritt led the men in a dash to the twenty-foot-high dyke containing the Lamone. The promised assault boats had never been delivered. "I crawled up the steep slope and got one quick glimpse of the river," Porritt recalled, "before bullets began to flick the earth about me. I was just able to roll back without being hit. My second-in-command, Captain [Oscar W.] Christiansen, was beside me and I saw his body go rolling down the slope, his beret flying past my head. He had been shot through the skull and was dead in a few minutes.

"The enemy was alerted now and his small-arms fire dominated the dyke crest and the river gulley completely. I tried to get through on the wireless to call for artillery support, but the set went out. There was nothing for it but to take the company back a hundred yards to the shelter of some buildings. At 1600 hours a messenger reached me with the news that the attack had been postponed."[18]

When Ketcheson explained the situation to Calder, the brigadier conceded that "the enemy was too strong to attempt a crossing with one battalion."[19] Calder seemed unaware that the hit had actually been made by just one company. The Hasty Ps were to try again with 'B' and 'C' Companies. The Royal Canadian Regiment would join the effort on the left flank. The attack was set for 0130 hours on December 5.[20]

Lacking any information about the Lamone, RCR Lieutenant Colonel Jim Ritchie sent Lieutenant James Edward Joice and three men forward on a "hazardous mission" to recce it. Gaining the river under cover of darkness, Joice and Sergeant George John Meadows swam into the rushing current to ascertain its width and depth. Just as the two men determined it was five feet deep and thirty-five feet wide, a grenade exploded in the water nearby. A machine gun then sprayed the water.[21] Joice was rendered helpless by a cramp as he swam for shore. Pulling him, Meadows gained the riverbank. Too weak to drag Joice clear of the water, Meadows crawled over the dyke to get help. By the time the three soldiers returned to Joice's position, the current had swept him away. A thirty-minute search failed to find any trace of the officer.

Returning to Ritchie's Tac HQ, Meadows reported the river's dimensions. He also said the dykes on both sides rose to forty-five feet on the side facing the river and twenty-five feet on the landward side.

Ritchie's sketch plan had called for the assault companies to swim the Lamone with the aid of ropes. That idea had been based on divisional intelligence claims that the river was three feet rather than five feet deep. The RCR war diarist reported that Ritchie told Calder "that since the current was strong, the water icy and the opposite dyke held by the enemy, it would be suicidal to attempt swimming the battalion across." Calder agreed and promised assault boats and strong supporting arms.[22] Despite these reassurances, neither Ritchie nor Ketcheson felt confident.

WHILE 1ST BRIGADE WAS cobbling together 1st Division's rushed assault, 5th Armoured Division operations in the area of Godo had thrown the German situation southeast of the Lamone into disarray.

At nightfall on December 3, the 4th Princess Louise Dragoon Guards and Lanark and Renfrew Scottish Regiment had cleared Godo—a task that entailed protracted skirmishes to eliminate pockets of Germans.

Originally, 12th Canadian Infantry Brigade's Brigadier John Lind had planned for the Plugs to cut the Piangipane–Russi road north of Godo. Once astride the road, they would then drive northeastward to the village of Piangipane and threaten the German line of retreat from Ravenna. With the fight in Godo dragging on, Lind decided to march the Westminster Regiment from San Pancrazio directly to Piangipane.[23] They would then turn right and follow the road to Highway 16. This would cut off any line of retreat for the Germans still in Ravenna.

From San Pancrazio to Highway 16 junction was almost seven miles.[24] "No two attacks are the same," Lieutenant James Oldfield wrote, "but this one was surely unique in the history of Westminster tactics. The enemy was known to be occupying the country to be traversed . . . in considerable strength. The roads were patrolled with enemy armoured vehicles and the Westminsters lacked adequate anti-tank protection, hence a circuitous and involved route was chosen entirely cross-country. In places the route followed forest trails and tracks, but major roads were avoided."[25]

As they would be on foot, the soldiers loaded up with everything that could possibly be needed for the battalion to survive a prolonged period without vehicle support. Lieutenant Colonel Gordon Corbould's Tac HQ was particularly heavily loaded. In addition to several No. 18 wireless sets, three No. 22 sets needed to be carried. The support company's No. 15 and No. 16 platoons were dragooned to help and also provide local defence. At 1600 hours, the Westies moved out with 'A' Company leading, followed by 'C' Company, Corbould's party, and then 'B' Company. Oldfield's 'A' Company scouts were on point. Major W.J. Neill was alongside Oldfield, carefully navigating a path through dense fog and a landscape devoid of landmarks. Behind the scouts, a section of the assault platoon under Sergeant G. Smith marked the route with tape and checked for mines.[26]

Whenever the lead party came to an abandoned German slit trench or weapon pit, Neill would use its shelter to check his map by flashlight. "It is one thing to follow a map over established roads, but quite another to follow it in unmarked country, sparsely settled with buildings, and a great share of the success of the 'night march' must be credited to Major Neill's painstaking accuracy," Oldfield concluded. "To make things more difficult, rains had made the ground slippery, and footing was abominable. Travel became a series of heavy slogging steps forward, then a slithering stop. It was tough for all, but probably worst for the company signallers who waded through mud, often almost knee-deep, impeded with bulky . . . sets. How they stayed on their feet was miraculous. Some of them didn't."

The Scolo Via Cupa proved too wide and deep to cross. Neill turned to a partisan along as a guide. "*Dove ponte?*" he asked. The partisan said there was a bridge a hundred metres distant, "so the long snaky file pushed forward again."[27] The hundred metres stretched to two and then three, but the bridge finally appeared—two thousand metres later.[28] Although demolished, enough masonry chunks remained to allow the Westies to clamber across.[29]

Backtracking to regain the assigned line of advance, Oldfield's scouts reported a man crying in pain from a house to the right. Familiar with this old trick, the Westies ignored the sounds. As the column passed by, inaccurate machine-gun fire erupted from the building. The Westies hurried on.

At about 2330 hours, having crossed some three thousand yards of "flat, muddy ground," the column reached a house beside the Godo–Ravenna road. While 'A' and 'C' Companies continued toward Piangipane, Corbould set up the Tac HQ in the building. As the signallers were netting in their wireless sets fifteen minutes later, Sergeant Paddy Clark reported tanks approaching from Ravenna. Extinguishing all lights, every man grabbed a weapon. Crouching by a window, Major Fred Shawcross counted fifteen armoured vehicles and forty to fifty infantrymen approaching. At first, it seemed the German force would pass by, but then someone moved and caught the attention of three German officers walking at the rear of the convoy. One started toward the house while calling out in German. Stepping into the open doorway, Corbould raised an MI .30-calibre carbine he had recently acquired. When he squeezed the trigger, however, the rifle failed to fire.[30] The German lunged at Courbould, and the two men grappled fiercely, until a soldier shoved the muzzle of a rifle under the lieutenant colonel's arm, pressed it against the German's chest, and shot him dead. While this struggle was under way, the convoy had obliviously continued on. Knowing the officer must soon be missed, Corbould ordered the Tac HQ to immediately withdraw to a nearby canal. It was midnight. Ten minutes later, clattering tracks of armoured vehicles signalled a return.

Having just arrived, 'B' Company hurriedly deployed. One No. 8 Platoon section occupied the building's second storey and a section of No. 5 Platoon the ground floor. The rest of the company spread out in the ditch. Just inside the doorway, Private Lloyd Leslie Brager manned No. 5 Platoon's PIAT. Corporal Ernie Dayton and Private Jimmy White set up with No. 8 Platoon's PIAT behind a two-foot stone wall lining the road.

"The first vehicle," Dayton recalled, "a halftrack, got by before we had a bomb ready. Brager didn't get a shot at it either. The next one, another halftrack, we both hit. It was going pretty fast and continued down the road until opposite the big house. There was a report down there and it may have been" another PIAT hitting it.

"The third vehicle was one of the bigger ones. I hit it in the rear just as it got by, and got it in the motor. There was a great cloud of smoke and steam. Brager also fired at it. It only went 30 to 40 feet before stopping. The fourth was hit the same as the one before and it went in the ditch on the south side of the road. By now Jimmy had all our bombs detonated, so I told him that he might as well get under cover and he left me.

"For a minute there were no more vehicles and now it was very foggy, perhaps partly due to our own shell bursts. The next thing I knew 2 Jerries ran right past me and inside the door where Brager was lying behind the PIAT. Another German stopped almost beside me. I don't know whether he saw me or not, but I grabbed the Tommy gun and shot him. There was a shot and flash inside the doorway and the next moment Brager staggered out. I helped him to the rear of the house where he died. Then there were Germans everywhere on foot. [Sergeant] Jack Laing shouted for us to use our grenades. This made them get into the ditches beside the highway. I shot another right across the road and Corporal George shot one in the shoulder and then took him prisoner. A moment later he and the wounded Jerry ran across the road and dragged the one I had just wounded into the house. One fired a flare and was immediately shot from an upstairs window . . . Things had quietened down now somewhat."

Scrounging three more PIAT rounds, Dayton readied for the next round. The three "remaining vehicles decided to make a run for it. They came by fast, but one at a time. I hit the first two and they both rolled to a stop. The last one, a big one, got through because we had lost one of the nipples that holds the detonator on the bomb head. I set the detonator in the bomb and fired but it just bounced off the side of the tank. Now most of the excitement was over. Jimmy White was badly wounded, but no one knew what with . . . He died as it was getting daylight. He showed a great deal of courage and was cheerful to the end."[31]

The knocked-out tanks proved to be two Italian 75-millimetre SPGs. Platoons led by Lieutenants Bruce Eaton and Vic Wilson quickly mopped up the area. Wilson, who with two of his men had earlier surprised and taken prisoner fifteen Germans, personally killed the gunner who opened fire on the Westies with an MG42 mounted on one of the disabled half-tracks. By 0200 hours it was all over—the entire action lasted fifty minutes. Both Italian SPGs and three half-track personnel carriers had been captured, ten Germans killed, and twenty-three taken prisoner.[32] Privates Brager, White, and Percy Edward Porter were dead and four other Westies wounded. Lieutenant Wilson's actions led to a Military Cross.[33]

WHILE THIS FIGHT raged along the Godo–Ravenna road, 'A' and 'C' Companies had continued toward Piangipane. German machine-gun positions and snipers fired randomly out of the fog—apparently just engaging any sounds of movement. Few casualties resulted. Then a volley of shells—obviously friendly 25-pounders because of the direction of approach—marched in precise single file along a road where the Westies were taking a break in a ditch. Not a single round strayed off the road.[34]

The Westies had no idea who had called for shelling along their assigned line of advance. Later it emerged that it had been the Princess
Louise Dragoon Guards. Having completed Godo's clearance, the
Plugs had advanced a short distance east on the Godo–Ravenna road.
When the leading 'A' Squadron came under fire from three tanks,
artillery was called in. The tanks, however, kept nimbly evading the
falling shot.[35]

As dawn was breaking, Lieutenant Oldfield and his Westie scouts
closed on Piangipane. A German guard ordered the men to halt.
Corporal Walter Myslicki—fluent in multiple languages—"shouted
back something unintelligible in German, and threw a 36 grenade
at the sentries." This silenced the German guards. Carrying on, the
scouts picked up three prisoners. Polish conscripts, they reported
that most of the garrison had decamped to Villanova, across the
Lamone. Dubious, Oldfield proceeded cautiously and soon saw that
those remaining "were apparently going to make a fight of it." Ahead,
a group of Germans were laying mines. After scattering them with
a burst of Bren gun fire, the scouts came under intense fire from an
88-millimetre SPG.

'A' Company deployed for a fight. Lieutenant Eddie Hoult's No. 2
Platoon moved to outflank the SPG. Having taken cover in a two-
storey house, the scout platoon was subjected to four SPG rounds
before Hoult's PIAT team silenced it. Two shots struck the second storey and wounded two snipers, one of whom was Myslicki. The third
round crashed into the ground floor and mortally wounded Private
Henry Hohenleitner. Just as Major Neill was ascending the stairs, the
fourth blast knocked him down to the ground floor—covering him
from head to foot in red brick dust.

As No. 2 Platoon silenced one SPG, another opened fire from
inside Piangipane. 'A' Company's two forward platoons and Neill's
headquarters section were pinned down. Neill urgently called for
tank support. Lieutenant Colonel Corbould reported that a squadron
of British Columbia Dragoons had arrived and he was sending it
Neill's way.[36]

At 0930 hours, the two leading troops of 'C' Squadron approached.
The Sherman on point, commanded by Sergeant Charles D. Inman,

was knocked out by an 88-millimetre round. Troopers Edward A. Lungstrum, Harry E. Petersen, and Duncan Young died. Despite serious wounds, Inman and Trooper Anton Daniar escaped before the Sherman erupted in flames.[37]

Hoping to take the pressure off 'A' Company and the tankers, Major Bert Hoskin led 'C' Company into the village. He soon found an abandoned SPG, assumed to be the one that had fired on 'A' Company and the BC Dragoon tankers. Both it and the one knocked out by No. 2 Platoon were brand new models freshly off an assembly line. Each had an 88-millimetre gun mounted on the chassis of an old Mark IV tank. Allied designation for this SPG type was Rhinoceros. One showed only fifty-eight kilometres on its odometer.

Hoskin's men moved warily through Piangipane, carefully checking each house. Coming upon a large pink building, No. 12 Platoon's Lieutenant Ron Mannering found the front door locked. He was preparing to shoot the lock apart when a woman speaking English in a very cultured voice said, "If you gentlemen will wait a moment, I'll open it for you." The woman granted Mannering and his men entrance.

'A' Company had also entered Piangipane and was advancing along the main street. Suddenly, a third SPG fired "directly down the middle of the street." Oldfield could "see the rounds, red hot, as they whizzed by. Like its mates, this gun caused considerable havoc. Major Neill's runner was wounded, as was Sergeant Nap Cormier of the 'A' Company mortars. The latter refused to be evacuated and was soon in the thick of things again. For some reason, after firing a few telling rounds, the crew of the third gun apparently decided they were cut off and turning their vehicle around, pushed off at the high port and made good their escape." The SPG fire killed Private Henry Lorne Andrews outright, while Private Elmer John Palmer succumbed to his wounds on December 9.

After the SPG withdrew, a few light skirmishes cleared Piangipane. The two companies then pushed on to the adjoining village of Borghetto.[38] By 1400 hours on December 4, the Westies were concentrated at Piangipane. Brigadier Lind arrived and congratulated Corbould on carrying out a six-hour night march and then "inflicting

a decisive blow on a strong enemy force."[39] Lind realized that after seventy-two hours without sleep and very little food, the Westies
were in no condition to continue to Highway 16 and the town of
Mezzano. This objective was four miles distant. He told Corbould
that 11th Canadian Infantry Brigade would take over. Both its Irish
and Perth regiments were to soon pass through Piangipane.[40]

ON THE NIGHT of December 3–4, Porterforce patrols south of the
Fiume Uniti (as the Montone and several small tributaries became
known as they flowed past Ravenna to the sea) had reported hearing
heavy explosions in the city. With 5th Canadian Armoured Division
already having cut many of their avenues for escape and threatening
most of the others, it seemed likely the Germans were preparing to
abandon the Lamone and make a run toward their next line.[41]

At the same time, British Eighth Army mobilized the partisans
gathered in the marshlands of the Valli di Comacchio. A signal to
28th Garibaldi Brigade's partisan Lieutenant Arrigo Boldrini, AKA
Major Bulow, read, "Attack. Good luck!" By 0300 hours, Bulow with
Captain Dennis Healy advanced 823 partisans who were armed with
one 47-millimetre anti-tank gun, four mortars, and a dozen heavy
machine guns. Following sandy footpaths, the force soon closed on
the major defensive fortifications north of the city, designed to meet
the threat of an amphibious attack on Porto Corsini and its adjacent
beaches. These fortifications consisted of heavy concrete bunkers
protected by tanks and artillery. Although each fort's garrison was
quite strong, morale was poor. At 0530 hours, partisan units attacked
various strongholds. Many of the troops surrendered as soon as the
partisans surrounded their fort.[42] The largest garrison, that at Porto
Corsini, was attacked by 300 partisans. After a brisk fight that resulted in several casualties on both sides, the partisans opted to contain the thoroughly trapped Germans.[43]

South of Ravenna, meanwhile, Porterforce's 27th Lancers Cavalry
Regiment had patrols across the Uniti by 1100 hours and advanced
unopposed. Simultaneously, other elements of the 27th Lancers,
accompanied by Popski's Private Army and a number of partisans,
moved inland from the coast on either side of the river.[44]

As Porterforce and the 28th Garibaldi Brigade pressed in on Ravenna from the north and south, 5th Division's Major General Bert Hoffmeister ordered 12th Infantry Brigade to send a force to the village of San Michele—about three miles west of Ravenna on the Godo–Ravenna road—and then patrol toward the city. At 0945 hours, the Princess Louise Dragoon Guards' 'B' and 'D' Squadrons, with 'C' Squadron of the British Columbia Dragoons, advanced along the road. By noon, after a short skirmish, San Michele was cleared. Anticipating that Ravenna might be wide open, Brigadier Lind immediately ordered the advance continued.[45]

Slowed by demolitions that had to be cleared, the Canadians were still well short of Ravenna when the 27th Lancers reported having already entered it. At 1530 hours, the column reached Ravenna's outskirts and was again delayed, this time by a larger than normal crater.[46] Then, nearing the junction with Highway 16, a Panther tank opened fire and pinned the Plugs down. Having got past the large crater, Lieutenant L.F.G. Borden's tank troop engaged the Panther. Although one tank was knocked out and a crew member killed, the Panther was also silenced. As the column reached the junction and turned on Highway 16 toward Ravenna, demolitions were so extensive that the tanks could go no farther.[47] Marching onward, the Plugs entered Ravenna at 1605 hours. The city was barely damaged, all its precious mosaic-rich churches and other buildings preserved. Bulow's determined efforts to pressure the Germans into evacuating the city without a fight had been successful.

The tankers returned to San Michele for the night, reporting that the push to Ravenna had cost only two fatal casualties. "One tanker and the other was one of our lads," the Plugs war diarist recorded. Because of the distance between battalion headquarters and the squadrons in Ravenna, wireless contact was lost. But the diarist thought "the men will be able to get fed in the town, so there is little to worry about."[48]

After the Plugs reached the city, Lieutenant Colonel Bill Darling wrote, "The BBC just about shocked the civilized world into stupor, when [its six o'clock news] came out with the statement that the Canadian 'Princess Louise Dragoon Guards had pulled a brilliant out-flanking movement, and occupied the town of Ravenna.' Little more can be said, except that the two squadrons concerned fought their way forward in a sea of mud without food or sleep, and liberated the town, and joined the Partisans in a short service in memory of those who had not quite made the grade, Partisan and Canadian.

"In the past, we have fought long and well, with little or no space in the newspapers, but this time we seem to have connected for we have been given our rightful share of the glory for a job that had lots of suffering and pain to be borne by the Unit.

"Everyone is high in the praise of the work of the Unit. We have yet to fail to reach our objective—once taken, we have not yielded ground. Casualties have been unusually high—fortunately, of late, many of these have been of a minor nature. We anxiously await the coming back of the 'old gang' [of wounded returning to duty], whom we feel certain will be eager to get a crack at the bastard again. Everything has been in his favour—ground and weather.

"To those who have laid down their lives, officers, NCOS, and men, we of the Regiment that are still here, share with their parents, wives, and relatives their loss. We are proud in their sacrifice. Not one has been in vain."[49]

15

A Ghastly Failure

A S RAVENNA WAS liberated in the late afternoon of December 4, 11th Canadian Infantry Brigade's Perth and Irish regiments reached Piangipane. At 1730 hours, both battalions passed through the Westminster Regiment lines and struck out for their respective objectives. Each was to cut Highway 16—the Perths at the junction of the road leading directly to it from Piangipane, and the Irish where the town of Mezzano spanned the Lamone River.[1] Before the Perths headed out, Lieutenant Colonel Maurice Andrew told his officers that if the lead company "bumped into opposition," all those following were to "bypass it to the left and continue on." At 1800 hours, the Perths started marching in a long, strung-out column.[2]

Tall pines lined the roadsides. Heavy fog reduced visibility to zero. "We had mixed feelings about the fog," Private Stan Scislowski wrote. "In one way we welcomed it because it hid us from enemy eyes. At the same time it gave us a feeling of uneasiness over not knowing what we might soon run into.

"The long tenuous column ghosted along . . . every eye fixed on the dim outlines of houses on the right side of the road. On our left was a fenced-in field, but we didn't expect to be fired on from this direction. What demanded more of our attention were the houses. There could be Jerries holed up in them ready to mow us down."

'D' Company's No. 16 Platoon led, and immediately after pass-ing through the built-up area—called Borgo Fusara—it came under fire from the rearguard of a retreating German formation. Although these Germans were quickly driven off, No. 18 Platoon's Sergeant Ken "Blackie" Rowe ordered Scislowski and his other men into the "soggy fields" left of the road. This way, if No. 16 Platoon encountered an-other roadblock, "we'd slide by and take them in the rear. In the time it took us to slog through four hundred yards of the stickiest mud we'd ever floundered our way through, the fog dissipated enough for us to see where we were going."[3]

No further opposition was encountered. By 0315 hours, 'D' Company was consolidating at Highway 16. The other companies soon dug in nearby. Casualties had been few: one man killed and five wounded.[4]

The Irish Regiment faced tougher going. Its advance to Mezzano fol-lowed a more circuitous network of roads to gain the Via della Lamone, which for two miles paralleled the river. Captain Tony Falzetta's 'C' Company led. Barely a hundred yards out of Piangipane, the men came to a small canal. As the company started wading it, German fire from the opposite bank caused several casualties. Falzetta pulled back, regrouped, and then forced a crossing. Captain Herb Hendrie then pushed 'B' Company through and continued the advance, with 'C' and 'D' Companies following. "The night was very dark," the Irish Regiment's war diarist recorded, so the companies "moved slowly, feel-ing out the country as they proceeded." At 0200 hours on December 5, 'B' Company reached the Via della Lamone. 'C' Company dug in, while 'B' and 'D' Companies continued toward Mezzano. As dawn broke, the two companies were spotted by Germans across the Lamone River and subjected to "constant fire from both small arms and mortars," inflicting some casualties. At 0800 hours, the Irish reached Mezzano. As they dashed forward to seize the Highway 16 bridge crossing, it blew up. The German demolition squad, however, was intercepted, with one man killed and the other two taken prisoner.[5]

With the Perths and Irish blocking any escape along Highway 16, the Germans caught south of the Lamone "struck off across the damp fields, hoping to skirt the roadblocks and strongpoints they rightly figured would be awaiting them," Scislowski wrote. "They couldn't have expected to run into any obstacle in open country, but when morning dawned, they ran smack up against 17 Platoon [of 'D' Company] deployed around a farmhouse in their path. From three Bren positions 17 Platoon opened fire, driving the greatcoat-clad Jerries to ground. The group got off some shots at our boys, but when 17 Platoon, throwing good sense to the wind, came charging out of their slit-trenches firing their weapons from the hips, the Jerries lost all heart for tangling with the crazy Canadians. They jumped up with their hands high, crying out in surrender."[6] An officer and thirty-eight other ranks were captured, bringing the Perth's total prisoner count to forty-five, with at least two other Germans killed.[7]

During the morning of December 5, the Cape Breton Highlanders advanced from Godo through Piangipane to come up on the Irish Regiment's left flank. A 'C' Company patrol checked that all houses immediately east of the Lamone were clear of enemy. The patrol also noted that the bridge at Villanova was blown. Germans were heavily concentrated on the river's other side, and tanks could be heard moving about.[8]

At 1400 hours, meanwhile, 'B' Company of the Westminster Regiment, supported by a squadron of Governor General's Horse Guards, came up alongside the Highlanders' left flank.[9] The Lanark and Renfrew Scottish Regiment also advanced 'B' and 'A' Companies to the river.[10] This left 5th Canadian Armoured Division holding a six-mile front of the Lamone, stretching from Traversara to Mezzano. Left of Traversara, the line was held by 1st Canadian Infantry Division. While 12th Infantry Brigade was just to hold the line to the right of 1st Division, Major General Bert Hoffmeister intended to win a crossing over the Lamone on the night of December 6, with the Perth Regiment attacking on the left and Cape Breton Highlanders on the right. The Irish Regiment would be in reserve. Even as this plan was being developed, however, corps meteorologists were predicting heavy rains in the Apennines that could render the Lamone impassable.[11]

THE HASTINGS AND Prince Edward Regiment's failure to win a crossing over the Lamone on the afternoon of December 4 had surprised
1st Division's acting commander Brigadier Desmond Smith. He realized, however, that the 'A' Company attempt had been launched with
no reconnaissance and little support in the hope of achieving surprise.

As Smith had ordered a renewed attempt, initially for 0130 hours
the following morning and then advanced to 0100 hours, surprise
was no longer possible. The Germans waited in strongly entrenched
positions concentrated on the dyke and in nearby buildings. Planning
was still rushed. With his 1st Brigade Tac HQ in transit to a location
near the river, Brigadier Allan Calder had to use 3rd Brigade's phone
to get the artillery support details from Smith. Four medium artillery
regiments would fire the initial barrage. Calder and his staff then
worked feverishly, preparing the firing plan and briefing the commanders of the Hasty Ps and Royal Canadian Regiment.[12]

Neither battalion commander had much time to plan. The Hasty Ps'
acting commander, Major Stan Ketcheson, held his Orders Group at
2000 hours. The attack would be put in by 'B' and 'C' Companies.
Medium artillery would fire concentrations along the line of the road
on the far side of the river for ten minutes prior to the attack. Then
1st Division's three field regiments would fire on the same stretch of
road with their 25-pounders for two minutes prior to the attack and
ten minutes following. The field artillery would then lift to engage
targets back from the river for another thirty minutes. Thereafter, the
guns would be on call. The assault companies were to be equipped
with both assault boats and the new Olafson bridges. Given the swift
current, the company commanders convinced Ketcheson to dispense
with the assault boats and just use Olafson bridging.[13]

The Royal Canadian Regiment's Lieutenant Colonel Jim Ritchie,
meanwhile, placed his bets on 'A' and 'B' Companies being able to
cross in assault boats to win a bridgehead. 'C' Company would then
cross by Olafson bridging. 'D' Company's job was to bring both the
assault boats and bridging materials to the river. Midnight found
'D' Company still lugging this equipment toward the river, and it was
0045 hours before 'A' and 'B' Companies reached their start line.[14]

Five minutes later, the medium artillery cut loose. At 0105 hours, Major Jim Houghton's 'A' Company on the right and 'B' Company under Major Eric Thorne to the left headed for the dyke where the assault boats were to be picked up. None had yet arrived. It was 0130 hours when 'D' Company delivered boats to Houghton's company. He sent Nos. 7 and 8 Platoons paddling across, and both were soon clearing houses close to the opposite dyke. "As soon as the boats came back," Houghton said, "I put Company HQ and 9 Platoon into them. A shell burst near my boat and killed or wounded all in it except myself. I reached the other side sans men and sans wireless set. On the far bank, I found 7 Platoon giving covering fire to the others taking on Casa Venturi." As soon as this large building was cleared, Houghton established his Tac HQ inside. The headquarters section now con- sisted of only Houghton, his runner, and a signaller lacking a wireless. Taking a No. 38 set from one platoon commander, Houghton was able to reach 'D' Company—who patched him through to Ritchie's Tac HQ. At 0215 hours, Houghton reported all company objectives secured.[15]

'B' Company had also sent two platoons across the Lamone in assault boats. Rather than wait for the assault boats' return, Captain Peder Hertzberg led his platoon to a partially destroyed railway bridge on the battalion's extreme left flank. As the men clambering across it gained the opposite shore, they were struck by a terrific mortar concentration. Hertzberg was killed. Eighteen of his twenty-one men were left either dead or wounded. Captain W.W. Hughes's platoon had, meanwhile, become entangled in a skirmish, and the officer—shot through the body—was evacuated. Despite these setbacks, by 0300 hours, both companies were firm on their objectives.[16] Twenty minutes later, 'D' Company reported one Olafson bridge installed and a second under construction. The battalion war diarist considered the operation to be "developing into a splendid success."[17]

Desperate for first-hand information, Ritchie sent Major Strome Galloway forward. Galloway took a wireless set for 'A' Company and orders for 'C' Company. Crossing on a footbridge, he soon encoun- tered 'C' Company's Captain Jimmy Wilkinson and his headquarters section. Wilkinson provided a guide to lead Galloway to Houghton's headquarters in the casa. Galloway had just delivered the wireless set to Houghton when Thorne arrived and pointed out 'B' Company's location on a map. Galloway told both officers their men were to stay put, while 'C' Company would advance 1,500 yards before digging in at dawn.

Returning to Wilkinson's position in a "soggy meadow," Galloway gave him the orders for 'C' Company. "In a parade ground manner, he saluted smartly," Galloway wrote. "His cane was tucked under his left armpit, his right hand properly poised at the rim of his helmet. I returned the compliment, my stick and cap act a duplicate of his. These little frills made the garment of war more wearable.

"I returned across the dykes, taking two docile prisoners with me, my pistol drawn and my walking stick tapping them on the shoulders to help them keep direction."[18]

Behind him, Wilkinson confidently advised battalion headquarters at 0430 hours that "his company would reach the objective in good time." He then led his men along the road while issuing a last report that "all [were] in good spirits."[19]

ABOUT 750 YARDS TO the right, meanwhile, the Hasty Ps had suffered a severe reversal shortly after reaching the dyke at 0100 hours. Flattening out on top of the dyke, Major Cliff Broad of 'B' Company heard the whistle of incoming medium artillery shells. He was half rising and shouting for his men to take cover, when the shells— fired on too low a trajectory—slammed into the dyke. "Most of the men were standing up . . . and for those who survived that initial blast, there was no cover and no place to hide," intelligence officer Lieutenant Farley Mowat wrote.

"Lying face down on the dyke, Broad stared with a despairing fascination at the luminous face of his watch, counting the seconds, the interminable seconds, until the barrage should end. Below him the earth shook and heaved and the red and yellow flashes of the shells illuminated a charnel scene."[20] When the guns fell silent, forty-eight men were dead or wounded. Both companies had been mauled, and their commanders told Ketcheson that neither could continue the attack.[21]

Ketcheson, Captain Max Porritt said later, contacted brigade at once and "stated flatly that the Regiment could not carry on." If he committed 'A' and 'D' Companies, there would be no reserve. Brigadier Allan Calder received the report with initial disbelief. But as the reality sank in, he contacted Brigadier Desmond Smith and asked either that the assault be postponed or the reserve battalion committed. Smith refused. 'A' and 'D' Companies were ordered forward.[22] Using Olafson bridging, 'D' Company crossed the Lamone at 0505 hours, and at 0530 hours Porritt's 'A' Company followed. Although 'B' Company had been reduced to platoon strength, it also entered the narrow bridgehead.[23]

FIRST LIGHT WAS approaching when 1st Division's war diarist remarked that "the attack appeared to be going well." The RCR had three companies across the Lamone and the Hasty Ps another two.[24] Brigadier Desmond Smith happily reported this to 1 Canadian Corps headquarters. Chief of Staff Brigadier George Kitching rushed to where Lieutenant General Charles Foulkes was resting in his caravan "to give him the good news. After studying the map for a moment," Kitching wrote, "he told me to drive as fast as I could to 1st Division Headquarters and order Brigadier Smith to ensure immediately that 6-pounder anti-tank guns were rafted or dragged across [the river] to give the infantry the necessary support in case of a German counter-attack."

Kitching started to leave the caravan, only to be called back. As "time was vital," Foulkes told Kitching to immediately phone Smith and give him the message. Kitching did this from the corps commander's caravan. "There was no time to waste," he later wrote. "I spoke personally to Brigadier Smith . . . and gave him the message . . . As I spoke to him, General Foulkes, who was sitting up in his bed, nodded his head to emphasize my remarks." Kitching ordered, "Get the anti-tank guns over immediately and let me know the minute they are there."[25]

Neither Kitching nor Foulkes fully comprehended the developing situation. The Lamone was running too swiftly for guns to be dragged across and there were no rafts robust enough to bear the weight of 6-pounder guns. While the RCR had been provided with two Little John anti-tank guns, the Hasty Ps had received none.[26]

In the RCR sector, 'D' Company had worked with the engineers through the night to get the footbridges installed and a raft capable of ferrying the Little Johns launched. Dragging the guns up the fifty-foot-high dykes was only possible by carving out ramps on both of their sides. It was 0430 hours before the ramps were finished and the raft floated. Both Little Johns and a jeep were ferried across. To "appreciate the task," a 'D' Company report stated, "it would be necessary to see the actual area, the heights of the dykes, the amount of digging required, the difficulty in dragging guns and jeep up the dykes so that when dawn came the men were utterly exhausted."[27]

THE SUCCESSFUL DELIVERY of the Little Johns into the RCR sector strengthened the perception that the Lamone bridgehead was consolidating smoothly. At first light, however—with fog cutting visibility to just fifty yards—German tanks and infantry counterattacked. The attack fell hard on 'C' and 'B' Companies. Captain Wilkinson's 'C' Company was advancing beyond the river, while Major Thorne's badly depleted 'B' Company had reached the raised railway on its left flank. The German infantry came pouring over the railway, and an SPG started firing through a gap carved out of it. Machine-gun positions along the top of the railway spat long bursts of fire into 'B' Company's exposed flank. In moments, Thorne's headquarters section was overrun and he was mortally wounded. The company's last platoon commander fell with a fatal wound, and all three platoon sergeants were killed or wounded. "Leaderless and reduced to less than thirty men," Major Galloway wrote, "the company as such ceased to exist and the survivors, many of them wounded, withdrew to the dyke."[28]

Sergeant Paul Hernandez, a No. 12 Platoon section leader, saw the building housing company headquarters blow up. A few minutes later, a bullet slammed into his platoon sergeant's shoulder with such force that he was flung twenty feet and landed in the middle of the road paralleling the river. With the sergeant down, Hernandez took over. Many men, like the sergeant, were wounded. Hernandez sent two runners to the destroyed company headquarters to fetch stretchers. When neither man returned, Hernandez decided to go himself.

Accompanied by a private, Hernandez soon came upon a knocked-out Jeep towing a Little John. The entire gun crew lay dead either inside the Jeep or alongside. Hernandez was just five feet from the Jeep when he saw a German ransacking it. The German responded first, drawing a pistol that clicked harmlessly when he tried firing. As the German took flight while yelling for help, the private called to Hernandez, "Shoot him." Hernandez snapped off a Thompson submachine-gun burst and the German fell dead. Suddenly, tanks rolled through a tunnel in the railway embankment. Diving into a ditch, Hernandez and the private watched them roll past. Some headed toward his platoon, while others followed the river road to penetrate deeper into the RCR lines. As Hernandez was assessing the situation, a German suddenly appeared above him. Hernandez and the private surrendered because "he was right there, so we had no choice." Both men were taken to a collection point, ferried across the Po River, and then loaded on freight cars that took them to a prison camp near Munich.[29]

'C' Company, meanwhile, had also been caught in the counterattack. Lashed by machine-gun fire from the railway embankment, Wilkinson led his men into a large stone house to make a stand. But another SPG emerged from a gap in the embankment and started knocking the building apart. Close behind, the SPG infantry put in an overwhelming assault. Wilkinson smashed his wireless set with a rifle butt as Company Sergeant Major M.R. Castello swallowed the codes. Both men were wounded and taken prisoner, as was Lieutenant L.G. Shore. Suffering two wounds, Lieutenant J.L.H. Campeau managed to escape. Sergeant John William Gray was dead, Sergeant F.G. Smith temporarily blinded by an eye wound. "Only some twelve men managed to extricate themselves and take up a new position slightly forward of 'A' Company."[30]

Many resisted bravely until their situation became hopeless, and then they surrendered. Others fought to the death. Days after the battle, the body of twenty-eight-year-old Corporal Robert Walter Russell was found in a ditch. His lone battle had been witnessed by hiding

Italian civilians. They testified that he killed or wounded thirteen Germans before finally being cut down.[31]

At 1000 hours, the RCR had just fifty-eight men of 'A' Company and remnants of 'B' and 'C' Companies in the bridgehead. An attempt by Captain J.E. Pickard's 'D' Company to cross was blocked when the Germans smothered the dyke with artillery and machine-gun fire that inflicted eleven casualties.[32]

To the right, the situation for the Hasty Ps was badly confused. 'B' Company's Major Broad had seen the counterattack maul the RCRs and reported the survivors withdrawing across the river. Hoping for more information, Major Ketcheson tried raising his 'A' and 'D' Companies by wireless but got only static.[33]

Both companies were heavily engaged in close-quarters fighting with infantry. When the sounds of approaching tanks or SPGs was heard, and with rumours swirling that the RCRs had retreated from the bridgehead, panic set in and both companies broke.[34] At 1110 hours, they were reported to have withdrawn across the Lamone.[35]

In fact, Major Houghton's 'A' Company of the RCRs was still hanging on with Nos. 7 and 9 Platoons concentrated around Casa Venturi. Houghton's headquarters and No. 8 Platoon had withdrawn across the bridge. The major had no intention of making a stand. As soon as the Germans put too much pressure on the two forward platoons, the lieutenant in charge was to fire a flare. Houghton would then lay down a smokescreen to cover their withdrawal. "Tanks and infantry came at them," Houghton said later, "and their PIATS were not effective, partly because of the heavy fog and poor visibility. I contacted the CO who confirmed my decision to pull the platoons out when they could no longer stay. Shortly after that, 7 and 9 Platoons came back using two Olafson bridges . . . and dug in on our own side of the river.

"There were still left on the enemy bank, 40-odd men of 'B' Company" of the Hasty Ps, Houghton noted. "They were dug in behind the dyke, but [high-explosive] from enemy tanks was exploding on top of the dyke . . . They stuck it out for a while and then I gave them 3 minutes of smoke to provide an opportunity for them to get out, which they did."

Houghton's final words on the fiasco were succinct: "This is an unhappy example of how a battle should not be fought."[36]

ALTHOUGH ALLIED INTELLIGENCE staff generally disparaged 114th Jäger Division's fighting ability, the counterattack launched by its Reconnaissance Battalion with supporting armour and engineer units of 356th Infanterie-Division had been expertly executed. A German divisional report noted how "the enemy bridgehead was first sealed off, then reduced, and, after particularly effective support from our own artillery, smashed."

Acting Commander-in-Chief Southwest Generaloberst Heinrich von Vietinghoff reported to Berlin that the "bridgehead over the Lamone which had been formed north-west of Russi was smashed in a determined counter-attack which was carried out in perfect co-operation with the artillery, and in which the enemy suffered considerable casualties."

In less than twelve hours, two Canadian battalions had lost 164 men. The three RCR companies that had crossed the Lamone had numbered only 205 instead of the 381 that constituted full strength. 'B' Company with 72 men had been the strongest. Only 31 came back across the river unscathed.[37] The battalion's total casualties were 29 killed or mortally wounded, 46 wounded, and 31 taken prisoner. Having attacked with equally depleted company strengths, the Hasty Ps counted 58 casualties. Forty-eight of these resulted from friendly fire.[38]

Both battalions lost more than just men. The loss of men, as Mowat wrote, "was the least of the hurt. For the first time the unit had been severely beaten in the field, and for the first time its spirit had broken. The one solid thing that had remained in the world of the infantryman had been destroyed.

"For the first time, men knew they had failed the Regiment, and in so doing knew that they had failed themselves.

"Knowledge of the failure was unbearable. It knifed into them . . . It is a measure of the appalling inner destructiveness of the failure that even in the first days of shock few of the men or the officers sought to lay the blame outside themselves. It was only by slow degrees that awareness returned, and with it the knowledge that the fault lay not alone with them, but that much of it lay on those shadowy figures in authority who had forced them to destroy, with their own hands, the one true thing that had remained in the chaos of their world."[39]

"The Lamone *débâcle*," Major Galloway declared, "was not the fault of the fighting troops. It was the result of stupid high-level planning by some planners unfamiliar with the Italian terrain and the realities of dykeland warfare . . . The Lamone operation had been a ghastly failure . . . The planning at Brigade, Division or somewhere could not have been worse. Both battalions were in a state of trauma. Somewhere, to shield the fault of others, the rumour was started that the troops had fought badly."[40]

Blame had to be placed. On December 9, Brigadier Allan Calder was sacked, reduced in rank to lieutenant colonel and sent to England. In a letter to recently promoted General Harry Crerar, Foulkes scapegoated Calder. "I thoroughly investigated this party and I have come to the conclusion it failed mainly because of the lack of inspired leadership and ability to command on the part of Calder. The consolidation was not properly buttoned up, and Calder was unable to read the battle properly and take the necessary action with his reserve when things were going badly . . . I'm afraid that Calder will not do as a brigade commander."[41]

Galloway considered the treatment of Calder "particularly brutal . . . Calder was a cool, calm and collected Brigade Commander. His experience was somewhat limited, as he had his command for only four months, but his subordinates had no apparent complaint about his low-key leadership and abilities during the breaking of the Gothic Line and subsequent successful operations leading to the capture of Rimini and the difficult succession of attacks which brought the Brigade up to the Lamone's bloody banks."[42]

After handing 1st Division command to Major General Harry Foster, who had arrived on December 6, Brigadier Desmond Smith was given 1st Brigade. Many officers in both battalions considered Smith the chief culprit behind the Lamone attack, so this was a bitter pill to swallow. The "Acting Divisional Commander became our Brigadier," Galloway wrote. "We had not deserved that. But such are the fortunes of war."

Not content to cease the cull at higher levels, Foulkes decided heads had to roll within both battalions. On December 7, the RCR's battalion liaison officer to 1st Brigade asked Lieutenant Colonel Ritchie "if he had an extra RCR cap badge and extra cloth shoulder flashes. He said a senior officer was visiting Brigade and had asked for a set. Ritchie said he was delighted to provide them and sent his batman to his kit bag to get the spare officer's pattern badge and flashes he kept there." When he asked the identity of the officer seeking these items, the liaison officer avoided answering. "Next morning he found out. The new Brigade Commander arrived with Ritchie's replacement [Lieutenant Colonel William Reid] in tow. He had belonged to another regiment in the 5th Division. Now he wore Ritchie's badges and flashes and was our new Commanding Officer! Ritchie left by jeep . . . within an hour . . . Ritchie, upon whose shoulders no blame could be laid, was fired in a most callous way."[43]

Had Major Ketcheson not been seriously wounded by a mortar round on December 9, he likely would also have been relieved.[44]

AS THE KNIVES had started being unsheathed by higher command in the late afternoon of December 5, the grim mundanity of war continued. The chief concern was that bridging in front of the Hasty Ps and RCRs still spanned the Lamone and could be used for German infiltration. Accordingly, brigade ordered their destruction.

The RCR immediately set about blowing their two Olafson bridges. Lieutenant W.C. Watson's pioneer platoon provided demolition parties. It was a dangerous task, for the Germans were immediately opposite and to actually collapse each span, one charge had to be emplaced twenty yards from the enemy positions. The right-hand bridge was easily destroyed, but when the pioneers started work on the left-hand bridge, the Germans opened up with small-arms fire and threw grenades at the men. Nevertheless, with a party of eight men, one manning a Bren gun, providing covering fire, Corporal Laurence Gibbins set out to destroy the bridge single-handedly. The moment Gibbins started crossing the dyke, the "enemy burst into activity, and the whole river was swept by heavy machine-gun fire. Paying no heed to this storm of lead," the citation for his subsequent Military Medal stated, "this imperturbable soldier slid down the dyke to the river's edge. As he did so, several grenades were tossed into the water. Three of the covering party were wounded, but [Gibbins] reached the bridge unharmed. He ran to the centre of the 45-foot span, placed the mine, and prepared the bridge for demolition. Meanwhile bullets and grenades fell all about him, but [Gibbins] succeeded in attaching the charge and lighting the fuse. Then rising to his feet, with the enemy making desperate attempts to kill him, he made his way up the dyke and succeeded in sliding to safety on our side just as the charge went off, destroying the bridge."[45]

Having resumed command of the Hasty Ps in the late morning, Lieutenant Colonel Don Cameron had spent several hours in conference with Ketcheson and the company commanders, seeking to understand the disaster that had befallen the regiment. He then set about planning the destruction of the regiment's Olafson bridges. The Hasty Ps pioneers tried to reach the bridges under cover of darkness at 2020 hours, but were driven back by heavy mortar fire. Cameron ordered another attempt at 0110 hours on December 6, but mortaring again forced the pioneers back. A standing patrol was positioned near the bridging, Lieutenant Mowat wrote, "to ensure that the enemy would not cross it."[46]

The expectation was that there would be a renewed attempt to win bridgeheads across the Lamone on the night of December 6, and plans were developed in both 1st Division's and 5th Division's sectors to do so. These were put on hold, however, when corps meteorologists reported that such bad weather was expected in the Apennines that the rivers might once again become impassable. "Not only was there the danger of a rise on the Lamone, which might cause great difficulty in the attack, but there was a danger of roads and bridges over the Montone being washed out. Beyond the Lamone, the water obstacles athwart the line of advance were more thickly concentrated than any others previously encountered. The strongly dyked Naviglio Canal (which linked Faenza to the sea), flanked on either side by small drainage canals—the Fosso Vecchio and the Fosso Munio— and further to the northwest the formidable areas of the flood-banked

Senio, all paralleled one another within a zone of three or four miles," one army report concluded.

Considering these dire predictions, British Eighth Army's Lieutenant General Richard McCreery told Lieutenant General Charles Foulkes to stand 1 Canadian Corps down "until such time as the operations could be ensured of reasonable success." On December 7, McCreery visited corps headquarters and then convened a meeting with Foulkes and his divisional commanders at 1st Division's headquarters. "It was decided that because the rain, particularly in the mountains, was causing the rivers to rise, thus increasing the difficulties of bridging, the operation would have to be postponed until the rivers had dropped."[47]

As 11th Brigade's Brigadier Ian Johnston wrote in a message to his battalion commanders, "The Army Commander says he will not have troops fighting the weather as well as the enemy." Until conditions improved, the corps would confine itself to active patrolling and reconnaissance along the Lamone and to conducting small actions against the few enemy pockets still found east of it.[48]

In truth, the enforced pause gave the front-line troops a badly needed rest and a chance to reorganize. For the RCR and the Hasty Ps, it was a challenge to find reinforcements to return rifle companies to anywhere near full strength. The RCR, Galloway wrote, "or what was left of it, clung to the near dyke and reorganized as best it could." There were still insufficient men to form four companies, so 'C' Company was blended in with support company personnel and branded 'X' Company.[49]

On December 6, as 'X' Company was establishing itself in a building facing the Lamone, an SPG opened up from the other bank. Several rapid shots collapsed the building. Private Douglas Lloyd Best was killed and three other regimental "old timers" were wounded. The following day, thirty-four reinforcements consisting of barbers, cooks, and shoemakers from the battalion's rear echelon were brought in, as Galloway noted in his diary, "to reinforce our shattered battalion."[50]

PART THREE

MONTONE TO THE SENIO

16

Exiled to Italy

BEING TRANSFERRED FROM Northwest Europe to Italy did not strike Major General Harry Foster as a career step in the right direction. Since the beginning of the war, his climb up the promotion ladder had been steady. The first-born son of Major General Gilbert Lafayette Foster—Director General of Military Services since February 11, 1918—Harry Wickwire Foster had been born in Halifax shortly after midnight on April 2, 1902. According to family lore, the timing was deliberate. Gilbert "Laffy" Foster had declared, "I'll not have our firstborn arrive on April Fools!" His wife, Janie, née Wickwire, managed to hold the baby in check until the clock chimed midnight.

A second son, Gilbert Lafayette, followed on February 16, 1905. While the two brothers were close, they were polar opposites. Harry's school performance was adequate, but he never excelled and often seemed aloof. "Gil," as his father noted, outpaced Harry in "brains, ability, and personality."[1] Both desired army careers, which meant attending Royal Military College in Kingston.

Gil's academic record ensured entry, but Harry's prospects were uncertain. To tip the odds, his father cashed in on a personal friendship with RMC's Commandant Archibald Cameron Macdonell. Reluctantly, Macdonell agreed to accept Harry, but at a third-and-final-year level. This would place Harry a year ahead of Gil, avoiding competition for popularity and academic achievement. Macdonell insisted on one caveat. Harry must enroll in McGill University's first-year science program. If he achieved an 80 per cent average, Harry would be welcomed into RMC.

Although he averaged only 67 per cent at McGill and failed one course, Macdonell opted not to jeopardize his friendship with Harry's father. In 1922, Harry was enrolled at the third-year level. Five months of studies did nothing to justify Macdonell's leniency. Efforts "satisfactory, albeit uneven," Macdonell wrote, despite Harry's failing grades in physics, chemistry, and English.

Academically lacklustre, Harry had also failed to fit into RMC's culture. Cadets, as one graduate noted, were "expected to grin and bear the consequences of military life." A cadet's demeanour was considered an accurate reflection of his potential ability to inspire and lead soldiers. Most of RMC's military instructors were veterans of the Western Front. They generally thought sad sacks made poor officers. Macdonell noted that Harry was "a fine type, but must cultivate cheerfulness."[2]

A classmate of Gil's, Major General Chris Vokes considered "Harry . . . a dour sonofabitch . . . He was a distant second in everything to his younger brother."[3]

"This cadet does not begin to do himself justice," Macdonell bemoaned at the first semester's end. His conduct was "fair." But he has "been slacking and drifting through life, not getting anywhere . . . Grade 'A' in Riding, 'C' in P.T., 'D' in Drill and Musketry. He could easily be 'A' in each one." He also disappointed peers. The December 1923 yearbook described Harry as "to some extent taking things too easily. When he wants to he can play a good game."

But Harry didn't *want to*. He was not interested and withdrew in July 1924. By withdrawing rather than failing RMC's third year, he still qualified to become a commissioned officer. Foster quickly joined the Lord Strathcona's Horse cavalry regiment.[4] With the regiment based in Calgary, he escaped both academia and his brother's shadow. The latter was destined to serve with an eastern Canadian regiment.

Foster proved ideally suited to regular army service. By the time he was promoted to captain in 1939, Foster was considered a rising star.

In late 1939, he attended Staff College—a necessary rung in the climb toward eventual brigade or divisional command. The war brought swift promotions—lieutenant colonel in 1941 and command in Britain of the newly formed 4th Princess Louise Dragoon Guards. By 1942, he was general staff officer 1 at 1st Canadian Infantry Division—another key appointment that provided staff management experience. Later that year, Foster took command of the Highland Light Infantry. This provided experience in leading infantry. Promotion to brigadier and command of 7th Canadian Infantry Brigade followed in 1943. Soon after assuming this duty, Foster returned to Canada to temporarily command Canadian forces committed to the Kiska Island invasion in the Aleutians.

As retaking the neighbouring island of Attu in a bloody campaign in May 1943 had left 1,000 American and about 2,500 Japanese troops dead, the Kiska operation was expected to be similarly costly. But the Japanese had since secretly abandoned Kiska, so the August 15 landings were unopposed. "I feel bloody silly having come all this way for nothing," Foster confided to his diary." The Americans, however, awarded him the Legion of Merit.

Returning to England, he resumed command of 7th Brigade and led it ashore at Juno Beach on June 6, 1944. As Foster proved to be a tough, hard-charging combat leader, First Canadian Army's Lieutenant General Harry Crerar marked him for a divisional command. On August 21, 1944, Foster replaced George Kitching as 4th Canadian Armoured Division's commander and led it competently through the Channel Port and Scheldt Estuary campaigns. As fighting wound down in the Scheldt, 11 Canadian Corps's Lieutenant General Guy Simonds took leave to Britain and appointed Foster acting corps commander during his absence. Being the second-highest-ranking officer in First Canadian Army for even a short period was a heady experience—dashed within a week when Crerar ordered him off to Italy and 1st Infantry Division command. Vokes would take over 4th Armoured Division. "A straight switch?" a dismayed Foster asked.

"A straight switch," Crerar agreed.

Foster thought he must have failed in some way. "May I ask why, sir?" Crerar's expression became more dour than usual. "It's rather a complicated story," he replied. Crerar was not going to tell Foster that he made the decision because of the bad blood between Vokes and Lieutenant General Charles Foulkes.

Going first to England, Foster dined with Vokes. "For one fucking week I was a lieutenant general and 1 Corps commander!" Vokes grumbled. "And then that purse-lipped sonofabitch showed up and took it all away."

"How the hell do you think I feel?" Foster replied. "I was sitting with command of 11 Corps when 'Uncle Harry' invited me to dinner. By the end of the evening I had lost the corps, my division, and was exiled to Italy to serve under Charles Foulkes!"

"Harry," Vokes offered, "you'll like Italy. It has good food, willing ladies, and pretty country—whenever it stops raining."

Foster's diary entry the day he arrived in Italy observed, "For my money it's not as good as Holland. But what could be?"

The immediate task was to establish himself as 1st Division's undisputed leader. "The division's three brigades consisted of an armoured car and ten infantry regiments," he wrote. "For the past 18 months they had been in the line more or less continuously. The regiments and battalions were tired, under strength and, in a few cases, badly led. A clique had developed between senior officers, starting with Vokes and [Major General Bert] Hoffmeister. It carried down to the regimental level. [Lieutenant General Tommy] Burns, the perfect staff officer, had lost control—if he ever had control—and the respect of his battlefield commanders. Foulkes said he intended to straighten the matter out quickly. He wanted my help . . . which seemed to me the beginning of another clique: Foulkes and I against everybody else."

Firing officers after 1st Infantry Brigade's December 5 failure on the Lamone River was the first step. But Foster disliked the overall strategic situation. "It was more of a standoff than a stalemate," he thought, "each side prepared to do a lot of shooting but without the devotion necessary for serious battle. But then perhaps my opinion had been coloured by the Battle of Normandy."

Aligning too closely with Foulkes, Foster would surely alienate himself from the division's veteran officers. Foster thought Foulkes competent enough. He also believed that their shared experience fighting in the Scheldt Estuary dyke-and-river country well-suited them to lead operations in the Emilia–Romagna. It was impossible, however, to set aside his dislike for Foulkes. "I thought Foulkes suffered from a sense of inferiority. He was not liked by any senior British or Canadian officer that I ever saw . . . To my knowledge he had few friends and, in a way, I felt sorry for him. He reminded me of someone who, knowing that he has overstepped his abilities, tries to bluff his way through . . . Our personalities clashed!"[5]

Foster was wise to distance himself from Foulkes. Replacing Vokes was not going to be easy. "When Chris went," Loyal Edmonton Regiment's Lieutenant Colonel Jim Stone said, "I thought I had lost a great friend. We had not seen eye to eye, but got along. We were both opinionated and didn't like backing down. Foster was a fine guy, but not flamboyant like Chris."[6]

Princess Patricia's Canadian Light Infantry's Lieutenant Syd Frost had welcomed the removal of Lieutenant General Tommy Burns, but losing Vokes was a nasty surprise. "He had been the 1st Division in body and spirit ever since he had assumed command in southern Italy. We all loved his rough, down-to-earth, soldierly approach to battle, even if at times we called him names for kicking us in the tail to fight harder."[7]

WHILE 1ST BRIGADE HAD been bloodily repulsed at the Lamone River on 1st Canadian Infantry Division's left, v British Corps and 11 Polish Corps were more successful on the night of December 4–5. Though operating in the rugged Apennine foothills with few roads for supporting armoured use, 46th British Infantry Division and 3rd Polish Carpathian Division had little trouble crossing the Lamone. And despite belatedly stiff resistance from 305th Infanterie-Division, by December 7 these divisions were midway between the Lamone and Senio Rivers.

Events during this period had semi-paralyzed Acting Commander-in-Chief Southwest Generaloberst Heinrich von Vietinghoff. All of British Eighth Army, from the Adriatic coast to the Apennines, appeared to be bearing down on LXXVI Panzer Korps. Unsure where the gravest threat lay, Von Vietinghoff refused to commit reserves anywhere. Not until December 8 did he recognize the temporary lull on the 1 Canadian Corps front. Knowing 305th Infanterie-Division was hard pressed, Von Vietinghoff drew 90th Panzer Grenadier Division out from behind Bologna and wedged it in south of Faenza between the 305th and 26th Panzer Divisions. This enabled the 305th to shorten its line. Panzer Grenadier doctrine called for aggressive counterattacks at the earliest possible moment. No sooner had they deployed than the panzer grenadiers struck the 46th Division violently across its front on December 9. The British, however, broke the counterattacks and mauled the Germans. Day's end saw the 90th and 305th Divisions so battered that a hard push by v Corps could have sent them reeling. The 46th Division's losses, however, had left it too weak to capitalize on the situation. Lacking reinforcements, Lieutenant General Charles Keightley ordered v Corps to cease offensive operations and regroup. Much of v Corps's problem stemmed from its reliance on a single seven-mile-long road that ran south from Highway 9 to move all supplies and reinforcements. In some places, the road deteriorated to nothing more than a rough track. A journey from one end to the other took twelve hours. As a result, the relief of the 46th Division was not completed until December 14.[8]

On the 1 Canadian Corps front, meanwhile, Foulkes was chomping at the bit to cross the Lamone but was held in check by the weather. When the break finally came, he had assigned 1st Infantry Division's new assault to be made by 3rd Brigade and the 5th Armoured Division effort by 11th Infantry Brigade. Both divisional commanders were told to make their own plans. Each decided on a uniquely different approach.

Neither underestimated the challenge. The Lamone was a formidable challenge. And beyond it, the country grimly duplicated what the Canadians had faced during the advance from the Montone River to the Lamone. The only significant difference that 12th Infantry Brigade staff saw was that between the Lamone and Senio Rivers there were more obstacles. Four watercourses were identified, "each within 500 yards of the next. These were the drainage ditches Fosso Vetro and Fosso Vecchio, the wider Canale Naviglio, and the Fosso

Munio. Due to the bareness of the flat ground and the height of the embankments, especially in the case of the Canale Naviglio, the enemy had a commanding view of all ground to his front. West of the Canale Naviglio cover was more plentiful."

In 5th Division's sector, only two roads ran from the Lamone to the Naviglio, and all their bridges were blown. With no cover, road movement and attempts to install bridges were certain to serve as magnets for German artillery and mortar fire.[9]

Eighth Army usually solved this problem with lavish use of its own artillery. Normal practice was to support any contested river crossing with a vast weight of guns battering the opposing shore. Such a repetitive strategy naturally served to alert the Germans to where the attack was to come. Realizing this, Major General Bert Hoffmeister decided to do things differently. Two 11th Brigade battalions—the Cape Breton Highlanders and Perth Regiment—would cross silently in assault boats. And on either side, 5th Armoured Brigade (to the right at Mezzano) and 12th Infantry Brigade (on the left at Traversara) would create a holy din to divert German attention.[10]

Although opting to use artillery, Foster's approach was also novel. As 3rd Brigade must cross where 1st Brigade had been defeated, surprise was impossible; the Germans would be waiting. To account for this, the divisional artillery plan was to open with a timed program of artillery concentrations—called Bingos—beginning fifty-five minutes prior to the attack and continuing for another thirty minutes. There was nothing unique about this part; the twist was that when the Bingos ended, the guns would cease firing for twenty minutes. If the Germans responded as usual, they would emerge from their shelters and set up to slaughter the Canadians crossing the river. The artillery, however, would then come back to life and, it was hoped, catch the Germans in the open.[11]

With two divisions attacking, the corps assault stretched across a four-mile front. In 5th Division's sector, 11th Brigade's attack would face the villages of Villanova and Borgo Villanova, two and three miles upstream from Mezzano respectively. The 1st Division assault would occur on a two-and-a-half-mile line running from Traversara on the right to a point nine hundred yards south of the

Russi–Bagnacavallo railway. To cause confusion, immediately to the division's left, the 43rd Indian Lorried Infantry Brigade in v Corps's sector would launch a mock attack shortly before the Canadian drive began.[12]

ON DECEMBER 7, I CANADIAN Corps recorded a quarter inch of rainfall. By evening, however, the heavy clouds had cleared, and the following day no precipitation was recorded.[13] "During late afternoon," 1st Division's war diarist reported, "a slight wind chased the clouds away and the evening and night were clear and fresh and we were treated to a starry sky." Although dubious that the improved weather would last, he noted on December 9, "the forecasters are optimistic about the near future and it wouldn't surprise us one bit if the op was resumed very soon."

The next morning, Foster convened an Orders Group in the divisional officer's mess and announced that the Lamone River would be crossed at 2130 hours that night by 3rd Brigade, with 1st Brigade's 48th Highlanders of Canada attached.[14] Hoffmeister simultaneously delivered a briefing at 11th Brigade's headquarters, scheduling the 5th Division assault for 1930 hours.[15]

To support 11th Brigade's assault, Hoffmeister placed the Westminster Regiment, tanks of the British Columbia Dragoons, the 16th Battery of 4th Anti-Tank Regiment, two platoons of 4.2-inch mortars from the Princess Louise Fusiliers, the engineers of both 10th and 14th Field Companies, and the divisional artillery under Brigadier Ian Johnston's direct command.[16] Because of the attack's silent nature, the artillery would come into play only when surprise was lost. At that time, either the Cape Breton Highlanders' or Perth Regiment's commander could send the signal "Bedlam" to the gunners with target coordinates.

At 1730 hours, the Perth's 'A' and 'D' Companies moved to their forming-up position about 1,500 yards from the Lamone. 'D' Company was to cross into the western edge of Borgo Villanova, while 'A' Company would be a hundred yards to the left.[17] About a half mile right of the Perths, the Highlanders' 'C' and 'D' Companies would cross next to Villanova.[18]

Reaching the river was anything but easy. With the Perth's 'D' Company, Private Stan Scislowski watched sympathetically as the battalion's support company personnel carried the collapsible canvas assault boats forward. The night was eerily still—not so much as a rifle shot disturbed the silence. Each boat was "heavy and cumbersome and had to be manhandled . . . across [mucky] fields . . . that sucked at the rubber galoshes everyone now wore. Halfway to the Lamone . . . the unwieldy . . . boats had to be lifted over [a] wire fence and then brought up as silently as possible" to the dyke.[19]

As the infantry gained the river, elements of 5th Division on both flanks let loose at 1845 hours with the rackety diversion. Facing Mezzano, where Highway 14 crossed the Lamone, the Lord Strathcona's Horse's Lieutenant Colonel Jim McAvity signalled his men to get "almost every weapon . . . firing: LMGs, dismounted Browning MGs, and rifles cracked off simultaneously all along the river dyke, while 9 troops of Shermans, only a few hundred yards from the river, fired on fixed lines on the roads leading away from the river on the enemy side, at suspected enemy HQs, mortar and gun positions—firing both 75-mm and .30-inch Brownings. The 105-mm battery fired . . . at a rapid rate . . . One troop of 40-mm Bofors was attached to the regiment for the night and they fired two streams of brilliant tracer—about 500 yards apart, parallel to the highway at Mezzano.

"Judging from the amount of defensive fire laid by the enemy, our object was certainly achieved. Major [R.J.] Graham estimated that over 200 mortar bombs landed along the 'A' Squadron stretch of road in one short session; from his slit trench behind a wire fence, he reported on the air that the fragments going through it sounded like, 'Home on the Range' played on a steel guitar! We were very lucky, however, and . . . received no casualties on that night."[20]

Both infantry battalions launched assault boats right on time. The Highlanders drew some scattered gunfire from the opposite side, but this seemed not to signal an alerted enemy. All 'D' Company was across the Lamone by 1955 hours.[21] As the company deployed over the dyke, it came under heavy mortar fire and its commander gave the "Bedlam" signal at 1952. The response was immediate, as "the full weight of the divisional artillery . . . [came] down on the perimeter bridgehead."22

'C' Company's crossing was slower because of insufficient boat numbers. But the company was fully across at 2045 hours. Having come upon a small rubber dinghy, Corporal Stan Watts and two privates of No. 13 Platoon were actually the first men across. The platoon's commander, Lieutenant Joe MacDonald, soon joined them. Seeing a light in a house on Villanova's outskirts, he knocked on the door and said, "Open up—*Canadesi!*" A large German swung the door open. "Oh-oh," MacDonald said, while shoving his rifle barrel into the man's stomach. Seconds later, 'C' Company had lined up eleven of the forty-three prisoners it was to take over a two-hour period.23

By 2140 hours, both companies had secured their objectives in Villanova. Lieutenant Colonel Boyd Somerville fed 'A' Company across. Its objective was the Via Aguta, a road about a thousand yards from the Lamone. At 2359 hours, 'A' Company was just short of the road, the battalion war diarist wrote, and was "having trouble with SP guns . . . running up and down the road between their platoons, firing at whatever they could see." Somerville ordered the PIAT anti-tank launcher section with 'C' Company to intervene and also dispatched 'B' Company to the Via Aguta.24

Left of the Highlanders, the Perths had lost the element of surprise just as 'D' Company's assault boats were being unfolded by the river's edge. Two "MG42s shattered the silence with bursts that ripped into the launching site," Scislowski wrote. "Although the range was almost point-blank only four men went down in the first two bursts as the boat-carriers scrambled for their lives. The enemy, alerted now to the assault, brought other weapons to bear, and from their converging streams of fire it looked almost certain the attack would die without a single boat getting across." Half of No. 16 Platoon, however, piled into a boat "and launched themselves into the fast-flowing current, pumping their oars with a skill they never knew they had. Behind them came the other half. Both boatloads made it to the far shore unscathed." The men scrambled up the dyke, "with guns blazing." Two men fell dead or wounded, but the rest crossed the dyke.

Two other boats, meanwhile, had gone adrift and were moving rapidly downstream. Ignoring machine-gun fire tearing up the ground around him, Company Sergeant Major Earl Weaver ran along the water's edge, grabbed hold of one boat, and steadied it while men of No. 17 Platoon boarded.

When No. 16 Platoon silenced the two German machine guns, the three remaining boats were soon shuttling back and forth, and the rest of the company crossed unmolested.[25] By 2030 hours, both 'D' and 'A' Companies were on the outskirts of Borgo Villanova. Lieutenant Colonel Maurice Andrew sent 'B' Company across the river to "mop up" the village. Half an hour later, 'C' Company reached the other shore. Resistance was easily eliminated or driven off.[26]

Scislowski and Private Gerry Curran formed the PIAT team for 'D' Company's No. 18 Platoon. They had almost lost the weapon while climbing out of their assault boat. Fumbling around for scattered PIAT bombs, Scislowski's helmet fell off and disappeared into the darkness. Before the crossing, the temperature had been slightly above freezing. Now it seemed to have dropped ten degrees, and frost whitened the damp fields. Three hundred yards from the Lamone, No. 18 Platoon swung to the right and followed a shallow drainage ditch that ran behind a row of houses.

Suddenly, and inexplicably to Scislowski, all the men around him stopped and sat down. As far as he knew, no order had been given. It was as if the platoon just ran out of steam. Then from the backyard of a house fifty yards away, a German mortar crew started firing. Scislowski "could see the silhouettes of the crew hard at work picking [rounds] up and laying them in. They were sitting ducks. Like everyone else, I [was] wondering why we showed no aggressive spirit. We sat there with cold asses and frozen trigger-fingers as the Jerries, suddenly out of ammunition, calmly packed up onto a horse-drawn wagon and went away at a gallop. What a beautiful opportunity to knock out a mortar team, and we let it go by! Somebody fumbled. Hell! We all fumbled! We sat there with our fingers up our asses and did sweet fuck-all. What a lousy bunch of infantrymen we turned out to be! Not what you'd call one of our prouder moments. No sooner did the Jerries disappear down the road than the command to advance came. Too late!"

'D' Company soon dug in on the east side of Via Cocchi around four low-slung houses. Borgo Villanova was about a quarter mile behind and being heavily shelled. Scislowski and Curran were just finishing a four-foot-deep slit trench when three men ran along the road shouting that Tiger tanks were approaching. Scislowski squeezed down behind the PIAT, ready to take on the behemoths. If he hit the frontal armour, the bomb would bounce harmlessly off. Hit the hull under the suspension then. Or let it pass and punch the bomb into the engine compartment.

Scislowski could hear the Tiger now. "Sounding very much like it was long overdue for a lubrication job, the tank lumbered on towards us." Another PIAT team engaged it first while the tank was still beyond Scislowski's range. Several hits were scored. Unable to pinpoint the PIAT team, the tank crew held fire, turned around, and trundled off into the night. Other than intermittent small-arms fire, the Perths spent the rest of the night undisturbed. "The battle of the Lamone River, which turned out to be little more than a skirmish, had come to an end, with the regiment suffering only eleven dead and a little less than twice that in wounded. A cheap price to pay for the quick victory—but only in the greater scheme of things. For the loved ones of those who died, it was a price far beyond what they could afford," Scislowski mused.[27]

WHILE 11TH BRIGADE HAD been attacking, 1st Division's 3rd Brigade had watched the artillery barrage pound the Lamone's opposite bank and then lift for the twenty-minute lull intended to lure the Germans out of their shelters. Twenty minutes later, the guns fired again. At 2130 hours, three battalions—48th Highlanders of Canada on the left, West Nova Scotia Regiment in the centre, and Carleton and York Regiment on the right—headed for the river. Each was equipped with assault boats and Olafson bridging.

The two flank battalions gained the Lamone without incident. But in the centre—with the Godo–Bagnacavallo Road to the right and the railway line on the left—the Germans had anticipated the attack.

'C' and 'A' Companies had just headed for the river when heavy mortar fire rained down. Caught in the midst of it, Major Gordon Leo French McNeil's 'C' Company suffered thirty casualties. "It had to reorganize and was temporarily out of the show," a West Nova account reported.

'A' Company, under Captain D.I. Rice, fared better, with only two casualties before gaining the river next to the destroyed railroad bridge. Heavy fire from supporting Vickers machine guns forced the Germans to keep low, and the engineers were soon pushing out Olafson bridging to facilitate the crossing. At 2200 hours, with the bridge halfway across the river, the swift current suddenly overturned it and swept it away. Having counted on the bridging, Rice was now forced to send a platoon for assault boats.[28]

At battalion headquarters, the situation seemed confused. The mortar fire had severed all phone lines, so reports reaching Lieutenant Colonel Al Saunders were sketchy. At 2230 hours, 'C' Company reported having pulled back from the river because of its losses and continuing heavy mortar fire. 'A' Company was still bringing up assault boats. Then Brigadier Paul Bernatchez sent a report at 2300 hours that the other two battalions "had made the crossing [while] meeting little opposition." On the West Nova's front, however, resistance seemed to be stiffening. When a 'D' Company patrol attempted to cross by clambering over the rubble of the railway bridge, it was driven back by heavy machine-gun fire that inflicted two casualties.

Bernatchez arrived at the battalion's headquarters at 0055 hours on December 11 to assess the situation. After Saunders explained what he knew, the brigadier told him to have 'B' and 'D' Companies "attain their objectives" by passing though the respective bridgeheads established by the Carletons and 48th Highlanders.[29]

Given the intense resistance the West Novas had met, the lack of opposition directed at the other two battalions was a welcome surprise. Crossing, however, had been no easy matter. In the Carletons' sector, events had been touch and go at first. 'D' and 'B' Companies had led. The men, already burdened with weapons, ammunition, and equipment, dragged the assault boats six hundred yards through ankle-deep mud. Even greater effort was required to haul them up the thirty-foot-high dyke and slide them thirty-five feet down the other slope to the water's edge.

During its approach, 'B' Company came under intense small-arms and mortar fire that slowed its progress. Gaining the Lamone right on schedule, 'D' Company launched two platoons. Although two machine guns were firing from positions directly across the river, their bursts passed over the soldiers' heads and seemed more directed at the pioneer platoon bringing Olafson bridging over the dyke.

The swift current immediately carried the boats downstream. Anticipating that this would happen, the Carletons had attached ropes to both ends of each boat. As the boats crossed, men paid out the lines to haul them back to the correct landing site. Both platoons spilled out of the boats, quickly climbed the dyke, and eliminated the two machine-gun positions with grenades.[30]

Major Rowland Horsey reported a successful crossing at 2148 hours.[31] When the two lead platoons hesitated on the top of the dyke to catch their breath, however, another machine gun opened fire from next to the ruined Godo–Bagnacavallo road bridge. As the men started going to ground, Horsey stood tall and shouted for them to follow him. Plunging down the landward slope, the two platoons cut through the German positions. Some enemy surrendered. The rest fled.[32] Horsey led two platoons through to the company objective a thousand yards up the road, while leaving the third to mop up any overlooked strongpoints.[33] This proved a simple task, the trick with the artillery having clearly achieved its purpose. "I have never seen so many wounded, maimed and dead Germans in another area of similar size," he wrote. "As we extended the bridgehead . . . we saw a good many killed by our arty fire, which after lifting from the river banks, had been laid on against possible counter attacking forces ahead of us."[34]

'B' Company, meanwhile, had also crossed the Lamone. By 2221 hours, its commander reported capturing prisoners. Deciding the moment had come to commit the entire battalion, Lieutenant Colonel Jack Ensor ordered 'A' Company over. By 2242 hours, this company had paddled across, scaled the dyke, and was consolidating in front of it. 'C' Company soon followed.[35]

While the rifle companies had been winning the bridgehead, the pioneers faced a hard task launching Olafson bridging. As they dragged the materials over the dyke, machine-gun fire wounded seven men. Among these was the platoon's commander, Lieutenant Mal Brown, who suffered his third wound. Despite their losses, the pioneers launched the bridge, only to have it overturned by the current so that one end sank. Not until daylight would they be able to rectify the situation and get the bridge operational.

The uncanny failure of the Olafson bridging—which had been successfully deployed in several contested crossings since its inception—proved to have been the fault of an adaptation. A shortage of kapok material had led to cork—five times less buoyant than kapok—being substituted to provide flotation. But with the swift currents and steep banks providing a difficult shoreline for anchoring, the cork floats' buoyancy proved insufficient.[36]

In the 48th Highlanders' sector, Captain Bill Leadbeater's 'B' Company was to have used the bridging on the right flank. But reconnaissance patrols on the night of December 9 reported that the bridge's forty-five-foot span was at least one fifteen-foot length too short for the bridge to be launched in that sector unless the river dropped. Accordingly, Lieutenant Colonel Don Mackenzie decided to have both 'A' and 'B' Companies cross in the former's sector. This was on 3rd Brigade's extreme left flank, where the 1st Division boundary met that of v Corps's 43rd Indian Lorried Infantry Brigade. Here the river was believed to be a little narrower and the bridge might work. If not, then both companies would just have to get over in the assault craft assigned to 'A' Company.[37]

Captain George Beal and two platoons of 'A' Company launched on schedule. Fifteen minutes later, he reported that they were across the dyke and that both Nos. 8 and 9 Platoons were also across and heading for their objectives.[38] That good news was followed almost immediately by the bad news that the Olafson bridging was still one span too short. Mackenzie ordered 'B' Company to fall back on the plan of using 'A' Company's boats.

By 2215 hours, all of 'A' Company was across the Lamone and reporting little opposition and many prisoners taken—Beal was, in fact, sending Germans back on the boats returning to the eastern bank. Leadbeater's men moved fast, the entire company across by 2230 hours. Then, just after midnight, 'C' Company entered the bridgehead. 'B' Company moved up alongside the raised railway and dug in on either side of the road that followed the river. 'A' Company was a short distance off to the left. Mackenzie was just starting to relax when Leadbeater reported a self-propelled gun (SPG) approaching on the road from the north. "The gun ran down the road, right through the company position and apparently turned around and came back up," the 48th Highlanders' war diarist reported. Leadbeater's men were waiting and hit it with a PIAT round, which failed to stop it. The SPG "disappeared up the road."

At 0200 hours, Bernatchez arrived to arrange for the company of West Novas to cross into the 48th's bridgehead. After that, the Royal 22e Régiment would follow with two companies and begin the advance to Bagnacavallo.[39]

By the time the West Nova's 'D' Company arrived, two of the three assault boats had been sunk by German shellfire. With only one boat, 'D' Company's crossing was "difficult and slow." The battalion's 'B' and 'A' Companies had, meanwhile, shifted to the Carleton and York sector and were crossing there. The badly battered 'C' Company was left to secure the West Nova side of the river.

Once across the Lamone, 'D' Company followed the river road to the raised railway. Shelling inflicted several casualties, and then the embankment and top of the railway was found to be heavily laced with mines, which injured more men. Finally crossing the railway and entering the battalion's assigned sector of the bridgehead, the company assaulted two large buildings. Taking about eight prisoners, the company reported it was consolidating at 0340 hours. At 0235 hours, meanwhile, 'B' Company had led the way across in the Carleton sector and started working along the road toward a building that had been 'C' Company's objective. 'A' Company soon joined 'B' Company, advancing through the ground between the road and riverbank.

As 'B' Company moved into the open, two SPGs tried to overpower it but were knocked out by its PIAT teams. Coming in from behind,

'A' Company overran one German dugout after another, all of which had commanding positions for firing across the river.[40] Every twenty feet or so, the West Novas came to deep and strongly timbered dugouts in the riverbank that would have been impervious to artillery fire and were well equipped—most even having electric lighting.[41] Together the two companies bagged eighteen prisoners and "killed a fair few" Germans. Reaching the objective building, 'B' Company halted while 'A' Company continued on to join 'D' Company. This was completed at 0440 hours. "The change in plan had one good result in that we surprised the enemy with a squeeze play," a West Nova report concluded.[42]

Dawn of December 11 saw the Germans fiercely shelling and mortaring 3rd Brigade's positions across the Lamone River. Nevertheless, at 0655 hours, the Van Doos advanced up the road toward Bagnacavallo with orders to cross both the Fosso Vetro and Fosso Vecchio. With the two leading companies of Van Doos facing ever-increasing resistance, the plan proved too ambitious, and a halt was called just after the Fosso Vetro was passed.[43]

Despite this setback, 1st Division's war diarist considered the bridgehead to be "well established." As early morning rain gave way to clearing skies, the entire 1 Canadian Corps operation received unprecedented support from Desert Air Force, with 350 sorties flown during the day.[44] The Van Doos reported receiving particularly heavy support from fighter-bombers.[45]

17

My Fucking Nerves

O N THE MORNING of December 11, Brigadier Ian Johnston decided to expand the bridgehead that the Perth Regiment and Cape Breton Highlanders had won across the Lamone River. He advanced 11th Canadian Infantry Brigade's last battalion—the Irish Regiment—through the Perth lines at the village of Borgo Villanova in a long hook to the left aimed at reaching the Naviglio Canal. The Perths, meanwhile, would advance directly up the Via Cocchi from Borgo Villanova to where the road dead-ended at Osteria on the Naviglio.[1]

To enter the bridgehead, the leading Irish company had to cross in assault boats. As Major George Macartney's 'A' Company started crossing at 0200 hours, it came under fire from positions southwest of Borgo Villanova. Rather than advancing cross-country as originally planned, Macartney led his men along the river road to engage the German positions dug in on the dyke. By 0600 hours, nine prisoners had been taken and the guns silenced. Captain Tony Falzetta's 'C' Company then leapfrogged through and dashed a thousand yards up the Via Cogollo, a road running northwest toward Bagnacavallo. The dash brought them to a bridge over the Fosso Vetro, where they surprised a German force, killing ten and taking twenty prisoners. Attempting to regain control of the bridge, the Germans counterattacked with two tanks in support. Falzetta broke this effort by calling in artillery.

As the Germans retreated, Captain Herb Hendrie's 'B' Company leapfrogged to the lead and seized the bridge intact. Half a mile ahead, a bridge crossed the Fosso Vecchio. Determined to maintain the regiment's momentum, Major Norman Hickling rushed 'D' Company toward it. Stiff opposition slowed the pace, however, and by the time they reached the Vecchio, the Germans had blown the bridge. The Vecchio was a narrow drainage ditch, but the Germans had obviously decided it was a sufficient obstacle on which to base a defence. 'D' Company was greeted with constant fire from machine guns and SPGS. Lieutenant Colonel Bobby Clark ordered 'D' and 'A' Companies to dig in and be ready to force a crossing during the night. Clark thought his Irish had done a good job, having conducted "a spectacular 3,000-yard advance."[2]

At 0900 hours, about the time the Irish Regiment reached the Vecchio, Lieutenant Colonel Maurice Andrew entered the bridgehead to plan the Perth's advance. Expecting that the straight-line push along the Via Cocchi would meet heavy resistance, he arranged for three field regiments to shell an intersection half a mile out from Borgo Villanova. The shelling started at noon, and Captain Robert Sydney Chamberlain led 'B Company forward. Despite heavy small-arms fire, Chamberlain's men won the crossroads two hours later. Major W.J. "Sammy" Ridge's 'D' Company and 'A' Company, commanded by recently promoted Major Robert Cole, soon arrived. Andrew decided to hold here, confident that the battalion could force crossings of the Vetro and Vecchio during the coming night.[3]

While these two advances had been under way, the Cape Breton Highlanders had handed control of the bridgehead to 12th Canadian Infantry Brigade's Westminster Regiment and gone into reserve. This fit with Major General Bert Hoffmeister's overall plan to have 12th Brigade assume responsibility for the north and northeast sectors of 5th Canadian Armoured Division's front, while 11th Brigade concentrated on winning a bridgehead across the Naviglio.[4]

Leaving their vehicles on the other side of the Lamone, the Westminster's 'A' and 'C' Companies moved across a footbridge at 0600 hours and relieved the Highlanders.[5] As soon as the relief in Villanova was completed, three hours later, the Westminster plan called for Major Bert Hoskin's 'C' Company to advance beyond the town on a northeasterly line away from the river. Major W.J. Neill's 'A' Company, meanwhile, would match 'C' Company's progress by moving through the ground bordered on one side by the river and the paralleling road on the other. 'A' Company had not yet left Villanova and 'C' Company had just exited on a farm road when, as Lieutenant James Oldfield wrote, the men "became acutely aware of the old, dread rumble and clanking that could only mean one thing—the approach of enemy armour."[6]

Bearing down was a hastily cobbled-together German combat group with orders to destroy the Lamone bridgehead. The Germans had long experience in creating ad hoc combat groups to counter localized crises. From LXXIII Korps formations around Faenza, this combat group included the 90th Panzer Grenadier Division's Reconnaissance Battalion, a battalion of 278th Infanterie-Division, and another from 98th Infanterie-Division.[7]

Any doubts as to what the Westies faced were "dispelled by the sight of Mark IV tanks approaching in column along both routes. The situation appeared a bit grim," Oldfield wrote, "since the bridge over the Lamone was under construction and still far from finished, and none of the Battalion's anti-tank guns could be moved forward to help the beleaguered companies. To make matters worse, a number of German infantry, overrun during the night attack, now took heart at the approach of their tanks, and joined . . . the battle with great gusto. 'C' Company was the first to be hit, and was subjected to both tank-gun and small-arms fire." A sniper's bullet killed thirty-five-year-old Company Sergeant Major Sydney Luard Salsbury. Sergeant Paddy Clark immediately took his place. Digging in, 'C' Company faced the enemy and used PIATs to keep the armour at bay.[8]

Despite repeated strafing by Desert Air Force fighters, the German armour kept coming.[9] They consisted mainly of Panthers and heavily-armoured SPGs. When the PIAT teams knocked two out, however, the others stood out of range and limited themselves to shelling 'C' Company.[10]

Inside Villanova, 'A' Company's situation was desperate. Several tanks and SPGs approached via the river road from Mezzano and crashed straight into the company's midst. Main gunfire started knocking houses apart. A Mark IV tank stopped outside the house sheltering No. 2 Platoon and opened fire on the company headquarters' building. When the crew commander opened the turret hatch to better observe the fire, Lieutenant Eddie Hoult shot him dead. Then three PIAT rounds broke a track and disabled the tank. Before Hoult's men could eliminate the rest of the crew, however, approaching German infantry opened fire. Private Richard Harrison was killed. The rest of the platoon scrambled to cover, creating a gap through which the infantry and several tanks passed to directly attack No. 3 Platoon's position between company headquarters and Hoult's men. Lieutenant Walter Tyler and Sergeant James Alton Thrasher attempted to engage a tank with a PIAT but were struck down. Thrasher was killed and Tyler severely wounded. Despite their losses, the Westies in Villanova responded with accurate small-arms fire. Sergeant Fred Koskaewich, meanwhile, found a Little John anti-tank gun left behind by the Cape Breton Highlanders. He started firing it single-handed. While the 2-pound anti-tank gun's rounds pinged uselessly off the armour, the rapidity of fire caused the tanks to withdraw from the village. Armour gone, the infantry also pulled back. As a standoff developed, Lieutenant Colonel Gordon Corbould sent 'B' Company across the Lamone to thicken the battalion's defences inside Villanova.[11]

As the battle raged, 5th Division engineers had worked feverishly on two bridge crossings. Lieutenant John Walter Young led a detail of 10th Field Squadron in installing a Floating Bridge Equipment crossing. Any movement on the dyke drew immediate mortar fire, which for one forty-five-minute period was continuous. Despite the fire, Young "refused to withdraw . . . and continually rallied his men back onto the job. By 1400 hours, mortar fire had subsided and given way to spasmodic but accurate shelling which caused further casualties." As the citation for his subsequent Military Cross reported, "Lieutenant Young's apparent contempt for danger and determination to complete his task was a great inspiration to his men who by this time were very tired and considerably shaken. The bridge was completed at 1845 hours 11 December, allowing badly needed supplies and supporting weapons to reach our troops in the bridgehead."[12]

Jeeps, Bren carriers, and anti-tank guns soon streamed in a continuous column over Young's bridge to reinforce the Westies. Opportunity lost, the German battle group slunk off into the darkness. By 0510 hours, the situation was further stabilized as 14th Field Company completed a bridge capable of supporting tanks.

Just before dawn, the 4th Princess Louise Dragoon Guards joined the Westies in Villanova. At 2020 hours, meanwhile, the Lanark and Renfrew Scottish had moved into Borgo Villanova. Major General Hoffmeister's immediate plan was to pass the British Columbia Dragoons over the tank bridge. One squadron would work with the Plugs, another with the Lanarks, and a third would be lent to 1st Infantry Division. To the east, the Lord Strathcona's Horse was to swing onto Highway 16 and seize Mezzano, then turn westward along the Lamone river road to meet an advance by the Westies from Villanova. Once Mezzano was secure, the 8th Princess Louise's New Brunswick Hussars would cut the highway north of the town with a force created by dismounting two squadrons to work as infantry, supported by one retaining its tanks.[13]

IN 1ST CANADIAN INFANTRY Division's sector, at about 1100 hours on December 11, Major General Harry Foster had passed two 1st Brigade battalions—the Royal Canadian Regiment and Hastings and Prince Edward Regiment—across the Lamone River. He also placed 3rd Brigade's Carleton and York Regiment under 1st Brigade command. Advancing from the Lamone at Traversara, the two 1st Brigade battalions marched to the Fosso Vecchio. Their job was to cross the Vecchio and advance to the Naviglio Canal. Once the canal was reached, the Carletons would pass through the RCR and win a crossing. The Hasty Ps would then come across on the right to extend the bridgehead.[14]

At 0200 hours on December 12, the RCR's 'A' Company quietly climbed up the four-foot slope to the top of the dyke beside the Vecchio and saw that on the other side the bank fell thirty feet to the water. Skidding down the slope, the men waded the ditch and clambered up the dyke on the other bank. At 0330 hours, 'A' Company reported a bridgehead secured. That was the cue for the other three companies to cross in turn and advance to the Naviglio.[15]

The Hasty Ps, meanwhile, had passed their 'A' Company over the Vecchio at 0300 hours. Meeting no resistance, the company hurried forward. By 0530 hours, it was on its objective—a group of houses three hundred yards from the Naviglio. As dawn broke, the Germans discovered the company's presence and began heavily mortaring the position. Twenty-five-year-old Captain Donald Edward Weese, who had just taken command of the company after serving as the battalion's 3-inch mortar platoon commander for two years, was killed.

As German artillery joined the mortars, 'D' Company passed through 'A' Company and headed for the Naviglio. Casualties mounting, the company fell back. Sergeant Marcel Octave Van Hende—who had received a Distinguished Conduct Medal for his gallantry in taking over No. 17 Platoon when its commander was wounded on September 20 at San Fortunato Ridge—was killed. Just twenty-two, as Lieutenant Mowat wrote, he "was quite literally idolized by the entire company. His death brought a kind of spiritual paralysis."[16] Private Norman Dalton Tysick was also killed, and several others suffered serious wounds.[17]

Because of the heavy enemy fire and the realization that the Germans were still established in buildings on the east side of the canal, Foster ordered the Hasty Ps and RCR to hold back. This would give room for 1st Division's artillery to support a night crossing by the Hasty Ps on the right and the Carletons on the left. With Bagnacavallo in German hands, it was evident that German artillery observers were using its numerous church towers and other tall buildings as observation points. This enabled them, the division's war diarist noted, to bring "down murderous mortaring and shelling of our forward positions." These posts were quickly marked for aerial attack by Desert Air Force. Although aircraft hovered over the battlefield, the heavy cloud cover "foiled any attempts to get at them."[18]

To the right of 1st Brigade's two forward battalions, 5th Division's Irish Regiment had come up alongside the Hasty Ps after crossing the Vecchio and moving cross-country. Whereas the 1st Brigade advance had been largely uncontested except by artillery and mortar fire, the Irish had been forced to fight for every building encountered. Captain Tony Falzetta's 'C' Company had led, followed closely by 'B' Company.

After contacting the Hasty Ps to his left, Falzetta sent one platoon at 1100 hours to clear a building on the Naviglio's east bank. The platoon killed seven Germans, wounded four others, and took two prisoners in a sharp fight. German artillery started hammering the building. Falzetta ordered the platoon to abandon it and fall back two hundred yards. Here the men dug in.

'B' Company, meanwhile, had advanced to the northeast of 'C' Company toward the dyke. Intense artillery fire stopped the company cold a thousand yards from the canal. A troop of tanks from the British Columbia Dragoons joined it, and plans started to be made for a renewed effort.[19]

ACROSS A BROAD front, 5th Division units had either gained the Naviglio Canal or secured ground between it and the Lamone River. After crossing the Fosso Vecchio, the Perth Regiment's 'B' Company, under Captain Robert Sydney Chamberlain, led the battalion advance along the Via Cocchi toward the Naviglio. As the company closed on the dyke, it was stopped by heavy artillery fire, and the men dug in. Any movement soon proved to be impossible. Chamberlain realized that the twenty-foot-high earthen dyke completely dominated the flat, treeless field where his men were stuck. An attempt to send a patrol forward to the dyke was driven back with one man wounded. Before Chamberlain could try a company-sized push, orders arrived to stand firm. The Lanark and Renfrew Scottish Regiment of 12th Brigade were to win a crossing under cover of darkness left of the Via Cocchi.[20] This attack would coincide with one launched by the Princess Louise Dragoon Guards a thousand yards to the right.[21]

Back at the Lamone River, meanwhile, the Westminster Regiment's 'B' Company had advanced out of Villanova in the early morning of December 12 and followed the river's western bank toward Mezzano.[22] No Germans were found, but the company was harassed by persistent mortaring and shelling. About a mile out, the Westies were met by a Lord Strathcona's Horse patrol led by Sergeant C.N. Macey. The patrol had crossed the Lamone. At dawn, Macey's men had entered Mezzano and learned from civilians that the

Germans had abandoned it an hour earlier. As Macey's patrol headed off to meet the Westies on the river road, another dismounted patrol was sent by 'B' Squadron up the coastal highway to make contact with the enemy. At the highway's junction with the Via Aguta, a party of Germans were found holding a building. A short fight drove them off and left the Strathconas controlling the junction.[23] They were soon met by the dismounted soldiers of 'A' and 'B' Squadrons of the 8th Hussars. Passing through the Strathconas, the Hussars continued a thousand yards up the coast highway to a position close to the Naviglio.[24]

On the afternoon of December 12, 12th Brigade's Brigadier John Lind personally delivered instructions to each battalion commander for the advance across the Naviglio. The general plan was for a two-battalion assault, with the Princess Louise Dragoon Guards on the right and the Lanark and Renfrew Scottish to the left. Lind expected the crossing to be easily won. Civilian reports indicated that a few days earlier, the Germans had dammed the canal at Faenza to create a water obstacle. Downstream of this point, the Naviglio should be drying up. Once the two battalions crossed the Naviglio, they were to advance a few hundred yards to the Fosso Munio—thought to be little more than a ditch—and cross that as well. This would put them less than a mile from the ultimate goal of the Senio River. The Westminster Regiment was to hold in reserve north of Villanova at the Fosso Vetro.[25]

The Lanarks set out at 2115 hours, with 'A' Company on the right and 'C' Company the left—advancing from the Fosso Vecchio. The other two companies were in trail.[26] Sergeant Fred Cederberg now commanded a three-man section that was part of a newly formed fourteen-man machine-gun group. At its core were two heavy Vickers .303 machine guns, each served by three men. The rest provided security for the gunners and were armed with an assortment of Bren guns, Thompsons, and rifles. Ideally, the group used a Bren carrier to move the Vickers to their deployment point. Because of the mud, they advanced this time on foot to the left of 'A' Company. Each ninety-four-pound Vickers had been broken down and its weight distributed. Cederberg carried one of the guns, Corporal Albert MacNeil the iron legs of its tripod, and new reinforcement Private Henri Boutlier the two ammunition cans that each held 250 rounds.

"We moved with a gentle hiss," Cederberg wrote, "heavy boots lifted up and lowered almost rhythmically in and out of the gumbo muck. It was a gentle sound, a repetitious sound . . . I could hear Albert swearing with each step. The forward pair of thick iron legs . . . was biting into his shoulders. Boutlier slogged alongside him. And we could actually smell the new man's fear and it bothered us because it heightened ours. And to a man we were repelled by it, because it could infect us, strip us of our self-imposed discipline, leaving only panic.

"It began to drizzle and a mist crept between the men . . . almost isolating four- and five-man clusters."

Next to Cederberg, Sergeant Eddie Kerr muttered that the recce patrol had reported no Germans holding the Naviglio. "Screw recce," Cederberg snorted back. He figured the Germans had let the recce patrol see what they wanted them to see. A flare burst overhead, reflecting light off the overhead cloud. It drifted "lazily below its tiny parachute, the burning magnesium chased the darkness away, fizzled and went out. The black of night clutched us again . . . It was cold. But not a man shivered. Each sweated profusely." Then before them, rising like a mountain, was the Naviglio dyke—"grass-covered and almost perpendicular."

Cederberg halted the men. Taking another man, he started climbing. "Wide-legged, clutching at heavier clumps of dying grass, we made it, gasping, to the dyke's broad, flat crown. Thankfully, we lay there, then bellied to the side of the canal. I peered into the black, almost dry channel. 'My fuckin' nerves!' I hissed. 'Germans!'"

The soldier beside him reacted instantly, snapping off shots from his rifle before the two surprised Germans could raise their Schmeissers. "First one, then the other, arms flailing, went over backward.

"At the same time, heavy gunfire shattered the night to our left. Long strings of tracers slit the darkness, followed by a series of detonating Jerry potato-masher grenades, the eye-blinking pinpoints of flame scarring the ground mists. Hoarse, maddened shouts were flung at the forbidding sky. The slow, rhythmic thump-thump-thump of a Bren gun, spouting incendiaries, sprayed the faint outline of the dyke, followed by the intermittent harsh crack of our own 36 grenades."

The firefight developed rapidly. German MG42s ripped at the exposed lines of the two companies lying on top of the dyke. From across the canal, 88-millimetre shells fired by an SPG ripped overhead or sent gushers of earth skyward.[27] 'C' Company was clinging to the dyke to the left of the Via Cocchi, 'A' Company was immediately to its right, and 'D' Company was farther over on that flank. As dawn broke, 'B' Company attempted to pass through 'D' Company and cross the Naviglio. Heavy mortar and artillery fire stopped it well short of 'D' Company's lines. The Lanarks were stalemated and taking heavy casualties when the Germans counterattacked at 0740 hours on December 13.[28]

Cederberg had just realized that the Germans were unaware of the machine-gun group's presence on the Lanarks' extreme left when the attack came in. Kerr "saw them first, a herky-jerky, ragged line of Germans, arms waving, machine-pistols spouting fire, potato mashers inside belts, on the crown of the far dyke. Sprinting, they crossed it, and, digging their heels in, charged down the canal side and splashed through the puddled canal bed."

The machine-gun group opened fire—both Vickers ripping out long bursts. Cederberg was firing his Thompson. "At less than thirty feet, I aimed straight at the belt buckle of the leading Jerry, his face straining beneath a coal-scuttle helmet. I ripped off two, quick single shots. The expression on his face didn't change when he went down sideways."

Mortar bombs and 88-millimetre shells hammered the Lanarks' line, as the Germans started clawing up the slope toward them. Unable to depress the Vickers barrel to bring them under fire, Kerr yelled at Boutlier to give him a Bren. The new soldier was lying face down beside a Bren, not moving. MacNeil shoved the man aside, grabbed the Bren, "pointed it straight into the line of crawling, stumbling Jerries and blew all twenty-eight rounds of steel-nosed .303s literally into their faces."

Cederberg was "vividly aware of the storm raging around me . . . I fired carefully without feeling. Out of the corner of one eye, I watched a potato masher go over our heads and explode at the foot of the dyke. Something glanced off my helmet. A German crawled laboriously out of his side of the dark Naviglio and began pulling himself up the face of the dyke. I put a short burst into his back and he shuddered and twitched before sliding down the slope until his legs jammed against another body.

"As abruptly as it had begun, it ended. Someone grunted. Only it sounded more like a long, sad sigh. The misty rain . . . thickened, swirling among the enemy sprawled like dirty heaps on the inside faces of the dykes."

Cederberg checked his men and then walked over to where Boutlier still lay, rolled him gently over, and saw "a small, darkish hole dead centre in his forehead. It was almost bloodless."[29]

Although the Lanarks had thrown back the counterattack, the December 13 battle, as one battalion report stated, "was still very furious" and showed no signs of abating.[30]

AT 2115 HOURS ON December 12, a thousand yards right of the Lanark and Renfrew Scottish, the Princess Louise Dragoon Guards had launched their assault. As there was only one viable ford over the Vecchio, all the squadrons had to cross in single file. Once across, 'A' Squadron moved to the left and 'C' Squadron came up alongside on the right. While 'B' Squadron followed, 'D' Squadron remained at the Vecchio to secure the ford.[31] The advance crossed "very open and flat" ground subjected to heavy mortaring and raked by machine-gun positions on the Naviglio dyke. All this fire seemed to be on fixed targets and set lines and not a result of the advance having been detected.[32]

At 2220 hours, 'A' Squadron's Captain Robert A. White reported his men had reached the canal. Finding it dry, 'A' Squadron lunged across and two minutes later had occupied a group of buildings about two hundred yards beyond the canal. At 2226 hours, 'C' Squadron's Captain Jack McNeil signalled that his men were also one hundred yards beyond the Naviglio. Surprise had been lost, and both squadrons were taking "lots of MG fire."

Further signals from the two companies were confused but indicated that they were heavily engaged. Three days earlier, Lieutenant Colonel Bill Darling had gone on leave to Florence for a week. And now the battalion's second-in-command, Major A.E. Langston, seemed unable to decide what action to take. At 0040 hours, two soldiers from the anti-tank platoon who had been attached to 'A' Squadron arrived at Tac HQ and reported that the entire squadron had been captured. Before they left the squadron, the two men had seen Burke's command section enter a house that was almost immediately approached by "Germans in great strength."³³

A few minutes later, 'C' Squadron signalled that thirty 'A' Squadron members had joined it. "In the forward positions, the regiment's historian wrote, "the three Squadrons were still engaged in a desperate struggle against attacks of increasing fierceness, but still held on grimly. Reports filtering back were the reverse of encouraging, one straggler affirming that few elements were still holding out."³⁴

At 0115 hours, 12th Brigade's intelligence officer advised that the Plugs were facing Field Marshal Kesselring's Machine Gun Battalion (Maschinengewehr-Bataillon Feldmarschall Kesselring). Formed in November 1944, it joined the 114th Jäger Division on December 11. The battalion comprised three 110-man companies, but it was the strength of arms each brought to battle that made them so formidable—16 machine guns, 40 submachine guns, and 20 Panzerfausts.

Across the Naviglio, remnants were still in the fight. Thirteen 'A' Squadron men were holed up in a stone building, but the situation was desperate. Although Trooper Raymond Jones's wireless could still receive, two bullets had destroyed its ability to send.

At about 0200 hours, the men ran out of ammunition just as Panzerfaust rounds started piercing the walls. A German officer shouted in English for the men to climb out of the windows and surrender. "We said no," Jones recalled. "We were soldiers, we come in through the door and that's the way we'd go out. So, we went out through the door and there was only thirteen of us left." Jones thought another thirty-three men from 'A' Squadron had been killed. "Most of those boys, it was their first time in action. They were reinforcements and it was really sad." Jones and the rest were led off to a prison camp in Germany.[35]

Remnants of the three forward companies were drifting into Tac HQ, but Langston thought they were too few to be reorganized and sent back to the Naviglio. He also rejected the idea of sending 'D' Squadron forward. Instead, Langston set off alone on foot to recce the situation. It was 0250 hours.

Langston was still out there somewhere when Brigadier Lind sent orders by wireless to send reinforcements to support a thirty-man platoon that brigade headquarters thought was still holding on the Naviglio's east bank. Brigadier Desmond Smith also demanded that Langston be found and returned to the TAC HQ. By the time Langston was brought in, Lind's chief of staff, Brigade Major D.M. Clark, had arrived. Relieving Langston, Clark and the battalion's medical officer agreed the man should be hospitalized for suspected battle exhaustion.[36]

At 0430 hours, Captain R.A. White and a sergeant from 'A' Squadron appeared. They had narrowly escaped their platoon being overrun. Then another lieutenant and twenty men drifted in. The lieutenant said this was the last of 'A' Squadron.[37]

Having assumed command, Clark told whatever number of Plugs were still at the Naviglio to fall back to the Vecchio. He also brought in a Westminster Regiment company to provide security and enable the Plugs to reorganize. Together, the three squadrons involved in the attack returned with just 89 men.[38] The battalion's losses were severe—21 killed, 21 wounded, and 46 lost as prisoners.[39] Save for 'D' Squadron, which had suffered few casualties, the Plugs were temporarily finished as a fighting formation.

WHILE THE GERMANS had decisively blocked 5th Canadian Armoured Division's attempts to cross the Naviglio Canal, 1st Canadian Infantry Division had better fortune. Although ostensibly a 1st Brigade attack, losses suffered earlier by its battalions resulted in the attached Carleton and York Regiment taking the lead. Lacking tank support, and knowing there was German armour across the canal, Major General Harry Foster delayed the attack until nightfall of December 12–13. This enabled the 51st Battery of 1st Anti-Tank Regiment to ford the Lamone River and be in place to support the assault.[40]

The Carletons were to secure an initial bridgehead through which the Hastings and Prince Edward Regiment would then pass. Planning the attack was rushed. Brigadier Smith only arrived at the Carletons' Tac HQ at 1700 hours, with instructions and details of support for an attack set to launch at 2200 hours.[41] Artillery provided by medium and field gun regiments, Lieutenant Colonel Jack Ensor wrote, would "pound the line of the canal for ten minutes, then the mediums [would] lift and the field guns [were] to come back . . . as a barrage behind which the infantry would advance at the rate of 100 yards in six minutes."[42]

'D' Company would go forward on the right, 'C' Company the left. Their objective was the road just beyond the Naviglio's west bank. Once this objective was secure, 'A' Company would advance between the two companies and expand the bridgehead to a depth of five hundred yards. This would give sufficient room for the Hasty Ps to enter the bridgehead and then push out to the right, while the Carletons' 'A' and 'D' Companies did the same to the left. 'A' Company would advance two hundred yards west to where the bordering river road intersected a rough track. 'D' Company would then move through to another junction three hundred yards farther west.

At 2200 hours, the creeping barrage started, and Captain Don Smith's 'C' Company followed it closely. 'B' Company, however, was ten minutes later reaching the start line, and its men had to sprint to catch up to the advancing barrage.[43] Both companies, the regiment's historian wrote, "swarmed across the dry bed of the canal" and came up alongside an abandoned water mill. Forty-five prisoners were taken from buildings and dugouts along the dyke.[44]

'A' Company started moving at 0045 hours on December 13.[45] Passing through the leading companies, it "reached its first objective with very little trouble." Soon thereafter, the Hasty Ps moved three companies into the bridgehead and started the rightward push.[46] Major William Oscar Stockdale's 'B' Company had the farthest to go— to a cluster of farmhouses identified as San Carlo, situated at a road junction about a thousand yards from the canal.[47] Moving quickly, and brushing aside "a small-arms battle on the way," 'B' Company had secured these buildings by 0130 hours.[48] 'C' Company, under Captain James Fraser, took up position midway between Stockdale's men and the canal. A sodden haystack provided the only cover. As the soldiers started digging slit trenches, they found the ground entirely saturated. 'A' Company, meanwhile, had struck out along the road paralleling the canal.[49] At 0600, the company reached its object-ive—a string of stone houses beside the canal—and reported vehicle movement to its front. Artillery was directed toward the sounds, but there was no evidence of damage caused.[50]

In the Carleton sector, 'A' Company had moved toward the road and track junction to the left. The lead platoon and company headquar-ters were separated from the following two platoons when a group of about twenty Germans fired on the company from positions behind it. "These enemy," Ensor reported, "were attended to and I ordered the commander of 'D' Company . . . to pass his company through to its objective, the junction in the road leading to Bagnacavallo and then to start feeling [his] way toward the town."[51]

Ensor thought 'A' Company had reached its objective, a mistake that 'D' Company's Major Rowland Horsey discovered when ap-proaching the road-and-track junction. After coming under heavy fire from Schmeissers and light machine guns, Horsey saw that only the lead 'A' Company platoon and its headquarters had reached the junction. The other two platoons had been driven across the can-al and were holding on the dyke there. Despite the incoming fire, Horsey attempted to carry on. "We tried every way we could to get forward to our objective, but were unable to," he wrote. At 0550 hours, 'D' Company stopped two hundred yards short of its objective. Horsey put two platoons and his headquarters beside the road paralleling the canal and had the other platoon set up across the Naviglio on the opposite bank.[52]

Although the bridgehead was not as broad as intended, by dawn the Carletons and Hasty Ps appeared to be solid on the west bank. Then, at 0700 hours, the Germans counterattacked the Carletons' 'B' Company on the battalion's right flank and 'A' Company in the middle with a mixed force of infantry and tanks. While the attack on 'A' Company was easily beaten back by artillery fire, Ensor had to leave 'B' Company "to rely more on its own weapons because we did not know exactly where the [Hasty Ps] were and so had to use arty cautiously on that sector." The counterattack on its lines was still repulsed. The Carletons identified the counterattacking infantry as troops of the same Field-Marshal Kesselring's Machine Gun Battalion that had mauled 5th Division's Princess Louise Dragoon Guards.[53] This was bad news, but even worse was the identification of tanks as the ominous Tigers of the 90th Panzer Grenadier Division's 190th Reconnaissance Battalion.[54]

Even as the Carletons fought off this counterattack, the same German battalion struck the Hasty Ps at 0735 hours. Major Stockdale's 'B' Company was hit first.[55] Stockdale's signaller reported, "Enemy C.A. with tank support coming in hard from the left . . . attacking from the front with Mark IV tanks . . . urgently need tank support . . . tanks closing in . . . " The wireless signal broke, then Stockdale came on. "We can't hold out," he said. "Do you wish us to remain or withdraw?"

Knowing that if Stockdale retreated the Germans could roll up the entire bridgehead, Lieutenant Colonel Don Cameron made a decision, his intelligence officer Lieutenant Mowat later wrote, "that ages men and withers up their hearts." Taking the microphone, Cameron said, "You must remain." There would be no tanks, as the engineers of 1st Field Squadron had still not bridged the Fosso Vecchio with anything sturdy enough to bear the weight of the waiting British Columbia Dragoons.[56] At 0915 hours, 'C' Company's Captain James Fraser reported that "he could see 'B' Company had been overrun with infantry and tanks and some of the men [were] surrendering."[57]

To Fraser's right, 'A' Company's three platoons had also been isolated from each other by infiltrating Germans. While the leading No. 9 Platoon, "reduced to a handful of men, held its position," the other two platoons fell back across the canal.[58] This left 'C' Company virtually surrounded. Inside a rapidly shrinking perimeter of exposed ground, Fraser "was constantly on the move and in the open, making the rounds of his company positions, and by his presence, his infectious cheerfulness and courage, maintained the morale of all at a high level," the citation for his subsequent Military Cross stated.[59]

With tanks and infantry closing from three sides, however, 'C' Company's situation was untenable. Cameron ordered Fraser to fight his way back to the canal under cover of high-explosive and smoke shells. Once he reached the dyke, Fraser was to hold at all costs. As Cameron gave the order, he learned help was on the way, with 2nd Brigade expected to cross the canal and pass through 'C' Company's dyke position at about 1600 hours.[60] First, however, Fraser had to reach the dyke. "Though hard-pressed by a foe superior in numbers and using armour, and under a never-ceasing rain of fire, Captain Fraser organized and successfully accomplished this very difficult task." At the canal, he "found elements of two other companies ['B' and 'A'] and, showing great initiative, promptly reorganized them and formed them into an effective fighting force to help in the holding of this crossing place."[61] Largely thanks to Fraser's gallant leadership, the Hasty Ps clung to the dyke on the Naviglio's west side.

Left of the Hasty Ps, meanwhile, the Carletons had also been hard pressed when a counterattack forced 'A' Company's headquarters section and the platoon still on the west bank to retreat to the other side. This isolated Major Rowland Horsey's 'D' Company out on the battalion's left flank and still across the canal. "From that time on until mid-afternoon all troops in the bridgehead area were subject to one counterattack after another," Horsey reported. "We could see these counterattacks and tanks coming in. Instantly arty and 4.2-inch mortar defensive fire was called for. The enemy on foot would go to ground, the tanks would keep on going, doing some shooting up, stop, because it had no infantry with it, and go back for them. This was the pattern of the counter attacks. Had we not had time to dig ourselves in extremely well, our casualties would have been much higher than they were. The companies were ordered to hold out, and told the tanks were on the way to support them. The situation by noon was critical."[62]

18

Well Done Indeed

BY NOON ON December 13, both Lieutenant Colonels Jack Ensor and Don Cameron had moved their Tac HQs close to the Naviglio Canal. Both were also pleading for tank support that could only come when the engineers finished bridging the Fosso Vecchio. The Carleton and York Regiment's three companies were dug in on the canal's west dyke. "There," Ensor said, "they fought it out."[1] The battered formation of Hastings and Prince Edward Regiment, made up of remnants from 'A' and 'B' Companies and Captain James Fraser's 'C' Company, was alongside and to the right of the Carletons' 'D' Company. Although a 2nd Canadian Infantry Brigade relief force was on the way, when it would arrive was unknown. Neither battalion commander thought his men could hold out without immediate tank support.

At 1300 hours, however, the bridge was completed, and the British Columbia Dragoons' No. 4 Troop of 'A' Squadron soon reported to Ensor. The troop leader, Lieutenant Donald Charles Wicklow, then had his three Shermans line up on the canal's east bank across from 'D' Company. Dismounting, Wicklow dashed across the canal and found Major Rowland Horsey's headquarters "in a large casa just off the road which ran along the side of the west bank . . . Captain Horsey's few troops were dug in and around HQ and due to the vegetation . . . unless you observed from the upstairs of HQ casa, visibility was very limited. Enemy armour was running up and down a road . . . at right angles from the canal road and this armour was firing point blank, although unseen, on the positions of ['D'] Company."

After a short huddle with Horsey, Wicklow found an unmarked ford apparently used by local farmers when the canal's bed was dry. The Shermans wallowed across and entered 'D' Company's narrow bridgehead. Dismounting again, Wicklow sneaked forward to a road on which the German tanks were motoring up and down and that intersected the river road. Peering around the corner of a farmhouse, Wicklow saw a Panther tank. As he considered how his out-gunned Shermans could tackle the heavier Panther, it opened fire on his troop. Its rounds, however, slammed harmlessly into an intervening dirt wall. Dashing back to his Sherman, Wicklow saw that the wall also prevented any flank shots at the Panther. A head-on encounter was one the Panther would surely win because of its more powerful gun and thicker armour.

"By standing up in my turret at discreet moments, I watched him backing up," Wicklow said. "I realized his plan was to get . . . into position to get a flank shot on me. Here the awkwardness of the Panther and the not too good driving gave me my chance, for as he swung broadside to change roads he exposed his flank . . . I had [Trooper] Bert Waite, my driver, move clear of the bend and [Trooper] Bill Buchan, my gunner, who was the very best in the business had an AP [armour piercing] up the spout and got his shot away . . . We had no more worry over that one." Wicklow's steady leadership this day led to a Military Cross.[2]

That the bridgehead was still imperiled became clear when a heavy counterattack struck the Carletons' 'B' and 'C' Companies at 1440 hours. Two Panthers and a Tiger approached via a road running toward the canal. Knowing they had mere minutes to save the situation, 'C' Company's commander, Captain Don Smith, and Royal Canadian Horse Artillery forward observation officer (FOO) Captain Peter Newell raced across the canal, pulled together a 6-pounder anti-tank gun crew, hooked the weapon to a jeep, and towed it to the west bank. As they were positioning the gun, large numbers of German infantry charged across a muddy field toward 'C' Company. Newell ran back to his wireless set to call in artillery, while Smith engaged the tanks. Smith sighted in on the leading Panther, his first round disabling it. Smith, as Ensor reported, then ran back to his company and "shot up the approaching infantry."[3] The Hasty Ps' Horsey was delighted to see the anti-tank gun knock out the Panther, as it squarely blocked the road and prevented the two other tanks from busting into the Carletons' position. He also thought that Newell's calling in "immediate and accurate [artillery] fire" saved the day. Although Wicklow's Shermans were "not able to cope with the Tigers," Horsey wrote, "their presence was a good morale booster to our men."

When two 17-pounder Fireflies entered the bridgehead at 1500 hours, the situation changed drastically. "From that time on," Horsey wrote, "the day was ours."[4] One Firefly halted next to the ruined house where Captain James Fraser and his Hasty Ps were making a final stand. Its mere appearance caused the Germans to fade away.[5] The result was the same when the second one joined the Carletons. Horsey noted that the "enemy fire eased off and no counterattack forces appeared after that. What saved the day? First, the determination of the men to stick it out."[6]

The Germans had counterattacked the bridgehead fourteen times. Surprisingly, the Carletons suffered relatively slight casualties—two killed and sixteen wounded. The Hasty Ps, however, had three killed, seven wounded, and fifty-nine lost as prisoners.[7] Most of the latter were from the overrun 'B' Company.

Hasty Ps intelligence officer Lieutenant Farley Mowat considered the regiment broken. "The survivors were told that their feat had been given prominence on the BBC . . . and they did not care. The Army Commander sent a personal message of congratulations . . . and they listened, and did not hear it . . . These men were beyond pride, beyond praise, beyond condemnation. They were empty of all emotions and knew nothing except a stupefying weariness. The medical officers had a term for individuals who had reached the end of their tether. They called it 'battle exhaustion.'"

The "entity that was the regiment lay like the last embers of a fire. Most of its substance had been consumed and there was little left save cooling ashes. Physically the exhaustion of the Regiment was just short of total. More than a hundred men had been lost at the Vecchio and the Naviglio." Companies mustered barely the fighting strength of platoons. "Spiritually, the wastage had been even greater."[8]

Lieutenant General Richard McCreery sent a personal message to each battalion commander. Ensor's read, "My congratulations on the splendid achievement of your battalion in capturing and holding a bridgehead over the Canale Naviglio against repeated infantry and tank counterattacks. Great gallantry and determination by all ranks went into this important success. The fierceness of the enemy's resistance clearly shows the importance of this ground to the enemy. Well done indeed."[9]

THE LOYAL EDMONTON Regiment's Lieutenant Colonel Jim Stone had learned at 0900 hours on December 13 that his 2nd Brigade battalion was to come under 1st Brigade command. He was to immediately assist the embattled Carletons and Hasty Ps in the Naviglio Canal bridgehead. Stone went directly to 1st Brigade headquarters, where Brigadier Desmond Smith declared, "We are in desperate straits. Been driven back . . . the whole brigade is exhausted. I have Carleton and York under command and they are holding the opposite bank. You're under command and I want you to attack right away."

Doubting the situation was as dire as Smith believed and thinking the man was panicking, Stone said, "Not right away, Brigadier. I've been in battle too long for that. I have to go up and have a look."

Smith blurted, "It's desperate." Unmoved, Stone went forward to speak with both battalion commanders. The Hasty Ps' Lieutenant Colonel Cameron said the Eddies were needed right away. Thinking Cameron too alarmed, Stone asked Lieutenant Colonel Ensor if his Carletons could "hold until four this afternoon."

"Sure," Ensor replied, "we've lots of artillery support. Have the place well covered." Stone said he was going to feed his men, then get them marching, and promised to come into the bridgehead at 1600 hours. Returning to 1st Brigade, Stone told Smith his intention. By 1600 hours it would be too late, the Brigadier argued. Stone, however, refused to be rushed. Using the brigadier's wireless, he ordered the Eddies' second-in-command, Major Alan MacDonald, to serve up a hot meal and then march the troops forward.

Stone was just leaving 1st Brigade's headquarters when 1st Canadian Infantry Division's senior artillery officer, Brigadier Bill Ziegler, walked in. Ziegler asked if Stone needed help. Stone said, "'The Germans are being stubborn, so let's put everything on them.' Right there, we devised the so-called 'fruit plan' for using artillery in concentrations rather than barrages. We designated target groups on the maps as Apple One, Apple Two, Apple Three, and Apple Four. Others were Pear. This enabled the man on the ground, usually a company commander, to just call in Apple One and that map area would get a fire concentration on it."[10] The B.C. Dragoons' 'C' Squadron was also to assist, with one troop assigned to each forward company. In addition to the "fruit plan," the artillery would fire an initial supporting barrage. The Saskatoon Light Infantry would weigh in with 4.2-inch mortars firing smoke rounds and Vickers medium machine guns sending bursts over the heads of the advancing infantry.

Two companies, 'B' on the right and 'C' the left, would lead.[11] At 1600 hours, just as promised, both companies crossed the Naviglio and contacted the Carletons. As the Eddies started emerging from the bridgehead, the tanks supporting 'C' Company were stopped by the Panther tank still blocking the road where B.C. Dragoons' Lieutenant Wicklow had knocked it out.[12] 'B' Company and the Dragoons' No. 3 Troop of 'A' Squadron, however, advanced quickly along the canal road. At 1640 hours, just short of its objective, a firefight for control of a row of roadside buildings broke out.[13] A hidden SPG slammed a round into Sergeant William P. Fleck's Sherman. Fleck and three crewmen were wounded, while Trooper Howard F. Lauzon was killed.[14]

'C' Company, meanwhile, had got past the Panther and reached its objective. Stone fed 'D' Company through it at 1635 hours to expand the bridgehead to the northwest. Although German tanks and SPGs kept appearing ahead of both 'C' and 'B' Companies' positions, infantry attempting to join them were driven off by the combined artillery, mortar, and medium machine-gun fire that Stone judged "excellent."[15]

The fight for the bridgehead had decisively shifted in favour of the Canadians. A tally of armour casualties counted only Fleck's Sherman as lost—in exchange for two SPGs, three Panthers, and one Tiger. With the ground in Canadian hands, the Dragoons could recover the Sherman for repair, while for the Germans' losses were permanent.[16]

As the heated battle in the Naviglio bridgehead slowed to a simmer, 1st Division reorganized to capitalize on the success. At 1700 hours, Major General Harry Foster arrived at 2nd Brigade headquarters with instructions for Lieutenant Colonel Pat Bogert to take óver the bridgehead from 1st Brigade "and restore it to the original size." As soon as the Eddies were firmly in control of their sector, they would return to 2nd Brigade command. In the meantime, the Seaforth Highlanders would concentrate on the Naviglio's east bank, opposite the bridgehead. The Princess Patricia's Canadian Light Infantry would be in reserve but ready to join the effort as necessary.

The fighting, 2nd Brigade's intelligence officer Captain Ed Bradish noted, "seemed to slack off . . . somewhat towards evening, although the area was still heavily shelled and mortared." At 2125 hours, Stone reported three companies of Eddies still in close contact with the enemy and the situation under control. Bogert ordered the Seaforths to cross the canal.[17]

Lieutenant Colonel Budge Bell-Irving sent all four infantry companies and a newly formed anti-tank company across. The Seaforth's tank-hunting platoon having proven so successful at the Savio River, Bell-Irving had expanded the Seaforth's tank-hunting platoon to a sixty-three-man-strong company. Two twenty-man platoons were each armed with two PIATs, while the third twelve-man platoon was equipped with two Little John anti-tank guns.[18]

When the Seaforths entered the bridgehead at about 2130 hours, they learned the Eddies had already secured two of their objectives. The objectives for 'D' and 'A' Companies—both alongside a road about seven hundred yards west of the canal—were, however, still dominated by German tanks. If taken, these objectives would push the bridgehead well out from the canal. Back at the Naviglio, the anti-tank company was using block-and-tackle equipment to try to lift the 2-pounders to the top of the dyke. On December 14 at 0045 hours, realizing this was going to be a long job, recently promoted Major D.G. Duncan of 'D' Company and 'A' Company's Major Oliver Herbert Mace decided not to wait.

Accompanied by the anti-tank company's two PIAT platoons, the force headed into the night. Several hours later, in the pre-dawn light, the Seaforths caught fleeting glimpses through the thick vineyards of tanks matching their pace at a distance of about five hundred yards. Never did the tanks remain stationary long enough for the PIAT teams to engage them.[19] By 0645 hours, the two companies had reached their objectives. 'A' Company held a crossroads and 'D' Company was in a nearby farm. At 0400 hours, the B.C. Dragoons—having withdrawn for the night to resupply—returned, with 'A' Squadron sending a troop to the Seaforths and 'C' Squadron a troop to the Eddies. Two 17-pounders roamed to wherever Panthers or Tigers were spotted.[20]

"SOME VERY BITTER fighting took place today, as the enemy attempted to hold the line of Canale Naviglio," 1 Canadian Corps's historical officer Captain Joe Wrinch wrote toward the end of December 13. While the bridgehead battle had raged, there had been other fighting across the corps front.[21]

To the left of the Naviglio bridgehead, 3rd Canadian Infantry Brigade—less the Carleton and York Regiment but with 1st Brigade's 48th Highlanders of Canada under command—had made little progress in crossing the Fosso Vecchio well left of the Godo–Bagnacavallo road. A few prisoners revealed that the area was being defended by a new battalion, the 289th Grenadiers Battalion of 98th Infanterie-Division—replacing the 356th Infanterie-Division's 870th Grenadiers. Intelligence staff considered these new troops "not good types, their morale was low, and their company strengths [were] low indeed." Despite this, when the Royal 22e Régiment's 'B' Company attempted to seize a crossroad just short of the Vecchio during the night of December 13–14, it reported the "enemy to be too thick on the ground" and pulled back. The West Nova Scotia Regiment was also blocked in an attack on another crossroads, and the 48th Highlanders failed to seize a farm identified as Casa Baldi. By 0900 hours on

December 14, a 1st Division report cited 3rd Brigade's positions as "relatively unchanged."[22]

In 5th Canadian Armoured Division's sector, in the late afternoon of December 13, the Cape Breton Highlanders' 'C' Company, under Irish Regiment command, had tried to gain the Naviglio to the left of the Lanark and Renfrew Scottish Regiment. It was driven back. Casualties were heavy and included the company commander.[23]

The Irish Regiment's 'D' Company, under Major Norman Hickling, did manage to get a platoon commanded by Lieutenant Norm Folliot up to the Naviglio to the left of the Highlanders. Folliot's men stormed a house beside the canal and prepared to hold it. Hickling, however, was unable to push the rest of the company through to the platoon, which was soon being shelled at close range by a German tank and was surrounded by infantry. All Hickling could do was lead one section of men within range to provide some fire support and to call in artillery fire. Luckily, that action broke the German attack. With the building crumbling around the platoon, however, he ordered it to withdraw from the "hopeless position."[24]

These setbacks for 12th Brigade proved that 5th Division could not break the stalemate with a direct attack. Consequently, Major General Bert Hoffmeister and 1 Canadian Corps's Lieutenant General Charles Foulkes turned their attention to 1st Division's bridgehead. At 0830 hours on December 14, Lieutenant Colonel Gordon Corbould received orders to move the Westminster Regiment into that bridgehead by 1000 hours. This would enable the Westies to swing back along the west bank of the Naviglio into 5th Division's sector. As the advance developed, the Lanark and Renfrew Scottish would punch across the canal from their embattled position on the eastern bank. At the same time, the Irish Regiment and the Cape Breton Highlanders company under its command would push along the east side of the Naviglio and secure that bank.

The Westies moved out with 'B' Company leading and 'A' and 'C' Companies trailing. En route, the lead company met up with Major R. J. Graham's 'A' Squadron of the Lord Strathcona's Horse.[25] As the infantry and tanks approached the crossing, Lieutenant James Oldfield wrote, the "situation was demoralizing in the extreme. The

approach was made through positions held by units . . . that had really
'had it' in the fighting of the previous day. They testified eloquently to
the enemy strength. Men and material, casualties of the bitter battles,
lay all about. But the Westminsters' spirit had never been broken.
Although no man could move through such a debacle unmoved, most
felt that this was just another job that the Regiment had been ordered
to accomplish and tackled it philosophically."[26]

Not far from the crossing, the lead Sherman was struck by a
heavy-calibre shell. It burst into flames, blocking the road so that the
following Shermans were unable to get past.[27] The Westies carried
on, crossed the Naviglio on the right side of the bridgehead, and then
started advancing along the western bank. Ahead, Desert Air Force
Spitfires strafed both sides of the canal. The strafing was so close
that on several occasions empty cartridges fell down on the Lanark
positions.[28]

Partly because of this close air support, German resistance was
weak and disorganized. By 1245 hours, 'B' Company was a thousand yards beyond the bridgehead. Catching up, 'A' Squadron joined
'A' Company in leapfrogging to the front. When 'A' Company reached
the Via Chiara, a road running west from the Naviglio's canal road, it
began to dig in. Major Bert Hoskin's 'C' Company passed to the front
and pushed up the Via Chiara with sights on winning a crossing
over the Fosso Munio, less than a half mile distant from the Naviglio.
Despite very open ground, lacking any cover, the company secured
several buildings a short distance from the Munio at 1900 hours.[29]

The company spread out among the houses. Sergeant Ron Hurley
set his platoon in one building and decided to check an adjacent one
that looked more defensible. Swapping his Thompson for a rifle so
his men would have more firepower, Hurley headed out. It occurred
to him that he actually knew little about handling a rifle—at about
the same time that a German soldier stepped around a corner and
jabbed a gun into him. "*Raus, Kamerad,*" the German snapped. A
ribbon-winning sprinter before the war, Hurley thought maybe he
could move fast and hit the German with his rifle. "I just took one
step and he fired right there." The bullet punched into Hurley's chest,
and he went down while the German ran.

"I was bleeding from my mouth. I tried to holler, must have made some noise because these fellows come running out and . . . they dragged me into this house. This one chap had a shell dressing on his helmet, but it [didn't work.] So [Private] Joe Leclair said, 'That's stupid, that isn't going to stop it.' Here they are arguing about me. And . . . there's some Italians . . . sleeping on this old mattress and Joe rips the sheet from under them and God knows how filthy it was . . . He said, 'Ron, this is going to hurt, but I got to do this.' And he kept shoving it into this hole about the size of my fist. I didn't care if it hurt or not. I just knew he was trying to help me . . . They rigged a stretcher out of blankets and stakes for grape vines. Four of these guys carted me out . . . and there's mortaring and shelling going on and I'm thinking I don't know if I'm going to make it out of this or not." The men carried him to company headquarters. Hurley was soon evacuated to a casualty clearing station, where he lost consciousness. He would only waken again on Christmas morning, in a hospital far behind the line, at Iesi, near Ancona.[30]

Back at the Munio, meanwhile, 'C' Company had become locked in a firefight. Twenty-two-year-old Sergeant Jim Keet was killed leading his section in a successful charge to eliminate a machine-gun position. Westminster casualties totalled 8 killed and 23 wounded. Despite being subjected throughout the advance to heavy mortar, artillery, and Nebelwerfer fire, the majority of the battalion's casualties were due to small-arms fire. Lieutenant Oldfield considered the losses light when compared with the 106 German prisoners taken and the "many dead" left on the battlefield.[31]

As night fell, the sky remained clear. That scotched the plan to create artificial moonlight to guide the Lanark assault across the canal. Instead, the searchlights brought into position during the day beamed straight over the Naviglio. The men of three companies—'C', 'A', and 'D'—and the heavy machine-gun platoon plunged into the canal's dry bed and clawed their way up the opposing bank. As he gained the summit, Sergeant Fred Cederberg "flinched, half expecting a withering storm of machine-gun fire. I looked to my left at the line of Lanarks, strung out, panting, slipping, and sliding as they crossed the flat ground, then in ragged confusion plunged down the far side.

"Tank shells slammed into the *osteria* on our right, driving long slivers of brilliant light through the eerie glow from the searchlights bathing the land. One building exploded in flames and burned fiercely.

"At a lope, eyes darting from one shifting shadow to another, we laboured forward toward a long, low shadow dominating the line where the black sky touched the rim of the earth.

"One hundred yards. Two hundred yards. The black, squat shadow began to take shape. A casa." Suddenly a tracer streaked out of the house into the gap that had opened between the machine-gun platoon and 'D' Company. Then "a dozen tongues of spitting flame seemed to erupt out of the casa wall. Hoarse shouts and curses mingled with angry cries. The night air was filled with singing and hissing bullets. Men fell in mid-step, as though driven into the soggy ground by flailing fists." Cederberg dove into a shallow fold of ground and started firing his Thompson at the house. The Lanarks were pinned in the open, the Germans securely ensconced in the building.

Cederberg figured the other companies would soon work around to take the building from behind, but worried that the entire platoon could be killed before that happened. He told Sergeant Eddie Kerr to take six men and crawl out to the left and then approach the rear of the building. "Use grenades and every automatic you got when you rush 'em," he said. "But get in as close as you can first, so you can lob the 36s inside the casa. When we hear 'em go off, we'll hit 'em from this side."

It seemed to take forever for Kerr and his men to get into position, with Cederberg and the other men hugging the ground and the Germans firing over their heads or into the little fold of earth protecting them. "But when we heard the grenades exploding in the casa, we gathered our legs underneath our heaving bodies and literally catapulted low through the air and straight at the building.

"It went off in perfect army pamphlet fashion . . . Five Germans died in the explosions and follow-up fire, three were wounded, and four survivors surrendered, still dazed by the ferocity of the short firefight."[32]

By first light on December 15, the Lanarks were all well across the Naviglio, and 'D' Squadron of the 4th Princess Louise Dragoon Guards arrived to establish a firm base on the east bank. The Strathcona's 'C' Squadron crossed over to support the Lanarks. "This bridgehead was made against heavy shelling, mortaring, and MG fire and close contact with the enemy was maintained," a 5th Division account reported.

Bridgehead well established, the Plugs sent three more squadrons through their 'D' Squadron to advance past the Lanarks toward the Fosso Munio. By 1050 hours, all had reached the Munio, except the left-hand squadron—stopped a hundred yards short by heavy German fire. When the Strathcona's tanks reached the battalion at 1445 hours, this squadron was also able to come up alongside the Munio. Shortly thereafter, the Westies and Plugs contacted each other. At the same time, the Governor General's Horse Guards crossed the Naviglio to the right of the Lanarks' bridgehead and headed east to where the Munio and Naviglio merged, just short of the coastal highway, to clear the narrowing ground. By late afternoon, 5th Division was firmly established before the Munio, along its entire frontage.[33]

THE SUCCESS OF 5th Division's breakout from the Naviglio Canal had been possible only because the Westminster Regiment had been able to carry out the bold hook from the bridgehead won by 1st Infantry Division. As December 14 developed, it became increasingly clear that the Germans still thought it possible to eliminate this thorn in their side. Artillery and Nebelwerfer fire thickened with each passing hour. In the Seaforth Highlanders' sector, the tank-hunting platoon led by Lieutenant Dave Fairweather that was supporting Major D.G. Duncan's 'D' Company spotted three German tanks next to the dirt track leading toward the canal. They were about six hundred yards away. Fairweather thought the tanks were either bogged down or "having very heavy going in getting back to the road." Realizing their vulnerability, Fairweather sent a runner to fetch the artillery FOO working with the Seaforths. When he arrived, at 0800 hours, the tanks were still in place. Fifteen minutes later, the FOO "had a shoot going and destroyed two of them. The third one pulled out and left the scene," Fairweather recalled.

As the morning progressed, the Germans massed several times for a full-press counterattack on the Seaforths. With the battalion's anti-tank guns and PIAT platoons in place and field artillery on call, Lieutenant Colonel Bell-Irving was sure the Seaforths could hold.[34] Beside them also were two troops of the British Columbia Dragoons' 'A' Squadron.

In the Loyal Edmonton Regiment's sector, the situation was much the same, and two troops of the B.C. Dragoons' 'C' Squadron were on hand. Lieutenant Colonel Stone had every confidence in his company commanders, even though Major George Brown of 'C' Company had been wounded in the early morning and replaced by a platoon commander—Lieutenant Keith MacGregor. Stone considered MacGregor "a very calm and collected man."[35]

At 1230 hours, 'D' Company's Major F.H. McDougall reported being heavily shelled by artillery. The shells continued to fall unabated for forty-five minutes. As the shelling eased, German armour could be heard moving just outside 'D' Company's lines. Soon four tanks, with a large force of infantry alongside, started closing in.[36]

In the Seaforth's sector, meanwhile, a smaller combined tank/infantry force was also headed for Duncan's 'D' Company. Instantly, the artillery FOO called in defensive fire against the German force, and within thirty minutes the enemy attacking the Seaforths were thrown back with heavy casualties.[37]

By 1330 hours, it was evident that the main weight of the German counterattack was focused on McDougall's 'D' Company. Stone had the battalion's 3-inch mortars and medium machine guns firing constantly in support, while the 4.2-inch mortars of the Saskatoon Light Infantry fired out to longer range to disrupt those forces still approaching the company. He also had both field and medium artillery pounding the German lines of approach. Fearing 'D' Company might be overrun, Stone ordered Captain Alon Johnson to get 'A' Company ready to restore the situation if necessary.[38]

A Dragoons' tank commanded by Corporal George L. White was supporting 'D' Company's No. 17 Platoon. White placed his Sherman squarely on the road that was serving as the axis of approach for the counterattacking force. Despite a rain of fire, White stood in his open turret hatch to better observe the enemy and accurately direct the tank's fire. As the fire thickened, the Eddies' platoon commander was unable to help direct White's fire. Realizing he needed the infantry officer to show him where his line was threatened, White descended from the Sherman five times to run through heavy fire and get directions. Each time, he dashed back to the tank "and gave perfect support by 'shooting up' the targets which had thus been indicated," his Military Medal citation noted.[39]

In the midst of the swirling battle, MacGregor calmly asked Stone by wireless, "How many rounds does a Panther carry?" Stone had no idea but was not inclined to admit that. "Sixty-six," he said. "Good," MacGregor replied. "This one has only sixty-four left," as two rounds had punched through the house his headquarters section was in, though without causing any casualties. A Sherman showed up moments later, and its fire caused the Panther to skulk away.[40]

At 1403 hours, all German activity in the Seaforth's area ceased, and the artillery supporting them swung to help the Eddies. Soon after, the artillery that had been assisting the Westminster's advance along the west bank of the canal was also redirected to the beleaguered battalion. 'D' Company's forward platoon came under direct fire from an SPG and had to evacuate houses being blown apart. The platoon fell back on the company's main position. While the artillery fire stopped a number of tanks approaching from the west, several SPGs came in from the south. Artillery fire, noted the Eddies' war diarist, was fired against these SPGs "and repeated again and again." At 1455 hours, McDougall said his company "was still holding the ground but had suffered heavy casualties and would need more men quickly if the ground was to be held." Stone ordered 'A' Company forward.

A message from Desert Air Force fighter-bombers circling overhead reported seven tanks closing on 'D' Company that were already too close to the Edmontons for the planes to engage them. Both medium and field artillery were immediately directed against these tanks. Stone ordered the Shermans with 'B' Company—which was not as hard pressed—to add their support to 'D' Company. Suddenly, at 1550 hours, the counterattack crumbled. 'D' Company's casualties numbered twenty-eight. Reports from prisoners were that the German losses had been "very heavy, particularly in their reserve company which was supposed to follow through the initial assault and hold the ground occupied by 'D' Company." One German tank was still lurking near the Edmonton lines at 1620 hours, before being driven off by several Shermans.[41]

By mid-afternoon, Lieutenant Colonel Bogert had considered the bridgehead sufficiently enlarged to accommodate the Princess Patricia's Canadian Light Infantry. At 1630 hours, Major Colin MacDougall's 'B' Company led its advance toward the Naviglio.[42] Lieutenant Syd Frost was close behind, at the wheel of a jeep overflowing with ammunition for his medium machine-gun platoon. Lieutenant Jim Horton of the pioneer platoon and the anti-tank platoon's Lieutenant Al Fairburn also rode in the jeep, while Frost's men lugged the three broken-down Vickers machine guns alongside on foot.

Frost's jeep was one of several "thin-skinned" vehicles and tanks in line on the road leading to the canal. Their presence quickly alerted the German observers in Bagnacavallo, and the road started being shelled. Immediately ahead of Frost, a Sherman was struck and burst into flames. Frost gunned the jeep "and shot past the burning tank as the ammunition started to explode inside.

"Now," Frost later wrote, "shells began to fall on the troops in the fields. Over the roar of our tanks and the firing of our guns, I could not hear the explosions but could see men hit the ground, quickly get up and continue the advance. No one stopped or hesitated unless he was wounded or killed. The wounded were left for the stretcher bearers who rushed forward and carried their charges to the rear."

With the vehicle column about four hundred yards short of the canal, the German fire switched back to the road. Three hundred yards ahead of his jeep, Frost saw "six dirty yellow flashes, as six mortar bombs exploded, one behind the other."

Frost heard Lieutenant Fairburn yell, "The next stonk may get us . . . watch out . . . Here comes . . . " The sentence went unfinished, as a mortar round "exploded in a blast of heat and dirt. A great rush of air seemed to bear me aloft. I felt I was going out of this world—like the sickening, spinning sensation of going down a long tunnel when given ether before an operation.

"I came back to earth . . . as soon as I hit the ditch. I got up a little dazed, but seemingly unhurt. Jim and Al were dusting themselves off." Their jeep was undamaged, but the vehicle in front of it was badly mangled, and two wounded men lay nearby. Stretcher-bearers were already running toward them. Frost saw that one of the downed men "had taken the full impact of a shell and was finished.

"I looked down at the shattered body, the limbs askew in grotesque patterns. I couldn't believe that minutes before it had been a man. He seemed so flattened out, so insignificant, lying there in the mud that had already begun to claim his remains."

As Frost walked toward the jeep, Horton said, "What happened to your pants? You've got a hell of a hole in the seat. For God's sake, you've been hit too!"

Frost put a hand inside his trousers and "felt something warm and sticky covering [his] right buttock. 'Christ sake, not again!'" he said. "Suddenly, I felt very tired." Frost was soon evacuated to the Patricia's Regimental Aid Post, where his wound was inspected by Medical Officer Captain Steve Worobetz. "Yeah, you've got a slug in there—deep, probably right to the bone, but you're lucky. Anywhere else in the back and you'd be a dead man." Bandaged up, Frost was sent down the line to hospital for surgery.[43]

The Patricias, meanwhile, had entered the bridgehead and had started pushing west toward Bagnacavallo. Opposition was light but persistent. Just before nightfall, 'D' Company's No. 16 Platoon under Lieutenant W.E. Harrington overran a machine-gun position, killing its two-man crew. Harrington then spotted a Panther nearby. Taking a PIAT, he closed on the tank and knocked it out. As the tank crew bailed out, they were taken prisoner.[44]

With night settling in, the Germans maintained a steady rate of harassing fire with artillery and Nebelwerfers. But the Canadians now had three infantry battalions, fifteen 75-millimetre Shermans, two 17-pounder Firefly tanks, and a troop of six-pounder anti-tank guns in the bridgehead, so 1 Canadian Corps's historical officer, Captain Joe Wrinch, considered it "reasonably secure." The Patricia's advance had also expanded it to within five hundred yards of Bagnacavallo. On the opposite flank, the Eddies had also greatly extended the bridgehead.

It stretched almost two miles along the Naviglio and was several hundred yards deep.[45]

AT 0810 HOURS ON December 15, another Panther growled toward the lines of Loyal Edmonton Regiment's 'D' Company. Blundering into a German minefield that the Eddies had left in place to provide some added protection, the tank triggered a mine, and the explosion broke one of its tracks. A PIAT platoon then rushed forward and "rendered it useless" with three rounds. Four of the crew were killed and its officer taken prisoner.

After this, the Germans seemed wary of approaching closer, but all companies "reported hearing continuous enemy movement in front of their areas." Reports from planes circling overhead also identified numerous tanks manoeuvring between one hundred and five hundred yards to the front of 'D' Company.[46]

At 0915 hours, enemy tanks and SPGs were also reported closing in on the Seaforth Highlanders. These were driven off by artillery fire directed by FOOs working from aircraft fitted out to serve as aerial observation posts. In the late morning, Lieutenant Colonel Bell-Irving was evacuated—suffering from a recurrence of malaria that he had first contracted in Sicily. The battalion's second-in-command, Major Howarth Glendinning, took over.[47]

In the Patricia's sector, meanwhile, a patrol led by Lieutenant Vaughan Stuart Allan came under fire while approaching buildings on Bagnacavallo's outskirts. Directing two sections to provide covering fire, Allan led the third in a charge on the German positions, only to have the section driven back by heavy fire. The patrol returned to the battalion lines, reporting Allan and three others as missing. Their graves were later discovered close to where this action had been fought.[48]

As the day progressed, both 2nd Brigade's Lieutenant Colonel Bogert and the Eddies' Lieutenant Colonel Stone focused on a Y-intersection about a thousand yards east of the Loyal Edmonton lines. The Via Guarno, a road running east from Bagnacavallo, intersected another one branching off the canal road. From this intersection, two roads provided separate approaches to the Senio

River. Aerial observation had alerted Bogert that there was significant German traffic flowing in all directions through the junction.
Bogert decided the junction needed to be closed off. At the same time,
'D' Company's Major F.H. McDougall had also reported increasing
enemy activity passing through it. Bogert's orders for Stone to seize it
coincided with his own thinking.[49]

"It's essential for us to get this crossroads," Stone told
'C' Company's Lieutenant MacGregor. "You must take it."[50] At
2000 hours, MacGregor led the company forward. Immediately, the
Germans opened up with heavy mortar fire. Machine guns also started firing from positions around the junction itself, and soon rounds
from Panzerfausts were flashing in. Seeing that the ground between
his men and the junction was devoid of cover, MacGregor realized
there was no chance to deploy for a measured advance. Spotting a
deep ditch that ran through to the junction, MacGregor sprinted to
the front of the company. Jumping into the ditch, he led the men in
a charge along it toward the junction—four hundred yards distant.[51]

"I was running along and suddenly tumbled head on into an MG
post that I hadn't seen at all," MacGregor later said. "I was thrashing
around and the Germans were thrashing around."[52] When the fight
ended, eight Germans were dead and fifteen taken prisoner, and
'C' Company had not only taken the junction but advanced two hundred yards beyond.[53] MacGregor's actions earned a Military Cross.
"I was surprised that I was described as being heroic," he said later,
by "taking out this MG in a direct charge. Which I did by accident."[54]
MacGregor, Stone wrote, "made a grand charge and was on his objective at 2105 hours."[55] However it played out, 'C' Company's winning of
the junction ended German efforts to eliminate the bridgehead. The
most they could do was try to contain the situation, which they did by
having armoured tanks prowl on the perimeters. These were kept at
bay with medium artillery shellfire.

19

No Braggadocio

B Y DECEMBER 15, 1 CANADIAN Corps had two decisive bridgeheads across the Naviglio Canal—the one won by 1st Canadian
Infantry Division's 1st and 2nd Brigades and another in 5th Canadian
Armoured Division's sector. To the left of the 1st Division bridgehead,
however, fierce resistance had prevented the division's 3rd Brigade
from even reaching the canal. Facing 3rd Brigade were elements
of the 98th Infanterie-Division—defending a line extending from
the eastern suburbs of Bagnacavallo south to the boundary between 1 Canadian Corps and v British Corps. Until December 14,
v Corps had also made little headway, prompting 1st Division's historical officer, Captain T.J. Allen, to observe that "the chief movers
from 1 Dec. to 14 Dec. seemed to be the Canadians."[1] The night
of December 14–15, however, brought a major v Corps assault by
2nd New Zealand Armoured Division and 10th Indian Division to
clear a ridge southwest of Faenza. At the same time, to the left of
v Corps, 11 Polish Corps punched through to the Senio River. After
suffering heavy casualties, both the 715th Infanterie-Division and
90th Panzer Grenadier Division had retreated behind the Senio
by sunset on December 15. The following day, Faenza was occupied without incident by 43rd Indian Lorried Infantry Brigade. On
December 17, 10th Indian Division won two small bridgeheads across
the Senio. Neither could be expanded, however, as the supply routes

for v Corps were by then so deteriorated that new offensive operations were unsupportable.[2]

Between Highway 9 and the coast, British Eighth Army was still well short of the Senio. Yet the Allied plan called for it to cross the river in strength in a move to coincide with U.S. Fifth Army's drive on Bologna before Christmas. Such a broad offensive—spanning virtually the entire line from Bologna to the coast—required the full attention of Allied high command, yet all of them were distracted by a major reorganization.

On December 12, General Harold Alexander had been promoted to field marshal and appointed Supreme Allied Commander Mediterranean. The promotion was backdated to June 4—the day Rome fell—to retain his rank seniority over Field Marshal Bernard Montgomery. The latter had risen to field marshal on September 1. Montgomery's fractious relationship with the American generals in Northwest Europe was such that Chief of the Imperial General Staff Field Marshal Sir Alan Brooke wanted Alexander in his back pocket. Should Montgomery's relationship with Supreme Headquarters, Allied Expeditionary Force General Dwight D. Eisenhower reach a breaking point, Brooke could make Alexander the SHAEF commander's deputy. With his congenial and diplomatic nature, Alexander could serve as a buffer between Montgomery and the Americans.

General Mark Clark succeeded Alexander at Headquarters Allied Armies in Italy, which was redesignated Fifteenth Army Group. U.S. Fifth Army command went to Lieutenant General Lucian K. Truscott Jr. of U.S. vi Corps. Lieutenant General Richard McCreery remained Eighth Army's commander.

Clark's reputation had never been fully redeemed after a disastrous decision during the First Battle of Cassino. On January 20, 1944, he had ordered the 36th U.S. Infantry Division to launch a cross-river assault directly into the sights of a string of German machine guns. In a fruitless forty-eight-hour battle, the division suffered 1,681 killed or wounded. As Alexander handed over command, he offered Clark the following cautionary comment: "Always at the back of my mind, when I make plans, is the thought that I am playing with human lives. Good chaps get killed or wounded and it's a terrible thing. The proudest thing I can say is that I am a frontline soldier myself. I fought in the last war with my battalion of Guards and was wounded three times. So, I do know what it means and I do not throw away lives unnecessarily."[3]

NOT SQUANDERING LIVES was precisely what Lieutenant Colonel Jean Allard was worrying about on December 15. His Royal 22e Régiment had been ordered to close up to within 1,500 yards of the Naviglio Canal by winning a brick factory on the Godo–Bagnacavallo road. The factory could then serve as a protected start point for attacking Bagnacavallo. From the Fosso Vecchio, where the Van Doos were formed up, to the factory was about 550 yards straight along the road. What probably seemed an easy task from the perspective of 3rd Brigade staff looking at a map seemed anything but when viewed through Allard's binoculars. He saw one ditch after another and knew that "the flat terrain complicated daytime movements and created risks that were unacceptable when weighed against the forces we were facing." Ahead, the Germans were heavily entrenched. A hard fight was certain. Past experience told him that once the Germans "destroyed the momentum of our advance, they would then withdraw to another likely obstacle." Allard normally disdained seeking supporting arms, believing his Van Doos could triumph alone. This time, however, he requested Desert Air Force strafing and bombing attacks and 4.2-inch mortar support from the Saskatoon Light Infantry.[4]

At 1530 hours, 'D' Company advanced, with medium artillery also firing concentrations aimed at sealing movement along any of the roads back to Bagnacavallo. Field artillery fire was blanketing the factory with shells. A troop of British tankers accompanied each 'D' Company platoon. "The tanks went in at the proper time," Van Doos' intelligence officer Lieutenant J. Richard wrote, "the arty support was effectively given, and, as the luck of war would have it, the Spitfires of the DAF came down strafing the known enemy positions as close as one hundred yards from our forward troops . . . At 1545 hours [D Company] called off the arty fire and by 1700 hours the brickworks were ours . . . A total of thirty prisoners were taken, as well as machineguns of all calibres, scores of rifles, grenades, a large amount of small-arms ammunition and countless pieces of equipment. The complete success of this operation can be attributed to the well-timed schedule and . . . complete co-operation between all arms involved."[5]

On the right flank of 'D' Company's main attack, 'A' Company had conducted a diversionary thrust. Lance Sergeant Joseph François Appleby headed up the leading platoon. Seeing a platoon behind falter in the face of heavy German fire from the flank, Appleby turned his platoon and struck the enemy position from behind. As 'A' Company dug in on its objective, the Germans counterattacked, only to be driven back by immediate fire from Appleby's platoon. Realizing the Germans were in disarray, Appleby charged out with his men, and ten prisoners were taken. Appleby's leadership resulted in a Military Medal.[6]

At the end of the day, the successes by the Van Doos failed to significantly improve 3rd Brigade's situation. The Germans had lost a little ground but seemed still solidly entrenched just ahead. Hoping to get some idea of the state of German opposition, Brigadier Paul Bernatchez dispatched two partisans on the night of December 15–16 to infiltrate Bagnacavallo. They found the town garrisoned by about three hundred enemy troops. These, however, had little or no transport. All road junctions within Bagnacavallo and on its approaches were mined. A number of light guns, mostly self-propelled or mounted in halftracks, continuously prowled the town's outskirts. That the Germans had withdrawn most artillery behind the Senio was a sign that they were loosening their grip.[7]

AS THE VAN Doos had been mounting their December 15 attack, Lieutenant General Charles Foulkes began to think that the German line in front of the Senio River might collapse if Bagnacavallo fell. Yet a direct attack on the town circled by an old defensive wall and with the Naviglio Canal like a moat guarding the southern approach would be costly and uncertain of success. Breaking the German line on either side, however, would threaten to surround the garrison and should lead to Bagnacavallo's abandonment. Foulkes decided to concentrate 1st Infantry Division's strength on forcing crossings of both the Fosso Vecchio and the Naviglio southwest of Bagnacavallo.

This push would start with 1st Brigade crossing the Vecchio and advancing to the Naviglio. While this was going on, 3rd Brigade would relieve 2nd Brigade in its bridgehead on the night of December 16–17. This would free 2nd Brigade to pass through 1st Brigade to complete Bagnacavallo's outflanking. As the 1st Division attack developed, 5th Armoured Division's 11th Infantry Brigade would force the Fosso Munio to the northeast and strike westward to link up with 2nd Brigade behind Bagnacavallo. The relocation of 3rd Brigade and concentration of the other two brigades would create a significant gap between 1 Canadian Corps and v Corps, which was to be filled by the Royal Canadian Dragoons.[8]

Southwest of Bagnacavallo, the Naviglio ran almost ruler-straight through the town of Granarolo to Faenza. The Vecchio, meanwhile, meandered toward and then away from the Naviglio until it crossed the canal just north of Granarolo. After that, the Vecchio sharply paralleled the Naviglio at a distance of about 750 yards to Faenza. German defences south of Bagnacavallo were anchored on the Vecchio with a secondary fallback line being the Naviglio to Granarolo. Past Granarolo, the Naviglio became the forward defended waterway.

At daybreak on December 16, 1st Brigade's Royal Canadian Regiment and 48th Highlanders of Canada prepared to cross the Vecchio. The RCR attack was to start from the railway that approached Bagnacavallo from Russi at the point about four hundred yards from the Vecchio. Because of the way the Vecchio meandered, the 48th Highlanders—starting from the village of Boncellino, just across the Lamone River—faced an advance of a mile over open ground.

Both battalions were badly depleted. The RCR attack was tasked to its 'X' Company, cobbled together from survivors of 'B' Company and the support company. Its objective was a six-building cluster on the Vecchio's south bank that was known to be in enemy hands. Support was provided by an M-10 17-pounder self-propelled gun. According to 'X' Company's after-action report, Lieutenant T.C. Miller's No. 2 Platoon "with great dash rushed the houses, firing from the hip as they charged and eight enemy were taken prisoner." No. 3 Platoon quickly passed the first house seized by Miller's men and took the next one along. This put the Germans in full retreat, and Lieutenant J.M. Carpenter's No. 1 Platoon joined in clearing the remaining houses. As soon as the houses were secured, the Germans counterattacked with infantry carrying machine guns and Panzerfausts. These were driven back over the Vecchio, the Germans suffering heavy losses. By 1400 hours, 'X' Company had consolidated its hold, with only one officer and two other ranks having been wounded.[9]

Left of the RCR, the 48th Highlanders had targeted two bridges over the Vecchio that intelligence reports claimed still stood. 'D' Company led on the right and 'C' Company the left. 'C' Company immediately came under heavy small-arms fire. Despite support by a 12th Royal Tank Regiment Churchill, the company fell back at 0900 hours to reorganize on its start line. 'D' Company had enjoyed initial success, its scout platoon bagging twelve prisoners before dawn in the process of infiltrating the German defences. By the time 'D' Company launched its main advance, however, the Germans were fully alerted and full of fight. Two enemy tanks appeared to take on the supporting 12th RTR Churchill. An initial exchange of rounds persuaded the German tanks to withdraw. The Churchill slipped into cover behind a haystack. When the haystack caught fire, the Churchill also "commenced to sink in the mud. The situation was made more awkward," the 48th Highlanders' war diarist wrote, "by the presence of an enemy tank some 200 yards away which was hiding behind a building. Both fired at one another through the building with no apparent effect." Mortar and artillery fire fell so thickly that 'D' Company could not move forward. Then Captain Bob Murdoch was shot in the foot and evacuated. Captain Lloyd Smith rushed forward to take over.[10]

'C' Company was again trying to win ground. Moving toward a brick shed, No. 14 Platoon came under almost point-blank fire from the right flank. Bren gunner Private Joseph Albert Bray was hit in the stomach by a Schmeisser round. When the section leader took a bullet in the neck, Bray, despite his painful wound, led a charge on the position. Killing two Germans with bursts of fire, he scattered the rest. The platoon was just recovering its breath when twelve Germans came charging in. Stepping into the open, Bray engaged them with the Bren—killing two and scattering the rest. Ten minutes later, a second attack developed. A bullet broke one of Bray's legs but, propping himself up, he kept firing until this attack broke. Bray then collapsed from loss of blood. His actions earned a Distinguished Conduct Medal. Bray's wounds were so severe, however, that the twenty-one-year-old succumbed to them on December 30.

By nightfall, the 48th Highlanders had gained only eight hundred yards at a cost of thirty-nine casualties, seven—not counting Bray—being fatal.[11] Between them, the RCR and 48th Highlanders had taken forty-two prisoners.[12]

At 2030 hours, Lieutenant Colonel Don Mackenzie ordered both companies to renew the advance by sending patrols to "feel out the enemy." By 0800 hours on December 17, 'D' Company's patrols reported the Germans holding a line about five hundred yards short of the Vecchio. Captain Lloyd Smith advanced the company toward the enemy. 'C' Company's commander reported his men would move within the hour. Mackenzie decided that once this company was halfway to the Vecchio, he would pass two platoons from 'B' Company through to continue the advance. Both companies were again supported by 12th RTR tanks. 'D' Company's support was impressive— two Churchills and M10s each. Just as Smith started forward, scouts reported the road ahead was mined. As the pioneer platoon came forward to lift the mines, its Lieutenant Ken Hudson lost a foot to a Schu-mine. Two other pioneers were also soon injured by mines.

The mine-clearing delayed the advance to 1000 hours. Attached to 'D' Company, Lieutenant John Milling's scout and sniper platoon led. Resistance was sharp, and Milling was soon wounded by a shell from an SPG. Then Lieutenant Richard Owen Buckland Williamson was killed. The advance bogged down. At 2200 hours, Brigadier Desmond Smith informed Mackenzie that he was going to pass the Hastings and Prince Edward Regiment through to gain the Vecchio and that the Royal Canadian Regiment would also push forward.[13]

At 0400 hours on December 18, these two battalions headed for the river behind a covering heavy artillery concentration. The Hasty Ps, still reeling and battered from their December 11–12 mauling at the

Naviglio, were in no shape for combat operations. As the German counter-artillery started falling, the battalion crumbled and went to ground.[14] On the right, the RCR had pushed 'A' and 'B' Companies forward. Major Jim Houghton's 'A' Company encountered little difficulty. The lead platoon quickly splashed across the Vecchio, overran a 298th Panzer Grenadier Regiment's battalion headquarters, and took thirty prisoners. Soon the entire company was across. At 0645 hours, however, the Germans counterattacked hard with tanks and infantry when the rest of the company was just past the headquarters. A withdrawal to where No. 8 Platoon had dug in began.[15]

During the withdrawal, Private Howard Otis went forward alone and attacked the tanks at point-blank range with his PIAT. The first bomb set the leading tank on fire. A second round failed to explode, while a third shot detonated amidst the following infantry and killed several of them. Otis returned to the company with a wounded comrade clinging to his back. His heroism garnered a Distinguished Conduct Medal.[16]

Otis's actions failed to deter the German counterattack. At 0715 hours, Lieutenant Colonel William Reid ordered 'A' Company back across the Vecchio. "This almost became disastrous," Houghton wrote, "because an enemy MG had set up in our rear and opened up as the company reached the river bank. Several men were wounded." Two infantrymen with rifles managed to silence the machine gun, and the company then escaped.[17]

'B' Company, meanwhile, had been hit hard by enemy fire from the outset. Disoriented in the darkness, its commander lost control of his platoons. At 0500 hours, only the company commander, two platoon commanders, and five privates reached the Vecchio. This party withdrew to the attack start line.[18]

After losing twenty-one men killed or wounded, the RCR was back where it had started. Another two officers and seventeen men were missing and assumed captured.[19]

In what the army's official historian termed a "fine display of initiative," 'D' Company of the 48th Highlanders had meanwhile pushed through to the Vecchio without any orders to do so.[20] Quickly passing through the disorganized Hasty Ps, Captain Lloyd Smith's men reached the more northerly of the two bridges, dashed across, and deployed to defend it. Although the bridge was wired for detonation, the surprised Germans fled before they could trigger the explosives. German mortar fire pounded the company, and a round killed Lieutenant Murray Hoffman. Lieutenant John Milling of the accompanying scout and sniper platoon had been wounded. This left just Smith and two lieutenants trying to control four platoons.

Smith was confident the bridge could be held, so long as reinforcements arrived soon. But at 1300 hours, Mackenzie ordered him to withdraw, as the brigade had decided to saturate the area with a heavy artillery concentration that might enable the RCR and Hasty Ps to get through.[21]

This was a bitter pill to swallow, and Smith and his men pulled out reluctantly. The artillery fire rained down, but neither battalion made any progress. When 'D' Company returned to within sight of the bridge, they saw that the Germans had detonated the charges and destroyed it.[22]

The loss of the bridge ended any hope that 1st Brigade's diminished and demoralized battalions could force the Vecchio. This turn of events delighted Acting Commander-in-Chief Southwest Generaloberst Heinrich von Vietinghoff. "Our own troops," he reported to Berlin, "thus achieved a complete defensive victory in which [98th Infanterie-Division] play[ed] a special part." Credit for effectively working with the infantry was given to the 504th Tiger Tank Battalion and 1st Panther Battalion, both of 4th Panzer Regiment.[23]

REALIZING THAT 1ST BRIGADE'S attack south of Bagnacavallo was beyond salvage, at 1000 hours on December 18, Lieutenant General Foulkes gathered his divisional, brigade, and senior supporting arms commanders in 5th Armoured Division's operations room to develop a new plan.[24] It entailed a two-brigade attack on the night of December 19. In the 5th Division sector, held by 12th Infantry Brigade, 11th Brigade would cross the Fosso Munio. At the same time, 1st Infantry Division's 2nd Brigade would advance out of the bridgehead west of the Naviglio Canal, which was now held by 3rd Brigade, to the right of Bagnacavallo. Foulkes envisioned 11th Brigade punching straight through to the Senio River, while 2nd Brigade wheeled leftward and isolated Bagnacavallo from the rear. Scheduled for 2000 hours, the attack would be silent, with no preceding artillery barrage. All objectives and intermediate advance points, however, were plotted and mapped. Once the attack was under way, artillery could be directed as required. The Irish and Perth Regiments would lead the 11th Brigade attack with support provided by the Lord Strathcona's Horse. Engineers would first construct a tank-bearing bridge and footbridges for the infantry. Leading 2nd Brigade's effort would be the Loyal Edmonton Regiment and Princess Patricia's Canadian Light Infantry.[25]

In 5th Division's sector, the Munio was thirty feet wide, with five-foot-high dykes on either side. On the German-held west side, a wide muddy field extended about six hundred yards to the first line of trees. In typical Italian fashion, the field had been deeply tilled into regularly spaced eighteen-inch furrows. Several houses stood near the tree line. Houses and tree line provided the Germans with excellent positions from which to sweep the open field. A road called the Via Chiara ran from the Munio to the Via Rossetta, which closely paralleled the Senio. The Perth Regiment was to follow the Via Chiara. About 1,200 yards to the north and 300 yards west of the Munio, the Via Sant' Antonio ran straight to the Via Rossetta and the Senio. The Irish Regiment was to follow this muddy farm track.[26]

In 2nd Brigade's sector, the Munio bent sharply northwestward before straightening out midway between the Naviglio and the Senio. This created a 1,000-yard swath of open ground between it and the attack start line. The Eddies and the Patricias were to clear this area of small tree-lined fields and vineyards, which were known to be heavily mined. Three lateral roads cutting across the advance line were also certainly mined and provided strong defensive positions. Many scattered farmhouses were believed to have been turned into fortified strongholds.

Both brigades were expected to face heavy resistance from Germans ordered to screen an ongoing orderly withdrawal to the Senio. Corps intelligence estimated there were eight opposing battalions—mostly from 98th Infanterie-Division—ranging in strength from eighty to two hundred men. All were well supported by Tigers, Panthers, SPGs, Nebelwerfer batteries, and artillery.[27]

Even as the attack plan was being finalized, 5th Division intelligence staff translated an intercepted December 18 operational order issued by 98th Infanterie-Division's Generalleutnant Alfred Reinhardt. Instead of defending a main line to the last man, Reinhardt ordered a "deep main sector of resistance. Therefore, every man must not be rammed into forward positions." Instead, "defence in the greatest possible depth [must] be organized through the conversion of all heavy weapon positions, HQs, etc., into nests of resistance." Reserves were to be close to the forward defensive lines "to exploit soonest the enemy's weakest moments, i.e. on canal and river crossings, and during the early stages of a breakthrough." Because of Allied air superiority, Reinhardt prohibited battalion counterattacks by close-company formations because "such attacks cost too much blood. Several simultaneous attacks on fighting patrol lines are much more certain of success."[28]

The Allied attack's silent nature was intended to surprise the Germans so their initial defences could be pierced. Once surprise was lost, the artillery would be called in and the supporting arms could rush forward. A diversionary plan was also initiated to convince the Germans that the main attack was actually happening where 1st Brigade's assault had failed, west of Bagnacavallo. The Royal Canadian Regiment was to launch a two-company raid across Fosso Vecchio to grab prisoners and then withdraw. To enhance the diversion's authenticity, the corps psychological warfare unit under Captain L.A. Hamer recorded two troops of tanks grinding about outside the hamlet of Cesenatico. The recording was then broadcast over loudspeakers, while sappers banged pieces of iron together to imitate bridge-building sounds. Gun-flash simulators were also fired. The German response was immediate, the 1 Canadian Corps war diarist recorded. "Heavy mortaring of forward positions of [1st Brigade] followed the playing of the recording, several heavy arty concentrations came down during the 'anvil chorus,' and the flash simulators drew some counter-battery fire."[29]

As this noisemaking was under way, four battalions formed on start lines for the true attack. In 5th Division's sector, the Irish Regiment disembarked from trucks and walked toward where it would attack through the Lanark and Renfrew Scottish Regiment lines. "A wretched drizzle of rain began to fall, to make the cold night colder," Captain Gordon Wood wrote.[30] Left of the Irish, the Perth Regiment gathered in muddy farmyards. Private Stan Scislowski watched his 'D' Company comrades as they "made last-minute adjustments to gear, checked weapons, and made sure their pouches were filled with either grenades or loaded Bren mags." There was no braggadocio: "they merely stood in the gloom of the evening, quiet and resigned, contemplating what lay ahead, each alone with his thoughts and apprehensions . . . They'd reached that point where it was no use worrying . . . There was no avoiding it. A battle awaited them, and they were ready, as ready as they ever would be."[31]

AT 2000 HOURS ON December 19, all four battalions advanced toward battle. In the 5th Armoured Division sector, both leading companies of the Irish and Perth Regiments crossed the Fosso Munio by assault bridges without attracting fire. On the right, the Irish Regiment's Captain Ted Charette's 'D' Company headed for a cluster of farm buildings next to the Via Sant' Antonio. Lieutenant Bob Crozier's platoon, the regiment's war diarist later wrote, progressed "nicely" until almost reaching the buildings. Then the Germans sprang their ambush—with "many MGs firing from well-dug in positions, cutting off the leading platoon on the objective and covering the open spaces with withering fire from enfiladed MGs inflicting some casualties and stopping the company."

Crozier rushed a guide back to Charette, who tried to push another platoon through to the objective, only to have it driven back. When heavy mortar fire started raining down, Charette withdrew most of the company almost to the Munio. Quickly reorganizing, he tried a hook to the right in order to reach the cut-off platoon. Heavy machine-gun and mortar fire stopped this attempt cold. Charette pulled back to the Munio and ordered the men to dig in. While some members of the cut-off platoon managed to fight their way clear, Crozier and six others were taken prisoner. When Major William Hayward Mitchell's 'C' Company attempted to take over the advance, it met the same wall of fire. After several men were killed or wounded, Mitchell withdrew to the canal.[32] 'D' Company then fell well back from the Munio to reorganize, while Captain Gordon Wood's 'B' Company dug in on the eastern bank to support Mitchell's company on the other side. "The shelling was by now of fearful intensity," Wood reported.[33] Its war diarist, meanwhile, lamented that the regiment "had failed to get onto the objective for the first time in twelve months of fighting."[34]

Left of the Irish, the Perth's advance had been led by Captain Robert Sydney Chamberlain's 'B' Company. No. 12 Platoon slipped into the cover provided by a drainage ditch on the right-hand side of Via Chiara. Four hundred yards ahead, the ditch entered a stone culvert. The leading section of No. 12 Platoon was just twenty-five yards from the culvert when an MG42 machine gun fired out of it. "In that first five-second burst 150 steel-jacketed rounds ripped down the length of the ditch," Private Scislowski wrote. "The first eleven men were knocked backward under the impact of the bullets smashing through flesh and bones. Most were dead even before they hit the ground." The next burst of fire "stitched a murderous path along the line of fallen and scrambling men. The wounded, the dying, and the dead lay piled in heaps of blood-splashed bodies, the trickle of cold water beneath them running red from the gallons of blood draining into it. The cries of the wounded rose about the whiplash of machine-gun bursts. Help, however, wouldn't reach them this night. Any move by a stretcher-bearer to reach the wounded would have only brought his . . . instant death. The ditch was an abattoir." Only a handful of men at the back of the platoon escaped unscathed to the Munio.[35]

A second 'B' Company platoon had also withdrawn to the Munio in the face of heavy fire, and both dug in there. Chamberlain, his headquarters section, and the third platoon were still forward, lost in the darkness and out of wireless contact. At the Munio, Major Robert Cole of 'A' Company was trying to sort out the confusion. Calling in artillery to suppress the German machine guns was impossible because he had no idea where the lost element of 'B' Company was. Finally, runners located Chamberlain, and all of 'B' Company withdrew through 'A' Company to the Munio's eastern bank. It was 2340 hours.[36]

The night battle was so chaotic that while the Perth and Irish Regiments were being shredded, the Loyal Edmonton Regiment's 'A' Company in the 2nd Brigade's sector met virtually no resistance just a short distance to the right of the Perths. By 2135 hours, the company had reached its objective—a farmhouse known as Casa Tasselli—without serious incident. To the left of 'A' Company, however, 'B' Company's push toward another farmhouse, called Casa Argelli, was greeted by fire from four heavy machine guns sighted in and around the farmhouse. Mortar and artillery fire rained down as the men tried to advance across an open field.[37] The same artillery and mortar fire also began to strike 'A' Company at Casa Tasselli, and its commander reported its strength being "considerably weakened." 'B' Company's situation was worse. Shortly after midnight and fielding no more than twenty-five men, however, it was still trying to reach Casa Argelli.[38]

Left of the Eddies, meanwhile, Major Sam Potts's 'C' Company had led the Patricia's advance toward Casa Toni, where the Via Guarno and two other roads intersected about a third of the way between the Naviglio Canal and the Munio. At 2030 hours, Lieutenant Bill Roach reported that his No. 13 Platoon was receiving heavy machine-gun fire from its right and also from straight ahead. Instructing Roach to keep pushing forward, Potts sent No. 15 Platoon to silence the guns to the right. By 2130 hours, the platoon had succeeded, killing six Germans and taking five prisoners. 'C' Company had one man killed and four wounded. An hour later, No. 13 Platoon reached Casa Toni, which turned out to consist of several buildings. Determining that the farm complex was a German company or battalion headquarters, Roach attacked at once with two sections of his men. No. 13 Platoon's other section and all of No. 15 Platoon provided covering fire. "In close fighting around the building two enemy were killed and twenty taken prisoner," Roach reported. "Our casualties were one killed and two wounded. The platoon then consolidated in all around defence."

Just after midnight, the Germans counterattacked—rushing in through their own mortar fire. 'C' Company broke the attack by killing two Germans and wounding two others. By 0015 hours on December 20, 'C' Company had finished clearing the buildings of opposition. But as Casa Toni was still being hammered by heavy mortar and artillery fire, the company's position remained precarious.[39]

WITH THE IRISH Regiment stopped cold at the Fosso Munio, the only hope in 5th Armoured Division's sector lay with the Perth Regiment. Accordingly, Lieutenant Colonel Maurice Andrew hurriedly organized a renewed effort. Teeing up support from two artillery regiments, the medium machine guns of the Princess Louise Fusiliers, and the Perth's own 3-inch mortars, Andrew ordered Major Robert Cole's 'A' Company forward. Having seen 'B' Company's advance along Via Chiara shredded, Cole led his men into the mud-soaked fields in a wide right hook at 0050 hours on December 20.[40] Despite crossing completely open ground lashed by intense artillery, mortar, and machine-gun fire, Cole kept his men close to the advancing friendly supporting fire. Bypassing any German "resistance nests" encountered, 'A' Company advanced four hundred yards to a farmhouse that was its intermediary objective.[41] Securing the house without a fight, Cole then led the company about six hundred yards farther, to an isolated farmhouse grandly called Casa della Congregatione, about two hundred yards north of Via Chiara. A sharp firefight yielded two German prisoners and an estimated thirty dead or wounded in exchange for a few light casualties. The Germans were identified as battle-experienced soldiers from the 98th Fusilier Battalion, the reconnaissance unit for 98th Infanterie-Division. Having won the casa, 'A' Company dug in. Cole's Perths were a thousand yards inside the German lines, completely isolated, and expecting a counterattack. It was about 0300 hours.

Lieutenant Colonel Andrew and 11th Brigade's Brigadier Ian Johnston knew the key to reinforcing 'A' Company was to push tanks through. That meant bridging the Munio, and 1st Field Squadron set to the task at 0430 hours.[42] With the ground on both sides of the Munio lacking any cover, the Germans quickly detected the arrival of the engineers and began shelling the bridging site. A nearby artillery observer estimated the site was subjected to 155 shell and mortar rounds per minute. An armoured D-7 bulldozer carving out a ramp to where the engineers were installing an Ark bridge was destroyed and its driver killed. Despite the relentless fire, by 0600 hours, the Ark bridge was in place. But the dim dawn light revealed that it lay askew. Where the bridge had been installed, the road it was to have connected to made a sharp turn that had gone undetected in the darkness. The bridge exited uselessly into a ditch.[43]

Standing in readiness was Lord Strathcona's Horse's Captain Jack Wilkin with two Shermans that were to have been first to cross. Wilkin took one look at the bridge and contacted 11th Brigade headquarters with the news. Major General Bert Hoffmeister, who was there conferring with Johnston, immediately put his chief engineer, Lieutenant Colonel Jack Christian, on the phone. Find the 1st Field Squadron officer, Christian snapped, and tell him, "For Christ's sake get bull-dozing!" Minutes later, 5th Division artillery began firing a smokescreen to cover the engineers, and several tanks of 'C' Squadron also pitched in with smoke rounds.[44]

The engineers installed fascines adjacent to the bridge to create an exit and then started grading ramps on either bank. It was a job that was going to take some hours to complete—hours that 'A' Company might not have.[45]

As soon as dawn revealed the bridge problem, the Germans that had struck Casa della Congregatione launched a counterattack supported by heavy machine-gun and artillery fire. Although he'd been painfully wounded in the face just before dawn, Major Cole continued to direct the defence. With artillery on call and his men told to hold fire until he instructed otherwise, Cole let the Germans close to within thirty yards before unleashing his men and the distant guns. The counterattack was shattered. The Germans reeled back with heavy losses and several men taken prisoner by 'A' Company.[46] For the present, as the Perth's war diarist wrote, 'A' Company's position was "not a happy one, but they were holding firm."[47]

[20]

Hard Going

O N DECEMBER 20, THE Germans mustered everything possible
to stop the Canadian advance toward the Senio River. In the
Princess Patricia's Canadian Light Infantry sector on the far left,
Major Sam Potts's 'C' Company clung to Casa Toni. At 0100 hours,
Potts moved his headquarters and an aid station into the main building held by Lieutenant Bill Roach's No. 13 Platoon. Ten minutes later,
an 88-millimetre self-propelled gun fired on it at close range with
armour-piercing and high-explosive shot. Eight shells collapsed the
upper storey. Potts hit the deck just as a shell went "through the wall
so close to my head that I saw the gun flash of the next round through
the hole, without taking my chin off the floor."[1]

Potts—a company commander with the regiment since its landing
in Sicily on July 10, 1943—was buried in rubble, his right leg so badly
injured that recovery would take months. Three men were killed and
another fifteen injured—four of whom continued to fight. Uninjured
and digging himself free from debris, Roach took command. The
company's No. 18 wireless set was knocked out, so his only link to battalion headquarters was through runners.[2] Roach's first concern was
to evacuate the wounded and dead from the crumbling building. As
he was overseeing this, two more armour-piercing shells tore through
its walls. Roach ignored the incoming fire, personally extricating and
evacuating several casualties.

This task was just completed when German infantry counter-attacked. "Quick to meet this new threat, [Roach] dashed outside the house and ran in the open from position to position and from trench to trench urging and directing his men to fight off the counterattack. During this action, he . . . killed two more of the enemy. Largely as a result of the inspiration of his presence and wonderful example, the enemy attack was unsuccessful and they withdrew, leaving their wounded and fifteen prisoners in 'C' Company's lines," read Roach's subsequent Distinguished Service Order citation.[3]

'C' Company's situation remained dire. In a building farthest from Roach, No. 15 Platoon was struck by fierce artillery and mortar fire. Lieutenant Mervyn Edward Garritty was killed and many of his men "swept . . . to ground." Corporal Jack McGrath took charge. Seventy-five yards away, a machine-gun was zeroing in. McGrath closed on it with his section, then he and Lance Corporal Harold James Fleming charged with fixed bayonets and killed the three-man crew. Fired on by a second machine gun, McGrath shouted for the rest of his men to provide covering fire. He and Fleming then charged the enemy while throwing grenades that killed the gunners.[4]

McGrath and Fleming had just returned to the section when they came under fire from a tank. Artillery and mortar rounds also began crashing down. Fleming was wounded. Hoisting the man on his back, McGrath led the section back toward the rest of No. 15 Platoon. A mortar round exploded directly behind McGrath, hurling him to the ground and killing Fleming. Badly dazed and suffering severe bruising, McGrath staggered to the platoon lines. Realizing his men were still being subjected to machine-gun fire, McGrath and another soldier set out to hunt down the suspected gun position. Moving through heavy shell and mortar fire, with the tank also pumping rounds at them, the two men spotted the German gun. After another charge, the three-man crew surrendered. McGrath returned to the platoon and continued to lead it, refusing all suggestions that he seek medical aid for his injuries. Credited with killing five Germans, wounding another, and taking three prisoners, McGrath received a Distinguished Conduct Medal.[5]

At 0730 hours, the Germans launched another counterattack against No. 15 Platoon's position, which was broken up with four Germans killed and fifteen taken prisoner. McGrath's men suffered no casualties.

While 'C' Company was fighting for its life, the Patricia's Lieutenant Colonel Slug Clark had decided at 0500 hours to send 'D' Company to reinforce it, with 'A' Company advancing behind. Once 'C' Company was reinforced, this following company was to pass through and push northwest along the Via Casalino to its junction with a road called Lo Stradello that ran northeast out of Bagnacavallo. Clark's intention was to then swing the Patricias southwest between this road and the Fosso Munio to cut off the Germans still holding Bagnacavallo.[6]

Coming forward to provide support, the British Columbia Dragoons' Nos. 1 and 2 Troops of 'C' Squadron were assured that the road had been cleared of mines. But at 1100 hours, all three Shermans of the leading No. 1 Troop were immobilized by mines a hundred yards from the intersection.[7] Clark's plan proved wildly ambitious. The attacking force came under close-range shelling from an spg short of 'C' Company's position and was unable to get through to it. Clark attempted to get the attack going again by directing artillery fire at the spg. When that effort failed, all three Patricia companies were left pinned down by intense machine-gun and spg fire.[8]

RIGHT OF THE Patricias, the Loyal Edmonton Regiment had entered the early morning hours of December 20 with 'A' Company relatively secure at Casa Tasselli. 'B' Company's situation at Casa Argelli, however, was critical. Shortly after midnight, the company had been badly battered by fire from an spg that reduced its effective strength to just twenty-five men. At 0330 hours, the company commander advised Lieutenant Colonel Jim Stone that his men could do nothing but sit tight. Stone agreed, moving to relieve the pressure by having 'C' Company bypass Casa Argelli to the south and seize the road junction where Via Pozzarda intersected Via Guarno. An hour after 'C' Company started its move, heavy fire halted it not far from the start line and a reorganization was required.

At 0215, meanwhile, German infantry had tried to surround 'A' Company at Casa Tasselli. Quick and accurate fire from the Eddies' 3-inch mortars and supporting artillery broke the attack. Several prisoners were taken.

Having teed up an extensive artillery support plan, Stone had 'C' Company renew its advance. Although meeting stiff resistance, the company slowly progressed toward the intersection and by 0530 hours were engaged in clearing the houses around it. Ninety minutes later, the company commander reported firmly controlling the intersection and sent a platoon to try to contact the Patricias to the right. The platoon soon reported that at least one German infantry platoon supported by a tank were blocking the road between the Eddies and the Patricias.

By 0900 hours, Stone understood what his battalion faced. 'C' and 'B' Companies were now in contact with each other. The Patricia's 'C' Company appeared firm just a short distance to the southwest. Immediately to the northwest of both the Patricias and Stone's Eddies, the Germans were deployed in a rough arrowhead formation, with two SPGs on their left flank, a force of infantry backed by a tank on the arrow's point, and more tanks on the right flank.[9] Given the German dispositions, Stone considered a counterattack against 'C' Company inevitable and was unsurprised when, at 1100 hours, an SPG began to systematically shoot up the buildings it was in, while another tank ground in from the north. 'C' Company immediately abandoned the buildings and fell back on 'B' Company's position in nearby fields. The two companies braced to meet the attack, while Stone had the battalion's mortars hammer the intersection. Artillery was out of the question because the Eddies and Germans were in too close contact.

At 1120 hours, the two companies reported that they had evacuated their positions and escaped into the fields to the northwest of the intersection. Both companies were taking casualties from intense armour and artillery fire. Then, shortly after noon, the German shelling ceased—indicating that they thought their counterattack had succeeded in shredding the two companies. 'C' Company immediately counterattacked and by 1425 hours had regained control of the intersection. By 1500 hours, both 'C' and 'B' Companies were back in position. The situation in the Eddies' sector appeared to have quieted down. There was little infantry activity, but tanks continued moving around west of the two companies.

When Stone explained the situation to Lieutenant Colonel Pat Bogert at 2nd Canadian Infantry Brigade headquarters, the two worked up a plan to send one platoon of the Eddies' 'D' Company with a troop of tanks through the Patricias to reinforce the two companies at the intersection. At 1530 hours, Lieutenant T.N. Adamson with a thirty-strong platoon and a troop of tanks from the B.C. Dragoons advanced. A heavy smokescreen covered the force's left flank. "Very shortly," the Eddies' war diarist wrote, "contact was made with the enemy and with the tanks firing on one side of the road and then the other, the infantry made good time and by 1635 hours had taken 25 POWs from . . . houses. 'C' Company, some 400 yards north, began to observe more infantry attempting to escape and mortar and arty fire was immediately called down in their area. By 1630 hours, this 'D' Company battle group had cleared the area and arrived at [the intersection]." Stone immediately funnelled Bren carriers and anti-tank guns through to the intersection, and as the enemy tanks deployed for another surge, 'C' Company pushed a standing patrol about seventy-five yards along the Via Guarno to close off this route. Stone realized the battle in 2nd Brigade's sector had turned, and the Germans were now on the back foot. He planned for 'D' Company to send them reeling at 2000 hours.[10]

At 1830 hours, No. 4 Troop of the B.C. Dragoons reported hearing "considerable enemy movement . . . to the west and southwest, becoming gradually fainter, apparently indicating a withdrawal. Shelling died down, and positions remained fairly quiet during the night; there were no enemy patrols into our areas."[11] Stone, who had pushed back the timing of 'D' Company's attack, soon had more good news. A push by the Patricia's 'A' Company, supported by artillery, had managed to get through to and secure its road junction objective after a short fight—capturing one SPG in the process.[12] This development, Stone wrote, made 'D' Company's "job relatively simple. At 0130 hours, 21 Dec., 'D' Company were within 300 yards of their objective and made contact with the enemy . . . All evidence in the area pointed to a very hasty withdrawal by the enemy and by 0600 hours the battalion was firmed up."

The Eddies suffered one officer and eleven other ranks killed, with four officers and fifty-one other ranks wounded.[13] For their part, December 20 cost the Patricias seventeen killed and twenty-eight wounded. This accounted for a large portion of the total losses during the Naviglio Canal fighting of twenty-five killed, fifty-seven wounded, and three missing.[14]

LATE MORNING OF December 20 had found the fate of 5th Canadian Armoured Division's 11th Infantry Brigade attack depending on 1st Field Squadron's engineers. If they failed to get a bridge capable of bearing the weight of tanks across the Fosso Munio, the battle was surely lost. Realizing this, the Germans sought to stop the work. By 1000 hours, Lord Strathcona's Horse commander Lieutenant Colonel Jim McAvity wrote that "the crossing place had attracted the full attention of every enemy weapon sited around the bare field beyond; machine guns, self-propelled guns, and tanks fired into our engineers literally from left, right, and centre." One 'C' Squadron Sherman, firing rounds to add to the smokescreen, was holed four times in rapid succession by a German SPG, and two 4th Anti-Tank Regiment M-10 anti-tank guns were knocked out.

McAvity's thoughts focused on the Perth Regiment's 'A' Company at Casa della Congregatione. Major Robert Cole's men, he knew, were certain to be "greatly reduced in numbers after their heroic advance through the plague of machine-gun lead during the night." Now they were surrounded by enemy infantry and tanks. "Their plight seemed hopeless. From his little Auster plane, an officer directing artillery reported "five enemy tanks on our side of the Senio in this sector; two of them were in positions on the straight road [Via Chiara] that was our Centre Line and these fired continuously into the bridge site; an SP gun was firing from a farm near the bridge . . . machine guns dug in all over the open field, some of them nearer than the 'lost' company, raked the dyke with streams of whining bullets . . . It seemed certain that, before long, the [enemy] would set about the obviously simple task of overrunning that company."[15]

At noon, the Germans struck with twenty-five to thirty men led by the commander of the 98th Fusiliers Battalion. Cole was ready. As the Germans closed in, he brought down a pre-arranged "box barrage" around the German formation that blocked its avenue of retreat. Having funnelled the Germans into a killing ground, Cole ordered his men to open up with small-arms fire that "cut the enemy force to pieces. Seven Germans survived—all taken prisoner. The commanding officer and the others were slain.[16]

At the bridging site, Brigadier Ian Johnston and McAvity agreed they could no longer wait for the bridge to be fully completed. McAvity ordered 'C' Squadron's Major J.F. Westhead to send a tank troop across it. Lieutenant A.S. Hutchings's No. 3 Troop drew the task, and Corporal M.H. Koffman led off at 1400 hours. Crossing the groaning bridge and chewing a path up the muddy ramp, Koffman's Sherman headed into the open field beyond. "Although his tank warded off mortar and shell fragments and small-arms bullets, no armour-piercing rounds found their mark," McAvity wrote. Ten minutes after exiting the bridge, Koffman reached 'A' Company's perimeter, with Hutchings following a few minutes later. The troop's 17-pounder Firefly, commanded by Sergeant D.R. Armstrong, bogged down in the already badly chewed-up, muddy ramp. Captain Jack Wilkin soon advised McAvity that his recovery tanks were unable to drag the Firefly free and it now blocked the bridge exit.

While the two tanks at Casa della Congregatione had bolstered the defence, strong opposition still lurked nearby. Clearing skies, however, brought the arrival of Desert Air Force Spitfires, which strafed German gun positions and anything moving on the road between the Munio and the Senio River.

At the bridging site, Wilkin conferred with the engineer driving the bulldozer. As the driver reversed the machine to a position on the dyke above the ramp, Wilkin's team strung heavy tow cable between it and the Firefly. A series of mud-slinging lunges wrenched the Firefly clear, opening the way for more tanks to reinforce 'A' Company.[17] Intense mortar fire, however, prevented Major Sammy Ridge's

'D' Company from crossing the bridge, until the fire suddenly lifted at 1830 hours. Ridge's Perths rushed forward and reached 'A' Company at 2000 hours "without incident."[18] The siege was lifted. Cole received a Distinguished Service Order for his unflinching leadership.

With the Perth position secure, the Irish Regiment passed two companies through Casa della Congregatione. On December 21, Captain Gordon Wood's 'B' Company led off at 0100 hours. Skirmishing lightly with an obviously retreating enemy, the company reached its objective on the Via Sant' Antonio.[19]

The 11th Brigade fight to cross the Munio had been costly—thirty-two Perths killed and forty-nine wounded.[20] Among the dead was Company Sergeant Major Earl Weaver. Ten days earlier, he had played a key role in 'D' Company's successful crossing of the Lamone River in assault boats.[21] The Irish Regiment suffered forty-two casualties, eight of them fatal.[22]

DURING THE NIGHT of December 20–21, 98th Infanterie-Division's Generalleutnant Alfred Reinhardt ordered a full withdrawal to the Senio River, and the Germans facing the Canadians melted away.[23] When 11th Brigade's Cape Breton Highlanders crossed the Fosso Munio at 2100 hours, they met no resistance during the two-company advance to the Senio. By mid-morning, the Highlanders were digging in opposite Fusignano and had swept clear a wide swath of ground to the town's right. "In almost every instance," a Highlanders report concluded, "the Boche had pulled out without much of a fight. They did not all get away, however, and we increased our 'bag' by another thirty-two PW."

By noon, all three 11th Brigade battalions and a squadron of Lord Strathcona's Horse tanks "were . . . facing up to the Senio." The Germans, however, still had several machine-gun and sniper positions along the dyke on the Canadian side. "With the able assistance of our supporting armour," the Highlanders report related, "the last of these were mopped up by the 23rd and from then until our relief on 27 December we remained in a holding role only. During this period our snipers had some excellent shooting from the top of the dykes and reported numerous hits."[24]

A similar story unfolded in the sector held by 1st Canadian Infantry Division's 2nd Brigade. At 0810 hours on December 21, the Seaforth Highlanders with 'A' Squadron of the B.C. Dragoons passed through the lines of the Patricias and Eddies during the early morning and crossed the Munio unopposed. Several deserters confirmed that the Germans had withdrawn to the Senio. What would have been a hard-fought slog the day before turned into a simple matter of marching. At 1630 hours, the advance was going so well that Major General Harry Foster ordered the Seaforths to push west along the Senio to cut the road running from Bagnacavallo to Lugo on the opposite bank. Except for an artillery shell strike on 'C' Company's headquarters that wounded everyone but the commander and a signaller, the advance was without incident. By the night of December 21–22, all Seaforths had reached the river and found the east dyke held by only a few staggered German positions. Just after dawn, patrols cleared all the houses near the river that were not occupied by the Seaforths. As soon as the patrols returned to their companies, however, the Germans slipped back across the river to reoccupy them. More patrols would then have to be sent out to clear them off.[25]

With the Seaforths threatening the escape route from Bagnacavallo, the Germans abandoned it on December 21. At 0115 hours, 'A' Company of the Carleton and York Regiment—which faced Bagnacavallo—fired all its Bren guns against the town's old walls to draw enemy fire. The response was fierce but was followed by sounds of much movement and then a brilliant display of flares. At 0645 hours, heavy explosions were heard. An hour later, 'A' Company ripped loose with its Bren guns. There was no return fire. At 0945 hours, 'D' Company warily advanced a platoon, which found the town abandoned. Bagnacavallo was declared clear at 1300 hours.[26]

West of Bagnacavallo, where 1st Infantry Brigade was deployed between the Fosso Vecchio and the Naviglio Canal, most of the Germans also withdrew on the night of December 20–21. Only small rearguards protecting engineer parties tasked with destroying the many bridges across these two waterways remained. On the brigade's right flank, the Royal Canadian Regiment pushed patrols across the Vecchio and confirmed the withdrawal. Just before midnight on December 21, the battalion reached a point five hundred yards east of the Senio and found Germans dug in on either side of it. In the centre, the Hastings and Prince Edward Regiment enjoyed similar success. But on the left flank, the 48th Highlanders met sterner resistance from a rearguard defending the Vecchio bridge on the road running northwest to the village of Cotignola.[27] A firefight followed, which ended with the German withdrawal in the mid-afternoon. The 48th then advanced to the Naviglio Canal. Few buildings here remained intact, the battleground striking their war diarist as "reminiscent of Ortona—pocked with shell craters and generally scarred by days of heavy arty fire."[28]

THE FIGHTING THAT I Canadian Corps had faced during its advance from the Lamone River to the Senio was aptly described by a December 21 5th Armoured Division report. It had been "characterized," the report stated, "by particularly heavy mortar and shell fire. The country was very open, little cover other than canals and ditches being available. This made accurate fire on the part of the enemy comparatively simple. Enemy MGs enfiladed the ditches and other cover was accurately registered by his mortars and arty. There were few routes forward and all of these with their defiles were well known to the enemy who kept constant harassing fire on them. Throughout most of the time he had good observation of the area, in many localities movement by day being almost impossible. Coupled to this was the fact that the forward troops had to remain in slit trenches in ground that would have been wet even without the rain that accompanied us throughout the operation.

"The enemy had intended holding this particular piece of ground at all costs. This had been proven by enemy orders captured. He yielded only after being thoroughly defeated by troops who had fought for many days under every disadvantage of ground and weather against an enemy whose supporting weapons provided him with an amount of supporting fire almost equal to ours. Ground and weather combined to reduce the effectiveness of our superiority in armour and air to a small portion of its normal effort."[29]

Assessing this battle, Lieutenant General Charles Foulkes wrote in a letter to be distributed to the troops on Christmas Day that they had "materially assisted in the forcing of the Montone and the Lamone and the capture of over 145 square miles of Italian territory— sufficient for a two and one-half acre allotment for each Canadian soldier in Italy. You have forced the enemy from three strong natural defence lines, liberated a city, Ravenna, four towns, thirty villages, and nearly one thousand smaller inhabited places, and you have materially assisted v Corps in the capture of Faenza. You have forced the enemy commander to withdraw a division from another part of the front in order to reinforce this sector and you have now severely mauled this new division.

"You have taken more than 1,500 prisoners and have killed or wounded probably twice that number of enemy. All arms and services have done their part in this task. The gunners have smashed the enemy's defences with over 1,200 3-ton lorry-loads of shells—184,000 rounds—and on more than one occasion have broken up enemy counterattacks. In addition to opening more than 200 miles of road, the sappers have erected more than a half mile of bridging. Many of the twenty-nine bridges were completed under hostile mortar and artillery fire. The Signals have laid some 2,600 miles of field cable, providing communications without which control of the battle would have been impossible. Despatch riders have delivered since 1 December no less than 28,000 packets.

"I fully appreciate that the going has been hard, the tempo fairly fast and tough, but your determination, skill at arms, and guts has again seen the Hun off. I am more than ever confident that you and I will see the next short stage of the operations to a successful conclusion."[30]

These successes had come at a high cost. In the twenty days of operations beginning December 2, 1 Canadian Corps had 548 officers and men killed, 1,796 wounded, and 212 taken prisoner.[31] Added to this was the psychological toll on the men still serving.

THE DECEMBER BATTLES, Lieutenant Colonel McAvity noted, "always had a definite beginning and a definite end; they began at one water obstacle and ended on the near bank of the next. Never was a fresh brigade committed simply to exploit between rivers. And now, again, the 'poor bloody infantry' had to hang on, taking their turn on patrol and sleeping in a crowded peasant's living-cum-dining room-cum-kitchen, waiting for someone to come forward to relieve them."[32]

On December 22, the Germans "still had some fairly strong dug-in positions along the dyke on our side of the river," an 11th Brigade report noted. "These required a systematic cleaning up."[33] Eliminating them fell to the Irish Regiment's 'B' Company and the Governor General's Horse Guards. The ground extended east from the Via Sant' Antonio to Highway 16—a distance of about four miles with the Via Rossetta bordering the Senio River forming one flank and the Naviglio Canal the other. Two miles wide at the Via Sant' Antonio start line, the ground narrowed to a width of just a mile, as the Via Rossetta bent toward the Naviglio and intersected Highway 16. Where the Via Rossetta drifted away from the Senio, a minor track continued along the dyke to the village of Alfonsine. The ground was typically flat, criss-crossed by lines of trees, hedgerows, and a maze of farm tracks and footpaths. The goodly number of buildings bordering the Via Rossetta provided many German strongholds. Happily for the tankers, the past few days of dry weather had hardened the fields sufficiently to permit cross-country manoeuvre.[34]

In the early morning of December 22, a Horse Guards 'A' Squadron patrol came under machine-gun fire from some of the buildings bordering the Via Rossetta. Deciding against a push directly along the road, Lieutenant Colonel Allan Jordan sent 'A' Squadron's No. 2 Troop "cross country to feel out the enemy position" where a farm road intersected Via Rossetta about a thousand yards east of Via Sant' Antonio. Setting out at noon, Lieutenant R.W. Murray's three tanks were immediately engaged by heavy machine-gun and mortar fire. The tankers fired back at the houses by the junction, which were being used by the Germans. An attempt to outflank this position brought No. 2 Troop to a farm track 750 yards south of the buildings and into 'B' Squadron's operational area—so far away that it was out of the fight. 'A' Squadron's No. 3 Troop, meanwhile, bypassed the buildings at the intersection and then cleared a cluster of farm-houses beyond it. No. 3 Troop was now also unable to work its way back to the intersection. Realizing the German position there was too strong to be eliminated by tanks operating alone, Jordan decided to wait for nightfall and then commit the Irish Regiment with Wasp flame-throwers in support.[35]

Early on December 23, Captain Wood's 'D' Company and the Wasps advanced and met heavy opposition at the intersection. The fire, however, was coming not from the buildings but from the Senio dyke. Charging forward, the Wasps eliminated these positions with bursts of flames.[36] Having received the Bren carrier mounted with flame-throwers only in late November, the Canadian infantry battalions were just beginning to realize their effectiveness. The Westminster Regiment had been the first, on December 16, when, supported by four Wasps, as Lieutenant James Oldfield wrote, they "so surprised [the Germans] they either threw down their arms and ran or surrendered as prisoners."[37]

The Wasps raised similar havoc working with the Irish's 'B' Company, and Wood was "most enthusiastic" about them.[38] However, this success was short-lived. When the Wasps exhausted their flaming fuel at 0220 hours, Germans in nearby houses hit the company with heavy fire from machine-guns and Panzerfausts. Jordan ordered Murray's No 2 Troop of 'A' Squadron to reinforce the embattled Irish. Grinding up from where it had laagered for the night with 'B' Squadron, the tank troop arrived at 0230 hours. Murray and Wood quickly allocated targets for the tanks, which were then "engaged continuously in the face of considerable [Panzerfaust] fire." The fight raged on until mid-morning, when one tank was knocked out. As the crew abandoned it, they were raked by machine-gun fire. Trooper Norman Loveland Cameron was mortally wounded.

Slowly, the Horse Guards and Irish kept gaining ground. In the afternoon, snow started "falling quite heavily and observation, which had been getting steadily poorer was now practically nil. 'A' Squadron tanks continued to engage the enemy and they in turn continued to engage us with heavy mortar concentrations."

At last light, Jordan decided to send Wood's Irish 1,600 yards along the Via Rossetta to a point halfway to Alfonsine. Expecting the Irish to reach this objective at daybreak, Jordan would then pass

'A' Squadron through to the town. To give the Irish some support, he assigned them two tank troops under command of Captain E.W. Taylor.

Beginning at midnight, the advance progressed well until the leading tank struck a mine. With the road blocked by a minefield, Taylor tried to move cross-country, only to have two more tanks run over mines. Deciding it was hopeless for the tanks to continue, Jordan ordered both Taylor and the Irish to sit tight until daybreak.[39] Shortly after dawn, the Irish's 'D' Company was brought in under Jordan's command to continue the advance. It soon became evident that the Germans were giving way, but the advancing force was halted about half a mile from Alfonsine by yet another minefield, which caused the Irish several casualties.[40] The Horse Guards also fell afoul of the mines, as No. 5 Troop of 'B' Squadron had been working with the tanks as supporting infantry. Troopers Gordon Elgin Hayward and William Sayers McLean were killed and three other men were wounded.[41]

December 24 closed with the Horse Guards and Irish a mile short of Highway 16 and Alfonsine. The junction was held by a German garrison too strong for Jordan's ad hoc force to overcome.[42]

BY CHRISTMAS EVE, the Germans had mostly fallen back behind the Senio River, yet they retained two salients, one on either flank of 1 Canadian Corps. The first was north of Ravenna in front of the Valli di Comacchio marshland, with its right flank anchored on Alfonsine. This salient's importance rested on the threat it posed to Ravenna and the German ability to maintain their garrison at Porto Corsini. The second salient extended from where the Senio bulged toward Cotignola to slightly east of the village of Granarolo. Eliminating these salients was deemed essential to the establishment of a fully secure front line.[43]

Currently, both salients were considered too robustly held to be easily won. Having been badly beaten up in its advance from the Montone River to the Senio, 1 Canadian Corps needed to recover and regroup. There was also no immediate thought of crossing the Senio—an imposing obstacle that provided the Germans with an ideal defensive barrier. The dykes on either side were 35 feet high with a flat 30-foot-wide top. On the river side, both dykes fell sheer to the water running through a 150-foot-wide channel.[44]

Across the Allied front, offensive operations were petering out, despite the wishes of Fifteenth Army Group's General Mark Clark. On December 20, he had announced that "the time is rapidly approaching when I shall give the signal for a combined all-out attack." British Eighth Army's Lieutenant General Richard McCreery was instructed to clear all the ground between the Fosso Munio and the Senio to prepare a launching pad for renewed operations. At Clark's signal, Eighth Army was to thrust hard over the Senio in conjunction with a U.S. Fifth Army advance from the Apennines to Bologna.[45]

The plan was doomed. By December 20, Eighth Army had run out of steam and Fifth Army was staggering. Recognizing this, Supreme Allied Command Mediterranean's Field Marshal Harold Alexander warned Clark that no significant offensive in December was possible. In November, when Alexander was still commanding all Allied forces in Italy, he had noted that any operation running into late December would be possible only with "an adequate spell" of good weather. No such spell was forecast. The most Eighth Army could achieve during this month, Alexander thought, was to straighten its line along the Senio by eliminating the two salients. After that, both Eighth Army and the facing Germans would settle into "an uneasy lull."

Such a lull suited Alexander. While Fifth Army had failed to take Bologna, he considered it and Eighth Army to have succeeded in the real mission—forcing the Germans to maintain their strength in Italy. Two divisions had left in November to meet a crisis in Hungary, but they had been immediately replaced. One replacement division had even transferred from Norway, passing through western Germany as the Ardennes offensive was under way nearby. As 1944 was drawing to a close, the Germans retained twenty-seven divisions in Italy, along with four Italian divisions and a Cossack cavalry division. As the battlefront stabilized, the Germans were forced to await a new Allied spring offensive while holding an "extended and uneconomical line."[46]

Any continuing illusions Clark may have had about the feasibility of a December offensive were shattered on Christmas Day, when McCreery formally requested that the planned two-army attack be cancelled. Reaching the Senio during the first fifteen days of December, he reported, had burned through a half million 25-pounder rounds. Eighth Army had just 612,000 rounds remaining—simply not enough to fight a major offensive.

Given the dismal weather, McCreery estimated that any air support would likely be on offer only one day out of every three. This would mean even more reliance on artillery to support any attack. "I am fully aware of the importance of the forthcoming operations and the issues at stake," McCreery wrote, "but feel it my duty to warn you that large scale operations . . . will not be practical unless the enemy carries out a withdrawal in front of Eighth Army." As the Germans were clearly strengthening their fortifications along the Senio, such a withdrawal was not to be expected.[47]

21

So Ended 1944

A S CHRISTMAS DAY approached, 1 Canadian Corps had begun to relieve as many units as possible from front-line duties. In 1st Canadian Infantry Division's sector, all of 3rd Brigade was withdrawn on December 24 to concentration points five to six miles south of the Senio River. The 2nd Brigade battalions—except the Seaforth Highlanders—also pulled back, with the Royal Canadian Dragoons filling their sections of line. Also left in place were 1st Brigade's Royal Canadian Regiment and 48th Highlanders.

"A major part of our infantry," the divisional war diarist wrote, "will thus have a chance to enjoy the Christmas festivities without having to worry about shelling, mortaring, or [small-arms] fire. We may be prejudiced that they deserve a rest; it is unfortunate that all cannot be withdrawn, because the fighting has been bitter and tough, ever since we moved into the line and launched the attack on 2 Dec . . . But this is war and . . . some have to stay . . . A good portion will at least be out—that's the best that can be done."

By the evening of December 24, most divisional staff officers were engaged in a raucous party. "The duty officer was frequently told where everyone was; that was a good thing because we are not sure that everybody knew where they were or where they had been or where they were going . . . The day ended as all Christmas Eves should end—with mutual wishes for a merry time and hopes that the next one may be spent in our homes. Outside, it was cold and the sun remained hidden behind clouds the whole day. We had some snow. The night was clear and bright, however, and it did look like a typical Christmas night."[1]

On the night of December 23–24, the Loyal Edmonton Regiment had boarded trucks and ridden to the seaside town of Cervia.[2] Being sent to Cervia was not by chance. The rest area had been carefully chosen by Lieutenant Colonel Jim Stone as part of a long-planned special treat for his men. The previous year, the Eddies and Seaforths had spent Christmas locked in the costly Ortona street fighting. Nevertheless, the Seaforth command had orchestrated an elaborate company-by-company rotation out of the front line on December 25 and served a full Christmas dinner at a church on Ortona's outskirts. Kept on the battle lines, the Eddies had received nothing extra but a cold pork chop eaten in whatever gun position they manned.

As soon as Stone had taken battalion command in early October, he resolved that the Eddies would celebrate Christmas 1944 properly. First step was commandeering a farm near Rimini, where he installed a battle-exhausted soldier and former farmer to care for an assortment of livestock. One of his chief duties was to track down and kidnap turkeys. Locating a granary nearby, Stone demanded its owner hand over a key so the Eddies' farmer could fatten his poultry. As Christmas approached, Stone had convinced 2nd Brigade's Lieutenant Colonel Pat Bogert to send the Eddies to Cervia for Christmas. While the farmer and some others were slaughtering turkeys, Stone went ahead of the battalion to Cervia. Stone warned the British officer serving as Town Major that he had five hundred to seven hundred men already en route that would need billeting, with a hotel for the officers. Impossible, the officer replied. The hotel was already housing his staff and there was no possibility of billeting the Eddies in the town's houses.

"If they aren't sent to billets," Stone growled, "I'll get my troops to march in with bayonets and take billets for themselves."

"Well, perhaps we can find them room," the officer conceded. Stone then demanded the hotel dining room for Christmas dinner. Again, the officer resisted. He had already arranged its use for a large Christmas Eve party. "So long as you invite all my officers, I'll let you have the party," Stone replied. "But tomorrow my soldiers will have the dining room and they will go in rotations, do you understand that?"

Nodding, the officer met the Eddies' convoy and soon had the men billeted throughout Cervia. Stone told the officers, "Get yourselves cleaned up, and there's a party tonight."

"My young men," he related later, "moved into the big party with magnificent food, lovely wine, and lovely women. They pushed the Englishmen out of the way and ate all the food, drank all the wine, and took all the women. Proprietor of the hotel was excellent. Put out his best linen and best silver for the men's Christmas dinner. I threatened to shoot anybody who took any of the silver. The proprietor insisted his staff would serve the men rather than the officers (who at such regimental dinners traditionally served the men). I had officers detailed to carve the turkeys. It was the best Christmas I ever had in my life. I never saw happier men. Having seen them for a year and a half in conditions of mud, dirt, and trenches and never having them sit down and eat together in all that time, and then making this possible."[3]

Meanwhile, in 5th Canadian Armoured Division's sector, the Westminster Regiment had withdrawn to billets in Ravenna. Lieutenant James Oldfield recorded that as "the carriers and White scout cars nosed their way down the narrow streets past the stately Roman and Byzantine buildings, little damaged for the most part, Ravenna seemed to be a wonderfully peaceful place.

"Christmas 1944, proved to be one of the most enjoyable the Westminsters had experienced since leaving home. Army fare was supplemented by a few beasts and fowl that had stepped on mines or otherwise became embroiled in the 'shooting war.' (We couldn't just leave them there to suffer, now could we?) In addition, the juice of the grape was available in many of the tastier Italian modifications until, as Lieutenant Leedham later remarked, 'It would have been unsafe to put anyone near an open flame after the first 48 hours.'" Dinner was held in an enormous garage. "The complete breaking of tension was undoubtedly the best medicine that the Regiment could receive, and after a day to recover, the companies returned to the fray at the Senio, refreshed in body and spirit."[4] The Westies relieved the

Irish Regiment so its troops could have a belated Christmas dinner on Boxing Day.

On the front lines, Christmas passed mostly without conflict. "A wary truce was observed on both banks of the Senio," the 1 Canadian Corps war diarist noted. In the Seaforth's sector, the Germans serenaded them with carols. Then one German raised his head above the dyke and wished the Seaforths "a guttural 'Merry Christmas.' Our troops replied with their version of 'Fröhliche Weihnacten.' Encouraged, the Germans tried a little propaganda, calling on our troops to surrender. Our counter-propaganda was an arty stonk on the German positions."[5]

The next day, the Eddies relieved the Seaforths. Even though a day late, the Seaforths were determined not to be outdone. On Christmas Eve, Lieutenant Colonel Budge Bell-Irving—recovered from his recurrence of malaria—had returned to find Christmas preparations well in hand. After the men moved to billets in Russi the morning of December 26, dinner was served company-by-company in a large banquet hall. From early afternoon until late at night, wrote the regiment's historian, "officers and sergeants were kept busy . . . serving turkey and pork with all the trimmings to the men. The hall had been decorated, the Pipes and Drums were in attendance, Padre [Roy] Durnford led the carol singing, and perhaps best of all, unlike the last Christmas when one company left to go back into the line to kill or be killed, the men could return in peace to their billets . . . After turkey and vegetables came the Christmas pudding with rum sauce and the mince pies washed down with beer. Then tea or coffee, apples and oranges, nuts and candy—indeed it was a feast."[6]

Not all of the Senio front was serene, however. In the sector held by the Governor General's Horse Guards, a half-track and two White scout cars of 'A' Squadron's No. 5 Troop (serving as mounted infantry) took a wrong turn and drove into the enemy lines near Alfonsine. The half-track struck a mine, and the Germans engaged the three vehicles with small-arms fire. German mortars soon pounded the Horse Guards' positions. "When the enemy had finally convinced himself that we were not assaulting his positions in White scout cars, he finally quietened down." An uneasy truce ensued.[7]

In the afternoon, meanwhile, the Royal Canadian Regiment—having had Christmas dinner early—was ordered to cross the Lamone River about three miles west of Russi. 'D' Company had a patrol across, closing on the Fosso Vecchio, when it was driven back by German machine-gun positions in a cluster of houses. The RCR began planning a stronger effort to clear these houses the next day at first light.[8]

Such incidences of violence were so rare they drew little notice. Christmas, the 1st Division war diarist wrote, "was quiet . . . there was little noise. It was strange not hearing the guns, but even they kept silent . . . Then with the moon half full, with a starry sky, and with cold, crisp temperature, Christmas Day came to pass. Tomorrow we return to the cold reality of war and all its ugliness but we won't forget Christmas 1944 because for twenty-four hours men became human again and war seemed very far away, almost forgotten."[9]

"ON BOXING DAY, the war came into prominence again," the 12th Canadian Infantry Brigade's war diarist wrote. "We hear that we will be relieving [11th Brigade.]" By 1400 hours, the brigade's battalion commanders were discussing with Brigadier John Lind the process for the relief to begin the next day.[10]

At first light on December 26, meanwhile, the Royal Canadian Regiment's 'B' Company, commanded by Captain C.V. Clark with a troop of Shermans in support, had attacked the Germans in the houses by the Vecchio that 'D' Company had been driven back from on Christmas Day. In short order, two 'B' Company platoons had cleared several buildings and taken eleven prisoners. As the men neared the last house, they saw a white flag hanging from a window. Suspicious, the platoon commanders agreed to encircle the building. With men covering it from all directions, two sections of one platoon advanced to take the occupants prisoner.[11] "No sooner had they done this," Major Strome Galloway recorded, "than they were mown down by cross-fire from machineguns. There ensued a fierce fight in which the RCR company assaulted the building, killing all the occupants, but three men who got out and ran down the road towards Cotignola were hotly pursued by a 'B' Company sergeant. He was last seen hurling grenades through the window of a chapel in which the enemy sought shelter, but was himself taken prisoner. Before the remnants of the platoon could reorganize the [building cluster] was ringed with a concentration of . . . mortar fire, and an enemy counterattack with sixty infantrymen fell upon them. In the course of this tussle, the eleven prisoners . . . were lost, two others were captured, and the platoons withdrew leaving twenty-two of their own number on the ground. The white flag trick had worked."[12]

An attempt to attack the same buildings was teed up by 'A' Company for 2200 hours, with its No. 7 Platoon advancing on the left and No. 9 Platoon to the right. Shermans and Crocodile flame-thrower tanks were in support. As the tanks tried to reach the start line, they were delayed by the rough ground, and the timed artillery bombardment ended just as the attacking force was ready to go. "It took the enemy about five minutes," 'A' Company's Major Jim Houghton wrote, "to pinpoint the sound of the attack. Then he shelled and mortared the area heavily. There was a considerable number of casualties caused in the right platoon." The attack bogged down and was eventually called off. Three members of No. 9 Platoon had been killed and seven wounded.[13] Among the dead was the platoon's commander, Sergeant James Ettels Bain. The twenty-two-year-old had been promoted to sergeant after so ably leading No. 9 Platoon through the Savio River fighting on October 17 while still a corporal.[14]

Outside of this action, engagements between the Canadians and Germans on December 26 and the days following largely consisted of each side harassing the other with machine-gun, sniper, and artillery fire.

ON THE U.S. Fifth Army's extreme left flank, however, December 26 saw a combined German and fascist Italian attack on a limited front in the Serchio Valley about fifty-five miles northwest of Florence. This sector was held by the segregated Black American 92nd Infantry Division. Responsible for a roughly twenty-mile-wide front that extended from the mountains to the Ligurian Sea, the 92nd's troops were thinly spread when struck by the Italian 4th Alpine Division and 3rd Marine Division and three German 148th Infanterie-Division battalions. Three days of fighting resulted in the Americans being driven back fifteen miles, until reinforcements from the adjacent 19th and 21st Infantry Brigades of the 8th Indian Division stemmed the offensive. The Axis force than pulled back to a new line little more than a mile in advance of its start line.[15]

Although the German offensive achieved little, a sufficiently alarmed Lieutenant General Lucian Truscott Jr. added his voice to British Eighth Army's Lieutenant General Richard McCreery's in opposing any immediate offensive operations. On December 30, Field Marshal Harold Alexander again intervened and decreed that both armies were "to go on the defensive for the present and to concentrate on making a real success of our Spring offensive."[16]

"The very near plan," 1st Division's war diarist wrote on December 30, "calls for this formation to close up to the Senio and consolidate there for the winter; the Senio is to be our 'winter line,' no less." In fact, he added, the entire Eighth Army was anchored on the Senio save for the two salients that 1 Canadian Corps was now to eliminate in the first days of the New Year.

"So ended 1944," Galloway wrote. "Although figures are not obtainable, it would seem that few indeed of the Royal Canadian Regiment . . . remained of the battalion which had left the mid-summer rest area . . . only five months before. In round figures the battalion's battle casualties since that date, not to mention the normal wastage from sickness and other causes, stood at nearly 525, of whom fifty were officers. During December changes in personnel had been so frequent that it would be an impossible task to list them . . . Reinforcements arrived in a continuous flow and streamed back from whence they came—only on stretchers[—]or were consigned to the sodden soil of the province of Emilia. In many cases the same day's return showed name after name of those who had been 'Taken on Strength' and 'Struck off Strength' in a matter of hours. Switches in the command of companies occurred frequently and to list them . . . would be but a dreary recital of names. Men became section commanders and platoon sergeants without ever sewing stripes on their sleeves and were wounded or dead before they could be officially promoted."[17]

DURING THE LAST days of December, rumours persisted that the Canadians were to be withdrawn and redeployed elsewhere or even moved to rest areas around Naples and Salerno. In fact, both prospects received attention at the higher command levels within 1 Canadian Corps. The more likely scenario was that the Canadians would shift westward. From positions immediately adjacent to Bagnacavallo, an advance on an axis running through Lugo, Massa Lombarda, and Medicina would threaten the Germans at Bologna from the north-west—possibly breaking their grip on the city. The realization that carrying out such an ambitious manoeuvre was unlikely for troops who were exhausted and when, as the 1st Division war diarist observed, there were "no sufficient replacements . . . available to crash through to Medicina" resulted in the plan being fully abandoned on December 30. Any withdrawal to Naples was also scuttled when it was learned that the only British corps capable of replacing the Canadians had been transferred to Greece.[18]

The fact that there was some high-level consideration of transferring the corps to the Naples–Salerno area had leaked far beyond corps headquarters. As a result, Lieutenant General Charles Foulkes felt it necessary to scotch such notions during a lecture delivered in Ravenna on New Year's Eve. Instead, he said, the Canadians would now eliminate the two salients. Then Eighth Army hoped to withdraw one division at a time for six weeks of training and rest in the Riccione area in similar fashion to what had happened in November. The idea, he stressed, was "hardening NOT softening" of the troops for a possible return to the offensive in February.

Foulkes then sternly announced that he was less than impressed by the corps's performance in December's fighting. He spelled out the casualties suffered, especially emphasizing the 22 officers and 420 other ranks gone missing and believed captured. The latter, he said, was "out of all proportion relative to our total casualties. There is something wrong with leadership."

Then he declared that winning river crossings had been badly handled. Although the initial assault was usually successful, getting supporting arms across to support the infantry took too long. Anti-tank guns should be across in no more than two hours and positioned by daylight to withstand the inevitable counterattack. Failing to do so had led routinely to the infantry abandoning the bridgehead.

Commanders at all levels, he continued, had not been where they were needed to exert leadership. "Commanders must be in right place and right time so that he knows when to take over battle . . . Company commanders should be within shouting distance of platoons, brigade commanders within five minutes of first assaulting battalion (in a jeep), but must control battle personally . . . On several occasions the battle 'stopped' and we lost our initiative. To wait for the enemy to move a tank into an open position or run out of ammunition is bad. We must force our will on the enemy until we win all the battles and run the Hun down."

Then there were the men taken prisoner. This Foulkes attributed to poor junior leadership and low morale. "It is a disgrace to give up and I am sure that if supplied with proper supporting arms and organized for defence roles . . . this will be cut considerably. This is a serious problem which we must face in the next few weeks, the question of getting and developing inspired leadership and morale until the Hun is licked." Units that achieved the most in the battles, Foulkes argued, had the least men going missing or being sent back as battle exhaustion cases. "A soldier must have confidence in himself, his weapons and you! . . . Let's start our next campaign here, or wherever we are, confident in the belief that we are fighting to win . . . and that capturing and killing the Hun tightens the noose around Germany."[19]

Bolstering the morale of battalions shattered by battle was a tough challenge. "Those last days of December," wrote Hastings and Prince Edward's Lieutenant Farley Mowat, "marked the lowest ebb to which the Regiment had fallen; but at the same time they marked the beginning of the turning tide and the first painful and uncertain steps toward regeneration.

"The exhaustion of mind and body could be dealt with—but only if the essential faith in the Regiment could be renewed." Instinct could have led the surviving Hasty Ps to blame leadership outside their battalion and beyond their control for the setbacks. "But enduring things cannot be rebuilt upon evasion, nor upon hatred.

"The real measure of the unit's greatness was to be found in its willingness to accept the fact that it had failed, and that much of the blame for failure rested on itself . . . the gnawing recognition that it was the individuals within the Regiment who had failed, was not to be denied. It was from the acceptance of its own humiliation that the Regiment was ultimately reborn."

Having either attended Foulkes's lecture or been briefed on it by 1st Brigade's Brigadier Allan Calder, Lieutenant Colonel Don Cameron personally drove his officers and non-commissioned officers to "rekindle the battalion's flickering spirit." Cameron was at times "ruthless. What could not be saved had to be cut out. Those soldiers, both officers and other ranks, who were beyond reclamation were quietly sent away for medical re-boarding. This was a drastic action, for the physical strength to the unit was now at a fraction of its operations level, and there were no indications that new reinforcements would be forthcoming."

To stop the men wallowing in misery, Cameron instituted a regime that saw the supposedly resting soldiers spilling out of billets at Bagnacavallo at dawn for physical training. After two years' absence, parade-ground drills were a daily affair. The initial resentment about this soon dissipated and "the old face of the unit began to reappear," Mowat wrote. Regimental pride was returning.[20]

While the Hasty Ps' morale might have been at a lower ebb than it was in most 1 Canadian Corps battalions, the grinding and costly December fighting had also left many others with shaken spirits. Brought out of the front line only on December 27 for a rest in Ravenna, the Perth Regiment's spirits were anything but festive. For the first two days, the war diarist wrote, the battalion "continued to wash away the mud and stains of battle. Clothing parades were held and the men began to take on the smart clean appearance that is characteristic of a soldier who is proud of his regiment and himself." But a distinct gloom pervaded, a fact addressed directly by 11th Brigade's Brigadier Ian Johnston in a talk to the Perth's officers on December 29. Events in the past month of fighting, he noted, had seldom conformed to the plans set out by corps and divisional command. This had, understandably, led to the soldiers feeling let down, and this "feeling must be wiped out as there was hard fighting ahead."

The following day, the Perths had "a belated Christmas dinner of turkey, chicken, vegetables, mince pies, etc. But in spite of the excellent food the spirit of Christmas was lacking." Largely, this was due to the news that the brigade would return to the front and almost immediately another combat operation.[21] The men were not surprised when ordered to gather their kit and board trucks soon after nightfall on January 1.[22]

"When word came down that we were on our way up to the line again," Private Stan Scislowski wrote, "everything went flat. How could anyone be expected to stay 'upbeat' when we knew what might be waiting for us up at the front? The bravado we'd taken into battle on that grim day the previous January had long since evaporated. We were much too wise now to look forward to glorious action. To a man, we had one goal, and that was to return to Canada and our families in about the same physical condition we had brought with us to Italy. Nothing more—nothing less. As far as most of us were concerned, those who handed out the medals could shove them!

"One hour before midnight, loaded down in full fighting gear, we stepped out into the biting cold and clear sky of the January night to climb aboard the battalion vehicles for the less-than-spirited ride to wherever battle awaited us. We damn near froze our butts and balls off on the short ride up to the drop-off point near a sugar factory a few miles north of Ravenna. Long johns, cardigans, battledress, leather jerkins and two pairs of socks simply didn't do the job of keeping out the well-below-freezing cold, especially when we had to sit near motionless on the cold steel benches of our three-ton Dodge trucks. It was a welcome relief when we were off-loaded at the [Forming Up Position] just short of a string of houses where the deep crump of mortar-bombs came to our ears." Scislowski and his mates were back in the war, and it was as if the few days of rest had never happened.[23]

22

Hordes of the Enemy

I N THE LAST days of December, Major General Bert Hoffmeister finalized plans for eliminating the German salient extending from Alfonsine to the Adriatic. With the Germans holding Alfonsine and the Senio River in strength, Hoffmeister decided to strike farther to the southeast and drive into a narrow gap bordered by the Fosso Vecchio to the left and the Lamone River to the right. Just beyond the start line, the Lamone had been diverted from its original course in recent years, so that it hooked hard right and flowed due east to Porto Corsini. The old channel—the Lamone Abbandonato—had not been filled in and extended northward to Sant' Alberto and a juncture with the Bonifica Canal. Sant' Alberto, situated between the Lamone Abbandonato and the Valli di Comacchio, was 5th Canadian Armoured Division's main objective. Just short of Sant' Alberto, the Bonifica was the only significant water obstacle. Offsetting the advantages of Hoffmeister's line of approach was the fact that his attacking force's left flank would be exposed throughout to potential counterattacks from Alfonsine.

The only alternative approach into the salient entailed advancing directly north from Ravenna into country that was semi-inundated and criss-crossed by myriad canals and ditches. Consequently, this avenue had been rejected as impassable.[1]

Hoffmeister's plan called for two phases. In the first, 11th Infantry Brigade's Perth and Irish Regiments advanced a short distance to Conventello. While the Irish secured the village, the Perths would occupy a farm called Casa Stasiol on the left flank. In the second phase, 5th Armoured Brigade would advance from Conventello to the Bonifica, establish a crossing, and then seize Sant' Alberto. The start line for the first phase was a ditch about half a mile from Conventello.[2] To free these units for the offensive, 9th British Armoured Brigade—brought under 1 Canadian Corps command on December 15—assumed responsibility for sixteen miles of 5th Division's front, extending from Porto Corsini to the Via Sant' Antonio. If the Germans facing this front began to withdraw in order to interfere with 5th Division's assault, the brigade would pursue them and prevent their organizing for a counterattack.[3]

By mid-morning of January 1, the assaulting force began gathering in Mezzano—about a mile south of the start line. At 1100 hours, 'A' and 'C' Squadrons of the British Columbia Dragoons arrived. It was a clear, cold day. Several frosty days had hardened the fields, so the tankers were looking forward to not being confined to roads. Squadrons of fighters and fighter-bombers were aloft, and at 1130 hours, a squadron of U.S. Army Air Force Thunderbolts suddenly swooped down and bombed Mezzano. 'C' Squadron's Trooper Ralph James Oldis was killed and another B.C. Dragoon wounded. About six civilians were also killed or injured.[4]

As the day wore on, despite intermittent harassing German artillery fire, Mezzano became increasingly crowded. "Everyone and everything was in position and ready—artillery, engineers, flame-throwing 'Crocodile' tanks, and other supporting arms of the service," noted the Dragoons' regimental historian.[5] As the initial advance would be in darkness, the infantry would start with no tank support. At first light, the 8th Princess Louise's New Brunswick Hussars 'B' Squadron would rush forward and attach two troops to each battalion.[6] As the attack developed, the Dragoons would take over supporting the Irish, while the Hussars backed the Perths.

Although frost had firmed the soil in the fields, these were small, "with fences at short intervals and many . . . were vineyards, with rows of wires and poles obscuring the view," the Perth's historian observed. This provided ideal ambush sites for infantry armed with Panzerfausts or anti-tank guns.[7]

The facing Germans were 3rd Battalion, 721st Jäger Regiment of 114th Jäger Division. It was believed to number about 250 men. The rest of the regiment was deployed nearby. A troubling intelligence report, meanwhile, also placed elements of 16th ss Panzer Grenadier Division just south of Alfonsine. This division had been redeployed from south of Bologna to strengthen German forces on the coast.

An extensive artillery plan was fixed to begin just before the attack launched at 0500 hours on January 2. Conventello and the farm were to be shelled until ten minutes after the infantry set out. The guns would then switch to firing at suspected and known German artillery and mortar positions for twenty minutes. Thereafter, the guns would be on call as needed. Weather permitting, the artillery would also screen the exposed left flank with smoke. Artificial moonlight was to be employed, while 5th Light Anti-Aircraft Regiment would fire tracer streams on the flanks to assist the infantry in staying on course.[8]

PRECISELY AT 0500 HOURS, the Irish and Perth Regiments advanced. The Irish had Captain Tony Falzetta's 'C' Company leading on the right and Major Norm Hickling's 'D' Company the left. Almost immediately, several short rounds struck 'C' Company, killing three men and wounding several others. Falzetta stopped to reorganize. 'D' Company carried on, heading for a building cluster near the Lamone River's tight rightward bend.[9] After a sharp fight, Hickling reported the buildings secure. The company had killed ten panzer grenadiers and captured four, also silencing two 75-millimetre anti-tank guns. Coming up alongside, Falzetta's men became heavily engaged in clearing houses. By 0800 hours the fight was over. Five Germans were dead, six were wounded, and ten others had surrendered. With these buildings taken, 'A' and 'B' Companies passed to the front. 'B' Company, under Captain Herb Hendrie, passed through 'D' Company and moved toward another building cluster just east of

Conventello. Major George Macartney's 'A' Company, meanwhile, cut over to the Lamone and set about eliminating dugouts cut into the side of the dyke.[10] Each of these companies was now supported by a troop from the 8th Hussars' 'B' Squadron. In the course of its fight, 'B' Company killed five more Germans and took twenty-seven prisoners. Once Hendrie declared the buildings cleared, Hickling leapfrogged 'D' Company through and started fighting in Conventello. When a Panther tank inside the village started firing, Hickling called down artillery and mortar fire. Desert Air Force fighter-bombers also swept in. Once the Panther was knocked out, 'D' Company quickly secured Conventello. It was 1800 hours, and the Irish had completed their immediate task.[11]

To the left, the Perth Regiment had crossed the start line with 'A' and 'B' Companies leading. There was little resistance, and forty-five minutes later, Major Robert Cole's 'B' Company reached its first objective. Shrapnel from an exploding artillery round, however, wounded Cole in the foot. Refusing to be evacuated until a replacement company commander could be sent forward, Cole limped onward. On the Perth's left flank, meanwhile, 'A' Company met increasing opposition, and its progress slowed dramatically despite the arrival of a tank troop. The battalion's advance was threatening to stall, until several fighter-bombers hammered the German positions. Pace quickening, 'C' Company moved out front and by 1050 hours had reached its objective, adjacent to Conventello. 'D' Company then took the lead, heading for Casa Stasiol.[12] Captain Pete Fisher's men advanced in arrowhead formation, with Lieutenant Dave Dooley's No. 18 Platoon on point. Private Stan Scislowski and the rest of the platoon were fifty yards into "a wide acreage of fallow farmland, lightly dusted with snow," when a flight of Thunderbolts "swooped in at no more than a couple hundred feet altitude off to our right, their wing guns yammering a deadly tune as they strafed a target somewhere on the far side of a cluster of houses."

During a second pass, the Thunderbolts fired rockets. A "thick column of black smoke shot skyward." Having never seen a rocket attack, 'D' Company was so distracted by the fireworks that nobody saw the mortar rounds being walked toward it, until No. 18 Platoon found itself right in the centre of explosions. There was no cover in the frozen field. The only solution was to run forward, which Scislowski and his mates did. Not a man was scratched. Just "another one of those unexplainable pieces of battle luck that came our way every so often." Sprinting onward, 'D' Company seized three clustered buildings. No. 18 Platoon then followed a narrow path adjacent to a grassy field. Ahead, Scislowski saw "the widely scattered and riddled bodies of [a] bicycle platoon. There had to be at least two dozen bicycles out there in the field, with riders sprawled either atop or underneath them. A couple of the Jerry cyclists . . . had dropped their bikes and made a run for it as the planes came swooping in with wing guns blazing, but the poor bastards got no farther than twenty feet away when the bullets slammed into their backsides. They lay face down in the grass, their backs crimson with blood."[13]

The Thunderbolt attack was just part of 176 aircraft sorties supporting 5th Division on January 2. In addition to the strafing runs by the fighters, fighter-bombers dropped about seventy-six tons of high-explosive bombs to assist the advance.[14]

Beyond the dead cyclists, No. 18 Platoon spread out in a shallow ditch and provided fire support as No. 16 Platoon rushed Casa Stasiol. The farm proved occupied by only a clutch of frightened civilians. As the company deployed around it, Scislowski climbed the stairs to the farmhouse's second storey to search for booty. Nothing was on offer until he opened an old shipping trunk and spied three dozen cans of Eagle Brand sweetened condensed milk. "My hands literally trembled as I used my clasp knife to open one. Never had I tasted such nectar since joining the army!" Gorging himself on two cans, Scislowski crammed the rest inside his tunic. Keeping six for himself, he shared the rest around. Before the night was through, he had drunk his additional six.[15]

AT 1230 HOURS ON January 2, Major General Hoffmeister ordered 5th Armoured Brigade to pass through 11th Infantry Brigade and drive to Sant' Alberto. 'C' Squadron of the B.C. Dragoons passed to the left of Conventello. Aircraft flying ahead reported large numbers of enemy tanks, self-propelled guns, and anti-tank guns between

Conventello and Sant' Alberto. Artillery forward observation officers in aircraft called shellfire on many buildings and small woods
suspected of concealing German armour, while fighter-bombers attacked others. Waiting until this support lifted, 'C' Squadron did not
renew the advance until mid-afternoon. As the tanks ground forward,
"houses, barns and haystacks—indeed anything liable to conceal or
protect enemy positions—were engaged with liberal machine-gun
and sometimes gun fire." As the Dragoons closed on the Strada
Molinazza, which crossed their path, they shot up a German half-
track. Then a Panther and SPG were both engaged just past the road
and quickly destroyed.[16]

To the left of the Dragoons, the 8th Hussars had passed through
the Perth Regiment. The country entered, however, proved "very
close and poor visibility made it difficult to see and engage the numerous SPs and Panthers that were in the area," 5th Brigade's Brigadier
Ian Cumberland wrote.[17] 'A' Squadron was leading when it moved
out into open ground backed by a row of trees at 1350 hours. "In the
tanks," the Hussars' historian wrote, "the crews braced and waited,
and the expected came. A German anti-tank gun barked, and then
another, and another. One tank [that of the lead troop's commander]
began to flame. The shells spat viciously at the others. In no time the
squadron was in a nasty spot.

"The worst might have happened except . . . for one man. He
was a lean, moustached Acting Sergeant named Jim McAskill."[18]
Seeing the muzzle flash of one gun, McAskill halted his Sherman
in the open field and engaged it at close range, while the rest of the
squadron dodged and ducked to reach a line of trees on one flank.
His fire destroyed the anti-tank gun. Still refusing to manoeuvre in
order to enable his gunner to fire more accurately, McAskill spotted a Panther zeroing in. McAskill's gunner got off a killing shot
before the German tank fired. Having also situated the remaining anti-tank guns, McAskill withdrew from the field to rejoin the
now sheltered squadron. As his wireless had failed, McAskill ran
across open ground raked by machine-gun fire to his squadron
leader's Sherman. Standing beside the tank, McAskill pointed out
the remaining enemy gun locations. This allowed 'A' Squadron

to outflank and destroy them from behind. As the citation for McAskill's subsequent Military Medal recognized, his "brilliant leadership . . . was directly responsible for destroying four anti-tank guns and one Panther, and his courageous action enabled the advance to continue without delay."[19]

While 5th Brigade's main thrust had been directed toward Sant' Alberto, the Dragoons' 'A' Squadron had moved east from Conventello toward the tight bend in the Lamone River. Here it was to marry up on the other side of the Lamone Abbandonato with the Irish Regiment's 'A' Company. After numerous delays, the tankers reached the marrying-up point to find that the engineers who were to have arrived earlier to carve a path through this natural anti-tank ditch had yet to appear. An hour later, an armoured bulldozer ground up and soon cut a gap in the two dykes, through which the tanks passed in single file. With dusk falling, Dragoons and Irish infantrymen settled down to pass the night.[20]

At 1555 hours, meanwhile, 'A' Company of the Cape Breton Highlanders had advanced in Bren carriers to join the Dragoons' 'C' Squadron. This force was then to establish another bridgehead across the Lamone Abbandonato, but well in advance of the Irish Regiment's. It was hoped the combined infantry/tank units could reach the Bonifica Canal before dark or at least push the advance out two thousand yards beyond Conventello.[21] At 1620 hours, the rest of the Highlanders started marching toward the Bonifica. In the end, only enough daylight remained for the battalion's main body to reach the two-thousand-yard objective. Farther out, having dismounted from its carriers, 'A' Company crossed the dyke, with 'C' Squadron's tanks alongside. The company commander soon reported being in contact with the enemy. Opposition was light, however, and ten prisoners were soon taken.[22] As January 2 ended, 5th Division had advanced three miles. "Our casualties during the day for both armour and infantry," 5th Brigade's Brigadier Cumberland wrote, "were almost negligible while the enemy counted rather a heavy toll both in equipment and PW."[23]

At 0500 hours on January 3, heavy German artillery fire struck all along the old channel from Conventello to where the Highlanders'

'A' Company held the most forward position. The shelling continued until 0630 hours. Fifteen minutes later, a fifty-strong force of infantry liberally armed with Panzerfausts struck 'A' Company's lines. In the years since the Lamone had been diverted, the wide bed of the old channel had become thickly overgrown with small trees, and the attackers used this cover to close to within fifty yards without being detected.[24]

The brunt of the attack—coming in two waves—fell on Sergeant Stuart MacDonald's platoon. Two shots fired at a house inside the platoon's perimeter preceded the attack. Led by a captain, the first wave came in from the right. The second wave, under a sergeant major's command, soon struck from the left. With the platoon at risk of being overrun, MacDonald ran from slit trench to slit trench through thickening small-arms fire to tie together the platoon's defences and direct the men's fire. When the Germans were just fifteen yards off, the Bren gun facing the main force jammed. "Realizing the desperate situation," MacDonald charged the Germans through a hail of bullets with his Tommy gun blazing. Then standing in the open, he proceeded to hold the enemy back with bursts of fire while shouting orders to his men. After personally gunning down the captain and two of his men, MacDonald turned to face the second wave. He seriously wounded the sergeant major before breaking this attack with bursts of fire that killed or wounded twenty men. Ten Germans were taken prisoner. The survivors fled in complete disorder. MacDonald's Distinguished Conduct Medal citation credited his actions with not only breaking the counterattack but paving the way for 5th Brigade's advance to continue toward Sant' Alberto.[25]

Counterattacks had also struck the lines of 'C' and 'D' Companies, but these were more easily repelled. In the midst of 'A' Company's fight, a jeep bearing the morning rations drove into the lines. A Panzerfaust round struck the jeep, killing the two men aboard and destroying the food.[26]

One troop of the Dragoons' 'C' Squadron had been caught in 'A' Company's fight. Before the Germans were driven off, a Panzerfaust round punched a hole in one Sherman, and four of its crew suffered minor burns.[27]

At the same time as the Highlanders had been counterattacked, German infantry supported by mortar fire also assaulted the Perth's front line. Failing to achieve surprise, the Germans were driven back while suffering heavy losses. Well out front of the main Perth line, a 'D' Company patrol consisting of six men led by Sergeant George Grant was cut off by the German counterattack. Taking refuge in a house, it was assaulted by about twenty-five infantrymen heavily armed with Panzerfausts.[28]

The German officer leading the attack wrenched the front door open and chucked in a stick grenade. As he charged in on the heels of the grenade's explosion, a Perth cut the officer down with a Bren gun burst. Outside, the Germans scattered to cover and began hammering the building with small-arms fire. Three Perths replied with Thompson submachine guns from windows upstairs. A ten-minute exchange of heavy fire followed. Then one of the Germans fired two Panzerfaust rounds. Both missed the farmhouse entirely, which struck the Perths as very poor marksmanship. Ammunition dwindling, however, the Perth's situation was becoming bleak. Because of the surrounding open ground, the platoon could not abandon the house and break free. Just after dawn, a burst of Bren gunfire struck the side of the house facing away from the Germans. Reinforcements had arrived, and their fire soon shifted toward the Germans.[29] Leaving six dead and seen to be helping several wounded, the Germans quit the battle. One man was taken prisoner and identified as a soldier of the 16th ss Panzer Grenadier Division, known to be deployed around Alfonsine.[30]

ONCE THESE ATTACKS ceased, Brigadier Cumberland ordered the 8th Hussars and B.C. Dragoons to head for the Bonifica Canal, with the Cape Breton Highlanders following as soon as possible. The canal was two thousand yards from the most advanced of the infantry companies. By 0830 hours, the Hussars' 'C' Squadron was on the move. "The country had not changed. The fields were lined with trees and between the trees the steel wires hung thick among the . . . vines. They were lucky at times to be able to see 40 yards ahead," the regiment's historian recorded. "The squadron bucked ahead, blazing away spasmodically at each house and haystack . . . In one retort, the Germans ripped the turret flap off one tank but just at a moment . . . when the tank commander had his head in."[31]

At 1235 hours, 'C' Squadron threw caution to the wind and began "bypassing a considerable number of small enemy pockets." An hour later, the lead troop reported being one hundred yards from the junction where the canal crossed the Lamone Abbandonato. A bridge crossing the canal was still intact, but fire from the other bank prevented the tankers from closing on it.[32] At 1530 hours, 'C' Squadron made a run for the bridge with one tank. As it closed in, the battalion war diarist wrote, a German soldier "ran onto the bridge and across it under heavy fire from our tank guns. This soldier climbed under the bridge and set the fuse which in a few seconds blew up one section of the bridge making it impassable. While running back to his own lines, again across the bridge, he was shot and killed by our fire. But the damage had been done."[33]

The Hussars stood on one side of the riverbed and the Germans on the other. As the Germans opposite were infantry in dugouts, the Hussars were able to inflict many casualties with main gun and machine-gun fire while enjoying virtual impunity. The one tank, a Panzer Mark IV, that tried to engage the Hussars was quickly knocked out. By the end of the day, sixty-seven Germans had surrendered— mostly taken when other squadrons cleaned out the strongpoints bypassed by 'C' Squadron. A further fifty enemy were estimated to have been killed. The Hussars had no casualties. By evening, the Highlanders were alongside the tanks.[34]

Soon after the morning counterattacks had been repelled, the B.C. Dragoons had also moved ahead of the infantry along the right-hand side of the Lamone Abbandonato toward the Bonifica. Initially following a road, Major J.C.P. Mills's 'A' Squadron was first away. 'C' Squadron soon followed, advancing along the left side of the Lamone Abbandonato toward the same bridge that had been the objective for the Hussars. The ground 'A' Squadron entered was again close, "being covered with low trees and grapevines. There were also numerous small houses, farm buildings, and haystacks, all of which afforded excellent cover to the enemy," a Dragoons account recorded. "For the first 2,000 yards the road had been prepared for mines. There were numerous holes dug and the mines were placed in readiness in the ditches, but very few had been laid. There were still a considerable number of enemy infantry about and all possible hiding places were sprayed with MG fire. The Boche did not seem to like this and numbers of them were seen beating a hasty retreat to the north." Seventeen Germans were taken prisoner, but Mills thought many more could have been captured if the tankers had been accompanied by infantry to oversee them. 'A' Squadron progressed steadily and without major incident, until it stopped for the night about half a mile short of the Bonifica.[35]

By contrast, 'C' Squadron had encountered stiff resistance soon after beginning its January 3 advance at 0850 hours—moving northward on a track paralleling the Lamone Abbandonato on its right. Major John Edward Cooke had two troops out front when the one to the left reported two Panthers approaching on a diagonal line about eight hundred yards ahead. As the leading right-hand troop was already four hundred yards closer, Cooke ordered its leader to halt and prepare to engage the Panthers. When the German tanks failed to appear, Cooke realized they had stopped in the cover of a vineyard in the hope of ambushing his squadron. Cooke decided on an immediate attack. He quickly assembled the squadron in echelon formation so one tank was covered by the one following it. Then Cooke advanced his Sherman well to the front of the column as a decoy. Feigning ignorance of the German tanks, Cooke pushed through the vineyard until he drew their fire. Having closed up on Cooke, the leading tanks in the column were able to fire at the muzzle flashes that exposed the German positions. One Panther was knocked out and the other retreated.[36]

Driving on, 'C' Squadron encountered five more groups of enemy armour, which consisted of SPGs, tanks, and anti-tank guns. Each time, Cooke offered his Sherman as a decoy. When it drew fire, the rest of the squadron was able to situate and engage the Germans. By the time 'C' Squadron reached its objective, parallel to 'A' Squadron, it had destroyed one Panther, two SPGs, and a 75-millimetre anti-tank gun. About twenty Germans had either been killed or captured.

Ahead, German infantry were spotted in and around the buildings of a farm with nearby haystacks. The squadron let loose, setting the haystacks ablaze and destroying the buildings. Cooke received a Distinguished Service Order for his actions that day.[37]

Nightfall on January 3 found 5th Armoured Brigade well positioned to force a crossing over the Bonifica. On the right flank, the Dragoons 'C' Squadron was east of the Lamone Abbandonato and 'A' Squadron on the western bank. The 8th Hussars stood to the left of the Dragoons and were closed up on the canal. Both tank regiments were supported by infantry—the Perths having come up beside the Hussars and the Highlanders beside the Dragoons.

While the force facing the Bonifica was considered secure from the front, its overall situation was shaky. Having advanced four miles over two days, the battle group's left flank was dangerously exposed to counterattack from Germans on the north banks of the Fosso Vetro and Fosso Vecchio. Recognizing the danger, Major General Hoffmeister had spent the day filling this gap. As the Perths moved north to join the Hussars, he replaced that regiment with the Westminsters under command of 11th Infantry Brigade. The Westminster line was established between seven hundred and nine hundred yards back from the Fosso Vetro. To the left of the Westies, the line was held by three companies of the King's Royal Rifle Corps and elements of the 12th Royal Lancers from the British 9th Armoured Brigade. Hoffmeister anticipated an attack on this front—and soon.[38]

HOFFMEISTER'S REALIGNMENT OF forces came in the nick of time. On the night of January 3–4, 36th ss Panzer Grenadier Regiment commander Sturmbannführehr Josef Maier assembled a battle group composed of 1st Battalion 36th Regiment, 16th Reconnaissance Regiment, and the 26th Reconnaissance Battalion. The latter battalion was in reserve and would be committed once the first two units breached the Canadian lines. All were units of the 16th ss Panzer Division. Maier's intent was to cut off 5th Armoured Brigade's armour by driving a wedge past Conventello to reach the Lamone River. Once the tanks and supporting infantry of 11th Infantry Brigade were isolated, they could be forced into the marshlands north of Ravenna.[39] Maier's battle group struck at 0430 hours on the heels of a thirty-minute artillery barrage. The attack immediately ran into trouble, the Germans finding it nearly impossible to move supporting arms—especially armour—quickly across the various waterways between their mustering area beside Alfonsine and the Canadian lines.

The main line of attack fell on the section of front held by 1st Battalion, King's Royal Rifle Corps (KRRC), and the Westminster Regiment. Unlike Hoffmeister, the Westies had not anticipated a hot front. Consequently, neither company was commanded by their regular leader. Instead, to gain some battle experience in a quiet area, Captain Jack Hall led 'B' Company and Captain Fred Cummins the support company—precisely the two Westminster companies facing the incoming Germans. Both men, however, were up to the task. During the night, Cummins had registered ranges for a series of defensive artillery fire tasks if needed. The moment the German artillery barrage lifted, Lieutenant James Oldfield wrote, the Westies looked up from their slit trenches, and "out of the slowly-lightening gloom poured veritable hordes of the enemy."[40]

Cummins had also earlier deployed one of the support company's Vickers medium machine guns. The crew manning it immediately ripped into the Germans with sustained bursts of fire. Moments later, the remaining Vickers were brought into action, while Cummins called down artillery. Being cut to pieces by the support company, the Germans shrank to the right to join those attacking 'B' Company.[41] While the left-hand ss battalion was stopped dead in front of the Westies, the one on the right succeeded in infiltrating the seam line between the Westies and the KRRC to the left. Cutting the Via Al Conventello, the ss battalion's leading elements soon reached a cluster of houses about three hundred yards from the Lamone. Canadian artillery, meanwhile, hammered the breach point between the Westies and KRRC—effectively sealing it shut. More artillery pounded the German rear to prevent further reinforcements entering the battle.[42]

Blocking the Germans in the breach was assigned to the Irish Regiment, in reserve at Conventello. At 0710 hours, Captain Herb Hendrie's 'B' Company, supported by a troop of 8th Hussars tanks, started moving and a half hour later were in contact with the leading Germans. Supported by "withering fire from the tanks," Hendrie's men "moved in and mopped up with great vigour, killing approximately 30 and capturing 65 PWs," the Irish Regiment's war diarist recorded.[43]

At 0815 hours, Desert Air Force fighters and fighter-bombers formed a cab rank over the battlefield and began strafing and bombing the Germans inside the breach. They also struck "occupied houses, dumps, company HQS, SPS, and half-tracks" from the German forward line back to the Senio River and Alfonsine.[44] The SS inside the breach were entirely isolated, being lashed by flanking fire from the Westies on one side and the KRRC the other, while Captain Hendrie's force rolled it up from the front. By 0900 hours, the threat was eliminated.[45] The SS troops had been thoroughly mauled—more than two hundred taken prisoner, many of whom were wounded, and an estimated two hundred killed.[46]

Even as the counterattack had been under way, 5th Armoured Brigade's advance on Sant' Alberto had been renewed. Patrols by the Cape Breton Highlanders and Perth Regiment had crept up to the Bonifica Canal during the night and determined it was about eighty feet wide from the dykes on either side, with icy water running in a twenty- to twenty-five-foot-wide channel bed. Numerous German positions were on the opposite bank, and aerial observation reported significant numbers of SPGs and tanks between the canal and Sant' Alberto. With the Canadians having reached the Bonifica, the Germans to the east were in a perilous situation. The gap between the canal and Sant' Alberto was a mere mile wide, and this was the only escape route for forces south of the Valli di Comacchio. There was also only one bridge still crossing the Bonifica. That it had not yet been demolished was taken by Brigadier Cumberland as proof that significant numbers of 114th Jäger Division were still south of the canal. Cumberland ordered the B.C. Dragoons to make an all-out effort to reach and secure this bridge.

Lieutenant Colonel Harry Angle's plan was straightforward. The four Honey tanks of the battalion's reconnaissance troop would lead 'A' Squadron to the Bonifica. Barring the path was a drainage ditch called Il Canalone, and the engineers provided two Arks to bridge this. Once Il Canalone was crossed, 'B' Squadron would come up alongside on the left and the entire force would converge on the bridge.

At 0700 hours, the tanks rolled. As they closed on Il Canalone, the bridge there was seen to have been blown. This had been expected. Not expected was the news that one Ark had been knocked out by shellfire and the other was badly delayed. Time and opportunity slipping away, Lieutenant J.C. MacKinnon—commanding the recce troop—called for 'A' Squadron to lay down suppression fire against German snipers banging away at the armour. He then set out on foot to find a crossing point. In short order, MacKinnon spotted an extremely narrow old brick bridge that proved just wide enough for 'A' Squadron's tanks to creep across one by one.

All this took time, though, and Angle decided to order 'B' Squadron to dash for the bridge without waiting for 'A' Squadron to come alongside on the opposite bank of Il Canalone. Major Richard Bartley Sellars advanced the squadron in a box formation. The bridge across the Bonifica was two miles distant, and the ground to be covered was open and becoming increasingly boggy as the day warmed. Lieutenant B.G. Hurst's troop led on the left. Repeatedly, he opted to use the road on the Lamone Abbandonato's dyke, despite this leaving his tanks completely exposed. Lieutenant A. Romanow's troop crowded up close to Hurst's to avoid being mired in muddy ground to the right. As the squadron closed on the bridge, it was increasingly pushed in on itself because of the narrowing and rugged ground. At 0850 hours, Hurst stopped his Sherman two hundred feet short of the bridge.

"I could see that it was heavily mined and wired. The wires actually were all over the roadway on the top of the bridge so there wasn't much question about whether the Germans had intended to blow it." Farther back, Sellars ordered Hurst and Romanow to cover the bridge with fire. This elicited an immediate response in the form of anti-tank guns and Panzerfaust fire. The Dragoons lashed back with machine-gun and main gun fire that quickly silenced the enemy. Both lieutenants were urging Sellars to let them try crossing the bridge. Fearing the Germans would blow the span, Sellars refused.[47]

The moment Sellars arrived on the scene, he jumped out of his Sherman. Under heavy small-arms fire, he then ran to the bridge and cut the lines running from detonators to charges. Scooping up as many detonators as possible, Sellars signalled Hurst and Romanow forward. Leaving them to finish neutralizing the demolition charges on the near side of the bridge, Sellars ran to the farther side and started cutting lines and gathering up detonators. All the time, bullets were snapping past the three men. Near the end, mortar rounds started falling around Sellars. Yelling at Hurst and Romanow to get back in their tanks and provide covering fire, Sellars continued working until the last charges were neutralized. The job took ninety minutes from start to finish. When Sellars returned to his tank, his clothes had been torn to shreds by mortar splinters. Yet, as his Distinguished Service Order citation reported, he suffered only minor scratches.[48] Although Sellars was eager to run the squadron over the bridge, Angle demurred. He had engineers on the way to ensure that the bridge was truly clear of demolition charges.

Realizing the Dragoons were out on a limb, Brigadier Cumberland ordered their 'C' Squadron to start shuttling the Perths to the bridge by having companies ride on the tank decks. By noon, the Perth's 'C' and 'D' Companies had been delivered, and the engineers declared the bridge clear. "Thus by 1200 hours," Cumberland noted, "we had performed the rare feat of capturing a bridge intact." 'B' Squadron and the Perths crossed it and established a strong bridgehead.[49]

At the blown bridge that the Highlanders and 8th Hussars had reached the day before, meanwhile, the infantry had crossed on the ruins and established another strong bridgehead. They were soon joined by the Dragoons' 'C' Squadron. By last light, engineers were working near the blown bridge to create a crossing for the Hussars to use in the morning.

The tide had turned. At 2355 hours, a Highlanders patrol crept out to Sant' Alberto and found no Germans. Later, the soldiers spotted a German patrol approaching the central square from the northwest. These troops soon withdrew. The general consensus among questioned civilians was that the enemy had abandoned the town. Returning at 0400 hours on January 5, the patrol leader's report prompted Lieutenant Colonel Boyd Somerville to send 'B' Company toward the town with the Dragoons 'C' Squadron at 0730 hours. By noon the force was inside Sant' Alberto, where they rounded up forty to fifty German stragglers, who surrendered without a fight.[50]

The Highlanders spent the rest of January 5 clearing the ground to the northwest of Sant' Alberto up to the Reno River—which ran past the bottom of the Valli di Comacchio—and closed the escape route to the north. 'A' Squadron of the Dragoons, with Perths riding on the tank hulls, had ground eastward on the road bordering the Bonifica Canal to the village of Mondriale, a distance of about three miles.[51] Pushing on another mile and a half, the force reached a ferry crossing over the Reno that tied into a road running north through the narrow and marshy ground on Valli di Comacchio's coastal flank. This was the last possible escape route for any Germans who had not yet managed to get north of the Reno. The ferry crossing had been under heavy aerial attack for several days, and many German dead lay around it. Milling about were sixty horses and mules that the Germans had been unable to evacuate.[52] A Perth patrol on the morning of January 6 reached Casal Borsetti on the coast and met the 12th Lancers advancing from Porto Corsini. The salient was closed. On January 7, 5th Armoured Brigade handed the entire area to the 7th Lancers.[53]

Trying to sustain the coastal salient had cost the Germans dearly. The five-day battle had resulted in more than 600 Germans taken prisoner, with a roughly equal number either killed or wounded. After the battle, the Canadians counted 310 German dead. By contrast, Canadians killed in this period numbered only 30, with about 200 wounded. The Germans also lost many heavy weapons, including eight Panthers, 20 anti-tank guns, four SPGS, four infantry guns, and one 88-millimetre gun.[54]

23

It Hasn't Been a Picnic

WHILE 5TH CANADIAN ARMOURED Division had been eliminating the coastal salient, 1st Canadian Infantry Division
assaulted the salient on the 1 Canadian Corps's left flank, which extended into v British Corps's sector. Clearing the Canadian portion
of the salient was tasked to 2nd Canadian Infantry Brigade, while
56th British Infantry Division would assign a brigade to do the same
in the British operational area.

Given the nature of the ground and weather conditions,
2nd Brigade's Lieutenant Colonel Pat Bogert considered the attack to
be "an infantryman's job and the function of armour was to follow
as closely as possible in an anti-counterattack role." The usual flat
fields and vineyards were dominated in this case by the Senio River's
dykes and the buildings in Cotignola. Despite recent frosts, Bogert
thought any tank moving off-road faced "a hazardous undertaking."
As the Fosso Vecchio looped across the Naviglio Canal just east of the
village of Granarolo, these two waterways provided obstacles. Most of
the bridges had been destroyed or were prepared for demolition, so
the speed by which the attack developed would be determined by the
division's engineers.

Bogert's January 1 orders set out three phases. The Princess
Patricia's Canadian Light Infantry would first advance two companies across the Naviglio and close up to the Vecchio. They would then

seize two still-intact bridges over this waterway. In phase two, the Seaforth Highlanders would pass through the Patricias and swing northeastward to clear the area between the Naviglio and Vecchio at the front of Granarolo. If another bridge could be won here, the Seaforths would then cross it and continue to the Senio. Phase three called for the Loyal Edmonton Regiment to win Granarolo.[1] The attack was to begin on January 3 at 1700 hours, with the Patricias advancing behind a creeping barrage.[2]

Northeast of the salient, the Germans held positions adjacent to the railway that ran from Bagnacavallo to cross the Senio opposite Lugo. In order to divert attention from the attack, 3rd Infantry Brigade was to drive these Germans behind the Senio. Brigadier Paul Bernatchez assigned the task to the Royal 22e Régiment. The Van Doos were provided with ten Wasps and six Lifebuoy flame-throwers.[3]

Lieutenant Colonel Jean Allard planned for a noon attack on January 3 by 'A' and 'C' Companies. In addition to the flame-throwers, twenty-six 2-inch mortars would lay down a covering smokescreen for thirty minutes—first firing two hundred smoke rounds and then five hundred high-explosive bombs. As Allard was finalizing the plan, the battalion's snipers reported that the enemy had positions in front of the Senio dyke that were fifty to a hundred yards apart and occupied by Germans manning machine guns and armed with Panzerfausts and rifles.

The Van Doos would attack with 'C' Company under Captain R. Desrivières on the right and 'A' Company under Major Henri Tellier on the left. Support fire would be provided by a medium artillery regiment and four M-10 SPGs from 1st Anti-Tank Regiment. Three Wasps would accompany 'A' Company and four would accompany 'C' Company. Once within range, the Wasps would flame the dyke on the Senio's east bank. Their fuel load would probably allow for a twenty-five-minute dousing. Once the Van Doos had secured the dyke, three additional Wasps would climb it and shoot flame across the river at the other dyke.

Starting on time at 1218 hours, Tellier reported having gained the Senio's east bank after the Wasps had drenched it with fire.

Thirty minutes later, however, Tellier signalled that he needed more stretchers for the wounded. Desrivières, meanwhile, reported that his No. 14 Platoon had three men wounded reaching the dyke. No. 15 Platoon, however, had been stopped by machine-gun fire when the covering smokescreen lagged behind its advance. Two Wasps rushed to support No. 15 Platoon. At 1336 hours, Tellier had both Nos. 7 and 8 Platoons dug in on the bank, but faced "plenty of Germans on the west bank." A sergeant commanding a Wasp warned that there were about fifteen enemy gun pits dug into the railway embankment on the right flank of the attacking companies. At 1430 hours, Tellier reported that his last platoon had reached the dyke, but with only one man still standing. The rest had been killed or wounded during the advance.[4] After that, the Van Doos' attack unravelled.

With night falling, the two companies withdrew from the bank at 1600 hours, leaving small outposts behind. Two Van Doos had been taken prisoner, five were killed, and eighteen were wounded—many by anti-personnel mines.[5]

NO SOONER HAD this battle died down than the artillery barrage supporting 2nd Brigade's main assault erupted at 1700 hours, with medium artillery targeting Granarolo to conceal the whereabouts of the real attack. At 1730 hours, the Patricia's 'A' and 'C' Companies marched toward the Naviglio Canal.[6] The moon was waning in a clear, starry sky. Major Ted Cutbill was leading 'A' Company and Captain J.D. Jones's 'C' Company. These lead companies were to advance on a parallel line to a road that led to the Fosso Vecchio. Thereafter, Major Colin McDougall's 'B' Company would pass through 'A' Company and swing over to where the road crossed the waterway. 'D' Company was in reserve.[7]

At 1930 hours, the companies advanced behind a creeping barrage intended to walk them up to the Vecchio. Both companies "hugged" the barrage closely, the battalion's Captain J.R. Koensgen reported, and crossed the Naviglio "very quickly." 'A' Company reached its objective first, achieving complete surprise and bagging twenty-one prisoners, including an officer. 'C' Company was not far behind, taking thirty-four prisoners. One was badly wounded and soon died. As the Germans had sheltered from the barrage in houses, they were unable to engage the Patricias.

When 'B' Company entered 'A' Company's perimeter, Cutbill warned McDougall that SPG fire was coming from the road crossing. Summoning a five-minute artillery concentration that started falling on the objective at 2130 hours, McDougall led the company in a wide sweep that brought them to the road by the Vecchio from behind. 'B' Company surprised and took prisoner five Germans and captured the SPG and a staff car. Finding the bridge intact, McDougall sent No. 10 Platoon 150 yards toward the Senio River to secure the position. The platoon established a strongpoint anchored on two houses beside the road.[8]

As the Patricias reported their success, Lieutenant Colonel Budge Bell-Irving ordered the Seaforth's 'D' Company to launch the second phase. Bell-Irving intended this phase to play out as follows. First, 'D' Company would clear ground along the west bank of the Naviglio. Passing through 'D' Company, 'A' Company would then clear a stand of woods and several large buildings immediately across the canal from Granarolo. Next, 'B' Company would advance to the Vecchio, and 'C' Company would then advance to the junction point of the Vecchio and Naviglio. The tank-hunting platoon would follow close behind 'D' Company, then 'A' Company, and finally 'C' Company, providing support as needed. A 2-pounder Little John anti-tank gun team was to join 'C' Company as soon as the road bordering the Naviglio was open for use.

But a serious problem with Bell-Irving's plan soon became clear. As 'D' Company crossed the Naviglio, pioneers warned that the road ahead was heavily mined. Until the mines were cleared, no supporting armour or anti-tank guns could be moved forward.[9] The Patricia's pioneer platoon and engineers working with them faced a potentially impossible task. But until supporting arms could be brought forward, the bridgehead was vulnerable to counterattacks.[10]

Lieutenant Jim Horton, commanding the pioneers, had crossed the Naviglio as soon as 'A' Company had started its attack. The road leading to the Vecchio was being raked by machine-gun fire and was badly cratered by demolitions. Horton had soon detected six mines in front of one crater. Twelve men hooked a rope to one, but were unable to budge it. Horton decided to blow the mine in place with explosives. Each mine had to be blown individually. The resulting blasts created enormous holes, leading Horton to believe that "the mines had been laid in threes, one on top of the other, and water placed around them to freeze them in." With the section of road reduced to one huge gaping crater, Horton summoned an Ark bridge to span the gap. When more cratering was found where the road crossed a railway track, Horton created a diversion by blowing the top off the railway embankment with a fifty-pound explosive charge. He then had a Sherman mounting a bulldozer blade plow through the dynamited section and carve out a level pathway.[11] All this was taking time, and Horton knew it was going to be morning before the way was clear for any supporting arms to get up to the forward Patricias and Seaforths.[12]

At about 0030 hours on January 4, meanwhile, the Seaforth's 'D' Company had headed forward, and immediately lost wireless contact. An hour later, its commander reported having become entangled in a sharp fight with German machine guns. These had been eliminated, and at 0215 hours the company declared its objective secure. Three Germans and an 88-millimetre SPG had been captured. Bell-Irving told Major Oliver Herbert Mace to advance 'A' Company for stage two.[13]

By now, the Germans were thoroughly alerted to the threat posed by 2nd Brigade. Precisely at the time the Seaforth's 'D' Company declared its objective secure, German infantry supported by an SPG and covering fire of heavy machine guns and mortars struck the Patricia's No. 18 Platoon of 'B' Company, which was holding the advance position across the Vecchio. About thirty yards in front of the platoon's position, Private Jacob Brown was dug in alone with a PIAT and Thompson submachine gun. As the SPG ground toward the platoon's position, its 88-millimetre gun set one of the two buildings and a haystack inside the perimeter on fire. The flames brightly illuminated the battlefield. Patiently, Brown allowed the SPG to move along the road, with the infantry following, until it was only forty yards away. Although the PIAT was normally fired from a prone position, intervening brush and small trees forced Brown to stand in order to see the SPG and then fire it from his shoulder. The first bomb exploded in one of the trees, sending a shower of wood splinters slashing at the infantry, killing some and scattering the rest. His position given away, Brown came under heavy fire. But he let the SPG close another ten yards before firing another round, which also detonated against a tree and created another shower of splinters. Reloading, Brown fired his last round. This time the SPG stopped dead, and "its crew appeared to have no more stomach for the fight."

Not so the infantry. Dropping the PIAT, Brown shouldered his Thompson. Opening up when the leading Germans were just ten yards distant, Brown shot two dead. This caused the rest to run.[14] Although Brown single-handedly broke the German counterattack in an act that earned a Military Medal, the final victory was postponed. No. 10 Platoon's Lieutenant William Anthony Groomes had been killed and five of his men wounded. As a second counterattack came in, Major McDougall ordered the platoon to abandon its exposed position. From the east bank of the Vecchio, 'B' Company then succeeded in breaking the second attack.[15]

By the time these counterattacks were stopped, at 0350 hours, the Seaforth's 'A' Company had begun clearing the ground facing Granarolo. The Seaforth's pioneers also began the slow task of sweeping the road bordering the Naviglio. It took until 0440 hours for the pioneers and supporting engineers to reach 'D' Company's position. At 0500 hours, Mace reported that 'A' Company had firmly closed any escape routes out of Granarolo. Bell-Irving signalled both 'C' and 'B' Companies to begin the operation's final two stages.[16]

'B' Company's recently promoted Major Tony Staples entered the bridgehead across the Naviglio and led his men toward the Vecchio. "The right-hand platoon had advanced to within about 200 yards of the [Vecchio] when they were pinned down by heavy fire from the bank," Staples recalled. "They suffered several casualties . . . As we moved forward towards the farm buildings that were our objective, one of the outbuildings was hit by a shell and burst into flames. In the semi-light, with the smoke and mist illuminated by the flames, ghostly figures appeared and the only way you could tell friend from foe was whether they fired at you or not.

"We took the building without too much trouble . . . Once the house was cleared, I went upstairs to see if I could find an OP [Observation Post] . . . and I entered a room that had had its whole window blown out. There, signalling to somebody on the other side of the canal, was the biggest . . . Jerry I had ever seen. In the best wild west style, I yanked out my pistol and let fly—and missed him by a yard. Fortunately for me, the German was so surprised he fell out the window and broke his leg.

"About this time, we heard obvious sounds of a counterattack being formed up out of sight beyond the canal. I called for an artillery stonk and in a few minutes a big column of black smoke rose into the sky and noises stopped for the time being.

"For a while things were pretty tense until the anti-tank guns came up."[17] As Staples was directing the guns into position, a bullet struck his head and something also struck him hard across the back. Staples fell to the ground and realized he was paralyzed. The company's first-aid man, he later wrote, was bandaging his head "up like mad . . . and I thought . . . if I'm hit that badly in the head, I had no hope. But as soon as I got down to the RAP . . . it was . . . realized the head wasn't causing [the problem], so [the medical officer] started looking . . . and I still swear at him because he ripped my leather jerkin all apart." Staples was found to have had not only one bullet graze his head but another pierce his back—both believed to have been fired by the same sniper.[18]

Evacuated in the same ambulance from the Regimental Aid Post to the brigade's casualty clearing station was 'C' Company's Major Stewart Lynch. Having successfully reached the objective where the Vecchio doglegged to cross the Naviglio, Lynch had been directing a new platoon leader in setting up his defences when a bullet ricocheted off his pistol and pierced his body. At the battalion's January 3 Orders Group, Staples, Lynch, and Mace—all having served with the Seaforths since January 1944 without being wounded—had figured that their mutual luck was surely running out. As Mace's company would enter the salient fight sooner than the others, they agreed he was most likely to get hit. Mace was now the last one of the three standing. Staples would not return to the battalion, and Lynch only after a prolonged recovery.[19]

At first light, 'C' and 'B' Companies staved off the inevitable counterattacks by calling in close artillery support. The Seaforths and Patricias, however, were too well dug in to be forced back, and their situation improved rapidly as the morning progressed. When 'B' Company came under renewed attack at 0900 hours, the road paralleling the Naviglio had had its mines cleared and its craters filled well enough to allow a troop of Royal Tank Regiment Churchills to get forward and help drive the Germans off.[20]

Early on January 4, despite the best efforts of pioneer Lieutenant Jim Horton, the road leading from the Naviglio to the Vecchio remained impassable. Knowing that German tanks could still potentially break into the Patricia's lines—particularly in the sector held by Major McDougall's 'B' Company—Lieutenant Colonel Bobby Clark decided it was imperative to get a 2-pounder Little John up to it. Summoning 'D' Company's Lieutenant Allan Bruce McKinnon, Clark pointed to a Little John and told him to "use his native wits in getting it forward." A thousand yards on the wrong side of the Naviglio, McKinnon decided that using the road was impossible because of the mines and constant targeting by artillery and mortars. Taking several men, McKinnon set off cross-country—a journey that required getting the jeep pulling the gun over a railway embankment and three bridges. McKinnon and his men bridged these obstacles by using logs, brush, and stones to make ramps or bridge crossings. They then manhandled the jeep and gun across each obstacle. At the Naviglio, there was no passable bridge. Ignoring thickening mortar and shellfire, McKinnon and his team dug ramps down the banks on either side, threw the resulting dirt into the canal, and topped it with brush to create a serviceable crossing. This job took two hours, and it was about 0230 hours when the gun was finally across. Hearing sounds of battle coming from 'B' Company's sector, McKinnon decided that continuing cross-country would take longer than McDougall's men could wait. Leading the way to the road, he proceeded to walk ahead of the jeep towing the gun so that he could guide it around suspected mines. At 0545 hours, McKinnon and the gun reached 'B' Company in time to help drive back the last counterattack.

It was later determined that the stretch of road McKinnon's team had travelled had been sown with twelve of the three-mine stacks. McKinnon's efforts earned a Military Cross, which also honoured a second act of gallantry. As McKinnon was returning from 'B' Company, a British fighter plane crashed into a nearby field and began to burn. Fearing exploding munitions and fuel, McKinnon shouted for his men to stay clear and then ran forward alone. Ripping the cockpit open, he dragged the badly burned pilot to safety.[21]

Securing 2nd Brigade's bridgehead proceeded rapidly during the morning of January 4. At 0430 hours, the Loyal Edmonton Regiment advanced toward Granarolo expecting a fight. They found the Germans gone. The battalion's only fatal casualty was Captain Douglas G. Fraser—a victim of shellfire. He had previously been wounded twice during the Gothic Line Battle. The twenty-six-year-old had risen from the ranks to attend officers' training back in Canada and then returned to the Eddies. Five other men were wounded when a grenade accidentally exploded.[22]

With Granarolo secure, 3rd Brigade launched the final Canadian phase in eliminating the salient during the mid-morning of January 4. The West Nova Scotia and Carleton and York Regiments advanced past 2nd Brigade's right flank toward where the Senio flowed past Cotignola. Left of 2nd Brigade, 56th British Infantry Division's 167th Brigade did the same. Both 3rd Brigade battalions came under such heavy mortar and shellfire that neither could get beyond their start lines. Small patrols discovered the German defence anchored on houses bordering the Vecchio—which in this sector was a half mile east of the Naviglio. Halting to tee up heavy artillery support, Brigadier Bernatchez planned a renewed attack for 2030 hours.

Advancing on the heels of the artillery, the two battalions progressed rapidly, and it was soon clear the Germans had withdrawn at nightfall.[23] By 0030 hours on January 5, the West Nova's 'D' Company had crossed the Vecchio and found the houses abandoned. Hampered only by mines, the West Novas reached the Senio at 1310 hours.[24]

To the right of the West Novas, the Carletons' leading 'C' Company met only scattered small-arms fire. Mortar rounds, however, dogged

it and several casualties resulted before the Senio was reached opposite Cotignola.[25]

Left of 2nd Brigade, meanwhile, 167th Brigade had advanced its
lead battalions in armoured personnel carriers. This enabled them to
cut across the apex of 2nd Brigade's bridgehead and reach the Senio
just west of the West Novas.

WITH THE BATTLES to eliminate the salients on both flanks of
1 Canadian Corps concluded on January 6, British Eighth Army finalized its establishment of a winter line anchored on the Senio River.
And yet, 1st Canadian Infantry Division's historical officer, Captain
T.J. Allen, noted, the Germans "were still very much alert and in
considerable strength along the river, nor was he entirely cleared out
from the east bank of the Senio." At 0400 hours on January 6, the
enemy attacked a Royal 22e Régiment outpost in buildings about
150 yards east of the river. Deploying flame-throwers, the Germans
drove the Van Doos out of the buildings and occupied them.

Throughout the day, v British Corps and 1 Canadian Corps reorganized to defend a static line. The 56th British Infantry Division
shifted rightward to allow 1st Division to anchor its left flank on the
railway crossing over the Senio to the west of Cotignola.[26] This enabled 2nd Infantry Brigade to disengage and move eastward to relieve the Royal Canadian Dragoons and Lanark and Renfrew Scottish
Regiment—extending 1st Division's right boundary to Fusignano.[27]

News that the Lanarks were to be relieved reached Sergeant Fred
Cederberg on January 7. By 1700 hours, he wrote, "our carriers were
packed—except for the Vickers, their barrels pointed through the
transverse slits at the ss positions on the dyke to our right. The Brens,
full mags in place, were stacked against walls." Cederberg had insisted the weapons be kept handy, "just in case, till the last minute."

A Seaforth Highlanders lieutenant arrived and asked how many
men Cederberg had. "Seven," he replied "two sergeants, a corporal,
and four other ranks . . . We started out with fourteen. And it hasn't
been a picnic, sir." Saying he had twenty-two men, the officer asked
how Cederberg had mounted a workable defence with only seven
men. Cederberg explained that they had sown captured Teller mines

in the fields, booby-trapped all the ditches, and scattered noisemakers made with ration tins to alert them of any approach.

"I'll be goddamned . . . the Lanyard and Slaughterhouse Regiment knows how to improvise!" the lieutenant declared.

"Lanyard an' what?" Cederberg asked.

"And Slaughterhouse. That's a kind of affectionate nickname you guys have earned, ever since the Naviglio."

As the section's Vickers were being placed in the carrier, Cederberg noticed one was still loaded with a belt of ammunition. He told Corporal Albert MacNeil to unload it. "He looked at me, grinning. 'There's only a touch left.'" Then MacNeil thumbed the triggers. "The barrel spouted fire. Thump! Thump! Thump! Until the trail of the belt wiggled, signalling the ammo was gone." The Seaforth lieutenant burst in, accusing Cederberg's men of trying to stir up the front in the middle of a relief. Runaway burst, he explained. Gun went off as they were trying to extract the belt. "Al didn't know it at the time," Cederberg wrote, "but we had fired our last shots in the Italian campaign."[28]

AS THE FIGHTING wound down, senior commanders offered the troops effusive praise. General Mark Clark sent a note congratulating Eighth Army for eliminating the salients. "The operation was thoroughly planned and executed. Despite strong resistance and counter-attacks [Canadian] Corps and 5th Corps pressed forward taking a heavy toll of enemy dead and many prisoners." Lieutenant General Richard McCreery wrote to Major General Charles Foulkes, "[H]eartiest congratulations to you and your corps on the very successful ops on both flanks, which has driven the enemy back over the Senio and secured valuable objectives on the right up to [Valli di] Comacchio. The op of both divs has been carefully planned and executed with splendid fighting spirit and great skill. Heavy casualties have been inflicted on the enemy in killed and prisoners . . . Well done indeed." Passing the message on to his men, Foulkes added his "sincere congratulations to all ranks of the . . . Corps and the 9 Armd Bde who have fought so well during this stage . . . You have shown what can be achieved by careful planning and speedy, determined execution of a sound plan. I appreciate very much the way that all the soldiers have conducted themselves during these ops."[29]

On January 4, Eighth Army had informed Foulkes that a two-regiment-strong Italian combat group—the Gruppo Cremona—was to come under 1 Canadian Corps command, enabling 5th Canadian Armoured Division's withdrawal to rest and regroup. Foulkes gave Gruppo Cremona responsibility for the right sector, extending from the main railway just east of Highway 16 to the coast. The 9th British Armoured Brigade took over the corps's centre from the railway to 1st Division's right flank at Fusignano.[30]

The Cremona traced its roots back to Lombardy and the 1848 War of Independence. In 1939, the Cremona had expanded from two infantry regiments to a division with the addition of an artillery regiment. When Italy surrendered to the Allies in September 1943, the Cremona was occupying Corsica. Brigadier Clemente Primieri switched sides and drove the Germans off the island. In October, the Cremona transferred to Sardinia and came under Allied command. Moved to the Italian mainland in September 1944, it was reorganized and equipped along British lines as a self-supporting brigade. On January 11, 1945, it moved into the 1 Canadian Corps front line.[31]

On the evening of January 13, one of the Cremona's infantry regiments relieved the Perth Regiment's 'D' Company. Private Stan Scislowski was freezing cold, exhausted, and worried that his six-man section might be overrun by Germans before they left the line. "With this in mind, it was only natural when our relief arrived . . . shortly before six, that I was more than a little glad to see them. I could have kissed every one of the scruffy, rough-bearded bastards. But since we were anxious to get our asses back to where we could thaw out in front of a fire and have a decent bite to eat, we wasted no time in idle chit-chat. We just gave them what little information we had as to the lie of the land, and away we went, leaving them to whatever fate had in store for them."[32]

Over the course of that day, 5th Armoured Brigade left the front line. The following day, its headquarters and all three regiments moved to Cervia. The next day, most of 11th and 12th Infantry Brigades' battalions also departed for rest camps.[33] Upon reaching

Cervia, British Columbia Dragoons commander Lieutenant Colonel Harry Angle announced that the regiment would likely be billeted there for more than a month, possibly even as long as three months. No return to combat was anticipated.[34]

Not so for 1st Division. "It is apparent," its historian, Captain Allen, wrote, "that the intention for the next month or two is to maintain a winter line. Differing from the winter line of last year there is no valley of No Man's Land between the opposing forces. In many cases our dyke positions on the east bank are a snow-ball's throw from the enemy on the west bank of the Senio. Differing also is the flatness of the land, making movement from forward positions difficult. Extensive camouflage work is being carried out and troops are being issued with white winter equipment. Different also is the enemy's mood and strength. It seems that he is expecting us to make a large attack in the direction of Lugo. Hence, he is defensively alert. Positions on the dyke are difficult to maintain because of the exposed situation."[35]

24

The Winter Line

O N THE SENIO River winter line, the Germans had the upper hand because of their greater numbers and almost imperme-able fortifications. Accordingly, 1st Canadian Infantry Division's in-itial efforts focused on establishing defensive strongpoints. At the same time, to keep the Germans off balance, the division undertook a number of patrols and small-scale raids. They made no attempt, how-ever, to cross the Senio. As the division's historical officer, Captain T.J. Allen, observed, the Germans "dominate the . . . Senio, his patrols and outposts on our side of the river us[e] foot bridges . . . Where our outposts are not on the dykes on the east side, the enemy's are. These enemy outposts are strongly held with wire, mines, and well-protected machinegun nests. These superior posts give him a field of observation over the lower ground ahead up to 300 yards deep, and such areas he has made into quite efficient killing grounds."[1]

The railway bridge on the division's left flank remained in German hands, and its wreckage provided a serviceable footbridge. Aerial re-connaissance photographs also revealed the presence of numerous other footbridges.[2]

On January 11, the Germans struck at the seam between the 4th Princess Louise Dragoon Guards—one of the last 5th Canadian Armoured Division units still in the line—and the Seaforth Highlanders. At 1910 hours, the Plugs' No. 7 Platoon, holding a farm on the left flank, adjacent to the Seaforths, came under heavy attack. Despite defensive fire by artillery and medium machine guns, ss panzer grenadiers wearing white camouflage burst from a tunnel dug through the dyke fronting the platoon's position. Surrounding the farm, the Germans blew the farmhouse's roof in with explosives. They then set the house and nearby barn on fire, forcing Lieutenant James Griffith to order a retreat to a reserve position seventy-five yards back.

When news of this action reached battalion headquarters, a counterattacking force of two tanks and a section of infantry moved to regain the lost ground. At 1945 hours, the force commander reported the situation "still obscure." At battalion headquarters, Lieutenant Colonel Charles Petch—who had replaced Lieutenant Colonel Bill Darling on December 19—had the situation on the front lines clarified somewhat when two ss prisoners were brought in at 2100 hours. One was a sergeant in possession of papers detailing the German plan. There was to have been a three-pronged assault against the left flank, but the sergeant said only the one against No. 7 Platoon had managed to cross the river. Each assaulting force had numbered about twenty-five men, and the overall force had included eighteen Italians. The objective had been to gain control of the Plugs' entire left flank.

At 0830 hours on January 12, the counterattacking force ousted the Germans from No. 7 Platoon's lost position, with the further loss of one tank, knocked out by a Panzerfaust round that also wounded a member of its crew. No. 7 Platoon's total casualties were one man killed and thirteen wounded. Lieutenant Griffith was among the wounded. The fight had cost the Germans dearly. They left behind twenty to thirty dead, and there were signs that many more had been wounded. With the buildings in ruins, the position was no longer tenable.[3]

Two days later, the Plugs were relieved by 9th British Armoured Brigade's 1st Welsh Regiment. By January 16, all 5th Division units had left the front lines. Its divisional headquarters was established in Riccione, 5th Armoured Brigade was in Cervia, 11th Infantry Brigade in San Giovanni, and 12th Infantry Brigade in Macerata.[4]

On the winter line, meanwhile, 1st Division had been seeking to even the balance of power between itself and the Germans. Major General Harry Foster's January 11 instructions required construction wherever possible of strong outposts along the Senio's east dyke that would be linked by telephone lines to battalion headquarters. These positions were to be fully manned during the night, with reduced garrisons in the day. Each battalion was to keep three companies forward, with the other and a troop of tanks in reserve to provide an immediate counterattack force. Forward defensive lines were established about three hundred yards behind the dyke and the open ground between turned into killing grounds. All companies were deployed so their platoons could mount inter-supporting and all-round defence. Extensive fields of anti-personnel mines were planted. At night, illumination flares and trip flares triggered by contact were used to cover all lines of approach.

Foster was particularly concerned that the untested Gruppo Cremona might be overwhelmed by a large-scale counterattack. As a precaution, he deployed the Carleton and York Regiment as a tactical reserve at Mezzano—just left of the Italians.[5]

Stretching almost fourteen miles, the Canadian line was thinly held. The 1st Division maintained its frontage with two brigades up and one in reserve. Two 21st British Tank Brigade regiments provided tank support. The 9th Armoured Brigade had four battalions forward with one tank regiment in support. Gruppo Cremona was the weakest link, but its front was expected to be the quietest.[6]

In fact, no sooner had the Italians deployed than the Germans subjected them to patrol and raiding activities supported by heavy mortar fire. The intent was to take prisoners and test morale. In a series of night attacks, the Germans overran several forward outposts. But the Italians launched vigorous counterattacks.

In mid-January, the Germans abandoned direct combat and began firing shells filled with propaganda leaflets, encouraging the Italians "to desert and enjoy the hospitality of the Germans in northern Italy. These pamphlets were supplemented by broadcasts of popular music and . . . appeals in Italian . . . by a female character known as Bianca." Several Italian cartoonists among the soldiers responded with caricatures of the supposed Bianca wearing a German uniform and clinging to a microphone while broadcasting from a slit trench. The cartoons were mimeographed and fired back at the Germans. Such humorous asides failed to diminish the fact that holding a defensive line remained deadly business. Twenty-eight days after entering the lines, Gruppo Cremona reported four officers and 52 other ranks killed and more than 190 wounded.[7]

In addition to Gruppo Cremona, the Canadians still had Major Bulow's partisans under command. In early January, they took responsibility for front-facing the section of the Reno River that looped along the south shore of Valli di Comacchio. At first numbering 209, by the end of January its ranks had risen to 319. Corps command found the partisans valuable for reconnaissance and used small parties across the Canadian front. Between the dykes of the Reno and the Comacchio lay a narrow, irregular strip of swampy and sandy ground where the partisans maintained regular patrols. They also established a strong outpost to block German attacks down a spit that thrust out into the Comacchio at Sant' Alberto. Much of the area for which the partisans were responsible had been mined earlier by the Germans. The partisan method of eliminating these mine fields was to drive flocks of sheep through the suspected areas. It proved a gory but effective technique.[8]

"THE FIGHTING ON the Senio bank was almost like bickering," Loyal Edmonton Regiment's Lieutenant Colonel Jim Stone recalled. "There was always something going on. We learned later that [Field Marshal Albert] Kesselring had ordered that there would be no live and let live. The fight would continue continuously, although not on a grand scale. So, we were constantly patrolling. They would come over and occupy a farmhouse on [our] side of the bank and we'd have another farmhouse, two hundred or three hundred yards from it, and we'd go and take [the German-held house] back and this just kept going on."[9]

Having recovered from his October 23, 1944, injuries, Kesselring had resumed command on January 16. He ensured that elements of four divisions faced the 1 Canadian Corps front. On the German right, part of 362nd Infanterie-Division was deployed from the

corps's far left flank to a road that ran directly from the Senio River
to Bagnacavallo. The line from here to Alfonsine was held by 16th ss
Panzer Grenadier Division. From Alfonsine, the 42nd Jäger Division
covered the ground south of Valli di Comacchio. Defending the narrow neck of ground between the Comacchio and the Adriatic were
elements of 710th Infanterie-Division.[10]

Although supposedly crack troops, 1st Division's Captain Allen
reported, the ss yielded "a constant dribble of deserters," especially
from the division's 35th Regiment. But even though the regiment
seemed "a poor specimen for an ss division," Allen wrote, there were
"still fanatics among" its soldiers. The truth of this had been demonstrated on January 15 in the Loyal Edmonton Regiment's sector.
To prevent German infiltrations, Stone decided to erect an eight-
hundred-yard-long barrier of barbed and concertina wire at the foot of
the dyke. Installation was assigned to the support company, and two
'D' Company platoons crawled up on the dyke to provide protection.
At 2030 hours, the Germans fired a shower of rifle grenades over
the dyke. Then a machine gun started firing from a position off to
the left that was beyond rifle range of the 'D' Company platoons. At
2200 hours, ss troops launched an attack from this position, which
was driven off. Shortly thereafter, the 'B' Company platoon on the battalion's extreme right was attacked. Four Germans armed with demolition charges rushed the house containing the platoon's forward
section.[11] Two Germans were cut down by Thompson submachine-
gun fire, but the other two kept coming. One shouted, "*Mein Führer!*"
repeatedly, as the two kicked in the door. Triggering the charges, both
men blew themselves up.[12] When the smoke cleared, the Eddies had
ten casualties.[13]

With the Germans firmly ensconced along the side of the Senio's
east dyke, the Canadians were seldom able to establish a presence on
its top. Major William George Robinson of 3rd Infantry Brigade headquarters noted that it was possible to establish a position on the dyke
"without much trouble by blasting our way in with lots of firepower.
But right behind the assaulting party must be a party to do digging,
mining, and wiring. Jerry is so active that he will flush the position
out if this is not done."[14]

The front soon settled into a routine. Generally clear and cold weather, Captain Allen believed, had provided the "best weather for fighting since September, for rain is a worse foe than frost." The daily pattern saw reconnaissance patrols sent to "a house or dyke position to find out if such is occupied by enemy. If not, an outpost is established for the night and possibly a listening post by day. If enemy are in occupation, either an ambush patrol or a fighting patrol is sent out the next night. In the first case to waylay enemy relief and other patrols, in the second to fight the enemy out of the position. If we find the position untenable, it is mined and in the case of a building blown up . . . Enemy patrols and raiding parties of 15 or 20 men are active nightly . . . He has been very busy blowing up buildings to clear fields of fire. The continuous sounds of demolitions in the middle of the month behind River Senio was finally judged to be not the blowing up of ammunition . . . dumps preparatory to withdrawal, but work . . . on defensive positions."

Although the fighting was constant, it was not intense. Casualties were steady but not heavy. This enabled the Canadian battalions to gradually return to normal strengths, as reinforcements came in. There remained, however, a shortage of non-commissioned officers.[15]

On the night of January 19–20, the West Nova Scotia Regiment replaced the Loyal Edmonton Regiment along the Senio near Bagnacavallo. The companies, the regiment's historian wrote, spread out "in an expanse of muddy fields and vineyards laid off in neat squares by a series of parallel farm lanes, some running north-east across the inner curve of the Senio, others crossing them at right-angles towards the southeast. The usual shattered farmhouses, barns and sheds were dotted along these lanes, each a potential strongpoint and each a target for the opposing mortars and artillery. The vineyards consisted of many rows of tall poles, each row strung with four wires on which the vines were trained, the first wire 3 feet from the ground and the others spaced about 18 inches apart above it. Between each row was a ploughed strip 15 to 20 feet wide in which the Italians planted vegetables and sometimes grain. In summer, when the vines had climbed and covered the wires, these green rows made a useful screen for troop movements. But in winter, when the leaves were gone and the vines cut back . . . the landscape was a monotony of bare poles and wires staggering across the flat, wet fields.

"Within this melancholy scene, crouching in soggy ditches and weapon pits, peering from loopholes in the upper stories of tottering farmhouses, both sides lay concealed with their rifles, machine-guns and mortars and their radios or telephone lines to the artillery. Every road and lane, every building, every clump of bushes, every possible vantage point was marked and ranged—and by day and by night a harassing fire of all arms was directed on each from time to time. All day snipers lay and watched for the slightest sign of human movement, each night, patrols crept forth on their deadly errands, each night the pioneers of both sides busied themselves in laying mines and wire."[16]

BOTH SIDES TRIED to improve their lot and develop new ways to harass or hurt the other. Staff at 3rd Canadian Infantry Brigade headquarters cooked up a scheme to convince the Germans that a patrol was closing on their position in order to lure them into opening fire. Position exposed, it could then be subjected to mortar fire.[17] Setting up a loudspeaker in the Royal Canadian Regiment sector, the staffers "broadcast the sound of a fairly noisy patrol," Major Galloway wrote. "Unfortunately, the recording had been made during a soft period and the sound of slushing through mud and water was broadcast on a night when the ground was frozen hard." Undeceived, the Germans held their fire.[18] When the same deception was attempted later in the Hastings and Prince Edward Regiment's sector, Lieutenant Farley Mowat considered the result inevitable—heavy artillery fire "lambasted" the front lines.[19]

On January 16, Galloway witnessed another 3rd Brigade staff "brainwave. A barrage of 2-inch mortar parachute flares was put up all along the Brigade front. The enemy responded to this display by mortar and MG fire. Supposedly they thought the flares were to indicate our direction for a night attack, which was the idea."[20]

The Germans also attempted to deceive the Canadians with forms of equally ineffective "sonic warfare." More realistic decep-

tions, however, sometimes yielded results. In late January, the Royal
22e Régiment carried out a noisy platoon relief of a forward position.
Then the troops left behind maintained strict silence throughout
the ensuing day. That night, a German patrol sent to determine
whether the position had actually been abandoned was ambushed
and eliminated.[21]

One sector into which the Seaforth Highlanders had moved on
January 10 saw the German-held east dyke no more than thirty feet
from the Canadian positions. Finding a spot on the dyke that was un-
guarded, a section from 'D' Company under Corporal A.C. Duncan
slipped into it. Having heard reports of other battalions managing to
destroy some German footbridges by lobbing PIAT rounds at a high
angle toward them, Duncan embarked on a failed attempt with several shots. Moving farther along the dyke to get a better angle of fire,
Duncan was surprised to see two coal-scuttle-helmeted heads pop out
of a hole almost precisely where his section had just been. Realizing
they had been spotted, the two heads promptly disappeared. Duncan
rushed over and lobbed a grenade into the hole, which produced the
emergence of two wounded ss panzer grenadiers.

That night, the Seaforths heard what sounded like a half-track
grinding along the German side of the Senio. After the vehicle
stopped opposite their positions, "there was a groaning sound like
a 'Moaning Minnie.' This was followed by a projectile with a trail
of smoke behind it coming into the . . . lines on a high trajectory.
It exploded with a crashing noise in a ball of fire," the Seaforth's
historian wrote, "and got the nickname 'casa cruncher.' Then the
vehicle moved on another 50 yards and let off another round. These
fell periodically into the Seaforth's lines and now and then caused
considerable damage."

All battalion 3-inch mortar crews were steadily engaged. Any
sounds of enemy movement or suspicion that the Germans occupied
a building within range drew their fire. "This was fine for targets
some distance from the dykes, but enemy positions across the tiny
river received attention from special weapons devised by some ingenious members of the battalion. Two worthy of special note were
called the 'v-2' and the 'Dagwood.' The 'v-2' was made from a crotch

of a tree and a piece of an inner tube. The stem of the crotch was planted firmly in the ground where, incidentally, it had a full traverse. Then a grenade with a seven-second fuse was placed in the pouch. The rubber band was stretched, the weapon aimed, the grenade's pin pulled, and the grenade was catapulted into the enemy's line with great satisfaction. It had a range of about 100 yards with a No. 36 grenade, or about half that distance with the heavier No. 75 Hawkins anti-tank grenade. The 'Dagwood' was a lethal sandwich made by putting a No. 36 grenade between two No. 75 grenades. These were tied together and placed in a sandbag which, whirled around once or twice, was thrown over to the enemy-held dyke where it exploded with a tremendous blast."[22]

On January 24, the Loyal Edmonton Regiment deployed a Wasp for the first time. Twenty Germans had reportedly occupied a ruined house the night before that was about three hundred yards from 'D' Company. After a morning patrol confirmed the German presence, a Wasp was requested. The flame-throwing Bren carrier arrived at 1945 hours and trundled to within thirty yards of the target. It then "put light hot-shots into it. The fire was completely satisfactory," an Eddies report noted. "The Wasp withdrew when through firing, and mortar smoke was put down to avoid silhouetting our troops as they closed in against the burning building. Unfortunately, the enemy had withdrawn."[23]

Although most Canadian infantrymen hated the Lifebuoy flame-thrower, it did sometimes prove effective. One divisional report cited the use of a Lifebuoy just south of Cotignola "to dissuade the enemy from using a tunnel he had built through the east dyke. Two enemy were burnt up and the tunnel was no longer used."[24]

Princess Patricia's Canadian Light Infantry's Lieutenant Syd Frost—wounded on December 15—returned to his unit and was posted as second-in-command of 'D' Company on January 30. The Patricias were again facing the Senio in front of Bagnacavallo, with 'D' Company's three platoons in fortified houses, two of which were only twenty yards from the German-held east dyke. With the Germans completely dominating the position, there could be no movement by day. Food- and ammunition-bearing parties shuttled back and forth at night, using carefully marked lines, as much of the surrounding ground was mined or otherwise booby-trapped. Various battalions had by the end of January held this ground and sown it with their own mines. The trace maps purporting to show minefield positions were untrustworthy, Frost found. More than one man was maimed or killed stepping on a "friendly" mine.

By this time, virtually every battalion was using v-2s and Dagwoods, most believing it had been one of theirs who first invented each one. One legend and a couple of nearly official reports credited the Dagwood invention to someone from 5th Division's Lanark and Renfrew Scottish Regiment. "Other means of terrorizing the enemy were more prosaic, but also more lethal, such as loading up a truck with bombs and mines and sending it careening down a road to greet the Germans, *sans* driver of course."

A favourite German tactic was "to roll Teller mines down the river embankment into our heavily sandbagged houses," Frost wrote. "Usually the mines became ensnarled in obstacles placed in front of the strongholds, or the mines simply didn't explode on contact. But when they did, they gave our *casas* a severe test." German snipers were constantly active during the day, but seldom was the rifle fire accurate. Deadlier were the MG42s firing on fixed lines. The house 'D' Company's headquarters was in had one corner that was routinely hammered by machine-gun fire every night according to some predictably fixed Teutonic timetable. Occasionally, the Germans dug tunnels through the dyke, creating "openings like portholes in a ship to fire heavy weapons at us." Sometimes the weapon was a 75-millimetre or 88-millimetre gun. After a few such incidents, the Patricias brought up a medium gun during the night. As the first glimmer of dawn lit the horizon, they fired a shot through the hole that blew the German gun apart.[25]

Throughout January, there had been little rain. Temperatures hovered around freezing. Occasional snow flurries kept the ground white, although the midday sun sometimes was warm enough to produce surface mud. Generally, however, the ground stayed frozen and the roads coated with ice or packed snow. Surface water in the fields froze, but the waterways remained open. Heavy rain reported in the

Apennines on January 26 caused a significant rise in the Senio's water levels, which reduced both German and Canadian patrolling.[26]

BY FEBRUARY 1, 5TH ARMOURED Division had been in reserve for nearly a month. From 1 Canadian Corps headquarters down, rumours had circulated in the last weeks of December that this was to prepare the division for an amphibious operation that would land it north of the Valli di Comacchio in order to turn the German line on the Senio River.[27] In reality, a plan of far more consequence for 1 Canadian Corps was afoot. On February 2, Supreme Allied Commander Mediterranean Field Marshal Harold Alexander was informed by the Combined Chiefs of Staff of their intention "to build up the maximum possible strength on the Western Front to see a decision in that theatre." Accordingly, five divisions were to be immediately withdrawn from the Mediterranean—two from Greece, the other three from Italy—and transferred to Northwest Europe. All of 1 Canadian Corps and 1st Canadian Armoured Brigade, which had served with British formations since January 1944, were included.

Alexander was given no time for complaint about a reduction in forces that would seriously hobble the effectiveness of the spring offensive in Italy. The following day, Allied Force Headquarters (AFHQ) delivered a complete program for the movement by ship of the designated formations from Italy to Marseilles. Embarkation was to begin on February 15. In meetings held in Paris on February 6 and 7, it was decided the transfer of troops would go through the ports of Leghorn and Naples.[28]

Brigadier W.G.H. Roaf, the Canadian AFHQ liaison officer, was verbally informed of the plan on February 4. The following day, he and other Canadian representatives attended an AFHQ detailed planning conference.[29] Although officially notified of the scheme at this time, Lieutenant General Charles Foulkes had been expecting this since meeting U.S. Chief of Staff General George C. Marshall in Florence at the Fifteenth Army Group headquarters following the Malta Conference's conclusion on February 3. During the conference, it was agreed to reduce strength in the Mediterranean in order to bolster the Allied Expeditionary Force in Northwest Europe. Marshall had told Foulkes in confidence that he expected the Canadians to be included. While keeping the reason to himself, Foulkes immediately instituted a series of corps staff exercises that created a theoretical preliminary plan that was well in hand when formal notification arrived on February 7.[30] Consequently, Operation Goldflake was able to be activated immediately.

A massive task still lay ahead. As 1st Infantry Division's Captain Allen wrote, "the speed of evacuation necessitated a high degree of administrative efficiency, good coordination, and felicitous cooperation between the various HQs concerned." The Canadian formations were widely scattered, and 1st Division was still on the winter line. The 5th Division had troops scattered from Rimini to Cattolica, and 1st Armoured Brigade regiments were serving with both the U.S. Fifth Army and British Eighth Army. Then there were the many subunits well to the rear, including hospital teams in six different communities. Some headquarter units, as far to the rear as Rome, were included in the move.

1 Canadian Corps, of course, was concentrated on the Adriatic coast between Cattolica and Ravenna. To get to either Naples or Leghorn necessitated a cross-country move by road and rail. Moving thousands of troops and immense amounts of equipment had to be carried out without upsetting the normal flow of maintenance traffic required to keep the war going. Nevertheless, on February 10, 5th Division started moving.[31] The entire division's move to Leghorn was expected to take until February 21. A total of almost 20,000 troops, 5,614 vehicles, 455 tanks, and 320 Bren carriers had to be moved.[32]

While the rest of 1 Canadian Corps was well along in the move before mid-February, 1st Division still manned the winter line. On February 10, Foulkes handed battlefront command to Major General Foster. From this point to when 1st Division withdrew, Foster reported directly to Eighth Army's Lieutenant General Richard McCreery. Foulkes and his corps staff were out of the picture.[33]

ON FEBRUARY 10, 2ND CANADIAN Infantry Brigade returned from a short rest out of the line to positions just opposite Fusignano on

1st Division's extreme right flank. The Germans here were even more aggressive than normal. Seaforth Highlanders' 'D' Company commander Captain J.D. Pierce wrote in his diary on February 13 that the day was extremely unlucky. Two of his privates had been wounded by shrapnel from a mortar round. Then nineteen-year-old Private Donald John Frederick Robinson ventured a peek over the top of the dyke he was behind. "He was shot instantly . . . In the afternoon, the other bank received an awful lacing . . . with PIATS on the sniper post . . . responsible for Robinson's death. A German was heard to scream for help on the opposite bank . . . the hate went on late into the evening."[34]

Having engaged in near static warfare for more than a month, it was easy to start getting slack. On February 16, heavy mortar fire struck the Royal Canadian Regiment's 'B' Company. Soon its commander, Captain Jimmy Quayle, reported to battalion headquarters that a German raiding party had "taken out the centre position in his company area. This house," Major Galloway recorded in his diary, "was an artillery and mortar OP guarded by a section from a 'B' Company platoon and with a section of [medium machineguns]. It was manned by 24 NCOs and men, of which 17 were captured . . . The enemy raid was daring and seemed thoroughly well prepared. Insufficient sentries outside the house, the heavy mortar concentrations, and the inky blackness of night allowed the enemy to take our post unawares." On either side of the raided house had stood two houses occupied by 'B' Company personnel, but the German mortar fire had made it impossible for any of them to assist in meeting the attack.

The next morning Galloway, temporarily in command of the battalion, was called to 1st Brigade's headquarters at 1100 hours and given a "going over" by Brigadier Desmond Smith. Knowing the dressing-down was deserved, Galloway went to every company position with the battalion intelligence officer, Lieutenant Jack David, in tow. He "blitzed" all the company officers and laid on a 50 per cent stand-to policy for every night thereafter.[35]

Like the Seaforths, the Loyal Edmonton Regiment was in the area near Fusignano. On the extreme right flank was a strongpoint house standing right next to the dyke. The building was too small for more than a platoon, and Lieutenant Colonel Stone considered it "always precarious. Never kept a platoon in there very long. It was a bit scary, nobody could sleep. The Germans would everyday try and put Teller mines against the house. Or they were rolling barrels of explosives at it or throwing grenades."[36]

On February 24, the house was held by No. 17 Platoon of 'D' Company. At 1740 hours, an SPG started firing at it. Soon the platoon leader reported a large force of German infantry mustering on the opposite side of the bank.[37] Moments later, a strong German force attacked the house, but even more Germans headed into the gap between the Eddies and the neighbouring Seaforths. By midnight, the attack was in full spate when Stone rushed forward to personally see what was going on. Both the Seaforths and the Eddies were pouring fire into the Germans trying to push through the gap. No. 17 Platoon was holding on, the men firing rapid bursts with their Bren guns. Three British Honey Stuart reconnaissance tanks were supporting the Eddies. Stone rushed to them and called up to the young subaltern in command, "Move those Honey tanks up the road to 'D' Company's headquarters and I hope you have lots of small-arms ammo." The officer replied that they hadn't fired in months and he'd love to get the opportunity to shoot. When the Honeys were in position, Stone directed their fire on to the top of the dyke about five hundred yards distant and had them rake it to prevent any further Germans coming forward.[38]

An hour later, the battle was over. No. 17 Platoon was still tight in the house, the building surrounded by German dead and wounded. The building itself was in ruins, the platoon almost out of Bren ammunition. Other Germans, who had rushed an unoccupied house in the gap that had been booby-trapped, were blown up and killed. When German stretcher parties came forward to collect their dead and wounded, the Eddies and Seaforths held their fire. In recent weeks, this had become an informal protocol—necessary to prevent the dead of both sides being left to rot in No Man's Land. The Eddies counted four men killed and another ten wounded. Prisoners reported that the attack had been more than a raid. Intending to seize the ground the two battalions held and keep it, the attack had been made by seven companies drawn from two battalions.

For the Eddies and all the remaining Canadians on the winter line, that night constituted their last fight in Italy. The following morning, a battalion of 10th Indian Division relieved the Eddies along with all of 1st Division.[39] The 2nd Infantry Brigade battalions were last to leave, the other brigades having departed a few days later. The Patricias were the last of 2nd Brigade to go, departing at 2110 hours on February 25.[40]

THROUGHOUT THE COURSE of Operation Goldflake, preventing the Germans from learning that the Canadians were leaving was a major challenge. There were legitimate fears that if the Germans realized the Allied force in Italy was being reduced, they would feel free to send some of their own divisions to other fronts. "Canadians have a distinct accent," one report noted, "are not unlikely to be loquacious, have many rather distinctive vehicles, look different from a Tommy, wear uniforms of peculiar cloth and colour and smoke their own brands of cigarettes. Further, the red and purple patches on the sleeves are, if not a hall-mark, at least striking signs; the sudden disappearance of these patches could not but be noticed." As the Canadians had done in other past moves, all identifying markers were removed from the vehicles and the distinctive shoulder patches were taken off.

An elaborate deception plan was undertaken to convince the Germans that the Canadians had been withdrawn from the front lines but remained in the theatre. This ruse included measures such as keeping all Canadian clubs, hostels, hotels, leave centres, hospitals, and administrative operations open. As the clubs and other accommodation facilities eventually closed, the ostensible reason was for "spring cleaning." The Canada Club in Rome and nearby Chateau Laurier only closed in late March. By then, the sole guests at the Chateau Laurier were British and other Allied officers. Under the code name "Penknife," a small unit of five officers and 229 men headquartered in Macerata travelled "hither and yon" to erect Provost Corps directional signs and then pull them down. Attached signallers were continually sending "dummy messages and keeping up the usual bulk of wireless traffic." That this ploy worked was indicated by German traffic intercepts that showed "the enemy had been listening, and upon occasion he attempted to jam the signals." Operation Penknife shut down on March 17.[41] So successful was the overall deception that German maps of Italy continued to include Canadian formations until April 19.

For 1 Canadian Corps, the Italian Campaign truly ended on February 25. It was the longest campaign undertaken by the Canadian army—slightly more than twenty months for those who waded ashore in Sicily on July 10, 1943. They, and the Allies beside whom they'd soldiered, had by February's end liberated almost the entire country. Although Allied casualties were severe, German losses were higher and the campaign succeeded in its strategy of pinning a significant number of enemy divisions in place. Total Canadian casualties in Italy tallied 408 officers and 4,991 all other ranks killed. A further 1,218 officers and 18,268 all other ranks were wounded and 62 officers and 92 men were captured. Another 365 died of other causes. Overall, Canadian casualties during the campaign were 26,254.[42] It was a high cost to pay, but the campaign was also a great victory—essential to the final fall of Germany, which came less than three months later.

JUST BEFORE HE left Italy, Lord Strathcona's Horse's Lieutenant Colonel Jim McAvity reflected, "This has been an education, never to be forgotten. We had seen Vesuvius after eruption; operas and concerts and ballets in Naples and Florence and Rome; Pompeii and Cassino—ruins old-style and new-style; scruffy women carrying their worldly goods on their heads on every highway and biway, smart women in the cities with their worldly goods enshrouded with furs and silks; oranges and olives growing on trees, lizards crawling, gray rocky hills topped with marshmallow clouds, mud and dust; and war with its dead and dying, its magic horror and its stark realism. We had smelt Neapolitan street scenes, medieval plumbing at its worst, sheep, pigs, goats, garlic and spice; and the sweet morning air in the valley of the Volturno. We had tasted 'Lacrima Christi,' cognac in Villanova, spaghetti and 'M&V,' legitimate turkey on Christmas Days, illegitimate turkeys and chickens and pork on the Senio, in the San Giustina 'mud-hole,' in Barchi.

"Despite your lack of hospitality, we had seen a lot, had experienced a lifetime of contrasts; the filthy thieving urchins in Naples, the immaculate choir-boys in Florence, the incredible poverty of your farms in the hills and over the south, the smartness that is modern Rome; the shrill call of roosters in the dawning in the Matera, the whine of mortars in the dawning in the Liri Valley; mepacrine and mosquito nets and anti-malarial cream, hot baths and crepe suzettes in Rome on a seven days' leave.

"Fun in Italy! Sure it was fun to have been there, now that we were going. During the long weeks and months there had been fun, but it was not real fun because there was no future in Italy. There was only the present and the past. We had been living from day to day and had become used to it; living in dusty olive groves, on baked hillsides, living in farm houses, dirty farm houses, always dirty farm houses; houses with three walls, houses with two walls, houses that had been collected by a bulldozer and pushed to one side. Poor blitzed Italy."[43]

The River Battles in Memory

O N A COLD, windy, late September day, I stand in the Villanova Canadian War Cemetery. Here, 205 Canadian and 6 British soldiers killed during the River Battles are buried. The cemetery's design is unusual—just three long rows with the Cross of Remembrance at the back, directly facing the entrance. Villanova Cemetery holds but a fraction of the Canadians who died between the opening of the River Battles on September 22, 1944, and their conclusion on February 25, 1945. Many more are buried at Ravenna Commonwealth Cemetery, on the city's outskirts, and in Cesena Commonwealth Cemetery. Smaller numbers are also buried in several other Commonwealth and community cemeteries near where 1 Canadian Corps fought its battles during these long months.

How many Canadians died, were wounded, or became prisoners during this phase of the Italian Campaign is not precisely known. This is primarily because statistics from September 22 to October 28, 1944, were not succinctly broken out. There is instead a five-day overlap between the last days of fighting during the Gothic Line Battle and the September 22 beginning of the River Battles. Further complicating matters, the data for that period only includes those suffered by 5th Canadian Armoured Division. No statistics for 1st Canadian Infantry Division were reported until October 1. This discrepancy is to some extent compensated for by the fact that 5th Division withdrew from the Gothic Line Battle on September 13—handing off to 1st Division. Consequently, it is largely safe to conclude that the majority of 5th Division losses from September 13 to October 27 (there appear to have been no Canadian casualties on October 28) occurred after the River Battles opened. In this period, 5th Division reported 1,290 casualties, with 267 being fatal and 82 listed as missing.

As most of the fighting in the early days of the River Battles fell to 5th Armoured Division—1st Infantry Division having gone into reserve after the Gothic Line Battle—the start of casualty reporting on October 1 also provides some separation between the two operations. The 1st Division casualties up to October 27 totalled 606, of which 122 died, 12 were missing, and 2 were reported captured.[1]

Data for October 29, 1944, to February 27, 1945, are clearer—and appalling. During that period, 1 Canadian Corps lost 61 officers and 826 other ranks killed, 206 officers and 3,889 other ranks wounded, and 15 officers and 311 other ranks taken prisoner. Thus, total losses during the advance from the Montone River to the Senio River and the period of holding the winter line were 5,318.[2] It needs to be remembered that neither Canadian division was involved in much fighting during November, so one is looking really at losses for four months.

When all the above numbers are collated, total 1 Canadian Corps Canadian casualties numbered 7,214, of which 1,276 were fatal. This amounts to more than a quarter of all Canadian Italian Campaign casualties.

The River Battles also had a cost for the Canadians that went beyond their casualties. Often the achievements of battalions and their men were dismissed by higher command—or worse, when operations failed, or succeeded only at heavy cost, the men were blamed. And again, at the end of the campaign when many soldiers were shattered, rebuilding their morale demanded they accept their personal failure. On the contrary, time and again as I was writing The River Battles, I was awed by the many accounts of heroism displayed by individual soldiers. And as these battles were so often fought by handfuls of men working together, it is hard not to think of them all as heroes. And so, I believe, they were.

Despite the small number buried in Villanova Cemetery, these statistics weigh heavily on me as I walk the rows of headstones. Over the past couple of weeks, I have been serving as a battlefield historian on a Liberation Tours Italian Campaign pilgrimage. Thirty-five Canadians have journeyed with us from the landing beach in Sicily to where the fighting concluded here at the nearby Senio River. We have walked battlefields and visited other cemeteries. Today, however, is unique for us. Unlike our visits to the other cemeteries, here we are not alone. With us today is a large group of local Italians. Most are members of Wartime Friends, an organization based in nearby Bagnacavallo that is dedicated to remembering the Canadian soldiers who liberated their region and town, and—in the case of those here in Villanova Cemetery—who remain. When we arrived at the cemetery, the Wartime Friends were here to greet us. A Canadian flag was attached to the railing next to the cemetery entrance. Although the leading force behind the organization is Mariangela Rondinelli, who had been involved in my invitation to Ravenna in 2004, the group seems to grow in size and number with each visit. This day, Bagnacavallo's mayor is present and stays for the entire cemetery ceremony.

The ceremony is short, leaving plenty of time to visit the headstones. I am drawn inevitably to a single headstone at the back row: VI c 6. This headstone is special to me and also to the Wartime Friends. Some years ago, a small contingent from the Osoyoos Indian Band of British Columbia's Okanagan Valley came to pay their respects before it. They left behind an official Osoyoos Indian Band flag and a small ceremonial eagle staff. Knowing these items, exposed to the weather, would soon deteriorate, Wartime Friends keeps them safely stored and deploys them whenever Canadians visit.

Buried here is Corporal Ernest Batiste George. He was twenty-six when the war took him, on December 13, 1944, while serving with the Lanark and Renfrew Scottish Regiment. Ernie, as he was known in my hometown of Oliver, was the son of Osoyoos Indian Band Chief Narcisse George. He enlisted with his best friend, Ernie Shaw, in late 1941. After training, they were to have gone overseas together. But just before they shipped out, Ernie Shaw fell ill. Ernie George went on alone. He died during the Lanarks' desperate fight at the Naviglio

Canal. The inscription on his headstone reads: "R.I.P. In loving memory. Father, mother, brothers and sisters." He was one of twenty-five sons of Oliver to die in World War II. This is the only time I have encountered one of their headstones. I vow to look for the others.

When I attempt to take a photograph, the stiffening wind is snapping the flag so hard that it is impossible to bring it into focus. Seeing the problem, one of the Italians comes over and holds the flag firmly so I can get the picture. He is the current guardian of the flag and eagle staff. When I thank him for caring for them, he shrugs it off. If I understood his Italian correctly, he said, "It is a small thing to do for him. A way to show respect."

"They liberated our towns and villages," Mariangela adds. "It is our duty and responsibility to not forget them." Every November II, Remembrance Day, Mariangela says, a significant crowd of nearby residents gathers in the cemetery for a formal remembrance ceremony.

As our coach departs the cemetery, I am comforted to know that the Wartime Friends remain to ensure that soldiers, like Corporal George, are remembered not only back in Canada but also in the land where they fell, so far from home.

APPENDIX A
PRINCIPAL COMMANDERS IN
THE RIVER BATTLES
(ONLY THOSE MENTIONED IN TEXT)

AMERICAN

U.S. Chief of Staff, Gen. George C. Marshall

Supreme Headquarters, Allied Expeditionary Force (SHAEF), Gen. Dwight D. Eisenhower

Fifteenth Army Group, Gen. Mark Clark (Replaced Alexander as theatre commander, Dec. 12, 1944, when AAI re-designated Fifteenth Army Group)

Fifth Army, Gen. Mark Clark, then Lt. Gen. Lucian K. Truscott Jr.

BRITISH

Chief of Imperial General Staff, Field Marshal Sir Alan Brooke

Supreme Allied Commander Mediterranean, Field Marshal Harold Alexander (Effective Dec. 12, 1944)

Allied Armies in Italy (AAI), Gen. Harold Alexander (Until Dec. 12 promotion)

Eighth Army, Gen. Sir Oliver Leese, then Lt. Gen. Richard "Dick" McCreery

CANADIAN

First Army, Lt. Gen. Harry Crerar

I Corps, Lt. Gen. Eedson L.M. "Tommy" Burns, then Maj. Gen. Chris Vokes, then Lt. Gen. Charles Foulkes

I Corps, Chief of Staff, Brig. Desmond Smith, then Brig. George Kitching

1st Infantry Division, Maj. Gen. Chris Vokes, then Brig. Desmond Smith, then Maj. Gen. Harry Foster

5th Armoured Division, Maj. Gen. Bert Hoffmeister
1st Infantry Brigade, Brig. Allan Calder, then Brig. Desmond Smith
2nd Infantry Brigade, Lt. Col. Pat Bogert
3rd Infantry Brigade, Brig. Paul Bernatchez
5th Armoured Brigade, Brig. Ian Cumberland
11th Infantry Brigade, Brig. Ian Johnston
12th Infantry Brigade, Brig. John Lind

NEW ZEALAND

2nd Division, Maj. Gen. C.E. "Steve" Weir, then Lt. Gen. Bernard
  Freyberg

GERMAN

Commander-in-Chief Southwest, Genfldm. Albert Kesselring, then
  Gen. Obst. Heinrich von Vietinghoff, then Genfldm. Albert
  Kesselring
Tenth Army, Gen. Obst. Heinrich von Vietinghoff, then Gen.
  d. Pztr. Joachim Lemelsen, then Gen. Obst. Heinrich von
  Vietinghoff
Fourteenth Army, Gen. d. Pztr. Joachim Lemelsen, then Gen. d.
  Artl. Heinz Ziegler
LXXVI Panzer Korps, Gen. d. Pztr. Traugott Herr

APPENDIX B
THE CANADIAN ARMY IN
THE RIVER BATTLES
(COMBAT UNITS ONLY)

I CANADIAN CORPS
7th Anti-Tank Regiment
1st Survey Regiment, Royal Canadian Army

NO. I ARMY GROUP, RCA
11th Field Regiment
1st Medium Regiment
2nd Medium Regiment
5th Medium Regiment

1ST CANADIAN INFANTRY DIVISION
RECONNAISSANCE TROOPS:
1 Canadian Armoured Car Regiment (Royal Canadian Dragoons)

BRIGADE SUPPORT GROUP:
The Saskatoon Light Infantry

ROYAL CANADIAN ARTILLERY:
Royal Canadian Horse Artillery
2nd Field Regiment
3rd Field Regiment
1st Anti-Tank Regiment
2nd Light Anti-Aircraft Regiment

CORPS OF ROYAL CANADIAN ENGINEERS:
1st Field Company
3rd Field Company
4th Field Company
2nd Field Park Company

1ST CANADIAN INFANTRY BRIGADE:
Royal Canadian Regiment (permanent force)
Hastings and Prince Edward Regiment
48th Highlanders of Canada

2ND CANADIAN INFANTRY BRIGADE:
Princess Patricia's Canadian Light Infantry (permanent force)
Seaforth Highlanders of Canada
Loyal Edmonton Regiment

3RD CANADIAN INFANTRY BRIGADE:
Royal 22e Régiment (permanent force)
Carleton and York Regiment
West Nova Scotia Regiment

5TH CANADIAN ARMOURED DIVISION
RECONNAISSANCE TROOPS:
3rd Canadian Armoured Reconnaissance Regiment (Governor
    General's Horse Guards)

BRIGADE SUPPORT GROUP:
Princess Louise Fusiliers

THE ROYAL CANADIAN ARTILLERY:
17th Field Regiment
8th Field Regiment (self-propelled)
4th Anti-Tank Regiment
5th Light Anti-Tank Regiment

5TH CANADIAN ARMOURED BRIGADE:

5th Canadian Assault Troop

2nd Canadian Armoured Regiment (Lord Strathcona's Horse)
(permanent force)

5th Canadian Armoured Regiment (8th Princess Louise's New
Brunswick Hussars)

9th Canadian Armoured Regiment (British Columbia Dragoons)

11TH CANADIAN INFANTRY BRIGADE:

Perth Regiment

Cape Breton Highlanders

Irish Regiment of Canada

12TH CANADIAN INFANTRY BRIGADE:

4th Princess Louise Dragoon Guards

1st Light Anti-Aircraft Battalion, then Lanark and Renfrew Scottish

Westminster Regiment (Motor)

CORPS OF ROYAL CANADIAN ENGINEERS

1st Field Squadron

4th Field Park Squadron

10th Field Squadron

1ST CANADIAN ARMOURED BRIGADE

11th Canadian Armoured Regiment (Ontario Tanks)

12th Canadian Armoured Regiment (Three Rivers Tanks)

14th Canadian Armoured Regiment (Calgary Tanks)

APPENDIX C
CANADIAN INFANTRY BATTALION
(TYPICAL ORGANIZATION)

HQ COMPANY

No. 1: Signals Platoon

No. 2: Administrative Platoon

SUPPORT COMPANY

No. 3: Mortar Platoon (3-inch)

No. 4: Bren Carrier Platoon

No. 5: Assault Pioneer Platoon

No. 6: Anti-Tank Platoon
   (6-pounder)

'A' COMPANY

No. 7 Platoon

No. 8 Platoon

No. 9 Platoon

'B' COMPANY

No. 10 Platoon

No. 11 Platoon

No. 12 Platoon

'C' COMPANY

No. 13 Platoon

No. 14 Platoon

No. 15 Platoon

'D' COMPANY

No. 16 Platoon

No. 17 Platoon

No. 18 Platoon

CANADIAN ARMY AND GERMAN ARMY ORDER OF RANKS
(LOWEST TO HIGHEST)

L IKE MOST COMMONWEALTH armies, the Canadian Army used the British ranking system. Except for the lower ranks, this system differed little from one service arm to another. The German Army system, however, tended to identify service and rank throughout most of its command chain. The translations are roughly based on the Canadian ranking system, although many German ranks have no Canadian equivalent, and there is some differentiation in the responsibility each rank bestowed on its holder.

CANADIAN ARMY	GERMAN ARMY
Private, infantry	Schütze
Rifleman, rifle regiments	Schütze
Private	Grenadier
Gunner (artillery equivalent of private)	Kanonier
Trooper (armoured equivalent of private)	Panzerschütze
Sapper (engineer equivalent of private)	Pionier
Signaller (signals equivalent of private)	Funker
Lance Corporal	Gefreiter
Corporal	Obergefreiter
Lance Sergeant	Unteroffizier
Sergeant	Unterfeldwebel
Company Sergeant Major	Feldwebel
Battalion Sergeant Major	Oberfeldwebel
Regimental Sergeant Major	Stabsfeldwebel
Second Lieutenant	Leutnant
Lieutenant	Oberleutnant

CANADIAN ARMY	GERMAN ARMY
Captain	Hauptmann
Major	Major
Lieutenant Colonel	Oberstleutnant
Colonel	Oberst
Brigadier	Generalmajor
Major General	Generalleutnant
Lieutenant General	General der (service arm)
(No differentiation)	General der Artillerie
	General der Infanterie
	General der Kavallerie
	General der Pioniere
	General der Panzertruppen
General	Generaloberst
Field Marshal	Generalfeldmarschall
Commander in Chief	Oberbefehlshaber

CANADIAN ARMY DECORATIONS

THE DECORATION SYSTEM that Canada used in World War II, like most other aspects of its military organization and tradition, derived from Britain. Under this class-based system, most military decorations can be awarded either to officers or to "other ranks" but not to both. The Canadian army, navy, and air force also have distinct decorations. Only the Victoria Cross—the nation's highest award—can be won by personnel from any arm of the service or of any rank. The decorations and qualifying ranks are as follows.

VICTORIA CROSS (VC): Awarded for gallantry in the presence of the enemy. Instituted in 1856. Open to all ranks. The only award that can be granted for action in which the recipient was killed other than Mentioned in Despatches, a less formal honour whereby an act of bravery was given specific credit in a formal report.

DISTINGUISHED SERVICE ORDER (DSO): Army officers of all ranks, but more commonly awarded to officers with ranks of major or higher.

MILITARY CROSS (MC): Army officers with a rank normally below major and, rarely, warrant officers.

DISTINGUISHED CONDUCT MEDAL (DCM): Army warrant officers and all lower ranks.

MILITARY MEDAL (MM): Army warrant officers and all lower ranks.

NOTES

For full source citations, see the bibliography. Sources are listed under five headings: Books, Journal Articles, Websites, Unpublished Materials, and Interviews and Correspondence. For abbreviations, see the top of the bibliography.

INTRODUCTION: ACE HIGH
1. Frost, *Once a Patricia*, 286–90.

PART ONE: THE PROMISED LAND

I GET AHEAD FAST
1. "Westminster Regiment (Motor) War Diary," Sept. 1944, 10.
2. Oldfield, *Westminsters' War Diary*, 126.
3. McAvity, *Lord Strathcona's Horse*, 144–45.
4. Burns, *General Mud*, 208.
5. Mowat, *The Regiment*, 234.
6. "CMHQ No. 187," 132.
7. Alexander, "Allied Armies in Italy, Chapter IV," 21–22.
8. Burns, *General Mud*, 208.
9. "CMHQ No. 187," 135.
10. Burns, *General Mud*, 209.
11. "12th Canadian Infantry Brigade War Diary," Sept. 1944, App. 3, 6–10.
12. Cederberg, *The Long Road Home*, 145.
13. "12th Canadian Infantry Brigade War Diary," Sept. 1944, App. 3, 7–9.
14. McAvity, *Lord Strathcona's Horse*, 150.
15. "General Burns, I Canadian Corps War Diary," Sept. 1944, 10.
16. McAvity, *Lord Strathcona's Horse*, 144.
17. Jackson, *Princess Louise Dragoon Guards*, 212.
18. McAvity, *Lord Strathcona's Horse*, 145–46.
19. Ibid., 265.
20. Ibid., 146.
21. "12th Canadian Infantry Brigade War Diary," Sept. 1944, App. 3, 10.
22. Kenneth William Eagan, "Canadian Army Overseas Honours and Awards," *National Defence and the Canadian Forces* (website).
23. "12th Canadian Infantry Brigade War Diary," Sept. 1944, App. 3, 11.
24. Oldfield, *Westminsters' War Diary*, 128.

25. McAvity, *Lord Strathcona's Horse*, 146.
26. John Armour Cambridge, "Canadian Army Overseas Honours and Awards," *National Defence and the Canadian Forces* (website).
27. Oldfield, *Westminsters' War Diary*, 128.
28. McAvity, *Lord Strathcona's Horse*, 146–47.
29. Oldfield, *Westminsters' War Diary*, 129.
30. McAvity, *Lord Strathcona's Horse*, 147.
31. "12th Canadian Infantry Brigade War Diary," Sept. 1944, App. 3, 12.
32. McAvity, *Lord Strathcona's Horse*, 147.
33. "12th Canadian Infantry Brigade War Diary," Sept. 1944, App. 3, 12.
34. "Lord Strathcona's Horse War Diary," Sept. 1944, 11.
35. Oldfield, *Westminsters' War Diary*, 129–30.
36. "Westminster Regiment (Motor) War Diary," Sept. 1944, 11.
37. Oldfield, *Westminsters' War Diary*, 129–30.
38. McAvity, *Lord Strathcona's Horse*, 148–49.
39. "12th Canadian Infantry Brigade War Diary," Sept. 1944, App. 3, 14.
40. Locke, *Governor General's Horse Guards, 1939–1945*, 128–30.

2 A FRIGHTFUL NIGHTMARE
1. "12th Canadian Infantry Brigade War Diary," Sept. 1944, App. 3, 15.
2. "Princess Louise Dragoon Guards War Diary," Sept. 1944, 9.
3. "12th Canadian Infantry Brigade War Diary," Sept. 1944, App. 3, 18.
4. Locke, *Governor General's Horse Guards*, 131.
5. McAvity, *Lord Strathcona's Horse*, 149.
6. "1st Light Anti-Aircraft Battalion War Diary," Sept. 1944, 8.
7. Locke, *Governor General's Horse Guards*, 132–33.
8. "Westminster Regiment (Motor) War Diary," Sept. 1944, 12.
9. "12th Canadian Infantry Brigade War Diary," Sept. 1944, App. 3, 18.
10. Cederberg, *Long Road Home*, 157–61.
11. "12th Canadian Infantry Brigade War Diary," Sept. 1944, App. 3, 18–19.
12. McAvity, *Lord Strathcona's Horse*, 149.
13. "Princess Louise Dragoon Guards War Diary," Sept. 1944, 10.
14. McAvity, *Lord Strathcona's Horse*, 150.
15. "Report of Ops: Lanark and Renfrew Scottish," DHH, DND, 4.
16. Locke, *Governor General's Horse Guards*, 134–36.
17. "Westminster Regiment (Motor) War Diary," Sept. 1944, 12.
18. Oldfield, *Westminsters' War Diary*, 132.
19. "12th Canadian Infantry Brigade War Diary," Sept. 1944, App. 3, 21–23.
20. McAvity, *Lord Strathcona's Horse*, 150.
21. Burns, *General Mud*, 208.
22. "AHQ No. 25," 4–5.
23. "GS 5 Canadian Armoured Division War Diary," May 1945, "12 CIB Report on Ops," 5.
24. Hinsley, *British Intelligence in the Second World War*, 342–43.
25. Nicholson, *Canadians in Italy*, 558.
26. Kesselring, *Memoirs of Field-Marshal Kesselring*, 216–17.

27. McAvity, *Lord Strathcona's Horse*, 143–44.
28. Orgill, *Gothic Line: Italian Campaign, Autumn 1944*, 12–13.
29. Kesselring, *Memoirs of Field-Marshal Kesselring*, 216–17.
30. Ellis, *Cassino: Hollow Victory*, 469.
31. "AHQ No. 25," 18.
32. Wood, *Story of the Irish Regiment*, 51.
33. "AHQ No. 25," 18.
34. "Irish Regiment of Canada War Diary," Sept. 1944, 6.
35. How, *8th Hussars*, 273–75.
36. "Cape Breton Highlanders War Diary," Sept. 1944, n.p.
37. "GS 5 Canadian Armoured Division War Diary," May 1945, App. 1, Part 2, 5.

3 NOT A LEADER
1. "Irish Regiment of Canada War Diary," Sept. 1944, 5.
2. "11th Canadian Infantry Brigade War Diary," Sept. 1944, "Log 27 Sep," 1.
3. "Irish Regiment of Canada War Diary," Sept. 1944, 6.
4. Wilbeck, "Swinging the Sledgehammer," 88–89.
5. How, *8th Hussars*, 275–76.
6. "Summaries of Ops 1 Sep/31 Dec 44 by Capt. Currelly," 4.
7. "Irish Regiment of Canada War Diary," Sept. 1944, 6.
8. How, *8th Hussars*, 276.
9. "Cape Breton Highlanders War Diary," Sept. 1944, n.p.
10. "AHQ No. 25," 21.
11. "Perth Regiment War Diary," Sept. 1944, 10.
12. Johnston, *Fighting Perths*, 99.
13. "GS 5 Canadian Armoured Division War Diary," May 1945, App. 1, Part 2, 6.
14. "Cape Breton Highlanders War Diary," Sept. 1944.
15. "General Burns, 1 Canadian Corps War Diary," Sept. 1944, 13.
16. "AHQ No. 25," 23–24.
17. "Perth Regiment War Diary," Oct. 1944, App. 8, 2.
18. "Cape Breton Highlanders War Diary," Sept. 1944.
19. "8th New Brunswick Hussars War Diary," Sept. 1944, 10–11.
20. How, *8th Hussars*, 276.
21. Burns, *General Mud*, 212.
22. Stacey, *Arms, Men and Governments*, 441.
23. Burns, *General Mud*, 213.
24. "Cape Breton Highlanders War Diary," Sept. 1944.
25. Morrison, *Breed of Manly Men*, 267.
26. Burns, *General Mud*, 212.
27. Nicholson, *Canadians in Italy*, 574.
28. Stacey, *Arms, Men and Governments*, 441–43.
29. Ryder, *Oliver Leese*, 191.
30. Jackson, *Mediterranean and Middle East*, 361–63.
31. Ryder, *Oliver Leese*, 191.
32. "Vokes Papers," "Adriatic Front—Winter 1944," 11.

33. Ryder, *Oliver Leese*, 193.
34. Delaney, *The Soldier's General*, 177.
35. Ibid., 175–76.
36. Don Smith correspondence.
37. Granatstein, *The Generals*, 198.
38. Ibid., 132.
39. Johnston, J.P. "E.L.M. Burns," 52–53.
40. Granatstein, *The Generals*, 135–36.
41. Vokes, "Summer of Dolce Vita," Vokes Papers, 6–7.
42. Granatstein, *The Generals*, 138.
43. Burns, *General Mud*, 218.
44. "8th New Brunswick Hussars War Diary," Oct. 1944, App. 7.
45. Alexander, "Allied Armies in Italy, Chapter IV," 27.
46. Mead, *Last Great Cavalryman*, 162.
47. Smith, "On Trust."

4 SOMEWHAT DEPRESSING

1. "Irish Regiment of Canada War Diary," Sept. 1944, 7.
2. "17th Field Regiment War Diary," Sept. 1944, 14–15.
3. "Irish Regiment of Canada War Diary," Sept. 1944, 7.
4. "GS 5 Canadian Armoured Division War Diary," May 1945, App. I: Part 2, 6.
5. "Perth Regiment War Diary," Oct. 1944, I.
6. Ibid., App. 8, 3.
7. "GS 5 Canadian Armoured Division War Diary," May 1945, App. I: Part 2, 6.
8. "11th Canadian Infantry Brigade War Diary," Sept. 1944, 7.
9. "GS 5 Canadian Armoured Division War Diary," May 1945, App. I: Part 2, 7.
10. "Irish Regiment of Canada War Diary," Oct. 1944, I.
11. "11th Canadian Infantry Brigade War Diary," Oct. 1944, I.
12. "GS 5 Canadian Armoured Division War Diary," May 1945, App. I: Part 2, 7.
13. "Royal Canadian Dragoons War Diary," Oct. 1944, I.
14. "Perth Regiment War Diary," Oct. 1944, I.
15. "Cape Breton Highlanders War Diary," Oct. 1944, 2.
16. "Princess Louise Dragoon Guards War Diary," Oct. 1944, I.
17. "Royal Canadian Dragoons War Diary," Oct. 1944, 1–2.
18. "GS 5 Canadian Armoured Division War Diary," May 1945, App. I: Part 2, 7–9.
19. Burns, *General Mud*, 213–14.
20. "GS 5 Canadian Armoured Division War Diary," May 1945, App. I: Part 2, 9.
21. "AHQ No. 25," 30–32.
22. "GS 5 Canadian Armoured Division War Diary," May 1945, "Hist. Cumb. Force," I.
23. "HQ 1st Canadian Infantry Division War Diary," Oct. 1944, 4.
24. "AHQ No. 25," 32.
25. Ibid., 29.
26. "1st Canadian Infantry Brigade War Diary," Oct. 1944, 3.
27. "AHQ No. 25," 33.
28. "1st Canadian Infantry Brigade War Diary," Oct. 1944, 3.

29. Beattie, *Dileas*, 676.
30. Mowat, *The Regiment*, 234.
31. "HPER War Diary," Oct. 1944, 3.
32. "1st Canadian Infantry Brigade War Diary," Oct. 1944, 3.
33. "HPER War Diary," Oct. 1944, 4–5.
34. Mowat, *The Regiment*, 236.
35. "HPER War Diary," Oct. 1944, 5.
36. "48th Highlanders of Canada War Diary," Oct. 1944, 8.
37. Beattie, *Dileas*, 677.
38. "48th Highlanders of Canada War Diary," Oct. 1944, App. 9: Part 2, 2.
39. Nicholson, *Canadians in Italy*, 577.
40. "Royal Canadian Regiment War Diary," Oct. 1944, 5.
41. Kerry and McDill, *History of Royal Canadian Engineers*, 241.
42. "HPER War Diary," Oct. 1944, 5.
43. Mowat, *The Regiment*, 239.
44. Kerry and McDill, *History of Royal Canadian Engineers*, 241.
45. Victor Alexander Moore, "Canadian Army Overseas Honours and Awards," *National Defence and the Canadian Forces* (website).
46. McAvity, *Lord Strathcona's Horse*, 155–56.

5 WHOLEHEARTED CO-OPERATION
1. "Irish Regiment of Canada War Diary," App. 11, 1–2.
2. "HPER War Diary," Oct. 1944, 6.
3. "HQ 1st Canadian Infantry Division War Diary," Oct. 1944, 7.
4. McAvity, *Lord Strathcona's Horse*, 155.
5. "HQ 1st Canadian Infantry Division War Diary," Oct. 1944, 7.
6. Mowat, *The Regiment*, 239.
7. "Account of Action HPER on 13 and 14 Oct. 44," 1.
8. McAvity, *Lord Strathcona's Horse*, 156.
9. "Account of Action HPER on 13 and 14 Oct. 44," 1–2.
10. McAvity, *Lord Strathcona's Horse*, 157.
11. "Account of Action HPER on 13 and 14 Oct. 44," 2.
12. Mowat, *The Regiment*, 242.
13. "HPER War Diary," Oct. 1944, 8.
14. McAvity, *Lord Strathcona's Horse*, 157.
15. "Account of Action HPER on 13 and 14 Oct. 44," 2.
16. "48th Highlanders of Canada War Diary," Oct. 1944, 12.
17. Beattie, *Dileas*, 679–80.
18. Edward Charles Ralph, "Canadian Army Overseas Honours and Awards," *National Defence and the Canadian Forces* (website).
19. Galloway, *Regiment at War*, 170.
20. Gordon Potts and Geoffrey Kenneth Wright, "Canadian Army Overseas Honours and Awards," *National Defence and the Canadian Forces* (website).
21. "Royal Canadian Regiment War Diary," Oct. 1944, 9–10.
22. Galloway, *Regiment at War*, 171.

23. "AHQ No. 25," 39.

24. "Freyberg Biography," *Encyclopedia of New Zealand* (website).

25. Burns, *General Mud*, 214–15.

26. "AHQ No. 25," 40.

27. Landell, *Royal Canadian Dragoons*, 120–21.

28. "GS 5 Canadian Armoured Division War Diary," May 1945, "Hist. Cumb. Force," 2–3.

29. "Royal Canadian Regiment War Diary," Oct. 1944, "Battle Narrative, 'C' Coy," 1.

30. Galloway, *Regiment at War*, 170.

31. Norman Rauta, "Canadian Army Overseas Honours and Awards," *National Defence and the Canadian Forces* (website).

32. "Royal Canadian Regiment War Diary," Oct. 1944, "Battle Narrative, 'C' Coy," 2.

33. Ibid., "Battle Narrative, 'B' Company," 2.

34. "48th Highlanders of Canada War Diary," Oct. 1944, 13.

35. Beattie, *Dileas*, 680–81.

6 WE'LL TAKE A CHANCE

1. "2nd Canadian Infantry Brigade War Diary," Oct. 1944, 16.

2. "2nd Canadian Infantry Brigade Ops": "Seaforth Acct. Pisciatello," 1–2.

3. "Seaforth Highlanders of Canada War Diary," 11–12.

4. "2nd Canadian Infantry Brigade War Diary," Oct. 1944, 17.

5. Roy, *Seaforth Highlanders*, 354.

6. "2nd Canadian Infantry Brigade War Diary," Oct. 1944, 17.

7. "2nd Canadian Infantry Brigade Ops": "Seaforth Acct. Pisciatello," 2.

8. "2nd Canadian Infantry Brigade War Diary," Oct. 1944, 17.

9. "Royal Canadian Regiment War Diary," Oct. 1944, 13.

10. Galloway, *Regiment at War*, 171–72.

11. William Bertrand, "Canadian Army Overseas Honours and Awards," *National Defence and the Canadian Forces* (website).

12. "Royal Canadian Regiment War Diary," Oct. 1944, 14.

13. "48th Highlanders War Diary," Oct. 1944, Part 3: App. A, 1.

14. Beattie, *Dileas*, 682.

15. "48th Highlanders War Diary," Oct. 1944, Part 3: App. A, 1–2.

16. Stone interview.

17. "2nd Canadian Infantry Brigade Ops": "LER Ops," 1.

18. "LER War Diary," Sept. 21, 1944–Mar. 15, 1945, 15.

19. "2nd Canadian Infantry Brigade War Diary," Oct. 1944, 17–18.

20. "2nd Canadian Infantry Brigade Ops": "LER Ops," 1.

21. Stone interview.

22. "LER War Diary," Sept. 21, 1944–Mar. 15, 1945, 15.

23. Gerald Elwood Kingston, "Canadian Army Overseas Honours and Awards," *National Defence and the Canadian Forces* (website).

24. Joseph Charles Bohemier," "Canadian Army Overseas Honours and Awards," *National Defence and the Canadian Forces* (website).

25. "2nd Canadian Infantry Brigade Ops": "LER Ops," 2.

26. "LER War Diary," Sept. 21, 1944–Mar. 15, 1945, 16.

27. Stone interview.
28. "LER War Diary," Sept. 21, 1944–Mar. 15, 1945, 16.
29. Stone interview.
30. "2nd Canadian Infantry Brigade Ops": "LER Ops," 2–3.
31. "Royal 22e Régiment War Diary," Oct. 1944, "Operations 18 Oct 44 to 29 Oct. 44," 1–4.
32. "3rd Canadian Infantry Brigade War Diary," Oct. 1944, 8.
33. "Royal 22e Régiment War Diary," Oct. 1944, "Ops 18 Oct 44 to 29 Oct. 44," 4–5.
34. "West Nova Scotia Regiment War Diary," Oct. 1944, 5.
35. "Royal 22e Régiment War Diary," Oct. 1944, "Ops 18 Oct 44 to 29 Oct. 44," 4–8.

7 ABSOLUTELY BROWNED OFF

1. "Carleton and York Regiment War Diary," Oct. 1944, 9.
2. Raddall, *West Novas*, 238.
3. "Carleton and York Regiment War Diary," Oct. 1944, 10.
4. Tooley, *Invicta*, 290.
5. "Royal 22e Régiment War Diary," Oct. 1944, 11–13.
6. "PPCLI: Ops from Savignano to the F. Ronco," 1–2.
7. "PPCLI War Diary," Oct. 1944, 19.
8. Stevens, *PPCLI*, 200–01.
9. "GS 5 Canadian Armoured Division War Diary," May 1945, "Hist Cumb. Force," 4.
10. "Governor General's Horse Guards War Diary," Oct. 1944, 5.
11. "GS 5 Canadian Armoured Division War Diary," May 1945, "Hist. Cumb. Force," 4.
12. "AHQ No. 25," 46–47.
13. Ibid., 52.
14. Burns, *General Mud*, 216.
15. Granatstein, *The Generals*, 141–43.
16. "AHQ No. 25," 63–64.
17. "2nd Canadian Infantry Brigade War Diary," Oct. 1944, 23.
18. Frost, *Once a Patricia*, 309–24.
19. "2nd Canadian Infantry Brigade Ops": "2 CDN INF BDE Savignano," 4.
20. "AHQ No. 25," 55–56.
21. Frost, *Once a Patricia*, 324–26.
22. Ibid., 327.
23. "PPCLI War Diary," Oct. 1944, 21.
24. Stevens, *PPCLI*, 202–03.
25. Frost, *Once a Patricia*, 327–28.
26. Stevens, *PPCLI*, 203–04.
27. "PPCLI War Diary," Oct. 1944, 23.
28. Frank Harris Sparrow, "Canadian Army Overseas Honours and Awards," *National Defence and the Canadian Forces* (website).
29. "PPCLI War Diary," Oct. 1944, 23.
30. "2nd Canadian Infantry Brigade Ops": "2 CDN INF BDE Savignano," 6.
31. Kerry and McDill, *History of Royal Canadian Engineers*, 242.

8 YOU MISS, YOU'RE DEAD

1. "Account by Lt.-Col. Bell-Irving: Assault," 1.
2. "Seaforth Highlanders War Diary," Oct. 1944, 17.
3. "Account by Lt.-Col. Bell-Irving: Assault," 1.
4. "Seaforth Highlanders War Diary," Oct. 1944, 17.
5. "LER War Diary," Sept. 21, 1944–Mar. 15, 1945, 18.
6. Stone interview.
7. "LER War Diary," Sept. 21, 1944–Mar. 15, 1945, 18.
8. Stevens, City Goes to War, 323.
9. "LER War Diary," Sept. 21, 1944–Mar. 15, 1945, 18.
10. "Crossing the Savio: 'A' Company Account."
11. Stevens, PPCLI, 205.
12. "Seaforth Highlanders War Diary," Oct. 1944, App. II: "'D' Coy's Action," 1.
13. Stevens, PPCLI, 205.
14. Roy, Seaforth Highlanders, 357–59.
15. "Seaforth Highlanders War Diary," Oct. 1944, App. II: "'D' Coy's Action," 1.
16. Ibid., "'B' Coy's Action," 1.
17. Gordon Victor Carrington, "Canadian Army Overseas Honours and Awards," National Defence and the Canadian Forces (website).
18. "Seaforth Highlanders War Diary," Oct. 1944, App. II: "'B' Coy's Action," 1.
19. Gordon Victor Carrington, "Canadian Army Overseas Honours and Awards," National Defence and the Canadian Forces (website).
20. "Seaforth Highlanders War Diary," Oct. 1944, App. II: "'B' Coy's Action at the Savio," 1.
21. Staples interview.
22. Gordon Victor Carrington, "Canadian Army Overseas Honours and Awards," National Defence and the Canadian Forces (website).
23. "Seaforth Highlanders War Diary," Oct. 1944, App. II: "'B' Coy's Action," 1.
24. Stevens, City Goes to War, 323.
25. "LER War Diary," Sept. 21, 1944–Mar. 15, 1945, 18.
26. Stevens, City Goes to War, 325–26.
27. Stone interview.
28. George Wallace Davies, "Canadian Army Overseas Honours and Awards," National Defence and the Canadian Forces (website).
29. "LER War Diary," Sept. 21, 1944–Mar. 15, 1945, 18.
30. George Wallace Davies, "Canadian Army Overseas Honours and Awards," National Defence and the Canadian Forces (website).
31. "LER War Diary," Sept. 21, 1944–Mar. 15, 1945, 18–20.
32. Stevens, City Goes to War, 324.
33. "LER War Diary," Sept. 21, 1944–Mar. 15, 1945, 20.
34. "Canadian Ops August–November 1944," "Bridging Difficulties Savio," 1.
35. Joseph Charles Portnuff, "Canadian Army Overseas Honours and Awards," National Defence and the Canadian Forces (website).
36. Roy, Seaforth Highlanders, 360–61.
37. "Italy to the Netherlands," Loyal Edmonton Regiment Military Museum (website).

38. Roy, *Seaforth Highlanders*, 362.
39. "Seaforth Highlanders War Diary," Oct. 1944, App. II: "'C' Coy's Action," 1.
40. Keith Philbrock Thompson, "Canadian Army Overseas Honours and Awards," *National Defence and the Canadian Forces* (website).
41. Roy, *Seaforth Highlanders*, 362–64.
42. Lockhart, *Last Man Standing*, 2.
43. Smith interview.
44. Ernest Alvia Smith, "Victoria Cross," *National Defence and the Canadian Forces* (website).
45. Roy, *Seaforth Highlanders*, 363–64.
46. "Seaforth Highlanders War Diary," Oct. 1944, App. II: "'C' Coy's Action," 1.
47. Robinson interview.
48. "2nd Canadian Infantry Brigade Ops": "2 CDN INF BDE Savignano," 7.
49. "LER War Diary," Sept. 21, 1944–Mar. 15, 1945, 20.
50. "AHQ No. 25," 56–57.
51. "Account by Lt.-Col. Bell-Irving: Assault," 3.
52. "Seaforth Highlanders War Diary," Oct. 1944, App. II: "'A' Coy's Action," 1.
53. Nicholson, *Canadians in Italy*, 588.

9 CARDINAL SIN
1. "2nd Canadian Infantry Brigade War Diary," Oct. 1944, 28.
2. "UK Military Bridging–Floating Equipment," *Think Defence* (website).
3. "Canadian Ops August–November 1944," "Bridging Difficulties Savio," 1–2.
4. "History of 1st Anti-Tank Regiment," 29–30.
5. "Canadian Ops August–November 1944," "Bridging Difficulties Savio," 1–2.
6. Locke, *Governor General's Horse Guards*, 149.
7. "Governor General's Horse Guards War Diary," Oct. 1944, 6–7.
8. Locke, *Governor General's Horse Guards*, 152–54.
9. Frost, *Once a Patricia*, 331.
10. "PPCLI War Diary," 25.
11. Frost, *Once a Patricia*, 333.
12. "PPCLI War Diary," 26.
13. "WNSR War Diary," Oct. 1944, 5–6.
14. Raddall, *West Novas*, 239.
15. "WNSR War Diary," Oct. 1944, 6.
16. Raddall, *West Novas*, 240.
17. "PPCLI: Ops from Savignano," 4.
18. Raddall, *West Novas*, 240.
19. "PPCLI: Ops from Savignano," 4.
20. Raddall, *West Novas*, 240.
21. "WNSR War Diary," Oct. 1944, 7–8.
22. Raddall, *West Novas*, 241.
23. John Keble Rhodes, "Canadian Army Overseas Honours and Awards," *National Defence and the Canadian Forces* (website).
24. Mitchell, RCHA–*Right of the Line*, 143.

25. "WNSR War Diary," Oct. 1944, 8.

26. "Major J.K. Rhodes Questionnaire," "Battle Experience Questionnaires."

27. Mitchell, RCHA–*Right of the Line*, 143.

28. "WNSR War Diary," Oct. 1944, 8.

29. Frost, *Once a Patricia*, 335.

30. "AHQ No. 25," 61.

31. "2nd Canadian Infantry Brigade War Diary," Oct. 1944, 32.

32. "Seaforth Highlanders War Diary," Oct. 1944, App. 11: "A' Coy's Action," 1.

33. Raddall, *West Novas*, 243–44.

34. "Canadian Ops August–November 1944," "Bridging Difficulties Savio," 3.

35. "2nd Canadian Infantry Brigade War Diary," Oct. 1944, App. 34, 1.

36. "AHQ No. 25," 64–66.

37. Stevens, *PPCLI*, 207.

38. "Irish Regiment War Diary," Oct. 1944, 7.

39. "GS 5 Canadian Armoured Division War Diary," May 1945, "Hist, Cumb. Force," 5.

40. Locke, *Governor General's Horse Guards*, 157.

41. "Perth Regiment War Diary," Oct. 1944, App. 9: "Ops of 'A' Coy," 5–6.

10 A SORRY MESS

1. Burns, *General Mud*, 218–19.

2. Granatstein, *The Generals*, 143.

3. Burns, *General Mud*, 221–22.

4. Granatstein, *The Generals*, 143.

5. Alexander, "Allied Armies in Italy, Chapter IV," 24–26.

6. Kesselring, *Memoirs of Field-Marshal Kesselring*, 218–19.

7. Alexander, "Allied Armies in Italy, Chapter IV," 26–29.

8. "Canadian Ops August–November 1944," "Bridging Difficulties Savio," 3–4.

9. "AHQ No.25," 71.

10. "Irish Regiment War Diary," Oct. 1944, App. 12, 2.

11. Wood, *Story of the Irish Regiment*, 54.

12. "Irish Regiment War Diary," Oct. 1944, App. 12, 2.

13. "AHQ No. 25," 71.

14. Ibid., App. B, 1–2.

15. "2nd Canadian Infantry Brigade War Diary," Oct. 1944, 39.

16. "AHQ No. 25," App. B, 2.

17. "Canadian Ops August–November 1944," "Seaforth Highlanders Account," 3.

18. "AHQ No. 25," App. B, 2.

19. "1st Canadian Infantry Division (G Branch) War Diary," Oct. 1944, 15.

20. "3rd Canadian Infantry Brigade War Diary," Oct. 1944, 17.

21. "PPCLI War Diary," Oct. 1944, 38.

22. "PPCLI War Diary," Nov. 1944, 1.

23. Frost, *Once a Patricia*, 345.

24. "PPCLI War Diary," Nov. 1944, 3.

25. "11th Canadian Infantry Brigade War Diary," Nov. 1944, 1.

26. "12th Canadian Infantry Brigade War Diary," Nov. 1944, 2.

27. "AHQ No. 31," 7–8.
28. "AHQ No. 25," 75.

PART TWO: TAKING RAVENNA

11 COMMAND SHUFFLE
 1. Alexander, "Allied Armies in Italy, Chapter IV," 32.
 2. Ibid.
 3. Ibid., Chap. 4, App. D, 58–60.
 4. Ibid., Chap., 4, 29.
 5. Ibid., Chap. 4, App. D, 60.
 6. Ibid., Chap. 4, 30.
 7. "Governor General's Horse Guards War Diary," Oct. 1944, 13–14.
 8. Landell, *Royal Canadian Dragoons*, 122–23.
 9. "AHQ No. 31," 14–15.
 10. Landell, *Royal Canadian Dragoons*, 123.
 11. "Royal Canadian Dragoons War Diary," Oct. 1944, 8.
 12. Allen Lucien Brady, "Canadian Army Overseas Honours and Awards," *National Defence and the Canadian Forces* (website).
 13. "Royal Canadian Dragoons War Diary," Oct. 1944, 8.
 14. Ibid., Nov. 1944, 1.
 15. "Royal Canadian Dragoons War Diary," Nov. 1944, 1.
 16. Charles Victor William Vickers, "Canadian Army Overseas Honours and Awards," *National Defence and the Canadian Forces* (website).
 17. James Morris Papps, "Canadian Army Overseas Honours and Awards," *National Defence and the Canadian Forces* (website).
 18. Charles Victor William Vickers, "Canadian Army Overseas Honours and Awards," *National Defence and the Canadian Forces* (website).
 19. "AHQ No. 31," 15–16.
 20. Peniakoff, *Private Army*, 482–83.
 21. Thomas Allan Smith, "Canadian Army Overseas Honours and Awards," *National Defence and the Canadian Forces* (website).
 22. "AHQ No. 31," 17.
 23. "Westminster Regiment (Motor) War Diary," Nov. 1944, 2.
 24. Oldfield, *Westminsters' War Diary*, 136.
 25. "I Canadian Corps GS War Diary," Nov. 1944, 1.
 26. Kitching, *Mud and Green Fields*, 230–31.
 27. "I Canadian Corps GS War Diary," Nov. 1944, 3.
 28. Granatstein, *The Generals*, 144.
 29. Kitching, *Mud and Green Fields*, 231.
 30. Granatstein, *The Generals*, 143.
 31. "I Canadian Corps GS War Diary," Nov. 1944, 2.
 32. Kitching, *Mud and Green Fields*, 232.
 33. "I Canadian Corps GS War Diary," Nov. 1944, 4–6.

34. Kitching, *Mud and Green Fields*, 232–33.
35. Vokes, *My Story*, 186.
36. "I Canadian Corps GS War Diary," Nov. 1944, 6.
37. Kitching, *Mud and Green Fields*, 233–34.
38. "1st Canadian Infantry Division (G Branch) War Diary," 6.
39. Kitching, *Mud and Green Fields*, 235–36.

12 VIRTUALLY UNENDING
1. "AHQ No, 31," 17–18.
2. "History of 3rd Canadian Field Regiment," 64–65.
3. "Westminster Regiment (Motor) War Diary," Nov. 1944, 3–4.
4. Oldfield, *Westminsters' War Diary*, 136.
5. "Westminster Regiment (Motor) War Diary," Nov. 1944, 4.
6. Oldfield, *Westminsters' War Diary*, 138.
7. "Westminster Regiment (Motor) War Diary," Feb. 1945, App. 6, 1.
8. "12th Canadian Infantry Brigade War Diary," Nov. 1944, 2.
9. "History of I CDN LAA Regiment, RCA (Lanark & Renfrew), 13–14
10. "Lanark & Renfrew Scottish Regiment War Diary," Nov. 1944, 4.
11. Cederberg, *The Long Road Home*, 173–85.
12. "Lanark & Renfrew Scottish Regiment War Diary," Nov. 1944, 7–8.
13. "AHQ No. 31," 18.
14. "Westminster Regiment (Motor) War Diary," Nov. 1944, 11.
15. Ibid., 12.
16. Oldfield, *Westminsters' War Diary*, 140–43.
17. "AHQ No. 31," 20–23.
18. "Westminster Regiment (Motor) War Diary," Nov. 1944, 24.
19. "AHQ No. 31," 19–20.
20. Oldfield, *Westminsters' War Diary*, 145–46.
21. "Westminster Regiment (Motor) War Diary," Nov. 1944, 24.
22. Granatstein, *The Generals*, 174–75.
23. "AHQ No. 31," 22.
24. "I Canadian Corps GS War Diary," Nov. 1944, 7.
25. Kitching, *Mud and Green Fields*, 236.
26. Galloway, *General Who Never Was*, 236–37.
27. Alexander, "Allied Armies in Italy, Chapter IV," App. B, 53–54.
28. "AHQ No. 31," 6.
29. Ibid., 10.
30. Marteinson and McNorgan, *Royal Canadian Armoured Corps*, 223–24.
31. Roy, *Sinews of Steel*, 330.
32. Marteinson and McNorgan, *Royal Canadian Armoured Corps*, 224.
33. "Cargo Carrier M29 Weasel," *Tank Encyclopedia* (website).
34. "3rd Canadian Infantry Brigade War Diary," Nov. 1944, 3.
35. "AHQ No. 31," 11.
36. "3rd Canadian Infantry Brigade War Diary," Nov. 1944, 6.
37. "AHQ No. 31," 12–13.

38. Tompkins, "OSS and Italian Partisans in World War II," CIA (website).

39. "I Canadian Corps GS War Diary," Nov. 1944, 8.

40. Tompkins, "OSS and Italian Partisans in World War II," CIA (website).

41. "I Canadian Corps GS War Diary," Nov. 1944, 8.

42. Dennis McNeice Healy, "Canadian Army Overseas Honours and Awards," *National Defence and the Canadian Forces* (website).

13 A GRIM TASK INDEED

1. Nicholson, *Canadians in Italy*, 612.

2. Dancocks, *D-Day Dodgers*, 388.

3. "1st Canadian Infantry Division (G Branch) War Diary," Nov. 1944, 11–12.

4. "AHQ No. 31," 24–25.

5. "12th Canadian Infantry Brigade War Diary," Dec. 1944, App. 1: "1 Dec 44–6 Dec 44, 2–3."

6. "AHQ No. 31," 24–25.

7. "Summaries of Ops: 1 Mar/31 Dec 44 by Div Hist Offr," 29.

8. "AHQ No. 31," 27.

9. "Summaries of Ops: 1 Mar/31 Dec 44 by Div Hist Offr," 29.

10. Allard, *Memoirs*, 102–03.

11. "AHQ No. 31," 26.

12. "1st Canadian Infantry Division (G Branch) War Diary," Nov. 1944, 13.

13. "3rd Canadian Infantry Brigade War Diary," Nov. 1944, 9.

14. Allard, *Memoirs*, 103.

15. "3rd Canadian Infantry Brigade War Diary," Nov. 1944, 9.

16. "AHQ No. 31," 28.

17. Nicholson, *Canadians in Italy*, 614.

18. "AHQ No. 31," 28.

19. "Account of Ops 29 Nov 44/11 Jan 45," 1.

20. "3rd Canadian Infantry Brigade War Diary," Nov. 1944, 10.

21. "AHQ No. 31," 29.

22. "3rd Canadian Infantry Brigade War Diary," Nov. 1944, 10.

23. "1st Canadian Infantry Division (G Branch) War Diary," Dec. 1944, 1–2.

24. "AHQ No. 31," 31.

25. Allard, *Memoirs*, 103.

26. Boissonault, *Histoire du Royal 22e Régiment*, 330.

27. "Royal 22e Régiment War Diary," Dec. 1944, 7.

28. Allard, *Memoirs*, 103–04.

29. Boissonault, *Histoire du Royal 22e Régiment*, 330.

30. Raddall, *West Novas*, 248.

31. "WNSR War Diary," Dec. 1944, 2–3.

32. "AHQ No. 31," 31.

33. "Princess Louise Dragoon Guards War Diary," Dec. 1944, App. A, 1.

34. "12th Canadian Infantry Brigade War Diary," Dec. 1944, App. 1: "1 Dec 44–6 Dec 44," 5–6.

35. Jackson, *Princess Louise Dragoon Guards*, 230.

36. Roy, *Sinews of Steel*, 332.
37. "Princess Louise Dragoon Guards War Diary," Dec. 1944, 2–3.
38. "Lanark & Renfrew Scottish War Diary," Dec. 1944, 1.
39. "Princess Louise Dragoon Guards War Diary," Dec. 1944, 3.
40. "Westminster Regiment (Motor) War Diary," Dec. 1944, 1.
41. Oldfield, *Westminsters' War Diary*, 148.
42. "Westminster Regiment (Motor) War Diary," Dec. 1944, 1–2.
43. Oldfield, *Westminsters' War Diary*, 148–49.
44. "Westminster Regiment (Motor) War Diary," Dec. 1944, 2.
45. Oldfield, *Westminsters' War Diary*, 149.
46. "Westminster Regiment (Motor) War Diary," Dec. 1944, 2.
47. "12th Canadian Infantry Brigade War Diary," Dec. 1944, App. 1: "1 Dec 44–6 Dec 44," 10–12.

14 CHEERFUL TO THE END

1. "Royal 22e Régiment War Diary," Dec. 1944, App. 13: "Battle Report 31," 2–3.
2. "Account of Ops 29 Nov 44/11 Jan 45 by 12 Bn Royal Tk Regt," 1–2.
3. Allard, *Memoirs*, 104.
4. Raddall, *West Novas*, 249.
5. "Reports on Ops in Italy by WNSR 1944/45," 2.
6. Raddall, *West Novas*, 249–50.
7. "WNSR War Diary," Dec. 1944, 3.
8. Raddall, *West Novas*, 250.
9. "Reports on Ops in Italy by WNSR 1944/45," 3.
10. Mitchell, RCHA–*Right of the Line*, 145.
11. "Account of Ops 29 Nov 44/11 Jan 45," 2.
12. "WNSR War Diary," Dec. 1944, 4.
13. "Reports on Ops in Italy by WNSR 1944/45," 3.
14. Tooley, *Invicta*, 308–09.
15. "1st Canadian Infantry Division (G Branch) War Diary," Dec. 1944, 3.
16. Mowat, *The Regiment*, 256–57.
17. "HPER War Diary," Dec. 1944, 3.
18. Mowat, *The Regiment*, 258.
19. "HPER War Diary," Dec. 1944, 3.
20. "1st Canadian Infantry Brigade War Diary," Dec. 1944, 3–4.
21. "Scales 40-Foot Italy Dyke," Jan. 9, 1945, *Toronto Star* (website).
22. "Royal Canadian Regiment War Diary," Dec. 1944, 2–3.
23. "12th Canadian Infantry Brigade War Diary," Dec. 1944, App. 1: "1 Dec 44–6 Dec 44," 12.
24. "Westminster Regiment (Motor) War Diary," Dec. 1944, 3.
25. Oldfield, *Westminsters' War Diary*, 150.
26. "Westminster Regiment (Motor) War Diary," Dec. 1944, 3.
27. Oldfield, *Westminsters' War Diary*, 150.
28. "Westminster Regiment (Motor) War Diary," Dec. 1944, 3.
29. Oldfield, *Westminsters' War Diary*, 151.

30. "Westminster Regiment (Motor) War Diary," Dec. 1944, 3–4.
31. Oldfield, *Westminsters' War Diary*, 153–55.
32. "Westminster Regiment (Motor) War Diary," Dec. 1944, 3–4.
33. Oldfield, *Westminsters' War Diary*, 153–55.
34. Ibid., 155.
35. Jackson, *Princess Louise Dragoon Guards*, 232.
36. Oldfield, *Westminsters' War Diary*, 157–58.
37. "B.C. Dragoons War Diary," Dec. 1944, 3.
38. Oldfield, *Westminsters' War Diary*, 158.
39. "Westminster Regiment (Motor) War Diary," Dec. 1944, 4.
40. Oldfield, *Westminsters' War Diary*, 159.
41. "AHQ No. 31," 46.
42. Tompkins, "OSS and Italian Partisans in World War II," CIA (website).
43. Nicholson, *Canadians in Italy*, 622.
44. "AHQ No. 31," 46.
45. "12th Canadian Infantry Brigade War Diary," Dec. 1944, 2.
46. "Princess Louise Dragoon Guards War Diary," Dec. 1944, 6.
47. Roy, *Dragons of Steel*, 333.
48. "Princess Louise Dragoon Guards War Diary," Dec. 1944, 6.
49. Ibid., App. 8, 4.

15 A GHASTLY FAILURE

1. "12th Canadian Infantry Brigade War Diary," Dec. 1944, 2.
2. "Perth Regiment War Diary," Dec. 1944, 2.
3. Scislowski, *Not All of Us Were Brave*, 306.
4. "Perth Regiment War Diary," Dec. 1944, 3.
5. "Irish Regiment War Diary," Dec. 1944, 3–4.
6. Scislowski, *Not All of Us Were Brave*, 307.
7. "Perth Regiment War Diary," Dec. 1944, 3.
8. "Cape Breton Highlanders War Diary," Dec. 1944, 3.
9. "Westminster Regiment (Motor) War Diary," Dec. 1944, 6.
10. "Lanark & Renfrew Scottish War Diary," Dec. 1944, 6.
11. "Perth Regiment War Diary," Dec. 1944, 6.
12. "1st Canadian Infantry Brigade War Diary," Dec. 1944, 3.
13. "HPER War Diary," Dec. 1944, 3.
14. "Royal Canadian Regiment War Diary," Dec. 1944, 3–4.
15. "Account by Major J.M. Hougton," DHH, DND, 1.
16. Galloway, *Regiment at War*, 176–77.
17. "Royal Canadian Regiment War Diary," Dec. 1944, 4.
18. Galloway, *Bravely into Battle*, 226.
19. "Royal Canadian Regiment War Diary," Dec. 1944, 4–5.
20. Mowat, *The Regiment*, 261–62.
21. "HPER War Diary," Dec. 1944, 4.
22. Mowat, *The Regiment*, 263.
23. "HPER War Diary," Dec. 1944, 4.

24. "1st Canadian Infantry Division (G Branch) War Diary," Dec. 1944, 3.

25. Kitching, *Mud and Green Fields*, 237.

26. Mowat, *The Regiment*, 260.

27. "Royal Canadian Regiment War Diary," Dec. 1944, App. 17: "Battle Narratives," 1–2.

28. Galloway, *Regiment at War*, 177–78.

29. Hernandez interview.

30. Galloway, *Regiment at War*, 177–79.

31. "Royal Canadian Regiment War Diary," Dec. 1944, 7–8.

32. Galloway, *Regiment at War*, 177–79.

33. "HPER War Diary," Dec. 1944, 4.

34. Mowat, *The Regiment*, 264–65.

35. "HPER War Diary," Dec. 1944, 4.

36. "Account by Major J.M. Hougton," DHH, DND, 2.

37. Galloway, *Sicily to the Siegfried Line*, 41.

38. Nicholson, *Canadians in Italy*, 617–19.

39. Mowat, *The Regiment*, 266–67.

40. Galloway, *Bravely into Battle*, 227.

41. Dancocks, *D-Day Dodgers*, 393.

42. Galloway, *Sicily to the Siegfried Line*, 43–44.

43. Galloway, *Bravely into Battle*, 227–29.

44. "HPER War Diary," Dec. 1944, 8.

45. Laurence Gibbins, "Canadian Army Overseas Honours and Awards," *National Defence and the Canadian Forces* (website).

46. "HPER War Diary," Dec. 1944, 5–6.

47. "AHQ No. 31," 62–63.

48. "11th Canadian Infantry Brigade War Diary," Dec. 1944, 3.

49. Galloway, *Regiment at War*, 180.

50. Galloway, *Sicily to the Siegfried Line*, 42.

PART THREE: MONTONE TO THE SENIO

16 EXILED TO ITALY

1. Foster, *Meeting of Generals*, 1–11.

2. Boire correspondence.

3. Foster, *Meeting of Generals*, 55.

4. Boire correspondence.

5. Foster, *Meeting of Generals*, 417–25.

6. Stone interview.

7. Frost, *Once a Patricia*, 363.

8. "AHQ No. 31," 61–62.

9. "GS 5 Canadian Armoured Div, War Diary," May 1945, "12 CIB Report on Ops," 1.

10. "AHQ No. 31," 80.

11. Nicholson, *Gunners of Canada*, 252.

12. "AHQ No. 31," 63–64.

13. "1 Canadian Corps GS War Diary," Dec. 1944, 7–8.

14. "1st Canadian Inf. Div. (G Branch) War Diary," Dec. 1944, 7–8.

15. "11th Canadian Infantry Brigade War Diary," Dec. 1944, 4.

16. "AHQ No. 31," 77–78.

17. "Perth Regiment War Diary," Dec. 1944, 7.

18. "Cape Breton Highlanders War Diary," Dec. 1944, 8.

19. Scislowski, *Not All of Us Were Brave*, 314.

20. McAvity, *Lord Strathcona's Horse*, 169.

21. "Cape Breton Highlanders War Diary," Dec. 1944, 8.

22. "AHQ No. 3 1," 80.

23. Morrison, *Breed of Manly Men*, 279.

24. "Cape Breton Highlanders War Diary," Dec. 1944, 8–9.

25. Scislowski, *Not All of Us Were Brave*, 314–15.

26. "Perth Regiment War Diary," Dec. 1944, 7.

27. Scislowski, *Not All of Us Were Brave*, 315–17.

28. "Report on Ops in Italy by WNSR," 5–6.

29. "West Nova Scotia Regiment War Diary," Dec. 1944, 7–8.

30. Tooley, *Invicta*, 314–15.

31. "Carleton and York Regiment War Diary," Dec. 1944, 9.

32. Rowland McDonald Horsey, "Canadian Army Overseas Honours and Awards," *National Defence and the Canadian Forces* (website).

33. Tooley, *Invicta*, 315.

34. "Account by Maj. R.M. Horsey, 'D' Coy of est Naviglio brhead," 4.

35. "Carleton and York War Regiment Diary," Dec. 1944, 9.

36. Tooley, *Invicta*, 315–16.

37. "48th Highlanders War Diary," Dec. 1944, 7.

38. Beattie, *Dileas*, 698.

39. "48th Highlanders War Diary," Dec. 1944, 7–8.

40. "Report on Ops in Italy by WNSR," 6–7.

41. Raddall, *West Novas*, 254.

42. "Report on Ops in Italy by WNSR," 7.

43. "3rd Canadian Infantry Brigade War Diary," Dec. 1944, 12–13.

44. "1st Canadian Inf. Div. (G Branch) War Diary," Dec. 1944, 8–9.

45. "Royal 22e Régiment War Diary," Dec. 1944, 24.

17 MY FUCKING NERVES

1. "Ops—11 Cdn Inf Bde period 2–27 Dec 44," 2.

2. "Irish Regiment War Diary," Dec. 1944, 5–6.

3. "Perth Regiment War Diary," Dec. 1944, 8.

4. "Summaries of Ops 1 Sep/31 Dec 44 by Capt. Currelly," 4.

5. "Westminster Regiment (Motor) War Diary," Dec. 1944, 9.

6. Oldfield, *Westminsters' War Diary*, 160.

7. Nicholson, *Canadians in Italy*, 626–27.

8. Oldfield, *Westminsters' War Diary*, 160.

9. Nicholson, *Canadians in Italy*, 627.

10. "Westminster Regiment (Motor) War Diary," Feb. 1945, App. 7.

11. Oldfield, *Westminsters' War Diary*, 160–62.

12. John Walter Young, "Canadian Army Overseas Honours and Awards," *National Defence and the Canadian Forces* (website).

13. "AHQ No. 31," 83.

14. "1st Canadian Infantry Brigade War Diary," Dec. 1944, 9.

15. "Royal Canadian Regiment War Diary," Dec. 1944, 12.

16. Mowat, *The Regiment*, 272–73.

17. "HPER War Diary," Dec. 1944, 11.

18. "1st Canadian Infantry Division (G Branch) War Diary," Dec. 1944, 9–10.

19. "Irish Regiment War Diary," Dec. 1944, 6.

20. "Perth Regiment War Diary," Dec. 1944, 9.

21. Jackson, *Princess Louise Dragoon Guards*, 237.

22. "Westminster Regiment (Motor) War Diary," Feb. 1945, App. 7, 2.

23. McAvity, *Lord Strathcona's Horse*, 170.

24. "8th New Brunswick Hussars War Diary," Dec. 1944, 3.

25. "GS 5 Canadian Armoured Division War Diary," May 1945, "12 CIB Report on Ops," 6.

26. "Lanark & Renfrew Scottish War Diary," Dec. 1944, 5.

27. Cederberg, *Long Road Home*, 199–202.

28. "GS 5 Canadian Armoured Division War Diary," May 1945, "12 CIB Report on Ops," 7.

29. Cederberg, *Long Road Home*, 203–04.

30. "GS 5 Canadian Armoured Division War Diary," May 1945, "Lanark & Renfrew," 3.

31. "Princess Louise Dragoon Guards War Diary," Dec. 1944, 13–14.

32. "GS 5 Canadian Armoured Division War Diary," May 1945, "12 CIB Report on Ops," 5.

33. "Princess Louise Dragoon Guards War Diary," Dec. 1944, 14.

34. Jackson, *Princess Louise Dragoon Guards*, 237–38.

35. "Veteran Stories: Raymond Jones," *The Memory Project* (website).

36. "12th Canadian Infantry Brigade War Diary," Dec. 1944, 6.

37. "Princess Louise Dragoon Guards War Diary," Dec. 1944, 14–15.

38. "GS 5 Canadian Armoured Division War Diary," May 1945, "12 CIB Report on Ops," 7.

39. "AHQ No. 31," 86.

40. Ibid., 70.

41. "Carleton and York Regiment War Diary," 10–11.

42. "AHQ No. 31," 70–71.

43. "Account by Lt-Col J.A. Ensor," 1.

44. Tooley, *Invicta*, 319.

45. "Carleton and York Regiment War Diary," 11.

46. "Account by Lt-Col J.A. Ensor," 1.

47. Mowat, *The Regiment*, 275.

48. "HPER War Diary," Dec. 1944, 12.

49. Mowat, *The Regiment*, 276.

50. "HPER War Diary," Dec. 1944, 12.

51. "Account by Lt-Col J.A. Ensor," 1.

52. "Account by Major R.M. Horsey, 'D' Coy of est Naviglio brhead," 1.

53. "Account by Lt-Col J.A. Ensor," 1.

54. Roy, *Sinews of Steel*, 337.
55. "HPER War Diary," Dec. 1944, 12.
56. Mowat, *The Regiment*, 276.
57. "HPER War Diary," Dec. 1944, 12.
58. Mowat, *The Regiment*, 277.
59. James Treadwell Fraser, "Canadian Army Overseas Honours and Awards," *National Defence and the Canadian Forces* (website).
60. "HPER War Diary," Dec. 1944, 12.
61. James Treadwell Fraser, "Canadian Army Overseas Honours and Awards," *National Defence and the Canadian Forces* (website).
62. "Account by Major R.M. Horsey, 'D' Coy of est Naviglio brhead," 1.

18 WELL DONE INDEED

1. "Account by Lt-Col J.A. Ensor," 2.
2. Roy, *Sinews of Steel*, 338–39.
3. "Account by Lt-Col J.A. Ensor," 2.
4. "Account by Major R.M. Horsey, 'D' Coy of est Naviglio brhead," 1.
5. Mowat, *The Regiment*, 280.
6. "Account by Major R.M. Horsey, 'D' Coy of est Naviglio brhead," 1.
7. Nicholson, *Canadians in Italy*, 630.
8. Mowat, *The Regiment*, 281.
9. Tooley, *Invicta*, 322.
10. Stone interview.
11. "LER: Enlarging & Consolidation," 1.
12. "LER War Diary," Sept. 21, 1944–Mar. 15, 1945, 34.
13. "LER: Enlarging & Consolidation," 1.
14. "B.C. Dragoons War Diary," Dec. 1944, 8.
15. "LER: Enlarging & Consolidation," 1.
16. "Ops—1 Cdn Inf Div, CMF, Summary of Ops," 41.
17. "2nd Canadian Infantry Brigade War Diary," Dec. 1944, 18.
18. "Org: Tank Hunting," 6.
19. Roy, *Seaforth Highlanders*, 379–80.
20. "Seaforth Highlanders War Diary," Dec. 1944, 14.
21. "Ops—1 Cdn Corps, Oct–Dec 1944," 26.
22. "Ops—1 Cdn Inf Div, CMF, Summary of Ops," 41.
23. "Cape Breton Highlanders War Diary," Dec. 44, 11.
24. "Irish Regiment War Diary," Dec. 44, 7.
25. "Westminster Regiment (Motor) War Diary," Dec. 1944, 12.
26. Oldfield, *Westminsters' War Diary*, 163.
27. McAvity, *Lord Strathcona's Horse*, 172.
28. "Lanark & Renfrew Scottish War Diary," Dec. 1944, 7.
29. "Westminster Regiment (Motor) War Diary," Dec. 1944, 12.
30. Hurley interview.
31. "Westminster Regiment (Motor) War Diary," Dec. 1944, 12–13.
32. Cederberg, *Long Road Home*, 218–20.

33. "GS 5 Canadian Armoured Division War Diary," May 1945, "12 CIB Report on Ops," 10.
34. Roy, *Seaforth Highlanders*, 380–81.
35. Stone interview.
36. "LER War Diary," Sept. 21, 1944–Mar. 15, 1945, 35.
37. Roy, *Seaforth Highlanders*, 381.
38. "LER: Enlarging & Consolidation," 1.
39. Roy, *Sinews of Steel*, 340.
40. Stevens, *City Goes to War*, 332.
41. "LER War Diary," Sept. 21, 1944–Mar. 15, 1945, 35.
42. "PPCLI War Diary," 11.
43. Frost, *Once a Patricia*, 373–74.
44. "PPCLI War Diary," Dec. 1944, 11.
45. "Bi-Monthly Summaries of Ops by Capt. L.A. Wrinch," 14.
46. "LER War Diary," Sept. 21, 1944–Mar. 15, 1945, 36.
47. "Seaforth Highlanders War Diary," Dec. 1944, 15.
48. Stevens, *PPCLI*, 214.
49. "LER War Diary," Sept. 21, 1944–Mar. 15, 1945, 36.
50. Stone interview.
51. Ernest Morgan Keith MacGregor, "Canadian Army Overseas Honours and Awards," *National Defence and the Canadian Forces* (website).
52. MacGregor interview.
53. Ernest Morgan Keith MacGregor, "Canadian Army Overseas Honours and Awards," *National Defence and the Canadian Forces* (website).
54. MacGregor interview.
55. "LER: Enlarging & Consolidation," 1.

19 NO BRAGGADOCIO

1. "Summaries of Ops: 1 Mar/31 Dec 44 by Div Hist Offr," 35.
2. "AHQ No. 31," 99.
3. Hilson, *Alexander of Tunis*, 173.
4. Allard, *Memoirs*, 106–07.
5. "Royal 22e Régiment War Diary, Dec. 1944," App. 13: "Battle Report," 4.
6. Joseph François Appleby, "Canadian Army Overseas Honours and Awards," *National Defence and the Canadian Forces* (website).
7. "3rd Canadian Infantry Brigade War Diary," Dec. 1944, 21–22.
8. Nicholson, *Canadians in Italy*, 633–34.
9. "Royal Canadian Regiment War Diary," Dec. 1944, "Battle Narrative, 'X' Coy," 3.
10. "48th Highlanders War Diary," Dec. 1944, 14–15.
11. Beattie, *Dileas*, 712–14.
12. "1st Canadian Infantry Brigade War Diary," Dec. 1944, 14.
13. "48th Highlanders War Diary," Dec. 1944, 16–18.
14. Mowat, *The Regiment*, 282–83.
15. "Royal Canadian Regiment War Diary," Dec. 1944, "Battle Narrative, 'A' Coy," 2.
16. Stevens, *Royal Canadian Regiment*, 177.
17. "Royal Canadian Regiment War Diary," Dec. 1944, "Battle Narrative, 'A' Coy," 2.

18. Ibid., "Battle Narrative, 'B' Coy," 2.
19. Stevens, *Royal Canadian Regiment*, 177.
20. Nicholson, *Canadians in Italy*, 635.
21. "48th Highlanders War Diary," Dec. 1944, 18.
22. Beattie, *Dileas*, 717–18.
23. Nicholson, *Canadians in Italy*, 635.
24. "5th Canadian Armoured Division War Diary," Dec. 1944, 11.
25. "AHQ No. 31," III.
26. Ibid., 109.
27. "Ops—1 Cdn Inf Div, CMF, Summary of Ops," 43.
28. "AHQ No. 31," III.
29. "I Canadian Corps War Diary," Dec. 1944, 17.
30. Wood, *Story of the Irish Regiment*, 56.
31. Scislowski, *Not All of Us Were Brave*, 327.
32. "Irish Regiment War Diary," Dec. 1944, 9–10.
33. Wood, *Story of the Irish Regiment*, 57.
34. "Irish Regiment War Diary," Dec. 1944, 9–10.
35. Scislowski, *Not All of Us Were Brave*, 329–30.
36. "Perth Regiment War Diary," Dec. 1944, 13.
37. "LER: Enlarging & Consolidation," 3.
38. "LER War Diary," Sept. 21, 1944–Mar. 15, 1945, 41–42.
39. "Breakout from Canale Naviglio brhead, 19/21 Dec 44," 2.
40. "Perth Regiment War Diary," Dec. 1944, 14.
41. Robert Cole, "Canadian Army Overseas Honours and Awards," *National Defence and the Canadian Forces* (website).
42. "Perth Regiment War Diary," Dec. 1944, 14.
43. Kerry and McDill, *History of Royal Canadian Engineers*, 257–58.
44. McAvity, *Lord Strathcona's Horse*, 174.
45. Kerry and McDill, *History of Royal Canadian Engineers*, 258.
46. Robert Cole, "Canadian Army Overseas Honours and Awards," *National Defence and the Canadian Forces* (website).
47. "Perth Regiment War Diary," Dec. 1944, 14.

20 HARD GOING
1. Frost, *Once a Patricia*, 379.
2. "Breakout from Canale Naviglio brhead, 19/21 Dec 44," 2.
3. William David Lewis Roach, "Canadian Army Overseas Honours and Awards," *National Defence and the Canadian Forces* (website).
4. Stevens, *PPCLI*, 216–17.
5. Jack McGrath, "Canadian Army Overseas Honours and Awards," *National Defence and the Canadian Forces* (website).
6. "PPCLI War Diary," Dec. 1944, 17.
7. "B.C. Dragoons War Diary," Dec. 1944, 14.
8. "PPCLI War Diary," Dec. 1944, 17.
9. "LER: Enlarging & Consolidation" 3–4.

10. "LER War Diary," Sept. 21, 1944–Mar. 15, 1945, 41.

11. "B.C. Dragoons War Diary," Dec. 1944, 14.

12. "PPCLI War Diary," Dec. 1944, 17.

13. "LER: Enlarging & Consolidation," 4.

14. Stevens, PPCLI, 219.

15. McAvity, Lord Strathcona's Horse, 174–75.

16. "AHQ No. 31," 114.

17. McAvity, Lord Strathcona's Horse, 175–76.

18. "Perth Regiment War Diary," Dec. 1944, 15–16.

19. "Irish Regiment War Diary," Dec. 1944, 10.

20. Nicholson, Canadians in Italy, 638.

21. Scislowski, Not All of Us Were Brave, 315.

22. Nicholson, Canadians in Italy, 638.

23. "AHQ No. 31," 114.

24. "Report on Ops by Capt. R.T. Currelly," 4.

25. "Seaforths: Exploitation from Brhead," 1.

26. "Carleton and York War Diary," Dec. 1944, 16.

27. "AHQ No. 31," 107.

28. "48th Highlanders War Diary," Dec. 1944, 21.

29. "GS 5 Canadian Armoured Division War Diary," May 1945, "History of Ops 5 CDN ARMD DIV," 4–5.

30. "1 Canadian Corps War Diary," Dec. 1944, "Attached letter to troops, Dec. 25," 1–2.

31. Nicholson, Canadians in Italy, 640.

32. McAvity, Lord Strathcona's Horse, 176–77.

33. "Ops—11 Cdn Inf Bde period 2–27 Dec 44," 5.

34. Locke, Governor General's Horse Guards, 180.

35. "Governor General's Horse Guards War Diary," Dec. 1944, 17–18.

36. "Irish Regiment War Diary," Dec. 1944, 11.

37. "Westminster Regiment (Motor) War Diary," Dec. 1944, 14.

38. "Irish Regiment War Diary," Dec. 1944, 11.

39. "Governor General's Horse Guards War Diary," Dec. 1944, 19–20.

40. "Irish Regiment War Diary," Dec. 1944, 11.

41. "Governor General's Horse Guards War Diary," Dec. 1944, 20.

42. "GS 5 Canadian Armoured Division War Diary," May 1945, "History of Ops 5 CDN ARMD DIV," 5.

43. "AHQ No. 31," 133–34.

44. Ibid., 117.

45. Nicholson, Canadians in Italy, 641.

46. Alexander, "Allied Armies in Italy, Chapter IV," 38.

47. "AHQ No. 31," 152.

21 SO ENDED 1944

1. "1st Canadian Infantry Division (G Branch) War Diary," Dec. 1944, 17–18.

2. "AHQ No. 31," 120.

3. Stone interview.

4. Oldfield, *Westminsters' War Diary*, 167.

5. "1 Canadian Corps War Diary," Dec. 1944, 22.

6. Roy, *Seaforth Highlanders*, 391.

7. "Governor General's Horse Guards War Diary," Dec. 1944, 21.

8. Stevens, *Royal Canadian Regiment*, 178–79.

9. "1st Canadian Inf. Div. (G Branch) War Diary," Dec. 1944, 19–20.

10. "12th Canadian Infantry Brigade War Diary," Dec. 1944, 9.

11. "Royal Canadian Regiment War Diary," Dec. 1944, 17.

12. Galloway, *Regiment at War*, 184–85.

13. "Royal Canadian Regiment War Diary," Dec. 1944, "Battle Narrative 'A' Coy," 4.

14. Stevens, *Royal Canadian Regiment*, 179.

15. Chen, Peter C. "Battle of Garfagnana, 26 Dec 1944–28 Dec 1944." *World War II Database* (website).

16. Nicholson, *Canadians in Italy*, 643.

17. Galloway, *Regiment at War*, 185–86.

18. "1st Canadian Inf. Div. (G Branch) War Diary," Dec. 1944, 22.

19. "1 Canadian Corps War Diary," Dec. 1944, App. 131, 1–3.

20. Mowat, *The Regiment*, 285–88.

21. "Perth Regiment War Diary," Dec. 1944, 22–23.

22. Ibid., Jan. 1945, 1.

23. Scislowski, *Not All of Us Were Brave*, 342.

22 HORDES OF THE ENEMY

1. "AHQ No. 31," 134.

2. "Report on Ops 11 Cdn Inf Bde for period 2 Jan to 13 Jan 45," 1.

3. "Ops—9 Brit Armd Bde, Op 'Syria' d/1 Jan 45," 1.

4. "B.C. Dragoons War Diary," Jan. 1945, 1.

5. Roy, *Sinews of Steel*, 350.

6. "Ops—5 Cdn Armd Div," "5 CDN ARMD REGT (8NBH) 2 Jan 45 to 14 Jan 45," 1.

7. Johnston, *Fighting Perths*, 109.

8. "AHQ No. 31," 135–36.

9. Wood, *Story of the Irish Regiment*, 58.

10. "Irish Regiment War Diary," Jan. 1945, 2.

11. "Ops—5 Cdn Armd Div," "Irish Regiment for period 2 Jan 45 to 16 Jan 45," 1.

12. "Perth Regiment War Diary," Jan. 1945, 1.

13. Scislowski, *Not All of Us Were Brave*, 343–44.

14. "Air Support–5 Cdn Armd Div, 26 Dec 44–11 Jan 45," 3.

15. Scislowski, *Not All of Us Were Brave*, 344–45.

16. Roy, *Sinews of Steel*, 351–52.

17. "5 Cdn Armd Bde, Account of Ops by Brig I.H. Cumberland," 4.

18. How, *8th Hussars*, 300.

19. John Daniel McAskill, "Canadian Army Overseas Honours and Awards," *National Defence and the Canadian Forces* (website).

20. Roy, *Sinews of Steel*, 352.

21. "5 Cdn Armd Bde, Account of Ops by Brig I.H. Cumberland," 4.

22. "Cape Breton Highlanders War Diary," Jan. 1945, 2.

23. "5 Cdn Armd Bde, Account of Ops by Brig I.H. Cumberland," 4.

24. "CB Highrs, Report on Ops 2/13 Jan 45," 2.

25. Stuart MacDonald, "Canadian Army Overseas Honours and Awards," *National Defence and the Canadian Forces* (website).

26. "Cape Breton Highlanders War Diary," Jan. 1945, 2.

27. "Ops—9 Cdn Armd Regt (BCD) 2/9 Jan 45," 2.

28. "Perth Regiment War Diary," Jan. 1945, 2.

29. Scislowski, *Not All of Us Were Brave,* 347–48.

30. "Perth Regiment War Diary," 2.

31. How, *8th Hussars,* 304.

32. "Ops—5 Cdn Armd Div," "5 CDN ARMD REGT (8NBH) from 2 Jan 45 to 14 Jan 45," 2.

33. "8th New Brunswick Hussars War Diary," 2.

34. "Ops—5 Cdn Armd Div," "5 CDN ARMD REGT (8NBH) from 2 Jan 45 to 14 Jan 45," 2.

35. "Ops—9 Cdn Armd Regt (BCD) 2/9 Jan 45," 2.

36. John Edward Cooke, "Canadian Army Overseas Honours and Awards," *National Defence and the Canadian Forces* (website).

37. Roy, *Sinews of Steel,* 354–55.

38. "AHQ No. 31," 141–42.

39. Ibid., 142.

40. Oldfield, *Westminsters' War Diary,* 172.

41. "Westminster Regiment (Motor) War Diary," Jan. 1945, 2.

42. "Report on Ops 11 Cdn Inf Bde," 2.

43. "Irish Regiment War Diary," Jan. 1945, 2.

44. "Air Support–5 Cdn Armd Div, 26 Dec 44–11 Jan 45," 2.

45. "Report on Ops 11 Cdn Inf Bde," 2.

46. Oldfield, *Westminsters' War Diary,* 172.

47. Roy, *Sinews of Steel,* 359–61.

48. Richard Bartley Sellars, "Canadian Army Overseas Honours and Awards," *National Defence and the Canadian Forces* (website).

49. Roy, *Sinews of Steel,* 361–62.

50. "Report on Ops: CB Highrs for 2 Jan to 13 Jan 45," 3.

51. "5 Cdn Armd Bde, Account of Ops by Brig I.H. Cumberland," 5.

52. "Report on Ops 11 Cdn Inf Bde," 2.

53. "5 Cdn Armd Bde, Account of Ops by Brig I.H. Cumberland," 5.

54. "AHQ No. 31," 146.

23 IT HASN'T BEEN A PICNIC

1. "Ops—2 Cdn Inf Bde, Attack," 1.

2. Stevens, PPPCLI, 221.

3. "3rd Canadian Infantry Brigade War Diary," Jan. 1945, 1.

4. "Royal 22e Régiment War Diary," Jan. 1945, 4–12.

5. "AHQ No. 31," 147.

6. "Report Capt. J.R. Koensgen, PPCLI on action 3/5 Jan 45," 1.

7. "PPCLI War Diary," 4.

8. "Report Capt. J.R. Koensgen, PPCLI on action 3/5 Jan 45," 1.
9. "Seaforths of c, Op Rept," 1–2.
10. Stevens, *PPCLI*, 222.
11. "Report Capt. J.R. Koensgen, PPCLI on action 3/5 Jan 45," 2.
12. "PPCLI War Diary," 5.
13. "Seaforth Highlanders War Diary," Jan. 1945, 5–6.
14. Jacob Brown, "Canadian Army Overseas Honours and Awards," *National Defence and the Canadian Forces* (website).
15. "Report Capt. J.R. Koensgen, PPCLI on action 3/5 Jan 45," 1.
16. "Seaforths of C, Op Rept," 3.
17. Roy, *Seaforth Highlanders*, 394–95.
18. Staples interview.
19. Roy, *Seaforth Highlanders*, 396.
20. "Seaforths of C, Op Rept," 4.
21. Allan Bruce McKinnon, "Canadian Army Overseas Honours and Awards," *National Defence and the Canadian Forces* (website).
22. Stevens, *City Goes to War*, 335.
23. "Ops—1 Cdn Inf Div, CMF, Summaries of Ops," "1 to 15 Jan 45," 3.
24. "WNSR War Diary," Jan. 1945, 6.
25. "Carleton and York War Diary," Jan. 1945, 4.
26. "Ops—1 Cdn Inf Div, CMF, Summaries of Ops," "1 to 15 Jan 45," 3–4.
27. "1st Canadian Infantry Division (G Branch) War Diary," Jan. 1945, 6.
28. Cederberg, *Long Road Home*, 256–57.
29. "Commendations," 1.
30. "AHQ No. 31," 155.
31. "Account of Ops of Gruppa Cremona," 1.
32. Scislowski, *Not All of Us Were Brave*, 358–95.
33. "5th Canadian Armoured Brigade War Diary," Jan. 1945, 20.
34. Roy, *Sinews of Steel*, 370.
35. "Ops—1 Cdn Inf Div, CMF, Summaries of Ops," "1 to 15 Jan. 45," 5.

24 THE WINTER LINE
1. "Ops—1 Cdn Inf Div, CMF, Summaries of Ops," "16 Jan–31 Jan. 45," 1.
2. Ibid., "1 to 15 Jan. 45," 3.
3. "Princess Louise Dragoon Guards War Diary," Jan. 1945, 9–13.
4. "Bi-Monthly Summary of Ops by Maj. L.A. Wrinch, Jan–Mar 45," "1–15 Jan 45," 1–2.
5. "Ops—1 Cdn Inf Div, CMF, Summaries of Ops," "1 to 15 Jan. 45," 5.
6. "AHQ No. 31," 161–64.
7. "Account of Ops of Gruppa Cremona," 1–2.
8. "Bi-Monthly Summary of Ops by Maj. L.A. Wrinch, Jan–Mar 45," "16–31 Jan 45," 2.
9. Stone interview.
10. "AHQ No. 31," 166.
11. "LER: Report on Operations," 1.
12. "Ops—1 Cdn Inf Div, CMF, Summaries of Ops," "1 to 15 Jan. 45," 5.
13. "LER: Report on Operations," 1.

14. "Ops—1 Cdn Inf Div, CMF, Summaries of Ops," "1 to 15 Jan. 45," 5.
15. Ibid., "16 Jan–31 Jan. 45," 1–2.
16. Raddall, *West Novas*, 271–72.
17. Galloway, *Bravely into Battle*, 236.
18. Galloway, *Regiment at War*, 187.
19. Mowat, *The Regiment*, 290.
20. Galloway, *Sicily to the Siegfried Line*, 67.
21. "Bi-Monthly Summary of Ops by Maj. L.A. Wrinch, Jan–Mar 45," "16–31 Jan 45," 2.
22. Roy, *Seaforth Highlanders*, 398–99.
23. "LER: Report on Operations," 2.
24. "Report on flamethrowers in action Jan 45," 2.
25. Frost, *Once a Patricia*, 392–96.
26. "Bi-Monthly Summary of Ops by Maj. L.A. Wrinch, Jan–Mar 45," "1–15 Jan 45," 1.
27. Ibid., "Feb & Mar 1945," 1.
28. "CMHQ No. 181," 3–4.
29. "Preliminary Report on Exercise 'Goldflake,'" 2.
30. Nicholson, *Canadians in Italy*, 660.
31. "Preliminary Report on Exercise 'Goldflake,'" 2–5.
32. "CMHQ No. 181," 11.
33. "1st Canadian Infantry Division (G Branch) War Diary," Feb. 1945, 6.
34. Roy, *Seaforth Highlanders*, 403.
35. Galloway, *Sicily to the Siegfried Line*, 71.
36. Stone interview.
37. "LER: Report on Operations," 3.
38. Stone interview.
39. "LER: Report on Operations," 3.
40. "2 Canadian Infantry Brigade: Report on Operations," 8.
41. "Preliminary Report on Exercise 'Goldflake,'" 2–12.
42. Zuehlke, "The Fight for Italy," 85.
43. McAvity, *Lord Strathcona's Horse*, 190–91.

EPILOGUE: THE RIVER BATTLES IN MEMORY
1. "AHQ No. 25," App. B, 1.
2. "AHQ No. 31," App. B, 1.

BIBLIOGRAPHY

Abbreviations: AHQ—Army Headquarters. CIA—Central Intelligence Agency. CMHQ—Canadian Military Headquarters. CWM—Canadian War Museum. DHH—Director of Heritage and History. DND—Department of National Defence. GS—General Staff. HQ–Headquarters. HPER–Hastings & Prince Edward Regiment. LAC—Library and Archives Canada. LER—Loyal Edmonton Regiment. PPCLI—Princess Patricia's Canadian Light Infantry. RCHA—Royal Canadian Horse Artillery. UVICSC–University of Victoria Libraries Special Collections. WNSR—West Nova Scotia Regiment.

BOOKS

Allard, Jean V. *The Memoirs of General Jean V. Allard*. Vancouver: University of British Columbia Press, 1988.

Beattie, Kim. *Dileas: History of the 48th Highlanders of Canada, 1929–1956*. Toronto: 48th Highlanders of Canada, 1957.

Boissonault, Charles-Marie. *Histoire du Royal 22e Régiment*. Québec: Éditions du Pélican, 1964.

Burns, E.L.M. *General Mud: Memoirs of Two World Wars*. Toronto: Clarke, Irwin, 1970.

Cederberg, Fred. *The Long Road Home: The Autobiography of a Canadian Soldier in Italy in World War II*. Toronto: Stoddart, 1985.

Dancocks, Daniel G. *The D-Day Dodgers: The Canadians in Italy, 1943–1945*. Toronto: McClelland & Stewart, 1991.

Delaney, Douglas E. *The Soldier's General: Bert Hoffmeister at War*. Vancouver: University of British Columbia Press, 2005.

Ellis, John. *Cassino: The Hollow Victory: The Battle for Rome January–June 1944*. London: André Deutsch, 1984.

Foster, Tony. *Meeting of Generals*. Toronto: Methuen, 1986.

Frost, C. Sydney. *Once a Patricia: Memoirs of a Junior Infantry Officer in World War II*. Ottawa: Borealis Press, 1994.

Galloway, Strome. *A Regiment at War: The Story of the Royal Canadian Regiment, 1939–1945*. Royal Canadian Regiment, 1979.

———. *The General Who Never Was*. Belleville, ON: Mika, 1981.

———. *Bravely into Battle: The Autobiography of a Canadian Soldier in World War Two*. Toronto: Stoddart, 1988.

———. *Sicily to the Siegfried Line: Being Some Random Memories and a Diary of 1944–1945*. Kitchener, ON: Arnold Press, n.d.

Granatstein, J.L. *The Generals: The Canadian Army's Senior Commanders in the Second World War*. Toronto: Stoddart, 1993.

Greenhous, Brereton. *Dragoon: The Centennial History of the Royal Canadian Dragoons, 1883–1983*. Ottawa: Guild of the Royal Canadian Dragoons, 1983.

Hilson, Norman. *Alexander of Tunis: A Biographical Portrait*. London, U.K.: W.H. Allen, 1952.

Hinsley, F.H, et al. *British Intelligence in the Second World War*. Vol. 3. Cambridge, U.K.: Cambridge University Press, 1988.

How, Douglas. *The 8th Hussars: A History of the Regiment*. Sussex, NB: Maritime Publishing, 1964.

Jackson, H.M. *The Princess Louise Dragoon Guards: A History*. Ottawa: The Regiment, 1952.

Jackson, W.G.F. *The Mediterranean and Middle East*. Vol. 6: Part 2. London, U.K.: Her Majesty's Stationery Office, 1987.

Johnston, Stafford. *The Fighting Perths: The Story of the First Century in the Life of a Canadian County Regiment*. Stratford, ON: Perth Regiment Veterans' Association, 1964.

Kerry, A.J., and W.A. McDill. *History of the Corps of Royal Canadian Engineers*. Vol. 2 (1936–46). Ottawa: Military Engineers Association of Canada, 1966.

Kesselring, Albert. *The Memoirs of Field-Marshal Kesselring*. London, U.K.: Greenhill Books, 2007.

Kitching, George. *Mud and Green Fields: The Memoirs of Major General George Kitching*. Langley, BC: Battleline Books, 1986.

Landell, K.D., et al. *Royal Canadian Dragoons: 1939–1945*. Montreal: The Regiment, 1946.

Locke, R.P., ed. *The Governor General's Horse Guards, 1939–1945*. Toronto: Canadian Military Journal, 1954.

Lockhart, Thomas Glen. *Last Man Standing: The Life of Smokey Smith, VC, 1914–2005*. Victoria: Friesen Press, 2013.

McAvity, J.M. *Lord Strathcona's Horse (Royal Canadians): A Record of Achievement*. Toronto: Bridgens, 1947.

Marteinson, John, and Michael R. McNorgan. *Royal Canadian Armoured Corps: An Illustrated History*. Toronto: Robin Brass Studio, 2000.

Mead, Richard. *The Last Great Cavalryman: The Life of Sir Richard McCreery*. Barnsley, U.K.: Pen & Sword Military, 2012.

Mitchell, G.D. RCHA–*Right of the Line: An Anecdotal History of the Royal Canadian Horse Artillery from 1871*. Ottawa: RCHA History Committee, 1986.

Morrison, Alex, and Ted Slaney. *The Breed of Manly Men: The History of the Cape Breton Highlanders*. Toronto: Canadian Institute of Strategic Studies, 1994.

Mowat, Farley. *The Regiment*. Belleville, ON: Hastings and Prince Edward Regimental Association, 2006.

Nicholson, G.W.L. *The Canadians in Italy: 1939–1945*. Ottawa: Queen's Printer, 1956.

———. *The Gunners of Canada*. Vol. 2. Toronto: McClelland & Stewart, 1972.

Oldfield, J.E. *The Westminsters' War Diary: An Unofficial History of the Westminster Regiment (Motor) in World War II*. New Westminster, B.C.: n.p., 1964.

Peniakoff, Vladimir. *Private Army*. London, U.K.: Jonathan Cape, 1950.

Raddall, Thomas H. *West Novas: A History of the West Nova Scotia Regiment*. n.p., 1947.

Roy, Reginald. *The Seaforth Highlanders of Canada 1919–1965.* Vancouver: Evergreen Press, 1969.

———. *Sinews of Steel: The History of the British Columbia Dragoons.* Kelowna, B.C.: The Whizzbang Association, 1965.

Royal Canadian Dragoons: 1939–1945. Montreal: The Regiment, 1946.

Ryder, Rowland. *Oliver Leese.* London: Hamish Hamilton, 1987.

Scislowski, Stan. *Not All of Us Were Brave: Perth Regiment—11th Infantry Brigade, 5th Canadian Armoured Division.* Toronto: Dundurn, 1997.

Stacey, C.P. *Arms, Men and Governments: The War Policies of Canada, 1939–1945.* Ottawa: Queen's Printer, 1970.

Stevens, G.R. *A City Goes to War.* Brampton, ON: Charters, 1964.

———. *The Royal Canadian Regiment.* Vol. 2, *1933–1966.* London, ON: London Printing, 1967.

———. *Princess Patricia's Canadian Light Infantry: 1919–1957.* Vol. 3. Griesbach, AB: Historical Committee of the Regiment, n.d.

Tooley, Robert. *Invicta: The Carleton and York Regiment in the Second World War.* Fredericton, N.B.: New Ireland Press, 1989.

Vokes, Chris. *My Story.* Ottawa: Gallery Books, 1985.

Wood, Gordon. *The Story of the Irish Regiment of Canada, 1939–1945.* Heerenveen, Holland: Hepkema, 1945.

JOURNAL ARTICLES

Johnston, Maj. J.P. "E.L.M. Burns—A Crisis of Command." *Canadian Military Journal,* Spring 2006.

Smith, Lt. Col. Jim. "On Trust: A Hard Look at Canadian Senior Officer Relationships during the Italian Campaign." U.S. Army Command and General Staff College, 2015.

Wilbeck, Christopher W. "Swinging the Sledgehammer: The Combat Effectiveness of German Heavy Tank Battalions in World War II." U.S. Army Command and General Staff College, 2002.

Zuehlke, Mark. "The Fight for Italy." Canada's Ultimate Story Series, *Legion* magazine, 2015.

WEBSITES

"Canadian Army Overseas Honours and Awards (1939–45)." *National Defence and the Canadian Forces.* DHH, DND. http://www.cmp-cpm.forces.gc.ca/dhh-dhp/gal/cao-aco/index-eng.asp.

"Cargo Carrier M29 Weasel." *Tank Encyclopedia.* http://www.tanks-encyclopedia.com/ww2/US/cargo-carrier-m29-weasel.

Chen, Peter C. "Battle of Garfagnana, 26 Dec 1944–28 Dec 1944." *World War II Database.* https://ww2db.com/battle_spec.php?battle_id=306.

"Freyberg Biography." *Encyclopedia of New Zealand.* https://teara.govt.nz/en/biographies/5f14/freyberg-bernard-cyril.

"Italy to the Netherlands." *The Loyal Edmonton Regiment Military Museum.* https://www.lermuseum.org/return-to-battle/italy-to-the-netherlands.

"Scales 40-Foot Italy Dyke, Braves Fire, Officer Missing." Jan. 5, 1945, *Toronto Star*. https://www.veterans.gc.ca/eng/remembrance/memorials/canadian-virtual-war -memorial/detail/2223019?James%20Edward%20Joice.

Tompkins, Peter. "The OSS and Italian Partisans in World War II," *Central Intelligence Agency*. https://www.cia.gov/library/center-for-the-study-of-intelligence/csi -publications/csi-studies/studies/spring98/OSS.html.

"U.K. Military Bridging–Floating Equipment." *Think Defence*. https://www .thinkdefence.co.uk/2011/12/uk-military-bridging-floating-equipment/.

"Veteran Stories: Raymond Jones," *The Memory Project*. http://www.thememoryproject .com/stories/1323:raymond-jones/.

UNPUBLISHED MATERIALS

"Account by Lt.-Col. Bell-Irving: Assault across the Savio 21–22.10.44." 145.2S5011(D3), DHH, DND.

"Account by Lt-Col J.A. Ensor on Est a Brhead over Canale Naviglio, night 12/13 Dec. 44." 145.2C6011(D1), DHH, DND.

"Account by Major J.M. Houghton Lamone Brhead Night 4/5 Dec." 145.2R13011(D1), DHH, DND.

"Account by Major R.M. Horsey, 'D' Coy of est Naviglio brhead, night 12/13 Dec 44." 1452C6011(D1), DHH, DND.

"Account by Major R.M. Horsey on establishing brhead over R. Lamone." 145.2C6011(D1), DHH, DND.

"Account of Action of HPER on 13 and 14 Oct. 44." 145.2H1013(D2), DHH, DND.

"Account of Ops of Gruppa Cremona." 224C1.011(D1), RG24, LAC.

"Account of Ops 29 Nov 44/11 Jan 45 by 12 Bn Royal Tk Regt." 234C1.012(D22), RG24, LAC.

"AHQ Report No. 25. Operations of 1 Cdn. Corps, 22 Sep 44 to 28 Oct 44: From the Marecchia to the Ronco." DHH, DND.

"AHQ Report No. 31. Operations of 1 Cdn. Corps, 28 Oct 44 to 27 Feb 45: The Capture of Ravenna, the Advance to the Senio and the Winter Line." DHH, DND.

"Air Support—5 Cdn Armd Div, 26 Dec 44–12 Jan 45." 244C5.013(D10), RG24, LAC.

Alexander of Tunis, Harold. "The Allied Armies in Italy, Chapter IV." MG27 AI, LAC.

"Battle Experience Questionnaires CDN ARMY 1939/45." 212C1.022(D1), RG24, LAC.

"Bi-Monthly Summary of Ops by Capt. L.A. Wrinch, 1 Sep 44/31 Mar 45." 224C1.013(D6), RG24, LAC.

"Bi-Monthly Summary of Ops by Maj. L.A. Wrinch, Jan–Mar 45." 224C1.013(D20), RG24, LAC.

"Breakout from Canale Naviglio brhead, 19/21 Dec 44, Acct of PPCLI action." 145.2P7011(D3), DHH, DND.

"British Columbia Dragoons War Diary," Dec. 1944, Jan. 1945. RG24, LAC.

"Canadian Ops August–November 1944, Extracts War Diaries and Memoranda." PPCLI Archives.

"Cape Breton Highlanders War Diary," Sept., Oct., Dec. 1944, Jan. 1945. RG24, LAC.

"Carlton & York Regt, Report on Ops in Italy, 1 Dec/23 Dec 44." 145.2C6009(D5), DHH, DND.

"Carleton and York Regiment War Diary," Oct., Dec. 1944, Jan. 1945. RG24, LAC.

"C.B. Highrs, Report on Ops 2/13 Jan 45." 145.2C5013(D1), DHH, DND.

"CMHQ Report No. 181. Operation 'Goldflake,' the Move of 1 Cdn Corps from Italy to North-West Europe, February–March 1945." DHH, DND.

"CMHQ Report No. 187. Operations of 1 Cdn. Corps, 4 Jun 44 to Sep 44: The Breaking of the Gothic Line and the Capture of Rimini." DHH, DND.

"Commendations." 224C1.016(D9), RG24, LAC.

"Crossing the Savio: 'A' Company Account." PPCLI Archives.

"8th New Brunswick Hussars War Diary," Sept., Oct., Dec. 1944, Jan. 1945. RG24, LAC.

"11th Canadian Infantry Brigade War Diary," Sept., Oct., Dec. 1944. RG24, LAC.

"5th Canadian Armoured Division War Diary," Dec. 1944. RG24, LAC.

"5 Cdn Armd Bde, Account of Ops 30 Nov 44/14 Jan 45 by Brig I.H. Cumberland." 274C5.011(D1), RG24, LAC.

"1st Canadian Infantry Brigade War Diary," Oct., Dec. 1944. RG24, LAC.

"1st Canadian Infantry Division War Diary (G Branch)," Oct., Nov., Dec. 1944, Jan. 1945. RG24, LAC.

"1st Light Anti-Aircraft Battalion War Diary," Sept. 1944. RG24, LAC.

"48th Highlanders of Canada War Diary," Oct., Dec. 1944. RG24, LAC.

"General Burns, 1 Canadian Corps War Diary," Sept. 1944. RG24, LAC.

"Governor General's Horse Guards War Diary," Oct. 1944. RG24, LAC.

"GS 5 Canadian Armoured Division War Diary," May 1945. App. I, RG24, LAC.

"Hastings and Prince Edward Regiment War Diary," Oct., Dec. 1944. RG24, LAC.

"HQ 1st Canadian Infantry Division War Diary," Oct., Nov., Dec. 1944, Jan., Feb. 1945. RG24, LAC.

"History of 1 CDN LAA Regiment, RCA (Lanark & Renfrew Scottish Regt): From 10 Mar 41 to 29 Jun 45." CWM.

"History of 1st Anti-Tank Regiment, Royal Canadian Artillery From 5 September 1939 to 31 July 1945." CWM.

"History of 3rd Canadian Field Regiment, Royal Canadian Artillery—September 1939 to July 1945." CWM.

"1 Canadian Corps War Diary," Nov., Dec. 1944. RG24, LAC.

"Irish Regiment of Canada War Diary," Sept., Oct. 1944, Jan. 1945. RG24, LAC.

"Lanark & Renfrew Scottish War Diary," Nov., Dec. 1944. RG24, LAC.

"Lord Strathcona's Horse War Diary," Sept. 1944. RG24, LAC.

"Loyal Edmonton Regiment: Enlarging & Consolidation of 1 Cdn Inf Bde brhead over the Naviglio Canal, 13/21 Dec 44." 145.2E2013(D1), DHH, DND.

"Loyal Edmonton Regiment: Report on Operations from Granarolo to the End of the Italian Campaign." PPCLI Archives.

"Loyal Edmonton Regiment War Diary," Sept. 21, 1944–Mar. 15, 1945. Loyal Edmonton Regiment Museum.

"Ops—1 Cdn Corps, Oct–Dec 1944." 224C1.013(D14), RG24, LAC.

"Ops—1 Cdn Inf Div, CMF, Summaries of Ops." 234C1.013(D4), RG24, LAC.

"Ops—1 Cdn Inf Div, CMF, Summary of Ops." 234C1.013(D15), RG24, LAC.

"Ops—2 Cdn Inf Bde, Attack 3/5 Jan 45 and 6 Jan/28 Feb 45." 264C2.013(D4), RG24, LAC.

"Ops—5 Cdn Armd Div." 244C5.013(D4), RG24, LAC.

"Ops—9 Brit Armd Bde, Op 'Syria' d/1 Jan 45." 274B9.016(D2), RG24, LAC.

"Ops—9 Cdn Armd Regt (BCD) 2/9 Jan 45." 141.4A9013(D1), DHH, DND.

"Ops—11 Cdn Inf Bde period 2–27 Dec 44." 264C11.013(D3), RG24, LAC.

"Org—Tank Hunting." 230C1(D94), RG24, LAC.

"Perth Regiment War Diary," Sept., Oct., Dec., 1944, Jan. 1945. RG24, LAC.

"PPCLI: Operations from Savignano to the F. Ronco, 14 Oct–28 Oct 1944."
    PPCLI Archives.

"PPCLI War Diary," Oct. 1944, Nov. 1944, Jan. 1945. PPCLI Archives.

"Preliminary Report on Exercise 'Goldflake.'" 224C1.013(D18), RG24, LAC.

"Princess Louise Dragoon Guards War Diary," Sept., Oct., Dec. 1944. RG24, LAC.

"Report Capt. J.R. Koensgen, PPCLI on action 3/5 Jan 45." 145.2P7011(D6), DHH, DND.

"Report of Ops: Lanark and Renfrew Scottish." 145.2L2013(D3), DHH, DND.

"Report on Flamethrowers in Jan 45." 224C1.013(D18), RG24, LAC.

"Report on Ops: 11 Cdn Inf Bde for period 2 Jan to 13 Jan 45." 264C11.011(D2),
    RG24, LAC.

"Report on Ops: C.B. Highlanders, 2/27 Dec 44 by Capt. R.T. Currelly."
    145.2C5013(D1), DHH, DND.

"Report on Ops: C.B. Highrs for 2 Jan to 13 Jan 45." 145.2C5013(D1), DHH, DND.

"Report on Ops in Italy by WNSR, 1944/45." 26003.009(D17), RG24, LAC.

"Royal Canadian Dragoons War Diary," Oct. 1944, Nov. 1944. RG24, LAC.

"Royal Canadian Regiment War Diary," Oct., Dec. 1944. RG24, LAC.

"Royal 22e Régiment War Diary," Oct., Dec. 1944, Jan. 1945. RG24, LAC.

"Seaforth Highlanders War Diary," Oct., Dec. 1944, Jan. 1945. Seaforth
    Highlanders Archives.

"Seaforths: Exploitation from Brhead over Canale Naviglio, 21–22 Dec 44." 145.
    S25013(D3), DHH, DND.

"Seaforths of 'C,' Op Rept on Capture of Granarolo and Senio Winter Line."
    145.2S5013(D1), DHH, DND.

"2nd Canadian Infantry Brigade Operations." PPCLI Archives.

"2 Canadian Infantry Brigade: Report on Operations, 6 Jan 45 to 28 Feb 45."
    PPCLI Archives.

"2nd Canadian Infantry Brigade War Diary," Oct., Dec. 1944. RG24, LAC.

"17th Field Regiment War Diary," Sept. 1944. RG24, LAC.

"Summaries of Ops 1 Mar/31 Dec 44 by Div Hist Offr." 231C1.013(D5), RG24, LAC.

"Summaries of Ops 1 Sep/31 Dec 44, Capt. R.T. Currelly." 244C5.013(D5), RG24, LAC.

"3rd Canadian Infantry Brigade War Diary," Oct. 1944, Nov. 1944, Jan. 1945.
    RG24, LAC.

"12th Canadian Infantry Brigade War Diary," Sept., Nov., Dec. 1944. RG24, LAC.

"Vokes, Chris. Vokes Papers." Royal Military College of Canada Massey Library.

"West Nova Scotia Regiment War Diary," Oct., Dec. 1944, Jan. 1945. RG24, LAC.

"Westminster Regiment (Motor) War Diary," Sept.–Dec. 1944, Jan.–Feb. 1945.
    RG24, LAC.

INTERVIEWS AND CORRESPONDENCE

Boire, Michael. Correspondence with author. Oct. 2004.

Hernandez, Paul. Interview by Ken MacLeod, undated. In the author's possession.

Hurley, Ron. Interview by the author, Vancouver, Oct. 4, 2000.

MacGregor, Keith. Interview by Ken MacLeod, undated. In the author's possession.

Robinson, Bill. Interview by Ken MacLeod, undated. In the author's possession.

Smith, Don. Correspondence with the author, December 12, 1998.

Smith, Ernest Alvia "Smokey." Interview by Ken MacLeod, undated. In the author's possession.

Staples, Tony. Interviewer unknown. Seaforth Archives.

Stone, Jim. Interview by William S. Thackray, Victoria, May 13 and 20, June 3, 10, and 17, 1980. UVICSC.

GENERAL INDEX

Ranks for individuals are highest attained as of February 28, 1945.

Adams, Sgt. George, 97
Adamson, Lt. T.N., 341
Adige River, 187–88, 190
Adriatic coast, 18, 30, 103, 122, 188, 218, 273, 405
Adriatic region, 218
Adriatic Sea, 59, 63, 80–81, 128–29, 133, 192, 223, 364, 398
Alamein, 28, 72
Albereto, 223, 226, 228
Alexander, FM Harold, 27–30, 51, 67, 70–72, 79, 130, 175–78, 187–90, 199, 214, 322, 351, 359, 404
Alfonsine, 348–50, 356, 364, 366, 372, 376–77, 398
Allan, Lt. Vaughan Stuart, 319
Allard, Lt. Col. Jean, 120–23, 125, 223, 228–29, 236–38, 323, 382
Allen, Capt. T.J., 321, 390, 393, 394, 398–99, 405
Allied Armies in Italy, 27, 175, 187, 322
Ancona, 312
Andrew, Lt. Col. Maurice, 74, 252, 279, 287, 335
Andrews, Pte. Henry Lorne, 248
Angle, Lt. Col. Harry, 248
Apennines, 25, 30, 50, 52–53, 97, 176–77, 187, 223, 254, 265, 273, 351, 404
Appleby, L/Sgt. Joseph François, 324
Appleton, Maj. H.W.F., 161
Argenta, 222
Armstrong, Maj. Bill, 55–56, 58–61
Armstrong, Sgt. D.R., 343
Asselstine, Lt. J.J., 59
Auchinleck, Gen. Claude, 72

Bagnacavallo, 2, 6, 212, 221–22, 225, 284–85, 286, 291, 300, 317–19, 321, 323–25, 329–31, 339, 345, 360, 362, 382, 398–99, 402, 413
Bagnolo, 180
Bain, Sgt. James Ettels, 109–10, 358
Ballam, Sgt. Ralph, 234
Ballard, Pte. K.W., 152–53
Bartoletti, Sgt. G., 208
Beal, Capt. George, 283–84
Bell-Irving, Lt. Col. Henry Ogle "Budge," 107–09, 113, 141–42, 146, 156, 308, 315, 319, 356, 384–86
Bernatchez, Brig. Paul, 120–21, 125, 225, 230, 239–40, 281, 284, 324, 382, 389
Bertrand, Pte. William, 110
Bérubé, CSM Pierre, 228
Best, Pte. Douglas Lloyd, 266
Bevano River, 170–72, 179–80, 191
Black, Lt. James John, 96
Bogert, Lt. Col. Pat, 106, 109, 113, 115, 131, 133–34, 139, 154–55, 158, 167–70, 308, 317, 319–20, 341, 354, 381
Bohemier, Pte. Joseph Charles, 117, 119
Boldrini, Lt. Arrigio, 217–19, 249–50, 397
Bologna, 3, 19, 26–27, 30, 53–54, 59, 79, 175–77, 187–88, 214, 222, 225, 274, 322, 351, 360, 366
Bone, Lt. S.W., 194–95
Bonifica Canal, 364–65, 370, 372–75, 377–78, 380
Borden, Lt. L.F.G., 250
Borghetto, 248
Borgo di Ronta, 158, 160, 162–64, 167–68
Borgo Fusara, 253
Borgo Pipa, 171
Borgo Villanova, 275–76, 279–80, 286–87, 290
Bouchard, Lt. C., 120
Boucher, Lt. X.W., 105
Boutlier, Pte. Henri, 294–96
Bradish, Capt. Ed, 106, 115, 308
Brady, Maj. Allen, 192–93

Brager, Pte. Lloyd Leslie, 245–46
Braithwaite, Maj. F.C., 36, 91–93
Brant, Pte. Huron Eldon, 95
Bray, Pte. Joseph Albert "Joe," 326–27
Broad, Maj. Cliff, 257, 261
Brooke, FM Sir Alan, 27–28, 31, 67, 70, 322
Brown, Capt. Chas, 40
Brown, Lt. Mal, 283
Brown, Maj. George, 315
Brown, Pte. Jacob, 385–86
Broz, Josip (Tito), 190
Buchan, Tpr. Bill, 304
Buchanan, Lt. Col. W.H. "Buck," 45–46,
    205–07
Bulgaria, 90–97, 101–02, 120–21
Bullock, Capt., 115–16
Bulow, Maj. See Boldrini, Lt. Arrigio
Burke, Maj. Douglas John, 296–97
Burns, Lt. Gen. Eedson L.M. "Tommy," 26,
    29–31, 33, 49–50, 54, 63–66, 69–72, 76,
    78–80, 101–02, 113, 129–30, 154, 167,
    174–75, 197–99, 201, 272–73

Calabrina, 129
Calder, Brig. Allan, 81–82, 85, 91–92,
    98–100, 240–42, 255, 258, 263, 362
Cambridge, Lt. Jack, 36, 38
Cameron, Lt. Col. Don, 82–83, 85–86,
    91–96, 240–41, 265, 301–02, 303,
    306, 362
Cameron, Tpr. Norman Loveland, 340
Campbell, Capt. Andy, 133–34
Campbell, Brig. C.A., 130
Campbell, Lt. Don, 238–39
Campeau, Lt. J.L.H., 260
Campiano, 203–04
Canale Naviglio. See Naviglio Canal
Canale Viserba, 33
Carrington, Pte. Gordon Victor, 145–46
Casa Argelli, 334, 339
Casa Baldi, 309
Casa Bettini, 210, 226–28
Casa della Congregatione, 335–36, 342–44
Casa Porcelli, 169
Casa Stasiol, 365, 367–68
Casa Tasselli, 334, 339–40
Casa Toni, 334–35, 337
Casa Venturi, 256, 261
Casablanca, 64
Casal Borsetti, 380

Casale, 34–35, 37, 41
Case Gentili, 148, 155
Cassino, 53, 71–72, 102, 409
Cassino, First Battle of, 322
Castellaccio, 102–03
Castello, CSM M.R., 260
Castiglione di Cervia, 172, 193
Caswell, Pte. George David, 83
Cattolica, 181–82, 216, 405
Cederberg, Sgt. Fred, 32, 43–44, 206–07,
    293–96, 312–13, 390–91
Cervia, 122, 128, 160–61, 172, 182, 193, 196,
    218, 354–55, 392–93, 395
Cesena, 79, 81, 101, 106, 109, 115, 121–23,
    124–26, 130, 132–33, 142, 151, 163, 167,
    170–71, 179, 181
Cesena–Cervia road, 122, 126, 129
Cesena Commonwealth Cemetery, 411
Cesena–Ravenna road, 142, 145, 149, 151,
    153, 156, 168, 192–94, 196, 204
Cesenatico, 128, 160, 197–99, 201, 331
Chamberlain, Capt. Robert Sydney, 287,
    292, 333
Chambers, Sgt. Alexander Ellwood, 172
Charette, Capt. Ted, 332
Chesney, Lt. James Lorne, 172
Chiesa di Pievesestina, 150–51
Christian, Lt. Col. Jack, 336
Christiansen, Capt. Oscar W., 241
Churchill, PM Winston, 67
Clapp, Lt. Frank Victor, 161
Clark, Lt. Col. Bobby, 55, 58, 61, 171, 287,
    388
Clark, Capt. C.V., 357
Clark, Maj. D.M., 298
Clark, Gen. Mark, 29, 72, 174, 176–77, 188,
    322, 351–52, 391
Clark, Sgt. Paddy, 244, 288
Clark, Maj. Robert, 107–08, 149–50,
    156–57, 168
Clark, Lt. Col. R.P. "Slug," 126–27, 132–34,
    137–39, 162–63, 339
Clark, Cpl. William Frederick, 168
Clifford, Lt. F.N., 37, 45
Coccolia, 225
Cole, Maj. Robert, 172, 287, 333, 335–36,
    342–44, 367
Conca River, 216
Conventello, 365–370, 375–76
Cooke, Maj. John Edward, 232, 374–75

Copper, Cpl. E.E., 34
Corbould, Lt. Col. Gordon, 25, 36, 47, 233, 243–45, 247–49, 289, 310
Coriano Ridge, 32
Cormier, Sgt. Nap, 248
Corsica, 392
Costello, Sgt. William John, 34
Cotignola, 222, 346, 350, 357, 381, 389–90, 402
Courtin, Capt. Len, 85
Crasemann, Gen. Lt. Eduard, 157
Crerar, Lt. Gen. Harry, 70–71, 175, 199–201, 212, 263, 271–72
Crofton, Maj. Pat, 126–27
Crozier, Lt. Bob, 332
Crutcher, Capt. D.A., 125
Cullation, Sgt. Arthur Charles, 171
Culliton, Lt. Frederick James, 62
Cumberland, Brig. Ian, 80, 104, 128, 173, 369–70, 372, 377, 379
Cummins, Capt. Fred, 376
Curran, Pte. Gerry, 279–80
Cutbill, Maj. Ted, 133–34, 136–39, 143–44, 383–84

Daniar, Tpr. Anton, 248
Darling, Lt. Col. Bill, 33, 35, 37, 46, 231–32, 250, 297, 395
Dauphinee, Lt. George Wharton, 193
Davidson, Tpr. H.E., 34
Davies, CSM Wallace George, 147–48
Dayton, Cpl. Ernest Frederick "Ernie," 48, 245–46
Deeks, Maj. D.B., 84, 87–88
Deniset, Capt. L., 120
Desrivières, Capt. R., 382–83
Dickinson, Lt. Sid, 151
Donegaglia River, 111
Dooley, Lt. Dave, 367
Drewry, Capt. Fred, 165–66, 239
Duncan, Cpl. A.C., 401
Duncan, Capt. D.G., 143–44, 156
Duncan, Maj. D.G., 309, 314–15
Durnford, Padre Roy, 356

Eagan, Capt. Kenneth William, 35
Eaton, Lt. Bruce, 246
Eatons, Lt. G.B., 211
Edgar, Capt. A.B., 216
Egan, Lt. A.D., 100, 104

Eisenhower, Gen. Dwight D., 175, 187, 190, 212, 322
Emilia–Romagna, 17, 273
Ensor, Lt. Col. Jack P., 125, 240, 282, 299–301, 303, 305–06

Faenza, 214, 225, 265, 274, 288, 293, 321, 325, 347
Fairburn, Lt. Al, 317
Fairweather, Lt. Dave, 314
Falzetta, Capt. Tony, 253, 286, 291–92, 366
Farrall, Cpl. M.J., 96
Featherstone, Capt. N., 126–27
Ferguson, Lt. A.M., 100
Ferrara, 30, 177
Fifteenth Army Group, 322, 351, 404
Firth, Lt. A.F., 147
Fisher, Capt. Pete, 367
Fiume, 190
Fiume Uniti, 249
Fiumicino, 55, 61–63
Fiumicino River, 5, 31, 50, 54–55, 57, 58–59, 61–63, 73, 75, 77–84, 89, 102–03, 128
Fleck, Sgt. William P., 307–08
Fleming, L/Cpl. Harold James, 338
Florence, 30, 51, 188, 202, 297, 358, 404, 409–10
Floyd, Brig. Harry, 201
Folliot, Lt. Norm, 310
Forli, 54, 169–70, 177, 197, 225–26
Fosso Ghiaia, 191–93, 196–97, 203–05, 207, 211
Fosso Munio, 265, 275, 293, 311–12, 314, 325, 329–30, 332–35, 339, 342–45, 351
Fosso Vecchio, 265, 274, 285, 287, 290–93, 296, 298, 301, 303, 306, 309, 323, 325–29, 331, 345–46, 357, 364, 375, 381–89
Fosso Vetro, 274, 285, 286–87, 293, 375
Foster, Lt. Bill, 116
Foster, Gilbert Lafayette, 269-70
Foster, Maj. Gen. Gilbert Lafayette, 269
Foster, Maj. Gen. Harry Wickwire, 199, 211, 263, 269–73, 275–76, 290–91, 298–99, 308, 345, 396, 405
Foulkes, Maj. Gen. Charles, 199–202, 211–13, 215–17, 258, 263–64, 266, 272–74, 310, 324, 329–30, 347, 360–62, 391–92, 404–05
Fraser, Capt. Douglas G, 389
Fraser, Capt. George, 97

Fraser, Capt. James, 300–02, 303, 305
French, Edward Andrew, 38
Freyberg, Lt. Gen. Bernard, 33, 101–02
Frisby, Lt. Jack, 38
Frocklage, Pte. A.L., 150
Frost, Lt. Syd, 17–21, 132, 134–35, 137–39,
    162–63, 167, 182, 273, 317–18, 402–03
Fusignano, 344, 390, 392, 405–06
Futa Pass, 51

Gallagher, Lt. George Alvin, 74
Gallipoli, 101
Galloway, Maj. Strome, 98–100, 104, 110–11,
    213–14, 256–57, 259, 263, 266, 357, 359,
    400, 406
Gambellera, 205
Gambettola, 83, 85–86, 91–93, 96, 98, 102
Gari River, 72
Garritty, Lt. Mervyn, 338
Gass, Lt. Dave, 60
Gatteo, 77
Gentles, Capt. Thomas Patrick, 116
George, Capt. Mike, 111
Ghiaia Canal. See Fosso Ghiaia
Gibbins, Cpl. Laurence, 264–65
Gibson, Brig. Graeme, 113
Gilbride, Lt. Col. W.P., 130
Gillies, Cpl. Adam, 38
Glendinning, Maj. Howarth, 319
Godo, 221, 225, 231, 234–35, 240, 242–43,
    247, 254
Godo–Bagnacavallo road, 237, 280, 282,
    309, 323
Godo–Ravenna railway, 235
Godo–Ravenna road, 244, 246–47, 250
Gorizia, 190
Gothic Line, 18, 26–30, 32, 48, 50–52, 54,
    67, 71–72, 112, 150, 263, 389, 411–12
Goucher, Lt. Len, 61
Graham, Maj. R.J., 277
Granarolo, 325, 350, 381–84, 386, 389
Granarolo River, 128
Grant, Sgt. George, 372
Gray, Sgt. John William, 260
Greengrass, Sgt. R., 151–52
Gregg, Capt. J.M., 98, 99–100, 105
Groomes, Lt. William Anthony, 386
Guest, Lt. Bill, 39

Hall, Capt. Jack, 376
Hamer, Capt. L.A., 331
Harrison, Pte. Richard, 289
Hayward, Tpr. Gordon Elgin, 350
Healy, Capt. Dennis, 219, 249
Heidrich, Gen. Fall. Richard, 128
Hendrie, Capt. Herb, 253, 287, 366–67,
    376–77
Hernandez, Sgt. Paul, 259–60
Herr, Gen. d. Pztr. Traugott, 52, 128
Hertzberg, Capt. Peder, 256
Hickling, Maj. Norman, 287, 310, 366–67
Highway 9, 19, 30, 35, 40, 59, 77, 79, 81–82,
    84–86, 89–93, 98, 100–01, 104, 106–07,
    109, 111, 120–21, 124–25, 128–29, 177,
    179, 181, 189, 212–13, 215, 274, 322
Highway 14, 277
Highway 16, 30, 33, 160, 172, 191–93,
    196–97, 203, 211–12, 221–22, 214, 243,
    249–50, 252–53, 290, 348, 350, 392
Highway 65, 176, 214
Highway 67, 192
Highway 71, 131
Hills, Capt. E.M., 98–99, 110
Hitler, Adolf, 51–52, 176, 238
Hitler Line, 131
Hoffman, Lt. Murray, 329
Hoffmeister, Maj. Gen. Bert, 31, 37, 43, 46,
    48, 57, 62, 68–71, 75, 78, 129–30, 171–72,
    221, 250, 254, 272, 275–76, 287, 290, 310,
    336, 364–65, 368, 375–76
Hohenleitner, Pte. Henry, 247
Horgan, Capt. G.S., 73, 75
Horsbrugh-Porter, Lt. Col. Andrew, 180,
    203, 211
Horsey, Maj. Rowland, 282, 300, 302,
    303–05
Horton, Lt. J.H. "Jim," 317–18, 384–85, 388
Hoskin, Maj. Bert, 233–34, 288, 311
Houghton, Maj. Jim, 256–57, 261–62, 328,
    358
Hoult, Lt. Eddie, 247, 289
How, Doug, 206
Hudson, Lt. Ken, 327
Hughes, Capt. W.W., 256
Hurley, Sgt. Ron, 311–12
Hurst, Lt. B.G., 378–79
Hutchings, Lt. A.S., 45–46, 343

Idice River, 50
Iesi, 312
Il Canalone, 378
Inman, Sgt. Charles D., 247–48

Jesshope, Sig. Kenneth William Bud, 105
Johnson, Capt. Alon, 315
Johnson, Maj. George, 47
Johnson, Sgt. Gordon Fraser, 96
Johnson, Lt. Thomas Ormond "Tommy,"
    204–05
Johnston, Brig. Ian, 55, 57, 62, 64, 69, 75,
    266, 276, 286, 335–36, 343, 362
Johnston, Capt. J.R., 61
Joice, Lt. James Edward, 242
Jones, Maj. D.E., 232
Jones, Maj. Harvey, 229–30, 238
Jones, Capt. J.D., 383
Jones, Sgt. J.D., 233
Jones, Tpr. Raymond, 297–98
Jordan, Lt. Col. Allan Kitchener, 43, 47, 128,
    160–61, 348–50

Keet, Sgt. Jim, 312
Keightley, Lt. Gen. Charles, 274
Kennedy, Lt. Don, 86
Kennedy, Capt. Franklin B., 62
Kenyon, Lt. Sydney Charles, 140
Kerr, Sgt. Eddie, 294–95, 313
Kesselring, Genfldm. Albert, 28–29, 51–54,
    157, 175–77, 297, 397
Ketcheson, Maj. Stan, 241–42, 255, 257–58,
    261, 264–65
King, PM Mackenzie, 66–67
Kingston, Cpl. Gerald Elwood, 116–17
Kitching, Brig. George, 198–202, 213, 220,
    258, 271
Knowles, Lt. Douglas, 165–66
Koblun, Pte. Albert, 205
Koensgen, Capt. J.R., 383
Koffman, Cpl. M.H., 343
Koskaewich, Sgt. Fred, 289

La Chiaviche, 127
La Parsota, 204–05
Ladiceur, Pte. W.O., 154
Laing, Sgt. Jack, 205, 245
Lake, Cpl. R., 34
Lamone Abbandonato, 364, 370, 373–75,
    378

Lamone River, 50, 210, 212, 215, 221–23,
    225, 228, 231, 235, 237, 239–42, 247, 249,
    252–54, 263–66, 272–76, 286, 292,
    299, 325, 344, 346–47, 357, 364, 366–67,
    370–71, 375–76
    1st Brigade's Dec. 5 assault, 255–63
    1 Corps's Dec. 10–11 assault, 276–85
    Expanding the bridgehead, 286–92
Landell, Lt. Col. Keith, 80, 191–93, 195
Langston, Maj. A.E., 297–98
Lauzon, Tpr. Howard F., 307
Lea, Sgt. Arnold, 111
Leadbeater, Capt. Bill, 283–84
Leclair, Pte. Joe, 312
Leese, Gen. Sir Oliver, 28–30, 66–71
Lemelsen, Gen. d. Pztr. Joachim, 177
LeMeseurier, Lt. Andy, 97
Leon, Sgt. R.P., 151–52, 154
Lessines, 101
Ligurian Sea, 358
"Lili Marlene," 26
Lind, Brig. John S., 25, 27, 33, 35, 37–39, 41,
    45–46, 205, 231–34, 243, 248–50, 293,
    298, 357
Liri Valley, 28, 31, 68, 70, 97, 99, 113,
    131, 410
Ljubljana, 190
Lloyd, Pte. Bruce, 105
Lloyd, Sgt. K.K., 140
Lo Stradello, 339
Lodwick, Cpl. H.J., 96
Lombardy, 392
Longhurst, Maj. Bill, 118, 146–47
Lugo, 212–13, 215, 222, 345, 360, 382, 393
Lungstrum, Tpr. Edward A., 248
Lynch, Maj. Stewart, 107–08, 149–52, 154,
    387

Mabbett, Pte. Bud, 234
Macartney, Maj. George, 286, 367
MacCulloch, Lt. D.G., 132, 135–36, 138–39,
    181–82
MacDonald, Maj. Alan, 307
MacDonald, Lt. G.L., 206
MacDonald, Lt. Joe, 278
MacDonald, Lt. John Albert, 86
MacDonald, Sgt. Stuart, 371
Macdonell, Archibald Cameron, 269–70
MacDougall, Maj. Colin, 126, 317
Mace, Maj. Oliver Herbert, 385–87

Macerata, 395, 408
Macey, Sgt. C.N., 292–93
MacGillvray, Lance Cpl. Jim, 60
MacGregor, Lt. Keith, 315–16, 320
Mackenzie, Lt. A.C., 164–65
MacKenzie, Lt. Alan, 141
Mackenzie, Lt. Col. Don, 84, 87, 105, 111, 283–84, 327, 329
MacKinnon, Lt. J.C., 378
MacLaren, Maj. F.G., 88, 97–98
Macmillan, Sir Harold, 67
MacNeil, Cpl. Albert, 32, 293, 295, 391
MacPherson, Maj. C.P., 61–63
Maier, Stubaf Josef, 375–76
Mannering, Lt. Ron, 248
Marecchia River, 17–18, 21, 26, 31, 35, 51–52, 132
Marignano, 182
Marseilles, 27, 404
Martorano, 131–32, 134–35, 141, 158–59, 163, 167, 178
Massa Lombarda, 222, 360
Mather, Pte. Maurice James, 118
McAdam, Maj. D.W., 164
McAskill, Sgt. Jim, 369–70
McAvity, Lt. Col. Jim, 25, 33–34, 39, 49, 91, 94, 96, 277, 342–43, 347, 409
McCormack, Lt. Laurence Edward, 162
McCreery, Lt. Gen. Richard "Dick," 71–72, 77–80, 129–30, 167, 170, 174, 179, 188–89, 192, 199, 201, 215, 218, 266, 306, 322, 351–52, 359, 391, 405
McDougall, Maj. Colin, 383–84, 386, 388
McDougall, Maj. F.H., 315–16, 320
McEwen, Maj. Cliff, 55–56, 59–61
McGrath, Cpl. Jack, 338–39
McKay, Lt. D.H., 143–44
McKechan, Capt. J.A., 172
McLean, Tpr. William Sayers, 350
McNaughton, Gen. Andrew, 67
McNeil, Maj. Gordon Leo French, 229, 281
McNeil, Capt. Jack, 296
Meadows, Sgt. George John, 242
Medicina, 221–22, 360
Mensa, 171–72, 179
Metauro River, 30
Mezzano, 221, 249, 252–54, 275, 277, 288, 290, 292, 365, 396
Miller, Lt. Art, 208
Miller, Lt. T.C., 325–26

Milling, Lt. John, 111, 327, 329
Mills, Maj. J.C.P., 373–74
Milnes, Sgt. John Goodwin, 147–48
Minard, Pte. Alan K., 165–66
Mitchell, Capt., 202
Mitchell, Maj. William Hayward, 333
Molinaccio, 210
Monte Belmonte, 177
Monte Cassino, 28, 102
Monte Cerere, 176
Monte Grande, 176
Montefiore Conca, 182
Montgomery, FM Bernard, 67, 212, 322
Montilgallo, 77
Montone River, 50, 180, 203, 208–12, 215, 221, 223, 225–26, 228, 231–33, 235, 249, 265, 274, 347, 350, 412
Moore, Lt. Victor Alexander, 88
Morciano di Romagna, 182
Morin, Pte. Eugene, 208
Moro River, 147
Mount Farneto, 77
Mowat, Lt. Farley, 81, 92, 257, 262, 265, 291, 301, 305, 361–62, 400
Murdoch, Capt. Bob, 326
Murray, Pte. D.S., 143
Murray, Lt. John Munro, 40
Murray, Lt. R.W., 161, 348–49
Myslicki, Cpl. Walter, 247

Naples, 64–65, 360, 404–05, 409–10
Naviglio Canal, 265, 274–75, 286–87, 290–300, 302, 303, 306–14, 317, 319, 321, 323–25, 328–30, 334, 342, 345–46, 348, 381–84, 386–89, 391, 413
Neill, Maj. W.J., 209, 243–44, 247–48, 288
Neuspiel, Tpr. G., 161
Newell, Capt. Peter, 304–05
Newton, Lt. Ross, 38
Nichols, Pte. Jim, 36

O'Brien, Capt. Pat, 55, 58–59
Office of Strategic Services, 217, 219
Ogilvie, Capt. Lorne, 41
Olafson, Capt. E.A., 216
Oldfield, Lt. James, 35, 38, 197, 204–05, 209, 211, 234, 243–44, 247–48, 288, 310, 312, 349, 355, 376
Oldis, Tpr. Ralph James, 365

Operations
Anvil, 27
Chuckle, 220–21
Dragoon, 27
Goldflake, 405, 408
Herbstnebel, 51–52
Husky, 112
Ortona, 53, 69, 82, 147, 346, 354
Osteria, 286
Osteriaccia, 129
Otis, Pte. Howard, 328
Ott, Capt. W.C., 125

Palmer, Pte. Elmer John, 248
Papps, Tpr. James Morris, 194–95
Payton, Cpl. Al, 111
Peniakoff, Lt. Col. Vladimir, 195
Pesaro, 18, 182
Petch, Lt. Col. Charles, 385
Petersen, Tpr. Harry E., 248
Pezzolo, 238
Piangipane, 243–44, 246–49, 252–54
Piangipane–Russi road, 243
Pickard, Capt. J.E., 261
Pieve Sestina, 131, 150, 167, 169
Pisciatello River, 81, 83, 100–02, 104–05,
106–09, 111–13, 115–21, 126, 128–29
Pitt, Lt. George, 56, 59–60
Plecas, Pte. Joseph, 38
Plow, Brig. E.C., 130
Po River, 30–31, 33, 49–53, 187, 190, 260
Po Valley, 25–26, 72, 188
Poirier, Lt. Alfred Hubert, 105
Ponte della Pietra, 106, 108, 113–14,
116–18, 126
Popplewell, Capt. T.A., 90
Porritt, Capt. Max, 94–96, 241, 258
Porter, Pte. Percy Edward, 246
Portnuff, MO Capt. Joseph Charles, 149
Porto Corsini, 219, 249, 350, 364–65, 380
Potts, Lt. Benny, 99
Potts, Maj. Sam, 18–19, 127, 133, 334, 337
Primieri, Brig. Clemente, 392

Quamme, Sgt. Ed, 38

Rabbi River, 197
Ralph, Sgt. Ed, 97–98
Ralston, Lt. Edward, 34, 37
Ralston, Col. J. Layton, 64–67, 70

Rauta, Pte. Norman, 104–05
Ravenna, 30, 142, 160, 177–78, 180, 183,
187–89, 191–93, 196–97, 203–04, 207,
212–15, 218–19, 220–21, 223, 225, 232,
234–35, 243–44, 249–51, 252, 347, 350,
355, 360, 362–63, 364, 376, 405, 413
Reid, Lt. Col. William, 264, 328
Reid, Lt. William Archibald, 86
Reinhardt, Gen. Lt. Alfred, 331, 344
Remple, Lt. W., 142
Reno River, 380, 397
Rhine River, 212
Rhineland, 212
Rhodes, Maj. John Keble, 164–66, 229,
238–39
Riccione, 90, 181–82, 199, 213, 218, 224,
360, 395
Rice, Capt. D.I., 229–30, 238, 281
Richard, Lt. J., 323
Richards, Lt. B.D., 93–96
Ridge, Maj. W.J. "Sammy," 287, 343–44
Rimini, 18–19, 30, 33, 50–51, 54, 67, 71, 160,
201, 224, 263, 354, 405
Rimini–Bologna railway, 79
Rio Baldona, 78, 86–87, 102
Ritchie, Lt. Col. Jim, 85, 98–99, 120, 242,
255–56, 264
Roach, Lt. Bill, 334, 337–38
Roaf, Brig. W.G.H., 404
Roberts, Capt. W.L., 109
Robinson, Capt. A.G., 133, 139, 162–65
Robinson, Pte. Bill, 154
Robinson, Pte. Donald John Frederick, 406
Robinson, Maj. William George, 398
Rocca Malatestiana, 124
Romagna, 21, 27, 175–78, 181, 183, 187
Romanow, Lt. A., 378–79
Ronco River, 50, 171, 179–81, 197, 203, 205,
208–11, 225
Rosa, Sgt. Warren, 60
Ross, Sgt. J.P., 161
Röttiger, Gen. d. Pztr. Hans, 157
Rowe, Sgt. Ken "Blackie," 253
Rowland, Padre David, 89
Royal Military College, 269
Ruffio, 101–02, 115, 118
Russell, Cpl. Robert Walter, 260
Russi, 212, 215, 221, 223, 225, 227–29, 231,
236–39, 262, 325, 356–57
Russi–Bagnacavallo railway, 276

Salerno, 72, 360
Salsbury, CSM Sydney Luard, 288
Salto River, 31, 42, 46, 48, 54–57, 61
San Carlo, 299
San Clemente, 182, 197
San Fortunato Ridge, 18, 25–27, 150, 291
San Giovanni in Marignano, 182–83, 395
San Giustina, 33–35, 41, 49, 410
San Martino, 129
San Mauro, 55–57, 58, 63, 76, 78
San Michele, 250
San Pancrazio, 209, 221, 223–25, 243
San Pietro in Campiano, 203
San Pietro in Vincoli, 180
San Stefano, 194–95, 204
San Vito, 31, 35–38, 40, 41, 45–47
Sant' Alberto, 364–65, 368–71, 377, 379–80, 397
Sant' Angelo, 77–78, 85, 102
Sant' Egidio, 126–27, 132, 162
Santerno River, 50, 215, 222–23
Sardinia, 392
Saunders, Lt. Col. Al, 163–66, 168, 229–30, 238–39, 281
Savignano, 63, 73, 76, 81–82, 85, 106
Savio River, 50, 79, 81, 101, 106, 119, 121, 123, 125–33, 135–36, 139, 141–46, 148–49, 152, 154–56, 158–60, 162–72, 178–82, 191, 193, 216–17, 224, 308, 358
Scheldt Estuary Campaign, 66, 212, 271, 273
Scislowski, Pte. Stan, 252–54, 277–80, 332–33, 363, 367–68, 392
Scolo Lama, 208
Scolo Rigossa, 75, 77–78, 83, 85–86, 88, 90–93, 98
Scolo Via Cupa, 228, 234, 236, 238, 244
Sellars, Maj. Richard Bartley, 378–79
Senio River, 50, 212, 215, 222–23, 266, 273–74, 293, 319, 321–22, 324, 330, 337, 342–46, 348–52, 353, 355–56, 359, 364, 377, 381–82, 384, 389–91, 393, 410, 412–13
    Winter Line on, 394–404
Shaw, Sgt. Bob, 97
Shaw, Ernie, 413
Shawcross, Maj. Fred, 244
Shone, Lt. Ernie, 164–65, 167
Shore, Lt. L.G., 260
Sillaro River, 50

Simonds, Lt. Gen. Guy, 66, 198, 200, 212, 271
Skrimshire, Lt. Pete, 38
Smith, Cpl. C.A., 191
Smith, Lt. C.H., 168–69
Smith, Capt. D.A., 75, 90
Smith, Brig. Desmond, 130, 198, 200, 220–23, 240, 255, 258, 263, 298–99, 306, 406
Smith, Capt. Don, 304–05
Smith, Pte. Ernest Alvia "Smokey," 152–54, 217
Smith, Sgt. F.G., 260
Smith, Sgt. G., 243
Smith, Cpl. H.R., 144
Smith, Capt. Lloyd, 326–29
Smith, Cpl. Thomas, 196–97
Smythe, Cpl. J.N., 160
Somerville, Lt. Col. Boyd, 57, 61–62, 171, 278, 380
Somme, the, 101
Sparling, Brig. H.A., 78
Sparrow, Sgt. Frank Harris, 137–39, 143
Spitsbergen, Norway, 112
Split, 190
Staples, Maj. Tony, 107, 145–46, 386–87
Stephens, Lt. Bert, 205
Stockdale, Maj. William Oscar, 299–301
Stone, Lt. Col. Jim, 112–16, 118–19, 142, 147–48, 151, 155, 273, 306–08, 315–16, 319–20, 339–41, 354–55, 397–98, 407
Stonefish, Tpr. Lawrence, 34
Strada Molinazza, 369
Stuart, Maj. Gen. Kenneth, 71

Taplin, Capt. L.E., 114
Taylor, Capt. E.W., 350
Tellier, Maj. Henri, 228, 382–83
Tennant, Pte. James, 152–54
Thiele, Capt. Alphonse Peter, 217–19
Thiessen, Cpl. F., 46
Thompson, Sgt. Keith, 150–54
Thompson, Lt. L., 62
Thomson, Lt. Col. Syd, 113
Thorne, Maj. Eric, 256–57, 259
Thrasher, Sgt. James Alton, 289
Threxton, Maj. R.G., 163–65
Ticino River, 187
Tito. See Broz, Josip
Traversara, 225, 254, 275, 290

Trudeau, Maj. Louis F., 120, 122, 228–29, 236–37
Trudel, Pte. Arthur, 112
Truscott Jr., Lt. Gen. Lucian K., 322, 359
Tucker, Maj. H.A., 114, 116
Tunisia, 72, 99
Turgeon, Lt. F., 122–23
Tyler, Lt. Walter, 289
Tyrrhenian Sea, 175
Tysick, Pte. Norman Dalton, 291

Uniti Canal, 192, 211, 249
Urbino, 182–83
Uso River, 31–32, 35, 37, 39–40, 41–43, 45–48, 50, 54, 56

Valli di Comacchio, 214, 218, 223, 249, 350, 364, 377, 380, 391, 397–98, 404
Van Hende, Sgt. Marcel Octave, 291
Variano, 34–35, 37
Vena, 55, 57
Ventena River, 216
Via Adriatica. See Highway 16
Via Aguta, 278, 293
Via Al Conventello, 376
Via Casalino, 339
Via Chiara, 311, 330, 333, 335, 342
Via Cocchi, 280, 286–87, 292, 295
Via Cogollo, 286
Via della Lamone, 253
Via Emilia. See Highway 9
Via Guarno, 319, 334, 339, 341
Via Pozzarda, 339
Via Rossetta, 330, 348
Via Sant' Antonio, 330, 332, 344, 348, 365
Vickers, Maj. Charles Victor William, 194–95
Villa Grappa, 57
Villa Pasolini, 225
Villanova, 247, 254, 275–76, 278, 287–90, 292–93, 409
Vincent, Lt. Paul Emile, 120, 229
Vincoli, 180
Vokes, Maj. Gen. Chris, 30, 68–71, 78, 81, 91–92, 101–02, 106, 109, 113, 129–31, 141, 154, 158, 163, 167, 171, 181, 198–202, 270–73

Volturona, 170
von Ribbentrop, Joachim, 51
von Rundstedt, Fldm. Gerd, 52
von Vietinghoff, Gen. Obst. Heinrich, 175–77, 262, 273–74, 329

Waite, Tpr. Bert, 304
Washburn, Capt. J.R., 147–48, 155
Watling, Maj. L.A., 124–25
Watson, Pte. Robert Thomas, 211
Watson, Lt. W.C., 264
Watts, Cpl. Stan, 278
Weaver, Sgt. Maj. Earl, 279, 344
Webb, Lt. Col. Ted, 158, 169–70, 178–79
Weeks, Brig. E.G., 65, 130
Weese, Capt. Donald Edward, 291
Weir, Maj. Gen. C.E. "Steve," 33, 78, 101
Wentzel, Gen. Maj. Fritz, 157
Westhead, Maj. J.F., 343
White, Cpl. George L., 315–16
White, Pte. Jimmy, 245–46
White, Capt. Robert A., 41
Wicklow, Lt. Donald Charles, 303–05, 307
Wilder, MO Ed, 38
Wilkin, Capt. Jack, 336, 343
Wilkinson, Capt. Jimmy, 256–57, 259–60
Williamson, Lt. Richard Owen Buckland,
Wilson, Lt. Vic, 210–11, 246
Wood, Capt. Gordon, 54, 180, 332–33, 344, 349
Woolley, Capt. Thomas Edwin, 108
Worobetz, MO Capt. Steve, 318
Wright, Maj. G., 74
Wright, Lt. Geoff, 99
Wrinch, Capt. Joe, 309, 318

Young, Tpr. Duncan, 248
Young, Lt. John Walter, 289–90
Yugoslavia, 190, 216

Zagreb, 190
Zavitz, Capt. Ross, 100, 109
Ziegler, Brig. Bill, 307
Ziegler, Gen. d. Artl. Heinz, 177

INDEX OF FORMATIONS, UNITS, AND CORPS

CANADIAN

Army

First Army, 66, 70, 175, 199, 211–12, 271

I Corps, 17–18, 21, 26, 30, 49, 63–65, 69, 71–72, 75, 77–80, 85, 101, 125, 129, 132, 142, 154, 160, 167, 179–83, 197–99, 203, 205, 209, 212–13, 215, 218, 220, 224, 231, 258, 266, 271, 274, 285, 309–10, 318, 321, 325, 331, 346–47, 350, 353, 356, 359–60, 362, 365, 381, 390, 392, 397, 404–05, 409, 411–12

II Corps, 198, 212, 271

Royal Canadian Provost Corps, 202, 408

DIVISIONS

1st Infantry, 19, 26, 30–31, 57, 66–69, 78–81, 87, 90–91, 99, 101–02, 106, 112, 121, 128–29, 131–32, 151, 167, 169–71, 178, 180–82, 198–200, 207, 211–12, 217, 220–22, 224–25, 227, 229, 240, 242, 254–55, 258, 263, 265–66, 271–76, 280, 283, 285, 290–91, 298, 307–08, 310, 315, 321, 325, 329, 345, 353, 357, 359–60, 381, 390, 392–93, 394, 396, 398, 405–06, 408, 411–12

2nd Infantry, 199

4th Armoured, 198–200, 271

5th Armoured, 20, 25, 30–31, 42, 50, 54, 60–61, 63, 69–70, 74–81, 101, 103, 129, 158, 167, 171, 176, 178–83, 209, 211–13, 215, 221, 231, 239, 242, 249–50, 254, 264–65, 274–77, 287, 289, 291–92, 298, 301, 310, 314, 321, 325, 329–32, 335–36, 342, 346, 355, 364–65, 368, 370, 381, 392, 394–95, 403–05, 411–12

BRIGADES

1st Armoured, 404

1st Infantry, 81, 84–85, 88, 90–91, 98, 100–01, 105, 106, 111, 115, 120, 222, 240, 242, 255, 263–64, 272–73, 275–76, 290–91, 298, 306–09, 321, 325, 329, 331, 345, 353, 362, 406

2nd Infantry, 69, 81, 101, 106, 108, 110, 113, 115, 119–20, 126, 129–30, 132, 139–40, 151, 154–55, 158, 160, 163, 167, 170, 181–82, 222, 302, 303, 306, 308, 319, 321, 325, 329–30, 334, 341, 345, 353–54, 381, 383, 385, 389–90, 408

3rd Infantry, 81, 115, 120–21, 124–26, 140, 163, 170, 181–82, 216, 221–23, 225–27, 231, 239, 255, 274–76, 280, 283, 285, 290, 309–10, 321, 323, 324–25, 329, 353, 382, 389, 398, 400

5th Armoured, 47, 80, 173, 182, 215, 275, 365, 368–71, 375, 377, 380, 392, 395

7th Infantry, 271

11th Infantry, 31–32, 48–49, 54, 61–64, 69, 73–78, 171–72, 179, 182, 198, 249, 252, 266, 274–76, 280, 286–97, 325, 329–30, 335–36, 342, 344, 348, 357, 362, 365, 368, 375, 395

12th Infantry , 25, 31–33, 38–41, 46, 48–50, 54, 58, 75, 77–78, 130, 182, 197, 205, 221, 231–32, 234–35, 243, 250, 254, 274–75, 287, 292–93, 297, 310, 329, 357, 392, 395

AD-HOC UNITS

Cumberland Force, 80–81, 102–04, 128, 160, 172–73, 180

Porterforce, 180, 191–92, 195–97, 203–05, 207, 209–11, 218, 221, 249–50

River Force, 203

Wilder Force, 80, 103

ARMOURED UNITS

5th Armoured Brigade Assault Troop, 47

8th Princess Louise's New Brunswick Hussars, 49, 54–56, 58, 61, 64, 290, 293, 363, 365, 367, 369, 372–73, 375–76, 379

British Columbia Dragoons, 103, 128, 216, 232, 247, 250, 276, 290, 292, 301, 303, 307–09, 315, 339, 341, 345, 365, 368–73, 375, 377–80, 393

Governor General's Horse Guards, 37, 40, 42–43, 47, 103–04, 128, 160, 162, 172, 180, 191, 210, 254, 314, 348–50, 356

Lord Strathcona's Horse, 25, 32–39, 42, 45–46, 49, 81, 88, 91–93, 95–96, 104, 270, 277, 290, 292–93, 310, 314, 330, 336, 342, 344, 409

Royal Canadian Dragoons, 57, 58–59, 76–77, 80, 102–04, 128, 180, 191–97, 204, 225, 227, 325, 353, 390

ARTILLERY UNITS

1st Anti-Tank Regiment, 96, 114–15, 118, 159, 217, 226, 299, 382

2nd Field Regiment, 100, 109, 192

3rd Field Regiment, 208

4th Anti-Tank Regiment, 276, 342

5th Light Anti-Aircraft Regiment, 366

5th Medium Regiment, 192

14th Field Regiment, 32

16th Anti-Tank Battery, 32, 39, 46

17th Field Regiment, 73–74

96th Anti-Tank Battery, 32

Royal Canadian Horse, 304

ENGINEER UNITS

1st Field Company, 85–86, 88, 91, 93, 178

1st Field Squadron, 301, 335–36, 342

3rd Field Company, 118–19, 140, 149, 158, 168

4th Field Company, 170, 226, 230, 234, 238

10th Field Company, 276

12th Field Company, 192, 194

14th Field Company, 32, 43, 290, 276

INFANTRY BATTALIONS/REGIMENTS

1st Light Anti-Aircraft Battalion. See Lanark and Renfrew Scottish

4th Princess Louise Dragoon Guards, 31, 33–35, 37, 41–42, 45–46, 57, 76, 81, 182, 221, 225, 227, 231–34, 243, 247, 250, 271, 290, 292–93, 296–98, 301, 313–14, 394–95

Canadian–American Special Service Force, 216

Cape Breton Highlanders, 32, 34, 55–57, 61–62, 64–65, 73–74, 76–77, 171–72, 254–55, 276–78, 286–87, 289, 310, 344, 370, 372–73, 375, 377, 379–80

Carleton and York Regiment, 120–21, 124–25, 170, 225, 237, 240, 280–82, 284, 290–91, 298–302, 303–07, 309, 345, 389, 396

48th Highlanders of Canada, 81, 84–85, 87–88, 97–98, 105, 107, 111, 120, 276, 280–81, 283–84, 309, 325–28, 346, 353

Hastings and Prince Edward Regiment, 81–88, 90–98, 100, 107, 120, 240, 242, 255, 257–59, 261–62, 264–66, 290–92, 299–303, 305–06, 327–29, 342, 346, 361–62, 400

Highland Light Infantry, 271

Irish Regiment, 54–57, 58, 60–61, 64, 73–75, 77, 81, 89–90, 98, 171, 180, 249, 252–54, 286–87, 291, 310, 330, 332–35, 344, 348–50, 356, 365–67, 370, 376–77

Lanark and Renfrew Scottish, 32, 37, 39, 41–43, 46, 75, 182, 205–07, 232–35, 243, 254, 290, 292–93, 295–96, 310–14, 332, 390, 403, 413

Loyal Edmonton Regiment, 106, 109–19, 121, 126, 137–140, 142–43, 146–48, 150–51, 154–57, 158–59, 168, 181, 273, 306–09, 315–19, 319–20, 330, 334, 339–42, 345, 354–56, 382, 389, 397–99, 402, 406–08

Perth Regiment, 57, 61–64, 73–74, 76–77, 172–73, 249, 252, 254, 275–78, 280, 286–87, 292, 330, 332–36, 342, 344, 362–63, 365–67, 369, 372, 375, 377, 379–80, 392

Princess Patricia's Canadian Light Infantry, 17–19, 106, 119, 121, 126–27, 131–32, 139, 141, 143–44, 155, 158–59, 162–71, 181, 273, 308, 317–19, 330, 334, 337, 339–42, 345, 381–85, 388, 402–03, 408

Royal Canadian Regiment, 85, 98–99, 104–5, 107, 109, 111, 120, 201, 242, 255, 258–64, 266, 290–91, 325–29, 331, 345, 353, 357, 359, 400, 406

Royal 22e Régiment, 120–23, 124–26, 139, 169–70, 223, 225–29, 236–40, 284–85, 309, 323–24, 382–83, 390, 401

Seaforth Highlanders, 69, 106–09, 115, 131, 137–140, 141–44, 146, 150, 152, 154,

156–57, 158, 168, 181, 308–09, 314–15, 319, 345, 353–54, 356, 382, 385, 387–88, 390, 394–95, 401, 406–07

Westminster (Motor) Regiment, 25, 31–32, 35–39, 41–43, 46–48, 180, 182, 197, 204–05, 208–12, 233–34, 243–44, 246–49, 252, 254, 276, 287–90, 292–93, 298, 310–12, 314, 316, 349, 355, 375–77

West Nova Scotia Regiment, 120–22, 163–68, 225–27, 229–30, 238–40, 280–81, 284–85, 309, 389–90, 399

OTHER UNITS

3rd Light Aid Detachment, 216

9th Light Field Ambulance, 226

SUPPORT UNITS

8th Princess Louise's New Brunswick Hussars, 49, 54, 58, 290, 365

Saskatoon Light Infantry, 109, 114, 131–32, 140, 143, 226, 307, 315, 323

BRITISH

Air

Desert Air Force, 91, 109, 222, 227, 229, 231, 241, 285, 288, 291, 311, 316, 323, 343, 367, 377

Army

Eighth Army, 21, 26, 28–30, 66–68, 71–72, 79–80, 112, 129–30, 167, 174–76, 178–79, 183, 189–90, 192, 195, 200–02, 209–10, 213–14, 217–18, 220, 222, 249, 266, 273, 275, 322, 351–52, 359–60, 390–92, 398, 405

CORPS

v Corps, 30, 63, 77, 79–81, 106, 125, 130, 167, 179–80, 183, 192, 197, 203, 210, 213, 215, 221–22, 226, 273–74, 276, 283, 321–22, 325, 347, 381, 390

x Corps, 72, 174

xii Corps, 176

xiii Corps, 176, 188, 214

King's Royal Rifle, 375–76

DIVISIONS

1st Armoured, 28, 189

4th Indian, 63

4th Infantry, 31, 33, 130, 167, 189

5th Infantry, 189

8th Indian, 189, 359

10th Indian, 77–78, 131, 210, 221, 224–26, 321, 408

46th Infantry, 63, 77, 81, 84, 87, 115, 121, 124–25, 130, 273–74

56th Infantry, 28, 63, 78–79, 82, 381, 389, 390

78th Infantry, 27, 79, 176, 188

BRIGADES

9th Armoured, 365, 375, 392, 395–96

19th Infantry, 359

21st Infantry, 359

21st Tank, 81

43rd Indian Lorried Infantry, 276, 283, 321

43rd Independent Gurkha Infantry, 78

BATTALIONS/REGIMENTS

1st Battalion/4th Essex Regiment, 197, 203, 205

1st Welsh Regiment, 395

2nd London Irish Rifles, 98

2nd Somerset Light Infantry, 33

6th Black Watch, 125

12th Royal Lancers Regiment, 180, 375

12th Royal Tank Regiment, 106, 114–15, 122, 126, 140, 215, 226, 237, 239, 326–27

24th Field Regiment, 192

27th Lancers Cavalry Regiment, 103–04, 128, 172, 180, 192, 196–97, 203, 211, 249–50

44th Reconnaissance Regiment, 82

145th Armoured Regiment, 140, 158

King's Dragoon Guards, 205, 207, 227

North Irish Horse Regiment, 33, 226–28

OTHER UNITS

151st Anti-Tank Battery, 192

Popski's Private Army, 195, 197, 203, 211, 218, 249

AMERICAN

Air

U.S. Army Air Force, 365

Army

Fifth Army, 29–30, 51, 53–54, 72, 79, 175–77, 188, 190, 214, 322, 351, 358, 405

CORPS
II Corps, 176, 188
VI Corps, 27, 322

DIVISIONS
34th Infantry, 176–77
36th Infantry, 322
85th Infantry, 176
88th Infantry, 176
91st Infantry, 176
92nd Infantry, 358

ITALIAN (ALLIED)
28th Garibaldi Brigade, 217, 249–50
Gruppo Cremona, 392, 396–97

OTHER ALLIED
2nd New Zealand Armoured Division, 19,
   21, 26, 30, 33, 54, 63, 76–79, 101–02, 106,
   128–29, 158, 167, 321
II Polish Corps, 183, 188, 215, 222, 273, 321
3rd Greek Mountain Brigade, 63, 80, 103
3rd Polish Carpathian Division, 273
4th New Zealand Armoured Brigade,
   127–129
5th New Zealand Infantry Brigade, 63, 76,
   81, 92, 98, 101–02, 104, 115
6th South African Armoured Division,
   188–89
22nd (New Zealand) Battalion, 76
French Expeditionary Corps, 27
People's Liberation Army, 190

GERMAN

Army
Fourteenth, 53, 175, 177
Tenth, 52–53, 157, 175, 177

KORPS
I Fallschirmjäger, 176
LI Gebirgskorps, 128, 177
LXXIII Korps, 288
LXXVI Panzer, 52, 128, 167, 273

DIVISIONS
1st Fallschirmjäger, 39, 128, 172
16th SS Panzer Grenadier, 366, 372, 375, 398
20th Luftwaffe Field, 49
26th Panzer, 59, 85, 92, 135, 152, 157, 274
29th Panzer Grenadier, 35, 61, 96, 176–77
42nd Jäger, 398
44th Infanterie, 176
65th Infanterie, 176
90th Panzer Grenadier, 84–85, 92, 274,
   288, 301, 321
98th Infanterie, 288, 309, 321, 329, 331,
   335, 344
114th Jäger, 172, 223–24, 231, 262, 297,
   366, 377
148th Infanterie, 358
278th Infanterie, 288
305th Infanterie, 273–74
356th Infanterie, 223, 231, 262, 309
362nd Infanterie, 397
710th Infanterie, 398
715th Infanterie, 321

BATTALIONS/REGIMENTS
1st Battalion, 36th Regiment, 375
1st Panther Battalion, 329
4th Panzer Regiment, 329
9th Panzer Grenadier Regiment, 85, 92, 135
16th SS Reconnaissance Regiment, 375
26th Reconnaissance Battalion, 375
36th SS Panzer Grenadier Regiment, 375
190th Reconnaissance Battalion, 301
289th Grenadiers Battalion, 309
361st Panzer Grenadier Regiment, 85, 92
721st Jäger Regiment, 366
870th Grenadiers Regiment, 309
Field Marshal Kesselring's Machine Gun
   Battalion (Maschinegewehr-Bataillon
   Feldmarschall Kesselring), 297
Schwere Panzer–Abteilung 504 Regiment,
   59 schwere Panzer–Abteilung 508
   Regiment, 59

ITALIAN (AXIS)
3rd Marine Division, 358
4th Alpine Division, 358

ABOUT THE AUTHOR

*T*HE RIVER BATTLES is the thirteenth volume in Mark Zuehlke's critically acclaimed Canadian Battle Series—the most extensive published account of the battle experiences of Canada's Army in World War II. The series is also the most exhaustive recounting of the battles and campaigns fought by any nation during that war to have been written by a single author. These best-selling books continue to confirm Zuehlke's reputation as the nation's leading popular military historian. In 2006, *Holding Juno: Canada's Heroic Defence of the D-Day Beaches* won the City of Victoria Butler Book Prize.

He has written six other historical works, including *For Honour's Sake: The War of 1812 and the Brokering of an Uneasy Peace*, which won the 2007 Canadian Author's Association Lela Common Award for Canadian History.

More recently, Zuehlke has been active in the graphic novel field, working with Renegade Arts on a number of projects based on Canadian history. In 2012, he was the co-author of *The Loxleys and the War of 1812*, and in 2013 wrote the script for a sequel, *The Loxleys and Confederation*, which garnered the Book Publishers Association of Alberta's Best Children's and Young Adult Book of the Year award.

Also a novelist, he is the author of the popular Elias McCann series, the first of which—*Hands Like Clouds*—won the 2000 Crime Writers of Canada Arthur Ellis Award for Best First Crime Novel.

Zuehlke is currently working on his next Canadian Battle Series book, which details the nation's involvement in the war against Japan. In 2015, he published a companion volume to the Canadian Battle Series—*Through Blood and Sweat: A Remembrance Trek Across Sicily's World War II Battlegrounds*—a memoir of his experiences in July 2013, when, over twenty days, he and a small contingent of Canadians marched 350 kilometres to retrace the routes taken by 1st Canadian Infantry Division through Sicily in 1943.

Zuehlke lives in Victoria, British Columbia. On the web, he can be found at www.zuehlke.ca and the Mark Zuehlke's Canadian Battle Series Facebook page.